DOCTRINE &

COVENANTS

ENCYCLOPEDIA

DOCTRINE &

COVENANTS

ENCYCLOPEDIA

HOYT W. BREWSTER JR.

DESERET
BOOK

SALT LAKE CITY, UTAH

First printing in hardbound 1988
First printing in paperbound 2004

Visit us at deseretbook.com

Library of Congress Catalog Card Number: 88-71860

ISBN 0-88494-669-X (hardbound)
ISBN 1-59038-362-1 (paperbound)

Printed in the United States of America   72076
Publishers Printing, Salt Lake City, UT

10   9   8   7   6   5   4   3   2   1

To Hoyt W. Brewster, my beloved father, who gave me a noble name which I am proud to bear and whose life has been such a worthy example that I gladly seek to follow in his footsteps; and to the memory of my saintly mother, Naomi Smith Brewster, who sought to bring up her children in light and truth.

The Book of Mormon brings men to Christ. The Doctrine and Covenants brings men to Christ's kingdom, even The Church of Jesus Christ of Latter-day Saints, 'the only true and living church upon the face of the whole earth' (D&C 1:30). I know that.

The Book of Mormon is the "keystone" of our religion, and the Doctrine and Covenants is the capstone, with continuing latter-day revelation. The Lord has placed His stamp of approval on both the keystone and the capstone.

President Ezra Taft Benson
CR, April 1987, p. 105

Acknowledgments

Gratitude is expressed to Russell Orton and Cory Maxwell of Bookcraft Publishers whose belief in the potential value of this work as a significant contribution to the literature of the Church has helped to make the dream a reality. Special thanks are expressed to Dan Hogan, whose capable and tireless editing skills have finely tuned a massive manuscript into a reference work of high quality. I'm also appreciative of the help George Bickerstaff gave to this project.

Thanks is expressed to the many who gave permission for copyrighted material to be used. Bookcraft Publishers and Deseret Book Company were particularly gracious in granting permission to quote liberally from dozens of books published by each company. General Authorities of The Church of Jesus Christ of Latter-day Saints were likewise generous in allowing their materials to be used.

Much love and appreciation is expressed to my eternal companion Judy and my children, Kimberly, Merrilee, Hillary and M. Hoyt. This work of some fifteen years of intensive research and writing could not have been accomplished without their loving support.

While I have tried to make this work representative of what I understand to be acceptable Church doctrine, it is not presented as an official interpretation of that doctrine.

Finally, although I accept full responsibility for this work, I feel to publicly acknowledge the guidance of the Spirit in bringing this material together. I thank my Father in Heaven for the divine assistance which I have so often felt in finding the answers and the resources I sought. Having said this, I hasten to borrow a phrase from an ancient prophet: "If there be faults [in this work] they be the faults of a man [the author]," and not of God. (Morm. 8:17.)

Key to Abbreviations

AA	*Ancient Apostles*, David O. McKay
ABL	*A Burning Light*, Robert J. Matthews
ACR	Area Conference Report, The Church of Jesus Christ of Latter-day Saints
AF	*Articles of Faith*, James E. Talmage
AGQ	*Answers to Gospel Questions* (5 vols.), Joseph Fielding Smith
ANW	*A New Witness for the Articles of Faith*, Bruce R. McConkie
APP	*Autobiography of Parley P. Pratt*
APTC	*Aaronic Priesthood Through the Centuries*, Lee A. Palmer
ASBY	*Acceptance of the Statue of Brigham Young*, United States Government
AWIH	*Adam: Who Is He?*, Mark E. Petersen
BD	Bible Dictionary, Pre-1979 editions of the Bible printed by Deseret Book, Co.
BLS	*Biography of Lorenzo Snow*, Eliza R. Snow
BMC	*Book of Mormon Compendium*, Sidney B. Sperry
BYUS	*BYU Studies*, Brigham Young University
CA 1978	*Church Almanac: 1978*, Deseret News Press
CBM	*Commentary on the Book of Mormon* (7 vols.), George Reynolds and Janne Sjodahl
CC	*Carthage Conspiracy*, Dallin H. Oaks and Marvin S. Hill
CE	*Cherished Experiences of David O. McKay*
CHC	*Comprehensive History of the Church* (6 vols.), B. H. Roberts
CHMR	*Church History and Modern Revelation* (1953 ed., 2 vols.), Joseph Fielding Smith
CN	*Church News*, The Church of Jesus Christ of Latter-day Saints
CR	Conference Report, The Church of Jesus Christ of Latter-day Saints
Cruden	*Cruden's Complete Concordance*, Alexander Cruden
DBY	*Discourses of Brigham Young*

DCC	*Doctrine and Covenants Compendium*, Sidney B. Sperry
DFS	*Devotional and Fireside Speeches*, Brigham Young University
DNTC	*Doctrinal New Testament Commentary* (3 vols.), Bruce R. McConkie
DOH	Diary of Oliver B. Huntington
DS	*Doctrines of Salvation* (3 vols.), Joseph Fielding Smith
DSY	*Devotional Speeches of the Year*, Brigham Young University
Dummelow	*The One Volume Bible Commentary*, J. R. Dummelow
ECH	*Essentials in Church History* (22nd ed.), Joseph Fielding Smith
En	*Ensign*, The Church of Jesus Christ of Latter-day Saints
ER	*Evidences and Reconciliations*, John A. Widtsoe
FPM	*Faith Precedes the Miracle*, Spencer W. Kimball
GD	*Gospel Doctrine*, Joseph F. Smith
GGG	*God's Greatest Gift*, Theodore M. Burton
GI	*Gospel Ideals*, David O. McKay
GK	*Gospel Kingdom*, John Taylor
GT	*Gospel Truth* (2 vols.), George Q. Cannon
HC	*History of the Church* (7 vols.), The Church of Jesus Christ of Latter-day Saints
HL	*The House of the Lord*, James E. Talmage
HR	*The Heavens Resound*, Milton V. Backman, Jr.
HSP	*Hyrum Smith: Patriarch*, Pearson H. Corbett
Hymns	Hymns of The Church of Jesus Christ of Latter-day Saints (1985 ed.)
IE	*Improvement Era*, The Church of Jesus Christ of Latter-day Saints
In	*Instructor*, The Church of Jesus Christ of Latter-day Saints
JD	*Journal of Discourses* (26 vols.)
Jenson	*LDS Biographical Encyclopedia* (4 vols.), Andrew Jenson
JI	*Juvenile Instructor*, The Church of Jesus Christ of Latter-day Saints
JST	Joseph Smith Translation of the Bible (Inspired Version)
KT	*Key to Theology*, Parley P. Pratt

LDS	*LDS Reference Encyclopedia* (2 vols.), Melvin R. Brooks
LDSBD	LDS Bible Dictionary, 1979 LDS Edition of the King James Version of the Bible
LF	*Lectures on Faith*, Joseph Smith
LHCK	*Life of Heber C. Kimball*, Orson F. Whitney
LJFS	*Life of Joseph F. Smith*, Joseph Fielding Smith
LJT	*Life of John Taylor*, B. H. Roberts
LMS	*History of Joseph Smith*, Lucy Mack Smith
LTG	*Look to God and Live*, Marion G. Romney
MA	*Mediation and Atonement*, John Taylor
MD	*Mormon Doctrine* (2nd ed.), Bruce R. McConkie
MF	*The Miracle of Forgiveness*, Spencer W. Kimball
MFP	*Messages of the First Presidency* (6 vols.), James R. Clark
Mill M	*The Millennial Messiah*, Bruce R. McConkie
MM	*The Mortal Messiah* (4 vols.), Bruce R. McConkie
MMM	*Moses: Man of Miracles*, Mark E. Petersen
MOD	*Man: His Origin and Destiny*, Joseph Fielding Smith
MS	*Millennial Star*, The Church of Jesus Christ of Latter-day Saints
MWW	*A Marvelous Work and a Wonder*, LeGrand Richards
NE	*New Era*, The Church of Jesus Christ of Latter-day Saints
OC	*Oliver Cowdery: Second Elder and Scribe*, Stanley R. Gunn
P	*Priesthood*, Deseret Book, Co.
PCG	*Priesthood and Church Government*, John A. Widtsoe
PC	*Program of the Church*, John A. Widtsoe
Peloubet	*Peloubet's Bible Dictionary*
PM	*The Promised Messiah*, Bruce R. McConkie
POC	*The Presidents of the Church*, Preston Nibley
Riciotti	*The Life of Christ*, Giuseppe Riciotti
RL	*Compendium*, Franklin D. Richards and James Little
SHP	*Stand Ye in Holy Places*, Harold B. Lee

SLS	*The Story of the Latter-day Saints,* James B. Allen and Glen M. Leonard
SMS	*Sermons and Missionary Services of Melvin J. Ballard,* Bryant S. Hinckley
SP	*Succession in the Presidency of the Church,* B. H. Roberts
SS	*Doctrine and Covenants Commentary,* Hyrum M. Smith and Janne M. Sjodahl
ST	*Signs of the Times,* Joseph Fielding Smith
SVOT	*Spiritual Values of the Old Testament,* Roy A. Welker
SWK	*Spencer W. Kimball,* Edward L. and Andrew E. Kimball, Jr.
SYE	*Seek Ye Earnestly,* Joseph Fielding Smith
TPJS	*Teachings of the Prophet Joseph Smith*
Talmage	*Jesus the Christ,* James E. Talmage
TRG	*Themes of the Restored Gospel,* Sidney B. Sperry
TS	*Times and Seasons,* The Church of Jesus Christ of Latter-day Saints
TYD	*Teach Ye Diligently,* Boyd K. Packer
UGHM	*Utah Genealogical and Historical Magazine*
UR	*The Upward Reach,* Sterling W. Sill
UTH	*Unto the Hills,* Richard L. Evans
VW	*Voice of Warning,* Parley P. Pratt
WAI	*Who Am I?,* Alvin R. Dyer
WOM	*Woman,* Deseret Book
WTP	*The Way to Perfection,* Joseph Fielding Smith
WW	*Wilford Woodruff,* Matthias F. Cowley
WWPTH	*We Will Prove Them Herewith,* Neal A. Maxwell
YC	*Youth and the Church,* Harold B. Lee
YLW	*Ye are the Light of the World,* Harold B. Lee

A

Aaron

Aaron was the great priesthood leader after whom the Aaronic Priesthood was named (D&C 84:18; 107:1). He was a Levite whose parents, Amram and Jochebed, also had another famous son—the prophet Moses (Ex. 6:16–20). Early in Moses' ministry, Aaron was called by the Lord to act as a spokesman for his younger brother in declaring the word of the Lord to the people (Ex. 4:10–16, 27–30). Aaron also stood beside his brother before Pharaoh and wielded his rod of faith before the eyes of Pharaoh's court (Ex. 7; 8; 9; 10; 11). He not only heard the voice of God speaking to him from the heavens but also was privileged to look upon his face (Ex. 24:9–10).

Elder John A. Widtsoe identified Aaron's original priesthood as being Melchizedek, which the book of Exodus also implies (PCG, 13; Ex. 18:12). When the Lord removed the Melchizedek Priesthood from the Israelites, Aaron and his sons were called to minister within the ordinances of the lesser priesthood, which was given Aaron's name (D&C 84:18–28; Ex. 28; 40:12–16). Aaron's ordination is used by the Lord and the Apostle Paul as an example of how one is to be called to the work of the ministry (D&C 27:8; 132:59; Heb. 5:4). He died on Mt. Hor at the age of 123 after having his presiding authority and keys conferred on his son, Eleazar (Num. 20:25–29).

The following summary is a fitting tribute to Aaron: "Aaron is not represented as a leader without human weakness. However, an objective overview of his mission and of his life brings him into full view as one of the most worthy and venerated leaders in Israel's history." (APTC, 52.)

See also: Aaronic Priesthood; Gift of Aaron; Sons of Aaron; Sons of Levi

Aaronic Priesthood

About forty years before his death, Aaron was given the responsibility of presiding over a lesser priesthood than that which the Israelites had previously enjoyed. He and his sons, assisted by all the sons of Levi, were the only ones designated to perform the rites and ordinances of the priesthood which bore his name—the Aaronic Priesthood. (Ex. 28; 40:12–16; Num. 18:1–6; D&C 84:18.) This priesthood is sometimes referred to as the lesser priesthood and includes the Levitical Priesthood (D&C 107:1).

Following the departure of Moses, the ecclesiastical affairs of Israel were governed by the

Aaronic Priesthood, for the people had proven themselves unworthy of the blessings of the greater or Melchizedek Priesthood (D&C 84:18–26). The Prophet Joseph Smith made an interesting observation in this regard: "All Priesthood," said he, "is Melchizedek, but there are different portions or degrees of it. That portion which brought Moses to speak with God face to face was taken away; but that which brought the ministry of angels remained." (TPJS, 180–81.) "That portion which . . . remained," according to Lee Palmer, "was the lesser priesthood, the priesthood of Aaron, or the Aaronic Priesthood as we know it today" (APTC, 78). It was to remain until the ministry of John the Baptist, who was to prepare the way for the one mightier than either himself or the lesser priesthood, for the Master's ministry would restore the power and blessings of the Melchizedek Priesthood (D&C 84:25–28). It should be remembered, however, that the Melchizedek Priesthood was not totally absent, for it was held by God's holy prophets during the years from Moses to Christ (DS 3:84–85).

The Aaronic Priesthood did not function among the descendants of the prophet Lehi. He was led from Jerusalem to the American continent shortly after 600 B.C. Speaking of Lehi and his family, President Joseph Fielding Smith said: "They were not descendants of Aaron, and there were no Levites among them. There is no evidence in the Book of Mormon that they held the Aaronic Priesthood until after the ministry of the resurrected Lord among them. . . . " (DS 3:87; AGQ 4:161; 1:123–26.)

John the Baptist held the keys of the Aaronic Priesthood and was the legal administrator for the kingdom of God at the time Jesus submitted himself for baptism (TPJS, 272–73). John understood that his was but a preparatory mission for the Savior, who would assume full control of that kingdom. Following the long night of darkness that resulted from the apostasy from the kingdom established by the Savior and his Apostles, John was called on to restore the keys and authority of the Aaronic Priesthood (D&C 13; 27:7–8). On May 15, 1829, "the veil was parted and the angel of God came down clothed with glory and delivered the anxiously looked for message, and the keys of the gospel of repentance" (HC 1:43). President David O. McKay said of this occasion: "If the world could but realize the full significance of the angel John's coming again to earth . . . , multitudes who are praying for the kingdom of God to be established among men would gratefully join in the commemoration of that heavenly manifestation" (GI, 167).

As a result of that restoration to Joseph Smith and Oliver Cowdery, the Aaronic Priesthood is with The Church of Jesus Christ of Latter-day Saints today. According to a heavenly proclamation, this priesthood "holds the keys of the ministering of angels, and of the gospel of repentance, and of baptism by immersion for the remission of sins" (D&C 13).

The callings that presently constitute this priesthood are bishop (the president of the Aaronic Priesthood) and the offices of priest, teacher, and deacon (D&C 20:46–60; 107:87–88; AF, 205).

See also: First Priesthood; Lesser Priesthood; Levitical Priesthood

Abase

"He that exalteth himself shall be abased," declared the Lord, "and he that abaseth himself shall be exalted" (D&C 101:42; see also 112:3; 124:114). To abase oneself is to humble oneself (Matt. 23:12; Luke 18:14). To be abased is the opposite of being puffed up in pride.

See also: Humility

Abel

One of two sons mentioned initially in the biblical account of Adam and Eve's posterity was Abel (Gen. 4). He and his brother Cain were not the firstborn children of our first parents, for they had older brothers and sisters (Moses 5:12). Abel was a keeper of sheep and, in contrast to his brother Cain, hearkened unto the voice of the Lord, offered

sacrifices in faith, and walked in holiness before the Lord (Moses 5:17, 26; TPJS, 58–59; Heb. 11:4).

Abel became the first martyr of the Church and the world when his brother slew him (D&C 138:40; Moses 5:32). Abel "magnified the Priesthood which was conferred upon him, and died a righteous man, and therefore has become an angel of God by receiving his body from the dead, holding still the keys of his dispensation; and was sent down from heaven unto Paul to minister consoling words, and to commit unto him a knowledge of the mysteries of godliness" (TPJS, 169; D&C 84:16).

Abolishment

Abolishment indicates complete destruction. An 1832 revelation warns of the "desolation and utter abolishment" which awaits the inhabitants of certain cities if they reject the gospel message (D&C 84:114). This is the only use of the word in the Doctrine and Covenants.

Abominations

An abomination is an object, practice, or teaching that is disgusting, detestable, and offensive. The hearts of the wicked are full of abominations (D&C 10:21). Moreover, any creed, doctrine, philosophy, precept, practice, ordinance, or teaching that deliberately or inadvertently leads people from the saving power of Christ and his gospel is an abomination (see JS—H 1:19). From all such things we should "turn away" (see 2 Tim. 3:1-5).

See also: Desolation of Abominations; Great and Abominable Church

Abraham

The history of Abraham, father of the faithful, is found in both the Old Testament and in the Pearl of Great Price (Gen. 11:26 to 25:9; Abr. 1-3). His given name of *Abram* was changed by the Lord to *Abraham*, signifying "father of a multitude" (Gen. 17:5). His father, Terah, was an idol worshipper whose attempt to have Abraham slain on the altar of sacrifice was prevented by an angel of the Lord (Abr. 1; TPJS, 260). It is therefore even more significant that Abraham was obedient to the command of the Lord to place his own covenant child, Isaac, on a similar altar (Gen. 22). Of this event the Prophet Joseph said: "The sacrifice required of Abraham in the offering of Isaac, shows that if a man would attain to the keys of the kingdom of an endless life; he must sacrifice all things" (TPJS, 322).

Elder Francis M. Lyman once declared, "Obedience is the first law of God" (CR, Oct. 1899, p. 35). It is because Abraham understood this principle that he prospered. For, declared the

Lord, "when we obtain any blessing from God, it is by obedience to that law upon which it is predicated" (D&C 130:21). Of Abraham's obedience, Joseph Smith wrote: "Abraham was guided in all his family affairs by the Lord; was conversed with by angels, and by the Lord; was told where to go, and when to stop; and prospered exceedingly in all that he put his hand unto; it was because he and his family obeyed the counsel of the Lord" (TPJS, 251-52). One of Abraham's sterling qualities was his great faith, regardless of the issues involved: "And he believed in the Lord," wrote Moses, "and he counted it to him for righteousness" (Gen. 15:6).

Before he was born, Abraham was chosen to serve the Lord, because he was one of the "noble and great" spirits of pre-earth life (Abr. 3:22-24). He received the Melchizedek Priesthood from the man whose name that priesthood bears (D&C 84:14). He had possession of a Urim and Thummim, *given him from the Lord*, through which he gained a knowledge of the abode of God, God's galaxy, and our system of stars (Abr. 3). He undoubtedly taught the Egyptians their knowledge of astronomy (TPJS, 251).

The Prophet Joseph saw him in the celestial kingdom (D&C 137:5) and was later informed that Abraham had received his exaltation and now sits on a throne as a god (D&C 132:37). Among the promises given to Abraham were the following: (1)

through his ministry the name of the Lord would be known in the earth forever (Abr. 1:19); (2) all members of the Church and kingdom would be of his *seed*, whether by lineage or adoption (Abr. 2:10; Gal. 3:29); (3) he would become a father of many nations (Gen. 17:2–4); (4) kings would come from his lineage —both earthly and heavenly (Gen. 17:6); (5) the earth would be blessed through his seed (Abr. 2:11); (6) his name would be great among all nations (Abr. 2:9).

See also: Seed of Abraham; Works of Abraham

Abridgment

See: Manuscript (116 pages); Plates of Nephi

Acceptable Year of the Lord

The term *acceptable year of the Lord* appears once in the Doctrine and Covenants (93:51), once in the Old Testament (Isa. 61:2), and once in the New Testament (Luke 4:19). The terms *acceptable day* (D&C 138:31; Isa. 58:5) and *acceptable time* (Isa. 49:8) are used in a similar fashion. "The acceptable year of the Lord," according to Elder Bruce R. McConkie, is *"the proper, designated, approved, appointed, or accepted time, in the divine order of things, for a particular work to be done."* As used in Luke, "Jesus is saying, 'This is the time and the day of Messiah's coming;

this is the acceptable year; this is the time designated by the Father for his Only Begotten to minister among men, and I am he.' " (DNTC 1:161–62; italics added.) Thus, its use in the Doctrine and Covenants denotes the imminence of Christ's coming; this is the time in which to receive his gospel of salvation, to prepare for his arrival.

Accountability

See: Accountable Before Me; Infant State; Little Children; Spirit of Man Was Innocent

Accountable Before Me

In 1830, the Lord decreed that "power is not given unto Satan to tempt little children, until they begin to become accountable before me" (D&C 29:46–47). The age of accountability was later defined as "eight years old" (D&C 68:27). Centuries earlier, however, this same principle was made known to Abraham: "Children are not accountable before me until they are eight years old," declared the great Jehovah (JST, Gen. 17:11). The Nephite prophet Mormon, though not mentioning a specific age, taught this same truth in his day: "But little children are alive in Christ, even from the foundation of the world. . . . And he that saith that little children need baptism denieth the mercies of Christ, and setteth at naught the atonement of him and the power of his redemption." (Moro. 8:12, 20.)

Parents are given the responsibility to bring up their children in "light and truth" and to teach them "to understand the doctrine of repentance, faith in Christ the Son of the living God, and of baptism and the gift of the Holy Ghost by the laying on of hands, when eight years old" (D&C 93:40; 68:25). If they fail, "the sin be upon the heads of the parents."

See also: Infant State; Little Children; Spirit of Man Was Innocent

Adam

"And the first man of all men," declared the Lord, "have I called Adam, which is many" (Moses 1:34). This noble man, on the basis of celestial criteria, was chosen to stand as the great patriarch of all mankind. His selection was not haphazard, for he had proven himself worthy of occupying such a patriarchal position to preside over his posterity. *"Adam was placed here, not a wild, half-civilized savage, but a perfectly developed man, with wonderful intelligence, for he helped to create this earth. He was chosen in pre-existence to be the first man upon the earth and the father of the human race. . . . The Lord did not choose a being that had just developed from the lower forms of life, to be a prince, an archangel, to preside over the human race forever! Adam, as Michael, was one of the greatest intelligences in the spirit world and he stands next to Jesus Christ."* (DS 1:94–95.)

Adam is he whom we knew in the spirit world as "Michael, the prince, the archangel" (D&C 107:54). Under the direction of the Lord, he presides over the human family and all angels who minister to this earth (HC 3:385–86; 4:207–8). He successfully led us in battle against the devil and the one-third of our brothers and sisters who chose to fight against our Father in Heaven (Rev. 12:7–9; D&C 29:36–37; Moses 4:3–4; Abr. 3:27–28; Jude 1:6). He shall bind the devil during the millennial period of earth's history and once again lead the forces of good to final victory over the forces of evil (D&C 88:110–15).

When Adam was 927 years of age (from the time of the Fall), he called the high priests and "the residue of his posterity who were righteous, into the valley of Adam-ondi-Ahman, and there bestowed upon them his last blessing" (D&C 107:53). While there, the Lord appeared and administered unto Adam, saying: "I have set thee to be at the head; a multitude of nations shall come of thee, and thou art a prince over them forever" (D&C 107:54–55). Prior to the second coming of the Lord, Adam will once again visit the valley of Adam-ondi-Ahman and receive a stewardship accounting of all who have held keys of authority during the history of this earth (TPJS 157; D&C 116; Dan. 7:9–14).

See also: Ancient of Days; Archangel; Battle of the Great God; Dispensation of the Fulness of Times; Fall, The; Father of All; First Flesh; First Man (Moses 1:34); Keys of Salvation; Michael; Prince; Seventh Angel

Adam-ondi-Ahman

On May 19, 1838, Joseph Smith and two companions visited an area known as Spring Hill, in Daviess County, Missouri, for the purpose of laying claim to a city plat. On this occasion, the Prophet Joseph Smith declared that "by the mouth of the Lord" the location was named "Adam-ondi-Ahman, because, said He, it is the place where Adam shall come to visit his people, or the Ancient of Days shall sit, as spoken of by Daniel the Prophet." (HC 3:34-35; D&C 116; Dan. 7:9-14.) On another occasion, wrote President John Taylor, "while standing on an elevated piece of ground or plateau near Adam-ondi-Ahman," the Prophet Joseph pronounced that the pile of stones he and his party were observing was an altar built by Adam whereupon he offered up sacrifices and that the valley that lay before them was the valley of Adam-ondi-Ahman, "or in other words, the valley where God talked with Adam" (MA, 69-70).

Specific scriptural references to this sacred valley are found only in the Doctrine and Cove-nants (D&C 78:15; 107:53; 116; 117:8, 11). It was in this valley that Adam gathered his posterity, three years before his death, and blessed them and was himself visited and blessed of the Lord (D&C 107:53-56). It is in this valley that "all that have had the keys must stand before him in . . . grand council" and render an accounting of their steward-ships. Father Adam, in turn, will deliver up his stewardship to Christ. (TPJS, 157-58.) This may well be the experience of which the Lord spoke when he declared "the hour cometh that I will drink of the fruit of the vine with you on the earth" (D&C 27:5-14).

Adultery

Echoes of the divine edict heard anciently on Sinai still reverberate from pulpits today: "Thou shalt not commit adultery" (Ex. 20:14; D&C 42:24). "This act between married people," said Elder Spencer W. Kimball, "is a most heinous transgression, so serious that it has been the subject of sermons by prophets and leaders in all gospel dispensations. The death penalty was exacted for it in the days of Israel . . . (Lev. 20:10). . . . Whatever the rationalizations and arguments, there are no circumstances which justify adultery. Regardless of what the world does, The Church of Jesus Christ of Latter-day Saints must continue to fortify its people against sin and to stand firm for total fidelity and solid home and family life." (MF, 67, 69.)

In its seriousness as a crime, adultery stands second only to blasphemy against the Holy Ghost and the shedding of innocent blood (Alma 39:5). Perhaps the Lord sadly reflected on David's demise when he counseled, "Thou shalt not covet thy neighbor's wife; nor seek thy neighbor's life" (D&C 19:25). Those who commit adultery either in lustful thought or in the flesh "shall not have the Spirit, but shall deny the faith and shall fear" (D&C 63:16; see also D&C 42:23; 3 Ne. 12:27–29; Matt. 5:27–28).

See also: Lust; Spirits of Men Who Are to Be Judged and Are Found Under Condemnation; Uncleanness

Advent

President Joseph F. Smith saw in vision the multitudes in the spirit world "awaiting the advent of the Son of God" (D&C 138:16). *Advent* means arrival or coming.

Adversary

See: Devil; Lucifer; Satan

Adversity

In revelation given while Joseph Smith was suffering under the cruel conditions imposed by his captors, the Prophet was given an eternal perspective on adversity. In spite of his months of confinement and life-long persecution (see JS—H 1:20–22), he was informed that his adversity and afflictions would "be but a small moment," and if he endured well, God would exalt him (D&C 121:7–8). He was also told that the adversity he suffered would give him experience and be for his good (D&C 122:7). It is of interest to note that both Christ and Melchizedek "learned . . . obedience by the things which [they] suffered" (Heb. 5:8; DNTC 3:157).

Elder James E. Talmage noted: "No pang that is suffered by man or woman upon the earth will be without its compensating effect . . . if it be met with patience" (FPM, 98). Similarly, Elder Orson F. Whitney wrote: "No pain that we suffer, no trial that we experience is wasted. It ministers to our education, to the development of such qualities as patience, faith, fortitude and humility. All that we suffer and all that we endure, especially when we endure it patiently, builds up our characters, purifies our hearts, expands our souls, and makes us more tender and charitable, more worthy to be called the children of God . . . , and it is through sorrow and suffering, toil and tribulation, that we gain the education that we come here to acquire and which will make us more like our Father and Mother in heaven." (FPM, 98.)

See also: Endure to the End

Advocate with the Father

The term *advocate* appears five times in the Doctrine and Covenants (29:5; 32:3; 45:3; 62:1; 110:4) and once in the New Testament (1 John 2:1). The dictionary defines an advocate as "one who pleads another's cause." The Savior described his role as our advocate with the Father in these words: "Listen to him who is the advocate with the Father, who is pleading your cause before him—Saying: Father, behold the sufferings and death of him who did no sin, in whom thou wast well pleased; behold the blood of thy Son which was shed, the blood of him whom thou gavest that thyself might be glorified; wherefore, Father, spare these my brethren that believe on my name, that they may come unto me and have everlasting life." (D&C 45:3–5.)

Through the Atonement, the Savior extends his arm of mercy to the penitent and satisfies the demands of justice (D&C 29:1; Alma 42:13–26). In the words of the Apostle John, "But if any man sin *and repent*, we have an advocate with the Father, Jesus Christ the righteous" (JST, 1 John 2:1; italics added).

See also: Jesus Christ

Affrighted

The old English word *affrighted* (terrified, especially suddenly) appears only occasionally in scripture (see Job 18:20; Mark 16:5; Alma 62:24; D&C 101:51).

Afloat

During dark days of persecution, the Prophet Joseph urged the scattered Saints to gather documents and data relating to their sufferings and abuses. Among these materials were "libelous publications that are afloat" (D&C 123:1–4). In this sense, the term applies to that which was circulating about the general public.

Age of a Tree

The unique phrase *age of a tree* appears only once (D&C 101:30) and has reference to the age to which men will attain during the Millennium. "Men shall live until they are the age of a tree or one hundred years old," said President Joseph Fielding Smith (CHMR 1:461). Isaiah does speak of the days of his people being as long as "the days of a tree" (Isa. 65:22).

Smith and Sjodahl, in commenting on the ages of trees, indicated that "when man lives in accordance with the laws of God, and is clean and temperate in all things, there is no reason, as far as we know, why he should not live to the same age as the Patriarchs before the flood." These venerable men lived upwards of nine hundred years. (SS, 644.)

Age of Man

In a series of verses that refer to millennial conditions, the Lord states that men who live at that particular time will "die at the *age of man*" (D&C 63:49–51; italics added). Speaking of this time period, the Prophet Isaiah proclaimed: "There shall be no more thence an infant of days, nor an old man that hath not filled his days: for the child shall die *an hundred years old*" (Isa. 65:20; italics added).

Commenting on this condition, President Joseph Fielding Smith said: "Men on the earth will still be mortal, but a change shall come over them so that they will have power over sickness, disease and death. Death shall all but be banished from the earth, for *men shall live until they are the age of a tree or one hundred years old* (See Sec. 63:50–51), *and then shall die at the age of man*, but this death shall come in the twinkling of an eye and mortality shall give way to immortality suddenly. There shall be no graves, and the righteous shall be caught up to a glorious resurrection." (CHMR 1:461; italics added.)

In ancient America, the term *age of man* was used in a different context. On the occasion of the Savior's visit as a resurrected being to the inhabitants of that land, he promised nine of his special disciples that they would live until the "age of man," which he defined as "seventy and two years old" (3 Ne. 28:1–3). This use, however, should not be confused with the different context in which the term is used in the Doctrine and Covenants.

Agency

The very principle over which warfare was waged in the premortal life was that of agency: man's inherent right to choose his course and accept the consequences thereof. Satan not only rebelled against God, but he also "sought to destroy the agency of man" (Moses 4:3). His followers exercised their agency by similarly pursuing the perditious path of evil, where they now wallow in wickedness (D&C 29:36).

"It is easy to see what a sad condition the world would be in if Lucifer's plan had succeeded," said Elder Joseph Fielding Smith. "Chaos would have ruled supreme. Every soul would have become a nonentity; individuality would have been destroyed and all righteousness, mercy, truth, would have passed away forever, and this would have brought destruction to the universe. How true are the words of the Lord: 'All truth is independent in that sphere in which God has placed it, to act for itself, as all intelligence also; otherwise there is no existence!' (D&C 93:30.)

". . . Force and compulsion are principles that obtain in Satan's realms. Upon these his kingdom was founded and because of these it shall fall.

"The great gift of agency is like fire: if properly controlled it becomes an *agency of life*; if improperly used it becomes the *agency of death*. The right to choose which has been given us, if we use it wisely, will bring *exaltation*. Through it we may become sons of God, enjoying the fulness of his kingdom. If improperly used it becomes the agency of *banishment* from the presence of God into outer darkness where we may become sons of Perdition, the slaves of sin." (WTP, 179–81; italics added.)

As previously mentioned, free will—man's agency or right to choose—also implies responsibility to accept the consequences of choice: condemnation and sorrow for sin or blessings and happiness for righteousness (D&C 93:31). Elder Neal A. Maxwell observed: "So many have erred, thinking that freedom included both freedom to obey or not to obey eternal laws and, wrongly, that it included freedom to change those laws. Not so. Ultimately, *freedom involves choice between eternal alternatives, but not the altering of the alternatives.* We can choose wickedness or happiness, but not wickedness with happiness." (DSY 1976, 199; italics added.)

The Lord made it clear that men are not pawns of forces extraneous to themselves, "for the power is in them, wherein they are *agents unto themselves*" (D&C 58:26–29; italics added). President Spencer W. Kimball has said: "There are those today who say that man is the result of his environment and cannot rise above it. Those who justify mediocrity, failure, and even weakness and criminality are certainly misguided. Surely the environmental conditions found in childhood and youth are an influence of power. But the fact remains that every normal soul has its free agency and the power to row against the current and to lift himself to new planes of activity and thought and development. Man can transform himself. . . . Abraham did. He came out of an idol-worshiping family; yet he headed a dispensation of worshipers of the true and living God." (DSY 1974, 239.)

"Next to life itself," declared President David O. McKay, "free agency is the greatest gift of God to man" (CR, Apr. 1952, p. 13).

Ahashdah

On six occasions in the Doctrine and Covenants, Newel K. Whitney was referred to as Ahashdah (D&C 78:9; 82:11; 96:2; 104:39, 40, 41; pre-1981 edition). The meaning of this name is not clear, but its use is explained by B. H. Roberts: "It was not always desirable that the individuals whom the Lord addressed in revelations should at the time be known by the world, and hence . . . the brethren were addressed by other than their own names. The temporary necessity having passed for keeping the names of the individuals addressed unknown, their real names were subsequently given in brackets." (HC 1:255; D&C 78:preface; pre-1981 edition.) In current editions of the Doctrine and Covenants, only the real name is given; thus, the name Ahashdah no longer appears in our modern scripture.

See also: Whitney, Newel K.

Ahman

See: Son Ahman

Alam

The name Alam was used in earlier editions of the Doctrine and Covenants as a pseudonym for Edward Partridge (D&C 82:11; pre-1981 edition). He was one of nine individuals whose true identity the Lord initially wanted to be kept secret from the world (HC 1:255). A year after this revelation was given, the Prophet again referred to Partridge as Alam in a letter dated June 25, 1833 (HC 1:363). The letter also referred to Newel K. Whitney as Ahashdah, by which name he was identified in earlier editions of section 82. Because in current editions of the Doctrine and Covenants only the real name is given, the name Alam no longer appears in modern scripture.

See also: Partridge, Edward

Albany, New York

In September 1832, Bishop Newel K. Whitney was specifically instructed to visit the cities of New York, Albany, and Boston, "and warn the people of those cities with the sound of the gospel" (D&C 84:114–15). Albany was a major city on the Hudson River, just south of where that river is joined by the Erie Canal in eastern New York. In the fall of 1832, Joseph Smith accompanied Bishop Whitney on a "hurried journey" to these cities and returned to Kirtland by November 6 (HC 1:295).

In 1866, Elder Orson Pratt predicted impending destruction on this triad of Albany, New York, and Boston (MS 28:633–34). It may be that these "great and magnificent cities," as Elder Pratt described them, are merely symbolic of the wicked cities of the world that will be destroyed and left desolate unless the inhabitants thereof repent.

All Heights and Depths

Those who enter into the new and everlasting covenant of marriage and are faithful to those covenants are promised that they "shall inherit thrones, kingdoms, principalities, and powers, dominions, all heights and depths" (D&C 132:19). This descriptive reward indicates that nothing will be withheld from such faithful followers of the Father. In the words of his Only Begotten Son, "all that my Father hath shall be given unto [them]" (D&C 84:38). "Then shall they be gods . . . because all things are subject unto them'' (D&C 132:20).

Almighty, The

The Lord is referred to as "the Almighty" twice in the Doctrine and Covenants (84:96; 121:33), although "Almighty God" (76:106–7), "Lord Almighty" (84:118), and "Lord God Almighty" (109:77) also appear. The title applies not only to Jesus the Son but also to Elohim the Father (D&C 20:21).

It signifies that Deity have all power and dominion. They are omnipotent. All things that can be done are within their power to do. They know all laws and control all elements. All things are created under their authority and are subject to that authority. They have all might. Each of the standard works refers to this title and the power it entails (for example, see Gen. 49:25; Rev. 1:8; Hel. 10:11; Moses 1:25).

See also: God; Jesus Christ

Alms

The word *alms* is mentioned in three of the standard works (see D&C 88:2; 112:1; 3 Ne. 13:1–4; Matt. 6:1–4). *Alms* comes from the Greek word meaning righteousness, or acts of religious devotion. Almsgiving is the act of donating to the poor, whether through organized religious and community activity or through one's own personal efforts.

Alpha and Omega

On thirteen occasions in the Doctrine and Covenants, Jesus refers to himself as "Alpha and Omega" (e.g., 19:1; 38:1; 63:60). In addition to these references, the title is also used in the Book of Mormon and the New Testament (3 Ne. 9:18; Rev. 1:8, 11; 21:6; 22:13). These terms represent the first and last letters of the Greek alphabet, the "beginning" and the "end." Christ's preeminent position among men is underscored by this title. All creatures are subject to him, first and last, for none shall be saved except in his name (Acts 4:12; 2 Ne. 25:20; Mosiah 3:17; 5:8).

See also: Beginning and the End, The; Jesus Christ

Alphus

The word *Alphus* is used to refer to the Lord in a revelation received June 1, 1833 (D&C 95:17). It is a derivative of the Greek word *alpha*, which is the first letter of that alphabet and denotes "the beginning." *Alphus* is the Greek word *alpha* with a Latin ending.

See also: Alpha and Omega; Beginning and the End, The; Jesus Christ

Altar That John Saw

Elder John Taylor, who was viciously wounded at the time of the martyrdoms of Joseph and

Hyrum Smith, wrote that the blood of these two martyrs was part of what John the Revelator saw under the altar of martyrs (D&C 135:7; Rev. 6:9–11). This altar was described in one Bible commentary as follows: "As the blood of the sacrificial victims slain on the altar was poured at the bottom of the altar, so the souls of those sacrificed for Christ's testimony are symbolically represented as under the altar in heaven" (DNTC 3:483).

In a sermon delivered in 1884, President John Taylor said that John, "under the inspiration of the Almighty, and filled with the light and intelligence of heaven, could gaze upon the position of things in the eternal worlds, and saw the souls of those who had been slain for the testimony of Jesus, and the word of God, etc. . . . His servants who have been called to lay down their lives, will come forth with crowns upon their heads and reign upon the earth." (JD 25:285.)

Amen

The word *amen* is familiar to all who have prayed or listened to prayers being offered. Jesus instructed his followers on two continents to conclude their prayers with the pronouncement, "amen" (Matt. 6:13; 3 Ne. 13:13). It is used over 150 times in the Doctrine and Covenants (e.g., sec. 1:39; 10:70; 20:4; 64:43; 136:42). It denotes acceptance or truthfulness (LDSBD, 607). Thus, Saints are encouraged to express

their acceptance of another's prayer, or words spoken under the influence of the Spirit, by uttering an audible amen at the conclusion of such words.

There is one particular usage of amen in the Doctrine and Covenants that denotes an ending or severance of previously held power and authority. Should a priesthood bearer fail to use his priesthood properly and then remain unrepentant, the Lord has declared, "Amen to the priesthood or the authority of that man" (D&C 121:37).

Amenable

An 1835 Declaration of Belief states: "We believe that religion is instituted of God; and that men are amenable to him" (D&C 134:4). Amenable in this passage means accountable or answerable.

America

While not mentioned by name in the Doctrine and Covenants, the Lord refers to America as a land which will be blessed because of the prayers of the faithful and in which the gospel might go forth and men might be free (D&C 10:49–51). This promise is *not* restricted to the United States or North America, but encompasses Central and South America as well.

Even though some citizens living in countries found in the Americas may be restricted in the exercise of political freedoms, the gospel will give them ultimate peace and freedom. The Church of Jesus Christ of Latter-day Saints, which had its birth in the land described by God as "choice above all other lands" (2 Ne. 1:5), is prophesied to become the greatest influence for good in the affairs of all nations.

See also: United States; Zion

Amherst, Ohio

While not directly mentioned in the revelations, Amherst, Ohio, is the location where section 75 was received. The town was in Lorain County, two counties west of the county in which Kirtland was located, and lay just south of Lake Erie. A conference of the Church convened at this site on January 25, 1832. "At this conference much harmony prevailed, and considerable business was done to advance the kingdom, and promulgate the Gospel to the inhabitants of the surrounding country," wrote the Prophet. (HC 1:242–43.) On this occasion, "Joseph Smith was sustained and ordained, by the will of the Lord, as President of the High Priesthood" (CHMR 1:274–75). Although Joseph held the keys of the priesthood, independent of a sustaining vote, the office of President belonged to the Church and necessitated a sustaining vote by the membership thereof (PCG, 255).

See also: President of the High Priesthood

Ancient of Days

Adam is referred to as the "ancient of days" in two revelations (D&C 116:1; 138:38). The Prophet Joseph Smith once declared: "Daniel in his seventh chapter speaks of the Ancient of Days; [Dan. 7:9]; he means the oldest man, our Father Adam, Michael, he will call his children together and hold a council with them to prepare them for the coming of the Son of Man. He (Adam) is the father of the human family, and presides over the spirits of all men, and all that have had the keys must stand before him in this grand council." (TPJS, 157.) Adam, the Ancient of Days, is "the first and oldest of all, the great, grand progenitor" (HC 4:207).

See also: Adam

Angel, The (#1)

In a great revelation on priesthood, it was revealed that John the Baptist "was ordained by the angel of God at the time he was eight days and unto this power, to overthrow the kingdom of the Jews, and to make straight the way of the Lord" (D&C 84:28). Regarding the identity of this angel, Smith and Sjodahl have written: "The angel who conferred upon John the power of the priesthood and the authority to overthrow the kingdom of the Jews, we do not know; but he was one commissioned with all the authority and power to confer these keys, and his name matters not'' (SS, 503).

Angel, The (#2)

In a revelation known as ''the appendix'' to the Doctrine and Covenants, the Lord said: ''For behold, the Lord God hath sent forth the angel crying through the midst of heaven, saying: Prepare ye the way of the Lord, and make his paths straight, for the hour of his coming is nigh'' (D&C 133:17). The footnote references to this verse refer to sections 13 and 27, the first of which specifically refers to John the Baptist and the second of which makes mention of him. Sidney B. Sperry wrote: ''That the angel referred to here as John the Baptist can scarcely be doubted in view of other scriptures (see 13:1; John 1:23; Isa. 40:3; Mal. 3:1; Matt. 11:7–10)'' (DCC, 303).

Angel Flying Through the Midst of Heaven

After quoting the prophecy that an ''angel . . . having the everlasting gospel'' was to appear on the earth (Rev. 14:6–7; see also D&C 133:6), Elder Rudger Clawson proclaimed: ''We believe and claim as a people, that that angel has come to the earth and appeared to Joseph Smith, in the person of Moroni, who delivered to the youthful Prophet a record familiarly known as the Book of Mormon, a record con-taining the fulness of the Gospel, with a message that [the] Gospel must be preached in every nation under the heavens before the end should come'' (CR, Apr. 1909, p. 92). The Lord affirmed that this angel had appeared to some, but would yet appear to *many*.

See also: Fifth Angel or Trump

Angel of God Who Was in Authority

The ''angel of God who was in authority in the presence of God'' is Lucifer (D&C 76:25–26). His pre-earthly status was of such significance that one-third of all our Father's spirit children were willing to cast their ballots in favor of his diabolical scheme to wrest total authority from God and assume the throne of ultimate power himself (D&C 29:36–38; Moses 4:1–4; Abr. 3:27–28). President Joseph Fielding Smith said, ''Just what authority Lucifer held before his rebellion we do not know, but he was an angel of light, his name, Lucifer, meaning torchbearer'' (CHMR 1:281).

See also: Angel of Light; Devil; Lucifer

Angel of Light

An unexplained incident is mentioned in section 128, in which Joseph Smith recounts an experience that occurred on the banks of the Susquehanna River: Michael, the archangel, detected ''the devil when he appeared as an angel of light" (D&C 128:20). This event might have occurred at the time John the Baptist, as a resurrected heavenly messenger, appeared to Joseph Smith and Oliver Cowdery to restore the Aaronic Priesthood (D&C 13). Satan, aware of the magnitude of this event and its consequent power in curtailing his demoniacal domain, may have appeared to fabricate a false and powerless priesthood. However, there is no revealed word as to what exactly took place, or when this event occurred.

Joseph Smith declared that not only the devil but also other ministering angels of his domain may appear as angels of light (TPJS, 162, 214; see also 2 Cor. 11:14–15). There are keys whereby these evil messengers might be discerned from true heavenly hosts. An angel from the devil may have colored hair and speak contradictory to previous revelation, although he may sprinkle his misleading message with elements of truth (TPJS, 214–15). Also, if you ask him to shake your hand, "he will offer you his hand, and you will not feel anything; you may therefore detect him" (D&C 129:8). Moses discerned Satan as a false angel of light: "Where is thy glory," he asked, "for it is *darkness* unto me?" (Moses 1:12–15; italics added). Perhaps this is why a prophet declared that the devil "transformed himself *nigh unto* an angel of light" (2 Ne. 9:9; italics added).

See also: Devil

Angels

The title of *angel*, or a derivative thereof, appears over eighty times in the Doctrine and Covenants. In some instances, the angel's identity is not made clear and is merely referred to as "another angel" (D&C 88:94). On other occasions, specific names are applied to angels, such as Michael and Moroni (D&C 88: 112; D&C 128:20). With the exception of references to Lucifer and his "angels" (e.g., D&C 29: 28, 37; 76:25; 129:8), the vast majority of references to angels refer to heavenly messengers with a divine commission to act in diverse assignments in behalf of Deity. They are "ministering servants of God" (TPJS, 312). The two types of heavenly angels presently ministering for the Lord are described in section 129.

In the hereafter, following the final judgment, those who qualify for exaltation shall be raised to the level of godhood, but others will qualify for a less exalted, eternal status as angels to the gods (TPJS, 312; D&C 132:15–21).

See also: Angel, The; Angel Flying Through the Midst of Heaven; Angel of God Who Was in Authority; Angel of Light; Angel's Time; Archangel; Destroying Angel; Fifth Angel; First Angel; Holy Angel, An; Innumerable Company of Angels; Keys of the Ministering of Angels; Ministering Angel; Ministering of Angels; Second Angel; Seventh Angel; Sixth Angel; Trump of the Angel of God

Angels' Time

In answer to the question as to how angels' time was reckoned, the Prophet Joseph said that it was according to the planet whereon they reside (D&C 130:4 −5). He further stated that "there are no angels who minister to this earth but those who do belong or have belonged to it." Therefore, the reckoning of time according to angels "who minister to this earth" would have to be according to the time frame of this earth; thus, twenty four hours equal one day, and 365 days equal one year. However, inasmuch as angels also traverse heavenly orbs and are in communication with God, whose reckoning of time is according to the celestial sphere known as Kolob—where a day is as one thousand of our years—they must reckon with at least a dual time frame (Abr. 3:1 −9; 2 Pet. 3:8).

See also: God's Time; Man's Time

Anger

An oft-repeated statement in scriptures is the Lord's declaration that his anger is kindled against the disobedient and wicked (e.g., Num. 11:33; 2 Kgs. 22:13, 17; 2 Ne. 15:25; Hel. 13:30; D&C 1:13; 56:1; 61:31; 84:24; Moses 6:27; 7:34). This is a figure of speech indicative of God's becoming angry or indignant.

A distinction should be made between the appropriate anger of God, which is a righteous application of the law of justice, and the unbridled anger of a fallible mortal. The Lord has consistently counseled his children against anger (Matt. 5:21−22; 3 Ne. 11:21−11); furthermore, we have been instructed that the devil "is the father of contention, and he stirreth up the hearts of men to contend with anger, one with another" (3 Ne. 11:29). One who is angry loses the Spirit and his love of his fellowman (Moro. 9:3−5).

In contrast, properly understood, God's anger is a divine display of his love. It is a manifestation of truth. (See 2 Ne. 1:24−27.)

See also: Contention; Justice; Stir Up the Hearts

Anointed

The word *anointed* has several usages as it appears in latter-day revelations. There are several instances in which the term is used to refer to the *authority* which has been or will be bestowed on certain individuals or holders of high offices in the Church. The office of Presiding Bishop is mentioned in this regard, as well as the position of counselor in the First Presidency (D&C 68:20; 124:91). The Lord spoke of Vinson Knight as having been "chosen and anointed," but no clarification is given of the particular meaning thereof (D&C 124:76).

In the dedicatory prayer of the Kirtland Temple, the Prophet Joseph prayed for "these, thine anointed ones" (D&C 109:80). A previously published cross-reference to this verse referred to verse 35 of the same section, which may have reference to those officially called to labor in the ministry. Another cross-reference referred to 124:39, which appears to speak of those who have received anointings within the temple.

There is a single reference to "thine Anointed," which specifically applies to the Savior, who interceded in behalf of his fallible brothers and sisters (D&C 109:53).

Finally, the Lord speaks of his prophet and the President of his church as "mine anointed" (D&C 132:7, 18, 19). Elder John Taylor compared Joseph Smith with "the Lord's anointed in ancient times" (D&C 135:3). It is in this capacity that the phrase is most often used in our day; that is, when we speak of "the Lord's anointed," we speak of his living prophet.

Anointings

The anointings referred to in Doctrine and Covenants 124:39 are sacred ordinances that pertain to exaltation in the celestial kingdom. These are performed only within holy houses of the Lord — temples — by authorized servants of God.

Antiquities

Section 124 speaks of building both a "house for boarding" (the Nauvoo House; see 124:23) and of "a house to my name [temple; see 124:27], for the Most High to dwell therein." In order to accomplish these building projects, the Lord asked that swift and chosen messengers be sent out to gather gold, silver, precious stones, antiquities, and the precious trees of the earth. Sperry says that antiquities are heirlooms. "Those who have knowledge of antiquities, such as rare pieces of furniture, tableware, art, and the like, are to come and bring with them such pieces as they can for the Temple, including rare woods from different parts of the world." (DCC, 650.)

Apocrypha

On March 9, 1833, while working on an inspired revision of the Bible, the Prophet Joseph inquired of the Lord regarding the authenticity of that body of writings known as the Apocrypha. In response to his inquiry, Joseph was told that "there are many things contained therein that are true, and it is mostly translated correctly." However, cautioned the Lord, "There are many things contained therein that are not true, which are interpolations by the hands of men." The revelation further pointed out that the means whereby man would know whether the apocryphal writings were true or false was to utilize the spirit of discernment. (D&C 91.)

Apocryphal writings are those which are of ancient origin but of doubtful authenticity. They have been grouped by biblical scholars into a collection which usually includes the following: 1 and 2 Esdras (sometimes called 3 and 4 Esdras); Tobit; Judith; additional chapters to the book of Esther; Wisdom of Solomon; Ecclesiasticus, or the Wisdom of Jeshua, Son of Sirach; Baruch and the Epistle of Jeremiah; Song of the Three Holy Children; History of Susanna; History of the Destruction of Bel and the Dragon; Prayer of Manasseh; and 1 and 2 Maccabees.

To those who contemplate studying the Apocrypha, the following admonition is given: "Obviously, *to gain any real value from a study of apocryphal writings, the student must first have an extended background of gospel knowledge, a comprehensive understanding of the standard works of the Church, plus the guidance of the Spirit* (MD, 42).

See also: Interpolations

Apollos

Speaking of the inhabitants of the telestial kingdom, the Lord said they were those who "are of Paul, and of Apollos, and of Cephas. These are they who say they are some of one and some of another." (D&C 76:99–100.) The only scriptural references to Apol-

los appear in the New Testament, where he is described as a Jew born at Alexandria, "an eloquent man, and mighty in the scriptures" (Acts 18:24). He had evidently been a disciple of John the Baptist and was devoted more to this *forerunner* of Christ than the *fulness of the Savior's gospel*. Once having been taught the fulness, he became a faithful follower of the Master and even proselyted with Paul (Acts 18:24–19:6; 1 Cor. 16:12).

The former position of Apollos typifies those who adhere to a small segment of the gospel plan while rejecting its fulness. These "received not the gospel, neither the testimony of Jesus, neither the prophets, neither the everlasting covenant. . . . Where God and Christ dwell they cannot come, worlds without end." (D&C 76:101, 112.)

In his later ministry, Apollos evidently brought into the fold some whom Paul had initially taught, and rivalry appeared to have arisen between the converts of Paul and the converts of Apollos. Paul reminded them that it mattered not who "planted" and who "watered," for "God gave the increase. So then neither is he that planteth anything, neither he that watereth." He cautioned these *disciples of men* that they were still caught up in carnality and must repent if they intended to reap the rewards of righteousness —even the kingdom of God. (1 Cor. 1:10–15; 3.)

See also: Cephas; Some of One and Some of Another

Apostates and Apostatize

The word *apostasy* does not appear in the Doctrine and Covenants; however, *apostate* (86:3), *apostates* (85:2), and *apostatize* (85:2, 11) are mentioned. Webster defines *apostasy* as "a renunciation or abandonment of a former loyalty." An apostate is one who follows such a course. "How does apostasy come about?" asked President Joseph Fielding Smith. "By neglect of duty, failing to keep in our souls the spirit of prayer, [dis]obedience to the principles of the Gospel; by failure to pay an honest tithing, or to observe the word of wisdom, and to absent one's self from sacrament meetings where we have been commanded to go and renew our covenants. Apostasy comes through the sins of omission as well as through sins of commission. Immorality is a deadly sin, and those who are guilty, if they do not repent, will lose the spirit and deny the faith. Apostasy does not come upon an individual suddenly, but it is a gradual growth in which darkness through sin crowds out the spirit of light from the soul. When a man who was once enlightened loses the Spirit of truth, the darkness which takes its place is overwhelming." (CHMR 2:125.)

Elder Thomas E. McKay quipped, "We do not lose our faith from a blowout—just by slow leaks" (En., Feb. 1971, p. 80). Criticism of Church leaders, according to Joseph Smith, was a sure sign one was "in the high road to apostasy" (TPJS, 156–57). "The basic cause of apostasy is sin," said Elder Bruce R. McConkie. "Men leave the Church because they are sensual and carnal. . . . The basic reason for rebellion against the truth is a desire to enjoy the lusts of the flesh. The choice is not between doctrinal concepts but between differing ways of life." (DNTC 3:426–27.)

Apostle

The Lord declared that Joseph Smith and Oliver Cowdery were Apostles by virtue of their having had the Melchizedek Priesthood conferred on them by the ancient apostolic First Presidency (D&C 20:2–3; 27:12). President Joseph Fielding Smith stated that the two men were not *ordained* to the specific office of Apostle within the priesthood, but rather received the priesthood out of which all offices pertaining to priesthood proceed. By virtue of that priesthood and their callings as "special witnesses of Jesus Christ," they were Apostles, *"the only men among men who could testify from knowledge and personal contact as did the Twelve in the meridian of time"* (DS 3:147). Joseph *"became a special witness for Christ, and thus an apostle,"* in the spring of 1820, when he became "the only *witness* among men who could testify with knowledge that God lives and Jesus Christ is verily his Son" (DS 3:146). Others, who have been sent forth with a special ministry, have been called Apostles by revelation but without specific ordination and keys (D&C 84:63–64; DS 3:144–46).

Various titles have been applied to men who are referred to as Apostles in the Doctrine and Covenants. An Apostle is one who takes upon him the name of Christ "with full purpose of heart" (18:27). He is an "elder" (20:38); he is a "special witness of the name of Christ" (20:2–3; 107:23–26); he is a "traveling high councilor" or a member of the "Traveling Presiding High Council" (102:30; 107:23, 33, 38; 124:139); he is one of "God's high priests," one whom the Father has given to Christ, and a "friend" of the Savior (84:63); he is one of "the Twelve" (18:26–36; 107:26, 33); and he is one of the "sowers of the seed" mentioned in the parable of the wheat and the tares (86:2; Matt. 13:24–43). An Apostle is one whose word is binding, for as he speaks "so shall it come to pass" (29:10). They who will not "give heed to the words of the prophets and apostles, shall be cut off from among the people," declared the Lord (1:14).

Anciently, the apostolic Quorum of the Twelve had been established by Jesus during his mortal ministry (Mark 3:14; Luke 6:12–13) and had been perpetuated after his death and resurrection (Acts 1:23–26). Paul was called as an Apostle, "though not one of the Twelve" (GT 1:250; D&C 18:9; Rom. 1:1). Barnabas (Acts 14:14) and James, "the Lord's brother" (Gal. 1:19), are also spoken of as Apostles in the New Testament. However, the original Church gradually drifted into apostasy and authorized apostolic authority was removed from the earth until such time as the Lord would sanction its return.

In June 1829, the Lord commissioned the Three Witnesses of the Book of Mormon to "search out the Twelve" (D&C 18:37). Finally, on February 14, 1835, the Quorum of the Twelve Apostles was organized anew upon the earth, never again to be removed (HC 2:185–200). Ordained members of this quorum are given every key necessary to preside over the kingdom of God here on earth. The Lord designated this quorum as "equal in authority and power" to the First Presidency (D&C 107:22–24). However, "the Twelve are equal to the First Presidency only when the First Presidency are absent" (GT 1:291).

This relationship is made clear in the following statement by Joseph Fielding Smith: "The Prophet [Joseph Smith], in anticipation of his death, conferred upon the Twelve all the keys and authorities which he held. He did not bestow the keys on any one member, but upon them *all*, so that *each held the keys* and authorities. All members of the Council of the Twelve since that day have also been given all of these keys and powers. But these powers cannot be exercised by any one of them *until*, if the occasion arises, he is called to be the *presiding officer* of the Church. The Twelve, therefore, in the setting apart of the President do not give him any additional priesthood, but *confirm* upon him that which he has *already* received; they *set him apart* to the office, which it is their right to do." (DS 3:155.) President George Q. Cannon made the same observation at an earlier date: "It is not necessary that an Apostle should be ordained to stand at the head of the people. When the exigency arises, he has already got the fulness of authority and the power of it." (GT 1:266-67.)

The "business" of the Twelve is always whatever "the president of the Church delegates" to them (SYHP, 156). For, "while the Twelve are associated with him, one in power, one in authority, they must respect him as their President, they must look to him as the man through whom the voice of God will come to them and to this entire people" (GT 1:266).

See also: Equal in Authority; President of the High Priesthood; Special Witnesses; Traveling Presiding High Council; Twelve, The

Appendages

Webster defines *appendage* as "something attached to a greater thing." The Doctrine and Covenants describes the position of the Melchizedek Priesthood, indicating that "all other authorities or offices in the church are appendages to this priesthood" (107:5). Thus, the Aaronic Priesthood "is called the lesser priesthood . . . because it is an appendage to the greater" (107:14).

In section 84, the Lord refers to the offices of bishop and elder as being "necessary appendages belonging unto the high priesthood," and the offices of teacher and deacon as being "necessary appendages belonging to the lesser priesthood" (84:29–30). Smith and Sjodahl state that "while it is here stated that these offices are 'necessary appendages' to the Priesthood, this does not signify, as some have supposed, that the other offices in the Priesthoods are not appendages. All the offices grow out of, and are appendages to the Priesthood as well as those mentioned here." (SS, 504.)

President Joseph F. Smith emphatically declared: "There is no office growing out of this Priesthood that is or can be greater than the Priesthood itself. It is from the Priesthood that the office derives its authority and power. No office gives authority to the Priesthood. No office adds to the power of the Priesthood." (GD, 148.)

Appointed unto Death

The Lord promises that those who have faith to be healed shall be healed if they are "not appointed unto death" (D&C 42:48). According to the Old Testament, "To every thing there is a season. . . . A time to be born, and a time to die." (Eccl. 3:1–2.) If the "times" of our "habitation" are determined by the Lord (Acts 17:26), it appears that, for the most part, the days of our earthly experiences—both arrival and departure—are known. President Joseph Fielding Smith proclaimed, "No righteous man is ever taken before his time" (CN, Nov. 6, 1971, C-3).

"I believe and know," declared Elder Gordon B. Hinckley, "that the death of no man of God is ever untimely. Our Father sets the time." (En., Feb. 1974, p. 90.) "The death of his servants," added President Spencer W. Kimball, "is in the power and control of the Lord" (CR, Oct. 1972, p. 29). This "appointed time" can, of course, be cut short by foolish actions on man's part, but it appears that as long as one is living faithfully and has a mission that must yet be fulfilled, his life will be preserved until he is "appointed unto death."

See also: Dead That Die in the Lord

Archangel

Adam, the first man on this earth, was known in pre-earth life as Michael, the archangel (HC 4:207–8; D&C 29:26; 107:54; 128:21). He successfully led the Lord's legions in battle against the devil and his evil forces (Rev. 12:7–9; D&C 29:36–37). The pre-

fix *arch* means chief or preeminent or "most fully embodying the qualities of his kind." Thus, Adam, in his role as the pre-earthly Michael, "was the chief angel, but not Deity. He embodied most fully the qualities of an angelic existence. He was preeminent among the angels. He was their leader." (AWIH, 7.)

However, he was subservient to Jesus Christ, for as Joseph Smith proclaimed, "Angels are under the direction of Michael, or Adam, who acts under the direction of the Lord" (HC 4:208; D&C 78:15–16). Having defeated the devil's designs for usurping authority on several occasions (D&C 29:36–37; 128:20), it is appropriate that this archangel, Michael, will proclaim the binding of Satan during the seventh period of earth's history, known as the Millennium (D&C 88:108-12). At the conclusion of this period, the archangel will lead the hosts of heaven to final victory over the devil and his hosts of hell (D&C 88:111–15).

See also: Adam; Michael; Seventh Angel

Ark of God, Steady the

The phrase *steady the ark of God* is found frequently in sermons dealing with authority and unauthorized attempts to usurp that authority. It originated in the Old Testament story of a man named Uzza, who "put forth his hand to hold the ark'' and was struck dead because of his unauthorized encroachment on the sanctity of this sacred symbol (1 Chron. 13:9–10).

The "ark of the covenant" was an oblong chest, built according to divine specifications, which contained the sacred "testimony" which God had given to Moses on Sinai (Ex. 25). It may also have held the rod of Aaron. Although Uzza's intentions to steady the ark were noble, he had no authority to do so. His death serves as a warning that the Lord will not tolerate forays into fields of labor in which we are unauthorized to serve.

"And thou shalt not command him who is at thy head," declared the Lord (D&C 28:6). Each is to stand firm within his designated stewardship, for therein lies accountability. This is the message the Lord was giving to Bishop Edward Partridge when he was cautioned about putting "forth his hand to steady the ark of God" (D&C 85:8). For a short time, this bishop had concerned himself with the business of the *Prophet*. These actions necessitated a reprimand and warning from the Lord that unless he repented, he would "fall by the shaft of death" and be replaced by "one mighty and strong" (D&C 85:7). It is to his eternal credit that he heeded the warning.

See also: One Mighty and Strong; Partridge, Edward; Shaft of Death; That Man

Arm

See: Arm of Flesh; Arm of the Lord; Arms of My Love; Bare His Holy Arm; Mercy

Arm of Flesh

In his preface to the Doctrine and Covenants, the Lord declared, "Man should not counsel his fellow man, neither trust in his arm of flesh" (D&C 1:19). Similarly, an ancient prophet proclaimed, "I know that cursed is he that putteth his trust in the arm of flesh" (2 Ne. 4:34). *The arm of flesh represents mortal man and the "wisdom of the wise" of this world* (D&C 76:9; 2 Ne. 9:28), and is thus contrary to the whisperings of the Spirit.

Elder Boyd K. Packer observed: "There are too many in the Church who seem to be totally dependent, emotionally and spiritually, upon others. They subsist on some kind of emotional welfare. They are unwilling to sustain themselves. They become so dependent that they endlessly need to be shored up, lifted up, endlessly need encouragement, and they contribute little of their own.

"It is critically important that you understand that you already know right from wrong, that you're innately, inherently, and intuitively good. When you say, 'I can't! I can't solve my problems!' I want to thunder out, 'Don't you realize who you are?

Haven't you learned yet that you are a son or a daughter of Almighty God? Do you not know that there are powerful resources inherited from him that you can call upon to give you steadiness and courage and great power?' '' (DSY, 1975, pp. 346, 355.)

Depending on the Spirit does not mean that counseling from our fellowmen should be avoided. Elder Packer noted that ''there should not be the slightest embarrassment on the part of any member of the Church who needs counsel to receive that counsel. At times it may be crucial that you seek and that you accept counsel.'' (Ibid, p. 354.) The key to accepting counseling appears in the Book of Mormon: ''Cursed is he that putteth his trust in man, or maketh flesh his arm, or shall hearken unto the precepts of men, *save their precepts shall be given by the power of the Holy Ghost*'' (2 Ne. 28:31; italics added).

See also: Wisdom of the Wise

Arm of Mercy

See: Mercy

Arm of the Lord

On several occasions the Lord has warned the wicked and rebellious that they shall know and feel the power of his arm if they remain unrepentant (D&C 1:13–16; 45:47; 56:1). In this sense, his holy arm is symbolic of the power with which he administers divine justice. In another sense, his arm represents the divine authority invested in his servants as they take the gospel to his children and gather scattered Israel to his fold (D&C 35:13–14; 1 Ne. 22:10–11). Thus, his arm may prove to be a blessing or a curse depending upon one's desire for and state of righteousness.

One thing is certain: none shall escape his arm, for it ''is over all the earth'' and ''is not shortened'' (D&C 15:2; 35:8). In the words of Elder Neal A. Maxwell, ''His grasp is galactic'' (CR, Apr. 1976, p. 39). There is no corner of the universe into which his arm cannot reach.

See also: Bare His Holy Arm

Arms of My Love

''Be faithful and diligent in keeping the commandments of God,'' the Lord declared, ''and I will encircle thee in the arms of my love'' (D&C 6:20). To be encircled in the arms of the Lord's love is to feel the warm and spiritually sustaining effect or influence of his love.

Army, The

In giving instructions to those pioneers who were to take their trek to the western part of the United States, the Lord reminded them of their obligation to take care of ''the poor, the widows, the fatherless, and the families of those who have gone into *the army''* (D&C 136:8; italics added). This latter group had reference to those families whose husbands and brothers had responded to the call for volunteers in the war between Mexico and the United States and became known as the Mormon Battalion. They were organized at Council Bluffs, Iowa, on July 16, 1846, and began their official march from Fort Leavenworth, Kansas, on August 12, 1846.

Brigham Young promised the battalion they would not have to fight the Mexicans; this prophecy was fulfilled. The battalion's only battle was with a herd of wild bulls that attacked them. By the time this faithful little army arrived in San Diego, California, on January 29, 1847, they had covered a distance of over two thousand miles. (LDS, 305; ECH, 347–55.)

Army of Israel

At a time when its meaning might have been misunderstood by enemies of the Church—the revelation having come at the end of the military march of Zion's Camp from Ohio to Missouri—the Saints were referred to as the "army of Israel" which would become "very great" (D&C 105:26). Though this is the only time it appears in the Doctrine and Covenants, this phrase is common in Mormon parlance. Members of The Church of Jesus Christ of Latter-day Saints are familiar with such hymnal phrases

as: "Behold! A royal army, With banner, sword, and shield,/Is marching forth to conquer On life's great battle field./It's ranks are filled with soldiers, United, bold, and strong,/Who follow their Commander And sing their joyful song." ("Behold! A Royal Army," *Hymns*, no. 251.) "Hope of Israel, Zion's army, Children of the promised day,/See, the Chieftain signals onward, And the battle's in array!" ("Hope of Israel," *Hymns*, no. 259.) "We are all enlisted till the conflict is o'er; Happy are we!/Happy are we! Soldiers in the army, there's a bright crown in store;/We shall win and wear it by and by. Haste to the battle, quick to the field;/Truth is our helmet, buckler, and shield." ("We Are All Enlisted," *Hymns*, no. 250.)

Perhaps a summary statement of the meaning of such phrases is found in the following remarks by Elder Bruce R. McConkie: "As members of the Church, we are engaged in a mighty conflict. We are at war. We have enlisted in the cause of Christ to fight against Lucifer and all that is lustful and carnal and evil in the world. We have sworn to fight alongside our friends and against our enemies. . . . In this war all who do not stand forth courageously and valiantly are by that fact alone aiding the cause of the enemy." (CR, Oct. 1974, 43–44.) Thus, the *soldiers* of the army of Israel are the *individual members of the Church*. Their actions upon the battle-fields of life will determine the "rank" and "medals of valor" which will be their inheritance in the hereafter.

Army with Banners

On three occasions in the Doctrine and Covenants the Church is described as "clear as the moon, and fair as the sun, and terrible as an army with banners" (D&C 5:14; 105:31; 109:73). This same terminology is used in the Old Testament in poetically describing a woman by the name of Shulamite (Song 6:4, 10).

According to one commentary, the phrase means that the Church is "indescribably beautiful, but at the same time inaccessible to flatterers, unconquerable, as an army under banners" (SS, 27–28). Though the phrase comes from a book which the Prophet Joseph described as uninspired, Smith and Sjodahl state that "this beautiful expression, it is reasonable to suppose, is not original with this uninspired book and, we may well suppose, was a current expression in ancient times."

Banners are symbolic standards that serve as rallying points for eager followers and often strike terror in the hearts of those who oppose the values for which they stand. They are often used for their emotional effect. For example, Captain Moroni used a banner known as the "Title of Liberty" to effectively rally his people to a righteous cause (see Alma 46).

In our day, a veritable army of missionaries goes forth throughout the earth seeking to rally people to the cause of Christ under the banner of his priesthood and Church. This banner is indeed "terrible" to the evil ones of the world, for it proclaims an end to their wicked ways.

Ashery

In an effort to initially disguise its identity from the outside world, the Lord referred to the ashery in Kirtland as "Shule" (D&C 104:39; pre-1981 edition). The ashery was a building where soap was made (DCC, 542). "Shule" no longer appears in current editions of the Doctrine and Covenants.

See also: Shule

Ashley, Major N.

At a conference held in Amherst, Ohio, in January 1832, a number of the elders expressed a desire to know what the Lord had in mind for them to do. In response to the inquiry of the Prophet Joseph, Major N. Ashley was informed that he was to take his missionary journey into the south, along with Burr Riggs (D&C 75:17). No additional mention of Ashley is found in the Prophet's subsequent writings.

Asia

In the Vision of the Redemption of the Dead, President Joseph F. Smith pondered on the "primitive saints scattered throughout . . . Asia" (D&C 138:5). In New Testament times this referred to "the Roman province that included the western parts of what is now called Asia Minor" (LDSBD, 615).

Assent unto My Death

See: Crucified Him unto Themselves

Atonement

A revelation given in January 1832 to Joseph Smith and Sidney Rigdon speaks of the "perfect atonement through the shedding of [Christ's] own blood" (D&C 76:69). The word *atonement* appears twice more in the Doctrine and Covenants (74:7; 138:4); a derivative appears once (29:1). Nevertheless, the doctrine of the Atonement is, in the words of Elder James E. Talmage, "the fundamental doctrine of all scripture, the very essence of the spirit of prophecy and revelation, the most prominent of all the declarations of God unto man" (AF, 77). Of course, the title *Redeemer* and variations of that word are generously sprinkled through the revelations of the Doctrine and Covenants.

"The structure of the word in its present form is suggestive of the true meaning; it is literally *at-one-ment*, 'denoting reconciliation, or the bringing into agreement of those who have been estranged'" (AF, 75). Through the fall of Adam, mankind became "estranged" from God, subject to both temporal and spiritual death (Alma 42:7). Of necessity, One was appointed to reconcile the demands of mercy and justice and pay the ransom of death and hell (2 Ne. 9:6–13; DS 1:124–26). "Not only did he redeem us from Adam's transgression, but he also redeemed us from our own sins, on condition that we obey the laws and ordinances of the gospel" (DS 1:121).

Christ was the only being qualified to pay such a ransom. He was qualified because it was his divine appointment, bestowed on him in the pre-earth life (1 Pet. 1:19–20; MA, 97). He became the Only Begotten of the Father, with power to retain or lay down his life (D&C 49:5; John 10:15–18); his could be the only sinless sacrifice, for he alone never succumbed to sin (D&C 20:22; 45:4; Heb. 4:15).

He voluntarily shed his blood in Gethsemane for our sins (Luke 22:44; D&C 19:15–20; DS 1:130) and likewise allowed his blood to be shed on Calvary in order that death might be conquered and the resurrection brought to pass (Mosiah 16:6–8). "To the last He had the means of terminating the tortures of His persecutors by the exercise of His inherent powers" (AF, 78; Matt. 26:51–54).

His supreme example of self-restraint is a model to those who selfishly struggle on smaller scales, such as is mentioned in the Sermon on the Mount (Matt. 5:38–44).

"The motive inspiring and sustaining Him through all the scenes of His mission, from the time of His primeval ordination to the moment of victorious consummation on the cross, was two-fold: first, the desire to do His Father's will in accomplishing the redemption of mankind; second, His love for humanity, of whose welfare and destiny He had assumed charge" (AF, 80; 3 Ne. 27:13; John 13:34).

The nature of this sacrifice was discussed by President John Taylor: "In some mysterious, incomprehensible way, Jesus assumed the responsibility which naturally would have devolved upon Adam; but which could only be accomplished through the mediation of Himself, and by taking upon Himself their sorrows, assuming their responsibilities, and bearing their transgressions or sins. In a manner to us incomprehensible and inexplicable, He bore the weight of the sins of the whole world; not only of Adam, but of His posterity; and in doing that, opened the kingdom of heaven, not only to all believers and all who obeyed the law of God, but to more than one-half of the human family who die before they come to years of maturity, as well as to the heathen, who, having died without law, will through His mediation, be resurrected without law, and be judged without law, and thus participate, according to their capacity, works and worth, in the blessings of His atonement." (MA, 148–49.)

See also: Advocate with the Father; Bitter Cup; Bleed at Every Pore; Eternal Life; Fall, The; Grace; Immortality; Jesus Christ; Justice; Justification; Mercy; Redemption; Resurrection; Resurrection of the Just; Resurrection of the Unjust; Rid Their Garments; Salvation; Saved; Shrink

Authority of the Priesthood

The prophet Isaiah admonished Zion to put on her "strength" (Isa. 52:1; D&C 113:7; 2 Ne. 8:24; 3 Ne. 20:36). According to Joseph Smith, this refers to her putting on "the authority of the priesthood" (D&C 113:8).

The authority of the priesthood is the authorization for duly ordained mortals to legally administer the affairs of God, to act as his authorized agent. An ordinance performed or declaration made by one acting fully within this authority would be as if the Lord himself were present. For example, in speaking to one to preach the gospel, he said: "And I will lay my hand upon you by the hand of my servant" (D&C 36:2). This authority comes *only* through proper channels; it is not self-initiated: "We believe that a man must be called of God, by prophecy, and by the laying on of hands, by those who are in authority to preach the Gospel and administer in the ordinances thereof" (Articles of Faith 1:5; AF, 179–97). The Apostle Paul stated this principle well in his epistle to the Hebrews: "And no man taketh this honour unto himself, but he that is called of God, as was Aaron'' (Heb. 5:4).

"The Priesthood," said Bishop H. Burke Peterson, ''is the authority to perform our duties in the same way the Savior would if he had our individual responsibility. Our authority is limited to doing it the way he would.'' (CR, Oct. 1974, p. 99.) In addition to this, it should be kept in mind that priesthood authority limits one to the particular area of stewardship over which one has jurisdiction. A word of caution, however—*authority* does not necessarily bestow *power* of the priesthood.

See also: Power of Priesthood

Ax Is Laid at the Root of the Trees

Alma declared that ''the Spirit saith: Behold, the ax is laid at the root of the tree; therefore every tree that bringeth not forth good fruit shall be hewn down and cast into the fire'' (Alma 5:52). A little over a century later, in a confrontation with the Pharisees and Sadducees—they who relied so heavily on their lineage back to Abraham—John the Baptist was to invoke the same statement. Furthermore, he reminded them that their lofty lineage would not secure a place for them among the branches of Abraham's tree, for the faithful would be the only foliage thereon. (Matt. 3:7–10; JST, Matt. 3:34–37.) The spiritually decayed branches would have the ax (judgmental decrees of Deity) laid at their roots, and they would be severed from Abraham's bosom and God's presence.

Centuries later, the Lord once again reminded the wicked that they will be severed by an ax laid at their roots unless they bring forth "fruit meet for repentance" (D&C 97:7).

B

Babbitt, Almon

The only mention of Almon Babbitt in the Doctrine and Covenants is very condemning, for the Lord proclaims his displeasure with him. Babbitt was inclined to establish his own counsel above that of the Presidency of the Church: "and he setteth up a golden calf for the worship of my people," declared the Lord (D&C

124:84). Of this rebuke, Smith and Sjodahl have written: "From these verses it may be gathered that his chief ambition was to make money, and that he advised the Saints to leave Nauvoo, contrary to the counsel of the Church leaders. Perhaps he was interested in the sale of land elsewhere. In any event, when the Saints left Nauvoo, he was appointed one of the real estate agents in whose hands the abandoned property was left, to be disposed of on the best terms obtainable. How he discharged this duty, we may infer from the following statement of Elder Heber C. Kimball: 'My house was sold at $1,700, intended to be used to help gather the Saints; but Almon W. Babbitt put it in his pocket, I suppose.' " (SS, 784; JD 8:350.)

Though he served as a member of Zion's Camp (HC 2:183), presided over the stake at Kirtland (HC 4:204, 361), and was presiding elder at Ramus, Illinois (HC 5:302-3), there were many evidences of his rebellion, which eventually led to his being officially disfellowshipped from the Church in October 1841. He was restored to full fellowship in April 1843. He became a member of the "utility committee" appointed to sell properties when Nauvoo was abandoned (HC 7:474), but, as previously mentioned, he appeared to violate that trust.

In 1846 Babbitt was one of the leaders in the Church at Kanesville, Iowa. He was actively involved in seeking to have Utah admitted to the Union as a state (BYUS 10:489).

Babes and Sucklings

A *babe* is an infant and a *suckling* is an unweaned child who is still feeding from the breast. The Prophet Joseph Smith stated that "things which never have been revealed from the foundation of the world, but have been kept hid from the wise and prudent, shall be revealed unto babes and sucklings in this, the dispensation of the fulness of times" (D&C 128:18). This metaphorical expression indicates that those whom the world might consider as immature or weak in knowledge will have revealed to them things which the wise and prudent in the world will not know.

Certainly the unlettered Joseph Smith was a *babe* in the eyes of the world, yet no man has provided the world with more recorded eternal truths, revelation, and scripture from God, than did he.

See also: Prudent; Smith, Joseph, Jr.; Understanding of the Prudent; Weak Things of the Earth/World; Wisdom of the Wise; Wise

Babylon

"Ancient Babylon was noted for its wickedness and cruelty among the peoples that it dominated. Therefore, it became a symbol of the wicked world of its day. The Lord uses it in . . . revelation to typify our modern world." (DCC, 289.) He defined the "midst of wickedness" as "spiritual Babylon" (D&C 133:14). The name *Babylon* is of Greek origin and signifies "confusion." Those who choose citizenship in Babylon, loving the ways of the world in preference to the light of the Lord, are "walking in darkness at noon-day" (D&C 95:6). Is this not confusion and folly? The plea to come forth out of Babylon (D&C 133:5, 7, 14) is the clarion call to modern Israel to escape from the Babylonian bondage of wickedness to the freedom and light of the gospel of Jesus Christ (D&C 45:9; 50:24; 88:86).

See also: Idumea; Kingdoms of the World; World

Backbiting

One responsibility of most priesthood bearers is to see that there is no "backbiting" (D&C 20:54). To backbite is to revile against one who is not present, to slander or speak evil of one who is absent. Thus, a backbiter attacks one whose physical absence denies him the opportunity of defending himself.

Baker, Jesse

In January 1841, Jesse Baker was called by revelation to serve as the second counselor in the elders quorum presidency in Nauvoo (D&C 124:137). More than two and one-half years later he was again sustained as a counselor in the presidency of the elders quorum at Nauvoo during the October conference of the Church, presided over by Brigham Young and the Twelve (HC 7:297). The only other mention of him in published documents is his participation in the Kirtland Camp, which was one of the last organized groups to leave Kirtland, Ohio, for Missouri in the summer of 1838 (HC 3:92).

Baldwin, Wheeler

One of the little-known men of early Church history is Wheeler Baldwin. He is mentioned but once in the Doctrine and Covenants, when he is called to take a mission to Missouri along with William Carter (D&C 52:31). This was in June 1831. His presence among the Saints is still evident in March 1840, when he is mentioned as a member of a committee of three, which included Lyman Wight and Abraham O. Smoot, who were "to obtain affidavits and other documents to be forwarded to the city of Washington" regarding the grievances and needs of the Saints (HC 4:94).

He did not remain true to the faith founded by the Prophet Joseph Smith and later affiliated with an organization founded by men rather than by God (*The Saints' Herald* 6:138).

Bands of Death

The phrase *band* or *bands of death* is found in both the Doctrine and Covenants and the Book of Mormon (D&C 138:16; Morm. 9:13) and refers to the bondage which a disembodied spirit experiences. *Bands of death* is synonymous with *cords of death* (D&C 121:44). President Joseph F. Smith, in his vision of the redemption of the dead, described the anxiousness with which the dead await the reuniting of their spirits with their bodies on their appointed day of resurrection. Because of the Atonement, death must yield her captives and the bands are forever broken (2 Ne. 9:11). Body and spirit will "be united never again to be divided, that they might receive a fulness of joy" (D&C 138:17).

Baneemy

The unique name of "Baneemy" is employed to refer to the elders of the Church in an 1834 revelation (D&C 105:27; pre-1981 edition). The use of such pseudonyms was common when the Lord wanted to hide the true identity of certain individuals from the world (HC 1:255). In current editions of the Doctrine and Covenants, this name no longer appears.

Banner of Liberty

In writing of the martyrdoms of Joseph and Hyrum Smith, Elder John Taylor said that their *"innocent blood* on the banner of liberty . . . of the United States, is an ambassador for the religion of Jesus Christ, that will touch the hearts of honest men among all nations." (D&C 135:7.) The "banner of liberty" is symbolic of the freedoms upon which America—the land of liberty—was founded and which are proudly unfurled and displayed to the rest of the world.

One of the constitutionally guaranteed rights of this nation is that of freedom of worship. Yet just and righteous men— prophets of God—were denied this right of worship, and their martyrs' blood stains the banner of liberty.

See also: Liberty

Banners

See: Army with Banners; Banner of Liberty

Baptism

"Baptism," said Joseph Smith, "is a sign to God, to angels, and to heaven that we do the will of God, and there is no other way beneath the heavens whereby God hath ordained for man to come to Him to be saved, and enter into the Kingdom of God, except faith in Jesus Christ, repentance, and baptism for the remission of sins, and any other course is in vain; then you have the promise of the gift of the Holy Ghost" (TPJS, 198).

Baptism by water is an ordinance as ancient as Adam, as far as this world is concerned (Moses 6:58–68). It fulfills at least the following purposes: it brings about a remission of sins (D&C 13; 19:31; 20:37; 33:11; 49:13; 68:27; 84:27, 64; 107:20); it admits the repentant person into the Church, or kingdom of God on earth (D&C 20:37, 71–74); it is the gate to the celestial kingdom (2 Ne. 9:23–24; 31:13–21; John 3:5; TPJS, 12); and it opens the way for one to receive the Holy Ghost and become sanctified or spotless before God (3 Ne. 27:20; 28:18; TPJS, 148; MD, 70).

Inasmuch as repentance is required for baptism (TPJS, 314), it follows that one must be *accountable* before God for his actions. The *age of accountability* has been defined by the Lord as eight years old (D&C 68:27; JST, Gen. 17:11). The Lord has severely rebuked the practice of infant baptism (Moro. 8). Of further necessity in validating one's baptism is the *authority* to perform such an ordinance. One doing the baptizing must be an authorized agent of the Lord, acting under a divine power of attorney, or the ordinance stands null and void (D&C 22; Acts 19:1–7). The baptism must also be performed by the prescribed method of total *immersion*, the same manner in which the Savior himself was baptized (D&C 20: 72–74; 3 Ne. 11:23–28; Matt. 3:13–17). Furthermore, the Prophet said, "Baptism by water is but half a baptism, and is good for nothing without the other half—that is, the baptism of the Holy Ghost" (TPJS, 314).

Joseph Smith and Oliver Cowdery were baptized for the remission of sins at the time the Aaronic Priesthood was restored (JS—H 1:66–73), but were again baptized when the Church was organized in order to become members thereof (DS 2:336). This same situation occurred among the Nephites who were baptized prior to the visit of the resurrected Savior and the establishment of his new church (3 Ne. 9:15–22; 11:10–40; 12:18–19; 15:4–10; 19:11–12).

The covenants one makes at baptism are described in both the Doctrine and Covenants (20:37) and the Book of Mormon (Mosiah 18:8–10). These are renewed each time one partakes of the sacrament. One should, therefore, be most attentive to the words of the sacramental prayers (D&C 20:77, 79; Moro. 4:3; 5:2).

See also: Baptism for the Dead; Baptism of Fire; Ordinance; Remission of Their Sins

Baptism for the Dead

Among the thousands of verses of scripture in the standard works of the Church, few are more important to Latter-day Saints than those found in three sections of the Doctrine and Covenants and in a single verse of Paul's writings (D&C 124:28–42; 127:6; 128:11–18; 1 Cor. 15:29). Each of these deals with the topic of baptism for the dead and, by extension, all vicarious ordinance work for our deceased ancestors.

Inasmuch as baptism is a requirement for salvation in the celestial kingdom (D&C 112:28–29; 3 Ne. 11:33; John 3:5), and because there are billions who have passed from this earth without that saving ordinance, God has set in place the means whereby the living may perform this ordinance in behalf of the dead. It is a labor of love performed within the House of Him who authorizes such saving service.

To the question as to whether we intend to perform this labor of love for *all* who have ever lived, the simple answer is "Yes!" "Why, that is impossible," say some. Elder Boyd K. Packer has responded, "Perhaps, but we shall do it anyway." Further: "And once again we certify that we are not discouraged. We ask no relief of the assignment, no excuse from fulfilling it."

He declared: "I say that no point of doctrine sets this church apart from the other claimants as this one does. Save for it, we would, with all of the others, have to accept the clarity with which the New Testament declares baptism to be essential and then admit that most of the human family could never have it.

"But we have the revelations. We have those sacred ordinances." (En., Nov. 1975, p. 99.)

It is significant that two revelations were canonized at the April 1976 general conference of the Church. Both dealt with the principle of redemption for the dead. (En., May 1976, pp. 19, 127–29; D&C 137, 138.) The further hastening of this work was emphasized in a revelation received in June 1978, wherein "every faithful, worthy man in the Church" was authorized to receive the priesthood (D&C OD—2). Not only did this affect the living, but also had great impact on the millions in the spirit world who had been awaiting the full blessings of the priesthood, including those of the temple. This revelation opened the way to doing the redemptive work for *every* man, woman, and child who had arrived at the age of accountability but died before receiving the saving ordinances of the gospel.

The significance of this work was stressed by one of the Lord's prophets, President Joseph Fielding Smith: *"It matters not what else we have been called to do, or what position we may occupy, or how faithfully in other ways we have labored in the Church, none is exempt from this great obligation. It is required of the apostle as well as the humble elder. . . .*

"Some may feel that if they pay their tithing, attend their regular meetings and other duties, give of their substance to the poor, perchance spend one, two, or more years preaching in the world, that they are absolved from further duty. But *the greatest and grandest duty of all is to labor for the dead."* (DS 2:148–49.)

Baptism of Fire

The "baptism of fire" is always associated with the Holy Ghost (D&C 20:41; 33:11; 39:6; 2 Ne. 31:13–14; Matt. 3:11). Of this baptism, Elder Bruce R. McConkie has written: "To gain salvation every accountable person must receive two baptisms. They are baptism of water and of the Spirit. (John 3:3–5.) The baptism of the Spirit is called the *baptism of fire and of the Holy Ghost.* . . . By the power of the Holy Ghost—who is the Sanctifier (3 Ne. 27:19–21)—dross, iniquity, carnality, sensuality, and every evil thing is burned out of the human soul as if by fire; the cleansed person becomes literally a new creature of the Holy Ghost. (Mosiah 27:24–26.) He is born again.

"The baptism of fire is not something in addition to the receipt of the Holy Ghost; rather, it is the actual enjoyment of the gift which is offered by the laying on of hands at the time of baptism. . . .

"There have been, however, exceptional and miraculous instances when literal fire has attended the baptism of the Spirit." (MD, 73; see also Hel. 5; 3 Ne. 9:20; 19:13–14; Acts 2:1–4.)

See also: Confirm; Gift of the Holy Ghost

Baptismal Font

The words *baptismal font* appear twice in the Doctrine and Covenants and refer in both instances to a font located within the walls of a temple (D&C 124:29; 128:13). In most temples the baptismal font is placed below the foundation, or the surface of the earth. "This is symbolical, since the dead are in their graves, and we are working for the dead when we are baptized for them. Moreover, baptism is also symbolical of death and the resurrection, in fact, is *virtually a resurrection from the life of sin, or from spiritual death, to the life of spiritual life.* (See D&C 29:41–45.) Therefore, *when the dead have had this ordinance performed in their behalf they are considered to have been brought back into the presence of God,* just as this doctrine is applied to the living. Other ordinances of the endowment and sealings, therefore, do not have to be performed below the surface of the earth as in the case of baptism." (CHMR 2:142.)

Bare His Holy Arm

In a revelation known as the Appendix to the Doctrine and Covenants, the Lord speaks of making bare his holy arm so that all nations shall see the salvation of their God (D&C 133:3). For God to "bare his holy arm" is to make his power known or manifest. This phrase is first found in Isaiah (52:10) and is repeated in the Book of Mormon (1 Ne. 22:10; Mosiah 12:24; 15:31). In looking at the context of these verses, it is evident that the fulfillment of this particular prophecy is in the latter days.

It is of interest to note that the resurrected Redeemer twice quoted this same passage to the Nephites (3 Ne. 16:20; 20:35), although in the latter instance he substituted the word *Father* for both *Lord* and *God*, adding, "and the Father and I are one."

See also: Arm of the Lord

Bassett, Heman

In a revelation received June 7, 1831, in Kirtland, Ohio (D&C 52:37), Heman Bassett is described as a transgressor whose previous blessing, or position, is to be taken from him and bestowed upon another. According to at least one source, Bassett was involved in some of the "strange visions" of which the Prophet Joseph Smith gave warning (TS 3:747). Bassett claimed to have received a revelation from an angel and showed many a picture of what he alleged was a group of angels (Autobiography of Levi Hancock, p. 41). No further mention is found of him in the annals of published history.

Bathed in Heaven

In preparation for executing judgment upon the wicked, the Lord will bathe his sword in heaven (D&C 1:13). Smith and Sjodahl suggest that "this is a very expressive term from Isaiah 34:5, where it is used to signify the pouring out of the indignation of the Lord upon all nations and His fury upon their armies, delivering them to destruction and slaughter" (SS, 7). Another possible interpretation is that the Lord will bathe (wash or clean) his sword in preparation for its use.

See also: Sword of Mine Indignation

Battle of the Great God

The "battle of the great God" is the last struggle between the forces of good and evil (God and the devil). This battle will take place at the end of the thousand-year period known as the Millennium and will pit the armies of Satan against the armies of Michael, or Adam, the seventh angel (D&C 88:111–16). All who have been associated with this earth—mortal beings, resurrected beings, and evil spirits—will take part in this great war.

Michael will lead the armies of righteousness to victory in this *last* war, the same as he did when he prevailed over the forces of evil in the *first* war (Rev. 12:7–9). The victory shall be climaxed by the celestialization of this earth, which shall then be inhabited by those who qualify for celestial crowns.

Baurak Ale

One of the names by which the Lord called Joseph Smith was

"Baurak Ale" (D&C 103:21, 22, 35; 105:16, 27; pre-1981 edition). This was done in order to hide Joseph's true identity from the world at a time when secrecy regarding some revelation was deemed necessary (HC 1:255). The name "Baurak Ale" is Hebrew, and, according to Elder Orson Pratt, it means "God bless you" (JD 16:156). The name does not appear in current editions of the Doctrine and Covenants.

Bear Him Up as on Eagles' Wings

An 1838 revelation promised that if Lyman Wight was faithful in his calling the Lord would "bear him up as on eagles' wings" (D&C 124:18). This is a figure of speech which conveys the idea that the Lord would lift or carry Lyman by his power as if on eagles' wings. When young eaglets first attempt to fly, the parents hover anxiously near. Should the young bird begin to falter from exhaustion, the parent bird is said to support the fledgling on its expanded, more powerful wings.

The phrase also symbolizes the strength and the ability of one so borne to soar beyond the grasp of man (see Ex. 19:4). In that same revelation William Law is told that through his faithfulness his thoughts would "mount up. . . . as upon eagles' wings," or in other words they would ascend to lofty heights (D&C 124:99; see also Isa. 40:31).

Beasts

With the possible exception of the symbolic creatures seen by John the Revelator (Rev. 4:6; D&C 77:2–4), the term *beasts* as used throughout the Doctrine and Covenants refers to creatures of the animal world. They have been placed on the earth "for the use of man for food and for raiment" (D&C 49:19; 89:12). Nevertheless, man is under strict charge not to waste flesh and to use it sparingly (D&C 49:21; 89:12–13). "I do not believe any man should kill animals or birds unless he needs them for food," declared President Joseph F. Smith, "and then he should not kill innocent little birds that are not intended for food for man" (GD, 266).

"Men must become harmless, before the brute creation," said the Prophet Joseph, "and *when men lose their vicious dispositions and cease to destroy the animal race, the lion and the lamb can dwell together*, and the suckling child can play with the serpent in safety" (HC 2:71; italics added). The day will come, according to President Joseph Fielding Smith, when "the animals and all living creatures shall be given knowledge, and enjoy happiness, each in its own sphere." They will inhabit kingdoms of glory just like man. (CHMR 1:298–99.) Is it inconceivable, therefore, to think that in some unknown fashion they could testify against any who might have abused them? "Let us be merciful to the brute creation," admonished President

Heber C. Kimball (JD 5:138). (For further information, see En., May 1978, pp. 47–48; En., Nov. 1978, pp. 44–45.)

Beautiful Garments

The Lord declared that "Zion must increase in beauty, and in holiness . . . [and] arise and put on her beautiful garments" (D&C 82:14). For Zion to "put on her strength is to put on the authority of the priesthood" (D&C 113:7–8; Isa. 52:1) and "what comes about as a result of exercising the Priesthood is equivalent to putting on 'her beautiful garments' " (DCC, 383).

See also: Priesthood; Zion

Beginning, The

Perhaps some of the most often read words of scripture are, "In the beginning God created the heaven and the earth" (Gen. 1:1). "The beginning" is spoken of a number of times in the Doctrine and Covenants and usually refers to the beginning of time as far as this world and its inhabitants are concerned. Speaking of the Savior, John said: "I saw his glory, that he was in the beginning, before the world was" (D&C 93:7). Smith and Sjodahl state that " 'The beginning' can hardly refer to any other moment of time than that with which the story of the creation in Genesis opens. At that moment our Lord 'was.' He existed then, and was,

therefore, before the world." (SS, 590–91.) At this point in time, man was innocent (D&C 93:38), the "new and everlasting covenant" was in existence (D&C 22:1), and a place had been prepared for the "devil and his angels" (D&C 29:38).

However, an occasional different meaning may apply to "the beginning," and one must read the verse carefully to see in what context the Lord is speaking. For example, when Joseph Smith was rebuked for "trampling" the counsel of God "from the beginning," this did not refer to the time of creation — at which time Joseph was one of the great premortal spirits — but rather to his rejecting God's initial counsel that Martin Harris not be allowed to take the 116 pages of manuscript, which he subsequently lost (D&C 3:15).

Beginning and the End, The

In connection with his title of Alpha and Omega, the Savior refers to himself as "the beginning and the end" (D&C 19:1). "These are English words having substantially the same meaning as the Greek Alpha and Omega. The thought conveyed is one of timelessness, of a being who is the Beginning and the End because his 'course is one eternal round, the same today as yesterday, and forever.' (D&C 35:1.) He was God 'in the beginning' (John 1:1); he is God now; he will be God in the 'end,' that is to all eternity. The beginning is the [premortal] eternity that went before; the end is the immortal eternity that is to come." (DNTC 3:439.)

Begotten Sons and Daughters unto God

Although Christ is the "Only Begotten of the Father" in the flesh (D&C 20:21), every babe born into this world came from a previous existence where he had been *spiritually begotten of Heavenly Parents*. The inhabitants of this world are "begotten sons and daughters unto God" (D&C 76:24; Heb. 12:9).

President Marion G. Romney has said: "We mortals are in very deed the *literal offspring of God*. . . . Members of The Church of Jesus Christ of Latter-day Saints accept this concept as a basic doctrine of their theology. The lives of those who have given it thought enough to realize its implications are controlled by it; it gives meaning and direction to all their thoughts and deeds. This is so because they know that it is the universal law of nature in the plant, animal, and human worlds for reproducing offspring to reach in final maturity the likeness of their parents. They reason that the same law is in force with respect to the offspring of God. Their objective is, therefore, to someday be like their heavenly parents." (En., July 1973, p. 12; italics added.)

In a different sense, men and women become "spiritually begotten" of Christ, the Son, by covenanting to follow his teachings (Mosiah 5:7). However, this latter instance has nothing to do with one's original spiritual birth nor with the physical birth.

See also: Father, The

Behoove

On several occasions in the Doctrine and Covenants the Lord uses the phrase, "it behooveth me" (21:10; 61:9; 124:49). This simply means that something is his desire, wish, or will. A slightly different use is found in several Book of Mormon passages where the word means an obligation or requirement (2 Ne. 9:5; Hel. 14:15).

Believers

Section 74 is a commentary on 1 Corinthians 7:14, in which the Apostle Paul speaks of believers and unbelievers. A believer is one who has accepted the gospel of Jesus Christ with all its attendant rites, principles, and ordinances. A believer follows not only the Master—he who was Jehovah of the Old Testament and came to earth as the Son of God in the New Testament—but also accepts and follows those whom he has placed as leaders in his church.

Those within the faith have always been counseled to avoid marriage with those who do not share these same beliefs. One of the earliest accounts of a parent's concern that a child not marry outside the faith was when Abraham sought a wife for Isaac (Gen. 24:1–4). Years later, Isaac and Rebekah suffered "grief of mind" when their son Esau married outside the faith (Gen. 26:34–35). The Lord specifically commanded Israel, his *holy* and *special* people, to avoid intermarriage with unbelievers, for such can result in a loss of faith for the believer (Deut. 7:1–6; see 2 Cor. 6:14).

However, where a marriage between a believer and unbeliever already exists, the counsel is for the believer to seek for the sanctification of the unbelieving spouse and the offspring of that union. The love of a patient, prayerful partner can help to work the miracle. Elder Boyd K. Packer once counseled women who were married to inactive or unbelieving partners to "never give up. If you have faith enough and desire enough, you will yet have at the head of your home a father and a husband who is active and faithful in the Church." (En., Feb. 1972, p. 69.)

See also: Unbelievers

Beneath

The word *beneath* generally means below or lower than someone or something (e.g., D&C 29:14; 84:100). In one instance, however, *beneath* refers specifically to the devil's domain and the consequences that accrue to those who disobey the Lord (D&C 58:32–33).

Benighted

In a prayerful petition, the Prophet Joseph Smith referred to the devil's abode as "the dark and benighted dominion of Sheol" (D&C 121:4). *Benighted* means to be darkened, without light, and could refer to the absence of both physical and spiritual light.

See also: Sheol

Bennett, John C.

An almost Davidic-like tragedy is expressed in the story of John C. Bennett, for like the ancient king of Israel, who had so much promise and yet threw it away in his adulterous descent to hell, so in like fashion John C. Bennett forsook his crown of glory.

Like David, the ancient king of Israel, John C. Bennett stood to receive untold blessings if he remained true to the Lord. Also like David, he turned from his duty to pursue the ways of adultery. (See 2 Sam. 11–12; D&C 132:39.) However, whereas David sought forgiveness of his iniquity, Bennett hardened his heart yet more and sought to bring down the kingdom of God on earth.

In 1841, the Lord promised a "crown . . . with blessings and great glory" to John C. Bennett, who was to labor with the Prophet Joseph, "and his reward shall not fail *if* he receive counsel" (D&C 124:16–17; italics added). Just sixteen months later Bennett was notified that because of his impurities his membership in the Church had been revoked. John Taylor wrote: "Respecting John C. Bennett: I was well acquainted with him. At one time he was a good man, but fell into adultery and was cut off from the Church for his iniquity." (HC 5:81.)

Though he had served as mayor of Nauvoo and traveled in the highest councils of the Church, even serving as an "assistant president" with the First Presidency for a time (HC 4:341) —a friend and confidant of prophets, seers, and revelators —he succumbed to the siren's call and wrecked his soul upon the reefs of adultery. "Then he became one of the most bitter enemies of the Church. His slanders, his falsehoods and unscrupulous attacks, which included perjury and attempted assassination were the means of inflaming public opinion to such an extent that the tragedy at Carthage became possible." (SS, 771.) Such is the tragic story of one who spurned spirituality and seared his soul in the fires of sensual passion.

Benson, Ezra T.

The only mention of Ezra T. Benson in the Doctrine and Covenants is in conjunction with his call to help organize a company of Saints for the move from Winter Quarters to the Salt Lake Valley (D&C 136:12). He had initially come in contact with the Church in 1839 when he moved to Quincy, Illinois. While favorably disposed to these "peculiar people," he did not join the Church until July 19, 1840. In October of that year, he was ordained a high priest by Hyrum Smith and was appointed as second counselor to the stake president at Quincy. He later served on the Nauvoo high council and presided over the Saints in Boston.

In the move west, he was called as a counselor in the presidency at Mount Pisgah. While serving in this capacity, he received notification from Brigham Young of his call to fill a vacancy in the Quorum of the Twelve Apostles, to which office he was ordained, July 16, 1846. He served a number of short-term missions, including one to Europe, and was with the group in Hawaii that experienced the miraculous saving of Lorenzo Snow's life after he apparently had been drowned.

Elder Benson also served in civic positions, including the territorial house of representatives and the territorial council. In 1860, he was appointed to preside in Cache Valley, which position he occupied until his death on September 3, 1869. (Jenson 1:99–102.)

Bent, Samuel

Although his only mention in the Doctrine and Covenants is as a member of the Nauvoo high council in 1841 (124:132), Samuel Bent had an illustrious career of Church service. Born July 19, 1778, he entered into religious service at an early age and was a "professor of religion for twenty-seven years previous to receiving the Latter-day work." His contact with the Church came through the Book of Mormon, about which he later received a vision and was shown that the fulness of the gospel would be revealed. He participated in Zion's Camp in 1834, and a year later took part in the School of the Prophets in Kirtland. In July 1836, near Liberty, Missouri, he was tied to a tree and whipped by a mob. Two years later he was taken as a prisoner to the Richmond jail, where he was confined for three weeks by the mob militia. Shortly thereafter, he was warned by a vision to leave his place of residence and had only been gone about two hours when mobocrats descended on his former abode. He served as a colonel in the Nauvoo Legion and as the senior member of the quasi-political group known as the "council of fifty."

Bent was appointed a captain of one hundred in the exodus from Nauvoo, and as the presiding elder at the camp known as Garden Grove in Iowa. Upon his death on August 16, 1846, the following sentiments were expressed regarding his loss: "Garden Grove is left without a president, and a large circle of relatives and friends are bereft of an affectionate companion and friend, and the Church has sustained the loss of an undeviating friend to the truth and righteousness. The glory of his death is, that he died in the full triumphs of faith and knowledge of the truth of our holy religion, exhorting his friends to be faithful; having three days previous received intimation of his approaching end by three holy messengers from on high." (Jenson 1:368.)

Bespeaketh

The only use of the archaic word *bespeaketh* appears in the Doctrine and Covenants when the Lord says that the day shall come that "all men shall know what it is that bespeaketh [signifies or indicates] the power of God" (D&C 60:4).

Betimes

The word *betimes* appears in the Doctrine and Covenants (121:43) and in the Old Testament (Prov. 13:24) and means "at the appropriate time."

See also: Reproving Betimes with Sharpness

Bible

In an 1831 revelation, the Lord declared that the principles of his gospel should be taught from the Bible and the Book of Mormon (D&C 42:12). "By the Bible we mean the collection of writings that contain the records of divine revelation. The word itself is of Greek origin, being derived from *ta biblia*, 'the books'. . . . By the word Bible therefore we must understand not a single book, but a divine library." (LDSBD, 622.)

The Bible, including the Old and New Testaments, is one of the accepted books of scripture for The Church of Jesus Christ of Latter-day Saints. However, "We believe the Bible to be the word of God as far as it is translated correctly" (Articles of Faith 1:9). The Prophet Joseph Smith declared, "I believe the Bible as it read when it came from the pen of the original writers. Ignorant translators, careless transcribers, or designing and corrupt priests have committed many errors." (HC 6:57; see also 1 Ne. 13:20–40.)

The vision found in Doctrine and Covenants 138 came as a result of President Joseph F. Smith's studying and pondering passages in the Bible, and the vision of the Father and Son which young Joseph Smith experienced was the direct result of his seeking answers from the Bible (JS–H 1:11–20).

See also: Testimony of the Jews

Billings, Titus

In a revelation received in August 1831, Titus Billings was directed by the Lord to dispose of some land in the Kirtland area and journey to Missouri—"the land of Zion" (D&C 63:38–39). Billings is reported to have been the second person baptized in Kirtland in November 1830. He endured all the persecution of the Missouri period of Church history and participated in the battle of Crooked River, in which three Saints lost their lives in defense of freedom.

Billings was set apart as the second counselor to Bishop Edward Partridge on August 1, 1837, and served in that capacity until the death of Bishop Partridge, May 27, 1840. He was called to be a "captain of fifty" in the Heber C. Kimball company that arrived in the Salt Lake Valley in 1848. In 1849 he was appointed to the Salt Lake High Council. He later became one of the first settlers of Manti, Utah, as a result of the First Presidency's request that he help to settle the Sanpete Valley. He died in Provo on February 6, 1866. (Jenson 1:242.)

Billowing Surge

Symbolically speaking, the Lord told the Prophet Joseph Smith that among the adversities which would come into his life was "the billowing surge" (D&C 122:7). A surge is something which rises and moves in waves or billows (rolling masses that resemble high waves). The billowing surges that came against the Prophet were the antagonisms, enmity, and hatred that rolled upon him and upon the cause he represented like unrelenting waves of a fierce storm.

Bind

See: Bind Up the Law/Testimony; Sealing and Binding Power

Bind Up the Law/Testimony

The phrases *bind up the law* or *testimony* and *seal up the law* or *testimony* are found in three volumes of scripture (D&C 88:84; 109:46; 133:72; Isa. 8:16; 2 Ne. 18:16). The law represents teachings, and the testimony represents the inspired utterances of God's messengers (see Isa. 8:16, fn. in LDS edition of the King James Bible). Dummelow indicated that the binding and sealing of the law is the process of actually tying up a parchment roll whereon the teachings of the prophets are recorded as a witness against those to whom the message was delivered (Dummelow, 420). Sperry suggested that this may be figurative in the sense of a document being signed in the hearts of the disciples (BMC, 104).

Bishop

The title *bishop* is applied to several categories of men in the Church: First, those "general bishops" who served in the early days of the Church when membership was small and scattered. These bishops had a jurisdiction which was "quite extensive or special, yet not over the whole Church" (PCG, 177). Edward Partridge, Newel Whitney, and George Miller were all early examples of this type of bishop (D&C 41:9–10; 72:5–8; 84:112–14; 124:20—21).

Second, the Presiding Bishop of the Church and his counselors, who serve as General Authorities, acting under the direction of the First Presidency and the Quorum of the Twelve.

Third, men who have previously served as bishops who continue to be referred to as "bishop" by many who associated with them in their previous ministry.

Fourth, men who are currently functioning as bishops. This last group of men have five main areas of responsibility in the wards in which they serve: (1) to preside over the Aaronic Priesthood and to serve as the president of the priests quorum (D&C 107:15, 87–88); (2) to serve as the presiding high priest of the ward, having all members of the ward "subject to his presidency" (GD, 185); (3) to "be a judge in Israel . . . to sit in judgment upon transgressors" (D&C 107:73–74); (4) to be the director of welfare services—he has the responsibility for caring for the poor and "is personally responsible for determining needs and resources" (*Bishop's Guide*, 1975, p. 11); (5) to serve as the administrator of finances, records, and properties, "for the office of a bishop is in administering all temporal things" (D&C 107:68).

In spite of the numerous responsibilities and concomitant demands on the time of one who faithfully serves as a bishop, the joy of his office knows no bounds. George Albert Smith, eighth President of the Church, stated: "There is no position in the Church that will bring a greater blessing to any man than the office of a bishop if he will honor that office and be a real father to the flock over whom he is called to preside" (CR, Oct. 1948, p. 186).

See also: Aaronic Priesthood; Bishopric; Common Judge; First-born; Literal Descendants of Aaron; Traveling Bishops

Bishopric

In one sense, "Any office or position of major responsibility in the Church, any office of overseership under the supervision of which important church business is administered, is a *bishopric*" (MD, 89). For example, there are several scriptural citations that use this term in conjunction with the apostolic calling of the Twelve (D&C 114; Acts 1:20–26). Bishopric can also refer to the specific office of a bishop (D&C 68:16).

The term is used most often in conjunction with the specific office of *a* bishopric, which is comprised of three high priests—a bishop and two counselors (PCG, 125; D&C 68:14–19; 107: 15–17, 69). Counselors in the bishopric do "not act as the bishop," but are "subordinate to the bishop, and [are] subject entirely to the bishop's direction" (GD, 185). Though the bishop presides, the three members of the bishopric act as a unified whole as they conduct the affairs of the ward (D&C 38:27).

See also: Bishop

Bitter Cup

In remembrance of their deliverance from bitter bondage in Egypt, Israel was commanded to eat the paschal lamb "with unleavened bread and with bitter herbs" (Ex. 12:8). The word *bitter* is used to express "intense feelings of disgust, displeasure, or anguish." Esau, for example, "cried with a great and exceeding bitter cry" for a forsaken birthright blessing (Gen. 27:34). And the barren Hannah "was in bitterness of soul" as she cried to the Lord for a child (1 Sam. 1:10).

The bitter cup is symbolic of the intense disgust, displeasure, or anguish one suffers as a consequence of his actions or something he has chosen to yet do. Sinners will sip the sediment of their "bitter cups" (Alma 40:26), and the Savior drank heavily from a "bitter cup" of anguish when he paid for our sins in Gethsemane (D&C 19:18). This was the cup his Father required him to drink (3 Ne. 11:11; John 18:11). His was a cup the contents of which produced not simple nausea but such total revulsion and anguish that they precipitated a porous letting of his holy blood. Those who refuse to accept the Savior's sacrifice must ultimately partake of their own cups of bitterness.

See also: Atonement; Bleed at Every Pore; Shrink

Blasphemy Against the Holy Ghost

The Lord defined this contemptuous crime as one in which "ye commit murder wherein ye shed innocent blood, and assent unto my death, after ye have received my new and everlasting covenant" (D&C 132:27; see also 76:35). President Joseph Fielding Smith stated: "It is a sin unto death, for it brings a spiritual banishment—the second death—by which those who partake of it are denied the presence of God and are consigned to dwell with the devil and his angels throughout eternity.

"All who partake of this, the greatest of sins, sell themselves as did Cain to Lucifer. They learn to hate the truth with an eternal hatred, and they learn to love wickedness. They reach a condition where they will not and cannot repent. The spirit of murder fills their hearts and they would, if they had the power, crucify our Lord again, which they virtually do by fighting his work and seeking to destroy it and his prophets.

"Before a man can sink to this bitterness of soul, he must first know and understand the truth with clearness of vision wherein there is no doubt. *The change of heart does not come all at once*, but is due to transgression in some form, which continues to lurk in the soul without repentance, until the Holy Ghost withdraws, and then that man is left to spiritual darkness. Sin begets sin; the darkness grows until the love of truth turns to hatred, and the love of God is overcome by the wicked desire to destroy all that is just and true. In this way Christ is put to open shame, and blasphemy exalted." (DS 1:49.)

"Wherefore I say unto you," said the Savior, "All manner of sin and blasphemy shall be forgiven unto men *who receive me and repent*; but the blasphemy against the Holy Ghost, it shall not be forgiven unto men" (JST, Matt. 12:26; italics added).

See also: Crucified Him unto Themselves; Sons of Perdition

Blazing Throne of God

In a vision in the Kirtland Temple, the Prophet saw the gate of the celestial kingdom "which was like unto circling flames of fire" and "the blazing throne of God" (D&C 137:2–3). An Old Testament prophet also saw the glowing glory of God's throne which had the "appearance of a sapphire stone" and the "appearance of fire" that surrounded the Being who occupied that exalted throne (Ezek. 1:26–27; see also Dan. 7:9). The Apostle Paul said, "Our God is a consuming fire" (Heb. 12:29). An explanation of the consuming fire surrounding God is provided by a latter-day prophet, President Joseph Fielding Smith: "God is full of energy, and should we mortals stand in his presence, unless his Spirit was upon us to protect us we would be *consumed*" (SYE, 275; italics added).

Emanating from the presence of Deity is an energy source of light that defies all description (see JS—H 1:19). Mortal man, with his limited understanding, can only refer to this as a substance similar to fire, perhaps with many of the same effects. Joseph Smith taught, "God Almighty himself dwells in eternal fire; flesh and blood cannot go there, for all corruption is devoured by the fire" (TPJS, 367).

See also: Fire; Throne

Bleed at Every Pore

In an 1830 revelation, the Savior recounted the agonizing experience which caused him to "bleed at every pore, and to suffer both body and spirit" (D&C 19:18). Luke recorded this incident in these words: "And being in an agony he prayed more earnestly: and his sweat was as it were great drops of blood falling down to the ground" (Luke 22:44). Of this experience, Elder Joseph Fielding Smith said: "We get into the habit of thinking, that his great suffering was when he was nailed to the cross by his hands and his feet and was left there to suffer until he died. As excruciating as this pain was, that was not the greatest suffering that he had to undergo, for in some way which I cannot understand, but which I accept on faith, and which you must accept on faith, he carried on his back the burden of the sins of the whole world.

. . . , and so great was his suffering *before he went to the cross*, we are informed that blood oozed from the pores of his body." (CR, Oct. 1947, pp. 147–48; italics added.)

According to Brigham Young, the total withdrawal of the Father's spirit in Gethsemane precipitated the sweating of blood (JD 3:206). "In that hour of anguish Christ met and overcame all the horrors that Satan, 'the prince of this world' could inflict" (Talmage, 613).

See also: Bitter Cup

Blindness of Heart

The phrase *blindness of heart* is found only in the Doctrine and Covenants (58:15) and in Paul's writings (Eph. 4:18). It is an attribute of the unrepentant sinner. According to Smith and Sjodahl it "means affections not guided by the light of the Spirit. Those who place their affection upon wrong objects, such as belong to the world, in preference to those that pertain to the Kingdom of God, are blind at heart, no matter how clear the physical or mental vision may be." (SS, 338.) Blindness of heart is to be equated with hardness of heart.

See also: Harden Their Heart

Blood

See: Bleed at Every Pore; Blood of Ephraim; Blood of This Generation; Innocent Blood; Man That Sheddeth Blood or Wasteth Flesh;

Moon Shall Be Turned into Blood; Murdered in Cold Blood; Perfect Frame; Sealed His Mission with His Blood; Shed Innocent Blood; Spiritual Body

Blood of Ephraim

Elder Bruce R. McConkie wrote: "In general, the Lord sends to earth in the lineage of Jacob [the grandfather of Ephraim] those spirits who in preexistence developed an especial talent for spirituality and for recognizing truth. Those born in this lineage, having the blood of Israel in their veins and finding it easy to accept the gospel, are said to have *believing blood*." (MD, 81.)

The Lord has specifically identified the obedient Saints of our day as having the blood of Ephraim, for "the rebellious" are not of that blood (D&C 64:36). The blood of Ephraim encompasses those believing and obedient Saints of literal descent from Ephraim and those who have been adopted into his tribe and thus become his posterity. These are they of whom the Savior spoke when he said, "My sheep hear my voice, and I know them, and they follow me" (John 10:27).

See also: Ephraim

Blood of This Generation

The Savior instructed those who labored within the kingdom that their efforts must be of such a nature that they would be "clean from the blood of this wicked generation" (D&C 88:74–75, 85). To be pronounced clean in this sense is to be free of guilt and the stain of sin. Those called to the ministry are cautioned that dereliction of duty will cause "the blood of this generation [to] be required at [their] hands" (D&C 112:33). Ezekiel warned that the Lord would require the "blood" of the wicked at the hands of those called to warn if that warning had not been issued (Ezek. 3:17–21; see also D&C 4:2; 88:81). President John Taylor promised those who had "performed their labors, and fulfilled their duties, [that] their garments are free from the blood of this generation" (JD 24:289).

Boarding House

In 1841, the Lord commanded the Saints to build a "boarding house" in his name for the "boarding of strangers" (D&C 124:56). This was the Nauvoo House, which "was to be dedicated to the Lord. The Prophet Joseph, or one of his descendants after him from generation to generation, was to live there. This does not imply that the Presidency of the Church should be transmitted as an inheritance from father to son. It refers only to the shares of stock in the Nauvoo House Association. The Prophet Joseph owned a portion of that stock that was transferable property, and it was perfectly proper that he and any of his descendants who owned the stock should have their residence in the House as part of the dividend on the money invested, when that condition was understood and agreed on from the beginning." (SS, 783.)

Boggs, Lilburn W.

The infamous name of Lilburn W. Boggs is mentioned in the preface to section 124. He left his mark of death and persecution on the early Latter-day Saints when, as governor of Missouri, he issued an order, dated October 27, 1838, which read in part, "The Mormons must be treated as enemies and *must be exterminated* or driven from the state" (HC 3:175). Boggs's order gave to mobocrats free license to pillage, plunder, and kill the Saints who had established homes in Missouri in their quest for a Zion society.

The Saints were successfully driven from the state. However, four years later on May 6, 1842, an unseen assailant shot and wounded Boggs through the window of his home in Independence, Missouri. Several months later he falsely accused Orrin Porter Rockwell, a close associate of Joseph Smith, of having done the shooting. He also accused the Prophet Joseph of being an accessory to the intended murder and tried to have the two men extradited from their homes in Illinois. The Prophet denied any complicity in the assassination attempt and also declared his friend to be innocent. Although Joseph was arrested on trumped-up charges, he was finally acquitted in a trial held in January 1843. (ECH, 322–31.) Rockwell was held in prison for nine months on false charges and finally released.

Several years later, Boggs emigrated with a group of Missourians headed for Oregon. Along the way his troublesome party tried to cause problems for the Mormons, but he was unsuccessful. (ECH, 443.)

See also: Missouri

Bondage of Sin

See: Chains of Darkness

Bond-servants

Bond-servants are slaves or those of indentured servitude. Joseph Smith said, "In my opinion, you will do well to search the Book of Covenants, in which you will see the belief of the Church, concerning masters and servants. All men are to be taught to repent; but we have no right to interfere with slaves, contrary to the mind and will of their masters. In fact, it would be much better, and more prudent, not to preach at all to slaves, until after their masters are converted, and then teach the masters to use them with kindness; remembering that they are accountable to God, and the servants are bound to serve their masters with singleness of heart, without murmuring." (HC 2:440.)

In a "declaration of belief regarding governments and laws in general," adopted by a general assembly of the Church on August 17, 1835, the inadvisability of interfering with bondservants was voiced (D&C 134:12).

See also: Servitude; Slaves

Book of Commandments

In the summer of 1830, the Prophet Joseph began compiling and arranging some of the revelations he had received up to that time. At a conference of the Church held in Hiram, Ohio, November 1, 1831, the decision was reached to print a book to be known as the Book of Commandments. This "book of revelations" was to be "the foundation of the Church in these last days, and a benefit to the world, showing that the keys of the mysteries of the kingdom of our Savior are again entrusted to man; and the riches of eternity within the compass of those who are willing to live by every word that proceedeth out of the mouth of God" (HC 1:235). During the conference the Lord revealed what is now section 1 of the Doctrine and Covenants, which he called "mine authority, and the authority of my servants, and my preface unto the book of my commandments" (D&C 1:6).

In the process of compilation, some of the "wise" objected to the wording in the revelations, claiming it was of Joseph Smith. The Lord issued to them a challenge to see if "the most wise" among them could write a revelation comparable to "even the least" that was in Joseph's revelatory repertoire (D&C 67). The "wise" failed, and the unlearned Joseph maintained his prophetic mantle. Oliver Cowdery and John Whitmer were appointed to take the compilation of revelations to Jackson County, where they were to be printed. However, on July 20, 1833, a mob destroyed the W. W. Phelps and Co. printing press at Independence, and the Book of Commandments, containing 65 revelations, was destroyed.

On September 24, 1834, the Kirtland high council made arrangements for printing a new edition, which was accepted by a conference of the Church held on August 17, 1835. This edition contained 102 sections and was renamed the Doctrine and Covenants. The reason for the name change is unclear, although this name is mentioned in Joseph's journal entry of November 3, 1831 (HC 1:229).

Book of Enoch

In discussing some of the history of the early patriarchs of our race, the Lord said that "these things were all written in the book of Enoch, and are to be testified of in due time" (D&C 107:57). Smith and Sjodahl have stated: "There is an alleged Book of Enoch extant, but it is no older than the second century B.C. Some time the genuine Book of Enoch will be revealed, from which some chapters in the Pearl of Great Price are copied, through the Spirit of Revelation." (SS, 706.)

Book of Lehi

See: Harris, Martin; Manuscript (116 Pages); Plates of Nephi

Book of Life

In an explanatory epistle, Joseph Smith spoke of the "book of life" which John the Revelator had seen (D&C 128:6–7; Rev. 20:12). He said that this book "is the record which is kept in heaven." Of this book, another has written: "Figuratively, it is our own life, and being, the record of our acts transcribed in our souls, an account of our obedience or disobedience written in our bodies. Literally, it is the record kept in heaven of the names and righteous deeds of the faithful." (DNTC 3:578.)

Those whose names are "written in heaven" (D&C 76:68) will find Christ confessing their names before his Father and the angels (Rev. 3:5). Their names will be written in the "Lamb's

Book of Life" (D&C 132:19; TPJS, 9). This is "the book of the names of the sanctified, even them of the celestial world" (D&C 88:2). In other words, it contains the names of the sanctified, celestialized Saints who have so lived as to make their calling and election sure (2 Pet. 1:10). They who reject righteousness will "be blotted out of the book of the living, and not be written with the righteous" (Ps. 69:27–28).

See also: Book of the Law of God

Book of Mormon

On November 28, 1841, Joseph Smith declared, "the Book of Mormon is the most correct of any book on earth, and the keystone of our religion, and a man would get nearer to God by abiding by its precepts, than by any other book" (HC 4:461). This book was preserved through the ages to burst forth with heavenly light upon the earth at a time when darkness prevailed. Not only did brilliant rays of celestial light illuminate the room of a young prophet as an angelic messenger told him of the book's existence (see JS—H 1:30–35) but rays of light from the same divine source have since penetrated the minds of millions through the pages of the Book of Mormon.

The history of the translation and publication of this volume of holy writ is particularly intertwined with the early revelations now contained in the Doctrine and Covenants. For example, the Lord's acceptance of the translation and his personal witness of the Book of Mormon is found among the revelations: "As your Lord and your God liveth it is true," he declared (D&C 1:29; 17:6). It contains "the fulness of the gospel of Jesus Christ . . . , proving to the world that the holy scriptures are true, and that God does inspire men and call them to his holy work. . . , showing that he is the same God yesterday, today, and forever" (D&C 20:8–12). The elders of the Church are commanded to teach from its pages (D&C 33:16; 42:12). By divine decree, those who purchased stock in the Nauvoo House had to be believers in the Book of Mormon (D&C 124:119).

It is of interest to note that during the years from 1823, when Joseph Smith was first informed of the existence of a "book written upon gold plates," until March of 1830, when that book reached the public in published form, that eighteen of the revelations now in the Doctrine and Covenants had been received. Most of these dealt in some way with the Book of Mormon or the principal characters who were striving to make its existence a reality. Section 2 of the Doctrine and Covenants contains words uttered by the angel Moroni on the night he first visited Joseph Smith (JS—H 1:28 –53). Sections 3 and 10 deal with the problem of the lost manu-script, containing the first 116 pages of translated writings from the plates entrusted to Joseph's care. Sections 5, 17, and 18 make particular reference to the calling of the three special witnesses to the Book of Mormon. Sections 6, 8, and 9 were given to Oliver Cowdery during the first month he served as a scribe in the work of translating. Section 13, concerning the restoration of the Aaronic Priesthood, was a direct result of a heavenly inquiry prompted by the work of translation. A number of the early revelations were received by means of the Urim and Thummim which Joseph had received along with the gold plates (see D&C 7, 11, 14–17).

A simplified definition of the Book of Mormon might be taken from Moroni's description of the record to Joseph Smith. It was a book "giving an account of the former inhabitants of this [the American] continent, and the source from whence they sprang . . . ; the fulness of the everlasting Gospel was contained in it, as delivered by the Savior to the ancient inhabitants" (JS—H 1:34). A more complete definition, written by Moroni, can be found on the title page of the Book of Mormon. Suffice it to say that *its major purpose is to bear witness to the divinity of Jesus Christ*, "for the right way is to believe in Christ and deny him not" (2 Ne. 25:28; see also 1 Ne. 6:4; 2 Ne. 26:12; Omni 1:26; Morm. 3:20–21; 5:14–15). In 1982 the First Presidency and Quorum of the Twelve Apostles added the subtitle "Another Testament of Jesus Christ" to the title of the Book of Mormon (En., Nov. 1982, p. 53).

The eternal significance of the Book of Mormon is stressed in the following inspired statements by Apostles of the Lord: "No member of this Church can stand approved in the presence of God who has not seriously and carefully read the Book of Mormon," counseled President Joseph Fielding Smith (CR, Oct. 1961, p. 18). Another destined to become a President of the Church, Harold B. Lee, said, "There is nothing better that we can do to prepare ourselves spiritually than to read the Book of Mormon" (IE, Jan. 1969, p. 13). Finally, President Ezra Taft Benson cautioned, "Every Latter-day Saint should make the study of this book a lifetime pursuit. Otherwise he is placing his soul in jeopardy and neglecting that which could give spiritual and intellectual unity to his whole life." (CR, April 1975, p. 97.)

See also: Angel Flying Through the Midst of Heaven; Book to Be Revealed; Branch of the House of Jacob; Breastplate; Brother of Jared; Cowdery, Oliver; Cumorah; Fayette, New York; Harris, Martin; Ishmaelites; Jacob Shall Flourish in the Wilderness; Jacobites; Josephites; King Benjamin; Laban; Lamanites; Lehi; Lemuelites; Line Running Between Jew and Gentile; Manuscript (116 Pages); Miraculous Directors; Mormon; Moroni; Nephi of Old; Nephites; Orange, Ohio; Page, Hiram; Plates; Plates of Nephi; Remnant of Jacob; Smith, Hyrum; Smith, Joseph, Jr.; Smith, Joseph, Sr.; Smith, Samuel H.; Stick of Ephraim; Sword of Laban; Testimony of Their Fathers; Urim and Thummim; Whitmer, David; Whitmer, John; Whitmer, Peter, Jr.; Work of Translation; Zarahemla; Zoramites

Book of Remembrance

The Saints were counseled as early as 1832 to keep a "book of remembrance" (D&C 85:9). Pre-1981 editions of the Doctrine and Covenants had footnote cross-references from this verse to verses 1, 5, and 11, wherein the record of all that transpires in the Church and the "book of the law of God" are mentioned. If one's name is not found in this book, President Joseph F. Smith said, "It means that you will be cut off from your fathers and mothers, from your husbands, your wives, your children, and . . . you shall have no portion or lot or inheritance in the kingdom of God, both in time and in eternity" (CHMR 1:107).

In a more modern sense, books of remembrance are family histories and records, which all Latter-day Saints have been counseled to maintain. President Spencer W. Kimball said: "I urge all of the people of this church to give serious attention to their family histories, to encourage their parents and grandparents to write their journals, and let no family go into eternity without having left their memoirs for their children, their grandchildren, and their posterity. This is a duty and a responsibility, and I urge every person to start the children out writing a personal history and journal." (En., May 1978, p. 4.)

See also: Book of the Law of God

Book of the Law of God

In 1832, the Lord warned the Saints in Zion that they must agree to abide by his laws or they would not be worthy to "have their names enrolled with the people of God" (D&C 85:1–5). In this connection he spoke of "the book of the law of God" in which their names should not be found. This book has been defined as follows: "Those records kept by the Church showing the names, genealogies, and faith and works of those to be remembered by the Lord in the day when eternal inheritances are bestowed upon the obedient are, taken collectively, called the *book of the law of God*. Such records contain both the law of God and the names of those who keep that law. They are in effect a church book of remembrance." (MD, 100.)

See also: Book of Life; Book of Remembrance

Book of the Names of the Sanctified

See: Book of Life

Book to Be Revealed

In recounting his many experiences with heavenly beings, the Prophet referred to Moroni's visit wherein he declared "the book to be revealed" (D&C 128:20). This book, announced to Joseph Smith in September 1823, would be revealed to the world almost seven years later when the Book of Mormon was published.

See also: Book of Mormon

Booth, Ezra

One of the infamous names of early Mormon history is that of Ezra Booth. He was a former Methodist minister whom a Campbellite publication referred to as a "preacher of much more than ordinary culture, and with strong natural abilities" (HC 1:215). He came into the Church as a result of witnessing a marvelous miracle when the lame, rheumatic arm of Mrs. John Johnson was healed by the Prophet Joseph, who said to her: "Woman, in the name of the Lord Jesus Christ I command thee to be whole." She "at once lifted it up with ease, and on her return home the next day she was able to do her washing without difficulty or pain." (HC 1:216.) Although appointed to go to Missouri with Isaac Morley (D&C 52:23), Booth and his companion evidently failed in some aspect of their mission, for the Lord severely rebuked the two of them in a later revelation (D&C 64:15–16).

Booth lost his faith and left the Church. A description of his apostasy is given in the following words: "Ezra Booth, who apostatized after his return from Missouri, did all in his power to injure the Church. He was responsible for the publication of the earliest attacks against the Church. He also caused articles to be published in the press among which were some scandalous letters published in the Ravenna *Ohio Star*, which created a bitter spirit on the part of many people." (CHMR 1:269.) As a result of this demented activity, the Prophet Joseph and his associate, Sidney Rigdon, were called on to take a short-term mission and refute the many falsehoods then circulating (D&C 71).

Elder B. H. Roberts identified Booth as the first apostate to publish against the Church (HC 1:216). George A. Smith claimed that Booth's "apostasy culminated in collecting a mob who tarred and feathered Joseph Smith, and inflicted upon his family the loss of one of its members" (JD 11:5).

Borders by the Lamanites

In September 1830, several prominent members of the Church were being led astray by the claims of one Hiram Page, who possessed a stone whereby he claimed to be receiving revelation regarding the affairs of Zion. As a result of this experience, the Lord made it clear that none but the President of the Church would be authorized to receive such revelations. (D&C 28:2–7.) Evidently, one of the things of which Page claimed knowledge was the location of the future city of Zion, for the Lord said, "no man knoweth where the city Zion shall be built, but it shall be given hereafter. Behold, I say unto you that it shall be on the borders by the Lamanites." (D&C 28:9.) Less than a year later, in July 1831, this location was revealed as Independence, Jackson County, Missouri. Furthermore, the "borders by the Lamanites" were referred to as "the line running directly between Jew and Gentile" (D&C 57:1–4).

See also: Line Running Between Jew and Gentile

Born of Me

The Savior promised that those who would believe his words would be "born of me, even of water and of the spirit" (D&C 5:16). To merely profess belief in Christ's words is insufficient to obtain this birth, for, as President Joseph F. Smith proclaimed, "if one 'believes,' he must also obey" (JD 23:170). The phrase *born of me* is elsewhere rendered as "born again" (John 3:1–8), "born of him" (Mosiah 5:7), "born of the Spirit" (Mosiah 27:24), and "born of God" (Alma

5:14). President Joseph Fielding Smith explained that those who are baptized and confirmed, with full purpose of heart, "are *born again* and thus come *back into spiritual life*, and through their continued obedience to the end, they shall be made partakers of the blessings of eternal life in the celestial kingdom of God" (DS 2:223).

To be born again is to be "spiritually begotten" of Christ and become "his sons and his daughters" (Mosiah 5:7). It is to have "the image of God engraven upon your countenance" (Alma 5:14–19), thus reflecting a godly image in everything one thinks, says, or does. Adding another dimension, President Harold B. Lee said, "It means to be quickened in the inner man . . . ; when our hearts are changed through faith on his name, we are born again" (SHP, 54–55).

The Prophet Joseph Smith added this inspired thought: "Whosoever is born of God doth not continue in sin; for the Spirit of God remaineth in him; and he cannot continue in sin, because he is born of God, having received that holy Spirit of promise" (JST, 1 John 3:9).

See also: Baptism; Baptism of Fire; Gift of the Holy Ghost; Holy Spirit of Promise; Sanctification

Bosom

The bosom has generally been seen as encasing the heart—the designated symbol of one's inner-most thoughts and feelings, the center of emotion. It is descriptive of closeness, intimacy, or affection. Christ's presence "in the bosom of the Father, even from the beginning" (D&C 76:13, 25, 39; 109:4) is illustrative not only of his close proximity to the Father but more particularly of his being in tune with the sacred thoughts and feelings held within the Father's bosom.

It is this type of "oneness" which can bring all mankind into the "bosom of the Father" (D&C 35:2; 50:43; John 17:20–26). Enoch's righteousness brought him and his city into the bosom of the Lord (D&C 38:4), and it is from the Lord's bosom (presence) that the holy scriptures have gone forth (D&C 35:20). God's throne is in the bosom of eternity; that is, his presence is at the very heart of the galactic bosom which encompasses his creations; he "is in the midst of all things" (D&C 88:13).

The bosom of the Church mentioned in an 1831 revelation had reference to the heart or center of Church activity at that time (D&C 38:38).

See also: Bosom Shall Burn

Bosom Shall Burn

In describing the process of revelation, the Lord told Oliver Cowdery that he must first "study it out in [his] mind; then . . . ask me if it be right, and if it is right I will cause that your bosom shall burn within you; therefore, you shall feel that it is right'' (D&C 9:8). In describing the nature of this feeling, Elder S. Dilworth Young said: "If I am to receive revelation from the Lord, I must be in harmony with him by keeping his commandments. Then as needed, according to his wisdom, his word will come into my mind through my thoughts, accompanied by a feeling in the region of my bosom. *It is a feeling which cannot be described*, but the nearest word we have is 'burn' or 'burning.' Accompanying this always is a feeling of peace, a further witness that what one heard is right." (En., May 1976, p. 23; italics added.)

See also: Feel; Prayer; Revelation; Speak Peace to Your Mind; Stupor of Thought; Testimony

Boston, Massachusetts

In the fall of 1832, the Prophet Joseph Smith accompanied Bishop Newel K. Whitney on a "hurried journey" to the cities of Boston, New York, and Albany (HC 1:295). This trip was made in accordance with the will of the Lord that the inhabitants of these cities should be warned and hear the gospel (D&C 84:114–15).

Boston, the capital of Massachusetts, though unusually small in geographical land mass, has an influence well beyond its borders. It lies strategically on Massachusetts Bay, an arm of the Atlantic Ocean. "As a city and as a name, Boston is a symbol of much that has gone into the development of the American con-

sciousness," says the *Encyclopedia Brittanica*. From the moment Puritans established the city in 1630, through the Revolutionary War and up to the present time, it has been a world-renowned center of concentrated activity. It is perhaps therefore symbolic of the "great and magnificent cities" which Elder Orson Pratt stated would be left desolate at some future date (MS 28:633-34).

Bowels

The Apostle Paul wrote that he longed after the Saints "in the bowels of Jesus" (Philip. 1:8). The Greek meaning of *bowels* is "affections" or "compassions." Cruden suggests that the word is used often to express "the seat of pity or kindness" (Cruden, 54). Paul admonished the Colossians to put on "bowels of mercies, kindness, humbleness of mind, meekness, longsuffering" (Col. 3:12).

The concept of kindness or compassion is inherent in the usage of the word *bowels* in the Doctrine and Covenants. For example, an anguished prophet pleaded from his prison that the Lord's bowels would be moved with compassion upon his suffering Saints (D&C 121:3–4). Joseph Smith also admonished his followers to "let thy bowels also be full of charity towards all men" (D&C 121:45). Speaking of some who were suffering, the Lord said, "My bowels are filled with compassion towards them" (D&C

101:9). In other words, the center of his emotions was directed towards them.

Occassionally the word *bowels* can refer to the womb (1 Ne. 21:1; 1 Kgs. 3:26).

See also: Brotherly Kindness

Box-Tree

Among the items the Saints were encouraged to bring to Nauvoo for the building of a house for the Most High was the box-tree (D&C 124:26). This is simply an evergreen tree that is also mentioned in the Old Testament (Isa. 41:19; 60:13). Its hard wood is particularly prized by engravers.

Boynton, John F.

Although he is not mentioned in the revelations contained in the Doctrine and Covenants, the name of John F. Boynton is affixed to the preface as one of the Twelve who bore witness as to the divine origin of the commandments and instruction contained in "the Book of the Lord's Commandments," the Doctrine and Covenants. Boynton was ordained one of the original members of the Quorum of the Twelve Apostles at the age of twenty-three, less than three years after he joined the fledgling faith of the Saints. Unfortunately, he did not remain faithful and was disfellowshipped from the Quorum of the Twelve in 1837 and shortly thereafter was excommunicated from the Church.

"Boynton later traveled through the United States giving lectures on natural history, geology, and other sciences. His name was in the patent office for some thirty-six patents." (LDS 2:46.) While he experienced these kinds of worldly successes, he never regained his spiritual stature and died October 20, 1890, outside the faith that held eternal rewards for him (CA 1978, 106).

See also: Those Who Have Fallen

Branch

One use of the word *branch* is as a unit of The Church of Jesus Christ of Latter-day Saints. From the time the Church was organized in April 1830, the Lord referred to these units (D&C 20:65–66). In our day, branches are generally the smallest units of the Church and are presided over by a branch president. Symbolically, a branch is a small extension from the main trunk of the tree representing the Church.

The word *branch* is also used in symbolic language to represent an extension of one's posterity (D&C 10:60) or the future existence of the individual himself. In the second instance, the wicked are warned that if they remain unrepentant they shall be wasted and left with "neither root nor branch" (D&C 109:50–52).

Branch of the House of Jacob

The term *branch* is used to denote the posterity of someone in the same sense that branches of a tree derive their existence from the trunk thereof. The specific phrase, *branch of the house of Jacob* is unique to the Doctrine and Covenants (10:60) and refers to a particular line of the posterity of Israel (Jacob). This specific branch was that body of people whom God led to the Americas shortly after 600 B.C. and whom we presently know as Lamanites. These people are descendants of the "other sheep" of whom the Savior anciently spoke and who received his resurrected presence (John 10:16; 3 Ne. 15:21–24). They are descendants of Jacob through his sons Joseph (1 Ne. 6:2) and Judah (D&C 19:27; Hel. 6:10).

See also: Remnant of Jacob

Bread

One of the earliest injunctions given to man was that he should "eat his bread by the sweat of his brow" (Moses 5:1; Gen. 3:19). Bread is the staff of life. To possess and partake of bread is to preserve life. The Lord promised William Law that if he would be faithful, his posterity would not "be found begging bread" (D&C 124:90). This promise may well have had spiritual as well as temporal implications.

Although other emblems may be used in the sacrament (D&C 27:1–2), it is significant that bread is most generally used in the sacrament of the Lord's Supper (D&C 20:40, 75–77; Moro. 4:1–3). It reminds us of the body of He who is the Bread of life (John 6:30–58), the spiritual staff of eternal life. By partaking of the gospel of Jesus Christ, we eat of the living Bread and ensure our eternal lives.

Breastplate

The three special witnesses to the Book of Mormon were promised that they would have a view of the "breastplate" (D&C 17:1). Joseph Smith first mentions this item in his review of his experience with the angel Moroni. Among the sacred artifacts being entrusted to his care were "two stones in silver bows—and these stones, fastened to a breastplate, constituted what is called the Urim and Thummim" (JS—H 1:35).

The Prophet Joseph allowed his mother to examine the breastplate, and from her we obtain this description: "It was concave on one side and convex on the other, and extended from the neck downwards, as far as the center of the stomach of a man of extraordinary size. It had four straps of the same material, for the purpose of fastening it to the breast, two of which ran back to go over the shoulders, and the other two were designed to fasten to the hips. They were just the width of two of my fingers . . . and they had holes in the end of them, to be convenient in fastening." (LMS, 111–12.) Evidently, the Urim and Thummim could be attached to the breastplate to free the hands of the translator (Ex. 28:30; Lev. 8:8).

Breastplate of Righteousness

Part of the "whole armor of God" is the "breastplate of righteousness" (D&C 27:15–16; Eph. 6:14). The breastplate is that piece of armor which protects one's heart. Righteousness provides one with a protective breastplate against the weapons of wickedness. President Harold B. Lee stated: "The righteous man, although far superior to his fellows who are not, is humble and does not parade his righteousness to be seen of men but conceals his virtues as he would modestly conceal his nudity. The righteous man strives for self-improvement knowing that he has daily need of repentance for his misdeeds or his neglect. He is not so much concerned about what he can get but more about how much he can give to others, knowing that along that course only can he find true happiness. *He endeavors to make each day his masterpiece so that at night's close he can witness in his soul and to his God that whatever has come to his hand that day, he has done to the best of his*

ability. His body is not dissipated and weakened by the burdens imposed by the demands of riotous living; his judgment is not rendered faulty by the follies of youth; he is clear of vision, keen of intellect, and strong of body. The breastplate of righteousness has given him 'the strength of ten —because his heart is clean.' " (SHP, 332–33, italics added.)

Breastwork of the Pulpit

When the Lord Jesus Christ appeared in the Kirtland Temple, he stood upon the "breastwork of the pulpit" (D&C 110:2). The Kirtland Temple had a stand on both the east and west ends. The east stand was reserved for the Aaronic Priesthood and the west stand for the presiding officers of the Melchizedek Priesthood. On each of these stands was a series of four pulpits, one rising above the other in terraced fashion and separated by a breastwork, which was a railing or decorative structure about breast high. "Each of these pulpits could be separated from the others by means of veils of painted canvas, which could be let down or rolled up at pleasure" (SS, 723–24; En., Jan. 1979, p. 48).

See also: Kirtland Temple

Bridegroom

In the parable of the ten virgins (Matt. 25:1–13), "the Bridegroom is the Lord Jesus; the marriage feast symbolizes His coming in glory, to receive unto Himself the Church on earth as His bride" (Talmage, 578–79). References to Christ as the "Bridegroom" appear in five verses of the Doctrine and Covenants (33:17; 65:3; 88:92; 133:10, 19).

Brimstone

See: Lake of Fire and Brimstone

Broad Seal

The word *broad* generally refers to something that is wide (D&C 132:25; Matt. 7:13; 3 Ne. 14:13; 3 Ne. 27:33; Moses 7:53). However, a different meaning is found in the account of the martyrdom. The spilled blood of Joseph and Hyrum Smith is described as "a broad seal affixed to 'Mormonism' " in the sense that this physical sign of their deaths is emphatic or conspicuous. The witness of their testimonies cannot be easily erased or avoided.
See also: Innocent Blood; Martyrdom; Sealed with His Blood

Broken Hearts

One of the requisites for baptism is that one should manifest a "broken heart" (D&C 20:37; 3 Ne. 9:20). It is usually associated with a "contrite spirit" (D&C 56:17, 18; 59:8; 2 Ne. 2:7; 3 Ne. 12:19; Morm. 2:14; Ether 4:15;

Moro. 6:2). "What is a broken heart?" asked Elder Joseph Fielding Smith. "One that is humble, one that is touched by the Spirit of the Lord, and which is willing to abide in all the covenants and obligations which the Gospel entails" (CR, Oct. 1941, p. 93). To one who offers the Lord such a heart will the "gates of hell be shut continually," and the "gates of righteousness" be open (2 Ne. 4:32).
See also: Contrite Spirit

Broome County

The only mention of Broome County, New York, appears as a reference point regarding the restoration of the Melchizedek Priesthood. It was in the wilderness between this county and Susquehanna County, Pennsylvania, that this restoration took place (D&C 128:20). Broome County was the site of Colesville, which figured prominently in the history of the Church from 1830 to 1831.
See also: Colesville

Brother

The word *brother* may refer to a male sibling, such as Hyrum being Joseph Smith's brother (D&C 135:3). In a general sense, "all men are brothers in the sense of being the spirit offspring of Deity" (MD, 105). Thus, the admonition that "every man esteem his brother as himself" (D&C

38:25) applies to all mankind (male and female), not merely blood brothers. The salutations of "brother" and "sister" within the Lord's Church are symbolic of the spiritual ties which bind the membership together (see Matt. 12:46–50).

Brother of Jared

The "brother of Jared" mentioned in Doctrine and Covenants 17:1 refers to an ancient prophet of great faith whose origin was in the days of the Tower of Babel (Ether 1:33–34). The history of his people is recorded in the book of Ether within the Book of Mormon.

His given name is not mentioned in the Book of Mormon, but was later revealed to the Prophet Joseph Smith in a most interesting way: "While residing in Kirtland Elder Reynolds Cahoon had a son born to him. One day when President Joseph Smith was passing his door he called the Prophet in and asked him to bless and name the baby. Joseph did so and gave the boy the name of *Mahonri Moriancumer*. When he had finished the blessing he laid the child on the bed, and turning to Elder Cahoon he said, 'The name I have given your son is the name of the brother of Jared; the Lord has just shown (or revealed) it to me.' Elder William F. Cahoon, who was standing near, heard the Prophet make this statement to his father; and this was the first time the name of the brother of Jared was known in the Church in this dispensation." (IE 8:705.)

See also: Cahoon, Reynolds

Brotherly Kindness

Those engaged in Christ's ministry must develop the quality of "brotherly kindness" if they are to succeed (D&C 4:6; 107:30). This trait is specifically mentioned in only one other place in scripture (2 Pet. 1:7), although the term *brotherly love* could be considered a synonym (Rom. 12:10; 1 Thess. 4:9; Heb. 13:1).

To be brotherly is to experience a warmth of feeling for another that transcends mere fraternal relationship. It is a genuine, sincere interest in another. Kindliness denotes benevolence, compassion, sympathetic forbearance, graciousness, and humaneness toward another. When one combines *brotherly kindness* into one term and cultivates the qualities symbolic of its meaning, a true saint in the household of God emerges (Eph. 2:19).

See also: Bowels

Brunson, Seymour

The name of Seymour Brunson first appears in the Doctrine and Covenants in a revelation given at the Amherst conference in January 1832. He, along with other brethren, was admonished to "be united in the ministry" (D&C 75:33). Brunson joined the

Church in January 1831 and was ordained an elder the same month by John Whitmer. He labored as a missionary in Ohio, Virginia, and several other states and experienced the persecution of the Missouri period of Church history. He was called to the Nauvoo Stake high council in October 1839, in which capacity he served until his death on August 10, 1840. (Jenson 3:331.) That he was a faithful follower of the Master is evidenced by the Lord's own testimony, given in January of 1841: "Seymour Brunson I have taken unto myself" (D&C 124:132).

Buckler

The word *buckler* is used only once in the Doctrine and Covenants (35:14). The Lord promises the faithful who go forth to teach his gospel that he will be "their shield and their buckler." The Old Testament speaks of God being the buckler of those who trust him and who walk uprightly (Ps. 18:2; Prov. 2:7). According to Webster, a buckler can either be a shield or "one that shields and protects." God is the One who shields and protects the faithful from the fiery darts of the adversary.

See also: Shield of Faith

Buffetings of Satan

"To be turned over to the *buffetings of Satan* is to be given into

his hands; it is to be turned over to him with all the protective power of the priesthood, of righteousness, and of godliness removed, so that Lucifer is free to torment, persecute, and afflict such a person without let or hindrance. When the bars are down, the cuffs and curses of Satan, both in this world and in the world to come, bring indescribable anguish typified by burning fire and brimstone. The damned in hell so suffer.

"Those who broke their covenants in connection with the United Order in the early days of this dispensation were to 'be delivered over to the buffetings of Satan until the day of redemption.' (D&C 78:12; 82:20–21; 104:9–10.) A similar fate (plus destruction in the flesh) is decreed against those who have been sealed up unto eternal life so that their callings and elections have been made sure and who thereafter turn to grievous sin. (D&C 131:5; 132:19–26.)" (MD, 108.)

One who is excommunicated from the Church is "turned over to the buffetings of Satan," for all priesthood power is removed. However, "through sincere repentance, a forsaking of sin, and the reordering of their lives to the divine will, there is a cleansing of soul and a feeling of forgiveness for their transgressions. Those renewed in faith testify that the period of their sinning was the unhappiest time of their lives. Paying the penalty for their mistakes has strengthened them to resolve with an unwavering faith to follow an undeviating path of righteousness." (Delbert L. Stapley, CR, Apr. 1970, p. 75.)

Burlington, Iowa

In 1841, William Law, Second Counselor in the First Presidency, was instructed to "proclaim [the] everlasting gospel with a loud voice, and with great joy, as he shall be moved upon by [the] Spirit unto the inhabitants of Warsaw, . . . Carthage, . . . Burlington, and . . . Madison" (D&C 124:88). Burlington was a town in Iowa located about thirty miles up the Mississippi River from Nauvoo.

Burn

Throughout scripture the Lord has consistently warned the proud and the wicked that unless they repent they shall be burned (D&C 29:9; Matt. 3:12; 2 Ne. 26:4). They have often been compared to a field, especially the tares or chaff thereof, that is ready to be burned and turned to stubble (D&C 32:4; 101:66; Luke 3:17). This may refer to an actual physical destruction or to a spiritual purification. This is one way in which God cleanses earth's environment of man's evil impurities.
See also: Bosom Shall Burn; Day That Shall Burn as an Oven; Earth Is Ripe; Fire; He That Is Tithed Shall Not Be Burned; Lamps Trimmed and Burning; Stubble; Tares

Burnett, Stephen

Stephen Burnett's name appears in two revelations given in 1832, both of which called him to be involved in the ministry (75:35; 80:1). A few years later he became critical of Church leadership and became one of the spiritual casualties who commence the strait and narrow path and then lose their way because of clouded vision and faltering faith (HC 1:405; see 1 Ne. 8:20–32).

Burroughs, Philip

The only mention of Philip Burroughs is in a revelation given to John Whitmer, constituting Burroughs's only footnote in official Church records (D&C 30:10). Whitmer is told to preach in the vicinity of "your brother Philip Burroughs' " home. Evidence indicates that Burroughs lived in Seneca County in western New York (APP, 42).

Bury Thy Talent

See: Talent

Butterfield, Josiah

Though mentioned but once in the Doctrine and Covenants (124:138), Josiah Butterfield was prominent in Mormon leadership circles from 1837 to 1844, when he served as one of the First Seven

Presidents of the Seventies. He assisted in the building of the Kirtland Temple as early as 1835, and on April 6, 1837, he received his appointment as one of the Seven Presidents. He traveled as one of the "commissioners" of the Kirtland Camp, which was an organized group of Saints who traveled from Kirtland to Missouri in 1838. Butterfield later assisted the poor in relocating from the strife-ridden lands of Missouri.

Though active in Church government in Nauvoo, Butterfield was excommunicated from the Church "for neglect of duty and for other causes, at the general conference held at Nauvoo, Oct. 7, 1844" (Jenson 1:192). Some years later he came through Utah on his way to California and expressed his faith in "Mormonism," though he never actively participated in the Church again. He died in Monterey County, California, in April 1871.

C

Caesar

The Roman emperor, or sovereign of Judea in New Testament times, was a man whose title was "Caesar" (John 19:12, 15). At the time Christ was born, this man was Caesar Augustus (Luke 2:1). Years later, in a confrontation with the Pharisees and the Herodians, the Savior was asked to declare the legality of paying tribute to Caesar.

"Render . . . unto Caesar the things which are Caesar's," was the Lord's reply, "and unto God the things that are God's" (Matt. 22:15–22; Mark 12:13–17; Luke 20:20–26). "That is, in this present world where wicked men will not repent and come unto the fulness of the Lord's perfect order of government, there must be two separate powers — ecclesiastical and civil — the one supreme in spiritual matters, the other in temporal. Neither power can dictate to the other. And men are subject to them both." (DNTC 1:600–601.)

In 1831, the Lord reminded the Saints that though he held ultimate title to the land of Zion, under present circumstances the land was to be purchased from the modern-day "Caesars" who held legal title to it (D&C 63:25–27).

Cahoon, Reynolds

Among the prominent names of early Church history was that of Reynolds Cahoon. He is mentioned four times in the Doctrine and Covenants (52:30; 61:35; 75:32; 94:14). In 1831, the Lord indicated his pleasure with the labors of Cahoon and Samuel Smith (D&C 61:35). He later received an inheritance in Kirtland from the Lord (D&C 94:14) and served as a member of the three-man building committee for the temple. He was a member of the Montrose, Iowa, high council (HC 4:16) and a counselor in the stake at Adam-ondi-Ahman, Missouri (HC 3:28).

Unfortunately, he was one of those who persuaded the Prophet Joseph to place his life in the hands of the authorities at Carthage, where his blood was shed (HC 6:549, 552). Cahoon served as a member of the bodyguard that accompanied the Prophet's body back to Nauvoo in what must have been a particularly painful journey for him (HC 7:135). Brigham Young appointed him captain of the sixth company of one hundred Saints that left Nauvoo in October 1845 (HC 7:482). He was later chosen as a counselor in the presidency of one of the emigrating camps (HC 7:626).

See also: Brother of Jared

Cain

Cain, a son of Adam and Eve, inscribed his indelible infamy on the pages of history when he inexorably sold his soul to Satan and killed his younger, more faithful, brother Abel (Moses 5:16–41; Gen. 4:1–16). Because of his crime, a mark was set upon him and he was "shut out from the presence of the Lord." He loved Satan more than God, and was referred to as "Perdition" and "Master Mahan."

Elder Joseph Fielding Smith has written: "The saddest story in all history is the story of Cain. Born heir to an everlasting inheritance in righteousness, with the promise of a crown of glory that would never fade away, and that too, in the morning of creation when all things were new—and he threw it away!" (WTP, 97.) The Lord told Cain that he would rule over Satan (Moses 5:23). Following the resurrection, this will become a reality because "they who have tabernacles, have power over those who have not" (TPJS, 190). However, this "power" will be a shallow victory to one consigned to suffer the fate of a son of perdition (D&C 76:31–43).

See also: Greediness; Offerings of Cain; Perdition; Sons of Perdition

Cainan

In a revelation on priesthood, the line of authority from Adam through the early patriarchs reveals that a great-grandson of Adam was a man named Cainan (D&C 107:45). The Lord "called upon Cainan in the wilderness in the fortieth year of his age," and he then received his ordination from Adam at the age of eighty-seven. He was among the great high priests accompanying Adam in the great council held in the valley of Adam-ondi-Ahman, three years before Adam's death (D&C 107:53). Cainan was born in the ninetieth year of his father Enos's life, and he himself begat his son Mahalaleel in the seventieth year of his life. A "land of promise" was named in his honor (Gen. 5:9–14; Moses 6:17–19). He is also mentioned as a forefather of Joseph, the husband of Mary (Luke 3:37–38).

Cainhannoch

In a revelation regarding the United Order at Kirtland, the Lord referred to the debts which were owed to their creditors in "Cainhannoch," which was later identified as New York (D&C 104:81, pre 1981-editions). Neither the nature of these debts nor the names and locations of the creditors were identified, but the Lord indicated his willingness to soften their hearts. That these debts were ultimately paid seems apparent from a statement made by President Brigham Young in 1874, when he declared, "We have sent East to New York, to Ohio, and to every place where I had any idea that Joseph had ever done business, and inquired if there was a man left to whom Joseph Smith, jun., the Prophet, owed a dollar, or a sixpence. If there was we would pay it. But I

have not been able to find one. . . . Consequently I have a right to conclude that all his debts were settled." (JD 18:242.)

The reason for the strange name of Cainhannoch being attached to New York was the desire to keep the world from knowing the true meaning of some of the early revelations (HC 1:255). This name does not appear in current editions of the Doctrine and Covenants.

See also: New York City

Caleb

The name of Caleb appears in the priesthood line of authority revealed in 1832 (D&C 84:7–8). He received his priesthood "under the hand of Elihu" and in turn conferred it on Jethro, who was the father-in-law of Moses. The Old Testament speaks of a contemporary of Joshua whose name was Caleb, but circumstances appear to eliminate his being the same Caleb mentioned in the Doctrine and Covenants. The Old Testament Caleb was one of the heads of tribes sent by Moses to search out the land of Canaan in the second year after the Exodus. This man and Joshua were the only ones from the original camp of Israel to survive the forty years in the wilderness (Num. 13; 14; 26:65). It seems unreasonable to believe that the Caleb who bestowed the priesthood on Jethro, who in turn conferred it on Moses, would be the same man who would later be under the jurisdiction of Moses and outlive that great prophet. Thus, we conclude that the Caleb of the Doctrine and Covenants is an unknown priesthood leader whose history is yet to be revealed.

Called

"Behold, there are many called, but few are chosen," declared the Lord (D&C 121:34). Those who "love God . . . are the called according to his purpose," said Paul (Rom. 8:28). Evidently, many of these callings came in councils held in premortality, when the Lord *foreordained* those with manifest talents to perform certain callings on the earth.

"These pre-existence appointments, made 'according to the foreknowledge of God the Father' (1 Pet. 1:2), simply designated certain individuals to perform missions which the Lord in his wisdom knew they had the talents and capacities to do. . . . By their foreordination the Lord merely gives them the opportunity to serve him and his purposes if they will choose to measure up to the standard he knows they are capable of attaining." (DNTC 2:268.)

Based on their performance in this life, many are called to the ministry. Unfortunately, however, many fail to perform and are found "walking in darkness at noon-day" (D&C 95:5–6). These will find themselves among those who are not chosen. Elder Joseph Fielding Smith said that "every man who is ordained to an office in the priesthood has been called" (CR, Oct. 1945, p. 97).

See also: Day of Calling

Camp of Israel

Doctrine and Covenants 136 provided instructions on how the Saints were to be organized in their trek across the terrain between Nauvoo, Illinois, and the Salt Lake Valley. The Lord referred to this body of exiles as the "Camp of Israel" (D&C 136:1). According to the official history, " 'Camp of Israel' was the name given to sections of the moving caravans, but more especially to the part of the encampment graced by the presence of President Brigham Young and his associate Apostles; from which headquarters instructions and orders were issued to the encampments along the whole line of march" (HC 7:606).

Canal, The

An 1831 revelation warned the Prophet Joseph and his companions not to continue traveling upon the waters they had previously traveled but to "journey . . . upon the canal" (D&C 61:23). "By this the Lord probably means canals, of which there were a number in the region concerned" (DCC, 258).

See also: Waters

Canker Your Souls

The Lord warns the rich who will not give of their substance to the poor that their riches will canker their souls (D&C 56:16). One of the definitions of canker is "to corrupt with a malignancy of mind or spirit." Those who greedily set their hearts on the temporal treasures of this earth, turning their backs on the needy, leave a festering sore on their spirits that, if not corrected, can consume them. Their substance will perish with their souls. (See Mosiah 4:16–23.)

Cappadocia

In pondering over the scriptures, President Joseph F. Smith reflected upon the areas of Asia where the early Saints resided (D&C 138:5). Among these areas was Cappadocia, which was the eastern district of Asia Minor and part of the ancient Roman empire. It is mentioned in the writings of Luke and Peter (Acts 2:9; 1 Pet. 1:1). The district can be seen on maps 11, 13, 19, 20, 21, and 22 in the LDS edition of the King James Bible.

Cares of the World

See: Honors of Men; Praise of the World

Carmel

See: Dews of Carmel

Carnal

The term *carnal* appears five times in the Doctrine and Covenants; three times in conjunction with the word *natural* (29:35; 67:10, 12). Elsewhere in this volume, the term *natural* is defined as the opposite of "spiritual" and is related to that which is physical or of the flesh. Webster defines *carnal* as that which relates to the body or is sensual. One who is carnal or sensual is one who spends his time striving to bring pleasure to his senses, indulging in bodily gratifications. To be so inclined is to remove oneself from the abode or presence of Deity. Thus, the Lord warns against seeking after "carnal desires" (D&C 3:4), for one cannot endure his holy presence with a carnal mind (D&C 67:10, 12). Well did the Psalmist state: "Who shall ascend into the hill of the Lord? or who shall stand in his holy place? He that hath clean hands, and a pure heart; who hath not lifted up his soul unto vanity, nor sworn deceitfully." (Ps. 24:3–4.)

Carter, Gideon

Though mentioned only once in the Doctrine and Covenants (75:34), Gideon Carter occupied a unique role in Church history, for he was one of the first martyrs for the faith. His history begins with his baptism by the Prophet Joseph on October 25, 1831, at Orange, Ohio. His confirmation occurred under the hands of Sidney Rigdon. He performed several short-term missions for the Church. Carter answered the call for help on the night of October 24, 1838, when news reached Far West, Missouri, of a mob uprising against the Saints. In the battle that ensued at Crooked River, he was one of three men who lost their lives in behalf of their brethren. His wounds were so devastating that he was defaced and his comrades did not recognize him. (Jenson 3:615–16.)

Carter, Jared

The name of Jared Carter appears six times in the Doctrine and Covenants in revelations received between June 1831 and February 1834. His ordination as a priest (D&C 52:38) and his call to the Kirtland high council are recorded (D&C 102:3, 34). The entire revelation in section 79 is addressed to him, and the Lord promised that "inasmuch as he is faithful, I will crown him again with sheaves." In Kirtland he was given a special inheritance by the Lord (D&C 94:14). In September 1835, a high council trial for Carter was held in Kirtland regarding some of his teachings. Joseph Smith indicated Carter had erred because of his "rebellious spirit" but had "not designed to do wickedly." A public apology was rendered, and Carter later served faithfully on high councils in Far West and Kirtland (HC

2:277–80, 510–11; 3:14). He also served on a three-man building committee for the erection of the Kirtland Temple. In July 1843, Carter served as a special missionary sent out to set right the public mind over the arrest of Joseph Smith by some Missouri sheriffs (HC 5:484–85). Though prominent in the affairs of the early Church, the last mention of him is in September 1844, when Brigham Young wrote of a confession rendered by Carter and of his promise to return to the Church (HC 7:271). How long he had been in disfavor and what he had done was not made clear. He remained in Illinois, where he died sometime prior to 1850.

Carter, John S.

The minutes of the organization of the first high council of the Church, at Kirtland, Ohio, reveal that John S. Carter was sustained as the fifth-ranking member of that body (D&C 102:3, 34). This occurred in February 1834. About a week later, he was called on a mission to the east with Jesse Smith (HC 2:35). He was a member of the famed Zion's Camp, where he lost his life. This event was described by the Prophet Joseph: "When the cholera made its appearance, Elder John S. Carter was the first man who stepped forward to rebuke it, and upon this, was instantly seized, and became the first victim in the camp. He died about six o'clock in the afternoon.'' (HC 2:115.) Perhaps John S. Carter was a modern-day Uzza who died from a divine rebuke when he "put forth his hand to steady the ark" (1 Chron. 13:9–10). Joseph Smith himself learned "that when the great Jehovah decrees destruction upon any people, and makes known His determination, man must not attempt to stay His hand'' (HC 2:114).

Carter, Simeon

In a revelation given at the Amherst, Ohio, conference, Simeon Carter was admonished to unite in the ministry with Emer Harris (D&C 75:30). The previous June, he had been called on a short-term mission with Solomon Hancock (D&C 52:27). Carter's name appears frequently in early Church documents. In 1831, he was appointed as a member of a six-man committee responsible for instructing the Saints in the techniques of conducting meetings (HC 1:219). He served as a branch president in Missouri and on high councils in two locations in that state (HC 2:124, 253; 6:409). Following the Missouri persecutions, Carter expressed his faith in the Prophet Joseph and indicated his own personal desire "to persevere and act in righteousness in all things, so that he might at last gain a crown of glory, and reign in the kingdom of God'' (HC 3:225). Carter was sent by Brigham Young to preside over a new unnamed district in the outlying areas of the Church in October 1844 (HC 7:305–7). He later served a mission to England and eventually migrated to the Rocky Mountains, settling in Brigham City, where he died February 3, 1869.

Carter, William

Following a conference in Kirtland, Ohio, in June 1831, William Carter was called to travel to Missouri with Wheeler Baldwin (D&C 52:31). There is some indication he did not fulfill this assignment and that he was stripped of his priesthood in September of that same year.

Several years later a man by the name of "Wm. Carter" is mentioned in the Prophet Joseph Smith's writings as one "who was blind" and who "was promised a restoration of sight, if faithful'' (HC 2:205–7). A man bearing that same name was listed as a member of the martial band that performed upon the return of the bodies of Joseph and Hyrum Smith from Carthage to Nauvoo (HC 7:135). According to one source Carter was "one of the Utah pioneers who put the first ploughs into the ground and planted the first potatoes in Salt Lake Valley'' (SS, 308). However, recent historians have questioned whether the pioneer named William Carter was the same individual as the one to whom the 1831 revelation was directed.

Carthage

A name that will forever elicit strong feelings among the Saints of God is *Carthage*. Initially mentioned as a location where the gospel was to be preached (D&C 124:88), its blood-stained borders later harbored those fiends whose foul deeds against the Prophet will live forever in infamy. Carthage, Illinois, the county seat of Hancock County, was located about fifteen miles southeast of Nauvoo. It became the stage whereupon one of the world's greatest dramas was portrayed. Masked with blackened faces, an estimated mob of 150 men attacked a state-guaranteed sanctuary, killing the Prophet Joseph Smith and his patriarch-brother Hyrum, leaving "the best blood of the nineteenth century" to stain the stage of the mob's actions (D&C 135).

Thus, a town with a population of only several hundred was placed on the mortal marquee of significant sites in history. Since the martyrdoms of Joseph and Hyrum Smith, scores of Saints have come within Carthage's borders as they have sorrowfully recounted the tragedy of June 27, 1844.

See also: Carthage Jail

Carthage Jail

On the northwest edge of the small town of Carthage, Illinois, stands a simple, two-story building. This structure is of far more significance to mankind than many shrines in which the world has sought spiritual solace. It was within the walls of this building that shouts and shots subdued the physical bodies of Joseph and Hyrum Smith, eternally sealing their testimonies and sending their spirits into the next dimension of their sacred work. Thus, an inconspicuous structure — Carthage Jail, a building constructed for purposes of confinement — became the setting where two noble spirits sealed a binding testimony that, if accepted, can set men eternally free. *"No man,"* said Joseph Fielding Smith, *"can reject that testimony without incurring the most dreadful consequences, for he cannot enter the kingdom of God"* (DS 1:190).

In the words of Elder John Taylor, "their innocent blood on the floor of Carthage jail is a broad seal affixed to 'Mormonism' that cannot be rejected by any court on earth, and their innocent blood . . . is a witness to the truth of the everlasting gospel that all the world cannot impeach" (D&C 135:7).

See also: Broad; Carthage; Escutcheon; Innocent Blood; Martyrdom; Sealed His Mission with His Blood; Smith, Hyrum; Smith, Joseph

Cause of Zion

One of the great purposes of God's servants throughout the

ages has been to "bring forth and establish the cause of Zion" (D&C 6:6; 11:6; 12:6; 21:7; HC 4:609-10). Speaking of this cause, President Joseph Fielding Smith said: "That is our work, to establish Zion, to build up the kingdom of God, to preach the gospel to every creature in the world, that not one soul may be overlooked where there is the possibility for us to present unto him the truth" (CR, Apr. 1951, pp. 152-53). Zion is "THE PURE IN HEART" (D&C 97:21), and the society of Zion is one in which the people live in such a state of purity and love that the Lord dwells in the midst of them.

See also: Zion

Celestial

In a marvelous revelatory instruction, the habitations of the hereafter were revealed to Joseph Smith and Sidney Rigdon (D&C 76). Among those kingdoms depicted was that of a celestial order. According to a later revelation, this kingdom, which is as the glory of the sun, is divided into three heavens or degrees (D&C 131:1-4). The highest heaven is only attainable by those who have paid the price of righteousness and entered into all ordinances of the gospel, including that of celestial marriage. "Those who receive a lesser degree in the celestial kingdom, will not be made equal in power, might and dominion, and many blessings of

the exaltation will be denied them" (CHMR 1:287).

The characteristics of the celestial Saints inhabiting this kingdom are outlined by the Lord and include the all-important "sealing by the Holy Spirit of promise" of individuals who were "valiant in the testimony of Jesus" and zealously accepted the laws of God (D&C 76:50-70). President George Q. Cannon observed that "the man who seeks for the possession of celestial glory is not content with treading the well-beaten road travelled in by the world, but his mind soars aloft with an intense desire to comprehend and put into practice every law pertaining to exaltation. . . . His continual struggle will be to obey those higher laws which can only be perceived and understood by those who attain into very powerful faith." (GT 1:106.) Furthermore, a celestial being must be "willing to sacrifice everything that he has for the cause of God," and before he attains such a glory, he "will be tried to the very uttermost" (GT 1:103; TPJS, 322).

The Lord decreed that "your glory shall be that glory by which your bodies are quickened" (D&C 88:28-32). Thus, those whose celestial spirits have manifested celestial works and have obeyed celestial laws will receive a resurrected body of a celestial order (D&C 88:22). President Brigham Young said, "Those who attain to the blessings of the first or celestial resurrection will be pure and holy, and perfect in body. Every man and woman that reaches to this unspeakable attainment will be as beautiful as the angels that surround the throne of God." (Contributor 9:40, cited in CHMR 2:359.) "These are they whose bodies are celestial, whose glory is that of the sun, even the glory of God" (D&C 76:70, 1 Cor. 15:35–42).

Following the Millennium, this earth will be sanctified, receive its celestial glory, and become the heavenly orb described by John as a "sea of glass" (Articles of Faith 1:10; D&C 77:1). It will be as a sacred seer stone to the celestial Saints who dwell thereon (D&C 130:8–9). In this connection, several statements by President Brigham Young are worth pondering: "When the earth is sanctified, cleansed, and purified by fire, and returns to its paradisiacal state, and becomes like a sea of glass, urim and thummim; when all this is done, and the Savior has presented the earth to his Father, and it is placed in the cluster of the celestial kingdoms, and the Son and all his faithful brethren and sisters have received the welcome plaudit, 'Enter ye into the joy of the Lord', and the Savior is crowned, then and not till then, will the saints receive their everlasting inheritance" (JD 17:117). "This earth, when it becomes purified and sanctified, or celestialized, will become like a sea of glass; and a person, by looking into it, can know things past, present, and to come; though none but celestialized beings can enjoy this privilege. They will look into the earth, and the things they desire to know will be exhibited to them, the same as the face is seen by looking into a mirror." (JD 9:87.)

See also: Church of Enoch; Church of the Firstborn; Glory; Just Men Made Perfect; Mansions of My Father; Presence of God the Father; Resurrection of the Just; Salvation; Saved; Sealed by the Holy Spirit of Promise; Sea of Glass

Celestial Kingdom

See: Celestial

Center Place

In 1831, Independence, Jackson County, Missouri, was designated as the "center place" (D&C 57:3). Smith and Sjodahl have noted: "It has become customary to speak of the 'Center Stake of Zion.' It might, therefore, be well to remember that no Stake was ever organized in Jackson County. Following the figure given by Isaiah ch. 33:20 and 54:2 we cannot speak of a 'center stake of Zion.' . . . Zion is the tent, and how can the tent be a stake?" (SS, 189, fn.) Ultimately, the New Jerusalem, or center place of Zion, will be established and from thence *"the law and the word of the Lord shall go forth to all peoples"* (DS 3:68–69).

See also: City of Zion; Independence, Missouri; Jackson County; New Jerusalem; Work of the Gathering; Zion

Cephas

The name *Cephas* appears but once in the Doctrine and Covenants (76:99). It is used in conjunction with the names of Paul and Apollos, both of whom labored in the ministry of the early Christian Church. The citation has reference to the incident when the Apostle Paul chastized the Corinthians for endeavoring to put a celestial weight on the position or prestige of the person who was responsible for bringing them into the Church. To those who said, "I am of Paul; and I of Apollos; and I of Cephas," Paul asked the penetrating question, "Is Christ divided?" (1 Cor. 1:10–15.)

Cephas, or the chief Apostle Peter, was a very prestigious person (John 1:42). To lay claim to baptism at his hands was evidently seen as a mark of social distinction. However, although the *authority* of the individual performing celestial ordinances is paramount, his *name* is not. Those who wish to be saved in the celestial kingdom must concern themselves with their commitment to Christ alone, otherwise they will fall short of their anticipated celestial abode. This is the message which Paul specified anciently and which the Lord reiterated in our day. (1 Cor. 3; D&C 76: 98–112.)

Chaff

See: Sift Him as Chaff

Chains of Darkness

The "wicked," we are told, are "kept in chains of darkness until the judgment of the great day, which shall come at the end of the earth" (D&C 38:5). Inasmuch as darkness is symbolic of the devil's domain (Rev. 16:10), it appears that "chains of darkness" are synonymous with "chains of hell," for those who "choose works of darkness rather than light . . . must go down to hell" (2 Ne. 26:10). An ancient Nephite prophet proclaimed: "They that will harden their hearts, to them is given the lesser portion of the word until they know nothing concerning his mysteries; and then they are taken captive by the devil, and led by his will down to destruction. Now this is what is meant by the chains of hell." (Alma 12:11.)

Those "angels that sinned" by rebelling and following Lucifer have already been bound in "chains of darkness," being eternally deprived of the light of the gospel (2 Pet. 2:4, Jude 1:6). For those who have traversed this earth with tabernacles of flesh, other than sons of perdition, and shackled themselves with sin, there is hope that they can yet "awake unto God," and have their "souls illuminated by the light of the everlasting word" of God, thus casting off their "chains of darkness" (Alma 5:7).

See also: Fetters of Hell

Chains of Hell

See: Chains of Darkness

Chamber of Old Father Whitmer

In recounting some of the glorious manifestations to which he had been exposed, the Prophet Joseph makes mention of having heard "the voice of God in the chamber of old Father Whitmer" (D&C 128:21). According to Elder B. H. Roberts, this has reference to an experience which Joseph and Oliver Cowdery shared in the spring of 1829 (HC 1:60–61, fn.). Following the visit of John the Baptist on May 15, 1829, Joseph and Oliver reflected often upon the Baptist's promise that if they continued faithful they would receive the Melchizedek Priesthood. Joseph's journal states: "We had for some time made this matter a subject of humble prayer, and at length we got together in the chamber of Mr. Whitmer's house, in order more particularly to seek of the Lord what we now so earnestly desired; and here, to our unspeakable satisfaction, did we realize the truth of the Savior's prom-ise—'Ask, and it shall be given you; seek, and ye shall find; knock, and it shall be opened unto you'—for we had not long been engaged in solemn and fervent prayer, when the word of the Lord came unto us in the chamber" (HC 1:60).

The "chamber" referred to was in the house of Peter Whitmer, Sr., the same house in which the Church would be organized less than one year later. At the time Joseph referred to him as "old Father Whitmer," Peter was sixty-nine years old, which in 1842 was a "ripe old age."

See also: Whitmer, Peter, Sr.

Chariots

In an 1831 revelation to some elders traveling to Missouri, the Lord declared his willingness to let them travel upon horses or mules or in chariots (D&C 62:7). "The use of the word *chariots* seems strange to us in this context. It generally refers to an ancient two-wheeled vehicle, but in this revelation, of course, it has reference to conveyances that were common in the Prophet's day. . . . The word *chariot* seems to have been used commonly in American literature between 1661 and 1828 in reference to a light four-wheeled carriage with only back seats." (DCC, 260.)

Charity

One of the cardinal virtues to be cultivated by those who claim kinship with Christ is *charity*. It is first mentioned in the Doctrine and Covenants among a list of traits necessary for service in the ministry (D&C 4:5–6). Significantly, its last mention is in the account of the martyrdom in which Hyrum Smith read aloud the prophet Moroni's commentary on charity (D&C 135:5; Ether 12:36–38). Addressing the Lord, Moroni said: "I know that *this love which thou hast had for the children of men is charity*; wherefore, except men shall have charity they cannot inherit that place which thou hast prepared in the mansions of thy Father" (Ether 12:34; italics added). The classic definition of charity is also found in the Book of Mormon: "But *charity is the pure love of Christ, and it endureth forever*; and whoso is found possessed of it at the last day, it shall be well with him." (Moro. 7:47: italics added). It is significant that the Spirit taught both Paul and Mormon the elements which help to make charity such a sought-after celestial quality (1 Cor. 13; Moro. 7).

See also: Love

Cheer

See: Good Cheer; Happiness; Joy

Children

See: Children of Disobedience; Children of Ephraim; Children of God; Children of Israel; Children of Jacob; Children of Judah; Children of the Kingdom; Children of Light; Children of Men; Children of Zion; Little Children

Children of Disobedience

The title "children of disobedience" is found in the Doctrine and Covenants (121:17) and in the New Testament (Eph. 2:2; 5:6; Col. 3:6). These are those individuals "who walk after the manner of the world, who are carnal, sensual, and devilish, who are subject to the lusts of the flesh" (DNTC 2:499).

See also: Servants of Sin

Children of Ephraim

As used in section 133, the term *children of Ephraim* refers specifically to those faithful members of the Church in the latter days who will minister to the spiritual and temporal needs of the other tribes of Israel as they return to the fold of the Great Shepherd. When the lost tribes return, for example, they shall receive their blessings at the hands of the latter-day Saints, who, for the most part, are the children of Ephraim. As President Joseph Fielding Smith has said, "It is Ephraim who is to be endowed with power to *bless and give to the other tribes, including the Lamanites, their blessings*" (DS 2:251).

See also: Ephraim; Tribes of Israel

Children of God

All men and women are the spiritual offspring of our Father in Heaven (Heb. 12:9). Yet, in the eternal sense, "only those who *obey* will be called . . . the children of God" (DS 3:250). Paul informed the early Saints that they were "children of God by faith in Christ Jesus" (Gal. 3:26). However, a verbal expression of one's belief is not sufficient to qualify one as a child of God. We must express faith by way of our good works (James 2:26; Mosiah 18:8–22). The children of God are his sons and daughters who qualify as joint-heirs with Christ for all that the Father possesses (Rom. 8:16–17; D&C 84:37–38). The various gifts of the Spirit are given "for the benefit of the children of God" (D&C 46:26).

See also: Church of the Firstborn; Fulness of the Glory of the Father; Sons of God

Children of Israel

See: Seed of Abraham

Children of Jacob

As used by Joseph Smith in his dedicatory prayer at the Kirtland Temple, the term *children of Jacob* appears to apply to all descendants of Jacob (D&C 109:61–69). He made particular reference, however, to those who had been "scattered upon the mountains for a long time, in a cloudy and dark day." Three years before the temple dedica-tion, the Prophet Joseph wrote the following: "Our western tribes of Indians are descendants from that Joseph which was sold into Egypt . . . ; the land of America is a promised land unto them, and unto it all the tribes of Israel will come, with as many of the Gentiles as shall comply with the requisitions of the new cove-nant. But the tribe of Judah will return to old Jerusalem. The city of Zion . . . will be built upon the land of America. . . . But Judah shall obtain deliverance at Jerusa-lem. . . . *The Good Shepherd will put forth His own sheep, and lead them out from all nations where they have been scattered in a cloudy and dark day, to Zion and to Jerusalem.*" (HC 1:315; italics added.)

See also: Children of Judah; Children of Israel; Cloudy and Dark Day; House of Israel; Resto-ration of the Scattered Israel; Seed of Abraham; Tribes of Israel

Children of Judah

The descendants of Judah, son of Jacob (Israel), are spoken of as the "children of Judah." In his dedicatory prayer at the Kirt-land Temple, the Prophet peti-tioned the Lord to allow these people to return to Jerusalem and the land of their inheritance (D&C 109:61–64).

See also: Children of Jacob; Jews; Judah; Tribe of Judah

Children of Light

As used in Doctrine and Cove-nants 106:5, the phrase *children of light* is similar to Paul's reference in his epistle to the Thessalonians: "But ye, brethren, are not in darkness, that that day should overtake you as a thief. Ye are all the children of light, and the children of the day: we are not of the night, nor of darkness." (1 Thess. 5:4–5.) Christ is *the Light*, and those who follow him are children of light, having been called out of darkness to walk in the light of his gospel (John 8:12; Eph. 5:8; 1 Pet. 2:9). He is the light his Saints are charged to shine before the world (3 Ne. 18:24).

In naming his Church in our day, the Lord specifically charged the members of The Church of Jesus Christ of Latter-day Saints to "arise and shine forth, that thy light may be a standard for the nations" (D&C 115:4–5). Anciently he charged the Saints on two continents to be a light unto the people of their societies (Matt. 5:14–16; 3 Ne. 12:14–16). Thus, the true followers of Christ, the faithful members of his Church, have always been identified as children of light; charged with the responsibility of letting that light shine. They are to be a "light unto the Gentiles" (D&C 86:11). Ultimately, through their righteousness, these faithful followers of Christ, these children of light, will be celestial Saints and "shine forth as the sun in the kingdom of their Father" (Matt. 13:43).

See also: Light and Life of the World; Light unto the Gentiles; Light to the World; Church of Jesus Christ of Latter-day Saints, The

Children of Men

The phrase *children of men* appears over three dozen times in the Doctrine and Covenants (e.g., 4:1; 43:15; 121:37). It is also found frequently in the Book of Mormon (1 Ne. 17:3; 3 Ne. 27:18), the Pearl of Great Price (Moses 1:41; JS—H 1:73), and the Old Testament (Gen. 11:5; Dan. 2:38), but not in the New Testament. "Children of men" appears to refer in general to all the posterity of Adam (Moses 1:8) and specifically to those who have not yet accepted the fulness of the gospel (D&C 5:6; 18:18, 44). The Lord himself drew a distinction between his disciples and the children of men (D&C 58:52). By making their covenants with Christ, the "children of men" change to "children of Christ" (Mosiah 5:7), or "children of light" (D&C 106:5).

Children of the Kingdom

Faithful members of The Church of Jesus Christ of Latter-day Saints could rightly be called "children of the kingdom." The kingdom refers to both the Church here on the earth and the ultimate kingdom that shall exist eternally. Only those who are valiant in the service of God will become children of that kingdom. In explaining the parable of the wheat and the tares, the Savior identified the "good seed" as the children of the kingdom (Matt. 13:38). Because of a mistranslation, another reference to the children of the kingdom appears to imply they are more like the tares than the wheat (Matt. 8:12). However, the Prophet Joseph corrected the verse to identify the children of the "wicked one" as being cast out rather than the children of the kingdom (JST, Matt. 8:12). The Lord made it clear that those who hold membership in his Church and who desire to be called the children of the kingdom will not be allowed to pollute his kingdom, but will be "cut off" (D&C 84:59; JS—M 1:55; JS—H 1:40).

See also: Holy Land

Children of Zion

The term *children of Zion* is used in three sections of the Doctrine and Covenants (84:56–58; 101:41, 81–85; 103:35). In the first instance, the Lord is chastening the members of the Church for having "treated lightly" those sacred things he had bestowed on them and calls on them to repent and remember their covenants. Here, then, the term is equated with membership in the Church. In the second instance, the Lord is specifically referring to members of the Church residing in the land of Zion, or Missouri (D&C 101: preface; 57:1–4). He chastens them for their transgressions and gives counsel regarding their receiving redress for the wrongs inflicted upon them by the mobs in Missouri (D&C 101:41, 81–85). In the third instance, the term again

applies to the Saints in Missouri. Joseph Smith was instructed to organize them upon the laws of God (D&C 103:35). However, in this instance the principle could apply to members of the Church in any locale. In a general sense, the true children of Zion would be those who fit the description of the Saints of an ancient Zion: "And the Lord called his people Zion, because they were of one heart and one mind, and dwelt in righteousness; and there was no poor among them" (Moses 7:18).

Chosen

A scripture which should be emblazoned on the minds of all who accept callings to serve in the Lord's kingdom is the statement that "there are many called, but few are chosen" (D&C 96:5–6; 121:34; see also Rom. 8:28). The Lord indicates that one fails to be chosen when he places his heart "upon the things of this world and [aspires] to the honors of men" (D&C 121:35). All who have been foreordained to serve and are given that opportunity in this life are called. If they prove faithful in their callings, they become chosen.

President Heber C. Kimball said: "If you live your religion and are faithful to the end of your days, that proves that you were chosen" (JD 5:34). Again, President Joseph Fielding Smith stated that "only those who serve and are faithful shall be chosen"

(CHMR 2:178). For what shall they be chosen? For exaltation in the celestial kingdom, to become kings and queens unto God and to reign with him throughout eternity (D&C 76:56). This concept is also taught in the parable of the marriage of the king's son (JST, Matt. 22:1–14).

See also: Day of Choosing

Chosen by the Body

In a revelation designating the three presiding quorums of the Church — First Presidency, Quorum of the Twelve Apostles, First Quorum of the Seventy — the Lord indicates that the First Presidency is ''chosen by the body . . . and upheld by the confidence, faith, and prayer of the church'' (D&C 107:22). Elder Harold B. Lee said this ''has been interpreted to mean President of the Church chosen by the Quorum of [the] Twelve Apostles and sustained by the vote of the membership of the Church'' (personal letter to Hoyt W. Brewster, Jr., dated January 19, 1968; see also CR, Apr. 1970, p. 123).

The President of the Church selects the counselors to serve with him in the First Presidency and this selection is ratified by the *body* of the Quorum of the Twelve Apostles.

See also: First Presidency of the Church; Man . . . Like Moses; Presidency of the High Priesthood; President of the High Priesthood

Chosen Seed

In a revelation on priesthood, the Lord indicated that the order of the patriarchal priesthood was to pass from father to son and ''rightly belongs to the literal descendants of the chosen seed, to whom the promises were made'' (D&C 107:40; see verses 39–52). The *chosen seed* is the birthright blessing of the firstborn male child, who has the right to the patriarchal office when properly called by recognized authority. In our day, this birthright belongs to the posterity of Hyrum Smith (D&C 124:91; IE, Nov 1956, pp. 789, 852).

See also: Patriarch; Smith, Hyrum

Christ

See: Jesus Christ

Church of Christ

In a revelation on Church organization and government given in April 1830, the same month in which the Church was organized, the Lord referred to the ''rise of the *Church of Christ* in these last days'' (D&C 20:1; italics added). This name was the same as that used by members of his church in ancient America (Mosiah 18:17; 3 Ne. 26:21; 28:23; 4 Ne. 1:26, 29; Moro. 6:4). It was used, along with several other derivations, to identify the Lord's church — ''the only true and living church upon the face of the whole earth" — until 1838, when the Lord decreed an official title: "For thus shall my church be called in the last days, even The Church of Jesus Christ of Latter-day Saints" (D&C 1:30; 115:3–4).

See also: Church of Jesus Christ of Latter-day Saints, The

Church of Enoch

The "church of Enoch" is spoken of once in sacred writ, that being in the Doctrine and Covenants (76:67). Of this, Elder Bruce R. McConkie has written: "All the inhabitants of Zion — being devoted members of the Lord's Church, with Enoch at their head — were translated and taken to heaven. (Moses 7:69.) Their callings and elections were made sure, and they were all assured of membership in the Church of the Firstborn and of an inheritance of exaltation in the eternal worlds. Those so favored were, of course, with Christ in his resurrection. (D&C 133:54–56.) They are spoken of as 'the general assembly and *church of Enoch*' (D&C 76:67), and all those who gain exaltation will be joined with them." (MD, 136.)

See also: Church of the Firstborn

Church of Jesus Christ of Latter-day Saints, The

Although The Church of Jesus Christ of Latter-day Saints was of-ficially organized on April 6, 1830, the revealed name of the Church was not *officially* given until April 26, 1838. "For thus shall my church be called in the last days," declared the Lord, "even The Church of Jesus Christ of Latter-day Saints." (D&C 115:3–4.) Smith and Sjodahl have informed us of the various names by which the Church had been previously known: "The world, from the beginning, gave to the Saints the name 'Mormons,' or 'Mormonites.' The Saints called their organization, 'The Church of Christ,' or 'The Church of Jesus Christ.' At a conference held at Kirtland, in May, 1834, it was called, 'The Church of the Latter-day Saints.'" (SS, 740.) It is of interest to note that the minutes of the high council meeting in which David Whitmer was excommunicated, dated April 13, 1838, reflect the correct name of the Church some two weeks before the aforementioned revelation was received (HC 3:19).

That the name of Christ's church should bear his name was made clear to the ancient inhabitants of the Americas. "And how be it my church save it be called in my name?" queried the Savior, adding, "if it be called in my name then it is my church, *if* it so be that they are built upon my gospel" (3 Ne. 27:1–9; italics added). The qualifying "if" is an important inclusion, for to merely attach Christ's name to a church does not make it his.

Elder James E. Talmage discussed the meaning of the other

components of the name of the Church: "We can understand, easily, what 'Latter-day' means—modern day, this day; but what does the word 'Saint' mean? . . . It means directly, used as an adjective, 'holy,' and when used as a noun, 'a holy one,' and we, therefore, profess to be a body of holy men, holy women. We proclaim ourselves in the name of Jesus Christ to be the holy ones of the last days, a significant proclamation, blasphemous in the extreme if it be not justified. But that name was given us of God. We do not apologize for it, nor do we preach the doctrines of the gospel, committed to the Church to be preached, in any apologetic manner. We preach in simplicity, in humility, but not by way of apology. . . . We have no apology to offer for our name nor for our membership in the Church, nor for our scriptures that have been given by revelation through the prophets of the Lord unto the people." (CR, Apr. 1922, p. 72.)

President Joseph Fielding Smith counseled members of this great Church regarding the usage of its name: "It is a very easy matter for us to adopt some other title, apparently for convenience, as the correct name is rather lengthy." However, he added, "Since the Lord felt it important to remind the councils of the Church of its correct name and inform them that by that name it should be known in the last days, we should endeavor to carry out this commandment more nearly

than it is the custom for many of us to do." (CHMR 2:86.)

This Church is, in the Lord's own words, "the only true and living church upon the face of the whole earth" (D&C 1:30). Its objectives, according to President Stephen L Richards, are "to bear witness to the divinity of the Lord Jesus Christ; to teach all men the principles of his Gospel; and to convert and persuade them to follow in his ways and keep the commandments of God, that they may thus advance the Kingdom of God in the earth to bring brotherhood and peace to men and nations, and even exaltation for themselves" (CR, Oct. 1956, 40–41).

See also: Church of Christ; Kingdom of God (on Earth); Mormonism; Saints; Stone Cut Out of the Mountain; Wheat

Church of the Devil

The Lord commanded several early leaders of his church to "contend against no church, save it be the church of the devil" (D&C 18:20). President Joseph Fielding Smith gave the following explanation of this exhortation: "We must understand that this is instruction to us to *contend against all evil, that which is opposed to righeousness and truth*" (CHMR 1:83; italics added). The Book of Mormon proclaims "that which is evil cometh from the devil" (Omni 1:25). Therefore, as we contend against evil we wage war against the "author of evil," the devil (Hel. 8:28). Smith and Sjodahl state that the devil's church "consists of those who adopt his plan and seek to destroy the free agency of man by brute force" (SS, 86).

See also: Babylon; Devil; Great and Abominable Church

Church of the Firstborn

The "church of the First-born," according to Elder Bruce R. McConkie, "is the Church which exists among exalted beings in the celestial realm. But it has its beginning here on earth. Members of The Church of Jesus Christ of Latter-day Saints who so devote themselves to righteousness that they receive the higher ordinances of exaltation become members of the Church of the Firstborn. Baptism is the gate to the Church itself, but celestial marriage is the gate to membership in the Church of the Firstborn, the inner circle of faithful saints who are heirs of exaltation and the fulness of the Father's kingdom. (D&C 76:54, 67, 71, 94, 102; 77:11; 78:21; 88:1–5; Heb. 12:23.)

"The Church of the Firstborn is made up of the sons of God, those who have been adopted into the family of the Lord, those who are destined to be joint-heirs with Christ in receiving all that the Father hath. (D&C 93:20–22.)" (DNTC 3:230–31.)

See also: Children of God; Church of Enoch; Firstborn, The; General Assembly and Church of the Firstborn; Sons of God

Cincinnati, Ohio

Following the dedication of the temple site at Independence, Jackson County, Missouri, in the forepart of August 1831, the Prophet and other brethren were instructed to return to Ohio. The Lord indicated the mode of travel was to be by water in a "craft made, or bought." Most of this journey took place on the waters of the Missouri River, which ran from Jackson County to St. Louis, from whence Joseph, Sidney Rigdon, and Oliver Cowdery were instructed to travel to Cincinnati, Ohio, where the wicked were to be warned (D&C 60:5–8; 61:30–33). Although accessible by water, Joseph's party took their journey by stage from St. Louis (HC 1:206).

Cincinnati is a major city along the Allegheny tributary of the Mississippi River, located in the southwest corner of Ohio. In September 1831, "W. W. Phelps was instructed to stop at Cincinnati on his way to Missouri and purchase a press and type, for the purpose of establishing and publishing a monthly paper at Independence, . . . to be called the *Evening and Morning Star*" (HC 1:217).

Circling Flames of Fire

See: Blazing Throne of God

Circumcision

See: Law of Circumcision

City of Enoch (Joseph)

During a period in which several revelations were given to individuals with disguised names, Joseph Smith was referred to as "Enoch," and his city, the city of Nauvoo, was called the city of Enoch (D&C 78:1, 4, pre-1981 edition). The reason for this secrecy was to avoid letting enemies of the Church know exactly of whom, or of what, the Lord was speaking at that time (HC 1:255). It seems appropriate that the city which Joseph (Enoch) founded, and in which he was striving so hard to bring the Saints to a perfect unity resembling the city founded by Enoch anciently (Moses 7:18–19), should be given the name of the "city of Enoch."

See also: Nauvoo

City of the Heritage of God

At the time the Saints moved the headquarters of the Church from Fayette, New York, to Kirtland, Ohio, the Lord promised to reveal to them at some future date the location of "the land of . . . inheritance" (D&C 38:18–20). This revelation did come six months later, when Independence, Jackson County, Missouri, was designated as the location for the city of Zion (D&C 57:1–4). Thus, the Lord is merely using descriptive language in a later revelation when he refers to "Zion . . . the *city of the heritage of God*" (D&C 58:13; italics added). This "heritage" is the right to oc-cupy the future location of the New Jerusalem, city of the sanctified Saints, "they whose garments are white through the blood of the Lamb" (Ether 13:4–10). To them the city shall be "the inheritance . . . while the earth shall stand, and [they] shall posses it again in eternity, no more to pass away" (D&C 38:20).

See also: City of the Living God; City of Zion; Holy City; New Jerusalem

City of the Living God

The only reference to the "city of the living God" appears in D&C 76:66. This city is the New Jerusalem, which is to occupy the site now known as Independence, Jackson County, Missouri (D&C 57:1–4; Ether 13:2–10; SS, 459).

See also: City of the Heritage of God; City of Zion; Holy City; New Jerusalem

City of Zion

In 1830, the Lord indicated that the location for the city of Zion was not yet revealed (D&C 28:9). One year later, the Lord made known that this holy city was to be located at the place known as Independence, Jackson County, Missouri (D&C 57:1–4). Although the Saints failed in their initial attempts to establish this special city, it will be built and become known as the New Jerusalem. It will be the "sanctified place from whence shall go forth the law" of the Lord during the Millennium (DS 3:67). This city is not to be confused with the ancient city of Zion, established by Enoch (Moses 7:18–19, 68–69).

See also: Center Place; City of the Heritage of God; City of the Living God; Holy City; Independence; New Jerusalem; Work of the Gathering; Zion

Clay County, Missouri

Extreme persecution and mobocracy resulted in the expulsion of the Saints from Jackson County, Missouri, in the latter part of 1833. "In Clay County, just across the [Missouri] river north of Jackson, they were received temporarily with some degree of kindness" (ECH, 139; see also HC 1:457). The only mention of Clay County in the Doctrine and Covenants is in the preface of section 101, a revelation received by Joseph Smith shortly after the arrival of the main body of exiled Saints within its borders. Because of the menacing actions of marauding mobbers from Jackson County, the citizens of Clay County requested the Saints to move to some part of the country where they could be by themselves, possibly in Wisconsin. Three days later, on July 1, 1836, the Saints expressed their willingness to comply with the request and thanked the citizens of Clay County for two and one-half years of hospitality. By December 1836, most had moved on to Caldwell County (ECH,

162–64). Clay County was later to be the repository of revelations received by the Prophet Joseph as he languished within the walls of Liberty Jail (see D&C 121, 122, 123).

See also: Liberty, Missouri

Cleanse Your Feet by Water

See: Shake Off the Dust

Clear as the Moon/Sun

See: Army with Banners

Cleave

The Lord counseled spouses to "cleave" unto each other and "none else" (D&C 42:22). President Spencer W. Kimball said, "Frequently, people continue to cleave unto their mothers and their fathers and their chums. Sometimes mothers will not relinquish the hold they have had upon their children; and husbands as well as wives return to their mothers and fathers to obtain advice and counsel and to confide, whereas cleaving should be to the wife in most things, and all intimacies should be kept in great secrecy and privacy from others. . . . *To cleave does not mean merely to occupy the same home; it means to adhere closely, to stick together.*" (DSY, 1976:151–52; italics added.)

In the same sense that husbands and wives should cleave together so should God's children adhere closely to their covenants and every good thing (D&C 25:13; 98:11; Moro. 7:28).

A totally different meaning of the word *cleave* refers to a dividing or splitting apart, such as when the Mount of Olives "shall cleave in twain" when the Lord returns (D&C 45:48).

Clothed with Light

For a servant of God to be "clothed with light for a covering" (D&C 85:7) is to be divinely endowed or enveloped with authority, power, and truth. "God is light" (1 John 1:5), and he will send forth his servants in light. "Where the gospel is there is light; where the gospel is not darkness prevails" (MD, 444).

Cloudy and Dark Day

The Prophet Joseph spoke of "the children of Jacob who have been scattered upon the mountains for a long time, in a cloudy and dark day" (D&C 109:61). This has reference to the scattered sheep of Israel who have been without the full light of the gospel and have been in dismal and gloomy circumstances. Anciently the Lord promised that he, as the great Shepherd, would "seek out [his] sheep, and will deliver them out of all places where they have been scattered in the cloudy and dark day" (Ezek. 34:12; see also HC 1:315).

See also: Children of Jacob

Cloven Tongues as of Fire

During the dedication of the Kirtland Temple, the Prophet importuned the Lord that "cloven tongues as of fire" might be poured out upon the Saints (D&C 109:36). Some spiritual outpouring, which evidently is manifested in a physical, visible form, is what has been described as "cloven tongues as of fire." It occurred on the day of Pentecost, when the ancient disciples first received the personage of the Holy Ghost (Acts 2:3–4). Similar manifestations are mentioned in the Book of Mormon, although the term *cloven tongues* is not used (Hel. 5:22–24, 43–45; 3 Ne. 19:13–14). An official declaration of the First Presidency has stated that "the *cloven tongues of fire were the sign of His [the Savior's] coming.* This manifestation was repeated in this dispensation at the endowment in the Kirtland Temple." (MFP 5:4; italics added.)

That which is cloven is split, and the imagery of cloven tongues of fire brings to mind the flickering tongues of flames of fire. During great spiritual outpouring, flickering flames of celestial light *may* be visible.

A more recent manifestation of like nature took place on June 1, 1978, in an upper room in the Salt Lake Temple. As the First Presidency and members of the Twelve Apostles were prayerfully petitioning the Lord, a marvelous outpouring of the Spirit occurred. One of their number, Elder Bruce R. McConkie, said: "The Spirit of the Lord rested mightily upon us all; we felt something akin to what happened on the day of Pentecost and at the dedication of the Kirtland Temple. . . . On this occasion, because of the importuning and the faith, and because the hour and the time had arrived, the Lord in his providences poured out the Holy Ghost upon the First Presidency and the Twelve in a miraculous and marvelous manner, beyond anything that any then present had ever experienced. . . . To carnal people who do not understand the operating of the Holy Spirit of God upon the souls of man, this may sound like gibberish or jargon or uncertainty or ambiguity; but to those who are enlightened by the power of the Spirit and who have themselves felt its power, it will have a ring of veracity and truth, and they will know of its verity. I cannot describe in words what happened; I can only say that it happened and that it can be known and understood only by the feeling that can come into the heart of man." (P, 126–37.)

See also: Upper Room

Coe, Joseph

The name of Joseph Coe appears three times in the Doctrine and Covenants; once in connection with his call to accompany the Prophet Joseph to Missouri (55:6), and twice in regards to his call as a member of the high council at Kirtland (102:3, 34). "He was one of eight men present when the Temple site, west of Independence, was dedicated, August 3rd, 1831. Unfortunately for himself, he did not remain in the Church. In the year 1837 he cast his lot with John F. Boynton, Luke S. Johnson, Warren Parrish, and others who had been disfellowshipped, and together they set up a church of their own, which they called the 'Church of Christ.' They alleged that Joseph Smith was a 'fallen prophet,' teaching false doctrines. For some time these dissenters took a leading part in the persecution of the Saints at Kirtland, but their efforts to build up a church came to naught. They were swept away, as chaff before the wind (Psalm 1:4)." (SS, 319–20.)

Colesville, New York

The town of Colesville, New York, is mentioned four times in the revelations (D&C 24:3; 26:1; 37:2; 128:20). It was the home of Joseph Knight, Sr., a faithful man for whom Joseph Smith had labored in 1826. Knight's farm was located about twenty miles above what was known as the "Great Bend," which is the bend where the Susquehanna River makes a dip into Pennsylvania and then hooks back up into New York (CHC 1:85). It is located about one hundred miles south of Fayette, and these two towns, together with Palmyra, were the focal points of Church activity in New York during its first year of existence.

It was here that the "first miracle" of the Church took place, when an evil spirit was cast out of Newel Knight. This was also the location where the Prophet Joseph suffered his first arrest, following the organization of the Church. He was charged with being a "disorderly person by preaching the Book of Mormon." (CHC 1:201–10.) About sixty Saints from this location went en masse to Ohio, where they settled at Thompson, sixteen miles northeast of Kirtland. However, they soon moved to Jackson County, Missouri, settling about twelve miles outside of Independence, in an area that is now part of Kansas City.

See also: Broome County; Thompson, Ohio

Coltrin, Zebedee

In June 1831, Zebedee Coltrin was admonished to take his journey up to the land of Zion — Missouri (D&C 52:29). He joined the Church soon after its organization and was soon ordained a high priest, "occasionally" serving as an alternate member of the Kirtland high council. As early as January 1834, he was mentioned as one who spoke in tongues and was reported to have enjoyed "spiritual gifts of the gospel in a great degree."

"At a meeting held at Kirtland, Ohio, Jan. 28, 1836, he had a vision of 'the Saviour extended before him, as upon a cross, and a little after, crowned with glory upon his head, above the brightness of the sun.' A few days later he saw the 'Lord's hosts' in another glorious vision."

He was called to serve as one of the first seven Presidents of the Seventy, where he labored from February 1835 until April 1837. His release was occasioned by his status as a high priest, which, at that time, was felt inconsistent with his calling.

Elder Coltrin served for a time in the Kirtland stake presidency under Almon W. Babbitt. He traveled west with the pioneers and settled in Spanish Fork, Utah County, Utah, where he died July 21, 1887. Upon his death, the *Deseret News* wrote the following editorial: "This respected and venerable man was one of the oldest members of the Church and was identified with many of its earliest incidents in the days of Kirtland. He was closely associated with the Prophet Joseph and has often testified to having been a witness of and participant in many marvelous spiritual manifestations. Father Coltrin has for many years past officiated as a Patriarch, and has left an excellent record for faithfulness." (Jenson 1:190.)

Comforter

The Comforter, promised to "those who labor in [the] vineyard" (D&C 21:9), is the Holy Ghost, for "no man can preach the Gospel without the Holy Ghost" (TPJS, 112). Joseph Smith described this Comforter as follows: "There are two Comforters spoken of. One is the Holy Ghost, the same as given on the day of Pentecost, and that all Saints receive after faith, repentance, and baptism. This first Comforter or Holy Ghost has no other effect than pure intelligence. It is more powerful in expanding the mind, enlightening the understanding, and storing the intellect with present knowledge, of a man who is of the literal seed of Abraham, than one that is a Gentile, though it may not have half as much visible effect upon the body; for as the Holy Ghost falls upon one of the literal seed of Abraham, it is calm and serene; and his whole soul and body are only exercised by the pure spirit of intelligence; while the effect of the Holy Ghost upon a Gentile, is to purge out the old blood, and make him actually of the seed of Abraham. That man that has none of the blood of Abraham (naturally) must have a new creation by the Holy Ghost. In such a case, there may be more of a powerful effect upon the body, and visible to the eye, than upon an Israelite, while the Israelite at first might be far before the Gentile in pure intelligence." (TPJS, 149–50.)

John 14 refers to the Holy Ghost as the Comforter in verses 16, 17, and 26, while referring to the Savior as the Second Comforter in verses 18, 21, and 23 (DS 1:55; TPJS, 150). The mission of the Comforter is to teach "the peacable things of the kingdom" (D&C 36:2; 39:6). He administers comfort and solace to those who forsake sin (3 Ne. 12:4; Matt. 5:4). "Peace of conscience" is a manifestation of the Comforter's presence (SHP, 62).

See also: Holy Ghost; Gift of the Holy Ghost; Peaceable Things of the Kingdom; Spirit of Truth

Comforter, Another

The Lord speaks of "another Comforter" in the great revelation known as the Olive Leaf (D&C 88:3–4). According to Smith and Sjodahl, "This is the Holy Spirit [of Promise], who gives to the Saints the assurance of eternal life. See also John 14:16." (SS, 541.)

See also: Comforter; Holy Spirit of Promise

Commandments of Men

The phrase *commandments of men* is found twice in modern-day scripture, once in the Doctrine and Covenants (46:7) and once in the Pearl of Great Price (JS—H 1:19). In the latter instance, the Savior specifically spoke of the corrupt creeds which were an abomination in his sight. These are those doctrines which deny the Holy Ghost and the power of God (2 Ne. 28:3–4).

The "commandments of men" are synonymous with the "precepts of men," or the false philosophies which prevent people from seeing the light of the gospel (D&C 45:28–29). These precepts cause people to speak of the Lord with their lips, but they never know him with their hearts (Isa. 29:13; JS—H 1:19; see also John 17:3 and JST, Matt. 7:21–23). The result of this approach is that men are "ever learning, and never able to come to the knowledge of the truth" (2 Tim. 3:7).

See also: Precepts of Men

Common Consent

The form of government used in the Church is based on the principle of "common consent" (D&C 26:2; 20:65). This has been explained as follows: "Every officer of the Priesthood or auxiliary organizations, though properly nominated, holds his position in the Church only with the consent of the people. Officers may be nominated by the Presidency of the Church, but unless the people accept them as officials, they cannot exercise the authority of the offices to which they have been called. All things in the Church must be done by common consent. This makes the people, men and women, under God, the rulers of the Church." (PCG, 238–39.) Elder Charles W. Penrose noted, "It is the voice of the Lord and the voice of the people together in this church that sanctions all things therein" (JD 21:45).

President Harold B. Lee identified this form of government as a "theocracy" (SHP, 150–52). This principle has been summarized by Smith and Sjodahl as follows: "In the Church of Christ where the government is that of the Kingdom of Heaven, neither autocracy nor democracy obtains, but government by common consent. That is to say, the initiative in all that pertains to the government of the Church rests with the Head of the Church, even our Lord Jesus Christ, and He exercises this sovereign function through his authorized servants, upon whom He has bestowed the Holy Priesthood: but it is the privilege of the people to accept, or reject, His laws and ordinances, for God has given every individual free agency. Obedience must be voluntary." (SS, 131.)

Common Judge

By revelatory delegation, the bishop is to serve as a "judge in Israel" (D&C 58:17; 107:72, 76), a "judge" (D&C 64:40), or a "common judge" (D&C 107:74). Of this responsibility, Elder Spencer W. Kimball has said: "Every soul in the organized stakes is given a bishop who, by the very nature of his calling and his ordination, is a 'judge in Israel.' . . . The bishop may be one's best earthly friend. He will hear the problem, judge the seriousness thereof, determine the degree of adjustment, and decide if it warrants an eventual forgiveness. He does this as the earthly representative of God, who is the master physician, the master psychologist, the master psychiatrist. If repentance is sufficient, he may waive penalties, which is tantamount to forgiveness so far as the church organization is concerned. The bishop claims no authority to absolve sins, but he does share the burden, waive penalties, relieve tension and strain, and he may assure a continuation of church activity. He will keep the whole matter most confidential." (FPM, 182.)

President Harold B. Lee counseled the priesthood of the Church to "teach those who are having problems to go to the father of the ward, their bishop, for counsel. No psychiatrist in the world, no marriage counselor, can give to those who are faithful members of the Church the counsel from one any better than the bishop of the ward." (CR, Oct. 1973, pp. 118–19.)

See also: Bishop

Commune

The verb *commune* is found only once in latter-day scriptures (D&C 107:19) and several score in the Bible (e.g., Ex. 25:22; Ps. 77:6; Luke 24:15). Although it has the connotation of conversing, it is generally thought to be more personal than mere conversation. To commune is to communicate *intimately* or to have a close relationship with another.

See also: Communion

Communion

The noun *communion* is found in Doctrine and Covenants 107:19. One of the blessings of faithful bearers of the Melchizedek Priesthood is to "enjoy the communion and presence of God the Father, and Jesus." In other words, they will enjoy a close relationship with these exalted Beings. Those who exercise faith and are not stiffnecked "have communion with the Holy Spirit, which maketh manifest unto the children of men, according to their faith" (Jarom 1:4).

See also: Commune

Compassion

One of the attributes of Deity is compassion (D&C 64:2; 101:9; 3 Ne. 17:6), and mortal man has been commanded to develop this trait also. "Execute true judgment, and shew mercy and compassions every man to his brother," declared the Lord (Zech. 7:9). Webster defines compassion as "sympathetic consciousness of others' distress together with a desire to alleviate it." The ministry of the Savior was marked by acts of compassion (Matt. 20:34; Mark 1:41; Luke 7:13). Truly those who show compassion to others do make a *difference* (Jude 1:22).

Concatenation

In an epistle written from Liberty Jail, the Prophet Joseph

Smith set forth the duty of the Saints in relation to their persecutors (D&C 123). He spoke of "the whole concatenation of diabolical rascality and nefarious and murderous impositions that have been practised upon this people" (D&C 123:5). Webster defines *concatenation* as "a series connected like links in a chain." In this instance, the Prophet was speaking of a string of diabolical (fiendish or devilish) deeds inflicted on the suffering Saints by nefarious (very wicked), murderous men, full of rascality (meanness and dishonesty).

See also: Imposition

Concubines

In a discussion of the nature of marriage, the Lord speaks of the "concubines" which Abraham, Isaac, Jacob, Moses, David, and Solomon had (D&C 132:1, 37–39). Concubines were wives of inferior social rank. Webster suggests that they were not legally a man's wives, although the posterity was legally recognized. Peloubet indicates that the "difference between wife and concubine was less marked among the Hebrews than among us." Generally, concubines would be from the following: "(1) a Hebrew girl bought of her father; (2) a Gentile captive taken in war; (3) a foreign slave bought; or (4) a Canaanitish woman bond or free. . . . Free Hebrew women also might become concubines. To seize on royal concubines for his use was often a usurper's first act." (Peloubet, 123.)

Conference

The Lord commanded at the onset of the Church's existence that it "meet in conference once in three months, or from time to time as said conferences shall direct or appoint" (D&C 20:61). Although initially these were priesthood conferences, the pattern of holding such meetings has evolved into quorum, auxiliary, branch, ward, district, stake, regional, area, and general conferences of the Church. The mention of "general conference" in the Doctrine and Covenants (20:67; 124:144) originally had reference to local conferences rather than to the worldwide conferences to which this title is presently applied.

According to President David O. McKay, there are four principal purposes for holding conferences of the Church: "(1) to transact current Church business; (2) to hear reports and Church statistics; (3) to approve, or disapprove, of those called to the ministry; and (4) to worship the Lord in sincerity and reverence, and to give and to receive encouragement, exhortation, and instruction" (CR, Oct. 1938, pp. 130–31).

President Joseph Fielding Smith added: "These conference sessions are solemn and sacred occasions on which we come together to wait upon the Lord, to seek his Spirit, and to be renewed in our desires to serve him and keep his commandments. All of our Church conferences are occasions to teach one another the doctrines of the gospel; to testify of the truth and divinity of those things which have come to us by the opening of the heavens; and to counsel together, and with the Lord, as to the things we should all do to fill the full measure of our creation." (En., July 1972, pp. 27–28.)

Finally, we view the words of another prophet as he closed a general conference of the Church: "I am not concerned about how much you remember in words of what has been said," noted President Harold B. Lee. "I am concerned about how it has made you feel." (CR, Oct. 1972, pp. 176–77.)

Confess

In a moving narrative of his suffering in Gethsemane, the Lord Jesus Christ commanded Martin Harris to repent and confess his sins lest he suffer in a small degree what the Savior experienced in his atonement (D&C 19:20; see verses 15–20). The Lord promises to forgive those who confess and forsake their sins (D&C 58:42–43).

To confess is to acknowledge. One may acknowledge his sins to God (D&C 64:7), to one whom he has offended (D&C 42:88–89), or to an appropriate priesthood leader. In this respect, Elder Marion G. Romney said: "Where one's transgressions are of such a nature as would, unrepented of, put in jeopardy his right to membership or fellowship in the

Church of Jesus Christ, full and effective confession would . . . require confession by the repentant sinner to his bishop or other proper presiding Church officer" (LTG, 106).

Ultimately every knee shall bow and every tongue confess that Jesus is the Christ, the promised Messiah, he who has ransomed us with his holy and innocent blood (D&C 76:110; 88:104; Philip. 2:9–11). The Lord has indicated his displeasure with those who do not confess (acknowledge) his hand in all things and obey his commandments (D&C 59:21).

Confirm

The word *confirm* is used in three different ways in the Doctrine and Covenants. Its initial appearance (20:10) is in the sense of verification, as a corroborative witness. It is possibly used in this same sense in several other scriptural citations (D&C 27:12; 84:42, 48), although in these instances, and in several others (D&C 84:18, 30; 107:40), an ordinance or ordination is implied.

The most common use of the term *confirm* in the Church today is in connection with the baptism of the Holy Ghost and "fire" (D&C 20:41; 33:11; 39:6). This is an ordinance, following the baptism of water, wherein one is confirmed a member of the Church by the laying on of hands. At this time the new member is commanded to receive the gift of the Holy Ghost (D&C 20:41, 43, 68; 33:15).

The Prophet Joseph said, "Baptism by water is but half a baptism, and is good for nothing without the other half—that is, the baptism of the Holy Ghost" (TPJS, 314). "The Gift of the Holy Ghost by the laying on of hands, cannot be received through the medium of any other principle than the principle of righteousness, for if the proposals are not complied with, it is of no use, but withdraws" (TPJS, 148). This gift is found only within The Church of Jesus Christ of Latter-day Saints (TPJS, 199; JD 14:304; CHMR 1:154).

See also: Baptism of Fire; Gift of the Holy Ghost

Confirmation Meetings

In addition to sacrament meetings, confirmation meetings are also mentioned in the Doctrine and Covenants (46:4–6). "By 'confirmation meetings,' " said Sidney B. Sperry, "is apparently meant meetings at which baptized persons are to be confirmed members of the Church" (DCC, 195). At the present time, confirmations may take place in sacrament meetings designated for testimony bearing and certain ordinances. In the early days of the Church, however, special meetings were conducted for the specific purpose of confirming members of the Church. These did not always follow immediately after the baptism of water.

Emma Smith, for example, was baptized in June 1830, yet was not confirmed until August (HC 1:87–88, 106, 108).

See also: Confirm

Congregations of the Wicked

On several occasions the missionaries have been admonished to preach "among the congregations of the wicked," raising the voice of warning (D&C 60:8, 13, 14). On another occasion certain brethren were admonished not to preach to such congregations in certain locations (D&C 61:30, 32). President Joseph Fielding Smith defined the "wicked" as "all who had not repented and received the Gospel." Then, he added, "Frequently the Lord refers to the people scattered abroad as 'congregations of the wicked.' We have good reason to believe that wickedness prevailed among the congregations. The elders were to seek out from among the people the honest in heart and leave their warning testimony with all others, thus they would become clean from their blood." (CHMR 1:258, 223.)

Connections

In his dedicatory prayer of the Kirtland Temple, the Prophet Joseph Smith prayed for himself, for his wife and children, and for "all their immediate connections" (D&C 109:68–70). According to the footnote reference in the 1981 edition of the Doctrine and Covenants, immediate connections referred to "close relatives."

Conscience

"We have a faculty by means of which we can pass judgment on our own conduct, either approving or condemning it, so anticipating the divine judgment on it. This faculty is called conscience." (LDSBD, 649.) It is based upon the Light of Christ, which is inborn with every human being and is a natural capacity to distinguish between right and wrong (see D&C 84:45–46; Moro. 7:16).

As the Prophet Joseph Smith resolutely faced martyrdom, he declared, "I have a conscience void of offense towards God, and towards all men" (D&C 135:4). In a similar vein, prior to his death, King Benjamin gave an accounting of his stewardship to his subjects that he might have "a clear conscience before God" (Mosiah 2:15).

See also: Light of Christ

Consecration

The principle of consecration is first mentioned in the section known as "the law of the Church" (D&C 42). "In this revelation the *Law of Consecration* is stated definitely as the law on which the New Jerusalem is to be built. This law is given for the benefit of the poor, for the building of Zion and the work of the ministry. The members of the Church should consecrate their properties, and then be appointed stewards in the service of the Lord. All surplus property was to be placed in the storehouse to be used as the Lord should direct, under the guidance of the bishop. . . . Through this celestial law (Consecration) the Saints are to become the covenant people of the Lord. We cannot enter into the fulness of the covenants pertaining to Zion until we have reached the point where we can live such a divine law. Those who cannot abide the law of tithing cannot partake of this law of consecration, or the higher law, and they will be deprived of an inheritance when the inheritances are divided." (CHMR 1:185.)

"Sacrifice and consecration are inseparably intertwined," said Elder Bruce R. McConkie. "The law of consecration is that we consecrate our time, our talents, and our money and property to the cause of the Church; such are to be available to the extent they are needed to further the Lord's interests on earth. The law of sacrifice is that we are willing to sacrifice all that we have for the truth's sake—our character and reputation; our honor and applause; our good name among men; our houses, lands, and families: all things, even our very lives if need be." (CR, Apr. 1975, p. 74.)

See also: United Order

Conspiring Men

See: Word of Wisdom #2

Constitution (#1)

The fundamental law of the United States, defining the principal organs of government as well as the rights of its citizens, is the Constitution. It was drafted by the Constitutional Convention in 1787 and declared in effect by Congress on March 4, 1789. Ratification of the first ten amendments, known as the Bill of Rights, occurred on December 15, 1791. The divine stamp of approval was placed on this sacred document when the Lord declared, *"I established the Constitution of this land, by the hands of wise men whom I raised up unto this very purpose"* (D&C 101:80; italics added). He has mandated that his people befriend the "constitutional law of the land" and has cautioned all to seek diligently for good and wise men who will uphold this basic document of free people (D&C 98:5–10).

Brigham Young once observed, "The spirit and letter of our Constitution and laws will always give us our rights, and under them we could have served God in Missouri and Illinois as well as in the courts of high heaven. But the administrators of the law trampled it under their feet, and wilfully and openly desecrated the holy principles held forth in the Constitution of our country." (JD 10:41.) Thus,

though the document is divine, the men who administer it are fallible mortals. Joseph Smith's declared feelings for this inspired instrument of freedom were: "The Constitution of the United States is a glorious standard; it is founded in the wisdom of God. It is a heavenly banner; it is to all those who are privileged with the sweets of its liberty, like the cooling shades and refreshing waters of a great rock in a thirsty and weary land. It is like a great tree under whose branches men from every clime can be shielded from the burning rays of the sun . . . ; the Constitution of the United States is true." (HC 3:304.) For further information on LDS theology, and even some mistaken mythology, regarding the Constitution, see the June 1976 *Ensign*, pages 60–65 and the September 1987 *Ensign*, pages 6–19.

See also: United States

Constitution (#2)

A revelation on health refers to wholesome herbs as being "ordained for the constitution . . . of man" (D&C 89:10). This simply means the physical makeup of the individual.

Consumption Decreed

The prophecy on war indicates that the inhabitants of the earth will be sorely vexed "until the *consumption decreed* hath made a full end of all nations" (D&C

87:6; italics added). This "consumption" is also spoken of in Isaiah's writings (Isa. 10:22, 23; 28:22; 2 Ne. 20:22, 23). It is the destruction declared for the wicked, or "the calamity which should come upon the inhabitants of the earth" prior to the Second Coming (D&C 1:7–17). The footnote references to "consumption decreed" refer to the numerous citations throughout the Doctrine and Covenants that touch upon premillennial upheavals of man's society and his physical environment.

Contend Against No Church

See: Church of the Devil

Contention

The Lord stated that he established his gospel so "that there may not be so much contention" (D&C 10:63). He further indicated that Satan stirred the people up to "contention concerning the points of my doctrine." While visiting the ancient inhabitants of the Americas, following his resurrection, he declared, "contention is not of me, but is of the devil, who is the father of contention, and he stirreth up the hearts of men to contend with anger, one with another" (3 Ne. 11:29–30). President Joseph F. Smith warned that "the spirit of contention" is found "only among apostates and those who have denied the faith." "We do not contend,"

he said. "We are not contentious, for if we were we would grieve the Spirit of the Lord from us, just as apostates do and have always done." (GD, 372.)

The Prophet Joseph Smith similarly admonished Church members to "avoid contentions and vain disputes with men of corrupt minds, who do not desire to know the truth" (TPJS, 43). More recently, Elder Marvin J. Ashton said: "Contention builds walls and puts up barriers. Love opens doors. . . . Ours is not only to avoid contention, but to see that such things are done away. . . . How important it is to know how to disagree without being disagreeable." (En., May 1978, p. 8.)

See also: Anger; Jarrings; Reviling Not Against Revilers; Standard of Peace; Stir Up the Hearts

Continuation of the Lives

In a revelation wherein the nature of the eternal marriage covenant was reviewed, the Lord spoke of the "strait gate" leading to "exaltation and continuation of the lives" (D&C 132:22). "The expression 'continuation of the lives,' " according to President Joseph Fielding Smith, "means the right and power of eternal increase or posterity" (CHMR 2:360). This procreative power is restricted to those celestial couples who qualify for the highest heaven and who will receive celestial crowns of glory and the "fulness of the glory of the Father'' (D&C 131:1–4; 132:6). All others will be partakers of the ''deaths,'' which means they will be denied posterity and the power of exaltation (D&C 132:25; CHMR 2:360).

See also: Continuation of the Seeds; Deaths; Eternal Lives; Gods; Fulness of the Glory of the Father; Increase

Continuation of the Seeds

Speaking of those sanctified Saints who will rise as husband and wife to dwell in the presence of God forever, the Lord said their ''glory shall be a fulness and a continuation of the seeds forever and ever'' (D&C 132:19). This phrase is described by Elder Harold B. Lee in the following words: ''If marriage . . . [is] for 'multiplying and replenishing the earth' on which we now live, surely there must likewise be a divine purpose in its being continued after the resurrection. This purpose is declared by the Lord to be for 'a continuation of the seeds forever and ever.' '' (YC, 128–29.) This ''continuation'' is ''the gift of eternal increase,'' or the procreative power of perpetual posterity.

''All who obtain . . . exaltation will have the privilege of completing the full measure of their existence, and they will have a posterity that will be as innumerable as the stars of heaven'' (DS 2:44). Brigham Young declared: ''After men have got their exaltations and their crowns — have become Gods . . . , they

have the power then of propagating their species in spirit; and that is the first of their operations with regard to organizing a world. Power is then given to them to organize the elements and then commence the organization of tabernacles.'' (JD 6:275.)

See also: Continuation of the Lives; Eternal Lives; Fulness of the Glory of the Father; Gods; Increase

Continueth in God

''That which is of God is light; and he that receiveth light, and continueth in God, receiveth more light,'' declared the Lord (D&C 50:24). To continue is to remain steadfast, to persist or endure. Thus, one who continues in God remains steadfast and faithful to him. He persists in keeping God's commandments.

See also: Endure to the End; Stand Fast; Valiant in the Testimony of Jesus

Contrite Spirit

Inseparably connected with a ''broken heart'' is a ''contrite spirit.'' Both are required of one who enters the waters of baptism and who desires to walk the path of righteousness (D&C 20:37; 56:17, 18; 59:8; 97:8). These terms are linked together in the Doctrine and Covenants and the Book of Mormon (2 Ne. 2:7; 4:32; 3 Ne. 9:20; Morm. 2:14; Ether 4:15; Moro. 6:2). Elder Joseph

Fielding Smith has said, "Every baptized person who has fully repented, who comes into the Church with a broken heart and a contrite spirit has made a covenant to continue with that broken heart, with that *contrite spirit, which means a repentant spirit.* He makes a covenant that he will do that." (CR, Oct. 1941, p. 93; italics added.)

Converted

"The greatest responsibility that a member of Christ's church has ever had is to become truly converted—and it is just as important to stay converted," said President Harold B. Lee (SHP, 91). The Lord promised the Twelve Apostles in 1837 that if they would not "harden their hearts" nor "stiffen their necks," they would be "converted" and "healed" (D&C 112:13).

Conversion is not mere entrance into the kingdom through the waters of baptism with a declared belief in Christ, for following such a declaration (Matt. 16:15–17) Peter was admonished by Jesus to be "converted" and "strengthen" others (Luke 22:32). President Lee said, "In effect the Lord is saying that the testimony we have today will not be our testimony of tomorrow. Our testimony is either going to grow and grow until it becomes as the brightness of the sun, or it is going to diminish to nothing, depending on what we do about it. Peter, somehow, was losing his testimony." (SHP, 91.)

To members of Christ's Church, President Lee offered the following insights: "Conversion must mean more than just being a 'card carrying' member of the Church with a tithing receipt, a membership card, a temple recommend, etc. It means to overcome the tendencies to criticize, and to strive continually to improve inward weaknesses and not merely the outward appearances." (CN, May 25, 1974, p. 2.) Elder Marion G. Romney added the following observation: "In one who is wholly converted, desire for things inimical to the gospel of Jesus Christ has actually died, and substituted therefor is a love of God with a fixed and controlling determination to keep his commandments. Paul told the Romans that such a one would walk in newness of life." (LTG, 109; Rom. 6:3, 4.)

Copley, Leman

In March 1831, Joseph Smith reported that Leman Copley, who had previously been a member of the Shaking Quakers sect, "embraced the fulness of the everlasting Gospel, apparently honest-hearted, but still retaining the idea that the Shakers were right in some particulars of their faith" (HC 1:167). In order to set Copley straight, Joseph inquired of the Lord and received the revelation found in section 49, which took to task many of the doctrines of the Quakers and called Copley on a mission to these people along with Parley P. Pratt and Sidney Rigdon. He was specifically admonished to teach according to that which the Lord's servants should teach him and not according to that which he had previously known. (D&C 49:4.)

Unfortunately, Copley later penned an infamous footnote in history for himself when he reneged on his agreement to share his property at Kirtland with emigrants from New York (HC 1:180). This action caused several hundred Saints to flee to Missouri in order to escape persecution from their enemies. In a scathing denunciation of the broken covenant, the Lord said: "And wo to him by whom this offense cometh, for it had been better for him that he had been drowned in the depth of the sea" (D&C 54:5).

Copley was subsequently excommunicated from the Church and was involved in a lawsuit wherein he testified against the Prophet Joseph. However, in March 1836, he sought Joseph's forgiveness and requested baptism into the Church. Joseph's journal reflects the action taken: he "was received according to his desire" (HC 2:433). The words of the Savior are appropriate in this instance: "joy shall be in heaven over one sinner that repenteth" (Luke 15:7).

See also: Covenant, The; Shakers; Thompson, Ohio

Cords of Death

See: Bands of Death

Corinthians

The book of 1 Corinthians is mentioned in two sections of the Doctrine and Covenants (77, 128). Ancient Corinth was the chief town of the Roman province of Achaia, in Greece. The Apostle Paul spent one and one-half years here during his second missionary journey (Acts 18:1–18) and raised up a branch that was occasionally split by differences. He evidently wrote them a reprimanding epistle (1 Cor. 5:9) to which they had made a reply. Both epistles are nonexistent today; however, 1 Corinthians is Paul's "reply to the reply."

Elder Bruce R. McConkie said that 1 Corinthians "is an inspired and inspiring recitation of some of the most glorious aspects of the doctrines of salvation. In it we read profound explanations of spiritual gifts, of the resurrection, and of degrees of glory in the world to come. We learn of baptism for the dead, are reminded that Christ is the God of Israel, and that there are gods many and lords many. We read of charity, unity, moral cleanliness, personal revelation, the sacrament, the spiritual powers of the saints, and much more. Truly the Lord's hand has been in the preservation of this storehouse of gospel knowledge, so needed for our edification and guidance." (DNTC 2:310.)

Cornerstone

The term *cornerstone* is descriptively used four times in section

124—verses 2, 23, 60, and 131—to refer to the Nauvoo Stake of Zion. Webster defines a cornerstone as ''a stone forming a part of a corner in a wall, especially one laid at the formal inauguration of the erection of a building; hence, something of fundamental importance.'' With the headquarters of the Church located at Nauvoo at the time of this revelation, the local stake was indeed a ''cornerstone'' for the rest of the Church—''something of fundamental importance.''

See also: Nauvoo; Stakes

Corrill, John

In May 1831, John Corrill was called to ''labor in the vineyard'' (D&C 50:38). The following month he was specifically called to travel to Missouri with Lyman Wight (D&C 52:7). Corrill ''took a prominent part in the affairs of the Church for some time . . . ; he was one of seven High Priests appointed to preside over the Saints of Zion. . . . In 1837, he was made keeper of the Lord's storehouse. . . . But notwithstanding the trust placed in him, when the fires of persecution raged with terrifying fury, he faltered, and signified his intention of publishing a booklet called *Mormonism Fairly Delineated*, the appearance of which the mob looked forward to with hopeful anticipation. . . . At a special conference at Quincy, Ill., March 17, 1839, he was excommunicated for acting against the interests of the Saints. Among others who were similarly dealt with at that time were Geo. M. Hinckle, Sampson Avard, W.W. Phelps, Frederick G. Williams, and Thomas B. Marsh—all of whom were, at one time, prominent in the Church.'' (SS, 294.) Truly, ''one sinner destroyeth much good'' (Eccl. 9:18).

Corrupt

In a sweeping condemnation, the Lord spoke of his corrupted vineyard and of the many who had ''corrupt minds'' (D&C 33:4). A similar statement was made during the First Vision, when Deity declared that ''those professors were all corrupt,'' speaking of the religious teachers of that day (JS—H 1:19).

An Apostle of the Lord, Hyrum M. Smith, discussed the meaning of this term: ''When I use the term 'corrupt' with reference to these ministers of the gospel . . . , I use it in the same sense that I believe the Lord used it when he made that declaration to Joseph Smith, the Prophet, in answer to the Prophet's prayer. He did not mean, nor do I mean, that the ministers of religion are personally unvirtuous or impure. I believe as a class they, perhaps in personal purity, stand a little above the average order of men. When I use the term *'corrupt'* I mean, as I believe the Lord meant, that *they had turned away from the truth, and have turned to that which is false.* A false doctrine is a corrupt doctrine; a false religion is a corrupt religion; a false teacher is a corrupt teacher. Any man who teaches a false doctrine, who believes in and practices and teaches a false religion is a corrupt professor, because he teaches that which is impure and not true." (CR, Oct. 1916, p. 43; italics added.)

When the Lord declared that "all flesh is corrupted before me; and the powers of darkness prevail upon the earth," he indicated that this is what causes "silence to reign" in the heavens (D&C 38:10–12). "When the heavens are sealed," declared President Spencer W. Kimball, "the spiritual darkness that follows is not unlike that physical darkness in Nephite history" (3 Ne. 8:21; En., May 1977, p. 77). Corrupted flesh (D&C 112:23) and corrupted hearts (D&C 10:21; 121:13) occur because of spiritual decay—the disease of darkness. Men either unwittingly or deliberately turn from truth to fable and darkness.

Council

The word *council* has several different meanings in the Doctrine and Covenants. For example, it is used on one occasion to describe a group of twenty-four high priests assembled temporarily under Joseph Smith's direction to consider matters of importance (D&C 102:1). A council may be a specific body, such as a high council or a bishop's council (D&C 102:2). The council of the Church (D&C 107:78) is "the supreme tribunal of the Church," consisting of the First Presidency and the Quorum of the Twelve Apostles (MD, 150). Section 120 speaks of a council that deals with the disposition of tithes (D&C 120:1). At the time of the revelation, the Kirtland High Council was part of this council, but at the present time it consists of the First Presidency, Quorum of the Twelve, and Presiding Bishopric (CR, Apr. 1948, pp. 116–17). President N. Eldon Tanner noted that "since its beginning, the Church has been governed by leadership councils. Priesthood councils are a fundamental order of the Church." (En. May 1979, p. 85.) President David O. McKay said, "As I conceive it, the genius of our Church government is government through *councils*" (CR, Oct. 1953, p. 86).

See also: High Council; Standing High Council; Traveling Presiding High Council

Council Bluffs

Mentioned in the preface of section 136, Council Bluffs, Iowa, was familiar to the Saints who followed the call of Brigham Young to head west. This is the modern-day name of what the pioneers called Kanesville, in honor of their friend, Colonel Thomas L. Kane (CHC 3:306). It is located on the eastern side of the Missouri River, opposite the settlement previously known as Winter Quarters, Nebraska, now known as Florence. It is perhaps most famous for being the place where the military body known as the Mormon Battalion was organized with five hundred men, in July 1846 (CHC 3:82–84). It was also the habitation for those Saints who abandoned Winter Quarters in the spring of 1848 but were unable to go west at that time.

Council of the Eternal God

Mention of the "Council of the Eternal God of all other gods" appears only in Doctrine and Covenants 121:32. This council was that grand gathering in the heavens wherein the plans were formulated for the creation of this earth. Joseph Smith proclaimed, "In the beginning, the head of the Gods [i.e., God the Father] called a council of the Gods; and they came together and concocted a plan to create the world and people it" (TPJS, 348–49). Abraham was reminded of this celestial council and informed that he was among those great spirits who were chosen to be rulers in God's kingdom (Abr. 3:22–28).

President Joseph Fielding Smith observed that "Adam helped to form this earth. He labored with our Savior Jesus Christ. I have a strong view of conviction that there were others also who assisted them. Perhaps Noah and Enoch; and *why not Joseph Smith*, and those who were appointed to be rulers before the earth was formed." (DS

1:74–75.) The plans formulated by this august group of noble spirits were joyfully accepted by all whose destiny was to be clothed in tabernacles of flesh on this earth, and "the morning stars sang together, and all the sons of God shouted for joy" (Job 38:4–7).

Countenance

Webster defines *countenance* as "the human face, especially as an indicator of mood or character." Although some may successfully wear masks of deceit in this life, the ultimate stamp of what one is will be plainly manifest on his eternal countenance. "There is no doubt that the life one leads, and the thoughts one thinks are registered plainly in his face," said President Spencer W. Kimball (En., May 1975, p. 81). To unrepentant sinners, Isaiah declared: "The show of their countenance doth witness against them, and doth declare their sin . . . and they cannot hide it" (Isa. 3:9; 2 Ne. 13:9). Perhaps this is the meaning behind the Lord's inquiry of Cain: "Why is thy countenance fallen?" (Moses 5:21–22). His visage revealed his real allegiance to the adversary. We are counseled to have the "image of God engraven upon [our] contenances" (Alma 5:14, 19). The Lord also admonished us to exhibit a "glad heart and a cheerful countenance" (D&C 59:15).

Those who serve him faithfully, will be "made glad" and

receive the "light of the countenance of their Lord" (D&C
88:51–61). Rays of illuminating
celestial light shall permeate their
entire beings. Like the heavenly
messenger, Moroni, their "countenance" shall be "beyond description . . . truly like lightning"
(JS—H 1:32).

Court of Last Resort

During the days of persecution
over the issue of polygamy, the
Church challenged the laws pro-
hibiting its practice and took their
case to "the court of last resort"
(D&C, OD—1). This had reference to the United States Supreme
Court, which is the highest court
to which a judicial appeal can
be made.

Covenant

At various times the Lord enters into celestial contractual
agreements, or covenants, with
men. For example, Martin Harris
was allowed to borrow 116 pages
of the translated manuscript from
the Book of Mormon, with a covenant that he would show them
only to a designated few. The violation of that covenant on Martin's part caused great sorrow to
him and to the Prophet Joseph,
with the result that millions have
been deprived of having additional insights from the Book of
Mormon, because of the loss of a
sacred manuscript (D&C 3; 10;
HC 1:20–28). Whenever men violate their covenants, they reap

sorrow, disappointment, and
condemnation (D&C 5:27; 54:4;
104:4; 132:4).

President Joseph Fielding
Smith defined a covenant as "a
contract and an agreement between at least two parties. In the
case of gospel covenants, the parties are the Lord in heaven and
men on earth. Men agree to keep
the commandments and the Lord
promises to reward them accordingly." (CR, Oct. 1970, p. 91;
D&C 82:10.)

See also: Covenant, The; Cove-
nant People; Doctrine and Cove-
nants; Everlasting Covenant;
Heirs According to the Covenant;
Immutable Covenant; New and
Everlasting Covenant; New and
Everlasting Covenant of Mar-
riage; New Covenant; Oath and
Covenant

Covenant, The

In section 54, the Lord chas-
tises those Saints in Thompson,
Ohio, who have broken "the covenant which they made unto
me" (D&C 54:4). In a footnote to
Joseph Smith's history, Elder
B.H. Roberts wrote: "It is difficult
to determine with exactness in
what the transgressions of the
Saints at Thompson consisted;
but it is evident that selfishness
and rebellion were at the bottom
of their trouble, and that Leman
Copley and Ezra Thayre were immediately concerned in it" (HC
1:180).

Church members from the
Colesville Branch in New York
had settled en masse at the town

of Thompson, Ohio, which was in the vicinity of Kirtland, the headquarters of the Church. Leman Copley, a recent convert, agreed to let them occupy "a considerable tract of land" which he owned, on the basis of a stewardship. This body of the Church had been granted permission to function under the law of consecration and stewardship (D&C 51). However, "it appears that Copley, who had not been fully converted, and some others in Thompson, violated their covenants, which caused confusion among the Colesville Saints and placed them at the mercy of their enemies. In their distress they sent Newel Knight, who was in charge of this branch, to the Prophet to learn what they should do. The Lord spoke to them by revelation (sec. 54) saying since their covenant was broken and of no effect, they would have to flee to Missouri or their enemies would be upon them." (CHMR 1:204–5.)

See also: Copley, Leman

Covenant People

The "covenant people" are those whom the Lord identifies as "my people," or the people of God (D&C 42:9, 36). These are they who have accepted membership in the Lord's church and kingdom and have taken upon themselves sacred covenants. "Among the covenants are these, that they will cease from sin and from all unrighteousness; that they will work righteousness in their lives; that they will abstain from the use of intoxicants, from the use of tobacco, from every vile thing, and from extremes in every phase of life; that they will not take the name of God in vain; that they will not bear false witness against their neighbors; that they will seek to love their neighbors as themselves; to carry out the golden rule of the Lord, do unto others as they would that others should do unto them" (GD, 107–8). Being a "covenant people" means that "we are subject to covenants and obligations as members of the Church" (DS 3:244).

True covenant people are not just those who have inherited promised blessings by lineage or outward ordinances but are those who are internalizing and cherishing their covenants. These are they whose worthiness warrants their receiving the promised blessings extended to the faithful followers of Christ. The prophet Nephi proclaimed, "as many . . . as will repent are the covenant people of the Lord" (2 Ne. 30:2).

In another sense, "covenant people," or "children of the covenant," refers to the seed of Abraham, through whom the Lord covenanted that the nations of the earth should receive the blessings of the priesthood and Church membership (Abr. 2:9–11; D&C 86:8–11; Gal. 3:26–29). These are they who are "armed with righteousness and with the power of God" (1 Ne. 14:14).

See also: Church of Jesus Christ of Latter-day Saints, The; Saints

Covet

One of the most detailed commandments revealed on Mount Sinai was, "Thou shalt not covet" (Ex. 20:17). This exhortation was repeated to the ancient Nephites (Mosiah 13:24) and again in our dispensation (D&C 19:25–26; 136:20). According to Webster, to covet is "to long inordinately for something that is another's." It is in this sense that it is expressly forbidden in the scriptures. On the other hand, Paul's counsel to "covet earnestly the best gifts" is a positive admonition to fervently desire something good (1 Cor. 12:31). This latter usage, however, is an exception to its usual common, negative connotation.

See also: Greediness; Lust

Covill, James

Of the 136 sections of the Doctrine and Covenants, two are given specifically to James Covill (39, 40). He "had been a Baptist minister for about forty years, and covenanted with the Lord that he would obey any command that the Lord would give to him" through the Prophet Joseph (HC 1:143). The Lord indicated his pleasure with the state of Covill's heart at that time and reminded Covill that he had previously rejected the Lord "many times because of pride and the cares of the world" (D&C 39:8–9). Although the revelation was received "with gladness, . . .

straightway Satan tempted him; and the fear of persecution and the cares of the world caused him to reject the word" (D&C 40:2).

The story of James Covill provides a tragic example of one who foolishly sought fleeting fellowship with the world at the expense of the constant companionship of the Spirit of God. "And the world passeth away, and the lust thereof: but he that doeth the will of God abideth for ever" (1 John 2:17).

Cowdery, Oliver

No man except the Prophet Joseph Smith had a more responsible position in the early days of the fledgling Church than did Oliver Cowdery. Coparticipant in receiving keys of authority from heavenly messengers, Oliver felt divine hands laid upon his head from the following angelic beings: John the Baptist (D&C 13; 27:7–8; JS—H 1:66–75); Peter, James, and John (D&C 27:12; 128:20); Moses, Elijah, and Elias (D&C 110).

At the time the Church was organized, Oliver was called as the "second elder" thereof. On December 5, 1834, he received the promised ordination as the Assistant President of the Church, which placed him ahead of the two counselors in the First Presidency (HC 2:176; DS 1:212). It is of interest to note that in the preface of the first edition of the Doctrine and Covenants, under date of February 17, 1835, Oliver's signature preceded those of the two counselors in the First Presidency.

Oliver came into the Prophet's life on April 5, 1829, when he arrived in Harmony, Pennsylvania, to inquire personally after Joseph's work on the Book of Mormon. The effect of that visit had eternal ramifications, for within two days he was serving as the scribe for Joseph Smith. He personally penned almost the entire first copy of the translation.

His first month with the Prophet brought to Oliver at least four revelations (D&C 6, 7, 8, 9). Among these was the reminder from the Lord that Oliver had been brought to Joseph's aid through the manifestations of the Spirit (D&C 6:14–24). Evidently Oliver desired to participate in the translating process but learned that great things do not come without great effort (D&C 9).

It was Oliver's contacts with the Whitmer family that made their home available for the completion of the translation. The Whitmer home later served as the setting for the organization of the Church, of which Oliver was a charter member. His testimony as one of the three special witnesses of the Book of Mormon can be found at the forepart of that sacred volume. Second only to Joseph Smith in being mentioned the most times in the Doctrine and Covenants, Oliver's life was an integral part of the restoration movement. Perhaps that led to overconfidence on his part regarding his indispensability to the divine work.

One of the early Apostles of the Church, George A. Smith, reported the following: "It is said, and I presume correctly, that Oliver Cowdery remarked at one time to Joseph Smith, 'If I should apostatize and leave the Church, the Church would be broken up.' The answer of the Prophet was, 'What and who are you? This is the work of God, and if you turn against it and withdraw from it, it will still roll on and you will not be missed.' It was not long until Oliver turned away, but the work continued. God raised up men from obscurity to step forth and shoulder the burdens, and it was hardly known when and where he went. In about ten years he came back again, came before a local conference at Mosquito Creek, Pottawattomie Co., Iowa, Oct., 1848, and acknowledged his faults. He bore testimony of the mission of the Prophet, Joseph Smith, and of the truth of the Book of Mormon; he exhorted the Saints to follow the authority of the Holy Priesthood, which he assured them was with the Twelve Apostles. He said, 'when the Saints follow the main channel of the stream, they find themselves in deep water and always right, pursuing their journey with safety; but when they turn aside into sloughs and bayous, they are left to flounder in the mud and are lost, for the Angel of God said unto Joseph in my hearing that this Priesthood shall remain on the earth until the end.'

"Oliver declared he took pleasure in bearing this testimony to the largest congregation of Saints he had ever seen together. He was rebaptized and made arrangements to come to the mountains, but died soon after, while on a visit to the Whitmers, in Missouri." (JD 13:347–8.)

Of particular interest regarding Oliver's detoured destiny is the following observation by President Joseph Fielding Smith: "I am firmly of the opinion that *had Oliver Cowdery remained true to his covenants and obligations as a witness with Joseph Smith, and retained his authority and place, he and not Hyrum Smith, would have gone with Joseph Smith as a prisoner and to martyrdom at Carthage*" (DS 1:219). Perhaps this is what the Lord alluded to in a revelation of April 1829, when the possibility of Oliver's death was pronounced (D&C 6:30). Thus, by his own choice, Oliver was denied the martyr's crown and a chance "to stand with the Prophet Joseph Smith through all time and eternity, holding the keys of the Dispensation of the Fulness of Times" (CHMR 1:121).

See also: Apostle; Book of Mormon; First Preacher; Gift of Aaron; Gift Possessed by Oliver Cowdery; Gifts . . . Once . . . Put Upon . . . Oliver Cowdery; Keys Whereby He May Ask and Receive; Olihah; Second Elder; Spokesman; Three Witnesses

Cowdery, Warren A.

Section 106 is a revelation given to Warren A. Cowdery, brother of Oliver Cowdery. War-

ren was called to lead the branch in Freedom, Cattaraugus County, New York. While presiding over the Church in Freedom, "he preferred charges against the Twelve Apostles for their alleged failure to teach the Saints while in Freedom, but he later made an apology" (OC, 16–17; HC 2:374–75). He moved to Kirtland, Ohio, and participated actively with the Church there, including serving on the high council. He became disaffected with Church leaders about the same time that Oliver was excommunicated from the Church. Warren remained in Kirtland after the Saints left; however, unlike his repentant brother Oliver, he never did reunite with the Church.

See also: Crafts of Men

Craftiness of Men

Some will miss an inheritance in celestial worlds because of the "craftiness of men" (D&C 76:75, see verses 71–79). To be crafty is to be adept in the use of subtlety and cunning, to be scheming or sly in seeking to deceive others. Men who resort to craftiness do not have righteous ends in mind but seek to serve selfish purposes and to take advantage of or destroy another.

The Lord has revealed the means whereby the faithful can avoid the craftiness or deception of men and the master deceiver, the devil himself: "For they that are wise and have received the truth, and have taken the Holy

Spirit for their guide . . . have not been deceived" (D&C 45:57).

Crafts of Men

The Lord expressed joy when Warren A. Cowdery "separated himself from the crafts of men" (D&C 106:6). Beyond its use as a synonym for a vessel that travels on water (D&C 60:5), the word *craft* generally refers to a skilled occupation. However, in the sense in which it is used with Cowdery it refers to something derogatory, an unrighteous activity.

See also: Cowdery, Warren

Created

As in other scriptures, the Doctrine and Covenants bears witness that God created the heavens and the earth and all things thereon (D&C 14:9; 20:18; 29:30; 76:24; 77:2). The Prophet Joseph Smith declared that "the word create came from the word *baurau* which does not mean to create out of nothing; it means to organize; the same as a man would organize materials and build a ship. Hence, we infer that God had materials to organize the world out of chaos—chaotic matter, which is element, and in which dwells all the glory. Element had an existence from the time he had. The pure principles of element are principles which can never be destroyed; they may be organized and re-organized, but not destroyed. They had no

beginning, and can have no end." (TPJS, 350–52.) Thus, "the Gods, organized and formed the heavens and the earth" out of those eternal elements which were available for such a "creation" (Abr. 4:1).

See also: Creation, The; Creator; Elements; Jesus Christ

Creation, The

The Creation refers to the process whereby those who were delegated the divine authority to do so brought this earth and the heavens surrounding it into existence. The scriptures are replete with revelation indicating that the premortal Jesus, or Jehovah, was the chief architect of this creation. For example, he declared to the remnants of an ancient civilization: "Behold, I am Jesus Christ the Son of God. I created the heavens and the earth, and all things that in them are." (3 Ne. 9:15.) Among those who helped the Great Jehovah in the creation of this earth were Michael, or father Adam, and "those who were appointed to be rulers before the earth was formed" (JD 1:51; DS 1:75). The story of the Creation is found in the Old Testament (Gen. 1–2) and in the Pearl of Great Price (Moses 2–3; Abr. 4–5). The Prophet Joseph Smith stated that "the word create came from the word *baurau* which does not mean to create out of nothing; it means to organize" (TPJS, 350).

See also: Created; Creator; Elements; Measure of Its Creation

Creator

In a revelation given June 1, 1833, the Lord referred to himself as "the Lord of Sabaoth, which is by interpretation, the *creator* of the first day, the beginning and the end" (D&C 95:7; italics added). In a doctrinal exposition by the First Presidency and Twelve Apostles in 1916, the meaning of the term *creator* was explained: "The Creator is an Organizer. God created the earth as an organized sphere; but He certainly did not create, in the sense of bringing into primal existence, the ultimate elements of the materials of which the earth consists, for 'the elements are eternal'. . . . Jesus Christ, whom we also know as Jehovah, was the executive of the Father, Elohim, in the work of creation. . . . He is very properly called the Eternal Father of heaven and earth." (MFP 5:26–27; see also Talmage, 32–41.) Ancient Apostles and prophets also understood this concept, such as John (John 1:3), King Benjamin (Mosiah 3:8), and Samuel the Lamanite (Hel. 14:12).

See also: Created; Creation; Elements; Jesus Christ; Worlds

Creatures

When one thinks of "creatures," the image of beasts, birds, and even insects usually comes to mind. However, as used throughout the Doctrine and Covenants, with the exception of one reference to animal life (D&C 77:2),

the term applies to *man*. "Preach my gospel unto every creature," the Lord proclaimed (D&C 18:28; 58:64; 68:8; 80:1; 84:62; 112:28; 124:128). In 1832, God revealed his desire to have the Church "stand independent above all other creatures beneath the celestial world" (D&C 78:14). "The term 'creature' is used here in its widest meaning, to signify *all that is created*, and refers especially to the various organizations in the world, whether ecclesiastical, political, financial, or industrial" (SS, 482; italics added). The ultimate destiny of the celestial Saints is to stand above all creatures and creations of lower orders.

Creeds

Joseph Smith wrote of the "damning hand of murder, tyranny, and oppression" which the Saints had suffered from those who were upheld and influenced by the lying "creeds of the fathers" (D&C 123:7). These creeds were the false philosophies or principles of men, often passed from parent to child, which led to confusion and contention in the world. The Prophet was informed during the First Vision that such creeds were abominable to Deity (JS—H 1:19).

Crooked

In consecutive revelations given in 1830, the Lord speaks of a "crooked and perverse generation" (D&C 33:2; 34:6). The same description is found in the Old Testament (Deut. 32:5) and a similar expression is in the New Testament (Matt. 17:17). To be crooked is to be bent or twisted, and to be perverse is to be turned away from what is right or good. Messengers of the gospel are being sent forth to proclaim the truth, striving to reclaim those who have become corrupted or crooked in their ways (D&C 33:2–6).

"God doth not walk in crooked paths," declare the scriptures (D&C 3:2; Alma 7:20), for "his paths are straight" (Alma 37:12). To walk in a crooked path is to be deceitful.

Cross, Take Up His

There are three occasions in the Doctrine and Covenants where individuals are admonished to "take up [the] cross" (D&C 23:6; 56:2; 112:14). Perhaps the most simple yet significant definition of this term is found in the Joseph Smith Translation of the Bible. Herein the Savior said: "And now for a man to take up his cross, is to deny himself all ungodliness, and every worldly lust, and keep my commandments" (JST, Matt. 16:26). A similar expression is found in the Book of Mormon (3 Ne. 12:30). Elder Neal A. Maxwell noted that "the *daily* taking up of the cross means *daily* denying ourselves the appetites of the flesh" (En., May 1987, p. 71).

In addition to the *denial* aspect of taking up one's cross, there is

another facet to consider. Elder James E. Talmage said: "We are apt to assume that self-denial is the sole material of our cross; but this is true only as we regard self-denial in its broadest sense, comprising both positive and negative aspects" (VM, 355). Thus, to "take up one's cross" is to magnify one's callings in the kingdom and to serve with full purpose of heart (D&C 4:2; 18:28). It is to bear the burden, even if occasionally the cross seems too heavy to bear.

Crown in the Mansions of My Father

See: Crown of Righteousness; Mansions of My Father

Crown of Eternal Life

See: Crown of Righteousness; Eternal Life

Crown of Righteousness

A "crown of righteousness" is promised to the faithful followers of the Lord (D&C 25:15; 29:13). This "crown" is elsewhere referred to as a "crown of eternal life" (D&C 20:14; 66:12; 124:55); a "crown of joy and rejoicing" (D&C 52:43); a "crown in the mansions of my Father" (D&C 59:2; 106:8); a "crown of glory" (D&C 58:4; 76:108; 88:19, 107; 104:7; 124:17; 133:32); a "crown of sheaves" (D&C 79:3); a "crown of immortality" (D&C 81:6; 124:55); a "crown of celestial glory" (D&C 101:65); a "crown of blessings" (D&C 124:17); a "crown of honor" (D&C 124:55); and, simply, a "crown" (D&C 75:28; 78:15).

An analogy of this crown was given by Smith and Sjodahl: "The victor at the Olympian games won, perhaps, a crown of olive branches, and he who was triumphant at the Pythian contests rejoiced in a laurel wreath; but those who conquer in life's conflicts, will wear a crown of righteousness. Their very righteousness in this life will be their glory hereafter." (SS, 150.) Just as the heads of royalty on earth wear crowns to signify their stature, so will celestial kings and queens, figuratively, if not literally, wear crowns symbolic of their royal stature, dominion, and authority. While earthly crowns will tarnish and perish, celestial crowns are "incorruptible" (1 Cor. 9:25) and "fadeth not away" (1 Pet. 5:4). Just as our Father in Heaven is a king, and our Heavenly Mother, therefore, a queen, all who physically traverse this earth have seeds of royalty in them. It behooves all to heed the admonition of the Apostle John: "Hold that fast which thou hast, that no man take thy crown" (Rev. 3:11).

Crucified Him unto Themselves

Those who deny the Holy Ghost thereby deny Jesus Christ and "[crucify] him unto them-selves and put him to an open shame" (D&C 76:35; see also Heb. 6:6). They have assented (agreed to or approved of) to his death (D&C 132:27). One "commits murder by assenting unto the Lord's death, that is, having a perfect knowledge of the truth he comes out in open rebellion and places himself in a position wherein he would have crucified Christ knowing perfectly the while that he was the Son of God. Christ is thus crucified afresh and put to open shame." (DNTC 3:161.)

See also: Blasphemy Against the Holy Ghost; Sons of Perdition

Cumbered

"Seek not to be cumbered," said the Lord to William E. McLellin (D&C 66:10). To be cumbered is to be troubled or burdened down with many concerns (see Luke 10:40). The parable of the wild and tame olive tree in the Book of Mormon speaks of the tree being cumbered (weighed down) with fruit; the Lord of the vineyard also expresses concern that the branches of the trees not cumber (clutter) the ground of the vineyard (Jacob 5:9, 30).

Cumorah

The only reference to Cumorah, a hill located outside Palmyra, New York, in the Doctrine and Covenants is in section

128, verse 20. The hill is not mentioned by name in the Pearl of Great Price, for Joseph Smith merely refers to it as "the place where the messenger had told me the plates were deposited," or a "hill of considerable size" (JS—H 1:50–51). Cumorah was the repository of the sacred records from which the Book of Mormon was translated.

The name *Cumorah* is first found in the Book of Mormon (Morm. 6; 8:2). It refers to a land and a hill where the final battle of the ancient Nephite civilization took place and where the sacred plates were originally deposited by Mormon, an ancient Nephite prophet and father to Moroni.

The Cumorah of the Nephite civilization appears to be the same one the Jaredite civilization referred to as the "hill Ramah" (compare Mormon 6:2 with Ether 15:11). However, Sidney Sperry suggested that the ancient "hill Ramah-Cumorah" was not the same as the one we presently call Cumorah. The first hill, he said, was probably located somewhere in middle America, whereas the present-day Cumorah is located in the northeastern part of the United States, three miles outside of Palmyra, New York (BMC, 6, 277, 299, 451). This latter hill probably received its name from Moroni, the resurrected Nephite prophet—who appeared to Joseph Smith as a heavenly messenger—in commemoration of the original hill. For a physical description of the hill, see HC 1:15.

Cup

See: Bitter Cup; Cup of Mine Indignation; Cup of Their Iniquity

Cup of Mine Indignation

The term *cup of mine indignation* is unique to the Doctrine and Covenants (29:17), but appears synonymous with such terms as "cup of the wrath of mine indignation" (D&C 43:26) and "cup of my fury" (2 Ne. 8:22). An ancient Nephite prophet spoke of those who do evil as having drunk from such a cup, because mercy had lost her claim on them (Mosiah 3:26). They drink of the wrath of God. Those who are obedient to the commandments of God need not drink the dregs of such a container (Mosiah 5:5). It appears, therefore, that this cup has a certain capacity to contain the sins of men and is drained through repentance. If, however, such divine draining does not take place, then a spillover of sins occurs. At this point, justice must intervene, and the Lord's "mopping up" takes place.

See also: Cup of Their Iniquity; Ripe; Sword of Mine Indignation

Cup of the Wrath of God

See: Cup of Mine Indignation

Cup of Their Iniquity

The Lord warns that his "indignation" will come on those

whose "cup of iniquity" is full (D&C 101:11). Because of divine patience, we are not immediately stricken each time we err. Were we instantaneously reprimanded or rewarded for each of our actions, we might have become mechanical men responding in robotlike fashion to the ring of an eternal Pavlovian bell. Because free agency allows us to perform without undue pressure, God patiently waits for perfection. In the meantime, however, if our level of iniquity becomes such that a spillover of sins occurs, then the Lord takes remedial action and his justice brings due retribution.

See also: Cup of Mine Indignation

Cursed the Land

In the beginning of man's mortal history, God told Adam that the ground would be cursed (Moses 4:23). In 1831 the Lord declared that in the last days he would bless the land, "in its time, for the use of my saints" (D&C 61:17). President Joseph Fielding Smith explained that the blessing of the land has occurred because of increased understanding of how to properly cultivate and care for the soil. "It matters not what the causes were, in those early days of world history there could not be the production, nor the varieties of fruits coming from the earth, and the Lord can very properly speak of this as a curse, or the lack of blessing, upon the land" (CHMR 1:224).

Cursed the Waters

See: Waters

Curtain of Heaven

Following an outpouring of tumultuous events preceding the Second Coming, a period of silence—described as half an hour in length—will occur in heaven "and immediately after shall the curtain of heaven be unfolded, as a scroll is unfolded after it is rolled up, and the face of the Lord shall be unveiled" (D&C 88:95; see also JST, Rev. 6:14; Isa. 34:4). The curtain of heaven is symbolic of the barrier which separates the earth and her inhabitants from the presence of God.

Commenting on this scripture, Elder Orson Pratt said: "Whether the half hour here spoken of is according to our reckoning—thirty minutes, or whether it be according to the reckoning of the Lord we do not know . . . ; the half hour during which silence is to prevail in heaven may be quite an extensive period of time. During the period of silence all things are perfectly still; no angels flying during that half hour; no trumpets sounding; no noise in the heavens above; but immediately after this great silence the curtain of heaven shall be unfolded as a scroll is unfolded. School children, who are in the habit of seeing maps hung up on the wall, know that they have rollers upon which they are rolled up, and that to expose the face of the maps they are let down. *So will the curtain of heaven be unrolled so that the people may gaze upon those celestial beings who will make their appearance in the clouds."* (JD 16:328; italics added.)

Cut Off

See: Excommunicate

Cutler, Alpheus

The only reference to Alpheus Cutler in the Doctrine and Covenants is in conjunction with his call to serve as a member of the Nauvoo high council in January 1841 (D&C 124:132). He was still sustained as a member of that body at the October conference, following the martyrdom, in 1844 (HC 7:296). Because his name appears in the high council minutes in Kirtland, dated August 28, 1834, it appears that Cutler also served in that body (HC 2:150–53).

He was designated as "the master workman" of the temple at Far West, Missouri, and on April 26, 1839, under the direction of the Twelve, he laid the foundation of this sacred edifice "by rolling up a large stone near the southeast corner" of the temple site (HC 3:337). "Thus," wrote the Prophet Joseph, "was fulfilled a revelation of July 8, 1838, which our enemies had said could not be fulfilled, as no 'Mormon' would be permitted to be in the state" (HC 3:339; D&C 118:4–5).

Cutler evidently had skills as a builder and architect, for he was designated for such tasks regarding a schoolhouse in Nauvoo (HC 4:18). He also served on the Nauvoo temple committee (HC 6:49), in which edifice he received his endowments, along with his wife, in December 1845 (HC 7:543). In the westward movement of the Saints, he was called to serve as a captain of one of the companies organized in October 1845 (HC 7:481).

Unfortunately, he later rejected the leadership of the Church and established an apostate organization, "The True Church of Jesus Christ," on September 19, 1853. His experience is a sad reminder that one cannot rest on past performance but must persevere and endure to the end (see 2 Ne. 31:16–20).

D

Damnation of Hell

In March 1839, Joseph Smith languished as a prisoner in Liberty Jail—confined yet not convicted; falsely accused, despised, and persecuted by the world—yet, withal, maintaining his prophetic mantle. In these circumstances the Lord revealed to him that "all those that discomfort my people, and drive and murder, and testify against them" shall "not escape the damnation of hell" (D&C 121:23). The Prophet later discussed the meaning of this phrase: "What is the damnation of hell?" he asked. "To go with that society who have not obeyed his [God's] commands." (HC 4:554–55.)

See also: Hell; Generation of Vipers; Damned; Eternal Damnation

Damned

The threat that one will be "damned" unless he abides by certain ordinances and principles is found several times in the Doctrine and Covenants. The disobedient and rebellious are warned of impending damnation (D&C 42:60; 132:4, 6, 27); the unbelievers, including they who reject saving ordinances, are admonished (D&C 49:5; 68:9; 84:74;

112:29); and the slothful are cautioned about their attitudes (D&C 58:29). President Spencer W. Kimball stated that to be "damned means stopped in progress" (DSY, 1976:154). Thus, those who, through the exercise of their agency, choose darkness over light are stopped in their progress of acquiring light and truth" (D&C 93:27, 39). They literally descend toward hell and darkness (2 Ne. 26:10). Joseph Smith taught that "if we are not drawing towards God . . . we are going from Him and drawing towards the devil. . . . As far as we degenerate from God, we descend to the devil and lose knowledge, and without knowledge we cannot be saved;" thus, we are "damned"! (HC 4:588.) In answer to the question, "Will everybody be damned, but Mormons?" the Prophet responded, "Yes, and a great portion of them, unless they repent, and work righteousness." (TPJS, 119.)

See also: Chains of Darkness; Damnation of Hell; Darkness; Devil; Eternal Damnation; Hell

Daniel

The words of the Old Testament prophet Daniel are referred to in Doctrine and Covenants 116 (see also Dan. 7:9–14; HC 3:386–87). Daniel was a man of indestructible integrity, sticking to his principles in spite of social pressure or threatened physical harm. For example, he refused to succumb to the king's prescribed diet and ultimately proved that his own inspired approach to health was superior (Dan. 1:3–16). He refused to cease praying to God, though commanded by kingly decree, and was cast into a den of lions for his actions; "and no manner of hurt was found upon him, because he believed in his God" (Dan. 6).

Daniel's book of scripture contains some powerful prophecies dealing with latter-day happenings, including the inspired interpretation of King Nebuchadnezzar's dream, which detailed the history of the world and the establishment of God's kingdom (Dan. 2). Daniel was a spiritual giant who "had understanding in all visions and dreams" (Dan. 1:17). He was among the "great and mighty ones" seen by Joseph F. Smith in his vision of the redemption of the dead (D&C 138:38, 44).

Darkness

Just as light is of God (1 John 1:5), darkness is of the devil, for he "is an enemy unto God, and fighteth against him continually" (Moro. 7:12). Darkness represents the evil influence of the devil's domain. It symbolizes that which does not edify (D&C 50:23). John declared that the devil's kingdom is full of darkness (Rev. 16:10). Those whose deeds are evil love darkness and reject light (D&C 10:21; 29:45; John 3:19). An ancient prophet proclaimed the fate of those who yield to the enticings of the devil and "choose works of darkness rather than light": they "must go down to hell" (2 Ne. 26:10).

Those who do not keep God's commandments find themselves "walking in darkness at noon day," for their sins have blocked the penetrating power of the gospel light (D&C 95:6). However, even from the darkest abyss the rays of repentance can dispel the darkness and once again admit the brilliance of the gospel light (Alma 26:3, 15). In answer to the query, "What shall we do that the cloud of darkness may be removed from overshadowing us?" an ancient Nephite said: "You must repent, and cry unto the [Lord], even until ye shall have faith in Christ" (Hel. 5:40–41).

See also: Chains of Darkness; Cloudy and Dark Day; Devil; Hell; Hidden Things of Darkness; Mind Became Darkened; Outer Darkness; Powers of Darkness; Region and Shadow of Death; Sun Shall Be Darkened

Daughters of Zion

The term *daughters of Zion* appears only in the Doctrine and

Covenants (124:11) and in Isaiah's writings (Isa. 3:16, 17; 4:4; 2 Ne. 13:16, 17; 14:4). Sperry suggested that the "daughters of Zion" represent Israel (BMC, 182), which is the name of the covenant people of God. Joseph Smith was instructed to write a "solemn proclamation" to all the mighty of the "four corners" of the world, in which they were to be admonished to awake and to bring their treasures "to the help of my people, to the house of the daughters of Zion" (D&C 124:1–11). As a king or president might bestow great gifts on regal heads of state, in like fashion the mighty of the earth are counseled to grant such gifts to the queens of the "royal Priesthood" of The Church of Jesus Christ of Latter-day Saints (1 Pet. 2:9).

David

David was the young shepherd boy whom the Lord called and whom the prophet Samuel anointed to become king of Judah, and ultimately of united Israel (1 Sam. 16:1–13; 2 Sam. 2:4; 1 Chron. 12:38). He was the son of Jesse, and the great-grandson of Boaz and Ruth (Matt. 1:5–6). In his youth he exercised such great faith in God that he slew both animal and human predators that preyed upon the "sheep" of his or of God's flocks (1 Sam. 17:32–51). Speaking of his forthcoming fight with the giant Goliath, David declared:

"The Lord that delivered me out of the paw of the lion, and out of the paw of the bear, he will deliver me out of the hand of this Philistine" (1 Sam. 17:37).

Though he prevailed over the mighty Goliath, clothed only in the armor of righteousness, he later lost the battle with Bathsheba for lack of such armament (cf. 1 Sam. 17; 2 Sam. 11–12). David's is the tragic story of one whose faith brought him to great heights yet who sold his eternal soul through his sinful seduction of another man's wife and the eventual murder of that faithful man. His heinous deed was so great that "he lost everything" (D&C 132:38–39; AGQ 3:145–46). The Prophet Joseph Smith stated that "David sought repentance at the hand of God carefully with tears, for the murder of Uriah; but he could only get it through hell: he got a promise that his soul should not be left in hell" (TPJS, 339). However, as President Joseph Fielding Smith observed, "Who wishes to spend a term in hell with the devil before being cleansed from sin?" (AGQ 1:74).

In spite of being eventually redeemed from hell, David has forever lost the crown of exaltation which he might have worn in the celestial kingdom, for "no murderer hath eternal life. Even David must wait for those times of refreshing, before he can come forth and his sins be blotted out . . . ; many bodies of the Saints arose at Christ's resurrection, . . . but it seems that David did not. Why? Because he had been a murderer." (TPJS, 188.) "For David is not ascended into the heavens," declared Peter (Acts 2:34).

See also: House of David; Uriah

Davies, Amos

On January 14, 1841, Amos Davies was reprimanded by the Lord and told to pay stock for the building of the Nauvoo House, to labor with his own hands, and to abase himself (D&C 124:111–14). Of this chastisement, Sperry said: "From the Lord's words one may deduce that Amos Davies was not a man of humble character, nor did he seem to have men's confidence, because he disdained to work with his hands" (DCC, 663). Less than two months later, under date of March 10, 1842, the Prophet made the following entry in his journal: "In the evening attended trial at Brother Hyrum's office, the City of Nauvoo *verses* Amos Davis, for indecent and abusive language about me while at Mr. Davis' the day previous. The charges were clearly substantiated by the testimony of Dr. Foster, Mr. and Mrs. Hibbard, and others. Mr. Davis was found guilty by the jury, and by the municipal court, bound over to keep the peace six months, under $100 bond." (HC 4:549.) He must have repented, for he is last mentioned in Joseph's writings as a missionary assigned to Tennessee in April 1844 (HC 6:338). He did not travel west with the Saints, spending most of his remaining years in Illinois.

Daviess County, Missouri

The only mention of Daviess County, Missouri, is in the preface of section 116. It was located directly north of Caldwell County, where the headquarters of the Church were temporarily located in 1838. Within its borders, Daviess County embraced the sacred ground of Adam-ondi-Ahman, where Adam and other ancient patriarchs once met and where all those who have held keys of priesthood authority shall meet at some future date (HC 3:34–35; Dan. 7:1–14). Ancient Nephites once worshiped within the borders of Daviess County.

The city of Gallatin, within the county, was the site of an election-day "battle" between bullies and the Mormons who tried to exercise their constitutionally guaranteed right to vote. "Many heads were broken in the conflict." (ECH, 181–83.) This led to many false rumors and the arrest of Joseph Smith and Lyman Wight, neither of whom were in Gallatin at the time of the trouble.

See also: Adam-ondi-Ahman; Spring Hill

Day

See: Ancient of Days; Cloudy and Dark Day; Day of Battle; Day of Calling; Day of Choosing; Day of Many Words; Day of Redemption; Day of Righteousness; Day of Transfiguration; Day of Warning; Earth . . . Like as It Was in the Days Before It Was Divided; Evil Day; Great and Dreadful Day of the Lord; Holy Day; Last Days; Lifted Up at the Last Day; Lord's Day; Perfect Day; Sabbath Day; Those Who Are to Remain Until the Great and Last Day; Today

Day of Battle

In the dedicatory prayer of the Kirtland Temple, the Prophet Joseph referred to the Lord's having fought for his people in the "day of the battle" (D&C 109:28). This may be an allusion to the many battles of the Old Testament or the Book of Mormon in which righteous Israel prevailed through the intervention of the Great Jehovah. The classic battle of Jericho is illustrative of this principle (Josh. 6). To his people, the Lord has declared, "I will fight your battles" (D&C 105:14). The words of Hezekiah to the troops of Israel are comforting. Speaking of the strength of the enemy, he said: "With him is an arm of flesh; but with us is the Lord our God to help us, and to fight our battles." (2 Chron. 32:7–8.) In a broader sense, the "day of battle" may refer to the everyday conflict in which the Saints are arrayed in battle against Satan. The Prophet's plea that the Lord would deliver his people "from the hands of all their enemies" could apply to anything that would subvert the ways of righteousness. Clothed with the spiri-

tual armor of the Lord (D&C 27:15–18), the Saints will survive this conflict. However, the *Sunshine Saint*, who retreats in the heat of battle, will lose the crown of victory promised to the righteous (see Bruce R. McConkie, CR, Oct. 1974, pp. 43–47).

Day of Calling

"There has been a day of calling, but the time has come for a day of choosing," declared the Lord in June 1834 (D&C 105:35). This day is the time period in which one receives the call to respond to the invitation to become "fellowcitizens with the saints and of the household of God" (Eph. 2:19). Although the "net" of the gospel catches many, some slip away and others are cast out because of their unworthiness (Matt. 13:47–50). Thus, while many Saints receive the call, some slip through sin back into the murky waters of the world and are lost. Only the faithful Saints were and are to be chosen for the promised endowment (D&C 105:12, 33; SS, 686; DCC, 550–51). The day of calling has not ceased, for the carriers of Christ's message, the "fishers of men," are covering the earth with the gospel net in search of the faithful.

See also: Called

Day of Choosing

At the time the revelation in section 105 was received, the

Kirtland Temple was under construction. The faithful were to receive "their endowment from on high" in this House of the Lord, for "the time [had] come for a day of choosing" (D&C 105:12, 33, 35). Those "chosen" for this blessing would be those whose works had manifest their worthiness (see SS, 686; DCC, 550–51). Although this original day of choosing has since passed, days of choosing occur daily as the faithful receive calls to serve and obey. From among those who call themselves "saints in the household of God," only the "wise virgins" among them will be ready for their day of choosing (D&C 45:56–57; 63:54; Matt. 25:1–13). Thus, "there are many called, but few are chosen" (D&C 121:34–40).

See also: Chosen

Day of Deliverance

See: Day of Redemption

Day of Judgment

See: Great and Dreadful Day of the Lord; Judgment

Day of Many Words

In 1831, the Lord proclaimed this to be a "day of warning, and not a day of many words" (D&C 63:58). The meaning of the latter part of this proclamation might be found in other admonitions. "Say nothing but repentance unto this generation" is the divine injunction found in several revelations (D&C 6:9; 11:9). Furthermore, the Redeemer admonishes those engaged in the ministry to avoid "tenets" and to speak only of "repentance and faith on the Savior, and remission of sins by baptism, and by fire, yea, even the Holy Ghost" (D&C 19:31).

The Apostle Paul said, "But foolish and unlearned questions avoid, knowing that they do gender strife" (2 Tim. 2:23). "It never ceases to amaze me," said President Harold B. Lee, "how gullible some of our Church members are in broadcasting sensational stories, or dreams, or visions, or purported patriarchal blessings, or quotations . . . supposedly from some person's private diary" (CR, Apr. 1970, pp. 55–56). His counsel was to avoid "these spurious writings and . . . purported revelations."

President Joseph Fielding Smith summarized the matter in these words: "The fundamental principles of the gospel—all that has to do with the salvation of man—are very clear and can be understood by those with ordinary intelligence. To spend time discussing useless questions which have no bearing on our salvation, and have no relationship to the commandments and obligations required of us by the plan of salvation, is just a useless pastime." (DS 1:305–6.)

Day of Pentecost

See: Pentecost

Day of Redemption

The phrase *day of redemption* is used six times in the Doctrine and Covenants (D&C 45:17; 78:12; 82:21; 104:9; 124:124; 132:26). This day, according to Joseph Fielding Smith, is the *day of resurrection* (DS 2:97). President Joseph F. Smith's vision of the redemption of the dead speaks of this day as the day of deliverance (D&C 138:16).

Until we are redeemed from the dead and have our spirits reunited with our resurrected bodies, we are in "bondage" (D&C 45:17). In fact, if there were no resurrection we would be in bondage to the buffetings of the devil, "to remain . . . in misery like unto himself" (2 Ne. 9:8–11). Smith and Sjodahl have written: "The separation of the spirits from the bodies is, even to those who are Christ's own, a 'bondage,' which is ended only by a glorious resurrection" (SS, 259).

Finally, the Lord himself declared that "the resurrection from the dead is the redemption of the soul" (D&C 88:16).

See also: Redemption; Resurrection; Year of My Redeemed

Day of Righteousness

Because of their having achieved a higher level of living than existed among other men on earth, Enoch and his brethren were separated from the earth and taken into the presence of God (D&C 45:11–12; Moses 7:69). Here they will remain "until a day of righteousness shall come." This day will be when the earth is cleansed of the wicked, preparatory for the second coming of Christ. (Moses 7:62–63; WTP, 309–10.)

See also: Enoch

Day of Sacrifice

See: Sacrifice

Day of the Lord

See: Great and Dreadful Day of the Lord

Day of Transfiguration

There is a difference between the "day of transfiguration" (D&C 63:20–21) and the day when "a new earth" (D&C 29:23) shall appear. The former, according to Elder Bruce R. McConkie, is the "regeneration" (Matt. 19:28), or "times of refreshing" (Acts 3:19–21), that will return this earth to its previous paradisiacal glory (DNTC 2:48–9; see also AF, 375–81). This doctrine is declared in our tenth article of faith. President Joseph Fielding Smith taught that "this earth will again appear as it did in the beginning. The sea will be driven back to the north; the islands will be joined to the mainland and the lands will be brought together as they were before the earth was divided.'' (CHMR 1:231; DS 1:84–88; D&C 133:22–24.) This terrestrial orb will exist for the duration of the Millennium, following which it shall die and be resurrected, becoming ''a new earth,'' a celestial sphere (D&C 88:26).

See also: End of the Earth; End of the World; New Heaven and a New Earth; Paradisiacal Glory

Day of Vengeance

See: Great and Dreadful Day of the Lord

Day of Visitation

See: Great and Dreadful Day of the Lord

Day of Warning

An 1831 revelation declared ''this is a day of warning, and not a day of many words'' (D&C 63:58). In earlier revelations, the Lord counseled his servants to ''say nothing but repentance unto this generation'' (D&C 6:9; 11:9; 19:21).

The day of warning is a day of repentance, a day in which to prepare to meet the Messiah, the resurrected Lord, when he returns to claim his earthly kingdom. It is a day when the message of the restoration of the

gospel — of keys of authority, additional scripture, and living prophets — is being proclaimed to the world.

In his preface to the Doctrine and Covenants, the Lord said, ''the *voice of warning* shall be unto all people, by the mouths of my disciples, whom I have chosen in these last days'' (D&C 1:4–5; italics added). One of these ''chosen disciples,'' President George F. Richards, said: ''I understand that the Lord expects every person who had received the gospel to be a missionary for him throughout his life — not necessarily to go abroad by special call only, but to seek opportunity to preach the gospel to his non-member neighbors as well.'' (CR, Apr. 1950, p. 24.)

Another of these ''chosen disciples,'' Elder Boyd K. Packer, has stated: ''We continually strive to share the gospel with others, but we cannot dilute it to suit their taste. We did not set the standards; the Lord did. It is his church. We ask those of you who are not yet members of the Church to be patient if we seem too anxious to share what we have. If we do not share it, we may lose it. That is one of the requirements if we are to keep it. Therefore, missionary work is not casual; it is very determined.'' (CR, Oct 1974, p. 125.)

This day of warning will continue until every creature has heard the gospel (Mark 16:15–16). The gospel shall be preached ''either to the convincing of them unto peace and life eternal, or unto the deliverance of them to the hardness of their hearts" (1 Ne. 14:7), in which case they shall be left without excuse before the judgment seat of Christ.

See also: Voice of Warning

Day of Wrath

See: Great and Dreadful Day of the Lord

Day That Shall Burn As an Oven

See: Great and Dreadful Day of the Lord

Days of Probation

The expression *days of probation* is not found in the Bible but is found once in the Doctrine and Covenants (29:43) and eight times in the Book of Mormon (e.g., 1 Ne. 10:21; 2 Ne. 9:27; Morm. 9:28). These days have reference to the period of testing in which man proves whether he "will do all things" which the Lord commands him to do (Abr. 3:24–25).

The days of probation are essentially confined to the span of one's mortal life, although this time period may vary according to the opportunities one has had to discover and abide by the principles and ordinances of the gospel. For example, Samuel the Lamanite told the wicked Nephites living in his day that their days of probation were past (Hel.

13:38). Similarly, Mormon saw that "the day of grace was passed" for the degenerate people of his time (Morm. 2:15). Amulek warned that "this life is the time for men to prepare to meet God" for "if we do not improve our time while in this life, then cometh the night of darkness [a time when one has lost the will or ability to repent] wherein there can be no labor performed" (Alma 34:32–35).

Deacon

The first office in the Aaronic Priesthood has been designated as that of a "deacon" (D&C 20:38–64; 84:30, 111; 88:127; 107:10, 62–63, 85; 124:142). The duties of this office, as described in revelation, are to assist the teachers and to warn, expound, exhort, teach, and invite all to come unto Christ (D&C 20:57–59). In modern times, bishoprics have delegated to deacons the responsibility of passing the emblems of the sacrament, collecting fast offerings, and performing other designated duties by special assignment.

Brigham Young once emphasized the importance of each priesthood office by asking, "Who . . . has the greatest power?" (JD 9:93.) Such a thought should be emblazoned in the mind of every deacon. Although his is the lowest office in the priesthood line, his power can be beyond comprehension if he does his best.

One is *ordained* to the office of deacon, which means that this office is retained throughout one's life, even when additional offices in the priesthood are bestowed on worthy bearers of this authority. President Spencer W. Kimball, a modern-day prophet, declared: "I am a deacon. I am always proud that I am a deacon. When I see the Apostles march up to the stand in a solemn assembly to bless the sacrament, and others of the General Authorities step up to the sacrament tables to get the bread and the water and humbly pass it to all the people in the assembly and then return their emptied receptacles, I am very proud that I am a deacon, and a teacher, and a priest." (CR, Apr. 1975, p. 117.)

See also: Aaronic Priesthood

Dead That Die in the Lord

Occasional reference is made to those who "die in the Lord" (D&C 29:13; 42:44, 46; 63:49; Rev. 14:13). This has reference to "the saints of God who have been true and faithful to every trust, who have kept the faith, who have endured to the end, who at their passing are prepared for an inheritance in the paradise of peace" (DNTC 3:534). "Death can be comforting and sweet and precious," said Elder Bruce R. McConkie, "or it can thrust upon us all the agonies and sulphurous burnings of an endless hell. And we—each of us individually—make the choice as to which it

shall be." (CR, Oct. 1976, p. 156; D&C 42:46–47.)

President Joseph Fielding Smith has offered the following additional explanation: "To some members of the Church the saying that those who die in the Lord shall not taste of death has been a hard saying. They have seen good faithful men and women suffer days and at times for months before they were taken. But here the Lord does not say they shall not suffer pain of body, but that they shall be free from the anguish and torment of soul which will be partaken of by the wicked, and although they may suffer in body, yet death to them will be sweet in that they will realize that they are worthy before the Lord. The Savior said to Martha: 'And whosoever liveth and believeth in me shall never die.' That is to say, they shall never die the second death and feel the torment of the wicked when they come face to face with eternity." (CHMR 1:186.)

See also: Appointed unto Death; Graves of the Saints

Dead Works

An 1830 revelation proclaimed that unauthorized baptisms, or "dead works," had no efficacy in God's kingdom (D&C 22:2). This same feeling had been expressed centuries earlier by an ancient Nephite prophet in respect to infant baptism (Moro. 8:22–26). Dead works are symbolic of that which has no life now nor power to grant life hereafter. Unauthorized baptisms—those performed without proper priesthood authority—are lifeless and do not have power to lead to eternal life. Participation in dead works has no saving power, no matter how sincere the recipient may have been.

Death

See: Baptism for the Dead; Bands of Death; Dead That Die in the Lord; Dead Works; Deaths, The; Dust of the Earth; First Death; Graves of the Saints; Last Death; Natural Death; Region and Shadow of Death; Second Death; Shadow of Death; Shaft of Death; Sinned unto Death; Spirit World; Spiritually Dead; Taken to Heaven Without Tasting Death; Taste of Death; Temporal Death

Deaths, The

The Lord decreed that "broad is the gate, and wide the way that leadeth to the *deaths*; and many there are that go in thereat, *because they receive me not*, neither do they abide in my law" (D&C 132:25; italics added). This is the opposite of the "continuation of the lives" promised to those who faithfully pursue the strait and narrow path (D&C 132:22). President Joseph Fielding Smith explained that "the term 'deaths' . . . has reference to the cutting off of all those who reject this eternal covenant

of marriage and therefore they are denied the power of exaltation and the continuation of posterity. To be denied posterity and the family organization, leads to the 'deaths,' or end of increase in the life to come." (CHMR 2:360.)

Deep

During the days of despair he spent unjustly incarcerated in a foul prison, Joseph Smith pled for relief from the Lord. Although the voice of the Lord reminded the Prophet that he was not forgotten, he was warned of other adversities that might befall him. Among these was the possibility of being "cast into the deep" (D&C 122:7), which was a metaphorical allusion to being cast into the depths of the seas, or suffering great personal discomfort and distress. When one thinks of a struggling soul sinking in the depths of the seas, one pictures a soul very much in distress. Such would be the lot of Joseph Smith.

Deep Water Is What I Am Wont to Swim in

In a moment of reflection on the many persecutions and privations he had suffered, Joseph Smith declared, "Deep water is what I am wont to swim in" (D&C 127:2). The Prophet was simply saying that he was accustomed to being in difficult surroundings that required him to be alert and active or he would not have survived. Elder Russell M. Nelson pointed out that "the expression *deep water* means danger" (En., May 1988, p. 33). The word *wont* is an alternate translation of the word *accustomed* from the Greek language (see Matt. 27:15).

Defense and . . . a Refuge

The Lord promises that the stakes of Zion will serve as a "defense, and for a refuge" to the faithful who gather to these protective canopies of Christ, there to be nurtured in his ways (D&C 115:6). A refuge is a shelter or protection from danger. Those who accept the gospel of Jesus Christ and gather to his stakes are shielded from spiritual danger and build spiritual strength and defenses to thwart attacks by the adversary. The congregations of the Saints become fortresses for the faithful. It is significant to note the promise that those who faithfully gather to worship and partake of the sacrament will "more fully" keep themselves "unspotted from the world" (D&C 59:9).

See also: Storm

Deign

On two occasions in the Doctrine and Covenants, the word *deign* is used. In an 1831 revelation the Lord said: "I . . . *deign* to give unto you greater riches, even a land of promise" (D&C 38:18; italics added). Ten years later he said: "I *deign* to reveal unto my church things which have been kept hid" (D&C 124:41; italics added). According to Webster, the verb *deign* means to esteem or treat as worthy, to condescend to give or bestow. Thus, the Lord esteemed the Saints as worthy to receive that which he was to bestow on them. He considered it appropriate.

Derision

While languishing in Liberty Jail, the Prophet was told that "fools shall have thee in derision" (D&C 122:1). The word is also found in the Old Testament where the Psalmist says of those who "take counsel together, against the Lord . . . , the Lord shall have them in derision" (Ps. 2:2–4). To have someone in derision is to ridicule, scorn, or mock him. While fools may mock Joseph Smith, they in turn shall be scorned by the Lord.

Desire of Their Hearts

Men will be judged not only for their works but also according to the desire of their hearts. The Lord declared that he "will judge all men according to their works, according to the desire of their hearts" (D&C 137:9). Although we may deceive mortal man, we cannot hide the true feelings and desires of our hearts from God, "for the Lord seeth not as man seeth; for man looketh on the outward appearance, but the Lord looketh on the heart" (1 Sam. 16:7). Alma taught that God "granteth unto men according to their desire, whether it be unto death or unto life" (Alma 29:4). He reminded his son that if the desires of men's hearts were good, at the last day they would "be restored unto that which is good" (Alma 41:3).

If one is prevented from doing something because of circumstances beyond his control, the Lord will judge him as if he had performed the desired righteous act. However, as noted by Elder Dallin H. Oaks, "Desire is a substitute only when action is truly impossible."

He further observed that "we should not assume that the desires of our hearts, which can apparently serve as compliance with a *law* of the gospel, can also serve as compliance with an *ordinance* of the gospel.

"There is no scriptural authority for the proposition that good intent can substitute for the performance of a required *ordinance*." (1985–86 DFS, 31.)

See also: Thoughts; Willing Heart

Desolation of Abomination

The phrase *desolation of abomination* appears twice in the Doctrine and Covenants (84:117; 88:85) and is similar to the terms *abomination of desolation* (Matt. 24:15; JS—M 1:12, 32) and *the abomination that maketh desolate* (Dan 9:27; 12:11). In pre-1981 editions of the Doctrine and Covenants, the footnote cross-references to these verses referred to the numerous calamities and judgments which are predicted to fall on the world prior to the Second Coming. The desolation of abomination is *the wrath of God . . . which awaits the wicked, both in this world and in the world to come*" (D&C 88:85; italics added). This is in keeping with Webster's definitions: "Desolation," the dictionary states, is the "act of desolating, or laying waste; the destruction of inhabitants." And *abominations* have been defined as "anything hateful, wicked or shamefully vile." Therefore, in what is known as the desolation of abomination, the Lord will destroy those things which are hateful, wicked, or vile.

The LDS Bible Dictionary indicates that "conditions of desolation, born of abomination and wickedness, were to occur *twice* in fulfillment of Daniel's words" (LDSBD, 601). The first of these was when Jerusalem was destroyed in A.D. 70, and the second is when the city will once again be besieged in the last days. It further states that "in a general sense, abomination of desolation also describes the latter-day judgments to be poured out upon the wicked wherever they may be."

See also: Abominations

Destroyed in the Flesh

The Lord declared that those who are "sealed up by the Holy Spirit of promise," and then violate their covenants, "shall be *destroyed in the flesh,* and shall be delivered unto the buffetings of Satan unto the day of redemption" (D&C 132:26; italics added). President Joseph Fielding Smith emphatically stated: "To be 'destroyed in the flesh' means exactly that. We cannot destroy men in the flesh, because we do not control the lives of men and do not have power to pass sentences upon them which involve capital punishment. In the days when there was a theocracy on the earth, then this decree was enforced. What the Lord will do in lieu of this, because we cannot destroy in the flesh, I am unable to say, but it will have to be made up in some other way." (DS 2:96–97.)

Brigham Young declared that "when people take the downward road, one that is calculated to destroy them, they will actually in every sense of the word be destroyed. Will they be what is termed annihilated?" he asked. "No, there is no such thing as annihilation, for you cannot destroy the elements of which things are made." (JD 2:302.) The *purchase* of sin is obviously not worth the *price* of the punishment.

Destroyer (#1)

In August 1831, on the banks of the Missouri River, at a place known as McIlwaine's Bend, W. W. Phelps saw in "open vision by daylight . . . the *destroyer* in his most horrible power, ride upon the face of the waters; others heard the noise, but saw not the vision" (HC 1:203; italics added). The following morning, after prayer, Joseph Smith received a revelation in which he was informed that "the destroyer rideth upon the face" of "these waters," referring particularly to the Missouri and Mississippi rivers (D&C 61:18–19; DCC, 255). "The 'destroyer' seen by William W. Phelps . . . was, in all probability, the Evil One himself." (SS, 361.) This disdainful title is in keeping with Satan's avowed intention of *destroying* the souls of men and making them as miserable as he is (2 Ne. 2:18, 27; Hel. 7:16; 8:28). The title is also used to refer to the individual who destroyed the Lord's vineyard (D&C 101:54).

See also: Devil

Destroyer (#2)

In 1834, the Lord warned that "the destroyer" would be "sent forth to destroy and lay waste mine enemies" (D&C 105:15). The identity of this destroyer was revealed by President Joseph Fielding Smith: "The Lord does send forth the destroyer in the shape of plague and famine, and also his angels to execute his authority from time to time upon those who blaspheme his name" (CHMR 2:4). In this sense the destroyer is something that ruins or damages, perhaps even kills.

Destroying Angel

In the revelation known as the Word of Wisdom, the promise is made that all who abide by the principles of health set forth therein by the Lord would find "the destroying angel" passing them by (D&C 89:21). In commenting on this promise, J. Reuben Clark, Jr., said: "This does not say and this does not mean, that to keep the Word of Wisdom is to insure us against death, for death is, in the eternal plan, co-equal with birth. . . . But it does mean that the *destroying angel, he who comes to punish the unrighteous for their sins*, as he in olden time afflicted the corrupt Egyptians in their wickedness (Ex. 12:23, 29), shall pass by the Saints, 'who are walking in obedience to the commandments,' and who 'remember to keep and do these sayings.' These promises do mean that all those who qualify themselves to enjoy them will be permitted so to live out their lives that they may gain the full experiences and get the full knowledge which they need in order to progress to the highest exaltation in eternity, all these will live until their work is finished and God calls them back to their eternal home, as a reward." (CR, Oct. 1940, pp. 17–18; italics added.)

Elder Spencer W. Kimball noted: "No promise is made through the Word of Wisdom that the faithful observer will not die. . . . With ancient Israel it was physical life or physical death. In our modern promise, it is spiritual life or spiritual death. If one ignores 'these sayings' and fails in 'obedience to the commandments' his death is certain, but if he obeys implicitly, his eternal life through perfection is assured. The angel of death cuts one short of mortal life for disobedience; the angel of light makes the way clear for the spiritual life eternal." (MF, 210–11.)

Elder Bruce R. McConkie said that while "such expressions as 'destroying angel' and 'sword of vengeance' may be figurative, they are intended to convey the reality that the Lord's hand is involved in what takes place and that he is using his powers to bring to pass his ends. Deity, for instance, slew the firstborn in all the houses of Egypt (Ex. 12:23, 29), and this is figuratively spoken of as having been done by 'the destroying angel.' (D&C 89:21.)" (DNTC 2:117—18.)

See also: Great and Dreadful Day of the Lord

Detroit, Michigan

An 1831 revelation instructed Hyrum Smith and John Murdock to take a missionary journey from Kirtland, Ohio, to Missouri by way of Detroit (D&C 52:8). The city of Detroit fronts the Detroit River where it connects Lake Erie with Lake St. Clair in Michigan. It was founded in 1701 by a French trader, Antoine de la Mothe Cadillac. At the time of the 1831 revelation it was the capital of the Territory of Michigan. It became a hub of early railroad operations in the 1830s, and this, combined with its accessibility for shipping, made it a prime place for industrial and commercial activity. Today, the metropolitan area of Detroit comprises one of the major industrial-commercial complexes in the United States. (See *Encyclopedia Brittanica*, 15th ed., vol. 5, pp. 621–22.)

Devil

He who was cast out of heaven for rebellion has become "the devil of all devils" (2 Ne. 9:37). He was formerly known as "Lucifer, a son of the morning" (D&C 76:26), who was desirous of exalting himself while debasing God. Now, rather than sitting on the coveted celestial seat of power, he occupies a temporary telestial throne. (D&C 29:36–38; Moses 4:1–4; Abr. 3:27–28; 2 Ne. 2:17–18; Rev. 12:7–9.) Among the titles whereby he is known in the Doctrine and Covenants are "devil" (1:35); "Satan" (10:5); "Perdition" (76:26); "Lucifer" (76:26); "a son of the morning" (76:26); "that old serpent" (76:28); "the adversary" (82:5); "that evil one" (93:37); "the prince of this world" (127:11); and "an angel of light" (128:20).

Joseph Smith said that the devil goes "up and down in the earth, seeking whom he may destroy—any person that he can find that will yield to him, he will bind him, and take possession of the body and reign there, glorying in it mightily, not caring that he had got merely a stolen body; and by and by some one having authority will come along and cast him out and restore the tabernacle to its rightful owner. The devil steals a tabernacle because he has not one of his own; but if he steals one, he is always liable to be turned out of doors." (TPJS, 297–98.)

Among his other objectives are "to destroy the souls of men" (Hel. 8:28), and to see "that all men might be miserable like unto himself" (2 Ne. 2:18, 27). His only power over man is that which is voluntarily yielded, for he cannot compel mankind to do evil (TPJS, 187). Elder James E. Faust noted that the devil "is really a coward, and if we stand firm, he will retreat" (En., Nov. 1987, p. 35). Where righteousness prevails, he has no power (1 Ne. 22:26). However, as the Prophet Joseph warned, "The moment we revolt at anything which comes from God, the devil takes power" (TPJS, 181).

Though his triumphs in our present world are evident in the sin and suffering we see, he and his followers will ultimately be banished and Satan's sceptre of power will be useless. Mankind will one day look on him with wonderment and proclaim, "Is this the man that made the earth to tremble, that did shake kingdoms" (Isa. 14:15–17).

An Apostle of the Lord, Elder James E. Faust, has given the following caution regarding curiosity about the devil and his evil ways: "It is not good practice to become intrigued by Satan and his mysteries. No good can come from getting close to evil. Like playing with fire, it is too easy to get burned. . . . The only safe course is to keep well distanced from him and any of his wicked activities or nefarious practices. The mischief of devil worship, sorcery, casting spells, witchcraft, voodooism, black magic, and all other forms of demonism should be avoided like the plague." (En., Nov. 1987, p. 33.)

See also: Angel of God Who Was in Authority; Buffetings of Satan; Chains of Darkness; Church of the Devil; Damnation of Hell; Damned; Darkness; Destroyer (#1); Doctrines of Devils; Eternal Damnation; Evil One, That; False Spirits; Fiery Darts; Gates of Hell; Hell; Hosts of Hell; Jaws of Hell; Lake of Fire and Brimstone; Lucifer; Outer Darkness; Perdition; Powers of Darkness; Prince of This World; Satan; Serpent, Old; Sheol, Benighted Dominion of; Son of the Morning; Sons of Perdition; That Wicked One; Third Part of the Hosts of Heaven; Vengeance of Eternal Fire; Vessels of Wrath

Devils

See: False Spirits; Hosts of Hell; Third Part of the Hosts of Heaven

Devouring Fire

See: Day That Shall Burn as an Oven; Ezekiel; Fire; Presence of the Lord Shall Be as the Melting Fire; Refiner's Fire

Dews of Carmel

It is assumed that the poetic mention of "the dews of Carmel" in an 1842 revelation has reference to Mount Carmel, "which forms one of the most striking and characteristic features of the country of Palestine . . . , the only headland of lower and central Palestine . . . , with a bold bluff promontory, nearly 600 feet high, almost into the very waves of the Mediterranean" (Peloubet, 110). The dew that would readily gather on such a place is compared by the Prophet Joseph to the way in which God would distill knowledge upon his faithful servants (D&C 128:19). "Give ear, O ye heavens, and I will speak; and hear, O earth, the words of my mouth," declared the Lord anciently. "My doctrine shall drop as the rain, *my speech shall distil as the dew*, as the small rain upon the tender herb, and as the showers upon the grass." (Deut. 32:1–2; italics added; see also D&C 121:45.)

Diabolical Rascality

See: Concatenation

Differences of Administration

Among the gifts of the Spirit enumerated in section 46 is "the differences of administration" (D&C 46:15). According to Smith and Sjodahl, "This is another special gift. The term as used by Paul (1 Cor. 12:5) means the different divisions or courses of the priests and Levites engaged in the temple service, and in this Revelation it may refer to the different duties and responsibilities of the Priesthood in its two divisions, the Melchizedek and Aaronic. To know this is a gift of the Spirit." (SS, 274.)

Moroni gave additional insight into this particular gift by stating: "And *there are different ways that these gifts are administered*; but it is the same God who worketh all in all; and they are given by the manifestations of the Spirit of God unto men, to profit them" (Moro. 10:8; italics added). Thus, while the origin of all gifts of the Spirit is common, the administration thereof may vary.

Discerning of Spirits

"Two spirits are abroad in the earth," wrote Elder Bruce R. McConkie, "one is of God, the other of the devil. The spirit which is of God is one that leads to light, truth, freedom, progress, and every good thing; on the other hand, the spirit which is of Lucifer leads to darkness, error, bondage, retrogression, and every evil thing. One spirit is from above, the other from beneath; and that which is from beneath never allows more light or truth or freedom to exist than it can help. . . .

In general, the more righteous and saintly a person is, the easier it will be for him to receive communications from heavenly sources; and the more evil and corrupt he is, the easier will it be for evil spirits to implant their nefarious schemes in his mind and heart." (DNTC 3:392–93.) An important gift of the Spirit, therefore, is the "discerning of spirits" (D&C 46:23; 1 Cor. 12:10).

To be discerning is to have revealing insight and understanding, to distinguish between that which is of God and that which is of the devil. It is to correctly perceive the right course of action (D&C 63:41) and to recognize subtle differences that may not be apparent to others (D&C 131:7). God is a "discerner of the thought and intents of the heart" (D&C 33:1), meaning he perceives and comprehends our every thought and desire.

Joseph Smith said, "No man knows the spirit of the devil, and his power and influence, but by possessing intelligence which is more than human, and having unfolded through the medium of the Priesthood the mysterious operations of his devices. . . . A man must have the discerning of spirits before he can drag into daylight this hellish influence and unfold it unto the world in all its soul-destroying, diabolical, and horrid colors; for nothing is a greater injury to the children of men than to be under the influence of a false spirit when they think they have the Spirit of

God." (TPJS, 205; see also 1 Cor. 2:10–16; 1 John 4:1–6.)

"The discerning of spirits is and can be practiced in righteousness only where the true Church and kingdom of God is found. In the final analysis, it takes apostles, prophets, priesthood, the gift of the Holy Ghost, and a knowledge of God's laws and the manner in which he operates, in order to separate the spirits into their two opposing camps. Only where these things are found can error be segregated from truth, because only there are the channels of revelation open." (DNTC 3:395.)

It is important to remember that revelation from God will be edifying, will not contradict that which has been revealed through the Lord's *authorized* and *recognized* servants, and will not concern an area over which we have no stewardship (HC 1:355; TPJS, 214–15; D&C 129). "We get our answers from the source of the power we list to obey," said President Harold B. Lee. "If we're following the ways of the devil, we'll get our answers from the devil. If we're keeping the commandments of God, we'll get our answers from God." (SHP, 138.)

Disciple

A disciple is a committed Christian, a faithful follower in the footsteps of Christ. "He that believeth on me," declared the Savior, "the works that I do shall he do also; and greater works

than these shall he do" (John 14:12). Elder Marion D. Hanks observed that *"the Lord expects more of the disciple than ordinary response* to need, to opportunity, to commandment" (CR, Oct. 1976, p. 41; italics added).

There are four different categories of disciples referred to in the Doctrine and Covenants. First are those disciples, including the Twelve, who followed Jesus in his mortal ministry (D&C 6:32; 10:59; 45:16, 34; 88:3). Disciples among the posterity of Lehi are spoken of in Doctrine and Covenants 10:46; the reference in Doctrine and Covenants 64:8 could apply to either of the above groups. The Apostles to be chosen in these last days are spoken of as disciples (D&C 18:27). Finally, there are general references to the members of the Church as disciples (D&C 45:32; 57:5, 8; 58:52; 63:38, 41, 45; 64:19; 84:91). The Savior gives his own definition to discipleship in these words: "He that receiveth my law and doeth it, the same is my disciple" (D&C 41:5). This basic statement was amplified by later revelatory remarks (D&C 52:40; 84:89–91; 103:28).

Dispensation

The word *dispensation* appears in seven sections of the Doctrine and Covenants (27:13; 110:12, 16; 112:30–32; 121:31; 124:41; 128:9, 18, 20, 21; 138:48). *"A dispensation of the gospel is defined as the granting to divinely chosen officers, by a commission from God, of power and authority to dispense the word of God, and to administer in all the ordinances thereof. However, a dispensation has frequently embraced additional power and included a special commission or warning to the people, the making of a special and definite covenant with man, and the conferring of special powers upon chosen prophets beyond what other prophets may have received."* (DS 1:160–61.)

President Joseph Fielding Smith identified the following dispensations: Adam, Enoch, Noah, Abraham, Moses, John the Baptist, the meridian of times or apostolic, Jaredites, Nephites, Lost Tribes, Lehi and Nephi—two brothers who lived at the time of the coming of the Savior—and our present dispensation, which is the dispensation of the fulness of times (DS 1:161–62). This was not intended to be a definitive list, for, stated this spiritual scholar, "I do not know how many dispensations there have been." He noted *"whenever the Lord has established a dispensation, there has been more than one witness to testify for him."* (DS 1:203.) For example, Noah was assisted by Methuselah and Lamech (Moses 8). Abraham was assisted by Elias (D&C 110:12), as well as by Melchizedek (D&C 84:14; JST, Gen. 14:36–37). Aaron assisted his brother, Moses (Ex. 3, 4). In more modern times, Joseph Smith was assisted by both Oliver Cowdery and Hyrum Smith (D&C 124:94–95).

See also: Dispensation of the Fulness of Times; Dispensation of the Gospel of Abraham; Dispensation of the Priesthood

Dispensation of the Fulness of Times

The dispensation which commenced with the restoration of keys of authority to the Prophet Joseph Smith, and which will continue until the second coming of Christ, is the "dispensation of the fulness of times" (D&C 27:13; 112:30; 121:31; 124:41; 128:18–21; 138:48). "God purposed in Himself that there should not be an eternal fullness until every dispensation should be fulfilled and gathered together in one," declared Joseph Smith (TPJS, 168).

Although Father Adam holds the keys of all dispensations (HC 4:207), Joseph Smith stands at the head of the dispensation of the fulness of times, which is a welding together of the keys, powers, and glories of all previous dispensations (D&C 90:3; 128:18; CHMR 1:388). Among the many messengers from past dispensations who appeared to Joseph Smith bearing sacred messages and keys of authority were the Father and Son, Moroni, John the Baptist, Peter, James, John, Gabriel (Noah), Raphael, Moses, Elijah, Michael (Adam), and other "diverse angels" (D&C 2; 13; 27:5, 8, 12; 128:20–21; JS—H:1; JD 16:161; 17:374; 18:47).

See also: Dispensation

Dispensation of the Gospel of Abraham

The dispensation of the gospel of Abraham was that period of time during which Abraham lived and in which the Lord had a dispensation of his gospel upon the earth. For some unknown reason Elias held the keys of this dispensation (D&C 110:12; DS 1:204). According to Elder Joseph Fielding Smith, these keys included "everything that pertains to that dispensation, the blessings that were conferred upon Abraham [and] the promises that were given to his posterity" (UGHM 27:100; see also Abr. 2:8–11).

Elder Bruce R. McConkie further elaborated on this dispensation: "Now what was the gospel of Abraham [restored by Elias]? Obviously it was the commission, the mission, the endowment and power, the message of salvation, given to Abraham. . . . It was a divine promise that both in the world and out of the world his seed should continue 'as innumerable as the stars; or, if ye were to count the sand upon the seashore ye could not number them. . . .'

"Thus the gospel of Abraham was one of celestial marriage; . . . it was a gospel or commission to provide a lineage for the elect portion of the [premortal] spirits. . . . This power and commission is what Elias restored." (MD, 219–20.)

See also: Abraham; Dispensation; Elias

Dispensation of the Priesthood

Inasmuch as a dispensation of the gospel requires that the priesthood be present to administer the ordinances of the gospel, we may assume that the terms *dispensation of the gospel* and *dispensation of the priesthood* are synonymous and may be used interchangeably. Adam holds the keys of salvation and the keys of the dispensation of the fulness of times (D&C 78:16; HC 4:207–8). The Prophet Joseph Smith said that the nature of the priesthood is that there are men who hold the presidency of the priesthood in each dispensation and that each is accountable to Adam, who holds the keys of the fulness of times and who in turn is accountable to the Lord (TPJS, 169; HC 3:385).

See also: Dispensation

Distil

In both the Old Testament (Deut. 32:2) and the Doctrine and Covenants (121:45) the Lord promises that something shall "distil as the dew." This is a figure of speech which means that the promised item would descend upon the recipient as gently and almost imperceptibly as the moisture of dew descends upon the earth.

See also: Doctrine of the Priesthood

Diversities of Operations

Among the "gifts of the spirit" is the "diversities of operations" (D&C 46:16; 1 Cor. 12:6). According to Smith and Sjodahl: "This refers to various spiritual influences at work, for instance such as are manifested in Spiritism, anarchism, and the numerous other 'isms.' To know whether an influence with a professedly moral, or reformatory, aim is from the Holy Spirit, or from another source, is a special gift." (SS, 274.)

Doctrine and Covenants

The Book of Commandments, intended for publication in 1833, was the name of the original volume of revelations which have since been incorporated into the Doctrine and Covenants. This latter volume has over twice as many revelations as the original book. The origin of the name is unclear, although it does appear in an entry in Joseph Smith's journal, dated November 3, 1831 (HC 1:229). It was first published under this name in 1835. It is a book containing "doctrine" and "covenants" given by the Lord to his people in these last days. " 'Doctrine' means 'teaching,' 'instruction.' It denotes more especially what is taught as truth, for us to believe, as distinct from precepts, by which rules, to be obeyed are given. 'Doctrine' refers to belief; precept to conduct. . . . The word 'covenant' is a term by which God indicates the settled arrangement between Him and His people." (SS, 14.)

President Joseph Fielding Smith made the following observations regarding the book and its title: "The *Doctrine and Covenants* . . . , how much more significant it is than the *Book of Commandments*. A Book of Commandments means, if we accept the title at its face value, that it contains only commandments. But this title which the Lord gave . . . is very significant and tells the story of what this book actually is. It contains the *doctrine* of the Church; it contains the *covenants* the Lord will make with the Church, if we are willing to receive them.

"In my judgment there is no book on earth yet come to man as important as the book known as the Doctrine and Covenants." (DS 3:198.)

The significance of the Doctrine and Covenants to the entire world was stressed in an early conference address by Elder Joseph Fielding Smith in the following words: "The Lord has given so many revelations, in our own day. We have this Doctrine and Covenants full of them, all pertaining unto the Latter-day Saints and to the world. For this is not our book alone. . . . The Lord has given it unto the world for their salvation . . . ; it belongs to all the world, not only to the Latter-day Saints, and they will be judged by it, and you will be judged by it . . . and if we fail to comprehend these things, if we will not take hold on the things which the Lord has revealed unto us, then his condemnation shall rest upon us, and we shall be removed from his presence and from his kingdom." (CR, Oct. 1919, p. 146.)

The Lord's admonition regarding this book of scripture is, "Search these commandments, for they are true and faithful, and the prophecies and promises which are in them shall all be fulfilled" (D&C 1:37).

See also: Book of Commandments

Doctrine of the Priesthood

Writing by way of revelation, a prophet promised that those whose bowels are full of charity towards all men and who garnish their thoughts with virtue unceasingly would find their confidence waxing strong in the presence of God and "the doctrine of the priesthood" would be distilled upon their souls "as the dews from heaven" (D&C 121:45).

An official explanation of this term appeared in print in 1961: "It is the doctrine that those who hold this power and authority will be chosen for an inheritance of eternal life if they exercise their priesthood upon principles of righteousness; if they walk in the light; if they keep the commandments; if they put first in their lives the things of God's kingdom and let temporal concerns take a secondary place; if they serve in the kingdom with an eye single to the glory of God. It is the doctrine

that even though men have the rights of the priesthood conferred upon them, they shall not reap its eternal blessings if they use it for unrighteous purposes; if they commit sin; if the things of this world take preeminence in their lives over the things of the Spirit. It is a fearful thing to contemplate this priesthood truth: Behold, many are called to the priesthood, and few are chosen for eternal life." (IE, 64:115.)

See also: Distil; Eternal Life; Melchizedek Priesthood

Doctrines of Devils

The Lord warned us against following either the "commandments of men" or the "doctrines of devils" (D&C 46:7). This latter term has been defined as *"false doctrines in which there is no salvation; doctrines which are contrary to the mind and will of God and which are encouraged and sponsored by Satan,* as for instance: That God is an immaterial Spirit essence filling all immensity; that revelation, gifts, and miracles ceased with the apostles; that infants must be baptized to be saved" (DNTC 3:85; italics added).

Elder Ezra Taft Benson identified "population control" as a specific doctrine of the devil (CR, Apr. 1969, p. 12). Joseph Smith described the teachings of a certain minister named Joshua as being doctrines of the devil (TPJS, 104–5), and identified the doctrine that one could know the fate of a son of perdition as being of the devil (TPJS, 24). Paul prophesied "that in the latter times some shall depart from the faith, giving heed to seducing spirits, and doctrines of devils" (1 Tim. 4:1). Additionally, the Lord warned us that "Satan doth stir up the hearts of the people to contention concerning the points of my doctrine; and in these things they do err, for they do wrest the scriptures and do not understand them" (D&C 10:63). Inasmuch as "contention is of the devil," it appears that those who pursue this course, regardless of their motive, are preaching "doctrines of devils" (3 Ne. 11:29).

Dodds, Asa

Among those called on a mission at the Amherst, Ohio, conference of January 1832 was Asa Dodds. He was called to accompany Calves Wilson on a journey to the west in proclaiming the gospel (D&C 75:15). Whether this mission was fulfilled is unknown, for no further mention is made of him or his companion in subsequent writings. Just as the New Testament immortalizes certain unknowns (Rom. 16), so the Doctrine and Covenants speaks of certain men whose deeds and destiny are at present unknown. Dodds is one of these.

Dogs

References to dogs in the scriptures frequently have nega-tive connotations. Wild packs of dogs devoured dead bodies in ancient Israel (1 Kgs. 14:11) and "became so fierce and such objects of dislike that fierce and cruel enemies were poetically called dogs" (see Ps. 22:16). "The dog being an unclean animal the name was used as a term of reproach, or of humility if speaking of oneself" (Cruden, 157; 1 Sam. 24:14; 2 Sam. 16:9).

The Savior admonished his followers to avoid giving holy things to dogs (D&C 41:6; Matt. 7:6; 3 Ne. 14:6).

See also: Pearls . . . Cast Before Swine

Dominion

To have dominion over someone or something is to have supremacy or controlling power. The Father and Son have dominion over the earth and its inhabitants (D&C 76:119; Ps. 24:1). Those who choose to rebel against God give the devil dominion (control) over them (D&C 1:35). Satan has no power over those who dwell in righteousness (1 Ne. 22:26). Elder ElRay L. Christiansen once noted that "in all his evil doings, the adversary can go no further than the transgressor permits him to go . . . , and when the Holy Ghost is really within us, Satan must remain without" (CR, Oct. 1974, p. 30). Those who endure "valiantly for the gospel of Jesus Christ" will receive "thrones and dominions, principalities and powers" (D&C

121:29). In other words, great areas of stewardship, including people and things, will be under their righteous control.

Dort, David

Although he is mentioned but once in the Doctrine and Covenants (124:132), the name of David D. Dort appears in several other prominent places on the pages of early Church records. He served on high councils at Kirtland, Ohio (HC 2:510—11); Far West, Missouri (HC 3:225); and Nauvoo, Illinois (HC 4:12). He was a member of the famed Zion's Camp, which went to the aid of fellow Saints in Missouri (HC 2:183), and later publicly covenanted to assist the Saints in their exodus from that land of persecution and mobocracy (HC 3:253). He is reported to have died in Nauvoo in 1841 at about age forty-eight.

Dove

See: Form of a Dove

Dust of the Earth

"For *dust* thou wast, and unto *dust* shalt thou return," declared Deity to Adam (Moses 4:25; Gen.

3:19; italics added). When Adam fell he became mortal or of the dust of this earth. Adam's corporeal body was created from the dust of this earth; in other words, it was *organized from those elements which belong to this planet Earth,* making it an "earthy" body (Moses 3:7; Abr. 5:7; Gen. 2:7; Alma 42:2; D&C 77:12; 128:14). Elder Russell M. Nelson noted that "compounds derived from dust—elements of the earth—are combined to make each living cell in our bodies" (En., May 1987, p. 10).

When man dies, "the dust return[s] to the earth as it was: and the spirit shall return unto God who gave it" (Eccl. 12:7). On the day of resurrection, the "sleeping dust" is restored to its perfect frame as the spirit is inseparably united with a glorified, heavenly body that is no longer quickened by mortal blood, but by spirit (D&C 138:17; Lev. 17:11; 1 Cor. 15:50; TPJS, 199–200, 326).

During the Millennium, "old men shall die; but they shall not sleep in the dust, but they shall be changed in the twinkling of an eye" (D&C 63:51). Thus, there will be no graves in the dust of the ground during this period of time, for those who die shall be instantaneously resurrected.

See also: Earthy; First Man; Flesh

E

Eagles' Wings

See: Bear Him Up as on Eagles' Wings

Eames, Ruggles

The only appearance of Ruggles Eames's name is in conjunction with the Amherst, Ohio, conference in January 1832. He, along with thirteen other brethren, was admonished to "be united in the ministry" (D&C 75:35). No further reference to him is found in published Church history.

Earth

See: Dust of the Earth; Earth Be Smitten with a Curse; Earth Is Ripe; Earth . . . Like as It Was in the Days Before It Was Divided; Earth Shall Tremble and Reel To and Fro; Earth Would Be Utterly Wasted; Earthy; Ends of the Earth; Fatness of the Earth; Four Corners of the Earth; Him Who Laid the Foundation of the Earth; Honorable Men of the Earth; Kingdom of God (on Earth); New Heaven and a New Earth; Salt of the Earth; Strangers and Pilgrims on Earth; Weak Things of the Earth/World; Whore of All the Earth

Earth Be Smitten with a Curse

See: Earth Would Be Utterly Wasted

Earth Is Ripe

Both the Doctrine and Covenants (29:9) and the New Testament (Rev. 14:15) speak of a time when "the earth is ripe." This is symbolic language representing a time of harvest. For the righteous it will be a day of gathering into the sheaves of the Master Harvester (see D&C 4:4; 6:3), but for the wicked it will be a day of destruction as they are treated as chaff and burned (1 Ne. 22:15; D&C 64:24).

See also: Burn; Field Is White Already to Harvest; Great and Dreadful Day of the Lord; Ripe; Stubble

Earth . . . Like as It Was in the Days Before It Was Divided

In the book of Genesis we read that in the days of Peleg, who was a great-great-great-grandson of Noah, the earth was "divided" (Gen. 9:18; 10:21–25). President Joseph Fielding Smith explained this momentous event as follows: "We are committed to the fact that Adam dwelt on this

American continent. But when Adam dwelt here, it was not the American continent, nor was it the Western Hemisphere, for all the land was in *one place*, and all the water was in one place. There was no Atlantic Ocean separating the hemispheres. . . .

"Then we read in Genesis that there came a time when the earth was divided. There are some people who believe that this simply means that the land surface was divided among the various tribes, but this is not the meaning; *it was an actual dividing of the surface of the earth*, and it was broken up as we find it now." (DS 3:74–75.)

Isaiah spoke of a time when the "land shall be married" (Isa. 62:4), which is what the Lord revealed when he said "the earth shall be like as it was in the days before it was divided" (D&C 133:24). Joseph Smith announced that "the Eternal God hath declared that the great deep shall roll back into the north countries and that the land of Zion and the land of Jerusalem shall be joined together, as they were before they were divided in the days of Peleg" (*Evening and Morning Star*, Feb. 1835).

Earth Rolls Upon Her Wings

To say that the earth and the stars roll upon their wings (D&C 88:45) is to indicate that these bodies move through the heavens as if they had wings.

Earth Shall Tremble and Reel To and Fro

The prophecy that "the earth shall reel to and fro like a drunkard" is found three times in the Doctrine and Covenants (45:48; 49:23; 88:87) and once in the Old Testament (Isa. 24:20). Isaiah states that following this reeling like a drunkard, which shall occur at the end of the Millennium, the earth "shall fall, and not rise again."

Regarding this statement, President Joseph Fielding Smith said: "The interpretation is that it [the earth] should not be restored to the same mortal or temporal condition. When the earth passes away and is dissolved, it will pass through a similar condition which the human body does in death. But, like the human body, so shall the earth itself be restored in the resurrection and become a celestial body, through the mercy and mission of Jesus Christ." (CHMR 1:143.)

"For after it hath filled the measure of its creation, it shall be crowned with glory, even with the presence of God the Father; that bodies who are of the celestial kingdom may possess it forever and ever; for, for this intent was it made and created" (D&C 88:19–20).

See also: New Heaven and a New Earth; Millennium

Earth Would Be Utterly Wasted

The prediction of Malachi that without the keys of Elijah the earth would be "utterly wasted" or "smitten with a curse" (Mal. 4:5-6; D&C 2:3; 27:9; 128:17) was discussed in this way by Elder Theodore M. Burton: The smiting of the earth with a curse, in essence, means that "the whole purpose of earth life will have failed in its purpose in exalting the children of God unless there is a welding link of some kind or other between the fathers and the children." (GGG, 208; D&C 128:18; see also DS 2:121-22).

"The spirit of Elijah", according to Joseph Smith, is "that we redeem our dead, and connect ourselves with our fathers which are in heaven, and . . . seal those who dwell on earth to those who dwell in heaven" (HC 6:252).

See also: Elijah

Earthy

The Prophet Joseph Smith used the writings of Paul to illustrate the relationship of "earthy" matters to "heavenly" matters (1 Cor. 15:46-48; D&C 128:13-14). "The first man is of the earth, earthy. . . . As is the earthy, such are they also that are earthy," wrote Paul, adding that "we have borne the image of the earthy" (1 Cor. 15:47-49).

The "image of the earthy," according to Elder Bruce R. McConkie, is the "image of Adam or mortality, which is the natural inheritance of all men from Adam" (DNTC 2:402). That which pertains to mortality is of the earth, or "earthy," and is subject to corruption, disease, and ultimately death.

See also: Dust of the Earth; First Man; Temporal Things

Eastern (Brethren, Countries, Lands)

In ten sections of the Doctrine and Covenants the Lord uses the phrase *eastern countries, eastern lands,* or *eastern brethren.* In those revelations given between 1831 and 1834, the term *eastern* applied to that area of the United States *east of the main settlements of the Saints in Ohio.* (D&C 39:14; 45:64; 48:2; 52:35; 75:6, 13, 14; 79:1; 99:1; 101:74; 103:29). The term *eastern lands,* as used in an 1841 revelation, however, refers to that area of the country which was east of Nauvoo, Illinois (D&C 124:83, 108).

Economy

The book which John the Revelator saw with seven seals (Rev. 5:1) is said to contain the "mysteries, and the works of God; the hidden things of his economy concerning this earth" (D&C 77:6). This has reference to God's efficient management of the affairs of this earth in accomplishing his divine objectives (see D&C 3:1-3).

Effectual

An 1837 revelation given through Joseph Smith to Thomas B. Marsh in his position as President of the Quorum of the Twelve Apostles promised that "an effectual door" would be opened up in places where the name of Christ was proclaimed (D&C 112:19). Similar promises were made in two other revelations (D&C 100:3; 118:3). The word *effectual* means effective, or producing the desired results. Thus the Lord promised Thomas Marsh the desired results — effectual doors would be opened —as he faithfully engaged in His ministry.

Egypt

The only mention of Egypt in the Doctrine and Covenants is contained in the Lord's testimony of the deliverance of Israel from bondage (D&C 136:22). According to Peloubet, "[Egypt] is probably the oldest country in the world still existing. . . . Egypt proper is bounded on the north by the Mediterranean Sea, on the east by Palestine and the Red Sea, on the south by Nubia, and on the west by the Great Desert." (Peloubet, 162.)

The significance of Egypt, in scriptural history, is its close proximity to Palestine, from whence came the children of Israel into bondage. Many years later, this land of pharaohs and pyramids provided a sanctuary for Joseph, Mary, and the Babe of Bethlehem (Matt. 2:13–15).

Elders

The office of *elder* is the first office within the Melchizedek Priesthood to which one is ordinarily ordained. Although there are other offices within that priesthood — namely, seventy, high priest, patriarch, and Apostle — each is an administrative call that possesses keys but not additional priesthood. "No office adds to the power of the Priesthood," declared President Joseph F. Smith (GD,148).

Three definitions by former Church Presidents of the office of elder follow:

President Joseph Fielding Smith said: "The designation 'Elder' is one applicable to the apostles and likewise to all others who hold the Melchizedek Priesthood. The use of this designation makes it needless to use unnecessarily sacred terms as 'Apostle,' 'Patriarch,' 'High Priest,' etc. It is proper in general usage to speak of the apostles, the seventies and all others holding the Melchizedek Priesthood as 'elders.' " (CHMR 1:95.)

"The term 'elder,' " said President Harold B. Lee, "which is applied to all holders of the Melchizedek Priesthood, means a defender of the faith. That is our prime responsibility and calling. Every holder of the Melchizedek Priesthood is to be a defender of the faith." (CR, Apr. 1970, p. 54.)

President John Taylor declared: "He is a herald of salvation. . . . Is there any greater position that man can occupy upon the earth than to be engaged as a herald of salvation?'' (GK, 153.)

See also: Melchizedek Priesthood

Elect Lady

The phrase *elect lady* was applied to Emma Smith by the Lord in July 1830 (D&C 25:3). President Gordon B. Hinckley said this meant ''she was a 'chosen vessel of the Lord' '' (En., Nov. 1984, p. 91; see Moro. 7:31). This was at a time when Emma was in complete harmony with the Spirit, for her sins had been forgiven.

This title is also used by the Apostle John in an epistle that appears to be addressed to his wife and family (2 John 1:1, 13). ''An *elect lady* is a female member of the Church who has already received, or who through obedience is qualified to receive, the fulness of gospel blessings. This includes temple endowments, celestial marriage and the fullness of the sealing power. She is one who has been elected or chosen by faithfulness as a daughter of God in this life, an heir of God, a member of his household. Her position is comparable to that of the elders who magnify their callings in the priesthood and thereby receive all that the Father hath (D&C 84:38.) . . . .

Just as it is possible for the very elect to be deceived, and to fall from grace through disobedience, so an elect lady, by failing to endure to the end, can lose her chosen status.'' (MD, 217.)

In a more specific sense, President John Taylor said that Emma's title of elect lady ''means that she was called to a certain work. . . . She was elected to preside over the Relief Society.'' (JD 21:367.) This is consistent with the Prophet Joseph's comment that ''the elect meant to be elected to a certain work.'' He said Emma's ''election to the Presidency of the Society'' was a fulfillment of revelation (HC 4:552–53.)

See also: Smith, Emma

Elect, Mine

The phrase *mine elect*, or the *elect of God*, appears in four verses within the Doctrine and Covenants (29:7; 33:6; 35:20; 84:34). Emma Smith is also described as an elect lady on one occasion (25:3). In a general sense, the elect are those both within and without the Church who love the Lord and are with full purpose of heart doing all within their power to live close to the directions of his spirit.

President George Q. Cannon said, ''All mankind are elected to be saved. No man is a tare unless his conduct makes him such.'' (GT 1:140.) The elect outside of the Church are the ''sheep'' who hear the voice of the Master Shepherd, obey that voice, and are received into the Church (Mosiah 26:21–28). These are the elect whom the missionaries are admonished to gather (D&C 29:7).

To the elect within the Church, the Lord directs this warning: "False Christs, and false prophets, . . . if possible, . . . shall deceive the very elect, who are *the elect according to the covenant*" (JS—M 1:22; italics added). Speaking of this verse, President Harold B. Lee said that " 'the elect according to the covenant' . . . means the members of the Church" (CR, Oct. 1973, p. 169).

Those who are ultimately "elected" for exaltation within God's kingdom will be those who righteously use their free agency and cast their ballots in God's favor, choosing to serve him faithfully to the end.

See also: Elect Lady

Elements

Joseph Smith stated that "God had materials to organize the world out of chaos—chaotic matter, *which is element*, and in which dwells all the glory. Element had an existence from the time he had. The pure principles of element are principles which can never be destroyed; *they may be organized and re-organized, but not destroyed*. They had no beginning, and can have no end." (TPJS, 350–52; italics added.) Brigham Young further said: "There is no such thing as annihilation, for you cannot destroy the elements of which things are made" (JD 2:302).

See also: Created; Creation, The

Elements Shall Melt with Fervent Heat

See: Mountains Flow Down; Presence of the Lord Shall Be as the Melting Fire

Eleventh Hour

The term *eleventh hour* is found only in the Doctrine and Covenants (D&C 33:3) and in the New Testament (Matt. 20:6, 9). The latter instance is in the context of the parable of the workers in the vineyard. President Joseph Fielding Smith wrote, "This is the 'eleventh hour.' The time in which we live is compared to the eleventh hour, and so it is in the Lord's reckoning, for we are in the *closing scenes of the present world.* Elder Orson F. Whitney referred to our dispensation as the 'Saturday night' of time. And, according to the parable of the men employed in the vineyard, we who labor in this hour will be rewarded if we are faithful, with equal compensation with those who labored in the previous hours, or dispensations, in the history of mankind." (CHMR 1:153; italics added.)

Elias

The name *Elias* appears in seven different references in the Doctrine and Covenants (27:6, 7; 76:100; 77:9, 14; 110:12; 138:45). In order to identify the sense in which the name is used, one must be aware of its multiple meanings. Elder James E. Talmage wrote that '' *'Elias' is a title of office; every restorer, forerunner, or one sent of God to prepare the way for greater developments in the gospel plan, is an Elias.* The appelative 'Elias' is in fact both a *personal name* and a *title.*'' (Talmage, 375; italics added.) Joseph Smith referred to the preparatory work as the ''Priesthood of Elias, or the Priesthood that Aaron was ordained unto'' (TPJS, 335–36).

President Joseph Fielding Smith identified Noah, Elijah, John the Baptist, and John the Revelator as prophets holding the scriptural title of Elias (AGQ 3:140–41). However, he specifically identified the prophet Noah, who is also the angel Gabriel, as the Elias referred to in Doctrine and Covenants 27:7 and 110:12 (AGQ 3:138–41). He also suggested that John the Revelator is the Elias spoken of in Doctrine and Covenants 77:14, whose mission it is to prepare the Lost Tribes ''for their return from their long dispersion'' (CHMR 1:265; HC 1:176).

On the other hand, in reference to Doctrine and Covenants 27:6 and possibly 77:9, President Smith suggested the likelihood of a composite picture of several men holding the title of Elias, rather than a single individual. ''The Lord has declared that Elias shall restore all things spoken of by all the holy prophets. (D&C 27:6.) This may have reference to all the prophets who were sent

with keys of authority to Joseph Smith and Oliver Cowdery.'' (CHMR 2:49.)

The ''spirit of Elias,'' as well as the ''spirit of Elijah,'' is to prepare mankind for the Messiah, the greatest of all, he who shall one day require an accounting of his forerunners.

See also: Elijah; Gabriel; John the Ancient Apostle; John the Baptist; Noah; Translated

Elihu

In 1832, the Lord identified a man named Elihu as part of a priesthood line of authority. This man received this power ''under the hand of Jeremy'' and in turn conferred it upon one named Caleb (D&C 84:8–9). The name of Elihu appears in the Old Testament as the great-grandfather of the prophet Samuel (1 Sam. 1:1, 19–20). However, this is not the same man, for this latter individual lived some years after the time in which the original Elihu lived. The original Elihu was a forerunner of Moses' line of authority, and the latter Elihu came long after the days of Moses. The history of the Elihu mentioned in the Doctrine and Covenants is yet to be revealed.

Elijah

Elijah the prophet is spoken of in seven different revelations in the Doctrine and Covenants, most of which refer to his special premillennial mission of restoring the promised sealing powers of the priesthood (2:1-3; 27:9; 35:4; 110:13-16; 128:17-18; 138:46-48). In only one section is he mentioned without referring to his special mission (133:55).

The Prophet Joseph described the mission of Elijah as follows: "Elijah was the last Prophet that held the keys of the Priesthood, and who will, before the last dispensation, restore the authority and deliver the keys of the Priesthood, in order that all the ordinances may be attended to in righteousness. It is true that the Savior had authority and power to bestow this blessing; but the sons of Levi were too prejudiced. 'And I will send Elijah the Prophet before the great and terrible day of the Lord,' etc., etc. Why send Elijah? Because he holds the keys of the authority to administer in all the ordinances of the Priesthood; and without the authority is given, the ordinances could not be administered in righteousness." (TPJS, 172.)

In a further clarification of Elijah's mission of "turning" the hearts of the fathers and children to one another, the Prophet said: "Now, the word *turn* here should be translated *bind*, or seal" (TPJS, 330). "Elijah shall reveal the covenants to seal the hearts of the fathers to the children, and the children to the fathers" (TPJS, 323).

Malachi's ancient prophecy (Mal. 4:5-6) which initially foretold of Elijah's special mission is found in each of the other standard works of the Church (D&C 2:1-3; 3 Ne. 25:5-6; JS—H 1:38-39; other passages already cited). The Jewish people still anticipate the arrival of Elijah, and each year during their Paschal service a place is set for the ancient prophet and the door is opened to admit him as the "forerunner" of the promised Messiah. It is of interest to note that on April 3, 1836, the Jewish people celebrated their Paschal service, opening their doors to Elijah's return (DS 2:100-101). On that very day, he did return to the Kirtland Temple, where he bestowed the long-awaited keys of the sealing power (D&C 110:13-16).

Elijah's power from God extends back to his "sealing" the heavens for a period of three years so that no rain or dew fell on the parched earth (1 Kgs. 17:1). His classic showdown with the wicked priests of Baal is another example of his extraordinary faith and power, and one would do well to contemplate Elijah's searing inquiry: "How long halt ye between two opinions? If the Lord be God, follow him: but if Baal, then follow him." (1 Kgs. 18:21.)

Elijah was taken to heaven in "a chariot of fire," without tasting death (2 Kgs. 2:1-11). In other words, he became a translated being with temporary power over death. This was necessary in order that he might return to the Mount of Transfiguration and bestow keys of authority on Peter, James, and

John, for he had to possess a tangible earthly body for that mission (DS 2:110–11; Matt. 17:3; Luke 9:30). Following the resurrection of Christ—the "first fruits" thereof—Elijah passed through death and was a resurrected being when he appeared to Joseph Smith and Oliver Cowdery in the Kirtland Temple.

See also: Earth to Be Utterly Wasted; Elias; Mount, The; Priesthood (#2); Translated

Empty

The Lord declared that if the inhabitants of the earth did not repent, a desolating scourge should go forth "until the earth is empty" (D&C 5:19). Similarly Isaiah spoke of the Lord making "the earth empty, and . . . waste" (Isa. 24:1–6). To make empty is to make bare or desolate. This was the state of the newly formed earth before God added light and began to beautify and fill the earth with his creatures and creations (Abr. 4:2).

End of the Earth

The "end of the earth" is the time when the earth shall pass away, be resurrected, and become a "new earth" (D&C 29:22–23; 43:31; 88:26; CHMR 1:143).

See also: Day of Transfiguration; End of the World; New Heaven and a New Earth

End of the World

The "end of the world" (D&C 19:3; 45:22; 132:49) is defined in Joseph Smith's inspired rendition of the twenty-fourth chapter of Matthew, as found in the Pearl of Great Price. The Savior's disciples asked, "What is the sign of thy coming, and of the end of the world, or *the destruction of the wicked,* which is the end of the world?" (JS—M 1:4; italics added.) The "end of the world" (or the end of the wicked) will actually occur in two phases: the first phase will be prior to the Second Coming as the earth is cleansed of all but celestial and terrestrial beings; and the second and final phase will be at the end of the Millennium, when Satan's hosts of hell will be defeated and banished to outer darkness.

See also: Day of Transfiguration; End of the Earth; Paradisiacal Glory; New Heaven and a New Earth

Endless Punishment

See: Everlasting Punishment

Endowment

To be endowed is to have received a special gift, power, or quality. On January 2, 1831, the Lord promised the Prophet Joseph that he was to go to Ohio, where he would be "endowed with power from on high" (D&C 38:32, 38). On June 1, 1833, the Savior commanded a house to be built "in the which house I design to *endow* those whom I have chosen with power from on high" (D&C 95:8; italics added). A year later, on June 22, 1834, the Lord again spoke of this *endowment of power* which "the *first elders* of [his] church" should receive in the Lord's house to be built in Kirtland (D&C 105:11–12, 33; italics added). The "first" and "second" elders of the Church were Joseph Smith and Oliver Cowdery (D&C 20:2–3). It was these "first elders" who were endowed with power as they received keys of authority under the direction of the Savior, Moses, Elias, and Elijah in the Kirtland Temple on April 3, 1836 (D&C 110). This endowment (D&C 110:9) was not the endowment which is received in the temples today.

On November 12, 1835, Joseph Smith told the Twelve, "The endowment you are so anxious about, you cannot comprehend now, nor could Gabriel explain it to the understanding of your dark minds" (HC 2:309). Time was needed to prepare their minds for such an event, and it was several years before such preparation was complete. On May 4, 1842, the Prophet instructed a select few in the "washings, anointings, endowments" and other pertinent matters pertaining to the plan of salvation. Joseph said, "the communications I made to this council were of things spiritual, and to be received only by the spiritual minded: and there was nothing made known to these men but what will be made known to all the Saints of the last days, so soon as they are prepared to receive, and a proper place is prepared to communicate them . . . ; therefore let the Saints be diligent in building the Temple, and all houses which they have been, or shall hereafter be, commanded of God to build." (HC 5:1–2.)

The definition of an endowment was given by President Brigham Young as follows: "Your endowment is, to receive all those ordinances in the House of the Lord, which are necessary for you, after you have departed this life, to enable you to walk back to the presence of the Father, passing the angels who stand as sentinels, being enabled to give them the key words, the signs and tokens, pertaining to the Holy Priesthood, and gain your eternal exaltation in spite of earth and hell" (JD 2:31).

See also: Fulness of the Priesthood; Temple

Endowment House

In his official pronouncement declaring an end to the practice of plural marriage in the Church, the Lord's prophet, Wilford Woodruff, referred to the Endowment House (OD—1). This was an adobe structure built on Temple Square in Salt Lake City wherein sacred rites normally reserved for the temple could be temporarily performed. This, like the portable tabernacle carried by the ancient Israelites (Ex. 25–31), was authorized until the temple could be completed. Because of persistent rumors that unauthorized marriages were being performed in the Endowment House, President Woodruff had the building torn down in the spring of 1899.

See also: Temple

Ends of the Earth

The Lord's voice will be heard "unto the ends of the earth" (D&C 1:11), and "the day cometh when the thunders shall utter their voices from the ends of the earth" (D&C 43:21). In other words, God's words shall go forth to the furthermost regions of the earth and will reach any who may have been driven to such places (D&C 109:67).

See also: Four Corners of the Earth; Voice of . . .

Endure to the End

"And, if you keep my commandments and *endure to the end* you shall have *eternal life,*" declared the Lord (D&C 14:7; italics added). The admonition to "endure to the end" is found frequently in holy writ (D&C 10:69; 18:22; 53:7; Matt. 10:22; 24:13; Mark 13:13; 1 Ne. 13:37; 2 Ne. 31:16, 20). Mormon's admonition was that we submit to baptism, partake of the sacrament, "do all things in worthiness . . . , and endure to the end" (Morm. 9:29).

To *endure* is to persist patiently, for partial performance is insufficient. In this encyclopedic reference, biographical sketches of men placed in high positions — witnesses to the Book of Mormon and Apostles of the Lord — illustrate the importance of this principle. To rest on past performance is to fail to meet the measure of celestial criteria. To "endure to the end" is to steadfastly traverse the strait and narrow path and obtain the fruit of the tree of life, even eternal life, which Nephi equated with enduring to the end (1 Ne. 8; 2 Ne. 33:4).

See also: Adversity; Continueth in God; Stand Fast; Valiant in the Testimony of Jesus

Enjoined

To be enjoined (D&C 123:6) is to have received an authoritative order or urgent admonition to take a specified course of action.

Enlarged

The word *enlarged* can have reference to expanding territory or influence, such as enlarging the borders of Zion and her stakes (D&C 82:14; 107:74), or it may have reference to expanding one's spiritual understanding, such as when one's soul is enlarged (D&C 121:42; Alma 32:28). Those who do not take a partner in the new and everlasting covenant of eternal marriage, and thereafter live faithfully to their vows, "cannot be enlarged," which simply means their eternal dominions will be restricted and they will have no family increase (D&C 132:17).

Enoch

The name of Enoch is recorded under several different circumstances in the Doctrine and Covenants, such as "book of Enoch" (D&C 107:57), "church of Enoch" (D&C 76:67), "order of Enoch" (D&C 76:57), and "Zion of Enoch" (D&C 38:4).

Enoch was twenty-five years old when "ordained under the hand of Adam," and sixty-five years of age when Adam "blessed him." "And he saw the Lord, and he walked with him, and was before his face continually; and he walked with God three hundred and sixty-five years, making him four hundred and thirty years old when he was translated." (D&C 107:48–49; Moses 7:68–69; 8:1.)

The Prophet Joseph explained the special mission of Enoch and the doctrine of translation as follows: "Now this Enoch God reserved unto Himself, that he should not die at that time, and appointed unto him a ministry unto terrestrial bodies, of whom there has been but little revealed. He is reserved also unto the presidency of a dispensation. . . . He is a ministering angel, to minister to those who shall be heirs of salvation, and appeared unto Jude as Abel did unto Paul; therefore Jude spoke of him (14, 15 verses). . . .

"Many have supposed that the doctrine of translation was a doctrine whereby men were taken immediately into the presence of God, and into an eternal fullness, but this is a mistaken idea. Their place of habitation is that of the terrestrial order, and a place prepared for such characters He held in reserve to be *ministering angels unto many planets*, and who as yet have not entered into so great a fullness as those who are resurrected from the dead." (TPJS, 170; italics added.)

Enoch and his people were separated from the earth because "the world in general would not obey the commands of God" and it was incompatible for those who were living a higher order to remain among those of a lower order (TPJS, 251; D&C 45:11–12). In the words of President Joseph Fielding Smith, they "were as pilgrims and strangers on the earth . . . due to the fact that they were living the celestial law in a telestial world" (CHMR 1:195). Thus, they were received up into the "bosom" of God; "and from thence went forth the saying, Zion is fled" (Moses 7:69).

This holy city will be brought once again to the earth, prior to the Second Coming (WTP, 309–10). In the meantime, according to President John Taylor, they could be performing missions to "various planets" created by the Savior (GK, 103). This is consistent with Joseph Smith's statement regarding their ministry to "many planets." Franklin D. Richards, who served as an

Apostle from 1849 to 1899, said he believed the three Nephite disciples who were translated (see 3 Ne. 28) were taken "into the heavens and endowed . . . with the power of translation, probably in one of Enoch's temples" (JD 25:236–37).

See also: Day of Righteousness; Enoch and His Brethren; Order of Enoch; Translated; Walked with God

Enoch (Joseph Smith)

In the early days of the Church the Lord occasionally used code names when revealing his will to specified individuals (HC 1:255). One of the names given to Joseph Smith was that of "Enoch," by which both the Prophet and his city of Saints—Nauvoo—were addressed (D&C 78:1, 4, 9; pre-1981 edition). It seems appropriate that the name of Enoch—one who was known for his great faith and valor—should be applied to Joseph Smith, who also exemplified these same virtues. In current editions of the Doctrine and Covenants, Joseph Smith's real name appears rather than the code name Enoch.

See also: Smith, Joseph, Jr.

Enoch and His Brethren

The citation to "Enoch and his brethren" being removed from the earth (D&C 45:11–12)

refers to those ancient inhabitants of the city of Zion. They became so righteous and unified that they were removed from this earth as translated beings (Moses 7:18–21, 68–69).

See also: Enoch

Enos

In a revelation on priesthood, it is mentioned that Adam bestowed the priesthood on his grandson, Enos, when the latter was 134 years of age (D&C 107:44). Enos was the son of Seth, born in the 105th year of his father's life (Gen. 5:6; Moses 6:13). He was taught "in the ways of God" and "prophesied also." He was one of the great high priests who was called by Adam into the valley of Adam-ondi-Ahman, three years prior to the death of the patriarch of our race. He is mentioned as an ancestor in the lineage of Mary's husband, Joseph (Luke 3:38). In his 90th year, Enos begat Cainan, after whom he named "a land of promise" (Gen. 5:9; Moses 6:17). Enos lived a total of 905 years and had "many sons and daughters" (Gen. 5:10–11; Moses 6:18).

Ensample

The word *ensample* appears eight times in the Doctrine and Covenants (68:2, 3; 72:23, 26; 78:13; 88:136; 98:38; 119:7). According to Webster, an "ensample" is "an example; a pattern or model for imitation or warning." The Church is a model for the world, and those who represent it must exemplify its principles. Thus, both people and programs become ensamples to the world.

Ensign

According to Webster's *Unabridged Dictionary*, an "ensign," as used anciently by Isaiah (Isa. 5:26), had reference to "a battle cry; a watchword; or, a signal." Its present meaning denotes a banner, flag, or standard. The "ensign" the Lord has raised to the world is Zion, or his Church (D&C 45:9; CR, Apr. 1961, p. 119). The "battle cry" is to "repent and be baptized, in the name of Jesus Christ" (D&C 18:41); to "stand . . . in holy places, and be not moved until the day of the Lord comes" (D&C 87:8).

See also: Church of Jesus Christ of Latter-day Saints, The; Standard for My People

Ensign of Peace

The proclamation that the "ensign of peace," or the "standard of peace," should be lifted up "unto the ends of the earth," is the injunction to take the gospel, the true message of peace, unto all nations (D&C 98:34; 105:39; Mark 16:15–16). "In the full

sense, only those who believe and spread the fulness of the gospel are peacemakers," observed Elder Bruce R. McConkie (DNTC 1:216).

The gospel, as taught by The Church of Jesus Christ of Latter-day Saints, is the "ensign of peace" which the Prince of Peace (Isa. 9:6) lifts up to the world. "The living of one protective principle of the gospel is better than a thousand compensatory governmental programs," observed Elder Neal A. Maxwell (CR, Oct. 1974, p. 15). The Nephite prophet Alma noted that "the preaching of the word [has a] more powerful effect upon the minds of the people than the sword, or anything else" (Alma 31:5). It is only within the framework of the gospel that ultimate peace will be found.

See also: Peaceable Things of the Kingdom

Ephraim

Ephraim was the second son born to Joseph, one of the twelve sons of Jacob, before the great famine in Egypt (Gen. 41:50–52). His mother was Asenath, daughter of the high priest of the state religion and descendant of Abraham (AGQ 1:170–71). Ephraim was given the birthright blessing by his grandfather Jacob in preference to his elder brother, Manasseh (Gen. 48; Jer. 31:9). Both brothers received a full portion of inheritance among the sons of Jacob and became the tribes of Ephraim and Manasseh (JST, Gen. 48:5–6).

When the united kingdom of Israel separated into two groups, Jeroboam, an Ephraimite, became king of the northern kingdom, which became known as the kingdom of Israel (1 Kgs. 11). The northern kingdom consisted of all but the tribes of Judah and Benjamin, who became the southern kingdom, known as the kingdom of Judah. Ephraim was one of those tribes led away into captivity, thus becoming a "lost tribe" (WTP, 130).

However, "Ephraim, he hath mixed himself among the people," declared the prophet Hosea (Hos. 7:8). Ephraim "was scattered more than any other among the people of other nations," and though he exists as a distinct tribe among the others of the ten lost tribes, yet he has posterity among the known nations of the earth today (DS 3:250–54). "At this present time," declared President Joseph Fielding Smith, "most of those who are receiving the gospel are of the tribe of Ephraim" (AGQ 5:70).

It is Ephraim's responsibility to preach the gospel to the inhabitants of the earth today, and when the lost tribes come back, "they will have to receive the crowning blessings from their brother Ephraim, the 'firstborn' in Israel" (DS 3:252–53). The Lord has said of this tribe that "the rebellious are not of the blood of Ephraim" (D&C 64:36). Those of this tribe might be said to have the "believing blood."

See also: Blood of Ephraim; Children of Ephraim; Stick of Ephraim; They Who Are in the North Countries

Epistle

The word *epistle* appears twice in the Doctrine and Covenants, once in connection with the writings of Peter (D&C 138:6) and once in relation to a letter to be written by Sidney Rigdon. An epistle is a formal or official letter, generally bearing some special message. A number of the books of the New Testament are epistles written by the early Apostles.

Equal

The word *equal*, as used in the scriptures, is often misunderstood. The "one-for-you and one-for-me" approach is not what the Lord had in mind when he commanded the Saints to be "equal . . . in earthly things" (D&C 70:14; 78:5–7). President Joseph Fielding Smith said, "To be equal did not mean that all should have the same amount of food, but each should have according to his needs. For instance, a man would receive in proportion to the number in the family, not according to the nature of his work." (CHMR 1:268– 69; see also D&C 51:3; 82:17.)

"Where there is no selfishness in the hearts of the people this desirable end can be accomplished, but it is bound to fail where jealousy and selfishness are not eliminated from the soul. *It is essential that we be able to keep the celestial law of equality."* (CHMR 1:307; italics added.) "Equality," according to President George Q. Cannon, "means to have an equal claim on the blessings of our Heavenly Father—on the properties of the Lord's treasury, and the influences and gifts of His Holy Spirit" (JD 13:99).

See also: Equal in Authority

Equal in Authority

The three major governing bodies of the Church—First Presidency, Quorum of the Twelve, and First Quorum of the Seventy—are described as quorums that are "equal in authority" (D&C 107:22–26). This *equality* is defined by Smith and Sjodahl: "There can never be two or three quorums of equal authority at the same time; therefore in the revelation where it reads that the Twelve Apostles form a quorum equal in authority with the First Presidency, and that the Seventies form a quorum equal in authority with the Twelve, it should be understood that this condition of equality could prevail only when the ranking quorum is no longer in existence, through death or otherwise. When the First Presidency becomes disorganized on the death of the President, then the Apostles become the presiding quorum, or council, of the Church with all the power to organize again the First Presidency, when they fall back again as the second ranking quorum of

the Church. So with the Seventies, they would become equal only on the condition that the first two quorums ceased to exist." (SS, 700.) It is in this same sense that counselors in a presidency are "equal," for they must uphold the right for the president to make the final decision (D&C 90:6).

Equal in Power (with Him)

See: Fulness of the Glory of the Father

Esaias

The name Esaias is the Greek form of Isaiah (LDSBD, 667). However, as used in the Doctrine and Covenants, it refers to a prophet who lived in the days of Abraham and who held the Melchizedek Priesthood (D&C 76:100 [note the cross-reference in the 1981 edition]; 84:111–13). The history of this prophet is yet to be revealed.

Escutcheon

Writing of the martyrdoms of Joseph and Hyrum Smith, John Taylor indicated that the stain of "their innocent blood" on the "escutcheon" of the state in which they were martyred would stand as "a witness to the truth of the everlasting gospel that all the world cannot impeach" (D&C 135:7). Webster defines an escutcheon as "a shield on which armorial bearings are depicted and displayed.'' The ''escutcheon'' of which John Taylor wrote was the shield of the state of Illinois, which displayed symbols depicting the things for which that state stood.

See also: Illinois

Especial Witnesses

In a revelation given in August 1830, Joseph Smith and Oliver Cowdery were designated ''apostles, and especial witnesses'' of the name of Christ (D&C 27:12). The Lord also called the ''Seventy,'' or those who are sustained as General Authorities in that particular calling, ''to preach the gospel, and to be especial witnesses unto the Gentiles and in all the world'' (D&C 107:25).

According to Webster, the term *especial* means ''not general, extraordinary or special.'' A distinguishable aspect is required to make one unique. In this sense, the Seventy join the Twelve Apostles in their unique calling as ''special witnesses,'' for the mission of both is to declare the divinity of Jesus Christ to the world.

Speaking of all members of the First Presidency, Quorum of the Twelve, First Quorum of the Seventy, and the Patriarch, President Spencer W. Kimball declared them all to be ''special witnesses'' (CR, Apr. 1976, p. 161). Elder Marion D. Hanks, in like fashion, spoke of the Seventy as ''special'' rather than ''especial'' witnesses when quoting from section 107 (CR, Oct. 1976, p. 40). The Seventy, the ''especial'' witnesses, are to act under the direction of the ''special'' witnesses, the Twelve, as decreed by the Lord (D&C 107:34).

See also: Special Witnesses; Seventy

Espouse

When a man desires to espouse a woman (D&C 132:61), he is desirous of taking her as a spouse—he wants to marry her. In current usage this is somewhat different from the ''espoused'' condition of Mary to Joseph, prior to their consummating their marriage (Matt. 1:18). Their espousal was merely the first of two stages in an official Hebrew marriage. It was a legally recognized, binding contract between the two that publicly declared their intentions to establish a family. In a legal sense, the two were considered as husband and wife, but they were not yet living together. This latter step occurred in a separate ceremony sometime later, usually a year if the bride was a virgin and one month if she was a widow. (Riciotti, 226; Cruden, 186.)

Another use of the word is found in an 1832 revelation in which the Lord speaks of ''the cause, which ye have espoused'' (D&C 78:4). In this instance the word refers to the cause which one has undertaken or for which one has been striving.

Essaying

Several revelations use the word *essaying* (e.g., D&C 124:84; 125:2). To essay is to try or to attempt to do something.

Eternal Damnation

The divine decree that disobedience and unrighteousness shall stop one's progress is known as "eternal damnation" (D&C 19:7; 29:44). Eternal means proceeding forth from God, for he is Eternal (D&C 19:10–12). And to be damned, said President Spencer W. Kimball, is to be "stopped in progress" (DSY 1976, 154).

See also: Damned; Damnation of Hell

Eternal King

The title "Eternal King" is applied to the Savior in section 128, verse 23. He is the King to whom we will give our allegiance eternally, he will reign with regal righteousness forever.

See also: Jesus Christ

Eternal Life

The greatest gift which God can bestow upon man is that of "eternal life" (D&C 14:7). Anciently, the Lord said to Moses: "This is my work and my glory —to bring to pass the immortality and eternal life of man" (Moses 1:39). Frederick G. Williams, a counselor to Joseph Smith, was promised "a crown of immortality, and eternal life" if he remained faithful (D&C 81:6).

Eternal life is synonymous with exaltation. Elder Bruce R. McConkie stated: "Eternal life is the name of the kind of life God lives. It consists, first, of the continuation of the family unit in eternity, and second, of an inheritance of the fulness of the glory of the Father." (En., Nov. 1977, p. 34.) Eternal life, by definition, can only be found in the highest heaven, or degree, of the celestial kingdom (D&C 131:1–4). On the other hand, "immortality," or life forever, is a gift that all who have tabernacled in the flesh shall receive, regardless of their kingdoms of inheritance (D&C 29:24–25; Alma 11:45; 1 Cor. 15:22; DS 2:4–10).

The Prophet Joseph Smith said that eternal life is "to know the only wise and true God; and you have got to learn how to be Gods yourselves, and to be kings and priests to God, the same as all Gods have done before you" (TPJS, 346; John 17:3; D&C 132:24). He further declared, "If you wish to go where God is, you must be like God, or possess the principles which God possesses" (HC 4:588).

See also: Eternal lives; Exaltation; Fulness of the Glory of the Father; Immortality

Eternal Lives

"Eternal lives," according to President Charles W. Penrose, "means more than life, more than mere existence, it means perpetual increase of posterity, worlds without end, and these blessings shall be ours if we will prove faithful to that which we have received of the Lord, and this is what we are for in the Church" (CR, Oct. 1921, p. 22). This term is synonymous with "continuation of the seeds" (D&C 132:19), "continuation of the lives" (D&C 132:22) and "increase" (D&C 131:4). It is bestowed on those who receive "eternal life" (D&C 14:7), "exaltation" (D&C 132:17), and the "fulness of the glory of the Father" (D&C 93:16), all of which mean joint heirship with the Father and Son in the highest heaven of the hereafter.

As the Lord decreed, "eternal lives" become available only to those who truly "know" God and Christ (D&C 132:24; John 17:3; see also JST, Matt. 7:23). To "know" the Father and Son is to become like them (TPJS, 346; HC 4:588).

See also: Continuation of the Lives; Continuation of the Seeds; Eternal Life; Fulness of the Glory of the Father; Gods; Increase

Eternal Punishment

See: Everlasting Punishment

Eternity

A favorite phrase among Mormons is *for time and for all eternity* (D&C 132:7). This is the framework within which temple mar-

riages are performed, meaning that they are valid both in this world and in the life hereafter. Eternity is a concept which does not reckon with parameters of time; it is forever.

Eternity has always been and will always be; but, for reference purposes, one may refer to various phases of existence in eternity. The first such phase was when we existed as intelligences, without spirit bodies. Next came spiritual creation within the heavenly mansions of God, to be followed by the physical creation here on this earth. Ultimately, we will reach the last, but everlasting, phase of eternity, wherein our resurrected bodies will either dwell eternally within kingdoms of glory or be consigned to everlasting darkness (DS 1:12).

Another use of *eternity* is found in the statement that "all eternity is pained" (D&C 38:12). This has reference to the totality of the creations in God's universe. (See also Moses 7:41.)

Eternity to Eternity

The phrase *from all eternity to all eternity* appears twice in the Doctrine and Covenants, although the second time it is slightly modified (D&C 39:1; 76:4). It is used in connection with the Savior, who, as a God, is "the same today as yesterday, and forever" (D&C 35:1). *"From eternity to eternity means from the spirit existence through the probation which we are in, and then back again to the eternal existence which will follow. . . . We are from eternity; and we will be to eternity everlasting, if we receive the exaltation. . . . Those who become like God will also be from eternity to eternity." (DS 1:12.)*

See also: Everlasting to Everlasting

Ether

Short hours before his name became eternally emblazoned among the martyrs of Christianity, Hyrum Smith quoted from the Book of Mormon. The particular verses he quoted were Ether 12:36–38. These verses were penned by Moroni, who was responsible for abridging the record known as the book of Ether, the fourteenth of the fifteen books within the Book of Mormon. It was named after the last prophet of the Jaredite people, whose history commenced at the time of the Tower of Babel and ended in America about thirty generations later (Ether 1:6–33).

Evangelical Ministers

The Prophet Joseph Smith declared that "an Evangelist is a Patriarch, even the oldest man of the blood of Joseph or of the seed of Abraham. Wherever the Church of Christ is established in the earth, there should be a Patriarch for the benefit of the posterity of the Saints, as it was with Jacob in giving his patriarchal blessing unto his sons, etc." (HC 3:381.) He holds the office of a high priest, which is an office within the Melchizedek Priesthood (DS 3:104–5). Upon the recommendation of a stake president, and with the approval of the First Presidency and Quorum of the Twelve Apostles, worthy men are ordained to serve in the office of patriarch in the stakes of Zion, which office "is one of blessing, not one of administration" (D&C 107:39).

There are three types of patriarchs: (1) the Patriarch to the Church, or he who receives his office by right of lineage as well as worthiness (D&C 107:40–52; 124:91–92; DS 3:160–69), who holds the "keys of this ministry and priesthood," and serves as a General Authority of the Church under the direction of the First Presidency; (2) those men called and ordained to serve in the stakes of the Church under the direction of the stake presidency; and (3) fathers, whose stewardship is restricted to their own families. The latter group do not receive their calling by *ordination*, but by marriage and fatherhood.

See also: Ministers; Order of This Priesthood; Patriarch; Patriarchal Blessing; Smith, Hyrum

Eve

She to whom we pay our respects as the mother of the human race is "our glorious Mother Eve" (Gen. 2:3; Moses 4:5; D&C 138:39). Her name means "the mother of all living" (Moses

4:26). "Without question she was like unto her mighty husband, Adam, in intelligence and in devotion to righteousness, during both her first and second estates of existence" (MD, 242). Elder Bruce R. McConkie suggests that Eve stood by her husband's side "before the foundations of the earth," and will continue to stand by his side through all eternity. "As Adam became the pattern for all his sons, so did Eve for all her daughters." (WOM, 67–68.) Words from a hymn give some indication of the praise she shall receive from her posterity: "Mother of our generations, Glorious by great Michael's side, Take thy children's adoration; Endless with thy seed abide" ("Sons of Michael, He Approaches," *Hymns*, no. 51).

Everlasting Covenant

On several occasions in the Doctrine and Covenants, the Lord speaks of his "everlasting covenant" (D&C 1:15; 45:9; 49:9; 66:2; 76:101). "The gospel is the everlasting covenant because it is ordained by Him who is Everlasting and also because it is everlastingly the same. In all past ages salvation was gained by adherence to its terms and conditions, and that same compliance will bring the same reward in all future ages. Each time this everlasting covenant is revealed it is *new* to those of that dispensation. Hence the gospel is the *new and everlasting covenant.*" (MD, 529–30.)

See also: New and Everlasting Covenant

Everlasting Fire

See: Lake of Fire and Brimstone

Everlasting Hills

The single reference in the Doctrine and Covenants to the "everlasting hills is in connection with the return of the Ten Lost Tribes (133:26–33). We are informed that the boundaries of these hills will tremble on this momentous occasion. This may be symbolic of the general physical manifestations that will occur throughout the earth; on the other hand, "everlasting hills" might have specific reference to that unbroken chain of mountains extending from the northern tip of North America to the southern point of South America. These "everlasting hills," the heritage of Joseph, are the Rocky Mountains (Gen. 49:22–26; MWW, 435).

Elder Richard L. Evans described the significance of these everlasting hills which have housed the headquarters of the Lord's church: "Those hills at the 'Crossroads of the West'—with their sure footings and their refusal to be moved by winds of strange doctrine—hills with their strength, their peace, and their quiet assurance—hills that do not run to and fro, chasing false utopias, following after blind leaders —hills that turn neither to the right hand nor to the left, but stand with calm majesty on rock foundations, no matter what storms may be raging around them'' (UTH, ii).

See also: They Who Are in the North Countries

Everlasting Order

According to Smith and Sjodahl, the ''everlasting order'' to which the Lord referred in Doctrine and Covenants 82:20 was the Order of Enoch, which was set up among nine early Church leaders. It was a ''united order.'' Orson Pratt said that this was ''a law inferior to the celestial law, because the celestial law required the consecration of all that a man had. The law of Enoch only required a part.'' (JD 16:156.) Elder Pratt emphasized that this ''order'' had reference to the days of Joseph Smith (who was called ''Enoch'' in the original wording of the revelation), and not the ancient ''Order of Enoch.''

See also: Enoch

Everlasting Punishment

The terms *eternal punishment, everlasting punishment,* and *endless punishment* are used interchangeably to express the nature of God's punishment (D&C 19:10–12; 76:44). The nature of this punishment is described by President George Q. Cannon: ''Because God's punishment is eternal punishment, it does not necessarily follow that the being who receives it is consigned to it eternally. For instance, a prison might stand for a hundred years. It might be a place of punishment. A person consigned to that prison might go in there and expiate his crime in the prison by suffering a certain punishment, and after the time pronounced as the punishment had expired he could emerge therefrom. Still the prison exists.

''So it is with God's punishment. His punishment is eternal punishment, because He is eternal; but it does not follow, as the Lord has said with great plainness, that a person who is consigned thereto will endure it eternally. The Lord Jesus Christ has died for all men, and He will draw all men unto Him. But there are degrees of punishment affixed to sin; and in proportion to men's crimes they will be punished. But they will not be consigned to endless punishment—that is, to suffer it eternally.'' (GT 1:144.)

Everlasting to Everlasting

The Lord is spoken of as being ''from everlasting to everlasting'' (D&C 20:17; 61:1; 109:77; Moro. 7:22). According to President Joseph Fielding Smith, '' 'Everlasting to everlasting' means from the eternity past to the eternity future as far as man's understanding is concerned, from the pre-existence through the temporal (mortal) life unto the eternity following the resurrection'' (AGQ 2:127).

See also: Eternity to Eternity

Evil Day

The Lord admonishes the Saints to put on the whole armor of God in order that they may be prepared "to withstand the evil day, having done all, that ye may be able to stand" (D&C 27:15; Eph. 6:13). "The evil day" is no particularly designated day but rather any day on which one might have a confrontation with the evil one and his hosts of hell. Thus, the phrase might be interpolated to read, be prepared "to withstand the evil *one*," regardless of the day.

Evil One, That

"Satan is the *Evil One*, a name-title signifying that he is the embodiment of all evil and all wickedness, that he is in opposition to all righteousness, and that he is the *father of lies* and the author of evil. (2 Ne. 4:27; 9:28; Alma 46:8; Hela. 12:4; Ether 8:25.)" (MD, 246.) Because the devil's domain is full of darkness (Rev. 16:10), "light and truth forsake that evil one" (D&C 93:37).

See also: Devil

Evil Speaking

One of the responsibilities of the priesthood is to see that there is no "evil speaking" in the Church (D&C 20:54). In the section the Prophet designated as the "law of the Church," the Lord commands all members to "not speak evil of thy neighbor, nor do him any harm" (D&C 42:27). Smith and Sjodahl state that "neither . . . backbiting, evil speaking, nor bearing false witness, [shall] be tolerated by the Lord. . . . It may be necessary when on the witness stand, or before an ecclesiastical court, to testify of one's sins, but to do so promiscuously is a sin. Even when called upon to testify, the testimony should be given in the spirit of brotherly kindness, not in the spirit of vindictiveness." (SS, 226.)

Evil Spirits

See: False Spirits; Hosts of Hell; Third Part of the Hosts of Heaven

Exaltation

The term *exaltation* is found throughout section 132, in which the Lord promises this gift to those who righteously qualify. It is reserved for those faithful followers of the Father and Son who do *all* that is required for such an inheritance (D&C 81:6; 88:22; 130:20–21). Exaltation is the gift of eternal life or life in the presence of the Father—forever—to receive a "fulness of His glory" (DS 2:24). The dictionary uses the following expressions to illustrate the word *exalt*: "to raise up, especially in rank, power, or dignity; to glorify; to elate the mind or spirit." Truly, one who receives exaltation inherits a celestial crown in the presence of Deity—receives rank, power, dignity, glory, and elation of mind and spirit.

See also: Fulness of the Glory of the Father; Eternal Life; Eternal Lives

Excommunicate

Although it is a frequently used term in religious circles, the only appearance of the word *excommunicate* in all of scripture is found in Doctrine and Covenants 134:10. To be excommunicated is to be overcome by the world and to be officially separated or cut off from the society of the Saints, to lose full fellowship in the household of God, to once again become a stranger and a foreigner to the faith (see Eph. 2:19–22). One who is excommunicated from The Church of Jesus Christ of Latter-day Saints loses all previously bestowed blessings and ordinances, which become as if they had never been bestowed. He may not perform priesthood ordinances, partake of the sacrament, pay tithing, or speak or pray in Church meetings.

Excommunication can come in two ways: (1) as an official act of the Church here upon the earth; or (2) as the result of a divine decree from Deity. Those who successfully hide their sins from priesthood leadership in mortality will prolong their spiritual suffering and will ultimately face God himself. He declared: "But the hypocrites shall be de-

tected and shall be cut off, *either in life or in death*, even as I will; and wo unto them who are cut off from my church, for the same are overcome of the world" (D&C 50:8; italics added).

Fortunately for all of us the principle of repentance offers a way back to God's presence and, for the excommunicant, to full fellowship in the Lord's church. Once the price has been paid, blessings can be restored, forgiveness can be found, and the Lord remembers the former sin no more (see Isa. 1:18; D&C 58:42–43).

Exigency

In a declaration of belief the Doctrine and Covenants states that "all men are justified in defending themselves . . . in times of exigency, where immediate appeal cannot be made to the laws" (D&C 134:11). Times of exigency are times of emergency, requiring immediate action.

Exterminating Order

See: Boggs, Lilburn W.; Missouri

Eye Single to the Glory of God

There are six instances in the Doctrine and Covenants when the Lord admonishes the Saints to keep their "eye single to the glory of God" (4:5; 27:2; 55:1; 59:1; 82:19; 88:67). The concept of keeping one's "eye single" is mentioned in the masterful sermons given by the Savior on both hemispheres: "If . . . thine eye be single," he admonished, "thy whole body shall be full of light" (Matt. 6:21–24; Luke 11:34–36; 3 Ne. 13:19–24). One's spiritual lenses can be darkened and split by sin. Eyes that are "single to the glory of God . . . are undimmed by sin and are focused solely on righteousness" (DNTC 1:240).

See also: Singleness of Heart

Eyes of . . . Understandings

As a result of fervent prayer, "the eyes of . . . understandings" (D&C 76:19) were opened in behalf of Joseph Smith and Sidney Rigdon, and the marvelous vision recorded in what is now section 76 was revealed. The "eyes of understanding" are one's spiritual eyes, which are activated when one is "quickened by the Spirit of God" (D&C 67:10–12). To have one's eyes so opened is to remove the "scales of darkness" from one's eyes (2 Ne. 30:6) and to be brought to "behold the marvelous light of God" (Alma 26:3). It is to have the "power of the Spirit" rest so mightily upon one's eyes that the unseen world of spiritual matters becomes visible (D&C 76:11–12). Such was the experience of the brother of Jared, whose virtue and faith allowed his "eyes of understanding" to penetrate the veil (Ether 3).

See also: See My Face

Ezekiel

The promised destruction of "the great and abominable church" as "spoken by the mouth of Ezekiel the prophet" is referred to in an 1830 revelation. Sperry suggests that while we may not know the exact words to which Doctrine and Covenants 29:21 refers, "the general effect could be as shown in Ezekiel 38:14–23" (DCC, 136). The reference in the Doctrine and Covenants to "devouring fire" is similar to Ezekiel's reference to "an overflowing rain, and great hailstones, fire, and brimstone." Ezekiel prophesied during a twenty-two year period from 592 B.C. to 570 B.C. and was one of the captives carried away by Nebuchadnezzar into Babylon (BD, 55). His book of prophetic writings covers forty-eight chapters and provides great insight into latter-day happenings.

Welker wrote the following biographical sketch: "Ezekiel was bold, and at times even severe. He was relentless in his fight against sin. . . . He was zealous for righteousness and moved by convictions too firm to be shaken. He was a man of keen vision, dramatic and intensely spiritual." (SVOT, 279.) Ezekiel was among "the great and mighty ones" whom President Joseph F. Smith saw assembled in the spirit world in his vision of the redemption of the dead (D&C 138:38, 43).

See also: Stick of Ephraim

Ezra

A revelation received November 27, 1832, reminded those who have "apostatized" or "been cut off from the church" that they "shall not find an inheritance among the saints of the Most High." It further mentioned that their lot shall be as that described in the Old Testment book of Ezra. (D&C 85:11–12; Ezra 2:61–62.) The fate of those ancients who were found unfaithful was to be unable to find their names on God's "register," to be "polluted" and "put from the priesthood." In other words, they would not find entrance into God's presence, for unhallowed and unworthy beings cannot abide such a glory (1 Ne. 10:21).

Ezra was a famous priest and scribe who authored the Old Testament book bearing his name, which covered the time period of about 536 B.C. to 457 B.C.. Along with Nehemiah, he made "the book of the Law" available to everyone instead of restricting its reading to the priests. This was a major departure in Jewish religious life and was hailed as "a new dispensation." (BD, 55–56.)

F

Faint

On several occasions the Lord has counseled his Saints to "pray always that ye may not faint" (D&C 75:11; 88:126; 101:81; 2 Ne. 32:9; Luke 18:1). This is essentially counsel to not be weary in praying but to importune God fervently and consistently (see Alma 34:17–27). Those who pray without fainting do not lose hope or weaken in their desire to communicate with Deity.

A common use of the word *faint* in its sense of becoming exhausted because of fatigue and even losing consciousness is found in the Word of Wisdom: the obedient are promised they shall "walk and not faint" (D&C 89:20).

The counsel to "let not your hearts faint" is an admonition to not lose courage or become timid or cowardly in one's course or conviction (D&C 103:19; 124:75; 2 Ne. 17:4; Deut. 20:2; Isa. 7:4).

Fair as the Moon/Sun

See: Army with Banners

Faith

President Ezra Taft Benson noted: "Faith is the foundation upon which a godlike character is built. It is a prerequisite for all other virtues." (En., Nov. 1986, p. 45.) "Every doctrine of the Church, every sermon that has been preached . . . has to do with faith in God and repentance from sin," said Elder Rulon S. Wells (CR, Oct. 1933, p. 48). Indeed, we proclaim in our fourth article of faith that the first principle of the gospel is "faith in the Lord Jesus Christ."

The basic principle of faith permeates every page of prophecy and revelation in the Doctrine and Covenants, as well as every other book of holy writ. Parents are specifically charged with the responsibility of teaching their children to *understand* the doctrine of "faith in Christ the Son of the living God" (D&C 68:25). "Faith," declared the Prophet Joseph, "comes by hearing the word of God, through the testimony of the servants of God; that testimony is always attended by the Spirit of prophecy and revelation" (HC 3:379).

Elder James E. Talmage provided the following explanation of faith: "The predominating sense in which the term *faith* is used throughout the scriptures is that of *full confidence and trust in the being, purpose, and words of God.* Such trust, if implicit, will remove all doubt concerning things accomplished or promised of God, even though such things be not apparent to or explicable by the ordinary senses of mortality; hence arises the definition of faith given by Paul: 'Now faith is the substance [i.e., confidence or assurance] of things hoped for, the evidence [i.e., the demonstration or proof] of things not seen.' " (AF, 96; italics added; see Heb. 11:1.)

"Faith is not a substitute for truth," said President Hugh B. Brown, "but a pathway to truth" (CR, Oct. 1969, p. 107).

"The terms *faith* and *belief* are sometimes regarded as synonyms; nevertheless each of them has a specific meaning in our language. . . . *Belief*, in one of its accepted senses, may consist in a merely *intellectual assent*, while *faith implies such confidence and conviction as will impel to action.* . . . Belief is in a sense passive, an agreement of acceptance only; faith is active and positive, embracing such reliance and confidence as will lead to works. Faith in Christ comprises belief in Him, combined with trust in Him. One cannot have faith without belief; yet he may believe and still lack faith. *Faith is vivified, vitalized, living belief.*" (AF, 96–97; italics added.)

In reminding Latter-day Saints of their obligation to declare the divine message of the gospel, President Ezra Taft Benson stated: "Our main task is to declare the gospel and do it effectively. We are not obligated to answer every objection. Every man eventually is backed up to the wall of faith, and there he must make his stand." (CR, Apr. 1975, p. 95.)

"Faith," said Elder Howard W. Hunter, "is the element that builds the bridge in the absence of concrete evidence" (CR, Apr. 1975, p. 57; see also Heb. 11:1; Alma 32:21).

Faithfulness upon His Loins

All who assemble upon the "land of Zion" should "take righteousness in [their] hands and *faithfulness upon [their] loins*" (D&C 63:36–37; italics added). Smith and Sjodahl offer the following explanation of this phrase: "The Israelites, when fleeing from Egypt, ate the paschal lamb, their loins girdled and their staffs in hand. (Ex. 12:11.) The Saints in their exodus, should also be prepared, but righteousness must be their 'staff,' and faithfulness their 'girdle.' No one should go to Zion unless so equipped." (SS, 381.)

Although this has specific application to those who are ultimately to inherit the land of Missouri—the site designated as the land of Zion (D&C 57:1–3)—the principle applies to all lands upon which the Saints of Zion dwell.

Fall, The

Upon placing our first parents, Adam and Eve, in the Garden of Eden, the Lord issued several directives. Among these were two that stood in apparent opposition to each other: (1) "Be fruitful, and multiply, and replenish the earth" (Gen. 1:28), and (2) don't partake of the "tree of the knowledge of good and evil" (Gen. 2:17).

At the time of their placement in the garden, Adam and Eve were in an *immortal state*; that is, they were not subject to death. Their bodies were "quickened by the spirit," for blood—the life-giving substance of mortal man —was not yet flowing in their veins (MOD, 362–64). Their Edenic status included the following conditions: (1) they were not subject to death (2 Ne. 2:22; Moses 3:15–17); (2) they enjoyed the presence of God (Gen. 3; Moses 4); (3) they had no posterity (2 Ne. 2:23); and (4) they had no knowledge of good and evil (Moses 5:11).

Because "he knew not the mind of God" and "sought to destroy the world," Satan beguiled mother Eve, who in turn enticed Adam (Moses 4:6–12). They partook of the "forbidden fruit," introducing mortality into their bodies and becoming separated from God's presence, thus becoming subject to both temporal and spiritual death (Alma 42:7). That this *transgression* was a necessary part of the eternal plan of progression is evidenced in several scriptural statements: "And now, behold, if Adam had not transgressed . . . all things which were created must have remained in the same state in which they were after they were created. . . . And they would have had no children . . . , having no joy . . . , doing no good. . . . Adam fell that men might be; and men are, that they might have joy." (2 Ne. 2:22–25.)

Both Adam and Eve rejoiced in the decision they had made, for, said Eve: "Were it not for our transgression we never should have had seed, and never should have known good and evil, and the joy of our redemption, and the eternal life which God giveth unto all the obedient" (Moses 5:11).

Though we may not fully understand all facets of the Fall, it should be kept in mind that "all things have been done in the wisdom of him who knoweth all things" (2 Ne. 2:24; DS 1:109–11). President Joseph Fielding Smith reminds us that "in no other commandment the Lord ever gave to man, did he say: ' . . . *nevertheless, thou mayest choose for thyself.* '" Thus, he refers to the violation of the commandment as a "transgression" rather than a "sin." (DS 1:114–15; see also D&C 29:40–41.) In like fashion, Elder Marion G. Romney said: "I do not look upon Adam's action as sin. I think it was a deliberate act of free agency." (LTG, 251.)

Brigham Young's encapsulating statement on this subject is worth pondering: "In my fullest belief, it was the design of the Lord that Adam should partake of the forbidden fruit, and I believe that Adam knew all about it before he came to this earth. I believe there was no other way leading to thrones and dominions only for him to transgress, or take that position which transgression alone could place man in, to de-

scend below all things, that they might ascend to thrones, principalities, and powers; for they could not ascend to that eminence without first descending, nor upon any other principle." (JD 2:302.)

The results of the Fall accruing to mankind are the inheritance of the seeds of death—corruptible flesh—and being denied immediate access to the presence of God (Alma 42:7; 1 Cor. 15:21–22; AF, 52–73). Both of these consequences, of course, are redeemable through the atonement of Christ (Articles of Faith 1:3).

See also: Adam; Atonement; Eve; Fallen Man; First Death; Forbidden Fruit; Garden of Eden

Fallen Man

King Benjamin taught that "the natural man is an enemy to God" (Mosiah 3:19). Some have interpreted that statement to mean that man is inherently inclined to evil by nature. However, in the same scripture just cited, Benjamin adds the qualifying statement that one is an enemy to God "unless he yields to the enticings of the Holy Spirit." Elder Marion G. Romney pointed out that one becomes an enemy to God "when he rejects the promptings of the Spirit and follows the lusts of the flesh. But he is not an enemy to God when he follows the promptings of the Spirit." (IE, June 1964, p. 506.)

President Brigham Young observed: "It is fully proved in all the revelations that God has ever given to mankind that they naturally love and admire righteousness, justice and truth more than they do evil. It is, however, universally received by professors of religion as Scriptural doctrine that man is naturally opposed to God. This is not so. . . . When we do an evil, we do it in opposition to the promptings of the Spirit of Truth that is within us. Man, the noblest work of God, was in his creation designed for endless duration, for which the love of all good was incorporated in his nature. It was never designed that he should naturally do and love evil. . . . I hold that it is easier to do right than wrong." (JD 9:305.)

Thus, fallen man (D&C 20:20) is one who has fallen from the higher plane and has become blind to the divine nature and inherent desire for righteousness bequeathed by God. To become "carnal, sensual, and devilish, by nature" (Alma 42:10) is to reap the natural consequences of disobedience. President Spencer W. Kimball noted: "The 'natural man' is the 'earthy man' who has allowed rude animal passions to overshadow his spiritual inclination" (En., Nov. 1974, p. 112).

Fallen People

In addition to the testimony it provides for Jesus Christ (1 Ne. 6:4; 2 Ne. 25:18–30), and the marvelous gospel teachings it contains, the Book of Mormon "contains a record of a fallen people" (D&C 20:9). These people lived in civilizations that existed in the ancient Americas; they were brought to these lands by the hand of God and later destroyed because they rejected God and turned to evil (see Ether 13:20–22; 15:19; Moroni 9).

These fallen people include the Jaredites, a group that originated at the time of the tower of Babel (Ether 1:33), and the Nephites, a group that came to the Americas from Jerusalem about 600 B.C. (1 Ne. 1). Intermingled with the Nephites was a people popularly known as the Mulekites but described in the Book of Mormon as the people of Zarahemla (Omni 1:1–19; Mosiah 25:13). These people were descendants and followers of Mulek, a son of the Jewish king Zedekiah (Mosiah 25:2; Hel. 6:10; 8:21).

See also: Nephites

False Brethren

The Lord intimated that Joseph Smith should be "in perils among false brethren" (D&C 122:5). These are they who feign friendship or loyalty to people or causes but secretly plot against them. They are as Judas who broke bread with the Savior yet secretly sold him for silver (Matt. 26:20–25, 47–50; Mark 14:10–11).

False Spirits

The term *false spirits* is used only in Doctrine and Covenants 50:2. "There are many spirits gone out into the world, and the false spirits are giving revelations as well as the Spirit of the Lord," declared Brigham Young (JD 3:44). These false spirits appear to be equated with those spirits who followed Lucifer in rebelling against God and all that is good (D&C 29:36–38). However, Lucifer's forces of false spirits are further augmented by "false brethren" (D&C 122:5; 2 Cor. 11:26), who are not true and faithful in keeping the commandments and their covenants.

In addition there are other men in the flesh, such as "false teachers" (2 Ne. 28:12), "false prophets" (Matt. 7:15), and even "false Christs" (Matt. 24:24) who supplement the ranks of false spirits.

It was revealed to Brigham Young that "in proportion to the spread of the Gospel among the nations of the earth, so would the power of Satan rise . . . ; if the people did not receive the spirit of revelation that God had sent for the salvation of the world, they would receive false spirits, and would have revelation" from the powers of darkness (JD 13:280–81).

See also: Devils; False Brethren; Hosts of Hell; Sons of Perdition; Third Part of the Hosts of Heaven

Far West, Missouri

"Let the city, Far West, be a holy and consecrated land unto me," said the Lord in an 1838 revelation (D&C 115:7). This city had been laid out near the center of Caldwell County, which was established in December 1836. It was northeast of Jackson and Clay counties, from whence the Saints had been either driven or asked to leave.

For a brief time, Far West became the headquarters of the beleaguered Church. Between March and July of 1838, seven revelations found in the Doctrine and Covenants were received within its borders (D&C 113; 114; 115; 117; 118; 119; 120). A temple site was dedicated, with the cornerstone being laid according to revelatory dictum on July 4, 1838 (D&C 115:8–10).

In like fashion, on April 26, 1839, a meeting of the Twelve Apostles took place at this site and fulfilled two divine decrees which their enemies had vowed would be impossible to do inasmuch as "no 'Mormon' would be permitted to be in the state" (D&C 115:11; 118:4–5; HC 3:336–39). The reason for such misplaced confidence by these enemies of the Church was that Far West had been ransacked and ravished in November 1838. The Prophet and other leaders had been incarcerated, and the flock had fled to Illinois or been scattered by the mobocratic wolves. Joseph and Hyrum Smith and several others had been ordered publicly executed in the town square at Far West by the commanding general of the state militia.

To the everlasting credit of Brigadier General Alexander W.

Doniphan, the lives of these noble men were spared. He refused to carry out the order, calling it "cold blooded murder," and threatened to hold the general who issued the order "responsible before an earthly tribunal" if such an order was carried out. (HC 3:187–99.)

Farm, This

In August 1831, the Lord counseled his disciples who dwelt on "this farm" to arrange their temporal concerns in order to be free to travel to Missouri (D&C 63:38–39). The farm mentioned is probably the Isaac Morley farm located in Kirtland, Ohio (see D&C 64:20).

Smith and Sjodahl offer the following commentary: "Among the prominent men who in the early days of the Church joined its ranks at Kirtland, was Isaac Morley. Previous to that time, he was one of the leaders of a society that practiced communistic principles and was sometimes called the 'Morley Family', because a number were living on his farm. He was ordained to the ministry at the same time as Sidney Rigdon, Lyman Wight, and Edward Partridge, by the brethren who passed through Kirtland on their Indian mission, and the newly baptized Saints in Kirtland and vicinity were left to their care. He passed through the many storms that swept over the Church and cast his lot with the Saints in Utah." (SS, 307.)

See also: Morley, Isaac

Fasting

In 1832, the Lord declared, "I give unto you a commandment that ye shall continue in prayer and fasting from this time forth" (D&C 88:76). The principle of fasting has existed on this planet from the time of Adam, and the Lord was here reemphasizing an eternal source of spiritual strength.

The term *fasting* is equated with "rejoicing" by the Lord, when applied to Sabbath day activities; in that sense, fasting may not mean abstaining from food and drink, although abstinence from activities pursued the other six days of the week is expected (D&C 59:13–14). This abstinence must be coupled with mighty prayer to make the fasting complete (3 Ne. 27:1). "To make a fast most fruitful," said President Ezra Taft Benson, "it should be coupled with prayer and meditation; physical work should be held to a minimum, and it's a blessing if one can ponder on the scriptures and the reason for the fast" (En., Nov. 1974, p. 67).

Some of the benefits accruing from fasting are gaining and strengthening a testimony (Alma 5:45–46); receiving revelation and the spirit of prophecy (Alma 17:3); eliminating contention (4 Ne. 1:12–13); gaining power to resist temptation (1 Cor. 7:5); and healing the afflicted (Mark 9:17–29). According to Isaiah, a proper fast is not merely going through the motions of bowing one's head and abstaining from food; it requires one "to loose the bands of wickedness, to undo the heavy burdens [of self and others], and to let the oppressed go free, and that ye break every yoke" (Isa. 58:5–6). "The greatest of all benefits" from fasting, said President David O. McKay, "is the spiritual strength derived by the subjection of physical appetite to the will of the individual" (CR, Oct. 1974, p. 19).

A monthly fast day is observed by the Saints of God. Brigham Young credited Joseph Smith with starting this procedure in Kirtland. The Prophet determined that the money or commodities saved by fasting one day a month should be contributed to the poor. It was not regularly practiced until about 1852, however, when the first Thursday of each month was set aside as a day of sacrifice. This continued until 1896, when the First Presidency changed the day from Thursday to the first Sunday of the month. (CR, Nov. 1974, pp. 17–19.) Accordingly, on this day, "Proper observance of the monthly fast consists of *going without food and drink for two consecutive meals, attending the fast and testimony meeting, and making a generous offering* to the bishop for the care of those in need. 'Without drink' applies to water as well as other liquids. A *minimum* offering is defined as the equivalent of the value of two meals." (NE, Sept. 1971, p. 18; italics added.)

Father, The

"Our Father in Heaven begat all the spirits that ever were, or ever will be, upon this earth," declared Brigham Young (JD 1:50). Just as Adam is the common father of all who have gained a tabernacle of flesh by living on this earth, so God is the common Father of our pre-earth spirit tabernacles (Heb. 12:9; D&C 93:23).

Of all the titles by which God might have chosen to be known, the fact that he has instructed us to address him as "Father" should underscore the reverence in which this name should be contemplated and uttered (Matt. 6:9). "After this manner therefore pray ye; Our *Father* who art in heaven, *hallowed be thy name*" (3 Ne. 13:9; italics added).

See also: Elohim; God; Lord

Father (Jesus)

In speaking to the brother of Jared, the Savior declared: "Behold, I am Jesus Christ. I am the Father and the Son." (Ether 3:14.) The implication of Christ's role as "Father" is found throughout the Doctrine and Covenants (see 9:1; 25:1; 34:3; 50:41; 121:7).

The First Presidency and the Twelve have declared: "Jesus Christ is not the Father of the spirits who have taken or yet shall take bodies upon this earth, for He is one of them. He is The Son, as they are sons and daughters of Elohim.'' (MFP, 5:34.) However, Jesus is the ''Father'' in three very distinct ways: (1) As the Creator of this earth, ''he is very properly called the Eternal Father of heaven and earth'' (MFP 5:27; Ether 4:7; Alma 11:38–39; Mosiah 15:1–4; Isa. 9:6; 2 Ne. 19:6).

(2) He is the ''Father'' of all who abide in his gospel and become heirs of eternal life in his kingdom (MFP 5:27–31). This concept is illustrated in the words of an ancient prophet: ''And now, because of the covenant which ye have made ye shall be called the *children of Christ*, his sons, and his daughters; for behold, this day he hath spiritually begotten you; for ye say that your hearts are changed through faith on his name; therefore, ye are born of him and have become his sons and his daughters'' (Mosiah 5:7; italics added; see also 15:10–13; D&C 39:4; 45:8; Matt. 13:38; 1 John 3:8–10).

(3) The third sense in which Jesus is the ''Father'' is by divine investiture of authority. A doctrinal exposition proclaimed: ''In all His dealings with the human family Jesus the Son has represented and yet represents Elohim His Father in power and authority'' (MFP 5:31–34). He is fully empowered to speak and act for the Father. ''I and my Father are one,'' proclaimed this divine Son (John 10:30; see also 17:22; D&C 50:43; 3 Ne. 20:35; 28:10).

See also: Jesus Christ

Father of All

Because of his unique position as the first man and first flesh on the earth, Adam is the father of all men who have inhabited this earth in tabernacles of flesh (D&C 27:11; Moses 3:7). All mankind have descended from our first parents, father Adam and his wife, mother Eve (1 Ne. 5:11).

See also: Adam

Fatness of the Earth

See: Feast of Fat Things

Fayette, New York

The Prophet penned the following entry in his journal in the spring of 1829: ''Shortly after commencing to translate, I became acquainted with Mr. Peter Whitmer, of Fayette, Seneca county, New York, and also with some of his family. In the beginning of the month of June, his son, David Whitmer, came to the place where we were residing, and brought with him a two-horse wagon, for the purpose of having us [Joseph and Oliver Cowdery] accompany him to his father's place, and there remain until we should finish the work. It was arranged that we should have our board free of charge, and the assistance of one of his brothers to write for me, and also his own assistance when convenient. Having much need of such timely aid in an undertaking so arduous, and being informed that the people in the neighborhood of the Whitmers were anxiously awaiting the opportunity to inquire into these things, we accepted the invitation, and accompanied Mr. Whitmer to his father's house, and there resided until the translation was finished and the copyright secured." (HC 1:48–49.)

Not only was the translation of the Book of Mormon completed at Fayette, but it was also here that the heavenly messenger Moroni showed the Three Witnesses the plates from which the record was translated, and the voice of God was heard bearing witness as to their authenticity. On April 6, 1830, the "kingdom" destined to "consume" all other kingdoms was organized at Fayette (Dan. 2:44; D&C 38:9). Two months later, the first conference of this fledgling kingdom convened at the same location. Between June 1829 and January 1831, twenty of the revelations found in the Doctrine and Covenants were received within the borders of Fayette (D&C 14–18; 20–21; 28–40). In obedience to the Lord's wishes (D&C 37:1), the Prophet moved the headquarters of the Church to Ohio in January 1831, and Fayette receded into the pages of history.

See also: Wilderness of Fayette, Seneca County

Fear God

"Fear God, and give glory to him" is the divine injunction to all mankind (D&C 88:104;

133:38). Speaking of the relationship between reverence and fear of God, Elder M. Russell Ballard has given us the following insights: "The root word *revere* also implies an element of fear. Thus reverence might be understood to mean an attitude of profound respect and love with a desire to honor and show gratitude, with a fear of breaking faith or offending." (En., May 1988, p. 57.)

Those who do not "fear God" are described as not keeping the commandments, building up churches to get gain, doing wicked acts, and building up the kingdom of the devil (D&C 10:56). The Psalmist wrote, "The fear of the Lord is the beginning of wisdom" (Ps. 111:10); and another Old Testament writer said, "Let us hear the conclusion of the whole matter: Fear God, and keep his commandments: for this is the whole duty of man" (Eccl. 12:13).

To "fear God," in the context of these scriptural admonitions, is to render him obedience, to reverence him and hold him in sacred awe. More important, however, is that when we "fear God" we love him with all our heart, might, mind, and strength (D&C 59:5; Matt. 22:36–38). The Lord delights to honor those who "fear" (love) him: "Great shall be their reward and eternal shall be their glory" (D&C 76:6).

Feast of Fat Things

In 1831, the Lord spoke of "a feast of fat things" (D&C 58:8). Sperry described the meaning thereof as follows: "The language here is both figurative and literal in its application. The feast prepared represents the restored Gospel or the Church in the latter days. (Cf. 2 Ne. 32:3.) The 'fat things' and 'wine on the lees' were to the ancient Hebrews a representation of prosperity . . . ; at the feast [they] are . . . a representation of the offering of rich things of the Gospel at the Lord's table. Nor do they by any means exclude the notion that those who partake thereof will experience literal prosperity in their basket and in their store. The feast thus explained would come in the latter days as foretold by the prophets. . . . It would indeed be a supper of the house of the Lord, well prepared . . . and intended for the humble, poor, and contrite of heart, but nevertheless one to which all nations would be invited. The first invited would be the rich, the learned, the wise, and the noble." (DCC, 237–38.)

President Joseph Fielding Smith has further clarified that the invitation to the feast "is to be given first to the rich and learned, the wise and noble—classes who do not readily embrace the Gospel and then in the day of his power, the poor, the lame, and the blind, and the deaf, should come in unto the marriage of the Lamb. In this manner the parable of the great supper (Luke 14) will be fulfilled." (CHMR 1:212.) "Feast upon that which perisheth not, neither can be corrupted, and let your soul delight in fatness," declared the prophet Jacob (2 Ne. 9:51). His brother Nephi admonished all to "feast upon the word of Christ" (2 Ne. 31:20; 2 Ne. 32:3).

See also: Good of the Land of Zion; Supper of the House of the Lord; Wine on the Lees

Feeble Knees

See: Hands Which Hang Down

Feel

The word *feel* can mean "to experience a physical sensation" such as described in the revelation on how to discern true messengers sent by God from those sent by the devil, whose purpose is to deceive (D&C 129:4–8). Further, selected individuals were invited to physically feel the nail prints in the body of the resurrected Redeemer (Luke 24:39; John 20:26–28; 3 Ne. 11:14–15; 18:25).

There is another type of feeling that can surpass any physical sensation one may have had. This is a spiritual sensation of Spirit speaking to spirit. It is an inner, intuitive or revelatory experience whereby one comes to know or understand something with great power. The Lord promised that when we study and pray about something that is true or correct we shall "feel that it is right" (D&C 9:8). However, this requires that one be in tune with the Spirit, for sin and neglect can corrode celestial channels of communication. The prophet Nephi noted that his wayward brothers "were past feeling, that [they] could not feel [God's] words" (1 Nephi 17:45).

Finally, to "feel after" someone or something is to grope or diligently search for the desired subject or object (D&C 101:8; 112:13).

See also: Bosom Shall Burn; Revelation; Speak Peace to Your Mind; Still Small Voice

Feet

See: Cleanse Your Feet by Water; Feet Shod with the Preparation of the Gospel of Peace; Footstool; Ordinance of the Washing of Feet; Shake Off the Dust of Thy Feet; Under His Feet; Wash Thy Feet as a Testimony

Feet Shod with the Preparation of the Gospel of Peace

What may appear to be the most insignificant components of a soldier's battle gear are his shoes. Yet, without adequate shoes to bear up the weight of the body, all the armament and weaponry will lose their effectiveness. Thus, the Lord suggested that part of our spiritual armament should be the spiritual sandals with which our feet are shod. Such shoes are called "the preparation of the gospel of peace" (D&C 27:16; Eph. 6:15).

"The feet," said President Harold B. Lee, "typify the course you chart in the journey of life . . . , your goals or objectives" (SHP, 331–34). If one's feet are kept on that narrow path that leads to the "strait gate," then eternal life will be found (3 Ne. 14:13–14; see also 1 Ne. 8:20). President Spencer W. Kimball has said that *strait* is "not the shortest distance between two points. Strait means hard, difficult, exacting, that kind of a gate." (DSY, 1973, p. 265.)

The "gospel of peace" is the plan of life which the Savior gave to us, his teachings and ordinances which, if obeyed, bring unspeakable joy and peace to our minds (John 14:27; 1 Ne. 8:10–12; Hel. 5:44; D&C 6:23). If the world would accept and live these teachings and ordinances, peace would reign supreme on the earth (see 4 Ne. 1:15–17).

Feigned Words

The Lord speaks of cursing those who "have broken the covenant through covetousness, and with feigned words" (D&C 104:4). Although this refers specifically to those who broke their covenants in the United Order at Kirtland, the principle applies to any who pronounce their agreement and loyalty to covenants and promises with feigned (pretended, insincere, or false) words. Such will bring down a cursing upon their heads.

In this respect it would be well to consider the words of

Jesus Christ in an 1831 revelation: "Wherefore, let all men beware how they take my name in their lips—For behold, verily I say, that many there be who are under this condemnation, who use the name of the Lord, and use it in vain, having not authority." (D&C 63:61–62.)

See also: Hypocrisy; Liars

Felicity

The word *felicity* is only found once in all of scripture (D&C 77:3). Webster states that it means "the quality or state of being happy," especially experiencing great happiness.

Fetters of Hell

The Prophet Joseph wrote of the weight of the world's iniquity and said that it is as "an iron yoke, it is a strong band; they are the very handcuffs, and chains, and shackles, and fetters of hell" (D&C 123:8). This is the only use of this description in all of scripture. Fetters are things, such as chains and shackles, that restrain movement (Judg. 16:21; 2 Kgs. 25:7; Mark 5:4). The fetters of hell are those shackles of sin that bind one to Satan himself.

One's movement to higher orders is thus restricted by such fetters, for no unclean thing can dwell in the presence of holy beings (1 Ne. 10:21; Moses 6:57).

See also: Chains of Darkness

Field Is White Already to Harvest

The Lord's observation that "the field is white already to harvest" is found frequently in early sections of the Doctrine and Covenants (4:4; 6:3; 11:3; 14:3; 31:4; 33:3, 7). Jesus used the same symbolic language in a discussion with his disciples in Samaria. He reminded them that though the time for the harvest of wheat was yet four months distant, the harvest of souls was imminent (John 4:31–42).

One knows when wheat is ripe because of the white appearance of the fields. The Lord has declared that this same condition now prevails where the human harvest of souls is concerned.

See also: Earth Is Ripe; Ripe; Sheaves; Stubble; Thrust in His Sickle; Wheat

Fiery Darts

The phrase *fiery darts of the adversary* is found once in Doctrine and Covenants 3:8 and once in the Book of Mormon (1 Ne. 15:24). Similarly, the phrase *fiery darts of the wicked* is found in two books of scripture (D&C 27:17; Eph. 6:16).

"Fiery darts" have reference to the burning arrows used in ancient warfare. Arrows were dipped in pitch and lighted before being shot from the archer's bow. Effective use of one's shield was necessary in order to avoid being struck with such "fiery darts." In similar fashion, the hosts of hell send forth their fiery darts of wickedness, which can only be warded off through the effective use of one's shield of faith.

Fifth Angel or Trump

A series of trumps, sounded by seven angels, will usher in significant world events surrounding the millennial era (D&C 88:98–110; Rev. 8:2). The fifth trump, sounded by the fifth angel, signifies the committing of the "everlasting gospel" to "all nations, kindreds, tongues, and people" (D&C 88:103).

The description of this particular angel's mission sounds very much like that which has been ascribed to the keeper of "the stick of Ephraim," Moroni (D&C 27:5; 133:36; Rev. 14:6–7; JD 14:257–59). However, Elder Bruce R. McConkie suggested that the angel flying through the midst of heaven with the everlasting gospel may be a composite angel, or group of angels, which includes Moroni (DNTC 3:527–31).

See also: Angel Flying Through the Midst of Heaven; Moroni

Fig Tree

The fig is a commonplace and highly prized food commodity in Palestine; therefore, it is not surprising that the Lord used it to symbolically represent principles he was teaching both in the New Testament and in the Doctrine and Covenants. For example, the falling of a fig from its tree is dramatically used to represent the falling of the stars from the heavens prior to the Second Coming (D&C 88:87). The parable of the fig tree is spoken of twice in the Doctrine and Covenants (35:16; 45:34–39). The Savior indicated that when the fig tree began to shoot forth its leaves, we would know that his coming was nigh.

Of this parable, Elder Melvin J. Ballard said: "One characteristic of a fig tree is that it does not put forth its leaves until relatively late in the year, long after most of the trees are in full leaf. The Savior used this feature in a parable concerning his second coming. Although the world will not know the day nor the hour of his coming, we should observe the signs of the times, for when the fig tree puts forth its leaves, we know that summer is nigh. In other words, when the signs of the second coming begin to be made manifest, we know that the second coming is nigh or near at hand." (CR, Oct. 1923, p. 32.) The parable is mentioned in the New Testament and also the Pearl of Great Price (Matt. 24:32–33; Mark 13:28–29; Luke 21:29–31; JS—M 1:38–43).

Filthy

To be filthy is to be spiritually unclean, to be unable to stand in the presence of God with a clear conscience and spotless raiment. Those who willingly seek to sin, whose desires are carnal, sensual, and devilish, "cannot be sanctified by law, neither by mercy, justice, nor judgment. Therefore, they must remain filthy still." (D&C 88:35.) The filthy "cannot dwell in the kingdom of God . . . , wherefore there must needs be a place of filthiness prepared for that which is filthy" (1 Ne. 15:33–34).

See also: Garments Spotted with the Flesh; Uncleanness

Fire

The world was once destroyed by water (Gen. 6–8). The next total destruction of the wicked will be by other means and elements, including fire (D&C 29:21; 45:41, 50, 57; 64:23–24; 133:41; JD 19:192). "As pertaining to the righteous, the term *fire* is used to indicate a purifying, cleansing agent, but where the wicked are concerned it is used to signify destruction and the severity of eternal torment" (MD, 279).

Joseph Smith taught that "some shall rise to the *everlasting burnings of God*; for God dwells in everlasting burnings, and some shall rise to the *damnation of their own filthiness, which is as exquisite a torment as the lake of fire and brimstone*" (TPJS, 361; italics added). The Lord's appeal for us to "come forth out of the fire" (D&C 36:6) has reference to that unquenchable fire to which the wicked are consigned.

The very eyes of the Savior are described "as a flame of fire" (D&C 110:3), and he and the Twelve Apostles shall appear "in a pillar of fire" at the Second Coming (D&C 29:12). The righteous will meet the Savior in the brightness of his glory (D&C 65:5) and ultimately join him in God's "everlasting burnings," basking in the rays of celestial light.

See also: Baptism of Fire; Blazing Throne of God; Burn; Cloven Tongues as of Fire; Ezekiel; Lake of Fire and Brimstone; Pillar of Fire; Presence of the Lord Shall Be as the Melting Fire; Refiner's Fire; Sea of Glass and Fire; Unquenchable Fire; Vengeance of Eternal Fire

Firmament

All references to the firmament in the Doctrine and Covenants are found in section 76 (D&C 76:70, 71, 81, 109). The firmament is the arch of the sky, or the heavens, in which heavenly bodies appear, such as the stars.

See also: Heaven

First Angel

John the Revelator saw seven angels stand before God and receive seven trumpets (Rev. 8:2). The successive sounding of these trumpets was to reveal significant events in the world's history. Joseph Smith's "Olive Leaf" also spoke of seven angels who would usher in significant events with the sound of their trumps (D&C 88:98–110).

The first angel will signal the resurrection of the first fruits at Christ's coming and will later "reveal the secret acts of men, and the mighty works of God in the first thousand years" of earth's history (D&C 88:98, 108). This angel's identity is presently unknown.

See also: First Thousand Years, Trump of the Angel of God

First Caught Up to Meet Him

See: First Fruits; Lifted Up

First Death

The "first death," which was suffered by Adam and Eve upon their banishment from the Garden of Eden, is described by Alma as being "cut off both temporally and spiritually from the presence of the Lord" (D&C 29:41; Alma 42:7–11). The parents of the human race were not the first to suffer such a "death," for it had been previously decreed for Lucifer and those spirits who chose to follow him in rebelling against righteousness (D&C 29:36–37; Rev. 12:7–9; 2 Ne. 2:17–18).

President Joseph Fielding Smith said this "death . . . has passed upon all men who have remained unrepentant and who have not received the gospel. Those who have suffered the *first*

spiritual death or departure, which is a shutting out from the presence of God, have the privilege of being redeemed from this death through obedience to the principles of the gospel. Through baptism and confirmation they are *born again* and thus come *back into spiritual life,* and through their continued obedience to the end, they shall be made partakers of the blessings of eternal life in the celestial kingdom of God." (DS 2:222–23; italics added.)

See also: Born of Me; Fall; Garden of Eden; Spiritually Dead

First Elder

The Lord himself called Joseph Smith to be an "apostle" and the "first elder" of the Church. This was the presiding position at the time the Church was organized on April 6, 1830 (D&C 20:2; HC 1:75–78). Joseph's "authority . . . originated in the Apostleship; and as he was the first Apostle, by virtue of that authority he presided in every place where there were Saints" (GT 1:258). The title "first elder" literally meant the "first President" of the Church (DS 1:212).

First Fruits

The "first fruits" who are spoken of as meeting the Savior at his return to usher in the Millennium are they who are worthy of the first resurrection and are heirs to celestial salvation (D&C 88:96–98).

Elder Orson Pratt described this event in the following words: "The face of the Lord will be unveiled, and those who are alive will be quickened, and they will be caught up; and the Saints who are in their graves will come forth and be caught up, together with those who are quickened, and they will be taken into the heavens into the midst of those celestial beings who will make their appearance at that time. *These are the ones who are the first fruits at the time of His coming.*" (JD 16:328; italics added.)

To refer to the celestial Saints as first fruits is symbolic of a practice of the Mosaic code. Anciently the Israelites offered the first fruits of their fields as a consecrated sacrifice to God (Ex. 23:19; 34:26).

Christ himself is referred to as "the firstfruits unto God" (2 Ne. 2:9), which is most appropriate in light of the total consecration of his life to his holy Father. It is also significant that the Firstborn Son of God should be called the firstfruits, because the firstborn sons of Israel were to be consecrated to God's service (Ex. 22:29).

See also: First Resurrection; Lifted Up; Trump of the Angel of God

First Man

"The first man," Paul declared, "is of the earth, earthy" (1 Cor. 15:47; D&C 128:14). Adam was the first man on this earth (Moses 1:34). His mortal body was created from the "dust" of this earth or those elements that belong to this particular planet (Gen. 2:7; Moses 3:7; Alma 42:2; D&C 77:12). Upon his death, his body returned to the "ground" from whence it came (Gen. 3:19; Moses 4:25).

The posterity of Adam—mortal mankind—is likewise "earthy," having been created from the "dust" of this earth and being subject to return to the "ground" at death (Moses 6:59). Thus, in a broader sense, the "first man," as used in Doctrine and Covenants 128:14, could refer to the body of earthly mortality; the telestial tabernacle of clay possessed by all who will ever dwell on this planet in the flesh. This "man" will be supplanted by the "second man," whose body will be of a resurrected, heavenly substance.

See also: Adam; Dust of the Earth; Earthy

First Preacher

The Lord's proclamation that Oliver Cowdery was to be the "first preacher of this church" (D&C 21:12) is not his designation as the presiding elder, for the Prophet Joseph was the "first elder" and Oliver the "second elder" (D&C 20:1–3). The meaning of "first preacher" is found in an entry in Joseph's journal. "On

Sunday, April 11th, 1830, Oliver Cowdery preached the first public discourse that was delivered by any of our number" (HC 1:81).

See also: Cowdery, Oliver; Gift of Aaron

First Presidency of the Church

By revelation, the Lord designated "three Presiding High Priests" to form a "quorum of the Presidency of the Church" (D&C 107:22). These three men, and the quorum they represent, are referred to by several designations in the Doctrine and Covenants: "First Presidency of the Melchizedek Priesthood" (D&C 68:15; see also 107:17); "Presidency of the High Priesthood" (81:2); "Quorum of the Presidency of the Church" (D&C 107:22); and "Presidency of the Church" (D&C 107:33).

The requirements for their selection, as revealed by the Lord, are summarized as follows: "First, it was requisite that there be three presiding high priests. Second, they were to be chosen by the body (which has been construed to be the Quorum of the Twelve Apostles). Third, they must be appointed and ordained by the same body—the Quorum of the Twelve. Fourth, they must be upheld by the confidence, faith, and prayers of the Church." (SHP, 165.)

When the President of the Church dies, his counselors are automatically released, for they cannot serve as counselors in a quorum that has no president

(TPJS, 106; see also GK, 165). "Immediately following the death of a President, the next ranking body, the Quorum of the Twelve Apostles, becomes the presiding authority," declared President Harold B. Lee, "with the President of the Twelve automatically becoming the acting President of the Church" (CR, Apr. 1970, p. 123; see also DS 3:156).

The only way one other than the senior Apostle could become the President of the Church is "if the Lord reveals to that President of the Twelve that someone other than himself could be selected" (CR, Apr. 1970, p. 123). It seems unlikely that such would ever happen, for as President Spencer W. Kimball has observed, "This is the way of the Lord, and he retains the leadership in his divine hands" (CR, Apr. 1970, p. 118).

In reorganizing the First Presidency, the Quorum of the Twelve sustain and set apart the new President of the Church, who in turn selects his two counselors. These counselors need not be Apostles, but they must be sustained by the Twelve as well as the body of the Church (GD, 173; DS 3:157). Once chosen and sustained, "the supreme governing power of the Church is vested in the President with his counselors. The First Presidency preside over all councils, all quorums, and all organizations of the Church, with supreme appointing power and power of nomination." (IE, Nov. 1966, p. 78.)

Although these men cannot claim infallibility (GT 1:206), nor have they ever asserted such to be the case, "what they say as a presidency is what the Lord would say if he were here in person" (Marion G. Romney, CR, Apr. 1945, p. 90). Joseph Smith noted that "revelations of the mind and will of God to the Church, are to come through the Presidency. This is the order of heaven." (TPJS, 111.)

"The voice of the First Presidency and the united voice of others who hold with them the keys of the kingdom shall always guide the Saints and the world in those paths where the Lord wants them to be," declared President Joseph Fielding Smith. "I testify," said he, "that if we shall look to the First Presidency and follow their counsel and direction, no power on earth can stay or change our course as a church, and as individuals we shall gain peace in this life and be inheritors of eternal glory in the world to come." (CR, Apr. 1972, p. 99.)

See also: Chosen by the Body; Presidency of the High Priesthood

First Presidency of the Melchizedek Priesthood

See: First Presidency of the Church; Presidency of the High Priesthood

First Priesthood

The "first priesthood" to be bestowed on man in this dispensation was the Aaronic, which incorporates the Levitical (D&C 13;

27:8; 107:1, 6). This priesthood was given to Joseph Smith and Oliver Cowdery near the banks of the Susquehanna River at Harmony, Pennsylvania, on May 15, 1829, under the hands of the resurrected John the Baptist (JS—H 1:66–72). The use of the term *first priesthood* in Doctrine and Covenants 27:8 (Aaronic Priesthood) is not to be confused with the "first" priesthood (Melchizedek Priesthood) referred to in Doctrine and Covenants 107:1–2. The Melchizedek Priesthood encompasses *all* other priesthoods (D&C 107:1–5; TPJS, 180). In fact, the Aaronic Priesthood is specifically referred to as the "second priesthood" in verse 13 of section 107.

See also: Aaronic Priesthood; Greater Priesthood; Lesser Priesthood; Levitical Priesthood; Melchizedek Priesthood

First Resurrection

The "first resurrection" is spoken of in several sections of the Doctrine and Covenants (45:54; 63:18; 76:64; 132:19, 26). It has been defined in the following terms: "While there was a general resurrection of the righteous at the time Christ arose from the dead, it is customary for us to speak of the resurrection of the righteous at the Second Coming of Christ as the *first resurrection*. It is the first *to us*, for we have little thought or concern over that which is past. The Lord has promised that at the time of his Second Advent the graves will be opened, and the just shall come forth to reign with him on the earth for a thousand years." (DS 2:295.)

"It is the opinion of some that the resurrection is going on all the time now, but this is purely *speculation without warrant in the scriptures*. It is true that the Lord has power to call forth any person or persons from the dead, as he may desire, especially if they have a mission to perform which would require their resurrection. For example, we have the cases of Peter, James, and Moroni.

"We are given to understand that the *first* resurrection yet future, which means the coming forth of the righteous, will take place at *one particular time*, which is when our Savior shall appear in the clouds of heaven, when he shall return to reign." (DS 2:299.)

If we look upon the resurrections which have already taken place as a prelude to the "first resurrection," as defined above, then there are three more phases of this "first resurrection" to consider. First, there will be the resurrection of the righteous who have died since the days of the Savior. These will join those worthy souls who are living on the earth at the time of Christ's coming in being "caught up to meet him" and accompany him in his descent to earth. This latter group will pass through an immediate "quickening"; that is, their death and resurrection will be instantaneous (D&C 88:96–98).

The second phase of the "first resurrection" will involve "those who are Christ's at his coming" (D&C 88:99). "In this resurrection will come forth those of the *terrestrial order*, who were not worthy to be caught up to meet him, but who are worthy to come forth to enjoy the millenial reign" (DS 2:296–97).

The third phase will involve those who live during the thousand years of peace, who shall "not sleep . . . in the earth, but shall be changed in the twinkling of an eye" when they reach "the age of a tree," or "an hundred years old" (D&C 101:29–31; Isa. 65:20).

See also: Celestial; Resurrection; Terrestrial; Those Who Are Christ's at His Coming

First Thousand Years

Two references to the "first thousand years" are found in the Doctrine and Covenants (77:6–7; 88:108). This period of time represents the first millennium from the time Adam and Eve were expelled from Eden, or the first one thousand years of earth's temporal history (D&C 77:6; DS 1:78–81). At the end of "time," prior to the last great battle of the forces of good and evil, seven angels will sound their respective trumps and reveal the "secret acts of men, and the thoughts and intents of their hearts, and the mighty works of God" during each of the seven millennia of earth's temporal history (D&C 88:108–15). The "first thousand years" is represented by the first "seal" on the book which John the Revelator saw containing the earth's temporal history (D&C 77:6–7; Rev. 5).

See also: First Angel

Firstborn

As used in Doctrine and Covenants 68:16–18, the term *firstborn* refers to the oldest male child among the descendants of Aaron who by lineage has the right to serve as the Presiding Bishop of the Church (DS 3:92). "The office of Presiding Bishop of the Church is the same as the office which was held by Aaron. . . . It was this office which came to John the Baptist. . . . The person who has the legal right to this presiding office has not been discovered; perhaps is not in the Church, but should it be shown by revelation that there is one who is the 'firstborn among the sons of Aaron,' and thus entitled by birthright to this presidency, he could 'claim' his 'anointing' and the right to that office in the Church." (CHMR 1:259.) However, it should be understood that such an office would always be appointed under the direction of the First Presidency of the Church.

See also: Aaron; Bishop; Literal Descendant of Aaron

Firstborn, The

In a revelation given to the Prophet Joseph in 1833, the Savior declared himself to be the "Firstborn" (D&C 93:21). In 1916, the First Presidency and Twelve Apostles pronounced the following: "Among the spirit children of Elohim the firstborn was and is Jehovah or Jesus Christ to whom all others are juniors. . . . Jesus Christ was 'the firstborn of every creature' and it is evident that the seniority here expressed must be with respect to antemortal existence, for Christ was not the senior of all mortals in the flesh. He is further designated as the 'firstborn from the dead' this having reference to Him as the first to be resurrected from the dead, or as elsewhere written 'the first fruits of them that slept' (1 Cor. 15:20; see also verse 23); and 'the first begotten of the dead' (Rev. 1:5; compare Acts 26:23)." (MFP 5:33.)

See also: Jesus Christ

Fishing River, Missouri

About twelve miles west of Richmond, Ray County, Missouri, was an elevated piece of ground between Little Fishing and Big Fishing rivers. These streams were formed by seven small tributaries. On June 19, 1834, Zion's Camp spent a most unusual night at this location. Their progress during the day had been impeded by an "act of divine providence," for they were undoubtedly prevented from falling prey to menacing mobocrats (HC 2:102–8; ECH 145–46). Members of the malicious mob force threatened the camp that they would "see hell before morning."

Through divine intervention, an estimated force of over 330 mobocrats were dispersed by a tremendous storm that "met them in great wrath, and soon softened their direful courage, and frustrated all their designs to 'kill Joe Smith and his army.'" They concluded "that when Jehovah fights they would rather be absent," said the Prophet.

The following morning the camp "drove five miles on to the prairie" in order to procure food and horses and be in a better defensive position. A Colonel Sconce, from Ray County, rode into camp and said: "I see that there is an Almighty power that protects this people, for I started from Richmond . . . with a company of armed men, having a fixed determination to destroy you, but was kept back by the storm, and was not able to reach you."

It was at this location that cholera broke out in the camp, as previously prophesied by Joseph Smith. Near this location, on June 22, the Prophet received the revelation contained in Doctrine and Covenants 105.

Flesh

The word *flesh* is used in a variety of ways in the Doctrine and Covenants, so one must look at the context of the reference to discern the exact meaning. Flesh may refer to the body of mortal man (D&C 61:15; 76:74); the meat of animals (D&C 49:21; 89:12); the bodies of either man or beast (D&C 98:17; 101:26); the mortal body of Christ (D&C 20:1, 26; 45:16; 93:4); one's lineage (D&C 86:9; cf. Abr. 2:9–11; HC 3:380); or marriage (D&C 46:16).

See also: Arm of Flesh; Destroyed in the Flesh; Dust of the Earth; Earth; First Flesh; Garments Spotted with the Flesh; Man That Sheddeth Blood or Wasteth Flesh; One Flesh

Flock

See: Good Shepherd

Fold

With the exception of the one instance in the Doctrine and Covenants in which the Lord referred to his followers in ancient Palestine as his fold (i.e., a group of people with a common faith; see D&C 10:59), the word *fold* is used in conjunction with a number, indicating increase to that degree (e.g., D&C 78:19; 98:25–26). When the Lord promises that he will reward righteousness "an hundredfold," it means the person will get one hundred times the increase for his effort.

Folly

Those who are "ever learning, and never able to come to the knowledge of the truth," who "resist the truth . . . , shall proceed no further: for their folly shall be manifest'' (2 Tim. 3:7–9; see also D&C 35:7; 63:15; see also 2 Ne. 9:28). Folly is a lack of good sense. It can be manifest in a foolish act or in evil, carnal conduct.

Foolish Virgins

See: Ten Virgins

Footstool

The Lord refers to the earth as his footstool (D&C 38:17; 1 Ne. 17:39; Moses 6:9, 44). A footstool is a low stool upon which to rest one's feet. It is symbolic of subjection, something beneath one and over which power is exercised. For example, God speaks of making a footstool of one's enemies (Matt. 22:44; Acts 2:35). James warns the Saints against treating the poor as one's footstool (Jas. 2:3).

Forbidden Fruit

A story known for centuries is the partaking of the forbidden fruit by Adam and Eve (D&C 29:40; Gen. 3:6; Moses 4:12). While popular belief refers to this fruit as an apple, the true nature of the forbidden fruit is unknown. What is known is that the eating thereof brought about a change in the bodies of Adam and Eve. Elder James E. Talmage taught, ''Therein consisted the fall—the eating of things unfit, the taking into the body of things

that made of that body a thing of earth'' (CR, Oct. 1913, pp. 118–19).

Elder Bruce R. McConkie has written that the tree from whence the forbidden fruit came, the tree of knowledge of good and evil, ''figuratively refers to how and why and in what manner mortality and all that appertains to it came into being.'' Adam and Eve ''complied with whatever the law was that brought mortality into being'' (ANW, 86).

See also: Fall; First Death; Garden of Eden

Forgiveness

One of the great promises of the gospel is found in the Lord's declaration that he will ''forgive sins unto those who confess their sins before me and ask forgiveness, who have not sinned unto death'' (D&C 64:7). While there are certain sins which can never be expiated, God alone being the judge of those sins, mortal man has been commanded ''to forgive all men'' (D&C 64:8–10; Mosiah 26:31).

The bruised and bleeding Redeemer, hanging from the torturous cross, was himself the epitomy of the virtues he had preached when he pleaded, ''Father, forgive them; for they know not what they do'' (Luke 23:34).

God's forgiveness carries with it the promise of divine forgetfulness: ''Behold, he who has repented of his sins, the same is forgiven, and I, the Lord, remember them no more" (D&C 58:42). Man's forgiveness of his neighbor's follies and transgressions should be no less magnanimous as he seeks to erase them from his memory.

Form of a Dove

See: Holy Ghost

Fornication

Paul warned the Corinthians that fornicators "shall not inherit the kingdom of God" (1 Cor. 6:9). The term *fornication* appears four times in the Doctrine and Covenants, thrice in connection with the cup of Babylon (see Wine of the Wrath of Her Fornication) (D&C 35:11; 88:94, 105).

Those who define fornication as sexual intercourse between unmarried individuals find the usage of the term in section 42, verse 74, somewhat unclear. Similar confusion results from a literal reading of several other passages of scripture (3 Ne. 12:32; Matt. 6:32). A clarification comes from Smith and Sjodahl: "This term is sometimes used for all kinds of sexual sins (See 1 Cor. 7:2; Matt. 5:32; 1 Cor. 5:1), and also figuratively, for idolatry (2 Chron. 21:11). But generally it stands for the sin of impurity when committed between unmarried persons." (SS, 236.)

"The body is not for fornication, but for the Lord," counseled Paul (1 Cor. 6:13).

See also: Uncleanness; Wine of the Wrath of Her Fornication

Foster, James

In a revelation that deals extensively with the organization of Church government, James Foster was mentioned as one of the seven Presidents of the Seventies in 1841 (D&C 124:138). He was born April 1, 1775, at Morgan County, Indiana, and became one of the seven Presidents on April 6, 1837, at the age of sixty-two (CA 1978:117).

His first appearance in the annals of Church history was on August 17, 1835, when he received a blessing at a meeting held in Kirtland (HC 2:244). He was a member of the famous Zion's Camp contingent (HC 2:88), as well as the group known as the Kirtland Camp (HC 3:91). In April 1841, some objection was raised regarding his standing in his priesthood quorum, but after an explanation by Foster he was sustained in his office (HC 4:341–42).

According to Jenson, although Foster is reported to have died on December 21, 1841, he was not removed from his presiding position until 1844 (Jenson 1:191–92). The official *History of the Church* mentions that at a conference in October 1844, Brigham Young said "that the Seventies (First Council) had dropped James Foster, and cut him off, and we need not take an action upon his case" (HC 7:297).

Foster, Robert D.

Four verses in section 124 are devoted to chastising Robert D. Foster (D&C 124:115–18). In particular, he was admonished to help in the building of the Nauvoo House. There are about three dozen references to him in Joseph Smith's history, with the majority of them mentioning his misdeeds.

Foster served as surgeon-general of the Nauvoo Legion, but one month following his excommunication in April 1844, he was court-martialed "for unbecoming and unofficer-like conduct" (HC 6:355, 362). The close proximity of this date to that of the martyrdom of the Prophet Joseph—June 27, 1844—appears to be no coincidence. A letter sent by Foster from Carthage, Illinois, dated June 20, 1844, makes reference to the "thousands of armed men" who were gathering for their unhallowed deeds (HC 6:520). He is mentioned as an "accessory" to the murders of Joseph and Hyrum on several occasions and even admitted as much (HC 7:146, 169, 513). The following is a reported conversation Foster had with Abraham C. Hodge in November 1845:

"I am the most miserable wretch that the sun shines upon," said Foster. "If I could recall eighteen months of my life I would be willing to sacrifice everything I have upon earth, my wife and child not excepted. I did love Joseph Smith more than any man that ever lived, if I had been present I would have stood between him and death." To this Hodge replied, "Why did you do as you have done? You were accessory to his murder." Foster then said: "I know that, and I have not seen one moment's peace since that time. I know that Mormonism is true, and the thought of meeting (Joseph and Hyrum) at the bar of God is more awful to me than anything else." (HC 7:513.) No further mention is made of Foster.

Foundation of the World

The phrase *foundation of the world* appears a score of times in the Doctrine and Covenants, in addition to one reference to the "foundation of the earth" (D&C 45:1). We are told that "little children are redeemed from the foundation of the world" (29:46); mysteries "have been sealed . . . from the foundation of the world" (35:18); "the ordinance of baptizing for the dead . . . was instituted from before the foundation of the world" (124:33); and the conditions whereupon blessings are received "were instituted from before the foundation of the world" (132:5).

This "foundation" was the creation, or organizing, of the earth. Known also as "the beginning of time," it included the pre-earth councils "when the morning stars sang together, and all the sons of God shouted for joy" (Job 38:4–7). It was that time period when Abraham (Abr. 3:22–23), Jeremiah (Jer. 1:5), and all other great ones who would traverse this earth were selected for their assignments (HC 6:364).

Four Corners of the Earth

Occasional reference is made to the four corners of the earth (D&C 124:3, 128; Isa. 11:12; 2 Ne. 21:12), the four quarters of the earth (D&C 33:6; 45:46; 135:3; Rev. 20:8; 1 Ne. 19:16), or the four winds (D&C 133:7; JS—M 1:37). This is figuration language which refers to the extremities or ends of the earth. The Church or kingdom of God will go forth in every direction under the direction of the Lord's anointed servants.

See also: Ends of the Earth

Four Quarters of the Earth

See: Four Corners of the Earth

Four Winds

See: Four Corners of the Earth

Fourth Trump

The fourth trump is the signal at the end of the Millennium that will "quicken" the "sons of perdition," bringing them forth from the depths of the grave to receive their resurrected bodies, which will tabernacle their tortured spirits throughout eternity. "They shall return again to their own place . . . because they were not willing to enjoy that which they might have received" (D&C 88:32, 102).

See also: Sons of Perdition; Those Who Are to Remain

Free Will

See: Agency

Freedom, New York

Freedom is a small town located about fifty miles southwest of Buffalo, New York, in Cattaraugus County. "On his journey among the churches to gather up the strength of the Lord's House (D&C 103:22–34), the Prophet came to the city of Freedom, N.Y., where he was entertained by Warren A. Cowdery. He held several meetings there. One of the converts was Heman Hyde, and shortly after his baptism, March 11, 1834, his parents and thirty or forty others were baptized and organized into a Branch, from which nucleus the light spread and souls were gathered into the fold in all the regions round." (SS, 689–90; HC 2:40–43.)

In November 1834, Warren A. Cowdery was called as a "presiding high priest over [the] church in the land of Freedom and the regions round about" (D&C 106:1).

French Farm

While not specifically mentioned in the context of a revelation, the preface to section 96 in 1981 editions of the Doctrine and Covenants mentions the French farm. It was named after Peter French. Over a score of years before Latter-day Saints began arriving in Kirtland, Ohio, French was one of the leaders of this small town. His job was to prevent families from remaining in Kirtland who were unable to pay their own way.

In 1833, agents for the Church purchased 103 acres from French for a sum of five thousand dollars; this land included the property upon which the Kirtland Temple was built. This property, along with other pieces of land, operated on the principle of stewardship and made a home available to those who otherwise might not be able to afford it. It is ironic that French, who earlier had driven the poor from Kirtland, was now responsible for providing the land whereupon the poor among the Saints might remain. (HR, 36–37, 73.)

Fruit of . . . Loins

"The loins," said President Harold B. Lee, "are those portions of the body between the lower ribs and the hips in which are located the vital generative organs" (SHP, 330). The fruit of the loins is the product of those procreative powers, that is, one's posterity (D&C 132:30; 2 Ne. 3:5).
See also: Offspring; Seed

Full Purpose of Heart

The Lord declared that the Twelve Apostles "are they who shall desire to take upon them my name with full purpose of heart" (D&C 18:27). To cleave unto God (Acts 11:23) or to turn to him with full purpose of heart (Mosiah 7:33) is to do so with one's entire being, without reservations. It is to set one's course and not look back or turn to the right or to the left (see Luke 9:62).
See also: Letter of the Gospel; Singleness of Heart

Fuller, Edson

One of a number of brethren residing in Ohio in June 1831 who received a call to "journey to the land of Missouri" was Edson Fuller (D&C 52:28). There is no evidence that Fuller fulfilled this mission call. Later that same year he was stripped of his priesthood and soon left the Church.

Fuller's Soap

The Savior shall be like a "refiner's fire, and like fuller's soap," declared the Prophet Joseph (D&C 128:24). This is a description which Malachi applied to the second coming of Christ

(Mal. 3:2), and which the resurrected Lord also quoted to the Nephites (3 Ne. 24:2).

Anciently, a fuller was one who cleansed and whitened garments. "The process of fulling or cleansing clothes consisted in treading or stamping on the garments with the feet or with bats in tubs of water, in which some alkaline substance answering the purpose of soap had been dissolved" (Peloubet, 203–4).

Christ's blood is the only "fuller's soap" strong enough to remove all stains of sin from those who repent and fully accept his atoning sacrifice (1 Ne. 12:11; Mosiah 3:11–18; Alma 5:27; 13:11). "Though your sins be as scarlet, they shall be as white as snow," declared the Lord (Isa. 1:18). However, the blood of Christ will have no cleansing effect upon the wicked, for the stain of sin shall remain on their garments (D&C 29:17).

Fullmer, David

The only mention of David Fullmer in the Doctrine and Covenants is in conjunction with his service as a high councilor in Nauvoo (D&C 124:132). However, his name was well known in the circles of the Saints of early days. He joined the Church on September 16, 1836, and to his dying day was devoted to duties therein. He first served on the Nauvoo high council in 1839, and later served as a member of the Nauvoo city council, the Council of Fifty, and "The Living Constitution"—a committee appointed to settle difficulties between different factions. He was one of the captains of hundreds appointed to lead the Saints in their westward trek and served in the presidency at Garden Grove, Iowa.

At the time of the martyrdoms of Joseph and Hyrum Smith, Fullmer was on an electioneering mission for the Prophet in the latter's quest for the United States presidency. Fullmer served as the first counselor in the Salt Lake Stake and served as acting president for four years while the president served a mission to England. He served in various civic functions in the valleys of the west, including being a member of the legislature.

Prior to his death on October 21, 1879, he was serving as a patriarch. One biographer gave the following tribute to Fullmer: "At the time of his decease he was in full fellowship, beloved and respected by all his associates." (Jenson 1:289–91.)

Fulness, A

See: Fulness of the Glory of the Father

Fulness, His

See: Fulness of the Glory of the Father

Fulness of My Glory

See: Fulness of the Glory of the Father

Fulness of My Scriptures

In 1831, the Lord informed Joseph Smith that he did not yet possess a fulness of the scriptures (D&C 42:15, 56–58). This was during the time in which the Prophet was preparing the "new translation," or "inspired version," of the Bible. The Book of Mormon had been published in 1830, but the Doctrine and Covenants and the Pearl of Great Price were yet to be either published or accepted as canonized scripture. It was not until 1880 that the four volumes constituting our present scriptures were accepted as standard works of the Church.

Revelation, of course, is an ongoing process, and scripture—such as the revelation on priesthood received by the First Presidency in June 1978—is constantly being unfolded to the Lord's prophets (see En., November 1978, p. 16). The developmental nature of revelation was stressed by Brigham Young, who said: "I do not even believe that there is a single revelation, among the many God has given to the Church, that is perfect *in its fulness*. The revelations of God contain correct doctrine and principle, so far as they go; but it is impossible for the . . . inhabitants of the earth to receive revelation from the Almighty in all its perfections. He has to speak to us in a manner to meet the extent of our capacities." (JD 2:314; italics added.)

We, therefore, anticipate that the future will find the heavens continuing to distill divine revelation upon the heads of the faithful Saints of God (D&C 121:33; Articles of Faith 1:9). The fulness of the scriptures is "the key of knowledge" (JST, Luke 11:53).

Fulness of the Earth

At the time of the creation, God gave man stewardship over all things to the end that he might use them wisely for his "food and for raiment, for taste and for smell, to strengthen the body and to enliven the soul" (D&C 59:19; see also D&C 49:19; 89; Gen. 1:27–31; Moses 2:20–31). The "fulness of the earth" (D&C 59:16) is everything God has ordained for the use of men which the earth provides. To paraphrase the psalmist, "The earth is the Lord's, and the fulness thereof" is his to give (Ps. 24:1; 1 Cor. 10:26, 28).

Fulness of the Glory of the Father

The "fulness of the glory of the Father" (D&C 93:16) is elsewhere expressed as "his fulness" (D&C 76:20), "fulness of the Father" (D&C 76:77), "fulness of his glory" (D&C 84:24), "a fulness" (D&C 93:12–13, 27), and "fulness of my glory" (D&C 132:6). It is also synonymous with, or applies to, those who receive "eternal life" (D&C 81:6), "his rest" (D&C 84:24), and "continuation of the seeds forever and ever" (D&C 132:19). Elder Bruce R. McConkie has written: "The 'fulness of the glory of the Father' consists in the possession of 'all power, both in heaven and on earth.' (D&C 93:16–17.) God is an exalted Man, and exaltation consists in having the fulness of all powers, all attributes, and all perfections. (D&C 76:93; 132.)" (MD, 300.)

President George Q. Cannon made the following observation: "I know that we are apt to think that heaven is a sort of spiritual place. It is spiritual; but God our Eternal Father is a *being of power.* He controls the earth and the inhabitants thereof; He controls the elements of the earth; and we are promised that we shall be sharers with Him. *He will give us an equal interest in all this power and authority.* . . . We will be His heirs; we will be (if I may use the term without irreverence) co-partners with Him in all this power and authority." (CR, April 1899, pp. 64–65; italics added.)

This promise of joint-heirship with the Father is made to those righteous Saints who do *all* that is required to inherit such a godly glory and position of power (D&C 76:50–70; 81:6; 84:33–38; 88:22; 93:27; 130:20–21). Joseph Smith described "joint heirs" as those who "inherit the same power, the same glory and the same exaltation, until you arrive at the station of a God, and ascend the throne of eternal power, the same as those who have gone before" (TPJS, 347).

The "fulness of the glory of the Father" will only be found among those who have received the necessary ordinances and lived lives worthy of an inheritance in the highest heaven or degree of the celestial glory (D&C 131:1–4; 76:58).

See also: Continuation of the Lives; Continuation of the Seeds; Eternal Life; Eternal Lives; Gods; Increase; Power of Godliness

Fulness of the Gospel

There are fourteen references to the "fulness of the gospel" in the Doctrine and Covenants. Of these, four of them specifically mention that the Book of Mormon contains this fulness (D&C 20:9; 27:5; 42:12; 135:3).

In response to the question as to what constitutes the fulness, President Joseph Fielding Smith said that the Lord "did not mean to convey the impression that every truth belonging to exaltation in the kingdom of God was recorded in the Book of Mormon. . . . Neither would this statement imply that every truth belonging to the celestial kingdom and exaltation therein was to be found within the covers of the Book of Mormon. There are many truths belonging to the exaltation that have not been revealed, nor will they be revealed to man while he is in mortality. . . .

"It is evident that there are many things that belong to the exaltation which are reserved for immortal glorified souls. The *ful-*

ness of the gospel then, as expressed in the Doctrine and Covenants, has reference to the *principles of salvation by which we attain unto this glory.* Therefore, the Lord has revealed in the Book of Mormon all that is needful to direct people who are willing to hearken to its precepts, to a *fulness of the blessings of the kingdom of God.* The Book of Mormon then, does contain all the truths which are essential for Gentiles and Jews or any other people, to prepare them for this glorious exaltation in the celestial kingdom of God." (AGQ 3:95–96; italics added.)

The Lord himself described the fulness of the gospel as "the covenant which I have sent forth to recover my people, which are of the house of Israel" (D&C 39:11). This recovery occurs as men, women, and children of the age of accountability accept the gospel and comply with its ordinances (Articles of Faith 1:4–5). President Harold B. Lee identified Doctrine and Covenants 39:6 as a "one-sentence" statement which defines the "fulness of the gospel" (SHP, 50–51).

Fulness of the Priesthood

From 1829 to 1836, the Prophet Joseph Smith received a series of sacred keys pertaining to the priesthood from such heavenly messengers as John the Baptist, Peter, James, John, Elijah, Moses, and Elias (D&C 2; 13; 27:12–13; 110). In January 1841, however, the Lord revealed that the "fulness of the priesthood" was not held by the Prophet, for there was no place yet on the earth where the Lord could "restore" such a blessing (D&C 124:28). Thus, the need for a temple at Nauvoo was revealed.

Joseph later stated that "if a man gets a fullness of the priesthood of God, he has to get it in the same way that Jesus Christ obtained it, and that was by *keeping all the commandments and obeying all the ordinances of the house of the Lord*" (TPJS, 308; italics added). President Joseph Fielding Smith declared, "You cannot receive the fulness of the priesthood and the fulness of eternal reward unless you receive the ordinances of the house of the Lord; and when you receive these ordinances, the door is then open so you can obtain all the blessings which any man can gain" (CR, April 1970, p. 58).

President Smith then added this observation: "Do not think because someone has a higher office in the Church than you have that you are barred from receiving the fullness of the Lord's blessings. You can have them sealed upon you as an elder, if you are faithful; and when you receive them, and live faithfully and keep these covenants, you then have all that any man can get."

See also: Endowment; Temple

Fulness of Times

See: Dispensation of the Fulness of Times

G

Gabriel

The angel Gabriel is mentioned but once in the Doctrine and Covenants (D&C 128:21). The Prophet Joseph indentified Gabriel as the prophet Noah, who "stands next in authority to Adam in the Priesthood" (TPJS, 157). This is the same being who announced the forthcoming birth of John the Baptist to his astonished father, Zacharias, in the temple (Luke 1:19).

In like fashion, Gabriel manifested the mission Mary was to perform as the mother of the Messiah (Luke 1:26–38). He undoubtedly was also the angel who counseled the troubled Joseph, earthly husband of Mary, giving him spiritual strength to perform his important role in this divine drama (Matt. 1:18–25).

According to Joseph Fielding Smith, Gabriel was the *Elias*, who appeared in the Kirtland Temple and restored the keys of the dispensation of the gospel of Abraham to the Prophet Joseph Smith and Oliver Cowdery (D&C 110:12; AGQ 3:139–40). Other sources are not as definitive in declaring Gabriel to be *the* Elias who appeared on that sacred occasion (LDSBD, 663).

See also: Dispensation of the Gospel of Abraham; Elias; Noah

Gad

The man Gad is an unidentified individual who received the priesthood from Esaias and in turn bestowed it upon Jeremy (D&C 84:10–11). He is *not* one of the sons of Jacob (Gen. 30:11) nor the Gad who was the prophet-friend of David (1 Sam. 22:5; LDSBD, 676).

Galatia

Among the Saints to whom the Apostle Peter wrote his first epistle were those residing in Galatia (1 Pet. 1:1). President Joseph F. Smith referred to this location in his vision of the redemption of the dead (D&C 138:5). Galatia was a Roman province in the center of Asia Minor and can be easily seen on maps 20 and 21 in the LDS edition of the King James Version of the Bible (see also LDSBD, 676–77).

Galland, Isaac

Of Isaac Galland, the Lord said: "I . . . love him for the work he hath done, and will forgive all his sins" (D&C 124:78–79). Galland was instructed to buy stock in the Nauvoo House and to accompany Hyrum Smith on an assignment given by the Prophet Joseph. He was baptized and ordained an elder on July 3, 1839, by Joseph Smith (HC 3:393). He is first mentioned in the Prophet's history on February 25, 1839, with the prefix "Dr." attached to his name.

Galland encouraged the Saints to settle at Commerce, Illinois, which was to become the site of Nauvoo and which Joseph mentions as "a providential introduction." His early sympathies for the Church are expressed in this excerpt from a letter written at that time: "I wish to serve your cause in any matter which Providence may afford me the opportunity of doing, and I therefore request that you feel no hesitancy or reluctance in communicating to me your wishes, at all times and on any subject" (HC 3:265–67).

According to a letter dated September 11, 1839, Galland moved his family to Kirtland, Ohio, and corresponded with the Prophet Joseph (HC 4:8–9). In March 1840, he was mentioned as one who would be qualified to testify in behalf of the Church before Congress (HC 4:97).

The last mention of Galland in published history indicates that he was in some difficulty with the Church, for on January 18, 1842, Joseph revoked the power of attorney he had previously given Galland; two days later at a special conference of the Church it was voted that the "trustee-in-trust (should) proceed with Dr. Galland's affairs in relation to the Church, as he shall judge most expedient" (HC 4:495–500). Galland did not return to Church activity.

Garden of Eden

The garden known as Eden was the sacred sanctuary created by God wherein the first man, Adam, and the first woman, Eve, were placed and joined together in holy matrimony (Gen. 2; 3; Moses 3; 4). Here Adam and Eve dwelt in innocence until, after partaking of the forbidden fruit, they were driven from the garden's lush surroundings into "the lone and dreary world" wherein their "bread" would come by "sweat" and arduous labor.

The location of this former paradise has been prophetically revealed. On March 30, 1873, Brigham Young announced that the Prophet Joseph had taught him "that the Garden of Eden was in Jackson County, Missouri" (WW, 481). Brother Brigham had previously identified the American continent as the land of the Garden of Eden (JD 8:195). This was consistent with the teachings of his apostolic colleague, Elder George Q. Cannon, who indicated that the garden was located in the spot designated for the "centre stake of Zion," or, Independence, Jackson County, Missouri (JD 11:336–37; D&C 57:1–3; 84:1–3).

President Joseph Fielding Smith emphatically announced that *"the Garden of Eden was on the American continent located where the City Zion, or the New Jerusalem, will be built"* (DS 3:74). Had Adam and Eve not transgressed, they would have remained in the garden "and they would have had no children; wherefore they would have remained in a state of innocence, having no joy, for they knew no misery; doing no good, for they knew no sin. . . . Adam fell that men might be; and men are that they might have joy." (2 Ne. 2:22–25.)

See also: Fall; First Death; Forbidden Fruit; New Jerusalem

Garments

See: Beautiful Garments; Garments . . . Pure and White; Garments Spotted with the Flesh; Marriage of the Lamb; Rid Their Garments; Unspotted

Garments . . . Pure and White

The angel Moroni's clothing is referred to as garments that are "pure and white above all other whiteness" (D&C 20:6; see also JS—H 1:31–32). This celestial clothing is symbolic of the spotless nature and utter cleanliness of those who dwell in the presence of Deity. Such spotlessness is a requirement of those who desire to serve God and gain his eternal presence (see D&C 61:34; 109:76; 135:5).

Elder Bruce R. McConkie noted: "We clean our garments by washing them in water. Filth, dirt, germs, odors, and whatever is unclean and offensive is thus removed; our wearing apparel becomes clean and spotless. A saved person is one whose soul is clean and spotless, one who is free from the filth and corruption of sin; and the prophetic way of describing such a person is to say that his garments are clean. Since the only way a human soul can be cleansed and perfect is through the atonement of Christ, it follows that the symbolic way of describing this process is to say that such a one has washed his garments in the blood of the Lamb." (PM, 251.)

See also: Garments Spotted with the Flesh; Holiness; Pure; Rid Their Garments; Unspotted

Garments Spotted with the Flesh

The Lord has commanded that we hate "the garments spotted with the flesh" (D&C 36:6). Similar expressions are found in the New Testament (Jude 1:23; Rev. 3:4). "This is symbolic language," said Joseph Fielding Smith, "yet is plain to understand. This is an untoward generation, walking in spiritual darkness, and the punishment for sin is spoken of as punishment in fire. Garments spotted with flesh are garments defiled by the practices of carnal desires and disobedience to the commandments of the Lord." (CHMR 1:163.)

"He that overcometh, the same shall be clothed in white raiment; and I will not blot out his name out of the book of life" (Rev. 3:5).

See also: Filthy; Garments Pure and White; Uncleanness

Gates of Hell

On a number of occasions the Lord promises protection to the Saints from the power of the adversary, stating that if they are faithful and build upon his rock, "the gates of hell shall not prevail against them" (D&C 10:69; 17:8; 18:5; 21:6; 33:13; 98:22; 128:10). "The gates of hell are the entrances to the benighted realms of the damned where the wicked go to await the day when they shall come forth in the resurrection of damnation. Those beckoning gates prevail against all who pass through them. But those who obey the laws and ordinances of the gospel have the promise that the gates of hell shall not prevail against them." (DNTC 1:388–89.)

See also: Hell

Gathering

"One of the most important points in the faith of the Church of the Latter-day Saints . . . is the gathering of Israel," said the Prophet Joseph (TPJS, 92–93). Shortly after the Church was organized, the Lord specified the responsibility of the members thereof to gather his elect (D&C 29:7). Several years later, the Prophet petitioned the Lord to appoint stakes of Zion in order that the gathering of the Lord's people would roll forth in great power and majesty (D&C 109:59).

As the people of the earth accept the gospel, they are gathered into stakes and wards where the celestial refining process continues. A modern-day prophet, Spencer W. Kimball, has said: "The 'gathering of Israel' is effected when the people of the faraway countries accept the gospel and remain in their native lands" (En., May 1975, p. 4).

In contrast to earlier days, in order for one to be gathered today, it is not necessary to take a long journey to some distant place. Saints are counseled to gather locally, to make their homelands "holy places" (D&C 101:22). "Verily . . . , where two or three are gathered together in my name . . . , there will I be in the midst of them" (D&C 6:32).

Whether through missionary endeavors for the living, or temple work for the dead, the work of gathering continues, for "there is no other way for the Saints to be saved in these last days, (than by the gathering)" (TPJS, 183).

See also: Work of Gathering

Gause, Jesse

The name of Jesse Gause does not appear in pre-1981 editions of the Doctrine and Covenants and only appears in the introduction to section 81 in the 1981 edition. Under the date of March 8, 1832, the Prophet Joseph Smith wrote: "Chose this day and ordained brother Jesse Gause and Brother Sidney [Rigdon] to be my counselors of the ministry of the high Priesthood" (Kirtland Revelation Book, p. 10; see also BYUS 15:362–64).

Gause evidently failed to fulfill his assignment and the appointment and promised blessings were transferred to Frederick G. Williams, whose name appears in the revelation, and to whom the revelation was then addressed (D&C 81).

See also: Williams, Frederick G.

Gazelam

In three different revelations, spanning a period of two years (1832–34), Joseph Smith was called "Gazelam" by the Lord (D&C 78:9; 82:11; 104:26, 43, 45, 46; pre-1981 edition). His name was disguised in order to prevent his enemies from discovering what plans the Lord had in mind at that particular time (HC 1:255).

In the Book of Mormon, Alma reveals the following use of the word *Gazelem:* "And the Lord said: I will prepare unto my servant Gazelem, a stone, which shall shine forth in darkness unto light, that I may discover unto my people who serve me" (Alma 37:23; italics added). The meaning of Gazelem is discussed by Reynolds and Sjodahl: "Gazelem

is a name given to a servant of God. The word appears to have its roots in Gaz—a stone, and Aleim, a name of God as a revelator, or the interposer in the affairs of men. If this suggestion is correct, its roots admirably agree with its apparent meaning—a seer." (CBM 4:162.) With this in mind, it is appropriate that such a name was applied to God's seer on earth—the Prophet Joseph Smith.

See also: Smith, Joseph, Jr.

Gems for the Sanctified

The names of the prophet-martyrs Joseph and Hyrum Smith shall "go down to posterity as gems for the sanctified," declared John Taylor (D&C 135:6). Just as a gem is a jewel to be prized, so are the names of Joseph and Hyrum Smith to be prized by the Saints through the generations. Their names are held in honor by the pure in heart.

General Assembly

The term *general assembly,* appearing without another qualifying component, is found only in Doctrine and Covenants 107:32. It has reference to a combined assembly of the General Authorities who comprise the three basic quorums of the Church; namely, the First Presidency, Quorum of the Twelve, and First Quorum of the Seventy (see D&C 107:22–35).

General Assembly and Church of the Firstborn

The phrase *general assembly and church of the Firstborn* appears three times in scripture (D&C 76:67; 107:19; Heb. 12:23). The "general assembly" appears to be the congregation of exalted beings who will inherit a celestial sphere and will comprise the church of the Firstborn.

See also: Church of the Firstborn

General Authorities

Although it is an often-used term among Latter-day Saints today, the term *general authorities* appears but once in the Doctrine and Covenants (102:32). At the time of this revelation, February 17, 1834, the First Presidency was the only "general" quorum of authority in the Church. That is to say, it was the only standing quorum with general jurisdiction over the entire Church. The minutes of the meeting during which this revelation was received speak of the "traveling high council composed of the twelve apostles" (D&C 102:30). However, these twelve "general authorities" were not chosen for another year.

Inasmuch as the revelation applies to the structure of the Church in our day, it is necessary to identify the meaning of General Authorities today. At the present time, those who receive this designation are the following: members of the First Presidency, Quorum of the Twelve, First Quorum of the Seventy, the Presiding Bishopric, and the Patriarch to the Church. This latter position was made emeritus in 1979 (CR, Oct. 1979, p. 25).

General Authorities are given general jurisdiction over the entire Church rather than being confined to a local area. Their authority is in a vertical descent from the First Presidency to the Twelve to the Seventy, with the higher quorum taking precedence over the lower one (D&C 107:22–34). One of their number has written: "Though general authorities are authorities in the sense of having power to administer church affairs, they may or may not be authorities in the sense of doctrinal knowledge, the intricacies of church procedures, or the receipt of the promptings of the Spirit. A call to an administrative position of itself adds little knowledge or power of discernment to an individual, although every person called to a position in the Church does grow in grace, knowledge, and power by magnifying the calling given him." (MD, 309.)

See also: Apostle; First Presidency of the Church; Seventy, The; Spiritual Authorities of the Church

General Church Book

From the beginning of the Church, the counsel has been to

maintain accurate records (D&C 20:83; 21:1; 47:1; 69:2–3; 85:1; 128:4). The "general church record," or "general church book," comprises all the recorded information stored by the Church in its archives. Both the Church and the individuals in it will be judged by the contents of these records. Therefore, "the matter of record keeping is one of the most important duties devolving on the Church" (CHMR 1:103).

See also: Book of the Law of God; General Recorder; Record

General Church Record

See: General Church Book

General Recorder

In September 1892, Joseph Smith wrote the Saints an epistle in which he instructed them to verify their ordinances by the use of "ward recorders," or as we now know them, ward clerks. These recorders would in turn present their records to a "general recorder" who would record the information received on the general Church book. (D&C 128:1–7.) The positions of "Church Recorder," "Church Historian," and "General Church Clerk" were apparently intermingled during the early period of the Church (ECH, 586–88). Oliver Cowdery was the first Church Recorder, pursuant to the request by the Lord that a "record" be kept (D&C 21:1). At the time of this revelation, James Sloan was serving as the General Church Clerk. Three months later, Willard Richards was appointed as the Church Historian and the following summer was named as the General Church Recorder. This responsibility is now under the direction of the Church Historical Department. (CA 1978, 250–51.)

See also: Book of the Law of God; General Church Book; Record

Generation

A "generation," according to Webster, is generally considered to be a "body of living beings constituting a single step in the line of descent from an ancestor." A question arises when one narrowly considers the 1832 proclamation that the temple in Zion "shall be reared in *this* generation" (D&C 84:4–5; italics added). President Joseph Fielding Smith noted that "this statement has been a stumbling block to some and there have been various interpretations of the meaning of a generation. It is held by some that a generation is one hundred years; by others that it is one hundred and twenty years; by others that generation as expressed in this and other scriptures has reference to a period of time which is indefinite. The Savior said: 'An evil and adulterous generation seeketh after a sign.' This did not have reference to a period of years, but to a period of weakness. *A generation may mean the time of this present dispensation. . . .* It is not our intention to place any interpretation on this expression, but to say that these matters are in the hands of the Lord and he will accomplish his purposes when he considers that the time has come." (CHMR 1:337; italics added.)

Smith and Sjodahl added, "It is quite possible that a complete explanation of it, cannot be obtained until it is fulfilled. That is the case with many divine predictions. When they are fulfilled they are clear." (SS, 497.)

To speak of "generation to generation" (D&C 127:9) or "to all generations" (D&C 109:24) means forever.

See also: Blood of This Generation; Generation of Vipers; Untoward Generation

Generation of Vipers

In a firm declaration of displeasure, the Lord referred to those who had discomforted, driven, murdered, and testified against his people as "a generation of vipers" (D&C 121:23). According to Webster, a viper is "a dangerous, treacherous, or malignant person." The name is taken from a poisonous snake that is common in Europe and whose name had generally been applied to various venomous creatures. The fiends who so mistreated the Saints in the early days would certainly qualify as "a generation of vipers" under this definition.

Gentiles

The term *Gentiles* is one of the most often used yet least understood words in Mormon culture. Its usage in scripture generally refers to those who are not of the house of Israel (descendants of Abraham through the lineage of Jacob and his twelve sons). However, the principle of adoption applies to all who join The Church of Jesus Christ of Latter-day Saints; they become of Israel regardless of their blood lines (Abr. 2:9–11; Gal. 3:26–29; TPJS, 149–50).

The term *Gentile* has been used in the following ways: (1) to refer to the descendants of Noah's son, Japheth (Gen. 10:1–5); (2) to identify those who have not descended from Abraham; (3) to classify those who have not descended from Jacob; (4) to identify those who have not descended from Judah; and (5) to distinguish the "non-Mormon." It is interesting to note that the term *Gentile* has been translated as "not of Judah" in both the German (*Nichtjuden*) and Dutch (*Niet-Joden*) editions of the Book of Mormon.

Elder Bruce R. McConkie has written: "After the Kingdom of Israel was destroyed and the Ten Tribes were led away into Assyrian captivity, those of the Kingdom of Judah called themselves Jews and designated all others as Gentiles. It is this concept that would have been taught to Lehi, Mulek and the other Jews who came to the Western Hemisphere to found the great Nephite and Lamanite civilizations. It is not surprising, therefore, to find the Book of Mormon repeatedly speaking of Jew and Gentile as though this phrase marked a division between all men; to find the United States described as a Gentile Nation (1 Ne. 13; 3 Ne. 21); and to find the promise that the Book of Mormon would come forth 'by way of the Gentile!' (Title page of Book of Mormon; D&C 20:9.)

"Actually, of course, the house of Israel has been scattered among nations, and Joseph Smith (through whom the Book of Mormon was revealed) was of the Tribe of Ephraim. At the same time the Prophet was of the Gentiles, meaning that he was a citizen of a Gentile Nation and also that he was not a Jew. Members of the Church in general are both of Israel and of the Gentiles. Indeed, the gospel has come forth in the last days in the *times of the Gentiles* and, in large measure, will not go to the Jews until the *Gentile fulness* comes in. (D&C 45:28–30.)" (MD, 311.)

See also: Times of the Gentiles

Gift of Aaron

In addition to the "gift of revelation" (D&C 8:3–4) which Oliver Cowdery possessed, he was promised the "gift of Aaron" (D&C 8:6–7). "Aaron was the elder brother of Moses. Being prompted by the Spirit of the Lord, he met his younger brother in the wilderness and accompa-

nied him to Egypt. He introduced him to the children of Israel in the land of Goshen. He was his spokesman before Pharaoh, and he assisted him in opening up the dispensation which Moses was commissioned to proclaim. (Exodus 4:27–31.) This was the gift of Aaron. In some respects Oliver Cowdery was the Aaron of the new and last dispensation." (SS, 44; see also CHMR 1:52.)

Oliver delivered the first public discourse after the organization of the Church (HC 1:81).

See also: Aaron; Cowdery, Oliver; First Preacher

Gift of the Holy Ghost

Joseph Smith announced, "there is a difference between the Holy Ghost and the gift of the Holy Ghost. Cornelius received the Holy Ghost before he was baptized, which was the convincing power of God unto him of the truth of the Gospel, but he could not receive the gift of the Holy Ghost until after he was baptized. Had he not taken this sign or ordinance upon him, the Holy Ghost which convinced him of the truth of God, would have left him." (TPJS, 199; Acts 10.)

The gift of the Holy Ghost, which is to be given by the laying on of the hands of the elders of the church" (D&C 49:14), is the second half of baptism. The Prophet proclaimed, "Baptism by water is but half a baptism, and is good for nothing without the other half—that is, the baptism of the Holy Ghost" (TPJS, 314). This gift "cannot be received through the medium of any other principle than the principle of righteousness, for if the proposals are not complied with, it is of no use, but withdraws" (TPJS, 148).

President Harold B. Lee declared that "the bestowal of the gift is actually . . . a command to so live that when we need and desire it, we may have the accompaniment of the power of the Holy Ghost." He further stated: "It's like all other gifts. If I have something to give you and you won't receive it, then I haven't given you a gift, have I? It's only a gift when you receive it." (SHP, 57; see also D&C 88:33.)

President Joseph Fielding Smith defined the gift of the Holy Ghost as "nothing more nor less than the right to the companionship of the Holy Ghost" (DS 1:40). "Every man may receive . . . a manifestation from the Holy Ghost when he is seeking for the truth, but not the power to call upon the Holy Ghost whenever he feels he needs the help, as a man does who is a member of the Church" (DS 1:42).

See also: Baptism of Fire; Confirm

Gift of Tongues

In the dedicatory prayer of the Kirtland Temple, the Prophet Joseph petitioned the Lord to "let the gift of tongues be poured out upon thy people" (D&C 109:36). This request was in the context of a reference to the outpourings of the Spirit on the ancient day of Pentecost when the disciples received the companionship of the personage of the Holy Ghost (Acts 2:1-17).

Five years later, the Prophet declared that "the gift of tongues by the power of the Holy Ghost in the Church, is for the benefit of the servants of God to preach to unbelievers, as on the day of Pentecost" (TPJS, 195). On another occasion he admonished the Saints: "Be not so curious about tongues, do not speak in tongues except there be an interpreter present; the ultimate design of tongues is to speak to foreigners" (TPJS, 247; 1 Cor. 14:27–28).

One of the evidences of the Lord's granting the Prophet's petition can be seen in the tens of thousands of missionaries who are "speaking in tongues" as they declare the message of the Restoration to the peoples of the earth. "For it shall come to pass . . . that every man shall hear the fulness of the gospel in his own tongue, and in his own language, through those who are ordained unto this power, by the administration of the Comforter" (D&C 90:11). The "gift of tongues" is one of the cardinal beliefs of the Latter-day Saints (Articles of Faith 1:7); (AF, 224–25).

See also: Interpretation of Tongues; Speak with Tongues

Gift, Possessed by Hyrum Smith

In Doctrine and Covenants 11:10, the Lord declared that Hyrum Smith possessed a "gift."

According to his grandson, "the great gift which he possessed was that of a *tender, sympathetic heart; a merciful spirit.* The Lord on a later occasion said: 'Blessed is my servant Hyrum Smith; for I, the Lord, love him because of the integrity of his heart, and because he loveth that which is right before me, saith the Lord.' (D&C 124:15.) This great gift was manifest in his jealous watch care over the Prophet lest some harm come to him." (CHMR 1:57; italics added.)

Smith and Sjodahl added, "His special gift . . . was the *possession, in an abundant measure, of the Spirit of Christ Jesus.* . . . Justice, humility, and righteousness, and, it may be added, a merciful disposition, were exemplified in the life of Hyrum Smith, because he had the Spirit of Christ and was guided by it." (SS, 62; italics added.)

See also: Smith, Hyrum

Gift, Possessed by Joseph Smith

The "gift" which Joseph Smith temporarily lost in the summer of 1828 was the seeric gift of translating the ancient Nephite records by the power of inspiration (D&C 10:2). His "mind became darkened" because he had lost the divine light which had previously illuminated his understanding. This came about as the natural consequence of his disobedience and willful neglect which led to the loss of 116 pages of translated manuscript.

See also: Book of Lehi; Smith, Joseph, Jr.

Gift, Possessed by Oliver Cowdery

The special "gift" which Oliver Cowdery possessed was the "spirit of revelation" (D&C 8:2–4; CHMR 1:43); it was the "special gift to understand the 'still, small voice' of the Spirit . . . if he would follow it" (SS, 43).

See also: Cowdery, Oliver

Gifts of the Spirit

See: Differences of Administration; Discerning of Spirits; Diversities of Operations; Healing; Interpretation of Tongues; Miracles; Patriarchal Blessing; Prophesy; Speak with Tongues; Word of Knowledge; Word of Wisdom (#1)

Gifts Once Given Oliver Cowdery

In 1841, Hyrum Smith was released from serving as second counselor in the First Presidency and called as Patriarch to the Church (D&C 124:91) and as Assistant President of the Church (D&C 124:94–95; 1978 CA, 101). In this latter capacity, he was given the "keys" and "crowned with the same blessing, and glory, and honor and priesthood, and gifts of the priesthood, that once were put upon . . . Oliver Cowdery."

Regarding this calling, President Joseph Fielding Smith wrote: "With many members of the Church Hyrum Smith was just the Patriarch. Hyrum Smith received a double portion. He received the office of Patriarch which belonged to his father and came to him by right, and also received the keys to be 'Second President' and precede the counselors as Oliver Cowdery had done. So he would have remained as President of the Church had he not died a martyr." (DS 1:221.)

See also: Cowdery, Oliver; Office of Priesthood and Patriarch; Smith, Hyrum

Gilbert, Algernon Sidney

"The Lord had few more devoted servants in this dispensation," said one historian of Algernon Sidney Gilbert (HC 2:118). His able business skills made him an invaluable asset to the early Church. Gilbert was called by revelation to serve as "an agent" for the Church in its business dealings (D&C 53). "Business talents," wrote Smith and Sjodahl, "when consecrated to the service of mankind, are just as good and necessary as so-called spiritual gifts. It is only when they are used to serve the purposes of selfishness and greed that they become a snare and a curse. In the service of the Lord they are a blessing. As an agent

he [Gilbert] could help in building up the Church." (SS, 313.)

Further mention of Gilbert throughout the Doctrine and Covenants is always in conjunction with his business stewardship for the Church (57:6, 8, 9; 61:7, 9, 12; 64:18, 26; 90:35; 101:96). Although he occasionally fell into human errors (D&C 90:35), for which he was chastized, his commitment to the Church was such that he not only sacrificed of his time but also offered his life as a ransom for his fellow Saints on one occasion (HC 1:394).

On June 23, 1833, the Prophet Joseph penned the following remarks: "Algernon Sidney Gilbert was called and chosen, and appointed to receive his endowment in Kirtland, and to assist in gathering up the strength of the Lord's house, and to proclaim the everlasting Gospel until Zion is redeemed. But he said he 'could not do it.' " (HC 2:113.) Three days later he died of cholera. Of this event Joseph wrote, "He had been called to preach the Gospel, but had been known to say that he 'would rather die than go forth to preach the Gospel to the Gentiles.' " Elder Heber C. Kimball added, "The Lord took him at his word" (HC 2:118).

See also: Mahalaleel (#1)

Gird Up Your Loins

To all who have sung the hymn, "Come, Come, Ye Saints," (Hymns, no. 30), the admonition to "gird up your loins" is a familiar phrase. There are eleven instances of the Lord giving this same admonition in the Doctrine and Covenants. In conjunction therewith, he has used such phrases as "be prepared" (38:9) and "be faithful" (75:22).

President Harold B. Lee has said, "The loins are those portions of the body between the lower ribs and the hips in which are located the vital generative organs . . . , the loins symbolize virtue or moral purity and vital strength" (SHP, 330–31). Cruden's *Concordance* indicates that "to gird up one's loins" is "an allusion to the custom of the Oriental nations, who wearing long loose garments were wont to gird them about their loins, that they might not hinder them in their traveling or working."

Webster defines *gird* as "to encircle or fasten . . . , surround . . . , clothe or invest with power . . . , prepare for a struggle." Thus, if one has girded up his loins, he has clothed himself with power in preparation for the ongoing struggle with Satan, that father of lies who would rob one of virtue and spiritual strength. To have girded up one's loins is to be prepared and protected by the power of God. One so "girded" is not encumbered with loose and ill-fitting principles or sins that might cause one to spiritually stumble and lose the battle for his soul.

Glory

Elder James E. Talmage has written: "The false assump-

tion . . . that in the hereafter there shall be but two places, states, or conditions for the souls of mankind—heaven and hell, with the same glory in all parts of the one and the same terrors throughout the other—is untenable in the light of divine revelation. Through the direct word of the Lord we learn of varied kingdoms or glories." (AF, 91.) The Doctrine and Covenants confirms the doctrine which Paul declared, namely, that there are various degrees of glory enthroned in resurrected bodies "and your glory shall be the glory by which your bodies are quickened" (D&C 76:70, 71, 81; 88:22–32; 1 Cor. 15:40–44).

These *glorified* individuals will be assigned to dwell in kingdoms of glory in like nature to their bodies. One's glory becomes the result of the way in which his life has been lived. If it has been lived in accordance with godly principles, then it will have gathered to it an abundance of celestial light, or glory. If principles have been violated, then darkness has replaced light and one's glory will be accordingly less brilliant. Thus, "God will give to every man a glory that will be suited to his condition" (GT 1:97).

Joseph Smith stated that God's whole purpose in placing us here upon the earth was to put us in a position where we could "advance like himself" and "be exalted with himself" so that we "might have one glory upon another" (TPJS, 354). President George Q. Cannon observed that "each one of us will receive glory far beyond anything that we can possibly conceive of, even if we have been sinners. But it is far better to repent of our sins and have them blotted out, so that we may receive the greater glory and the greater exaltation." (GT 1:121.)

Only the sons of perdition will be resurrected without a condition of glory (D&C 88:24, 32).

See also: Celestial Kingdom; Eye Single to the Glory of God; Fulness of My Glory; Fulness of the Glory of the Father; Intelligence; Kingdom Which Is Not a Kingdom of Glory; Paradisiacal Glory; Telestial; Terrestrial

Gnashing of Teeth

The description of the wicked as "weeping, wailing and gnashing of teeth" upon their receiving the divine decrees pronounced upon them is common in scripture (D&C 19:5; 85:9; 101:91; 124:8, 52; 133:73; Alma 40:13; Moses 1:22; Matt. 8:12).

"In the literal sense, the *gnashing of teeth* consists in grinding and striking the teeth together in anger. This expressive act, indicative of hate and violent animosity was adopted by the prophets as the proverbial way of portraying the intensity of the weeping, wailing, and sorrow of the ungodly. Wicked men gnash their teeth at the anointed of the Lord in this life. (Job 16:9; Ps. 35:16; 37:12; 112:10; Mark 9:18; Acts 7:54; Alma 14:21.) Then in eternity the wicked are cast into hell where there is weeping, and wailing, and gnashing of teeth." (MD, 315.)

God

In the introduction to the Doctrine and Covenants, the following phrase is found: "Behold, I am God and have spoken it; these commandments are of me" (D&C 1:24). The God who speaks on this occasion is Jesus Christ. However, he is speaking in behalf of God the Father; therefore, it is as if the Father were speaking himself. Though one in purpose, yet they are two separate personages. (D&C 130:22–23; Articles of Faith 1:1.)

Joseph Smith proclaimed: "I have always declared God to be a distinct personage, Jesus Christ a separate and distinct personage from God the Father, and that the Holy Ghost was a distinct personage and a Spirit; and these three constitute *three distinct personages and three Gods*" (TPJS, 370; italics added).

The context in which the title of "God" is used must be studied in order to determine to whom it refers. However, inasmuch as the Godhead functions with total unity, this does not pose a major obstacle, for what One speaks is the "mind" and "voice" of Another (1 John 5:7).

See also: Father, The; Father, Jesus as; God of Enoch; God's Time; Gods; Holy Ghost; Israel's God; Jehovah; Jesus Christ; Lord

God . . . Is in the Midst of All Things

See: Bosom

God of Enoch

Jesus Christ refers to himself only once as "the God of Enoch, and his brethren" (D&C 45:11). In the context of this statement, the Lord refers to this title as having originated with the people of the Church: "Ye say [I am] the God of Enoch, and his brethren."

The "God of Enoch" is the same God who was the God of all Old Testament people, he who came to earth in the meridian of time as Jesus the Christ. He it was who proclaimed himself to be the "Great I Am" to Moses and the children of Israel (Ex. 3:2–15); who claimed that identity while in the flesh (John 8:57–58); and who revealed himself as such to a latter-day prophet: "Hearken and listen to the voice of him who is from all eternity to all eternity, the Great I Am, even Jesus Christ" (D&C 39:1).

He is not only the God of "Enoch, and his brethren" but also of all the great patriarchs and peoples of past, present, and future ages.

See also: Great I Am; Jesus Christ

God of Israel

See: Israel's God

Godliness

The principle of godliness is mentioned as a cardinal virtue of one who desires to serve in the ministry (D&C 4:6; 107:30). The power of godliness, we are informed, is in the ordinances of the priesthood (D&C 84:18–22). "Godliness," said President Joseph Fielding Smith, "means that we should try to be as nearly like God as we can. If we keep that in mind, that will help to keep us humble." (SYE, 356.)

Borrowing a phrase from Elder Carlos E. Asay, one might say that to possess the virtue of godliness is to carry on a "lifetime courtship with the Holy Ghost, that member of the Godhead that has power to sanctify and purify and quicken all of us" (DSY 1976, 341).

Gods

The plural term *gods* is found nine times in the Doctrine and Covenants. Those who attain this exalted station are they who have done all that is required to merit eternal life, which is the kind of life our Eternal Father lives. Of them the Lord declared, "Then shall they be gods, because they have no end; . . . then shall they be above all, because all things are subject unto them" (D&C 132:20).

These "gods" are husbands and wives who inherit the highest heaven of the celestial kingdom (D&C 131:1–4) and who will have a "continuation of the seeds" (procreative power) throughout the eternities (D&C 132:19). In 1916, the First Presidency and the Twelve declared: "Only resurrected and glorified beings can become parents of spirit offspring. Only such exalted souls have reached maturity in the appointed course of eternal life; and the spirits born to them in the eternal worlds will pass in due sequence through the several stages or estates by which the glorified parents have attained exaltation." (MFP 5:34.)

Anciently, the Apostle Paul admonished the Philippians to "Let this mind be in you, which was also in Christ Jesus: Who, being in the form of God, thought it not robbery to be equal with God" (Phil. 2:5–6). Of this inspired insight, another prophet, Lorenzo Snow, wrote:

"Dear Brother [Paul]:
Hast Thou not been unwisely bold,
Man's destiny to thus unfold?
To raise, promote such high desire,
Such vast ambition thus inspire?

Still, 'tis no phantom that we trace
Man's ultimatum in life's race:
This royal path has long been trod
By righteous men, each now a God;

As Abra'm, Isaac, Jacob, too,
First babes, then men—to gods they grew.
As man now is, our God once was;
As God now is, so man may be, —

Which doth unfold man's destiny. . . ."
(IE, June 1919, p. 660.)

The mention of Abraham, Isaac, and Jacob has reference to the Lord's statement that these three "have entered into their exaltation . . . and sit upon thrones, and are not angels but are gods" (D&C 132:37; see also D&C 138:51).

Of this great truth, the Prophet Joseph Smith said: "*God himself was once as we are now, and is an exalted man, and sits enthroned in yonder heavens! That is the great secret. If the veil were rent today, and the great God who holds this world in its orbit, and who upholds all worlds and all things by his power, was to make himself visible, —I say, if you were to see him today, you would see him like a man in form—like yourselves in all the person, image, and very form as a man.*" (TPJS, 345.) He further stated, "If men do not comprehend the character of God, they do not comprehend themselves" (TPJS, 343).

The Pearl of Great Price makes it very clear that a council of Gods helped organize, or create, this earth (Abraham 4, 5). In this council, however, was "the Eternal God of all other gods," or the Father to whom we should give our obedience (D&C 121:32). In this respect, Joseph Smith declared: "I say there are Gods many and Lords many, but to us only one, and we are to be in subjection to that one" (TPJS, 371).

For an excellent discussion on the subject of the plurality of

Gods and man's potential destiny, see Elder Boyd K. Packer's talk, "The Patterns of Our Parentage" (En., Nov. 1984, pp. 66–69).

See also: Continuation of the Lives; Continuation of the Seeds; Eternal Lives; Fulness of the Glory of the Father; Increase

God's Time

In an item of instruction issued by the Prophet Joseph in 1843, he indicated that "God's time" was reckoned according to the planet on which he resided (D&C 130:4–5). The planet of God's residence is Kolob, where one day's revolution of that sacred sphere is as one thousand years upon earth (Abr. 3:1–9; see also Ps. 90:4; 2 Pet. 3:8).

See also: Angel's Time

Golden Calf

The reference to the golden calf with which Almon Babbitt was enticing the people of Nauvoo apparently refers to his counseling the Saints to leave that place, contrary to divine counsel, in order to seek for worldly gain (D&C 124:84; DCC, 658).

The golden calf is a symbol of worldly worship as contrasted to true divine devotion. It originated in the days of the exodus of the children of Israel from Egypt, when Aaron was persuaded to fashion an image of a calf out of gold as an object of worship. The people wanted something tangible to worship rather than developing the faith necessary to worship the true and living God. Moses destroyed the original golden calf by burning it, grinding it into powder, and then strewing it upon the water, which he then made the people drink. (Ex. 32.)

"Ye cannot serve God and mammon" (Matt. 6:24).

Good Cheer

The Lord has invited all his people to "be of good cheer" (D&C 61:36; 68:6; 78:18; 112:4; John 16:33; 3 Ne. 1:13). "Good cheer," said Elder Marvin J. Ashton, "is a state of mind or mood that promotes happiness or joy. . . . With God's help, good cheer permits us to rise above the depressing present or difficult circumstances. It is a process of positive reassurance and reinforcement. It is sunshine when clouds block the light." (En., May 1986, p. 66.)

See also: Happiness

Good of the Land of Zion

The "willing and obedient" are promised that they "shall eat the good of the land of Zion in these last days" (D&C 64:34). Similarly, the reward of the righteous shall be to receive the "good things of the earth" (D&C 59:3). Although these statements could be interpreted to mean that the soil of the earth would bring forth its produce in abundance, there is a greater application to consider.

Our thirteenth article of faith states, "If there is anything virtuous, lovely, or of good report or praiseworthy, we seek after these things." Saints of God follow the admonition to come to Christ and "eat and drink of the bread and the waters of life freely" (Alma 5:34; John 4:14; 6:35, 51). We seek after that spiritual soil which produces good wholesome food, keeping the gardens of our minds clear of the weeds of wickedness and the clutter of carnality. We "feast upon that which perisheth not, neither can be corrupted," which is the "word of Christ" (2 Ne. 9:51; 31:20; 32:3). Surely these things represent the "good of the land of Zion" and the "good things of the earth."

See also: Feast of Fat Things

Good Shepherd

The Lord refers to his people as his *sheep* (D&C 10:59, 60; 112:14; 3 Ne. 15:24), his *flock* (D&C 6:34; 35:27), and his *fold* (D&C 10:59), and to himself as the "good shepherd" (D&C 50:44; Hel. 7:18; John 10:14). According to Webster's *Unabridged Dictionary*, a scriptural shepherd is "one charged with the religious care and guidance of others." One with this title safeguards the flock from wolves, or spiritual predators (Acts 20:29).

Our relationship to the good shepherd was described by Alma: "I say unto you, that the good shepherd doth call you; yea, and in his own name he doth call you, which is the name of Christ; and if ye will not hearken unto the voice of the good shepherd, to the name by which ye are called, behold, ye are not the sheep of the good shepherd. And now if ye are not the sheep of the good shepherd, of what fold are ye? Behold, I say unto you, that the devil is your shepherd, and ye are of his fold." (Alma 5:38–39.)

See also: Jesus Christ; Sheep; Shepherd

Good Things of the Earth

See: Good of the Land of Zion; Fulness of the Earth

Goodly Land, The

In August 1833, John Murdock was promised that "after a few years," if he desired, he might "go up also unto the goodly [choice] land, to possess thine inheritance" (D&C 99:7). Two years prior to this, the Lord had identified Missouri as the place of Zion (D&C 57:1–4); evidently Murdock had some desires to leave Ohio and go up to the "promised" or "goodly land" in Missouri. However, this desire was to be deferred until he had served the mission for which the Lord had called him (D&C 99:1). The Lord uses the term *goodly land* in several other revelations (D&C 97:9; 103:20, 24). In each instance it appears to refer to the land of Zion, or Missouri.

See also: Independence, Missouri; Jackson County, Missouri; Zion

Gospel

The word *gospel* appears in sixty-six sections of the Doctrine and Covenants, but, of course, the whole book is the gospel itself. Elder Bruce R. McConkie has provided us with an excellent summary statement, or definition, of this important word: "The *gospel* of Jesus Christ is the plan of salvation. It embraces all of the laws, principles, doctrines, rites, ordinances, acts, powers, authorities, and keys necessary to save and exalt men in the highest heaven hereafter. It is the covenant of salvation which the Lord makes with men on earth.

"Literally, gospel means good tidings from God or God-story. Thus it is the glad tidings or good news concerning Christ, his atonement, the establishment of his earthly kingdom, and a possible future inheritance in his celestial presence." (MD, 331.)

The Prophet Joseph recorded these words: "And this is the gospel, the glad tidings which the voice out of the heavens bore record unto us—That he came into the world, even Jesus, to be crucified for the world, and to bear the sins of the world, and to sanctify the world, and to cleanse it from all unrighteousness; That through him all might be saved whom the

Father had put into his power and made by him." (D&C 76:40–42.)

See also: Dispensation of the Gospel of Abraham; Feet Shod with the Preparation of the Gospel of Peace; Fulness of the Gospel; Gospel of Peace; Gospel of Repentance; Letter of the Gospel; Preparatory Gospel

Gospel of Peace

See: Feet Shod with the Preparation of the Gospel of Peace; Peaceable Things of the Kingdom

Gospel of Repentance

The "gospel of repentance" (D&C 13; 84:27) is the preparatory gospel, "which is the Gospel of faith, repentance and the remission of sins by baptism by immersion" (SS, 68).

See also: Preparatory Gospel

Gould, John

The single reference to John Gould appears in the context of an assurance by the Lord that he and his missionary companion, Orson Hyde, are safe (D&C 100:14). The two men had been sent as special messengers from the First Presidency, in Kirtland, to the Saints in Jackson County, Missouri, where they arrived the latter part of September 1833.

On April 6, 1837, at the age of twenty-eight, he became the

eighth man to be sustained as one of the Seven Presidents of the Seventy but was released several months later to serve in the high priest's quorum (Jenson 1:191). He once accompanied the Prophet Joseph on a mission (HC 2:41), and the last mention of his service is when he was called on a mission in April 1844 (HC 6:340). He died on May 9, 1851.

Grace

According to Webster, *grace* means "help given man by God, as in overcoming temptation; freedom from sin; relief from payment; or, approval and acceptance." The doctrine of grace has long been debated by misled ministers who endeavor to pit the Apostle Paul against his colleague James. Paul, for example, declared to the Ephesians that "by grace are ye saved. . . . Not of works, lest any man should boast." (Eph. 2:8–9.) James, on the other hand, emphasized "that faith without works is dead" (James 2:14–26). One must realize that Paul was denouncing those who were steeped in tradition and felt that the law of Moses was sufficient for salvation. James, however, was preaching to those who, in essence, cried, "All is well in Zion" (2 Ne. 28:21), feeling that God's gift of grace left them without personal responsibility.

The Savior's declaration that his "grace is sufficient" (D&C 17:8; 18:31) must be understood as the final divine payment on our debts to the laws of justice. Our "notes of indebtedness" cannot be "retired" through our repentance alone, but require the grace of God to free us from bondage. This is essentially what Nephi was saying in his observation that "it is by grace that we are saved, *after* all we can do" (2 Ne. 25:23; italics added).

President Joseph Fielding Smith wrote: "*We must believe that it is through his grace that we are saved, that he performed for us that labor which we were unable to perform for ourselves, and did for us those things which were essential to our salvation, which were beyond our power; and also that we are under the commandment and the necessity of performing the labors that are required of us as set forth in the commandments known as the gospel of Jesus Christ*" (DS 2:311). Through disobedience, "there is a possibility that man may fall from grace and depart from the living God" (D&C 20:32). In the words of Elder Francis M. Lyman, "it is possible for men to repent and then to unrepent, and to fail to keep their repentance good" (CR, Oct. 1897, p. 16).

The grace of Christ offers redemption from the grave to all (1 Cor. 15:20–23). This is a gift free to all. On the other hand, the gift of grace regarding one's sins can only be purchased through repentance (D&C 19:15–20).

The grace which is in the Father (D&C 66:12; 93:11), and in which the Son continued to grow (D&C 93:11–12), is probably the total and perfect goodness that permeates their beings, freeing them from the shackles of sin and temptation. Not only are they personally set free but they are also thereby enabled to offer expiating grace to others. We are commanded to follow their examples and "grow in grace and in the knowledge of the truth" (D&C 50:40), in order that we may meet their approval and be accepted into their presence.

Granger, Oliver

The Lord is very complimentary in a revelation mentioning Oliver Granger: "His name shall be had in sacred remembrance from generation to generation, forever and ever, saith the Lord" (D&C 117:12–15). His biography is found in the Prophet's journal: "He was the son of Pierce and Clarissa Granger, born in the town of Phelps, Ontario county, New York, 7th February, 1794; received a common school education, was two years a member of the Methodist Church and was a licensed exhorter. On the 8th September, 1813, he married Lydia Dibble; in the year 1827, he in a great measure lost his sight by cold and exposure; he was sheriff of Ontario county, and colonel of the militia. He received the Gospel on reading the Book of Mormon, which he providentially obtained, and was baptized at Sodus, Wayne county, and ordained an Elder by Brigham and Joseph Young, they being the first Elders he saw, and immediately devoted his time to preaching and warning the people.

"In the year 1833 he moved to Kirtland, and then took a mission to the east with Elder Samuel Newcome; returned and was ordained a High Priest; took another mission in the spring of 1836 to New York with John P. Greene; and after his return built up a branch at Huntsburg, Geauga county, Ohio; also a branch at Perry, Richfield county, where he baptized Bradley Wilson and his seven sons and their wives. When the Church left Kirtland he was appointed to settle the Church business.

"In June, 1838, he went to Far West, and returned in August of same year; in October he again started, taking his family; he went seventy miles into Missouri, and was driven back by the mob; in the spring of 1839 he went to Nauvoo; in 1840 removed to Kirtland with his family, where he remained until his death.

"He was a man of good business qualifications, but had been for many years nearly blind." (HC 4:408–9.) He died in August 1841 in Kirtland, where he had been looking after the affairs of the Church.

Graves of the Saints

The "graves of the saints" (D&C 133:56) are those resting places containing the remains of those who have "died in the Lord" (D&C 29:13; 42:44, 46; 63:49; 124:86; Rev. 14:13). These Saints are they who were true and faithful to their covenants while in mortality and shall rise from the grave in immortality to meet the Son of Man upon his return in clouds of glory. The opening of these graves will repeat what took place following the resurrection of the Lord, when the ancient Saints came forth from their tombs (Matt. 27:52–53; Hel. 14:25; 3 Ne. 23:9–11; D&C 138:12–17, 50–52).

See also: Dead That Die in the Lord

Great and Abominable Church

The ancient American prophet Nephi spoke of "the great and abominable church" sixteen times in his writings, but the specific name appears only once in the Doctrine and Covenants (29:21), although reference is made to it elsewhere as "the church of the devil" (18:20) and the "great church, the mother of abominations" (88:94). This church will ultimately be destroyed. Its identity is more readily understood when one contemplates the ramifications of the scriptural statement that "there are save two churches only; the one is the church of the Lamb of God, and the other is the *church of the devil*; wherefore, whoso belongeth not to the church of the Lamb of God be-

longeth to that *great church, which is the mother of abominations*; and she is the whore of all the earth" (1 Ne. 14:10; italics added).

Thus, according to Elder Bruce R. McConkie, "the great and abominable church," or "*the church of the devil is the world*; it is all the carnality and evil to which fallen man is heir; it is every unholy and wicked practice; it is every false religion, every supposed system of salvation which does not actually save and exalt man in the highest heaven of the celestial world. *It is every church except the true church, whether parading under a Christian or a pagan banner.*" (DNTC 3:551; italics added.)

In light of this definition, however, words of caution must be considered. Speaking of the membership of The Church of Jesus Christ of Latter-day Saints, Elder James E. Talmage said: "We are ofttimes charged with being very exclusive, and we admit the charge; we are exclusive, but in a rational sense. How can we solemnly testify that this is the Church of Jesus Christ and then ascribe that same high title to other organizations that have been formed not under the direction of Jesus Christ, but according to man's thoughts and plans? . . . Now when we say that the Lord is not pleased with those churches, we do not mean that he is not pleased with the members thereof. . . . But the Lord is not pleased with those churches that have been constructed by men and then labeled with his name. He is not pleased with those doctrines. . . . The church as such may be wholly corrupt because of the false claims that are being made for it, and yet within that church as members there may be people who are doing their best. They have been deceived." (CR, Oct. 1928, p. 120.)

Perhaps it would be well to consider another observation by the Lord. Speaking of the Church which he established through the Prophet Joseph Smith, he said: "[It is] the only true and living church upon the face of the whole earth, with which I the Lord, am well pleased, *speaking unto the church collectively and not individually*" (D&C 1:30; italics added). Thus, even members of record in The Church of Jesus Christ of Latter-day Saints (church of the Lamb of God) must abide by their covenants or they become part of that "other" church, "which is the mother of abominations."

Elder McConkie has said: "We are either for the Church or we are against it. We either take its part or we take the consequences. We cannot survive spiritually with one foot in the Church and the other in the world. We must make the choice." (CR, Oct. 1974, p. 44.) "They who are not for me are against me, saith our God" (2 Ne. 10:16).

See also: Abominations; Babylon; Church of the Devil; Whore of All the Earth; Wine of the Wrath of Her Fornication

Great and Dreadful Day of the Lord

It is of interest to note that the prophecy recorded by Malachi regarding the coming of Elijah, "before the coming of the great and dreadful day of the Lord" (Mal. 4:5–6), is quoted in the Book of Mormon (3 Ne. 25:5–6), the Doctrine and Covenants (2:1–2; 128:17–18), and the Pearl of Great Price (JS—H 1:38–39).

This "great and dreadful day" has reference to Christ's second coming and is referred to by the following terms in the Doctrine and Covenants: "day when the Lord shall come" (1:10); "day of my coming" (29:12); "great day" (34:7–9); "day of the Lord" (45:42); "day of visitation, and of judgment, and of indignation" (56:16); "day of his coming" (61:39); "day of wrath" (63:6); "day of vengeance" (133:51); and "day . . . that shall burn as an oven" (133:64). It will truly be a *great* day to those who righteously await its onset; but, to the wicked, it shall be a *dreadful* day of exquisite sorrow.

Nevertheless, Joseph Smith raised a flag of caution regarding the "coming of the Son of Man; . . . it is a false idea," said the Prophet, "that the Saints will escape all the judgments, whilst the wicked suffer; for all flesh is subject to suffer, and 'the righteous shall hardly escape;' still many of the Saints will escape, for the just shall live by faith; yet *many of the righteous shall fall a prey to disease, to pestilence, etc., by reason of the weakness of the flesh, and yet be saved in the Kingdom of God. . . . So* that it is an unhallowed principle to say that such and such have transgressed because they have been preyed upon by disease or death, for all flesh is subject to death; and the Savior has said, 'Judge not, lest ye be judged.' " (HC 4:11; italics added.)

Elder Orson Pratt defined "the great and dreadful day of the Lord" as "the day in which wickedness should be entirely swept from the earth, and no remnants of the wicked left, when every branch of them and every root of them should become as stubble, and be consumed from the face of the earth" (JD 7:76–77).

See also: Destroying Angel; Healing; Stubble

Great and Marvelous Work

See: Marvelous Work

Great Britain

The "mother Gentile," Great Britain, who had been referred to in ancient prophecy regarding the destiny of America (1 Ne. 13:16–19), was once again an item of prophecy in the 1800s. On December 25, 1832, the Prophet Joseph declared that a divisive war would rupture the seams of the United States and that the Southern States would call upon "other nations, even the nation of Great Britain" for assistance (D&C 87:3).

"Did the South appeal to Great Britain and other nations for aid? Historians tell us that in May, 1861, the Southern States sent commissioners abroad to seek recognition of the Confederacy. Mr. William L. Yancy, of Alabama, was sent to England; Mr. P.A. Rost, of Louisiana, to France; and Mr. A. Dudley Mann, of Virginia, to Holland Belgium. In October, the same year, James M. Mason and John Slidell were appointed ambassadors to England and France, respectively, to induce those countries to aid the Southern cause. That their mission failed was due to the firm stand taken by the working men of the United Kingdom, who regarded the cause of the North as a righteous cause, even though they suffered greatly through the Northern blockade of Southern ports, especially on account of the 'cotton famine' resulting therefrom." (SS, 535–36.)

Great Church

See: Great and Abominable Church; Church of the Devil

Great I Am

When the premortal Lord spoke to Moses from the burning bush on Mt. Horeb, he identified himself as "I Am." By this name he was to be known among the children of Israel. (Ex. 3:14.) Many years later, during his mortal ministry, the Savior once again identified himself by this title during a confrontation with the Jews (John 8:56–58). And we find him addressing himself as "the Great I Am" in latter-day revelation (D&C 29:1; 38:1; 39:1).

The meaning of the name "is expressed in the saying that God is 'omnipotent, omnipresent, and omniscient; without beginning of days or end of life; and that in him every good gift and every good principle dwell' (Lectures on Faith, No. 2)" (CHMR 1:166).

See also: God of Enoch; Jesus Christ

Great Sign in Heaven

The "great sign in heaven" shall appear just prior to the second coming of Christ (D&C 88:93). Jesus referred to it as the "sign of the Son of man" (Matt. 24:30). "What this sign is has not been revealed, but there will be no uncertainty about it, when it appears. In 1843 one Mr. Redding, of Ogle County, Ill., claimed to have seen the sign. The Prophet Joseph then wrote to the *Times and Seasons:* 'Notwithstanding Mr. Redding may have seen a wonderful appearance in the clouds one morning . . . he has not seen the sign of the Son of Man, as foretold by Jesus; neither has any man, nor will any man, until after the sun shall have been darkened and the moon bathed in blood; for the Lord hath not shown me any such sign; and as the Prophet saith, so it must be— "Surely the Lord God will do nothing, but he revealeth his secret unto his servants the prophets." (See Amos 3:7.) Therefore, hear this O earth! The Lord will not come to reign over the righteous, in this world, in 1843, nor until everything for the Bridegroom is ready.' (HC 5:291.)

"It may be gathered from this that when the sign appears, God will make its meaning known to the Prophet, Seer and Revelator who at that time may be at the head of the Church, and through him to His people and the world in general." (SS, 560.)

Great Treasures of Knowledge

See: Hidden Treasures; Knowledge; Riches of Eternity; Treasures; Wisdom; Word of Wisdom (#2)

Great Waters, The

The "great waters" referred to in Doctrine and Covenants 118:4 means the Atlantic Ocean. These waters were to be crossed by the Twelve Apostles as they carried the gospel message to the shores of Great Britain (CHMR 2:194).

Greater Priesthood

The "greater priesthood" (D&C 84:19) refers to the "priesthood which is after the holiest order of God," (D&C 84:18), which is the Melchizedek Priesthood (D&C 107:1-3). It is "greater" in comparison to the "lesser," or Aaronic, priesthood in that the Melchizedek encompasses the Aaronic.

See also: First Priesthood; Holy Priesthood After the Order of the Son of God; Melchizedek Priesthood

Greediness

The Lord has warned against those "whose hands are not stayed from laying hold upon other men's goods, whose eyes are full of greediness" (D&C 56:17). Those who are full of greediness do not seek the things which matter most—the riches of eternity (D&C 68:31). To be driven by greediness is to have an excessive or reprehensible desire to acquire temporal things that cannot be transported through the veil into eternity.

Cain's motive in killing his brother, Abel, was greed. Elder Dallin H. Oaks observed: "The motive of Cain is at the headwaters of wickedness. Cain's sin was murder, but his motive was personal gain. That motive has produced all manner of wickedness, including murder, thievery, and fraud. That motive is also at work in the legal but immoral practices of those who get gain by preying on the weaknesses or ignorance of their neighbors." (En, Nov. 1986, pp. 22-23.)

See also: Cain; Covet

Griffin, Selah J.

The name of "Selah J. Griffin" appears in two revelations, both of which were given in June 1831 (D&C 52:32; 56:5-6). Initially he was called to accompany Newel Knight on a mission to Missouri, but this call was shortly thereafter revoked because of the "stiffneckedness" of the Saints in Thompson, Ohio, where Newel Knight was told to remain. Griffin received a new assignment to accompany Thomas B. Marsh to Missouri.

Following his mission, he moved his family to Missouri and suffered with the Saints during those days of persecution. He remained in the East when the Saints moved west, and nothing more is known of him.

Grover, Thomas

A man of impeccable character who exemplified the principles of charity, consecration, and trust was Thomas Grover (D&C 124:132). He is one who epitomizes the truth of J. Reuben Clark's statement that "in the service of the Lord, it is not where you serve but how" (CR, Apr. 1951, p. 154).

Although he served faithfully on high councils in Kirtland, Far West, Nauvoo, and Utah, his real achievements in life were in the unheralded acts of charitable service to others. For example, after his arrival in Kirtland, he called on the Prophet. "As he knocked at the door the Prophet opened it and said, putting out his hand: 'How do you do, Brother Grover. If God ever sent a man he sent you. I want to borrow every dollar you can spare for immediate use.' Brother Grover entered the house and conversed with the Prophet about the situation, offering to let Joseph have what money he needed. Brother Joseph accepted the offer and told Brother Grover to look around and find a location that suited him for a home and then return, when the money he had advanced would be returned to him. In a short time the place was selected, but Brother Grover refused to receive back his money, saying, 'I have sufficient for my needs without it.' " From that day the devotion of Thomas Grover to Joseph Smith never wavered.

On another occasion, the son of Widow Brown came to Grover to buy "a little flour." "Brother Grover sent his son to fill a grain sack full of flour and put it on the boy's wagon. The flustered youth asked how much a whole sack of flour would cost, adding that he had only a little money. To which Brother Grover replied, 'I do not sell flour to widows and fatherless children.' As the sack was placed upon the wagon the happy boy drove away in tears."

Grover once refused to sell a harvest of seven hundred bushels of wheat at the market price of five dollars a bushel, but instead "loaned or sold every bushel of it, except enough for his own family, for the tithing office price of two dollars a bushel." Numerous are the accounts of his providing goods and service to those in need without any thought of recompense.

Brigham Young paid tribute to Grover in these words: "Brother Grover, if every Latter-day Saint would do as you have done there would be no need of a tithing among this people."

Grover's personal philosophy was expressed in this motto he coined: "A debt can never be outlawed; a dollar is due until it is paid. If I were going to be hanged I should go on time."

His daughter rendered the following tribute to him: "My father was loved by all who knew him. He never spoke evil of anyone; he did not boast, and he did not take honor unto himself. Many times he has divided his last meal with a sufferer. His word was as good as his bond. He could neither be bought or sold. He was incapable of a little mean or treacherous trick. Not one of his children has apostatized."

In addition to his acts of charity, Grover was a man of physical courage. He served as one of the Prophet's bodyguards and was instrumental in releasing Joseph when he had been kidnapped by a couple of renegade sheriffs from Missouri. Grover was serving a mission in June 1844 when he was warned in a dream to return to Nauvoo. He arrived in time to join the procession carrying the slain prophets back to Nauvoo and helped in preparing the bodies for burial.

He died true to the faith on February 20, 1886, following a lifetime of service to the Church and his fellowmen. "About the last Sunday in the life of Thomas Grover he attended the sacrament meeting in Farmington Ward. As the amen was spoken and the people were about to move, Brother Thomas suddenly raised his hand and said, 'Wait a minute, Bishop.' Then he added, that he could not go home until he had borne testimony that the Gospel was true and that Joseph Smith was a true Prophet of God." (Jenson 4:137–42.)

Guile

On two different occasions, almost two centuries apart, the Lord spoke of his ancient Apostle Nathanael as being without guile (John 1:47; D&C 41:11). He applied the same description to at least two other early leaders of his restored church (D&C 41:9–11; 124:20), and admonished all priesthood bearers to be without guile (D&C 121:41–42).

Elder Joseph B. Wirthlin said: "To be without guile is to be free of deceit, cunning, hypocrisy, and dishonesty in thought or action. . . . A person without guile is a person of innocence, honest intent, and pure motives, whose life reflects the simple practice of conforming his daily actions to principles of integrity."

He further noted: "I believe the necessity for the members of the Church to be without guile may be more urgent now than at other times because many in the world apparently do not understand the importance of this virtue or are indifferent to it." (En., May 1988, pp. 80–81.)

See also: Nathanael; Partridge, Edward

H

Hagar

Hagar was the Egyptian handmaid of Sarah who became a wife, or concubine, of Abraham. She bore him his first child, a son named Ishmael. She was given to Abraham by his first wife, Sarah, because the latter had been barren and desired Abraham to have posterity. (Gen. 16.)

Hagar was given to Abraham in accordance with the will of God, and from her "sprang many people" (D&C 132:34–35, 65). This was a partial fulfillment of the promise given Abraham that he would be the "father of many nations" (Gen. 17:4–5).

Hagar also received promises from angelic visitors that her descendants would be multitudinous (Gen. 16:10; 21:17–18). This posterity is believed to include much of the present-day Arab world.

See also: Law of Sarah

Hancock, Levi W.

The name of Levi W. Hancock appears twice in the Doctrine and Covenants, once in connection with a mission call (D&C 52:29) and once in conjunction with his position as one of the seven Presidents of the Seventy (D&C 124:138). He served in this latter capacity from February 1835 to June 1882, with a short period of interruption because of a misunderstanding regarding his priesthood office (CA 1978, 117).

Levi Hancock was baptized on November 16, 1830, and served as a member of two famous Mormon miliary movements—Zion's Camp and the Mormon Battalion. He was the only General Authority of the Church to serve in this latter capacity, and he served as the Battalion's chaplain.

His susceptibility to the spirit of inspiration is illustrated in the following incident: "A non-Mormon by the consent of the Battalion joined the company and soon after required baptism. Elder Hancock, in company with others of the brethren, took him down to the Missouri river and performed the ceremony. On raising him from the water he said, as if wrought upon by the spirit, 'If I have baptized a murderer, it will do him no good.' His words had such an effect upon the stranger that he soon afterwards confessed that he was a murderer, having killed his own brother."

Upon arriving in Utah, he continued his labors as a Seventy and also served in the Utah legislature. In addition to his calling as a General Authority, he was ordained as a patriarch, in which capacity he served about the last ten years of his life. He died in Washington, Utah, on June 10, 1882. (Jenson 1:188–89.)

Hancock, Solomon

In June 1831, Solomon Hancock was called to leave Kirtland for Missouri and to "preach by the way" (D&C 52:27). His name appears frequently in the journal of Joseph Smith. He was among a small group whose names were manifested to the Prophet "by the voice of the Spirit and revelation, to receive their endowments" at Kirtland in June 1834 (HC 2:112–13).

Hancock served on three high councils and was particularly active in Church affairs in Missouri (HC 2:124, 523; 3:225, 252; 5:427). During the exodus from Nauvoo, he was appointed to the "Utility Committee," whose responsibility was to sell the property of the Saints (HC 7:474).

Earlier, he had been appointed to preside over a new district for the Church (HC 7:305).

Solomon Hancock died on December 2, 1847.

Handmaid

On two occasions, a woman mentioned in the Doctrine and Covenants is referred to as a handmaid of the Lord (D&C 90:28; 132:51–56). A handmaid is a personal female servant. In the same sense in which John the Baptist referred to Joseph Smith and Oliver Cowdery as his "fellow servants" in the ministry of the Messiah (D&C 13:1), women who so serve are often referred to as handmaidens.

Hands

See: Hands Which Hang Down; Left Hand; Right Hand

Hands Which Hang Down

There are two instances in scripture where the admonition is given to "lift up the hands which hang down, and strengthen the feeble knees" (D&C 81:5; Heb. 12:12). A related reference is found in Isaiah: "Strengthen ye the weak hands, and confirm the feeble knees" (Isa. 35:3).

Sidney B. Sperry said these "clauses mean . . . to help sustain persons who are either weak of body or in a position where they find it difficult to help them-

selves" (DCC, 377). The description also applies to those who suffer discouragement, despair, and loneliness.

Happiness

Although the word *happiness* appears only once in the Doctrine and Covenants (D&C 77:2), it is the core of the gospel of Jesus Christ, which is itself "the great plan of happiness" (Alma 42:8).

"Happiness is the object and design of our existence," declared the Prophet Joseph Smith, "and will be the end thereof, if we pursue the path that leads to it; and this path is virtue, uprightness, faithfulness, holiness, and keeping all the commandments of God" (TPJS, 255–56). This course is what Nephi called living "after the manner of happiness" (2 Ne. 5:27; see also Mosiah 2:41).

Another prophet, Ezra Taft Benson, noted that one "cannot do wrong and feel right. It is impossible! Years of happiness can be lost in the foolish gratification of a momentary desire for pleasure. Satan would have you believe that happiness comes only as you surrender to his enticements, but one only needs to look at the shattered lives of those who violate God's laws to know why Satan is called the Father of Lies." (En., Nov. 1977, p. 30.)

"Wickedness," we are reminded, "never was happiness" (Alma 41:10–11; see also Hel. 13:38).

See also: Good Cheer; Joy

Harden Their Hearts

Throughout the scriptures the Lord warns of the dire consequences accruing to those whose hearts are hardened and consequently grow cold, rejecting the warm whispers of the word of God. Just as the hardening of one's physical heart's arteries can cause death to the body, so, in like manner, can the hardening of one's spiritual arteries lead to spiritual death—the departure of God's Spirit from one's presence—for he cannot remain in unholy tabernacles (D&C 93:35; 1 Cor. 3:16–17).

The Lord pronounces condemnation on those who harden their hearts (D&C 5:18; 20:15), and promises conversion and healing to those who do not (D&C 112:13). Those whose hearts are hardened are labeled as "wicked" (D&C 38:6), while those who do not harden their hearts are those who "hear" his voice and are characterized as the Lord's "elect" (D&C 29:7).

It appears that the hardening of one's heart impairs one's capacity to hear with spiritual ears, for Amulek once confessed that he "was called many times," yet he "would not hear" because he hardened his heart (Alma 10:6). Perhaps this is the spiritual numbness of which the ancient prophet Nephi spoke when he castigated his errant brothers with these words: God "hath spoken unto you in a still small voice but ye were past feeling, that ye could not feel his words" (1 Ne. 17:45). Surely, as a man hardens his spiritual arteries, a numbness sets in that impairs all aspects of his spiritual sensitivity and leads ultimately to spiritual death.

See also: Blindness of Heart; Heart; Open Hearts; Soften the Hearts

Harmony, Pennsylvania

The town of Harmony, Pennsylvania is located in the northeast corner of the state at a point where the Susquehanna River first leaves the borders of New York. Although fifteen of the revelations in the Doctrine and Covenants were received in Harmony, Pennsylvania, the only mention of this city is in section 128, verse 20.

The first mention of Harmony by the Prophet Joseph is in October 1825, when he went there to work. He boarded with the Isaac Hale family, which led to his marriage of Emma Hale in January 1827. (JS—H 1:56–58.) The following December, Joseph and Emma returned to Harmony, where they resided on her father's property until June 1829. It was during this time that the initial efforts at translating the Book of Mormon were undertaken.

The restoration of the Aaronic Priesthood occurred on the banks of the Susquehanna River near Harmony, and the Melchizedek Priesthood was restored in the wilderness between Harmony and Colesville, New York (D&C 13; 128:20).

See also: Pennsylvania; Susquehanna County

Harris, Emer

The only mention of Emer Harris occurs in the revelation received at the Amherst, Ohio, conference in January 1832 (D&C 75:30). He is admonished to be united in the ministry.

In October 1831, he had been appointed as one of six men to be responsible to instruct "the several branches of the Church" on the manner in which meetings should be conducted (HC 1:219). He was a brother to Martin Harris, one of the Three Witnesses to the Book of Mormon. In December 1835, the Prophet Joseph listed him as one of almost two dozen men who came to his aid in a moment of financial need (HC 2:327).

He later served as a member of the Nauvoo Legion and came west with the Saints to Utah, where he died on November 28, 1869.

Harris, George W.

In 1841 George W. Harris was called to serve as the third member of the high council in Nauvoo, "the corner-stone of Zion" (D&C 124:131–32). He is initially mentioned in Joseph Smith's writings on March 14, 1838, when the Prophet writes that he was "received under the hospitable roof of Brother George W. Harris, who treated us with all possible kindness" (HC 3:9). Several days later, he was called to the high council in Far West, Missouri, and ordained a high priest (HC 3:14–15).

He was one of nine men who signed a resolution in December 1838, sent to the Missouri legislature in behalf of the citizen Saints of Caldwell County, regarding their grievances (HC 3:217–24). Harris was called as the ranking member of the high council at Commerce, Illinois, in October 1839, and was appointed by the Prophet to go on a fund-raising mission to the East (HC 4:161, 164, 199).

In October 1841, he was selected as an alderman in Nauvoo and was serving as the "President pro tem" of the city council at the time of the martyrdoms of Joseph and Hyrum. In fact, Harris signed the document declaring the *Nauvoo Expositor* a "public nuisance," which event triggered the momentum that led to that fateful day of June 27, 1844, when "the best blood of the nineteenth century" was spilled (D&C 135:6; HC 7:63).

Harris was appointed commissary of the first encampment of pioneers headed to the Salt Lake Valley (HC 7:586). He did not go west with the Saints, preferring to remain in Iowa, where he died in 1857.

Harris, Martin

Outside of the Smith family itself, Martin Harris was one of the earliest supporters of Joseph Smith's divine work. In the fall of 1827, shortly after Joseph received the gold plates from the angel Moroni, Martin made a present of fifty dollars to the young Prophet which enabled him to get to Pennsylvania where he could pursue the work of translation without the severe hindrance he suffered in New York.

In February 1828, Martin visited Joseph and persuaded the latter to allow him to copy from the plates some of the characters, which Harris then took to New York City to show some learned professors. The result was that an ancient prophecy by Isaiah was fulfilled (Isa. 29:11-14; 2 Ne. 27:15-22; JS—H 1:61-65).

Martin's role as a chief participant in the fulfillment of further prophecy was again brought to the forefront when he was responsible for losing the first 116 pages of translated writings from the Book of Mormon plates. The Lord, having foreseen this eventuality, had prepared a second set of plates which Joseph was later allowed to translate, following a severe rebuke for his carelessness in losing the first manuscript (HC 1:20-28; 1 Ne. 9; Words of Morm. 1:3-7). This event was the setting which precipitated the revelations found in sections 3 and 10 of the Doctrine and Covenants. For his role in becoming a dupe of the devil, Martin was labeled "a wicked man" by the Lord (D&C 3:12; 10:7).

Although his loss of the sacred manuscript denied him further participation as a scribe for Joseph Smith, Martin's repentance allowed him to serve as one of the three special witnesses to the Book of Mormon (D&C 17; HC 1:52-57). In this capacity, he saw the gold plates from which the sacred book was translated; saw the heavenly messenger who brought the plates; viewed the sword of Laban, the Urim and Thummim, and the Liahona; and heard the voice of God declaring the record to be true.

Martin mortgaged his farm in order to help finance the first printing of the Book of Mormon and was cautioned by the Lord not to "covet [his] own property, but [to] impart it freely" (D&C 19:26). He served on the first high council of the Church at Kirtland (D&C 102:3, 34) and was one of the select few first called to participate in a united order (D&C 58:35). In order to keep his identity secret on several occasions, the Lord referred to him as "Mahemson" (D&C 82:11; 104:24, 26; pre-1981 ed.).

The month prior to Joseph Smith's fleeing Kirtland for fear of his life, Martin Harris and other disaffected Mormons were excommunicated from the Church (IE, March 1969, p. 36). Martin remained in Kirtland for the next thirty-two years until he was persuaded to come to Utah. Edward Stevenson was instrumental in raising funds to accomplish this purpose, and Martin arrived in Salt Lake on August 30, 1870. Five of the Quorum of the Twelve witnessed his rebaptism, and one of them, Orson Pratt, confirmed him a member of the Church.

Although far removed from Church activity for many years, Martin was true to his witness of the divinity of the Book of Mormon. On one occasion, when some of his acquaintances deliberately got him "tipsy," he was questioned about the truthfulness of his declaration of belief regarding the Book of Mormon. "Now, Martin," they cajoled, "do you really believe you did see an angel when you were awake?" To the delight of the crowd, Harris replied, "No! I do not believe it." However their glee was short-lived, for he then said: "Gentlemen, what I have said is true, from the fact that my belief is swallowed up in knowledge; for I want to say to you that as the Lord lives I do *know* that I stood with the Prophet Joseph Smith in the presence of the angel, and it was in the brightness of day."

He died in Clarkston, Utah, on July 10, 1875, shortly after taking the beloved book in his hands and bearing final testimony of its truthfulness. (Jenson 1:271–76.)

See also: Mahemson; Three Witnesses; Wicked Man, A

Harvest

See: Earth Is Ripe; Field Is White Already to Harvest; Ripe; Sheaves; Tares; Thrust in His Sickle

Haws, Peter

In 1841, Peter Haws was appointed as one of a four-man committee to see that the Nauvoo House was built (D&C 124:62, 70; HC 4:301–2). He was also appointed a member of the "Nauvoo Agricultural and Manufacturing Association," whose purpose was "the promotion of agriculture and husbandry in all its branches, and for the manufacture of flour, lumber, and such other useful articles as are necessary for the ordinary purposes of life" (HC 4:303). Haws's participation in constructing the Nauvoo House was still being mentioned in Joseph Smith's history as late as April 1843 (HC 5:369).

Haws is also mentioned as a companion of the Prophet during one of his arrests and later served a mission to Alabama (HC 5:210, 370). In October 1844, he was called to preside over a new district of the Church, and in the westward movement of the Saints he served as a captain of one of the companies (HC 7:306, 482).

Although he remained actively involved in Church affairs following the martyrdoms of Joseph and Hyrum Smith, he later became critical of the Twelve Apostles' leadership. His apostate attitude led to his being cut off from the Church early in

1849. He is an example of Brigham Young's warning that "if the Spirit of God whispers . . . to His people through their leader, and they will not listen nor obey, what will be the consequences of their disobedience? Darkness and blindness of mind. . . . until they apostatize entirely from God and His ways." (JD 12:117.)

He That Is Tithed Shall Not Be Burned

In good-humored jest, one will occasionally hear the law of tithing referred to as "fire insurance." The basis for this is the Lord's promise that "he that is tithed shall not be burned at [my] coming" (D&C 64:23). "What does that mean?" asked Elder Rudger Clawson. "Does it mean that if a man will not pay his tithing, that the Lord is going to send a ball of fire down from heaven and burn him up? No: the Lord does not do that way. The Lord works on natural principles. This is what it means, if I read correctly: a man who ignores the express command of the Lord, by failing to pay his tithing, it means that the Spirit of the Lord will withdraw from him; it means that the power of the priesthood will withdraw from that man, if he continues in the spirit of neglect to do his duty. He will drift away into darkness, gradually but surely, until finally (mark you) he will lift up his eyes among the wicked. That is where he will finally land; and then

when the destruction comes and when the burning comes, he will be among the wicked and will be destroyed; while those who observe the law will be found among the righteous, and they will be preserved." (CR, Oct. 1913, p. 59.)

See also: Tithing

Healing

"We believe in the gift of . . . healing," states our seventh article of faith. This spiritual gift is mentioned throughout the Doctrine and Covenants (e.g., 24:13; 35:9; 42:43–52; 46:19–20; 84:65–73). Although the major method whereby healings are accomplished is through the laying on of hands by Melchizedek Priesthood bearers (James 5:14–15; D&C 42:44), healings have occurred in other ways. For example, the command of a priesthood bearer, without the accompanying laying on of hands, has effected healings (John 11:43–44; Acts 3:1–8). This latter approach has been used even in the physical absence of the afflicted person (John 4:46–53).

Touching an article belonging to one of great faith and priesthood power has also brought about healings (Luke 8:43–48; Acts 19:11–12). Of course, fasting and prayer is a most efficacious method of healing (Mark 9:25–29).

Smith and Sjodahl distinguish between two types of healing: mental and spiritual. "Mental healing is as old as the race. It is done through 'suggestion.' . . . The spirit within is an intelligent being and is greatly helped, in its efforts to repair tissue or withstand the attacks of adverse agencies, by the suggestion of others who have great will-power. . . . Spiritual healing is by the Spirit of God, through the Priesthood. It is healing effected by the Holy Spirit imparting the strength necessary to overcome the causes of diseases, and it often operates instantaneously. . . . Spiritual healing is divine healing. It is part of the gospel. Mental healing is human. It is good in its place, but it is not part of the gospel." (SS 402–3.)

The use of natural laws in healing is explained by Elder Parley P. Pratt: "To heal a person by the touch, or by the laying on of hands, in the name of Jesus Christ, is as much in accordance with the laws of nature, as for water to seek its own level, an apple to fall to the ground when loosened from the tree where it grew, or quicksilver to attract its own affinities. A person commissioned of Jesus Christ, and filled with this spiritual substance, can impart of the same to another, provided there is a preparation of heart, and faith on the part of the receiver. Or if, as in cases of healing, casting out devils, etc., it happens that the receiver has no command of his own mind — as in cases of little children, persons swooned, fainted, deranged, or dead, then the *faith* of the administrator alone, or in connection with other friends and agents, on

his behalf, is sufficient, in many cases, to perform the work." (KT, 107–8.)

See also: Destroying Angel; Great and Dreadful Day of the Lord; Miracles

Health in Their Navel

Those who observe the Word of Wisdom are promised that they "shall receive health in their navel and marrow to their bones" (D&C 89:18). The navel is representative of the inner organs of the body; thus, the promise of "health in their navel" suggests that they will receive blessings of health to their inner organs.

See also: Marrow to Their Bones; Word of Wisdom

Heart

"The heart suggests our daily conduct in life," said President Harold B. Lee (SHP, 331). Indeed, the Master taught that "out of the abundance of the heart the mouth speaketh" (Matt. 12:34). And the author of Proverbs wrote: "For as he thinketh in his heart, so is he" (Prov. 23:7). Thus, the heart is symbolic of one's thoughts, feelings, and actions. They who are pure in heart (D&C 97:21) and have open hearts (D&C 64:22) and broken hearts (D&C 20:37) are receptive to the warm glow of spiritual light radiating from the Source of all truth and righteousness. To those who harden their hearts, this eternal life–giving substance is restricted and spiritual heart failure results.

Elder Delbert L. Stapley said: "'The word *heart* is used in scripture as the core of life and strength; hence it includes mind, spirit, and soul, and one's entire emotional nature and understanding. One of the dictionary definitions states: 'Heart is the center of the total personality with reference to intuition, feeling, or emotion: the center of emotion, in contrast to the head as the center of intellect.'

"In many statements it is regarded as the central source of one's mental faculties or capacities. . . . It is also the seat of one's affections, moral life, and character. In addition, heart is defined as having spirit, courage, and enthusiasm. Thus, when we love the Lord with all our heart and soul, we love him in spirit, with courage, enthusiasm, and profound earnestness of purpose." (*CR*, Oct. 1968, pp. 27–28.)

See also: Blindness of Heart; Bosom; Broken Heart; Desire of Their Hearts; Full Purpose of Heart; Harden Their Hearts; Hearts . . . Shall Turn to Fathers; Lay It to Heart; Lowliness of Heart; Murmurings of His Heart; Open Your Hearts; Pure in Heart; Singleness of Heart; Soften the Hearts; Stir Up the Hearts; Upright in Heart

Hearts . . . Shall Turn to Fathers

The promise of turning the hearts of the children to their fathers through the restoration of the keys held by Elijah is an oft-quoted scriptural phrase (D&C 2:2; 27:9; 110:15; 128:17; Mal. 4:5–6; 3 Ne. 25:5–6; JS—H 1:38–39). *To turn one's heart to the fathers is to seek after one's dead, and to perform the saving ordinances of the gospel in their behalf.* "The greatest responsibility in this world that God has laid upon us," said the Prophet Joseph, "is to seek after our dead." (TPJS, 356).

The restoration of Elijah's keys in 1836 (D&C 110:13–16) has literally turned the hearts of the children to the fathers. Elder Joseph Fielding Smith observed "that in 1836 there were no genealogical societies in this land or in Europe. Save for the keeping of pedigrees of royal and noble families, very little attention was being paid to the records of the dead in any Christian country. The first organized effort to collect and file genealogies of the common people was made shortly after the coming of Elijah. This was the formation of the New England Historic and Genealogical Society. In 1844, this society was incorporated." Since then, "A great many societies have also been organized, . . . but all of them since the keys of the Priesthood were returned to the earth which planted in the hearts of the children the promises made to their fathers." (WTP, 168–69; see also MWW, 189–92.)

See also: Elijah; Promises Made to the Fathers

Heathen

The "heathen" is spoken of three times in the Doctrine and Covenants (D&C 45:54; 75:22; 90:10). According to the Bible Dictionary, a heathen is a gentile. Elder Bruce R. McConkie defined heathens as "those who do not even profess a knowledge of the true God as record is borne of him in the scriptures. They worship idols or other gods that are entirely false as distinguished from so-called Christian peoples who attempt to worship the Lord, but who have totally false concepts of the nature and kind of being that he is." (MD, 347.)

See also: Heathen Nations

Heathen Nations

The term *heathen nations* is employed twice in the Doctrine and Covenants (D&C 45:54; 90:10) and refers to those nations which worship false gods and idols who are generally represented by some tangible material. Heathen nations are the antithesis of Christian nations, or those nations who profess a belief in Jesus Christ.

See also: Heathen

Heaven

The word *heaven* often refers to the dwelling place of God and those who abide his holy presence (D&C 1:17; 110:13; 129:1–3; Alma 18:30). The plural *heavens* may symbolically represent the inhabitants of heaven (D&C 76:1; 1 Ne. 21:13) or the power of God (D&C 121:33). On the other hand, heavens may refer to the expanse of sky above the earth (D&C 67:2; Morm. 9:11; Moses 2:20). The term *end of heaven* (D&C 133:7; 2 Ne. 23:5) refers to perceived limits of the horizon rather than to an actual end of the firmament.

See also: Celestial; Fire; Firmament; Heavenly; Sea of Glass and Fire

Heavenly

Joseph Smith wrote "that all things may have their likeness . . . —that which is earthly conforming to that which is heavenly" (D&C 128:13). Paul's writings to the Corinthians are then quoted, wherein he stated, "As is the earthy, such are they also that are earthy; and as is the heavenly, such are they also that are heavenly" (1 Cor. 15:48; D&C 128:14).

"The heavenly" evidently appears to be that which emanates from the Lord of heaven and earth, the Savior Jesus the Christ. "The image of the heavenly" of which Paul speaks (1 Cor. 15:49) is the "image of Christ or immortality, which is the natural inheritance of all men from Christ" (DNTC 2:402).

See also: Heaven

Heirs According to the Covenant

Following a conference of the Church held in Kirtland in June

1831, the Lord revealed that the next conference would "be held in Missouri, upon the land which I will consecrate unto my people, which are a remnant of Jacob, and those who are heirs according to the covenant" (D&C 52:2).

While the footnote references indicate "the covenant" is the "everlasting covenant" of the gospel—that which the "faithful children of Abraham" take upon themselves (Gal. 3:7–9)—there appears to be a broader application. When the resurrected Lord appeared to the "remnant of Jacob" living in the Americas, he said: "This is the land of your inheritance; and the Father hath given it unto you" (3 Ne. 15:13). He further declared, "This people will I establish in this land, unto the fulfilling of the covenant which I made with your father Jacob; and it shall be a New Jerusalem" (3 Ne. 20:22). Jacob's son Joseph—"a remnant of Jacob"—was given an inheritance "unto the utmost bound of the everlasting hills" (Gen. 49:22–26). His posterity has occupied portions of this land of inheritance since shortly after 600 B.C. (1 Ne. 5:14; 13:30).

Inasmuch as the location for the New Jerusalem, or the city of Zion, has been identified as Independence, Jackson County, Missouri (D&C 57:1–3), it would seem that the rightful heirs of this land are those members of the Church ("remnants of Jacob") who are called to possess this land of inheritance and build the city of Zion and its promised temple. This "remnant" would not be restricted to only those who are descendants of the people whom Jesus visited in this "land of promise," for the promise was to all of Joseph's posterity. (DS 2:247–51.)

See also: Remnant of Jacob

Hell

The term *hell* is used in the Doctrine and Covenants in basically two senses: (1) to illustrate the forces of the devil who use their pernicious power to fight against God and all that is good (D&C 6:34; 122:1); and (2) to indicate the actual place of the devil's domain or the place to which he and his followers will be confined (D&C 10:26; 29:38; 63:4; 76:84; 76:106; 104:18; 121:23; 123:10). The phrases *gates of hell* (D&C 10:69; 17:8; 18:5; 21:6; 33:13; 98:22; 128:10), *hosts of hell* (88:113), *jaws of hell* (122:7), and *handcuffs, chains, shackles, and fetters of hell* (123:8) are further descriptions of these two basic meanings.

However, there is a third meaning of the term: a state of mind. President George Q. Cannon said that heaven and hell are "not altogether a question of locality," for we carry them with us. "Hell is with the individual that deserves it." (GT 1:95.) Brigham Young taught that one who through his wicked ways grieves the Spirit of the Lord sufficiently to cause the withdrawal of that Spirit is "shut out from the presence of the Lord, . . . does not hear His voice, sees not His face, receives not the ministering of His angels or ministering spirits, and . . . must surely be in hell'' (JD 2:137).

Furthermore, speaking against the idea of universal salvation and death-bed repentance, he said: ''Were the wicked, in their sins, under the necessity of walking into the presence of the Father and Son, . . . their condition would be more excruciating and unendurable than to dwell in the lake that burns with fire and brimstone'' (JD 8:153–54). King Benjamin gave a graphic description of the suffering experienced by those whose sins have consigned them to hell (Mosiah 2:36–39).

Hell, as a place, is basically divided into three phases: (1) The present domain of the devil and his hosts, where they seek souls in their war against mankind on this earth (D&C 29:36–37); (2) the spirit prison in which the wicked remain in torment until the day of redemption (Alma 40:11–14; D&C 38:20–22, 29–30; Moses 7:36–39; DS 2:229); and (3) that future place of exquisite suffering and everlasting punishment where the devil, his angels, and all whom they have led away to misery as sons of perdition will be eternally consigned (D&C 29:38; 76:43–47). All who receive residence in any of these locations do so because they *choose to go there.*

''There is no power on earth or in hell that can compel a man to go to hell or to be damned if in the exercise of his agency he chooses to serve God'' (GT 1:139).

See also: Chains of Hell; Damnation of Hell; Fetters of Hell; Gates of Hell; Hosts of Hell; Jaws of Hell; Lake of Fire and Brimstone

Helmet of Salvation

Elder Bruce R. McConkie has said: ''As members of the Church, we are engaged in a mighty conflict. We are at war. We have enlisted in the cause of Christ to fight against Lucifer and all that is lustful and carnal and evil in the world. . . . The great war that rages . . . is resulting in many casualties, some fatal.'' (CR, Oct. 1974, pp. 43–44.)

In order to protect us from becoming casualties in this war, the Lord has prepared spiritual armament with which our bodies should be clothed. Among this protective armor is a ''helmet of salvation'' (D&C 27:18).

President Harold B. Lee noted that ''our head or our intellect is the controlling member of our body. It must be well protected against the enemy, for 'as a man thinketh in his heart, so is he.' (Proverbs 23:7.) . . . With the goal of salvation ever in our mind's eye as the ultimate to be achieved, our thinking and our decisions which determine action will always challenge all that would jeopardize that glorious future state. Lost indeed is that soul who is intellectually without the 'helmet of salvation'. . . . Our intellects, so protected, must always measure learning by the gospel criteria: Is it true? Is it uplifting? Will it benefit mankind? . . . Our thoughts must 'smell of the sunshine.' " (SHP, 334–35.)

Hen Gathereth Her Chickens

The Lord, who is a master at using analogies and symbolism, has indicated his willingness to gather his people "as a hen gathereth her chickens under her wings" (D&C 10:65; 29:2; 43:24; 3 Ne. 10:4–6; Matt. 23:37; Luke 13:34). Just as a mother hen provides safety and security for the chicks beneath her protective wings, so will the Savior provide peace and eternal safety to those who gather under his protective arms. However, just as safety will not come to the chick who refuses to respond to his mother's plea, there is no spiritual security for those who refuse the call of the Savior to gather to him.

There is a need for those who have already so gathered to assist the Savior in his work of gathering the lost and wayward. Elder Marvin J. Ashton suggested the text might read, "How often would I have gathered thy children together, even as a hen gathereth her chickens under her wings, and ye would not *help me!*" (En., Dec. 1971, p. 101.)

Herbs

Twice in the Doctrine and Covenants herbs are referred to as something that can have a positive effect on the body. The sick should be "nourished with all tenderness, with herbs and mild food" (D&C 42:43). And "all wholesome herbs God hath ordained for the constitution, nature, and use of man" (D&C 89:10).

A clarifying footnote in the 1981 edition of the Doctrine and Covenants indicates that herbs refers to plants. Although it is common to think of herbs strictly in the sense of actual or alleged medicinal properties they possess, Sperry indicates that there is a broader meaning to the word: "For most practical purposes 'wholesome herbs' may be defined as edible plants or vegetables as they are commonly known" (DCC, 454).

See also: Word of Wisdom (#2)

Herriman, Henry

The only mention of Henry Herriman in the Doctrine and Covenants is in connection with his appointment as one of the seven Presidents of the Seventy (D&C 124:138). He served in this capacity from February 1838, until his death on May 17, 1891, at Huntington, Utah (CA 1978:117). Elder Herriman was the senior president of that body during the last nine years of his life and served a total of fifty-three years in the council.

He was a member of Zion's Camp in 1834 and was a leader of the Kirtland Camp in 1838. This latter group left Ohio in 1838 and traveled approximately one thousand miles to Adam-ondi-Ahman. He was present "when the Prophet Joseph declared that the remnants of an altar found on the top of the hill, near Grand river, were what was left of the identical altar upon which Father Adam offered sacrifice" (Jenson 1:194).

He suffered all the persecutions heaped upon the Saints in Missouri and was one of the few authorized to travel in Daviess County, Missouri, during the height of troubles in that land (HC 2:184; 3:210). He actively participated in building up Nauvoo and served missions to Canada, Maine, and Great Britain (HC 2:35; 6:335; Jenson 1:193).

Elder Herriman crossed the plains originally in the Heber C. Kimball pioneer company in 1848, and later "acted as the president of the only company of missionaries, who ever crossed the plains with handcarts. Though fifty-two years of age," observed Andrew Jenson, "he pulled his handcart [as] faithfully and ably as his younger missionary companions."

Hicks, John A.

In January 1841, the name of John A. Hicks was given as the president of the elders quorum in Nauvoo (D&C 124:137). He is next mentioned in the minutes of a Church meeting held April 8 of that same year, when objections were raised to his continuing as a presiding officer (HC 4:341). On October 5, 1841, conference minutes reflect the following: "President Brigham Young presented an appeal from the decision of the Elders' quorum on a charge made against Elder John A. Hicks by Dimick B. Huntington for a breach of the ordinances of the city, for falsehood and schismatical conversation. After hearing the testimony in the case it was voted that Elder John A. Hicks be cut off from the Church." (HC 4:428.)

The tragic fall of Hicks did not end with this action, for he is mentioned as a member of the apostate mob at Carthage and is credited with having stated that he and others had "determined to shed the blood of Joseph Smith . . . whether he was cleared by the law or not" (HC 7:560).

Hid from the World

An 1832 revelation spoke of the faithful as being "hid from the world with Christ in God" (D&C 86:9). The Apostle Paul used this same phrase in writing to the early Saints in Colosse (Col. 3:3). The Prophet Joseph Smith gave an interpretation to this phrase. Placing his hands upon one of the faithful members of the Church, he said: "Your life is hid with Christ in God, and so are many others. Nothing but the unpardonable sin can prevent you from inheriting eternal life for you are sealed up by the power of the priesthood unto eternal life, having taken the step necessary for that purpose." (HC 5:391.) Thus, to be hid from the world is to be assured of eternal life or to have one's calling and election made sure.

Hidden Things of Darkness

There are two instances in which the Lord speaks of the "hidden things of darkness" (D&C 123:13; 1 Cor. 4:5). A footnote in the Doctrine and Covenants refers to the subject of secret combinations in the Topical Guide, which implies that these hidden things of darkness were of an evil nature; i.e., no man's secret combinations or sins will remain hidden but will ultimately be revealed. Sperry's commentary also indicates that these hidden things of darkness are things of iniquity to be eventually unmasked (DCC, 644–45).

According to one Bible commentator, the phrase as used by the Apostle Paul refers to "the things that are at present unknown. There is no suggestion of evil in the phrase." (Dummelow, 898.)

See also: Secret Combinations

Hidden Treasures

Those who keep the Word of Wisdom are promised "great treasures of knowledge, even hidden treasures" (D&C 89:19). One who keeps his physical body free from the ill effects of harmful substances is likely to be more alert and capable of understand-

ing and assimilating knowledge. One who keeps his spiritual senses sharp will discover treasures of knowledge hidden from the world.

Commenting on living the Word of Wisdom, President Ezra Taft Benson said: "Living the commandments of God is a condition of worthiness for entrance into the House of the Lord. There wisdom and 'great treasures of knowledge' are given that relate to our happiness in this life and joy throughout eternity.

"The Lord will increase our knowledge, wisdom, and capacity to obey when we obey His fundamental laws. This is what the Prophet Joseph Smith meant when he said we could have 'sudden strokes of ideas' which come into our minds as 'pure intelligence' [TPJS, 151]. This is revelation." (En., May 1983, p. 54.)

Speaking of hidden treasures of knowledge, Elder Spencer W. Kimball said: "The treasures of both secular and spiritual knowledge are hidden ones—but hidden from those who do not properly search and strive to find them. The knowledge of the spiritual will not come to an individual without effort any more than will the secular knowledge or college degrees. Spiritual knowledge gives the power to live eternally and to rise and overcome and develop and finally to create.

"Hidden knowledge is not unfindable. It is available to all who really search. . . .

". . . The coming of the Father and the Son to a person is a reality—a personal appearance—

and not merely dwelling in his heart. . . .

"This personal witness, then, is the ultimate treasure." (CR, Oct. 1968, p. 129.)

See also: Riches of Eternity; Treasures; Word of Wisdom (#2)

Higbee, Elias

In March 1838, Elias Higbee asked the Prophet Joseph to explain the meaning of several verses in the 52d chapter of Isaiah. The answers to these questions are found in Doctrine and Covenants 113:7–10.

Higbee was the Church Recorder from 1838 to 1843. He first heard of the Church in the spring of 1832 and traveled from Ohio to Jackson County, Missouri, to be baptized later that summer. He was ordained a high priest on August 7, 1834, by Elder Orson Pratt and later served as a missionary.

Higbee helped in the construction of the Kirtland Temple and received his endowments there. He suffered the persecution of the Missouri period of Church history and later settled at the site of Nauvoo, where he was appointed to serve on the committee charged with building the temple.

Higbee died in full fellowship, true to the faith, on June 8, 1843, in Nauvoo. "He endured much persecution for the gospel's sake, both in Missouri and other places. In his official capacities he was always just and trustworthy and manifested great zeal for the prosperity of the latter-day work." (Jenson 1:253.)

High Council

The earliest date on which revelatory mention of a "high council" appears is Februry 9, 1831 (D&C 42:34). Although this body is mentioned earlier in Doctrine and Covenants 20:67, that particular verse was added five years after the original revelation had been received, following the establishment of a permanent high council in Kirtland on February 17, 1834. Prior to this there had been "several Councils of twelve High Priests called for special cases" (JD 11:7).

The procedural pattern of operations of all high councils — their "form and constitution" — is outlined in section 102 (HC 2:31). "The Stake High Council consists of twelve High Priests, presided over by the Stake President, assisted by his two counselors" (PCG, 216). "The functions of a Stake High Council are largely judicial, yet important legislative and executive powers are conferred upon it. And in the establishsment of various committees within it, in representing the Stake Presidency in visiting wards, Priesthood quorums, auxiliary groups, and assisting the Presidency in any manner called upon, the Council is seen as an important administrative body." (PCG, 299.)

See also: Standing High Councils; Traveling High Priests

High Priesthood

The term *High Priesthood* appears in the Doctrine and Covenants with both capitalized initial letters (D&C 107:64) and uncapitalized letters (D&C 84:29). Its meaning was officially declared by the First Presidency in 1902: "It is well to remember that the term 'High Priesthood,' as frequently used, has reference to the Melchizedek Priesthood, in contradistinction to the 'Lesser,' or Aaronic Priesthood" (IE 5:551).

See also: Melchizedek Priesthood

High Priests

In June 1831, at a conference in Kirtland, nineteen men were the first to be ordained to the office of high priest in modern times (ECH, 106). This office of the Melchizedek Priesthood had been mentioned in a revelation received several months earlier (D&C 42:31, 71). Reference to this office can also be found in section 20, but in verses that were added five years after the original revelation was received (D&C 20:66).

Although it is a separate office in the priesthood, it is often used to designate men who hold yet other offices. For example, bishops must be high priests unless lineal descent from Aaron can be ascertained (D&C 68:14–21). Apostles are designated as high priests (D&C 84:63), as are members of the First Presidency of the Church (D&C 107:22). High councilors must be high priests (D&C 102:1).

The office of high priest is an appendage to the Melchizedek Priesthood and derives its authority from that priesthood (D&C 107:2–5). One who holds the office of high priest would do well to ponder these words of President Joseph F. Smith: "Every man who holds the office of high priest in the Church, or has been ordained a high priest, whether he is called to active position in the Church or not—inasmuch as he has been ordained a high priest, should feel that he is obliged—that it is his bounden duty, to set an example before the old and young worthy of emulation, and to place himself in a position to be a teacher of righteousness, not only by precept but more particularly by example—giving to the younger ones the benefit of the experience of age, and thus becoming individually a power in the midst of the community in which he dwells. . . . There is no body of priesthood in the Church who should excel, or who are expected to excel, those who are called to bear the office of high priest in the Church." (GD, 182.)

Those who belong to the high priests quorum "should have a lively union with it, not a dead connection" (PCG, 125).

High Tower

Anciently, after being delivered from danger, David spoke of the Lord as being his rock, fortress, deliverer, strength, buckler, horn of salvation, and high tower (2 Sam. 22:3; Ps. 18:2). In modern times the Lord promised to be the salvation and high tower of Zion (D&C 97:20).

A tower is symbolic of strength or readiness to repel incursions by the enemy. The higher the tower, the more territory that can be watched. God is the ultimate High Tower. His omniscience and omnipotence can keep one safe from enemies by giving sufficient warning so that appropriate defenses can be made ready.

See also: Watch Towers

High-Mindedness

As used in Doctrine and Covenants 124:3, *high-minded* is an adjective denoting honorable, principled, and fair. However, as used in an 1833 revelation, the noun *high-mindedness* means arrogant and haughty, full of pride (D&C 90:17).

Highway Cast Up in the Midst of the Great Deep

See: They Who Are in the North Countries; Ice Shall Flow Down at Their Presence

Him Who Laid the Foundation of the Earth

Jesus Christ, as a premortal God, clothed in a tabernacle of spirit, created the earth upon which we dwell (D&C 45:1; John 1:1–5, 14; 3 Ne. 9:15). In an epis-

tle issued by the First Presidency and Council of the Twelve Apostles in 1916, the role of Jesus as Creator was defined: "Scriptures that refer to God in any way as the Father of the heavens and in the earth are to be understood as signifying that God is the Maker, the Organizer, the Creator of the heavens and the earth.

"With this meaning, as the context shows in every case, Jehovah, who is Jesus Christ, the Son of Elohim, is called 'the Father,' and even 'the very eternal Father of heaven and earth.' (See . . . Mosiah 16:15.) With analogous meaning, Jesus Christ is called 'The Everlasting Father' (Isa. 9:6; compare 2 Ne. 19:6.) The descriptive titles 'Everything' and 'eternal' in the foregoing texts are synonymous.

"That Jesus Christ who we also know as Jehovah, was the executive of the Father, Elohim, in the work of creation is set forth in the book *Jesus the Christ*, Chap. 4. Jesus Christ, being the Creator, is constantly called the Father of heaven and earth in the sense explained above; and since his creations are of eternal quality, he is very properly called the Eternal Father of heaven and earth." (CHMR 1:168; also IE 19:34.)

See also: Jesus Christ

Hiram, Ohio

Joseph Smith's journal entry of September 12, 1831, reads: "I removed with my family to the township of Hiram, and commenced living with John Johnson. Hiram was in Portage county, and about thirty miles southeasterly from Kirtland. From this time until the forepart of October, I did little more than prepare to re-commence the translation of the Bible." (HC 1:215.)

Of this move, Joseph Fielding Smith wrote: "It was for the purpose of correcting these scriptures [the Bible], in large part, that Joseph Smith and Sidney Rigdon moved to Hiram where they could be at peace and able to pursue their work. It was also their intention to prepare for publication the revelations which had been given up to this time, as soon as the printing press was ready in Independence, Missouri. The revision of the Bible had been delayed by command of the Lord, while the Prophet was in Fayette, because of the pressure of other duties." (CHMR 1:242.)

It was in this little town of Hiram that fourteen revelations were given the Prophet Joseph. Among these were the preface (D&C 1) and appendix (D&C 133) to the Doctrine and Covenants, as well as the magnificent manifestation entitled "A Vision" (D&C 76).

At a special conference in Hiram in early November 1831, the decision was made to print the revelations which now comprise part of what we have as the Doctrine and Covenants (HC 1:221–37).

Hoar Frost

In a moment of despair and discouragement, Joseph Smith was promised that those who falsely charged him should have "their prospects . . . melt away as the hoar frost melteth before the burning rays of the rising sun" (D&C 121:11). The word *hoar* denotes something white; the hoar frost is the white frozen dew produced when once humid air is frozen.

Holiness

Members of The Church of Jesus Christ of Latter-day Saints are commanded to walk "in holiness before the Lord" (D&C 20:69; 21:4). Furthermore, Zion, which represents the "pure in heart" (D&C 97:21), is to "increase in beauty, and in holiness," extending her borders and strengthening her stakes (D&C 82:14).

To be in a state of holiness is to be set apart for holy or sacred purposes and to avoid that which is common, worldly, or profane (LDSBD, 703). To have "holiness of heart" is to be spiritually pure (D&C 46:7). One who walks in holiness walks in concert with Christ and has the companionship of the Spirit. One who walks in holiness eschews anything that is sordid and sinful, having "no more disposition to do evil, but to do good continually" (Mosiah 5:2; see also Alma 13:12).

See also: Garments Pure and White; Pure; Pure in Heart; Sanctification; Unspotted

Holy Angel, An

At the time the Church was organized, the Lord reminded Joseph Smith that following his cleansing experience during the First Vision, wherein he saw and conversed with the Father and Son, he again became entangled in the ways of the world. "But after repenting, and humbling himself sincerely, through faith, God ministered unto him by an holy angel" (D&C 20:5-6). This was the angel Moroni, who gave him power to bring forth and translate the Book of Mormon and anciently had hidden the sacred records which he was now authorized to bring forth (JS—H 1:28-54; Ether 5; Moro. 10).

See also: Moroni

Holy City

The faithful who "die in the Lord" are promised an inheritance in the "holy city" (D&C 63:49). This sanctified city of Saints is the New Jerusalem (TPJS, 86; Ether 13:5). This is the "city of Zion" (D&C 57:1-3); the "city of the heritage of God" (D&C 58:13); the "city of the living God, the heavenly place, the holiest of all" (D&C 76:66).

This "City Eternal" was seen in a dream by Elder David O. McKay, and described in the following terms: "a beautiful white city . . . , trees with luscious fruit, shrubbery with gorgeously-tinted leaves, and flowers in perfect bloom abounded everywhere. The clear sky above seemed to reflect these beautiful shades of color." Each inhabitant of the city "wore a white flowing robe and a white headdress," and above their heads, written in gold, were these words: "These Are They Who Have Overcome the World—Who Have Truly Been Born Again!" (CE, 101-2.)

See also: City of the Heritage of God; City of the Living God; City of Zion; New Jerusalem

Holy Day

See: Sabbath Day

Holy Ghost

"The Holy Ghost has not a body of flesh and bones, but is a personage of Spirit," declared the Lord through his prophet (D&C 130:22-23). This third member of the Godhead, in whom we declare our belief (Articles of Faith 1:1), *"is a Spirit, in the form of a man"* (DS 1:38). Whether he will ever have a physical body has not been revealed, and, in the words of a prophet, "It is a waste of time to speculate" on this subject (DS 1:39). He has a specific size and dimension and "can no more be omnipresent in person than can the Father or the Son, but by his intelligence, his knowledge, his power and influence, over and through the laws of nature, he is and can be omnipresent throughout all the works of God" (GD, 61).

Some become confused about the personage of the Holy Ghost

because prophets and gospel writers have written that following Jesus' baptism, "the Holy Ghost descended upon him in the form of a dove" (D&C 93:15; 1 Ne. 11:27; 2 Ne. 31:8; Matt. 3:16; Mark 1:10). Joseph Smith said: "The sign of the dove was instituted before the creation of the world, a witness for the Holy Ghost, and the devil cannot come in the sign of the dove. The Holy Ghost is a personage, and is in the form of a personage. It does not confine itself to the *form* of the dove, but in [the] *sign* of the dove. The Holy Ghost cannot be transformed into a dove; but the sign of a dove was given to John to signify the truth of the deed, as the dove is an emblem or token of truth and innocence." (TPJS, 276.)

President Harold B. Lee suggested that the office of the Holy Ghost involved pronouncing "one free from guilt or blame . . . to absolve" one from the stain of sin (SHP, 51). This is what was meant when the Lord proclaimed, "by the Spirit ye are justified" (Moses 6:60).

A major mission of the Holy Ghost is to testify of the reality of Jesus as the Christ. As Paul wrote to the Corinthians, "no man can *know* that Jesus is the Lord, but by the Holy Ghost" (JST, 1 Cor. 12:3; italics added). Additionally, the Doctrine and Covenants states that "to some it is given by the Holy Ghost to know that Jesus Christ is the Son of God, and that he was crucified for the sins of the world" (D&C 46:13; see also Moro. 10:6–7).

The power of the Holy Ghost —the ability to receive revelation—is based upon faith in Christ and righteousness (1 Ne. 10:17). The effect of this upon man is to expand his mind and his whole soul with "pure intelligence" (TPJS, 149–50).

See also: Blasphemy Against the Holy Ghost; Comforter; Gift of the Holy Ghost; God; Holy Spirit of Promise; Spirit; Spirit of the Lord; Spirit of Truth; Unspeakable Gift of the Holy Ghost

Holy House

In three places in the Doctrine and Covenants the term *holy house* refers specifically to the Kirtland Temple (D&C 96:2; 109:13; 110:8). However, reference to "my holy house" in Doctrine and Covenants 124:39 is an allusion to temples in general. A temple is a holy house of God.

Elder James E. Talmage provided the following understanding of the term *temple*: "Both by derivation and common usage the term 'temple,' in its literal application, is of restricted and specific meaning. The essential idea of a temple is and ever has been that of a *place* specially set apart for service regarded as sacred, and of real or assumed sanctity; in a more restricted sense, a temple is a *building* constructed for and exclusively devoted to sacred rites and ceremonies. The

Latin *Templum* was the equivalent of the Hebrew Beth Elohim and signified the abode of Deity; hence, as associated with Divine worship, it meant literally the HOUSE OF THE LORD." (HL, 1.)

See also: House

Holy Land

An 1832 revelation states the Lord will not allow the children of the kingdom (the Lord's own people) to pollute his holy land (D&C 84:59). Sperry suggests the land referred to is Missouri, which at that time had been designated as the land of Zion, the gathering place for God's Saints (DCC, 399; see also HC 1:318; D&C 57:1–4). Six years later the Lord referred to the city of Far West, Missouri, as a "holy and consecrated land" (D&C 115:7).

Perhaps there is a broader meaning to holy land that extends beyond the borders of a single state, for any place where the Saints are gathered and the Lord's Spirit is present could be designated as a holy land or place (D&C 6:32; Matt. 18:20).

See also: Children of the Kingdom; Holy Places

Holy Men That Ye Know Not Of

In Doctrine and Covenants 49:8, reference is made to "holy men that ye know not of." According to President Joseph Field-ing Smith, these men "who were without sin, and reserved unto the Lord, are translated persons such as John the Revelator and the Three Nephites, who do not belong to this generation and yet are in the flesh in the earth performing a special ministry until the coming of Jesus Christ" (CHMR 1:209; see also SS, 284).

Holy One

"Christ is the *Holy One*," declared Elder Bruce R. McConkie, "a designation signifying that he is a holy, pure, sanctified Person, One who was and is without sin, who had no reason for repentance, and who stands perfect in all things" (MD, 360; see also D&C 78:16; Isa. 43:15; 49:7; Ps. 16:10; Acts 2:27; 3:14; 13:35; 2 Ne. 9:20, 41; 3 Ne. 26:5; Morm. 9:5, 14).

See also: Jesus Christ

Holy One of Zion

The use of the title "Holy One of Zion" (D&C 78:15) has been defined as follows: "To speak of Christ as the *Holy One of Zion* is to point attention both to his holiness and to the especial and personal relationship that exists between him and his Zion. . . . When the perfect Zion—composed solely of the pure in heart (D&C 97:21)—is again established on earth, then the presence of the Lord will be felt there as his presence was found in the ancient city of that name. (Moses 7:16–19, 62–64.)" (MD, 361.)

See also: Zion

Holy Places

"My disciples shall stand in holy places, and shall not be moved," declared the Lord (D&C 45:32; 87:8). According to Elder Harold B. Lee, holy places are to be found in Zion, which, according to the scriptures, is where the pure in heart dwell (D&C 97:21). Therefore, "the all-important thing is not where we live but whether or not our hearts are pure" (CR, Oct. 1968, pp. 61–62).

Latter-day Saints are to gather upon "holy places" (D&C 101:64); in other words, wherever members of Christ's church are located that place should be holy, as befits the dwelling places of saints. Temples are, of course, designated as special holy places (D&C 124:39); however, should not the *home* be just as holy a place?

See also: Holy Land

Holy Priesthood

The Holy Priesthood which the Lord took out of the midst of ancient Israel (D&C 84:25) was the Melchizedek Priesthood, or "the Holy Priesthood, after the Order of the Son of God" (D&C 107:3).

President Joseph Fielding Smith said the following: "The Lord offered to Israel in the days of Moses the fulness of the Gospel with the Higher Priesthood and its keys, intending to give unto them the blessings of exaltation and make of them a royal Priesthood. When Moses went up into the sacred Mount Horeb and received the writings which the Lord made with his own finger, he received the fulness of the Gospel with its ordinances and covenants, but when Moses returned after his absence of forty days and found the Israelites reveling in idolatry, he broke the tables. Later the Lord gave unto him other tables but changed some of the commandments, and took away the Higher, or Melchizedek Priesthood, and gave to the people the carnal law." (CHMR 1:338–39.)

See also: Melchizedek Priesthood

Holy Priesthood After the Order of the Son of God

In 1835, the Lord revealed the original name of the Melchizedek Priesthood as being "the Holy Priesthood, after the Order of the Son of God," who is Christ (D&C 107:1–4). This name ceased to be used in order "to avoid the too frequent repetition of his name."

The original name is alluded to in other scriptural references. Section 84, for example refers to "the priesthood which is after the holiest order of God" (84:18). Jacob and Joseph, ancient Nephite priesthood bearers, were "ordained after the manner of his holy order." (2 Ne. 6:2, see also

AGQ 1:124–25). Another Nephite, the prophet Alma, spoke of God having "ordained priests, after his holy order, which was after the order of his Son" (Alma 13:1–11).

See also: Melchizedek Priesthood; Order of the Only Begotten Son

Holy Spirit of Promise

With the exception of a single occurrence in the New Testament (Eph. 1:13), the only other scriptural references to the "Holy Spirit of Promise" are all in the Doctrine and Covenants (D&C 76:53; 88:3; 124:124; 132:7, 18, 19, 26).

"*The Holy Spirit of Promise is the Holy Ghost* who places the stamp of approval upon every ordinance: baptism, confirmation, ordination, marriage. *The promise is that the blessings will be received through faithfulness.*

If a person violates a covenant, whether it be of baptism, ordination, marriage or anything else, the Spirit withdraws the stamp of approval, and the blessings will not be received." (DS 1:45.)

See also: Comforter, Another; Holy Ghost; Sealed by the Holy Spirit of Promise

Honorable Men of the Earth

The Lord informs us that among the inhabitants of the terrestrial world will be "honorable men of the earth, who were blinded by the craftiness of men" (D&C 76:75). These are they who "failed to comply with the requirements of exaltation" (AF, 92).

According to Webster, an "honorable" person is one who is noble, commendable, and respectable. Thus, the inhabitants of the terrestrial kingdom will be *good* men and women of the earth.

Elder Alvin R. Dyer said: "Many noble and great bodies will possess the terrestrial kingdom. . . . These, for the most part, will be men who, during earth-life existence, sought the excellence of men; and some who gave of their time, talents and endeavors to the ways of man-made ideals of culture, science, and education, but thought not to include God and his ways in their search for a complete life. They received more of the spirit of the world and of the wisdom which men teach . . . , neglecting that spirit which is of God." (WAI, 552–53.)

See also: Terrestrial

Honors of Men

One reason why men lose the power of their priesthood is that they seek after the things of the world and the honors of men (D&C 121:35). To seek the honors of men is to set aside the things of God and place priority upon the praise of the world (D&C 58:39).

Nephi saw the wicked destroying the Saints of God for the praise of the world (1 Ne. 13:9).

He also saw the practice of priestcraft whereby men preached for gain and the praise of the world rather than for the welfare of Zion (2 Ne. 26:29).

Another ancient Nephite prophet indicated that seeking such praise cankers the soul and brings a misery which never dies (Morm. 8:38). Whenever the applause, accolades, and praise of the world take precedence over the things of God, one is seeking the honors of men.

Hope

Inseparably connected with faith is the principle of hope (D&C 18:19; Ether 12; Moro. 7; 1 Cor. 13). Hope is a qualification for those who labor in the ministry (D&C 4:5; 12:8). The true meaning of hope has been provided by the Nephite prophet Moroni, who taught that hope consists of the faith that through one's righteousness and the atonement of Christ, one will not only be resurrected but also "raised unto life eternal" (Moro. 7:40–42).

A modern-day Apostle said, "Hope enables men to have faith in the first instance and then because of faith the hope increases until salvation is gained." Thus, "as used in the revelations, hope is the desire of faithful people to gain eternal salvation in the kingdom of God hereafter. It is not a flimsy, ethereal desire, one without assurance that the desired consummation will be received,

but a desire coupled with full expectation of receiving the coveted reward." (DNTC 2:263–65.)

"The hope of the righteous shall be gladness," wrote the author of Proverbs (Prov. 10:28; see also 14:32).

Horah

On various occasions the Lord deemed it wisdom to disguise the identities of individuals to whom he revealed his will. Once the necessity for the secrecy had passed, the true identities were made known (HC 1:255). One of the unnamed individuals in a revelation given April 26, 1832, was a person designated as "Horah" (D&C 82:11). Recent editions of the Doctrine and Covenants identify Horah as John Whitmer.

See also: Whitmer, John

Hosanna

Teachers and preachers of the gospel have been exhorted to cry, "Hosanna, hosanna, blessed be the name of the Lord God!" (D&C 19:37.) In his dedicatory prayer of the Kirtland Temple, the Prophet pleaded that we might mingle our voices with those of the angels in "singing Hosanna to God and the Lamb!" (D&C 109:79.)

The word *Hosanna* is "of Hebrew origin, meaning literally, *save now*, or *save we pray*, or *save we beseech thee* [and] is both a chant of praise and glory to God and an entreaty for his blessings" (MD, 368). As an entreaty, it is a plea to show one the way to salvation. It was used in both senses by the crowds who shouted "Hosanna to the son of David" as the Savior rode humbly yet triumphantly into Jerusalem (Matt. 21:1–11).

The Nephites uttered the same plea of salvation to the resurrected Christ (3 Ne. 11:17), whereupon he taught them the basic principles of the gospel and commanded them to be baptized.

Hosts of Heaven

The "hosts of heaven" (D&C 38:1; 45:1) or "heavenly hosts" (D&C 84:42) are those who inhabit celestial spheres. Unfortunately, one-third of the hosts of heaven who dwelt in the Father's presence *prior* to the creation of this earth chose to forsake their celestial mansions and became "hosts of hell" (D&C 29:36–38; 88:113).

Those who choose to follow the teachings of the Lord Jesus in this life, doing all that is required of them, will qualify to become subjects of the Lord of Hosts, or the Lord of the hosts of heaven.

Hosts of Hell

As described in the Doctrine and Covenants, the "hosts of hell" consist of (1) those spirits who forfeited their place among the "hosts of heaven" and chose to follow Lucifer in his rebellion against God in the spirit world (D&C 29:36–37; Abr. 3:27–28; Rev. 12:7–9) and (2) those individuals who received a tabernacle of flesh upon this earth but who knowingly and willfully rejected righteousness and committed the unpardonable sin— blasphemy against the Holy Ghost (D&C 76:31–38; 132:27).

These demented devils will follow their leader into a battle reminiscent of the premortal war (D&C 88:110–15; Rev. 12:7–9). However, as before, Satan and his soldiers shall be defeated by Michael and the "hosts of heaven" in a struggle that will end in the triumph of righteousness and the eternal banishment of the "hosts of hell" to outer darkness and endless punishment (D&C 76:43–46).

See also: False Spirits; Hell; Sons of Perdition; Third Part of the Hosts of Heaven

Hot Drinks

One of the items prohibited by the Word of Wisdom is the use of "hot drinks" (D&C 89:9). These beverages were defined by Joseph Smith as "tea and coffee" (TS 3:799–801). Furthermore, President Joseph Fielding Smith has written: "Patriarch Hyrum Smith delivered an address to the Saints in Nauvoo, in 1842, in which he declared that hot drinks include tea and coffee, and this interpretation was accepted by the Church. However, all hot drinks, whether they are stimulants or not, are harmful to the body." (CHMR 1:385.)

More recently, under the heading of "Cola Drinks," an official publication of the Church stated: "The leaders of the Church have advised, and we do now specifically advise, against use of any drink containing harmful habit-forming drugs" (CR, Apr. 1975, p. 102).

See also: Word of Wisdom (#2)

House

The use of the word *house* varies widely within the Doctrine and Covenants, and one must look beyond the word to the context in which it is used in order to ascertain the meaning thereof. For example, "house" may refer to one's dwelling (D&C 41:7) or to the family that occupies it (D&C 75:18–22). The word *house* can also be symbolic of the faithful who are living in such a way that they have membership in God's house (D&C 58:9; 85:7; 101:55; 132:8–18).

On the other hand, God will divinely discipline those who claim such membership but whose lives are not in accord therewith (D&C 112:25). Those whose houses are in order in this life will inherit the eternal mansions of the Father (D&C 81:6; 98:18).

A temple is a "house of the Lord." Among the temples mentioned are the Kirtland Temple (D&C 88:119; 94; 95; 96; 97; 109; 117:16); the Far West Temple (D&C 115:8–14; 118:5; 119:2); the Independence Temple, or Temple of Zion (D&C 57:1–3; 84:5, 31–32); the Nauvoo Temple (D&C 124; 30–31); and the temple at Jerusalem (D&C 45:18).

The counsel in Doctrine and Covenants 88:119 regarding the establishment of a house of prayer, fasting, faith, learning, glory, order, and God, though referring to the Kirtland Temple (D&C 95:3; 109:8), also has implications to the necessity of establishing personal houses of godliness and orderliness.

Elsewhere in section 88, the house of which the Lord speaks refers to the school of the prophets (D&C 88:119–37).

See also: Holy House

House for Boarding, A

See: Nauvoo House

House of David

The term *house of David* refers specifically to those who have descended through the loins of David and who are therefore automatically children of his forefathers — Judah, Jacob, Isaac, and Abraham. The yoke of bondage (D&C 109:63) which has been upon the house of David has evidently been the dispersion and persecution which has followed his descendants, especially since the destruction of Jerusalem by the Romans in A.D. 70. The prophet Zenos declared that "they shall wander in the flesh, and perish, and become a hiss and a by-word, and be hated among all nations" (1 Ne. 19:14).

In the dedicatory prayer of the Kirtland Temple, the Prophet Joseph Smith pleaded with the Lord to allow both the persecution and dispersion to be lifted from these descendants of David and his patriarchal fathers (D&C 109:61–64).

There are several significant prophecies affecting the house of David. One has been fulfilled and the second is yet to come. The first was fulfilled when the promised Messiah, Jesus the Christ, was born in the house of David, according to prophetic and divine utterances (Ps. 132:11; Luke 1:31–33; Acts 2:29–30; Rom. 1:3; 2 Tim. 2:8). His mortal mother, Mary, was of Davidic descent and her genealogy is recorded in the third chapter of Luke (Talmage, 86). Jesus himself responded to the title "son of David" (Matt. 9:27; 15:22; 20:30–31; 21:9).

The second significant prophecy regarding the house of David was when the Prophet Joseph Smith declared that "the throne and kingdom of David is to be taken from him and given to another by the name of David in the last days, raised up out of his lineage" (TPJS, 339). This is yet to come to pass.

See also: David; Israel

House of Israel

House of Israel appears only five times in the Doctrine and Covenants (D&C 14:10; 18:6; 29:12; 39:11; 42:39), but it is synonymous with "Israel" (D&C 35:25), "children of Israel" (D&C 8:3), "nations of Israel" (D&C 90:8), and "tribes of Israel" (D&C 77:9–11). It can denote one of the following: (1) a literal descendant of Jacob (Israel) through his children, or (2) the covenant people of the Lord who have wholeheartedly accepted the gospel and become heirs to all the promises bestowed upon the patriarchal fathers—Abraham, Isaac, and Jacob.

Faithful followers of Christ become the true seed of Abraham. Lineage of the flesh does not qualify one for eternal membership in his hallowed household. Paul instructed the Galatians on this matter when he said, "They which are of faith, the same are the children of Abraham. . . . For as many of you as have been baptized into Christ have put on Christ. . . . And if ye be Christ's, then are ye Abraham's seed, and heirs according to the promise." (Gal. 3:7, 26–29.)

Joseph Smith said, "The effect of the Holy Ghost upon a Gentile, is to purge out the old blood, and make him actually of the seed of Abraham" (TPJS, 150).

See also: Children of Israel; Israel; Seed of Abraham; Tribes of Israel

House of Joseph

Those who are descendants of Jacob's son Joseph, through either of the latter's two sons, Ephraim or Manasseh, are of the house of Joseph. Section 113 speaks of a servant of Christ who will be of mixed descent, coming both through Ephraim, son of Joseph, and through Jesse, a descendant of Judah. President Joseph Fielding Smith has declared: "We, each and all, have descended through a mixed lineage. No one can lay claim to a perfect descent from father to son through just one lineage." (AGQ 3:61.)

See also: Joseph; Israel

House of Prayer

The "house of prayer" to which the Saints are commanded to go each sabbath day is the location where the sacrament service and other sacred sabbath meetings are held (D&C 59:9). This may be within the walls of a beautiful chapel dedicated to the purpose of worship, or in a humble home where "two or three are gathered in [the Lord's] name" (D&C 6:32).

However, regardless of location, the only authorized "house of prayer" is the place designated by the proper priesthood authority: "For all things must be done in order" (D&C 28:13). All meetings are to be conducted under the direction of the presiding priesthood authority.

Of course, each individual is responsible for maintaining his own personal "house of prayer," making his own abode a house of daily worship (D&C 88:119).

House of the Daughters of Zion

See: Daughters of Zion

Household of Faith

The term *household of faith* is found only in the Doctrine and Covenants (121:45) and in Paul's writings (Gal. 6:10). It appears to be synonymous with the term *household of God*, which is found only once in scriptural writings (Eph. 2:19) and has been defined as "those who dwell together as brethren (of like-minded faith) under one roof, the roof of the gospel (DNTC 2:504).

Housetops

Speaking of the rebellious, the Lord stated that "their iniquities shall be spoken upon the housetops, and their secret acts shall be revealed" (D&C 1:3). In essence, the wicked will have their sins spoken of publicly—they shall not be hidden (Morm. 5:8).

In a positive vein, the prophet Nephi speaks of the day when "the words of the book which were sealed [Book of Mormon] shall be read upon the house tops" [spoken of publicly] (2 Ne. 27:11). One can also visualize this occurring through radio or television antennae attached to housetops.

How Beautiful upon the Mountains . . .

Joseph Smith wrote of a voice of gladness which both the living and the dead should hear and then quoted a verse of scripture from Isaiah: "How beautiful upon the mountains are the feet of those that bring glad tidings of good things, and that say unto Zion: Behold thy God reigneth!" (D&C 128:19; Isa. 52:7.)

This particular passage is also referred to in the Book of Mormon (1 Ne. 13:37; 3 Ne. 20:40). According to the prophet Abinadi, *all* who have proclaimed the peace and glad tidings of the gospel are the "seed of Christ" and are those who are "beautiful upon the mountains" (Mosiah 12:21; 15:15–18). Their beauty is symbolic of the message of Christ which they bear.

Humility

One of the cardinal virtues to be cultivated by the Saints of God is humility. All who desire to serve God must possess this attribute (D&C 4:6; 12:8; 118:3; Col. 3:12). Humility involves freedom from pride or arrogance; to be humble is to be meek and teachable.

Christ was thus the meekest of men (Matt. 11:29). Even as we are commanded to model our lives after the Master (Matt. 5:48; 3 Ne. 12:48), so we are commanded to be humble (D&C 105:23; 112:10; 124:97, 103). Humility is required of all who wish to rend the veil and see God (D&C 67:10).

See also: Abase

Humphrey, Solomon

Among those called to missionary service in June 1831, was Solomon Humphrey (D&C 52:35). Humphrey was born September 23, 1775, and his name is occasionally rendered as *Humphreys* or *Humphry* (HC 1:285; 2:73–74, 184). In September 1832, at Potsdam, New York, he confirmed George A. Smith a member of the Church. The latter was to become an Apostle and member of the First Presidency.

Humphrey served as a member of the famous Zion's Camp contingent and was revered for his bravery and love of wildlife. The following is Joseph Smith's account of an occurrence on May 27, 1834: "This afternoon, Elder Solomon Humphrey, an aged brother of the camp [Zion's Camp] having become exceedingly weary, lay down on the prairie to rest himself and fell asleep. When he awoke, he saw, coiled up, within one foot of his head, a rattlesnake lying between him and his hat, which he had in his hand when he fell asleep. The brethren gathered around him saying: 'It is a rattlesnake, let us kill it;' but Bro. Humphrey said 'No, I will protect him, you cannot hurt him, for he and I have had a good nap together.'" Humphrey died in September of that same year, in Clay County, Missouri. (Jenson 4:689–90.)

Hundred and Forty-four Thousand

When the Lamb of God returns to earth to stand upon Mount Zion, he will be accompanied by "a hundred and forty-four thousand, having his Father's name written on their foreheads" (D&C 77:1; 133:18; Rev. 7:4; 14:1). Although an explanation of these servants is given in section 77, Elder Orson Pratt provides further information regarding the name of the Father that is sealed in their foreheads: "Will it be simply a plaything, a something that has no meaning? Or will it mean that which the inscriptions specify? — that they are indeed Gods — one with the Father and one with the Son." (JD 14:242–43.)

Joseph Smith taught that the selection of this body of redeemed souls, twelve thousand from each of the tribes of Israel, had already commenced (HC 6:196). One commentary describes these select Saints as "kings and priests . . . converted, baptized, endowed, married for eternity, and finally sealed up unto eternal life, having their calling and election made sure" (DNTC 3:491; 2 Pet. 1:1–19).

Huntington, William

The name of William Huntington surfaces in the Doctrine and Covenants as a member of the Nauvoo high council in 1841 (D&C 124:132). However, this faithful Saint was known in the circles of the Church for some time prior to this. Before the Church was organized, it was revealed to him that he would live to see the true Church, which he boldly proclaimed. When he first heard of "Mormonism" in the winter of 1832–33, he "read the Book of Mormon, believed it with all his heart and preached it almost every day, to his neighbors and everybody he could see." He was finally baptized in 1835, after which his home became a meetinghouse for the Saints. He lived in Kirtland for some time, where he suffered the persecution heaped upon the members who were faithful. "His house was a hiding place for Father Joseph Smith, Hyrum, Samuel and Don Carlos, while they were trying to escape from the persecutions in Kirtland. The Egyptian mummies were also hid in his house for a long time, and many of the pursued and persecuted Saints found a retreat there and a hiding place from apostates' persecution."

He served as a high councilor in Kirtland and as commissary for the Saints in Far West. He worked on the Nauvoo Temple as a stone cutter, and later within its sacred walls as an ordinance worker. He helped lay one of the corner stones of this edifice on April 6,

1841. Huntington served as one of the leaders of the pioneer companies and presided over the Church at the Mt. Pisgah, Iowa, settlement. "In this place his labors were extreme and unremitting for the good and welfare of the people, and the comfort of the sick of which there were a great many." He died on August 19, 1846, while serving his people. Huntington's biographical epitaph reads: "In life he was beloved by all the Saints. His love and zeal for the cause of God were unsurpassed by any. His judgment was respected and his conduct never questioned; he never had a trial or difficulty with any person in the Church." (Jenson 1:368–70.)

Hyde, Orson

One of the more frequently mentioned men in the Doctrine and Covenants is Orson Hyde. He is first mentioned in connection with his call to "proclaim the everlasting gospel" in 1831 (D&C 68:1, 7). Several months later, in January 1832, he is told to accompany Samuel Smith on a mission "into the eastern countries" (D&C 75:13), where he traveled over two thousand miles without purse or scrip. Almost three years later, the Prophet was assured that Orson was safely performing a special mission for the First Presidency (D&C 100:14).

He was mentioned as a member of the Kirtland high council as well as one of its two clerks (D&C 102:3, 34). Still another missionary journey is mentioned in D&C 103:40, and the last reference in the Doctrine and Covenants to Elder Hyde is as a member of the Quorum of the Twelve Apostles (124:129).

Prior to joining the Church, he affiliated with the Campbellite movement because of the influence of the then Campbellite preacher, Sidney Rigdon. Initially, he preached against "Mormonism" and the "golden Bible," but upon further investigation became convinced of the error of his former ways and was baptized into this new faith.

In February 1835, he was called to join with two of his brothers-in-law, Lyman and Luke Johnson, as they all became members of the Quorum of the Twelve Apostles. He occupied the position of president of that quorum from December 27, 1847 until April 10, 1875, when President Brigham Young changed the seniority status based upon Hyde's having been dropped from the quorum many years previous to that for a period of almost two months—May 4, 1839 to June 27, 1839. He died on November 28, 1878, while serving faithfully within his apostolic calling.

"Elder Hyde was a man of great natural ability, and by industrious application had acquired a good education, which, with his great and varied experience and extended travels, rendered him a powerful instrument in the hands of God for the defense and dissemination of the gospel and the building up of the Latter-day Work."

He performed numerous missions, the most famous of which was his trip to Palestine where on Sunday morning, October 24, 1841, he climbed the Mount of Olives and dedicated that land to the return of the scattered of Judah. (Jenson 1:80–82; CA 1978:105–6.)

Hypocrisy

An undesirable character trait which the Lord has frequently denounced is hypocrisy (Matt. 6:1–18; 7:1–5; 23:23–29; 3 Ne. 16:10). Hypocrisy is to publicly pretend or profess to believe in principles but to privately practice otherwise. Hypocrites will ultimately "be detected and shall be cut off, either in life or in death" (D&C 50:6–8; 101:90; 124:8).

See also: Feigned Words; Liars

Hyrum

There are fourteen instances in which the name *Hyrum* is used without a surname in the Doctrine and Covenants, and each refers to Hyrum Smith. These instances are found in sections 11, 23, 112, 115, 124, and 135.

See also: Smith, Hyrum

I

Ice Shall Flow Down at Their Presence

One of the prophecies connected with the return of the ten lost tribes from the north countries is that "they shall smite the rocks, and the ice shall flow down at their presence" (D&C 133:26). Some have conjectured that this refers to the breaking down of ice masses that might be barring the way of the returning tribes. However, one scholar suggested a different approach: "Presumably, when our sphere becomes a new earth; when every valley is exalted and every mountain is made low; when the islands become one land, and the great deep is driven back into the north countries — when all these and other changes occur, then there will also be changes in the climate, and the ice masses of the polar areas will no longer be as they are now" (Mill M, 326–7).

See also: They Who Are in the North Countries

Idolatry

The Lord has warned against the practice of idolatry (D&C 52:39; 3 Ne. 30:2; Lev. 19:4; 1 Cor. 10:14). Idolatry is not confined to the worship of idols made in the image of some false and powerless god but extends to the unnatural worship or pursuit of anything that displaces God as the first and foremost thought of one's heart. The Savior counseled, "Seek ye first the kingdom of God" (3 Ne. 13:33) for "no man can serve two masters. . . . Ye cannot serve God and Mammon [riches or the things of this world]." (3 Ne. 13:24.)

Idumea

"Idumea is equivalent to Edom, the nation so despised by the prophets of the Old Testament. Edomites were descendants of Esau and their actions made them a symbol of crass materialism and wickedness towards the servants of God." (DCC, 15.) Therefore, Idumea, or the world against which the Apostle John warned us (1 John 2:15–17) and which shall be harshly judged by the Lord (D&C 1:36), is representative of everything that is in contrast to the Lord's revealed ways.

See also: Babylon; Kingdoms of the World; World

Ignorance

See: Knowledge

Illinois

The *Encyclopedia Brittanica* states that "Illinois is a state that long has been profoundly divided within itself." Although this statement has direct reference to the basic division between the metropolitan area of Chicago and "downstate" Illinois, the divisiveness between the Saints of Nauvoo and their Illinois neighbors was in large part responsible for the stain of *"innocent blood* on the escutcheon" of that state (D&C 135:7).

In the early 1840s, the political climate in western Illinois was such that "no election could occur without the opposing Whig and Democratic candidates courting or denouncing the Mormon vote" (CC, 12). The Saints became the proverbial political hot potato. Unfortunately, "Mormonism" was handed over to the mobs, and the "best blood of the nineteenth century" now stains the soil of Illinois (D&C 135:6).

The impact of Joseph Smith on Illinois was not to be removed with the burial of his physical remains beneath her soil. The work of God which rolled forth from Nauvoo between 1839 and 1846 has continued its charted course. Temples and stakes are now found in far-off lands, and missionaries continue to preach the glad tidings throughout the earth. Nauvoo, as a city, has long since been eclipsed by Chicago in size and worldly fame; yet, the scope of the work once espoused and envisioned in Illinois continues to spread to the ends of the earth.

See also: Carthage; Escutcheon; Martyrdom; Nauvoo; Nauvoo House; Northern States; Ramus; Warsaw

Immanuel

See: King Immanuel

Immortality

The terms *immortality* and *eternal life* have frequently been associated with one another (D&C 29:43; 81:6; Moses 1:39), but their separate meanings must not be confused. Eternal life is a restricted reward for righteousness that is bestowed upon inhabitants of the highest heaven, or kingdom of glory, which is celestial (D&C 131:1–4).

Immortality is a gift of grace granted by God to all who have received tabernacles of flesh here on earth, regardless of the kingdom which they inherit in the hereafter (DS 2:4–10). "*Immortality* is to live forever in the resurrected state with body and spirit inseparably connected" (MD, 376). According to revelation, immortality will be granted to every living thing (D&C 29:24–25).

The term *immortal* has occasionally been applied to the condition of Adam and Eve before the Fall. "We use the term 'immortal' meaning that they could have lived forever in that state in which they were created if they had not fallen," declared President Joseph Fielding Smith. In this case "the term 'immortal' does not mean that they had passed through a resurrection and thus become immortal, for we are taught that a resurrected being cannot die again." (CHMR 1:292; Alma 11:44–45; D&C 63:49; John 11:26.)

See also: Atonement; Grace; Resurrection

Immutable Covenant

There are two occasions in the Doctrine and Covenants in which the Lord uses the word *immutable*. In one instance he speaks of an immutable covenant (D&C 98:3), and in the second he speaks of a promise that is immutable and unchangeable. (D&C 104:2.) Webster defines immutable as "not capable of or susceptible to change." The Lord's covenants and promises are irrevocable, unchanging guarantees that are not susceptible to change.

See also: Covenant

Impositions

The Prophet Joseph spoke of the "nefarious and murderous impositions that have been practiced upon this people" (D&C 123:5). Impositions are wrongful acts practiced by one person or group upon another.

See also: Concatenation

In the Season Thereof

The phrase *in the season thereof* is used under different circumstances, but all such usages have a common thread of meaning. For example, the Lord speaks of using the produce of the earth "in the season thereof" (D&C 59:18; 89:11). "Some have stumbled over the meaning of the expression . . . and have argued that grains and fruits should only be used in the season of their growth and when they have ripened. This is not the intent, but any grain or fruit is out of season no matter what part of the year it may be, if it is unfit for use." (CHMR 1:385.)

The term *in the season thereof* refers to "the appropriate time." The Lord admonishes us to offer prayers "in the season thereof" (D&C 68:33). "The season of prayer," said Elder Joseph Fielding Smith, "is in the morning before the family separates" (CR, Oct. 1919, p. 143). Of course, this "season" extends throughout the day inasmuch as one should constantly be involved in prayer (Alma 37:37; 3 Ne. 18:15–25).

In summary, one should consider eating, praying, and all things at the appropriate time (season). "To every thing there is a season, and a time to every purpose under the sun" (Eccl. 3:1).

See also: Season

Inalienable Rights

A declaration of belief speaks of the "inalienable rights" of citizens (D&C 134:5). This simply means rights that are beyond the power of anyone or anything to change or withhold.

Increase

The Lord warns that those who do not achieve the highest order of the celestial glory cannot have an increase (D&C 131:1–4). While *increase* has reference to eternal offspring, it appears to also have connotations in terms of one's eternal progression towards Godhood, which is available only to those who inherit eternal life, or life in the presence of the Father and Son (D&C 132:17–24). The ultimate destiny of these righteous ones will be to follow in the footsteps of the Father and increase in glory through bringing to pass the immortality and eternal life of their own eternal offspring (Moses 1:39).

See also: Continuation of the Lives; Continuation of the Seeds; Fulness of the Glory of the Father; Gods

Inculcate

President Wilford Woodruff used the word *inculcate* in the document known as the Manifesto (D&C OD—1). To inculcate is to teach and impress by frequent admonition.

Incumbrances

In 1833 the Lord told John Johnson "to seek diligently to lift incumbrances upon a certain house known to the brethren, in order that he may dwell therein" (D&C 96:9; DCC, 491). An incumbrance is a legal claim such as a mortgage or lien attached to a property which shows that money is owed to the holder of the incumbrance.

Independence, Missouri

In July 1831, the Lord revealed Independence, Jackson County, Missouri, as the "center place" for the "city of Zion" and "spot for the temple" (D&C 57:1–3). On August 3 of that year, Joseph Smith dedicated the temple site and the Saints proceeded to build up Zion (HC 1:199). During the next two years, however, circumstances prevented their accomplishing the desired objectives, and they were ruthlessly driven from the county in the latter part of 1832.

Although the Saints looked upon the expulsion as temporary, over a century has passed since the Lord's decree. President Joseph Fielding Smith has said, "Some of the members of the Church seem to be fearful lest the word of the Lord shall fail. Others have tried to convince themselves that the original plan has been changed and that the Lord does not require at our hands this mighty work which has been predicted by the prophets of ancient times. *We have not been released from this responsibility, nor shall we be.* The word of the Lord will not fail.

"If we look back and examine his word carefully, we will discover that nothing has failed of all that he has predicted, neither shall one jot or tittle pass away unfulfilled. It is true that the Lord commanded the saints to build to his name a temple in Zion. This they attempted to do, but were prevented by their enemies, so the Lord did not require the work at their hands *at that time.* [D&C 124:49–54.] The release from the building of the temple did not, however, cancel the responsibility of building the City and the House of the Lord, *at some future time. When the Lord gets ready for it to be accomplished, he will command his people, and the work will be done.*" (DS 3:78–79.)

"It should be remembered that the great temple, which is yet to be built in the City Zion, will not be one edifice, but twelve. Some of these temples will be for the lesser priesthood." (DS 3:93; see also HC 1:357–59.)

Thus, the seat of Jackson County — Independence — located on the Kansas-Missouri border, almost as a suburb of Kansas City, will one day rise in glory and fame under the title of the "New Jerusalem."

See also: Center Place; City of Zion; Goodly Land; Jackson County; Missouri; New Jerusalem; Work of the Gathering; Zion

Infant State

The Lord declared that the redemption of Christ makes it possible for man to return to his "infant state, innocent before God" (D&C 93:38). Commenting on this verse, President Joseph Fielding Smith said: "Every spirit was innocent in the beginning. When Lucifer rebelled because of his agency, he persuaded others to follow him, then their innocence came to an end, for they were in rebellion before God and had to be cast out. . . . It seems very reasonable that others were not valiant in that premortal state, and they may have led to the gradations upon the earth. However, the Lord declared that every spirit coming into this world is innocent. That is to say, *so far as this life is concerned the spirit coming here is innocent.* Nothing is to be laid to its charge; this is a correction of the false doctrine which prevails in some religious organizations, that children are born with the taint of 'original sin' upon them. Such false doctrine denies the mercies of Jesus Christ and declares ignorance of the atonement of our Lord." (CHMR 1:402; italics added.)

Innocent Blood (#1)

See: Shed Innocent Blood

Innocent Blood (#2)

In recounting the tragedy at Carthage, John Taylor spoke of the "innocent blood" of the martyrs, Joseph and Hyrum Smith (D&C 135:7). Their innocence stems not from living lives of perfection, for they too fought occasional failings in mortal moments. However, their victorious struggles had won for them a degree of spirituality unequaled by the majority of mankind. The innocence of Joseph and Hyrum is expressed in Joseph's own prophetic proclamation, as he resolutely faced the road to martyrdom. "I am going like a lamb to the slaughter," he said, "but I am calm as a summer's morning; I have a conscience void of offense towards God, and towards all men. I *shall die innocent, and it shall yet be said of me—he was murdered in cold blood.*" (D&C 135:4.)

The Prophet's uncle, John Smith, was later to state: "I was in jail with him [Joseph] and his brother Hyrum a few hours before they were killed, and I can testify before God, that *they died innocent of any crime*, and that they sealed their testimony with their blood" (CR, Apr. 1927, p. 85; italics added).

See also: Blood; Martyrdom; Murdered in Cold Blood; Smith, Hyrum; Smith, Joseph, Jr.

Innumerable Company of Angels

The future inhabitants of the celestial kingdom are described as having "come to an innumerable company of angels, to the general assembly and church of Enoch, and of the Firstborn'' (D&C 76:67).

"How many people by actual number shall be saved and exalted in the heavenly Jerusalem? Though the gate is strait and the way narrow and though comparatively few of earth's present inhabitants shall be so rewarded, yet the total number who actually do so obtain shall be large beyond comprehension. John speaks in one place of 'ten thousand times ten thousand, and thousands of thousands,' which is a hundred million, plus unspecified millions (Rev. 5:11), and in another of 'a great multitude, which no man could number.' (Rev. 7:9.) It should be remembered that this host shall include the millions of children who have died before they arrived at the years of accountability as well as the unnumbered hosts who pass through their mortal probation in that millennial day when 'children shall grow up without sin unto salvation.' (D&C 45:58.)'' (DNTC 3:230.)

See also: Angels

Intelligence

A revelation of 1833 declared, "The glory of God is intelligence, or in other words, light and truth" (D&C 93:36). Elder John A. Widtsoe said, "The word *intelligence*, as used in common speech, means readiness in learning, quickness of mind. Its higher gospel meaning is more profound. The intelligent man is he who seeks knowledge and uses it in accordance with the plan of the Lord for human good. . . . Intelligence, [is] but another name for wisdom. In the language of mathematics we may say that knowledge, plus the proper use of knowledge, equals intelligence, or wisdom.'' (CR, Apr. 1938, p. 50.)

Elder Joseph Fielding Smith wrote that "there is a vast difference between the meaning of intelligence and that of knowledge. The former, while it includes the latter, is more potent and has a great significance. Intelligence is more than the capacity to understand and communicate truth. The *intelligent man glories in righteousness* not only does he *know* truth, but wisely *applies* it in all his actions.'' (WTP, 227.)

The same revelation mentioned above proclaims that light and truth, or intelligence, "forsake that evil one.'' (D&C 93:37). Therefore, as President Joseph F. Smith declared, "Satan possesses knowledge, far more than we have but he has not intelligence, or he would render obedience to the principles of truth and right'' (WTP, 231). "*A man who has intelligence will worship God and repent of his sins; he will seek to know the will of God and follow it.*'' (DS 1:290–91.) God "is perfect intelligence,'' or, in other words, his every thought and act is in perfect harmony with truth and right (TPJS, 55).

A second meaning for intelligence is implied in Doctrine and

Covenants 93:29, wherein it is stated that "intelligence, or the light of truth, was not created or made, neither indeed can be." Joseph Smith taught that "the spirit of man is not a created being; it existed from eternity, and will exist to eternity. Anything created cannot be eternal." (TPJS, 158; 373.) In commenting on this statement, Elder Joseph Fielding Smith wrote: "In saying the spirit of man is not created the Prophet without any doubt had in mind the intelligence as explained in the Doctrine and Covenants, Sec. 93:29. . . . From this we gather that the intelligence in man was not created, but the Prophet taught very clearly that man is in very deed the offspring of God, and that the spirits of men were born in the spirit world the children of God." (TPJS, 158, footnote.) When Abraham wrote of the "intelligences that were organized before the world was," he spoke of the spirit children of our Father in Heaven begotten from an eternal intelligence (Abr. 3:22).

Interest

See: Tithing

Interpolations

Speaking of the apocryphal writings, the Prophet Joseph Smith said "many things contained therein . . . are not true, which are interpolations by the hands of men" (D&C 91:2). Interpolations are words or phrases not found in original manuscripts but inserted at a later time. These may be deliberate efforts to corrupt the original text (1 Ne. 13:24–26; Morm. 8:33; HC 6:57).

See also: Apocrypha

Interpretation of Tongues

"We believe in the . . . interpretation of tongues," states our seventh article of faith. This gift is one of those spiritual manifestations mentioned in section 46 (D&C 46:25). The ability to comprehend the meaning of what another is saying in a strange or foreign tongue is the gift of interpretation of tongues.

"Be not so curious about tongues," Joseph Smith cautioned, "do not speak in tongues except there be an interpreter present; the ultimate design of tongues is to speak to foreigners" (TPJS 247). If an unknown tongue were being spoken, such as occurred when Brigham Young first met the Prophet Joseph, one blessed with the gift of interpretations of tongues would be present (HC 1:296–97).

Elder James E. Talmage wrote, "The gift of interpretation may be possessed by the one speaking in tongues, though more commonly the separate powers are manifested by different persons" (AF, 225).

See also: Gift of Tongues; Speak with Tongues

Inviolate

According to a declaration of belief, laws should be held inviolate if governments are to exist in peace (D&C 134:2). To be held inviolate is to hold something sacred, to respect and honor it.

Iowa

The westward trek of the Saints from Illinois to Utah took them across the state of Iowa (see map no. 4 on page 298 of the 1981 edition of the D&C). The area of Iowa was first explored by non-Indians in about 1673, but permanent settlement did not take place by white men until the early 1830s, although Spanish land grants were briefly occupied before this time. The area was included in the Louisiana Purchase from France in 1803. The French and Indian influence is readily found today in such city names as Des Moines, Keokuk, and the name of the state itself.

The Territory of Iowa was established in 1838, and in 1846 Iowa was granted statehood. This was the year the great exodus of Saints took place across her soil.

See also: Burlington, Iowa; Council Bluffs, Iowa; Madison, Iowa; Nashville, Iowa; Territory of Iowa

Isaac

Isaac was the miracle child promised to Abraham, then in his hundredth year, and Sarah, then in her ninetieth year (Gen. 17:17). His name, given him by the Lord, allegedly means "laughter," which may have reference to Abraham's reaction to the announcement that in his old age he would sire a son. Abraham's laughter should not be mistaken to imply mockery or doubt that such an event should transpire, but should be seen as the *laughter of rejoicing and happiness* (JST, Gen. 17:23). Sarah likewise spoke of the laughter which Isaac's birth had brought into her life (Gen. 21:6).

Isaac was the focal point in the test of Abraham's faith, when the latter received a commandment to offer his son on the sacrificial altar. Isaac was saved at the last moment by an angel of God (Gen. 22). He received the birthright and patriarchal promises and blessings from his father (Gen. 25:5). When Isaac was sixty, his wife, Rebekah, bore him twin sons—Esau and Jacob. Esau became the father of the Edomite nation, and Jacob became the father of the Israelite nation.

He was "a peace-loving shepherd of great personal piety, full of affection for the members of his own family" (BD, 82), and lived to the age of 180 (Gen. 35:28–29). Because of his strict obedience to the commandments of the Lord, he has already entered into his exaltation and sits upon a throne as a god (D&C 132:37).

Isaiah

The name of the great prophet Isaiah is recorded in three sections of the Doctrine and Covenants (D&C 76:100; 113; 138:42).

Isaiah, the son of Amoz, was a prophet in Israel from about 740–701 B.C., and is responsible for having written a scriptural record containing many Messianic prophecies as well as the history and destiny of Israel (BD, 82). The Savior himself said, "Search these things diligently; for *great are the words of Isaiah*" (3 Ne. 23:1; italics added).

The Book of Mormon quotes 32 percent of Isaiah's writings, which writings "delighted" the soul of the prophet Nephi. They "are plain unto all those that are filled with the spirit of prophecy." (2 Ne. 25:1–5.) A modern-day Apostle, Bruce R. McConkie, has said of Isaiah, "Personally, I feel about Isaiah and his utterances the same way Nephi felt and think that if I expect to go where Nephi and Isaiah have gone, I had better speak their language, think their thoughts, know what they knew, believe and teach what they believed and taught, and live as they lived" (En., Oct. 1973, p. 78).

Contrary to the theory espoused by some, Latter-day Saints believe there was but one Isaiah who was responsible for having written the entire book bearing his name. He was one of the "great and mighty ones" visited by the Redeemer in the spirit world following his sacrifice on Golgotha (D&C 138:38, 42).

Ishmaelites

Originally the Ishmaelites (D&C 3:18) were those people who descended from the sons of Ishmael, a man who joined his family with that of the Book of Mormon prophet Lehi as the Lord led them away from Jerusalem around 600 B.C. (1 Ne. 7). Ishmael was a descendant of Ephraim, and his sons married into Lehi's family (JD 23:184–85). His sons joined forces with Lehi's rebellious sons, Laman and Lemuel, and ultimately became known as Lamanites (1 Ne. 7:6; 2 Ne. 4:13; Jac. 1:13–14; Alma 3:7–8; 47:35; Morm. 1:9). Ishmaelitish ancestry, through intermarriage, is found among the Lamanites today.

Islands of the Sea

In the opening verse of the Doctrine and Covenants the Lord calls upon all men, including those upon the islands of the sea, to give heed to his voice (D&C 1:1). Scattered Israel will be gathered from the isles of the sea (1 Ne. 22:4; 2 Ne. 10:8; Isa. 11:11). Good and evil will both reach to the islands of the sea (D&C 88:94; 133:8) and the Lord's second coming will be witnessed there (D&C 133:20).

In general, islands of the sea refer to distant countries (Dummelow, 424). When the ancient inhabitants of America referred to their land as an isle of the sea (2 Ne. 10:20), it was in the perspective of their being on a mass of land separated by great waters from their orignal homeland (CBM, pp. 214, 319).

Israel

The name *Israel* appears over forty times in the Doctrine and Covenants. It is the name initially given to Jacob, the father of the twelve sons who became the twelve tribes of Israel (Gen. 32:28; 35:10).

Elder Bruce R. McConkie said, "Literally, the name Israel means *contender with God*, the sense and meaning indicating one who has succeeded in his supplication before the Lord, who has enlisted as a *soldier of God*, who has become a *prince of God*" (MD, 389). By extension, and by promised blessing to Abraham's posterity, the name *Israel* applies to the faithful in all ages and not just a single man or nation (Abr. 2:10; Gal. 3:29).

The Prophet Joseph Smith taught that "one of the most important points in the faith of the Church of the Latter-day Saints, through the fullness of the everlasting Gospel, is the gathering of Israel" (TPJS, 92–93). This gathering is proceeding for both the living and the dead as worldwide missionary and temple activity continues to increase and intensify. The Lord declared, "My arm is stretched out in the last days, to save my people Israel" (D&C 136:22).

Historically, the name *Israel* has been used in the following ways: (1) a personal name for Jacob; (2) a name applied to all of Jacob's descendants; (3) the titular name bestowed on the faithful followers of Christ; (4) the name whereby the northern tribes were known, especially after the division of the United Kingdom (1 Sam. 11:8); (5) the name whereby Judah, the nation of Jews, has been known, whether as a distinct body occupying a land called *Israel*, or as a group of scattered people. A careful reading of each reference in the Doctrine and Covenants should readily identify the sense in which it is being used.

See also: Army of Israel; Camp of Israel; Children of Israel; Children of Jacob; Covenant People; God of Israel; Heirs According to the Covenant; House of Israel; Israel's God; Jacob; Judge in Israel; Keys of the Gathering of Israel; Remnants of Israel; Remnants of Jacob; Restoration of the Scattered Israel; Sons of Jacob; Stone of Israel; Tribes of Israel

Israel's God

The term *Israel* in this case is the special name applied to the faithful Saints of God in all lands and is not meant to denote a specific nation. Wherever the

Church is established on this earth, and the members thereof are living in righteousness, there is Israel.

Israel's God (D&C 127:3) — the Mighty One of Israel (D&C 36:1) or the Holy One of Israel (Omni 1:26) — is the same God who created and rules over this earth. He is Jehovah, the Great I AM, the God of Abraham, Isaac, and Jacob. He came to this earth as Jesus the Christ, the Son of the Eternal Father (D&C 38:1–3; John 1:1–3, 14; 8:51–59; 1 Ne. 19:7–17; 3 Ne. 11:7–17; Ex. 3:14).

He is the God to whom all mankind should give obedience as they worship him in truth and righteousness. However, many reject him through false teachings and unrighteous living, thus establishing their own false gods. Therefore, Israel's God is worshipped in truth only by those who truly know him and abide his teachings. All others will one day hear those fateful words, "Ye never knew me; depart from me ye that work iniquity" (JST, Matt. 7:33).

See also: God of Israel; Jesus Christ; Mighty God of Jacob

J

Jackson County, Missouri

Jackson County, Missouri, is destined, perhaps, to become the most famous county in the entire world. As The Church of Jesus Christ of Latter-day Saints continues to spread stakes of Zion throughout the earth (Isa. 54:2; 3 Ne. 22:2; D&C 109:59), the name of Jackson County will continue to gain recognition. Within its borders the sacred city of Zion, the New Jerusalem, will be established, "from whence the law and the word of the Lord shall go forth to all peoples" (DS 3:66–79).

"The monument to Mormonism will stand in Jackson County, Missouri," declared Elder Orson F. Whitney. "There the great City will be built: There Zion will arise and shine, 'the joy of the whole Earth,' and there the Lord will come to His temple in His own time, when His people shall have made the required preparation." (SS, 147.)

This county is specifically mentioned in four revelations (D&C 101:71; 105:28; 109:47; 124:51). It will obviously be of major import in some future revelations yet to be received through the Lord's prophet. Though it was a place of persecution for the Saints of the early Church, it shall be a refuge of righteousness when the city of Zion is established (D&C 101:1–3, 16–20).

See also: Center Place; City of Zion; Independence, Missouri; Missouri; New Jerusalem; Work of the Gathering; Zion

Jacob

A grandson of Abraham, Jacob was the father of the twelve sons who became the twelve tribes of Israel. He was one of the twin boys born to Isaac and Rebekah. His lifelong struggle with his twin brother, Esau, was foreseen while they were yet within the womb of their mother, who was informed that the children within her would form two nations, with the elder one serving the younger (Gen. 25:22–26). Esau, the firstborn, sold his birthright to Jacob and lost his father's blessing to his younger brother (Gen. 25:29–34; 27).

One of the more significant events in Jacob's life was his dream of the ladder reaching from heaven to earth (Gen. 28:12). The Prophet Joseph compared the three degrees of glory to the "three principal rounds of Jacob's ladder," and referred to Jacob as a prophet and seer (TPJS, 12–13, 304–5).

Jacob had numerous spiritual experiences and at one time proclaimed, "I have seen God face to face" (Gen. 32:30). That his life must have been accordant with God's will is evidenced by the Lord's statement to Joseph Smith that Jacob had entered into his exaltation and was now sitting enthroned as a god (D&C 132:37).

See also: Branch of the House of Jacob; Children of Jacob; Israel; Jacob Shall Flourish in the Wilderness; Mighty God of Jacob; Remnants of Jacob; Sons of Jacob

Jacob Shall Flourish in the Wilderness

In March 1831, the Lord promised that "Jacob shall flourish in the wilderness and the Lamanites shall blossom as the rose" (D&C 49:24). This has reference to the descendants of Jacob (Israel) whose forefathers came to the Americas shortly after 600 B.C. and whose record is contained within the pages of the Book of Mormon. These are those we know today as the Lamanites, or American Indians, who can be found from the northern tip of Alaska to the southern tip of Chile.

The rapid growth of The Church of Jesus Christ of Latter-day Saints among these people is evidence that the promised blossoming and flourishing has commenced. In an area conference of the Church in Chile, for example, an Apostle of the Lord uttered a remarkable prophecy regarding that land of Lamanites: "I foresee the day," said Elder Bruce R. McConkie, "when The Church of Jesus Christ of Latter-day Saints will be the most powerful influencing leaven in this entire nation."

Another of the Lord's special witnesses, President Marion G. Romney, promised those people of Jacob in Bolivia that they would "live to see the day when millions of Indians will join The Church of Jesus Christ of Latter-day Saints." ("The Day of the Lamanite," devotional address at the Salt Lake Institute of Religion by Duane V. Cardall, April 1, 1977, pp. 5–6.)

At a special area conference of the Church in Mexico City in February 1977, President Spencer W. Kimball related a dramatic dream to the people of that great land. "Maybe it was a vision," he declared, speaking of this special spiritual experience of three decades earlier. In this "vision" the prophet saw the "flourishing" and "blossoming" of the Lamanite people in Mexico as they rose to responsible positions within the community and Church. He saw "stakes by the hundreds" and "a temple." (CN, Feb. 19, 1977, C–3.) Thus, at general conference in 1947, he declared, "The Lamanites must rise in majesty and power" (CR, Oct. 1947, p. 22).

That this has occurred was well documented in an address by Elder J. Thomas Fyans in which the details of this "blossoming" were described. (CR, Apr. 1976, pp. 16–19.) The "flourishing" has only begun, for declared the Lord's prophet to the assembled Saints in Mexico, "I look forward to another thirty years of tremendous progress. I can see things unbelievable almost which will happen to you and your children." (CN, Feb. 19, 1977, C–3.)

See also: Lamanites; Line Running Between Jew and Gentile

Jacobites

The Jacobites spoken of in Doctrine and Covenants 3:17 are descendants of Jacob, a faithful son of Lehi (1 Ne. 18:7). The term *Jacobite* was a family name used not only in the days of Jacob but also hundreds of years later, even though in a broader sense they were also referred to as Nephites (Jac. 1:13–14; 4 Ne. 1:36; Morm. 1:8).

Jacob beheld the glory of the Lord in his youth and also beheld angels (2 Ne. 2:3–4; 2 Ne. 10:3; 2 Ne. 11:3; Jac. 7:5, 12). He was a prophet among his people and wrote the book of Jacob in the Book of Mormon. His sermons are also found in his brother Nephi's records (2 Ne. 6, 9–11). His descendants, or those having his blood lineage, can be found among some of the Lamanites of our day.

James

The ancient Apostle, James, was a brother to his fellow Quorum of the Twelve member, John (Matt. 10:2). He is referred to as a "son of Zebedee," "Boanerges," and "son of thunder" (Mark 3:17). These latter titles may have had reference to the *thunderous* reaction of James and his brother John to the refusal of a Samaritan city to host the Savior. They cried out, "Lord, wilt thou that we command fire to come down from heaven, and consume them, even as Elias did?" (Luke 9:51–56.)

His ministry must have tempered him, for he is reported to have readily forgiven the man whose accusations brought him to the executioner's sword, saying: "Peace, my son, peace be unto thee, and pardon of thy faults" (AA, 96).

During his life he served as the second of the three-man inner circle that constituted the First Presidency of the early Church (TPJS, 158; DS 3:152). In June 1829, he appeared as a resurrected being to Joseph Smith and Oliver Cowdery and helped ordain them to the holy apostleship (D&C 27:12; 128:20; MD, 478). The Prophet Joseph declared that James's name should be correctly translated as "Jacob" (TPJS, 349).

James, George

One of the little-known individuals of early Mormon history is George James. He was called by revelation to the office of a priest in 1831 (D&C 52:38) and was later mentioned as a traveling companion with the Prophet Joseph on one of his missionary journeys (HC 1:369). The only other times he is mentioned in early Church history is when he is having problems with the Church.

The minutes of the high council in Kirtland, April 4, 1834, reflect that he had been charged with not attending his meetings, not going on an assigned mission, and treating "lightly some of the weak" (HC 2:47). James gave an explanation and rendered a confession to the council whereupon he was extended the hand of fellowship.

On November 10, 1834, Joseph Smith and Sidney Rigdon cosigned a letter sent to James in which he was admonished to come to Kirtland and face charges rendered against him. The correspondence mentioned that he was in an "important and interesting station in the Church" and that he was suspended from acting within the authority of his office until the matter had been resolved. (HC 2:170.) No further mention is made of the matter involved. James remained in Ohio where he died in 1864.

Jaques, Vienna

One of the few women mentioned in the Doctrine and Covenants, Vienna Jaques was counseled to go from Kirtland to Missouri after she had received money "to bear her expenses" (D&C 90:28). Almost two months later, the Prophet Joseph made this notation in his journal: "It was . . . decided that Sister

Vienna Jaques should not proceed immediately on her journey to Zion, but wait until William Hobert was ready, and go in company with him" (HC 1:342). A letter sent from the First Presidency in July 1833 acknowledged their pleasure that Sister Jaques and Brother Hobert had arrived safely in Missouri (HC 1:368).

The last mention of this woman is in a letter the Prophet wrote to her on September 4, 1833. In this correspondence the Prophet said: "I have often felt a whispering since I received your letter, like this: 'Joseph, thou art indebted to thy God for the offering of thy Sister Vienna, which proved a savor of life and pertaining to thy pecuniary concerns. Therefore she should not be forgotten of thee, for the Lord hath done this, and thou shouldst remember her in all thy prayers and also by letter, for she oftentimes calleth on the Lord, saying, O Lord, inspire thy servant Joseph to communicate by letter some word to thine unworthy handmaiden, and say all my sins are forgiven, and art thou not content with the chastisement wherewith thou has chastised thy handmaiden?' Yea, sister, this seems to be the whispering of a spirit, and judge ye what spirit it is." (HC 1:407–9.)

She evidently continued faithful in the Church, for she received her endowment in the Nauvoo Temple and moved west with the Saints to Salt Lake City, where she died on February 7, 1884.

Jared

Perhaps one of the greatest compliments ever paid a man was the following statement of a father-son relationship: "And Jared taught Enoch in all the ways of God" (Moses 6:21). Jared is mentioned in the Doctrine and Covenants as having been "ordained under the hand of Adam who also blessed him" at the age of 200 (D&C 107:47). He was one of the seven great high priests called by Adam into the valley of Adam-ondi-Ahman, three years before our great progenitor's death (D&C 107:53). At the age of 162, Jared begat his noble son Enoch and afterwards lived to the age of 962 (Gen. 5:16–20; Moses 6:20–21). His father was Mahalaleel and Jared was a great-great-great-grandson of Adam.

Jarrings

In December 1833, the Lord chastised some of the Saints. "Jarrings and contentions" were listed among their transgressions (D&C 101:6). Jarrings are contentious disputations and arguments. They are harsh quarrels, squabbles, or altercations.

See also: Contention

Jaws of Hell

The uniquely descriptive yet foreboding words that "the very jaws of hell shall gape open the mouth wide after thee" were given to the Prophet Joseph as he languished in the Liberty Jail. (D&C 122:7.) It appears that even before the moment of their first recorded encounter (JS—H 1:15-17) Satan sought to destroy this chosen and anointed vessel of the Lord (JS—H 1:20).

"Few men have been called on to suffer more than did Joseph Smith," said one of his successors. "His entire life was spent in the midst of persecution by the hands of his enemies." (CHMR 2:181.)

Elder Bruce R. McConkie observed that "such are the ways of Satan that when the God of heaven seeks to send the greatest light of the ages into the world, the forces of evil oppose it with the deepest darkness and iniquity of their benighted realm" (CR, Oct. 1975, p. 24). Surely the very "jaws of hell," symbolic of the monstrous mouth of perdition's pit, extended their hellish width to the utmost in an attempt to physically destroy, and spiritually swallow, the Prophet and the divine work he had been ordained to perform.

See also: Devil; Hell

Jehovah

When the Lord Jesus Christ appeared to Joseph Smith and Oliver Cowdery in the Kirtland Temple in 1836, he was identified as Jehovah (D&C 110:1-4). This same personage was known to the ancient patriarchs as the God of the Old Testament: "And I appeared unto Abraham, unto Isaac, and unto Jacob. I am the Lord God Almighty, the Lord JEHOVAH. And was not my name known unto them?" (JST, Ex. 6:3.)

"*Jehovah* is the Anglicized rendering of the Hebrew, *Yahveh* or *Jahveh*, signifying the Self-existent One, or The Eternal. This name is generally rendered in our English version of the Old Testament as LORD, printed in capitals." (Talmage, 36.) "The Jews regarded *Jehovah* as an ineffable name, not to be spoken; they substituted for it the sacred, though to them the not-forbidden name, *Adonai*, signifying the Lord" (Talmage, 37).

Though variations of this sacred name appear in the Old Testament (Gen. 22:14; Ex. 17:15; Judg. 6:24), the name itself, as the name of the Lord, appears only four times (Ex. 6:3; Ps. 83:18; Isa. 12:2; 26:4). The name can also be found in the Book of Mormon (2 Ne. 22:2; Moro. 10:34).

See also: Great I Am; Jesus Christ

Jeremy

The only mention of Jeremy in all of scripture is in a priesthood line of authority revealed in 1832. He is mentioned as having received this power "under the hand of Gad"—

himself a little-known figure—and in turn Jeremy conferred the priesthood upon another unknown individual, Elihu (D&C 84:9–10). Undoubtedly, we will learn the history of these men when "those things which never have been revealed from the foundation of the world, but have been kept hid from the wise and prudent, shall be revealed" (D&C 128:18).

Jerusalem

Unless the qualifier *New* precedes the word *Jerusalem*—in which case it means the city to be established at the site now known as Independence, Missouri—when the name of Jerusalem appears in the Doctrine and Covenants, it refers to the renowned city of the Old World. However, reference may be to the ancient city (D&C 5:20; 29:12; 45:18, 24; 95:9) or to the city as it now stands or will yet become prior to the Millennium (D&C 77:15; 109:62; 124:36; 133:13, 21, 24).

The Bible Dictionary gives the following information on Jerusalem: "It lay on the frontier line between Judah and Benjamin, and was chosen by David to be his capital. Until then it had been merely a mountain fortress, about 2,600 feet above sea level, surrounded by deep valleys on all sides except the north. . . . After the division of the kingdoms, Jerusalem remained the capital of Judah. It was frequently attacked by invading armies."

Jerusalem became one of the focal points of Christ's ministry and harbored the hill on which he gave his life, following his eternal expiation in Gethsemane. Less than four decades later, it was destroyed by invading Romans, in fulfillment of a prophecy uttered by the Savior (Luke 21:20–22). During the next eighteen hundred years it was literally "trodden down of the Gentiles."

With the creation of the state of Israel in 1948, Jerusalem—although partitioned by the United Nations—once again became the habitat of Judah. Two decades later, in the famous "six-day war," the divided city became one. However, it is yet to play a major role in future pre-Millennial events, and shall be one of the Lord's capitals during the one-thousand-year reign of Christ on this paradisiacal planet (DS 3:67–71).

See also: New Jerusalem

Jesse

Jesse, a descendant of Judah, was the father of David, king of Israel (1 Chron. 2:3–12). He was, therefore, one of the earthly forefathers of Jesus, for Mary, the mother of the Babe of Bethlehem, was of this lineage (Talmage, 86). According to section 113, Jesse will have designated descendants who will have great power in furthering the work of the Lord (D&C 113:1–6).

See also: David; Root of Jesse

Jesus Christ

"*Jesus* is the individual name of the Savior, and as thus spelled is of Greek derivation; its Hebrew equivalent was *Yehoshua* or *Yeshua*, or, as we render it in English, *Joshua*. In the original the name was well understood as meaning 'Help of Jehovah,' or 'Savior.'" (Talmage, 35.) The name was divinely prescribed by the angel Gabriel in a *vision* shown to Joseph, the husband of Mary (JST, Matt. 2:3–4).

"*Christ* is a sacred title, and not an ordinary appellation or common name; it is of Greek derivation, and in meaning is identical with its Hebrew equivalent *Messiah* or *Messias*, signifying the *Anointed One*." All other scriptural titles applied to Jesus "are expressive of our Lord's divine origin and Godship." (Talmage, 35–36.)

An ancient prophet declared, "For the right way is to believe in Christ and deny him not. . . . Jesus is the Christ, the Eternal God." (2 Ne. 25:28; 26:12.) Adding to that witness is the confirming observation of twentieth century Apostle, James E. Talmage: "The solemn testimonies of millions dead and of millions living unite in proclaiming Him as divine, the Son of the Living God, the Redeemer and Savior of the human race, the Eternal Judge of the souls of men, the Chosen and Anointed of the Father—in short, the Christ" (Talmage, 1–2). All must bear in mind the prophetic pronouncements from two continents that "there is none other name given under heaven save it be this Jesus Christ . . . whereby man can be saved" (2 Ne. 25:20; Acts 4:12).

The central role of Jesus Christ in the theology of the Latter-day Saints was expressed by the Prophet Joseph: "The fundamental principles of our religion are the testimony of the Apostles and Prophets, concerning Jesus Christ, that He died, was buried, and rose again the third day, and ascended into heaven; and all other things which pertain to our religion are only appendages to it" (HC 3:30). The Church of Jesus Christ of Latter-day Saints is "Christocentric," said Elder Neal A. Maxwell, who then humbly proclaimed: "I gladly and unashamedly acknowledge Jesus of Nazareth, Savior and King! . . . *I witness that he lives*—with all that those simple words imply. I know I will be held accountable for this testimony; but *as . . . readers, you are now accountable for my witness*—which I give in the very name of Jesus Christ." (En., May 1976, pp. 26–27; italics added.)

It is significant that the Doctrine and Covenants serves as yet another witness for the reality of Him who gave so much, who suffered the greatest of pain to atone for our sins (D&C 19:16–19). "And now after the many testimonies which have been given of him, this is the testimony, last of all, which we give of him: That *he lives!*" (D&C 76:22; italics added.) "The death on Calvary," said Elder Orson F. Whitney, "was no more the ending of that divine career, than the birth at Bethlehem was its beginning" (CR, Apr. 1927, p. 101).

See also: Advocate with the Father; Ahman; Almighty, The; Alpha and Omega; Alphus; Atonement; Beginning and the End; Bleed at Every Pore; Bridegroom; Creator; Eternal King; Father, Jesus As; Firstborn, The; God; God of Enoch; God of Israel; Good Shepherd; Grace; Great I Am; Him Who Laid the Foundation of the Earth; Holy One; Immanuel; Israel's God; Jehovah; King Immanuel; Lamb; Light of Christ; Lord; Lord of Sabaoth; Lord of Hosts; Messenger of Salvation; Messiah; Mighty God of Jacob; Most High; Omegus; One God; Only Begotten of the Father; Only Begotten Son; Pillar of Heaven; Presence of the Son; Prints of the Nails; Red in His Apparel; Redeemer; Resurrection; Rock; Savior; Son, The; Son Ahman; Son of God; Son of Man; Stone of Israel; Supreme Being; Well of Living Water; Word, The; Word of My Power

Jethro

"Among the scholars who are uninspired, there is doubt as to who Jethro was. In Exodus 3:1, he is called the father-in-law of Moses, but these scholars say the name may mean any male relative by marriage. In Exodus 2:18,

Reul, or Raguel, appears as the name of the father-in-law of Moses. Then it is maintained that the transaction related of Jethro in Exodus 18:12–27, is told of Hobab in Numbers 10:29. These may have been names given to Jethro by different scribes, or in different countries." (SS, 500.)

Jethro was a Midianite, a descendant of Abraham, and evidently received the priesthood through this lineage. Jethro, in turn, conferred it upon his son-in-law, Moses (D&C 84:6–7).

Jewels

Twice in the Doctrine and Covenants the Lord speaks of the day when he shall make up his "jewels" (D&C 60:4; 101:3). "This is an expression found in Malachi 3:17, where 'jewels' refers to the people of God, and where the meaning seems to be that when God segregates His people from the world, His power, as that of a monarch wearing a crown of jewels, will be made manifest to all men. But the testimony concerning the truth must be given to the world before the coming of that day, in order that, when it comes, its portent may be known to all." (SS, 358.)

Jews

The term *Jews* has multiple meanings, and the context in which it is used should be scrutinized to determine which applies.

A Jew was originally a descendant of Judah, one of the twelve sons of Israel (Jacob). It has been used in a much broader context to include those who have been part of the kingdom ruled over by Judah. For example, 2 Nephi 30:4 calls the Nephites "descendants of the Jews," and in modern revelation the Lord identifies the Lamanites as Jews (D&C 19:27; 57:4).

Since Lehi and Ishmael, the fathers of the Nephite and Lamanite nations, were descendants of Joseph through Manasseh and Ephraim, respectively (1 Ne. 5:14; Alma 10:3; JD 23:184–85), an explanation is in order. President Joseph Fielding Smith said: *"Lehi was a citizen of Jerusalem, in the kingdom of Judah. . . . and all of the inhabitants of the kingdom of Judah, no matter which tribe they had descended through, were known as Jews."* "The Nephites were of the Jews, not so much by descent as by *citizenship*, although in the long descent from Jacob, it could be possible of some mixing of the tribes by intermarriage." (DS 3:263.)

It should also be remembered that the Nephites and Lamanites intermixed with the descendants of Mulek, who was a son of the king who ruled Judah at the time it was destroyed by the Babylonians (Omni 1:14–19; Hel. 6:10; 8:21; 1 Ne. 1:4; 2 Chron. 36; 2 Kgs. 24, 25). Thus, the literal blood of Judah was mixed with that of Joseph.

In the New Testament, the Apostle Paul identified himself as "a Jew of Tarsus" when addressing the citizens of Jerusalem (Acts 21:39). In writing to the Romans and the Philippians, however, he claimed his lineage through the tribe of Benjamin (Rom. 11:1; Phil. 3:5). Thus, in one instance he is proclaiming his citizenship, and in another his lineage.

See also: Children of Judah; House of David; Israel; Kingdom of the Jews; Lamanites; Tribe of Judah

Job

One of the ultimate compliments which can be paid an individual is to tell him that he possesses the "patience of Job." The Lord himself uses Job as an example of long-suffering and patience in reminding the Prophet Joseph that his trials, up to that point, had not yet been as severe as were those of Job (D&C 121:10).

Although this righteous man of Old Testament times was severely tried and tempted, the tragic loss of his family, friends, wealth, and health did not cause him to lose faith in his God: "Naked came I out of my mother's womb, and naked shall I return thither: the Lord gave, and the Lord hath taken away; blessed be the name of the Lord. . . . Though he slay me, yet will I trust in him." (Job 1:21; 13:15.)

The great Jehovah spoke well when he said of Job, "There is

none like him in the earth, a perfect and an upright man, one that feareth God, and escheweth evil" (Job 1:8).

John

The following are the references to the name *John* in the Doctrine and Covenants, followed by the person to whom they have reference. (For further information, see "John the Apostle," "John the Baptist," "Whitmer, John," and "Gospel of John."

D&C Reference and Identity

7:1

Apostle John, sometimes referred to as the "revelator" (128:6; 77:2), or the "beloved" (7:1; 3 Ne. 28:6).

13:Preface

Apostle John

15:1

John Whitmer

20:35

Apostle John

27:7-8

John the Baptist

27:12

Apostle John

30:9

John Whitmer

35:4

John the Baptist

47:1

John Whitmer

61:14

Apostle John (see Rev. 16:4 and DCC, 364-5)

76:15

Gospel of John, the Apostle

76:100

John the Baptist

77:1, 2, 3, 5, 6, 14

Apostle John

84:27

John the Baptist

88:3, 141

Gospel of John the Apostle

93:6-18, 26

There is not total agreement on the part of scholars as to the identity of this John (see the listing under "John the Baptist" and "John the Beloved" in the index of the 1981 edition of the D&C). John Taylor, Orson Pratt, Bruce R. McConkie and Sidney Sperry all suggest that the passages in section 93 refer to John the Baptist (ABL, 80-81; DCC, 473).

128:6

Apostle John

128:20

Apostle John

130:3

Gospel of John

133:55

John the Baptist

135:7

Apostle John

John the Ancient Apostle

The ancient Apostle John is referred to by this title in the preface of section 13, in conjunction with his fellow Apostles Peter and James. These three Apostles were given the keys of presidency and constituted the First Presidency of the early Church (D&C 7:7; TPJS, 158; DS 3:152). In this capacity, John helped deliver the keys of the kingdom to the Prophet Joseph Smith (D&C 27:12; 128:20).

In addition to his being mentioned as an Apostle and member of the First Presidency, John is referred to by several other titles in the Doctrine and Covenants: "my beloved" (7:1); "my servant" (61:14); and "the Revelator" (77:2; 128:6). Other titles by which he is known are "son of Zebedee" and "Brother of James" (Matt. 4:21; Mark 1:19); "Boanerges" and "son of thunder" (Mark 3:17).

His writings are referred to in several places in the Doctrine and Covenants: 20:35; 76:15; 88:3; 130:3; and 135:7. John is the author of five New Testament books: the Gospel of John; 1, 2, and 3 John; and the book of Revelation. He was granted his request to remain upon the earth as a "ministering angel" and has continued his ministry to this day (D&C 7; John 21:20–24; HC 1:176).

See also: Elias; John; Ministering Angel; Revelations of John

John the Baptist

"Among those that are born of women," said the Savior, "there hath not risen a greater than John the Baptist" (Matt. 11:11).

He was, in a sense, a miracle child, for he was born to Elisabeth and Zacharias at a time when they were "well stricken with years." His was a birth foretold not only by angelic announcement (Luke 1:13) but also by prophetic pronouncements on two separate continents (Isa.

40:3; 1 Ne. 10:7–10). When only eight days old, he received an "ordination" from "the angel of God" which empowered him "to overthrow the kingdom of the Jews, and to make straight the way of the Lord before the face of his people, to prepare them for the coming of the Lord" (D&C 84:28).

Regarding this ordination, Elder Bruce R. McConkie stated that it was "not to the Aaronic Priesthood, for such would come later, after his baptism and other preparation" (DNTC 1:89). What he received was "the divine commission to serve as the greatest forerunner of all the ages," the prophet who would prepare the way for the Lord. That John understood his secondary position to that of Jesus is well illustrated by his own declarations: "He that cometh after me is mightier than I, whose shoes I am not worthy to bear." (Matt. 3:11.) "He must increase, but I must decrease" (John 3:30).

Both the Savior and the Apostle John identified the Baptist as an Elias, or as one who prepares the way for something greater (John 1:20–28; Matt. 17:12–13; D&C 27:7). The Prophet Joseph Smith declared: "The spirit of Elias is to prepare the way for a greater revelation of God, which is the priesthood of Elias, or the priesthood that Aaron was ordained into. And when God sends a man into the work to prepare for a greater work, holding the keys of the power of Elias, it was called the doctrine of Elias." (TPJS, 335–36.)

Though it was claimed that "John did no miracle" (John 10:41), yet his greatness is unquestioned by those who understand his ministry. Joseph Smith enumerated on the reasons for his greatness as follows: (1) "He was entrusted with a divine mission of preparing the way before the face of the Lord. Whoever had such a trust committed to him before or since? No man." (2) "He was entrusted with the important mission, and it was required at his hands, to baptize the Son of Man. Whoever had the honor of doing that? Whoever has so great a privilege and glory? Whoever led the Son of God into the waters of baptism. . . ?" (3) "John, at that time, was the only legal administrator in the affairs of the kingdom there was then on the earth, and holding the keys of power. The Jews had to obey his instructions or be damned, by their own law; and Christ Himself fulfilled all righteousness in becoming obedient to the law which he had given to Moses on the mount, and thereby magnified it and made it honorable, instead of destroying it. The son of Zacharias wrested the keys, the kingdom, the power, the glory from the Jews, by the holy anointing and decree of heaven, and these three reasons constitute him the greatest prophet born of a woman." (TPJS, 275–76.)

John was given additional keys which were not held by any of the priests of his day, including his faithful father, Zacharias (AGQ 5:2). In addition to those powers mentioned above, John held the keys of presidency in the Aaronic Priesthood (TPJS, 272–73, 319; DS 3:88–89). Though he was beheaded by those whose sins he openly denounced (Mark 6:17–28), yet he returned to earth, on May 15, 1824, as a complete resurrected being to give those keys to Joseph Smith and Oliver Cowdery (D&C 13; 27:8; 133:55).

Thus, John was not only the forerunner for the earthly ministry of the Savior, but, through the first restoration of priesthood keys in nearly two centuries, he has likewise prepared the way for His second coming.

See also: Elias; John

John the Beloved

See: John; John the Ancient Apostle

John the Revelator

See: John; John the Ancient Apostle

John the Son of Zacharias

See: John; John the Baptist

Johnson, Aaron

The appointment of Aaron Johnson as a member of the high

council at "the cornerstone of Zion" (Nauvoo) is the only mention of him in the Doctrine and Covenants (D&C 124:132). At the October conference in 1844, following the martyrdoms of Joseph and Hyrum, he was again mentioned as a member of that body (HC 7:296). His name appears among those who left Kirtland in the summer of 1838, following the flight of the Prophet from that area to avoid his enemies (HC 3:93).

Johnson is also listed among those who covenanted to assist the Saints in removing from Missouri in January 1839 (HC 3:252). He was a lieutenant in the Nauvoo Legion (HC 6:350) and was loyal to Joseph and Hyrum in the face of false accusations against the latter (HC 6:495). He was a delegate to the political convention that nominated Joseph Smith for president of the United States (HC 6:390) and later served as an officiator in the Nauvoo Temple (HC 7:548).

Jenson's *Biographical Encyclopedia* mentions an "Aaron Johnson" who was ordained a high priest in Nauvoo in 1847, but this is not the same man, for the first Johnson was a high priest in 1841 when he served on the Nauvoo high council. Johnson came west with the Saints and served as a bishop in both Garden Grove and Springville. He was active in the territorial government in Utah, serving in the legislature and as a chief justice in Utah County. He died on May 10, 1877.

Johnson, John

John Johnson is mentioned five times in the Doctrine and Covenants, though in three instances his name was originally disguised as "Zombre" (D&C 96:6; 102:3, 34; 104:24, 34). He was described as "one of the highly favored men in the early days of this dispensation, who did not remain faithful to the end, though at one time he was valiant in the cause.

"He had seen his wife miraculously healed by the Prophet Joseph. He opened his home at Hiram to Joseph and his family, while the Prophet was engaged in his great Biblical work. He defended Joseph against a murderous mob, risking his own life. In fact, his collar bone was broken in the conflict, but he was instantly healed under the hands of David Whitmer. He became a member of the first High Council, and he saw two of his sons, Luke S. and Lyman E., rise to the exalted position of members of the Council of the Twelve Apostles. And yet, when the spirit of apostasy possessed so many Church members in Kirtland, in 1837 and 1838, he as well as his sons were affected by it. He died in Kirtland, July 30th, 1843, at the age of 64 years." (SS, 607.)

See also: Zombre

Johnson, Luke

One of the prominent men of early Mormon history was Luke

S. Johnson. The Lord revealed his will to Johnson in a revelation given in November 1831 (D&C 68:7). He was called on a mission to the South in 1832 (D&C 75:8–9) and was called as the fourth highest ranking member of the Kirtland high council in 1834 (D&C 102:3, 34).

Jenson wrote that Luke S. Johnson, "one of the original pioneers of Utah, was born Nov. 2, 1807, in Pomfret, Windsor Co., Vermont. He was baptized by the Prophet Joseph Smith May 10, 1831. He was a member of Zion's Camp, and on Feb. 15, 1835, was ordained one of the Twelve Apostles. After a while he indulged in speculation and devoted more of his attention to his financial interests than to his duty in the Church and was excommunicated from the Church for apostasy at Far West, Mo., April 13, 1838. He continued friendly relations with the saints, however, and was baptized in Nauvoo and came to the 'Valley' as one of the pioneers in July, 1847. In 1858 he settled at St. John, Tooele County, Utah, and was appointed Bishop when that ward was organized. On Dec. 9, 1861, he died at the home of his brother-in-law, Orson Hyde, in Salt Lake City." (Jenson 4:709.)

A fitting capstone comment to his life's story is expressed in Doctrine and Covenants 18:13: "And how great is [God's] joy in the soul that repenteth!"

See also: Those Who Have Fallen

Johnson, Lyman

The name of Lyman Johnson appears twice in the Doctrine and Covenants, once when he is called to the ministry (D&C 68:7) and several months later when he is specifically called to preach in the "eastern countries" (D&C 75:14). He was born October 24, 1811, in Pomfret, Vermont, and baptized in February 1831 by Sidney Rigdon. In 1834 he traveled to Missouri with Zion's Camp and was one of those called from that body to serve in the first Quorum of the Twelve Apostles in this dispensation.

Jenson provides the following details of Johnson's life: "He studied the Hebrew language in the winter of 1835–36, and after returning from another mission to the East in the fall of 1836 he entered into merchandising and soon after apostatized. At a conference held in Kirtland September 3, 1837, he was disfellowshipped, but as he made confessions he was restored to his former standing, a few days later. His repentance, however, not being genuine, he was excommunicated from the Church at Far West, Mo., April 13, 1838. Until his death he remained friendly to his former associates, making frequent visits to Nauvoo, after the Saints had located there. He relinquished his business of merchandising and commenced to practice law, locating himself at Davenport, Iowa. A few years later he removed to Keokuk, where he continued his practice, and was finally drowned in the Mississippi river at Prairie du Chien, Wis., December 20, 1856." (Jcnson 1:92.)

See also: Those Who Have Fallen

Joseph

Most instances in which the name *Joseph* appears in the Doctrine and Covenants refer to the Prophet of the restoration (e.g., D&C 3:9; 5:7; 6:18). However, there are several instances in which the name *Joseph* refers to the Old Testament prophet-leader (D&C 27:10; 98:32). Joseph was the eleventh son born to the ancient patriarch Jacob, and first son of Rachel. As a great-grandson of Abraham, he became heir to the promises given by God to the patriarchal fathers, Abraham, Isaac, and Jacob. His history can be found in chapters 37–50 of the book of Genesis.

Joseph's life was characterized by his unwavering fidelity to God, regardless of the circumstances in which he found himself. For example, following his being sold as a slave into Egypt by his jealous brothers (Gen. 37), Joseph suffered himself to be wrongfully cast into prison rather than to submit to the seductive advances of his master's wife. His classic answer to her should be repeated by all when faced with the trials of temptation: "How then can I do this great wickedness, and sin against God?" (Gen. 39:9.)

Joseph's two sons, Ephraim and Manasseh, were born to him by his wife, Ascnath, who was the daughter of Potipherah, the priestly head of the state religion. She was a descendant of the Hyksos, Semitic shepherds who were ruling in the land of Egypt during Joseph's sojourn in that country. This marriage brought Joseph into the "very heart of the royal circle," and placed him on a "footing of equality with the highest nobles of Egypt" (AGQ 1:169–71). Additionally, Pharaoh placed Joseph next to him in authority throughout the land of Egypt. From this position of power, he was able to save both the Egyptians and his own family, the Israelites, from the destructive forces of a famine (Gen. 41–47).

Just as his spiritual strength and prophetic foresight saved an ancient people from temporal starvation, so shall the strength of his sons and daughters save a modern-day people from spiritual starvation. Through his lineage the Prophet Joseph Smith was born, and through his posterity the world is receiving the teachings and saving ordinances of the gospel of Jesus Christ (2 Ne. 3; AGQ 5:70–71).

Of Joseph, Pharaoh said that "there is none so discreet and wise" and that he was a man in whom the spirit of God resided (Gen. 41:38–39).

See also: Ephraim; House of Joseph; Israel; Josephites; Seth (Joseph); Smith, Joseph Jr.

Josephites

The Josephites to whom a knowledge of the Savior was promised are descendants of Joseph, youngest son of Lehi and Sariah, who were the progenitors of the people whose history is recorded in the Book of Mormon (D&C 3:17; 1 Ne. 18:7). The term *Josephite* was a family name used not only in the days of Joseph but also centuries later (4 Ne. 1:36–37; Morm. 1:8).

However, in a much broader sense, the descendants of Joseph were usually referred to as "the people of Nephi," according to the system of government under which they lived (Jacob 1:13–14; 4 Ne. 1:36; Morm. 1:8). Joseph received a promise that his seed would never be completely destroyed, and thus his blood has been intermingled and preserved with the posterity of his brethren known as the Lamanites (2 Ne. 3:3, 23).

Joy

"Men are, that they might have joy," declared an ancient prophet (2 Ne. 2:25). More recently the Lord spoke of "that which bringeth joy," enumerating such things as revelation, knowledge, mysteries, peaceable things, and life eternal (D&C 42:61). True joy is an intense inner peace and happiness that can only come from righteous living.

The Book of Mormon reminds us that "wickedness never was happiness" (Alma 41:10) and refers to the gospel as "the great plan of happiness" (Alma 42:8). The Savior declared that he experienced a fulness of joy because of the righteousness of his people (3 Ne. 27:31). Resurrected beings are capable of receiving a fulness of joy (D&C 93:33).

See also: Happiness

Judah

The name *Judah* appears three times in the Doctrine and Covenants, each time in reference to the descendants of the ancient son of Jacob (109:64; 133:13, 35). Judah was the fourth son of Israel's (Jacob's) first wife, Leah. His patriarchal blessing included the promise that "thy father's children shall bow down before thee" and that "the sceptre shall not depart from Judah . . . until Shiloh [Christ] come" (Gen. 49:8, 10). Through his loins the Savior would be born; One to whom "every knee shall bow" (Rom. 14:11; Mosiah 27:31).

"The Shiloh prophecy," according to President Joseph Fielding Smith, "has reference to the authority which should in course of time be conferred upon the descendants, or tribe of Judah, when Israel became established in the land of their inheritance. This authority was to be that of kingly rule or exercise of authority in making and enforcing the law." (DS 1:21.)

Judah's leadership among his own brothers is evident on several occasions, such as when he acted as spokesman for them before Joseph in Egypt (Gen. 44). He was earlier responsible for saving Joseph's life when he suggested the young man be sold into slavery rather than left to die (Gen. 37:23–28).

See also: Children of Judah; Israel; Jews; Tribe of Judah

Judge in Israel

See: Bishop; Common Judge

Judgment

Judgment is the decreed status of an individual by justice with its accompanying retribution or reward. In the Doctrine and Covenants, the Lord speaks of the "last great day of judgment" (D&C 19:3), which has reference to that final judging before the "judgement-seat of Christ" (D&C 135:5). This will occur at the end of the Millennium. However, there will also be a "judgment" passed on the wicked of the world when Christ comes to usher in his thousand-year reign of righteousness (D&C 1:36; 43:29; 84:114–15; 99:5; 133:2).

There is also that "judgment" which comes more immediately upon the unrighteous, either directly from the Lord or through his authorized servants (D&C

82:11; 107:71–74). In this latter instance, the bishop passes regular judgment on members of his ward through personal interviews. Thus, the "hour" or "day" of judgment" is in at least this way an ongoing process, an everyday occurrence, through which Saints and sinners alike are sifted.

"When we come to stand before the bar of God, to be judged out of the things which are written in the books," cautioned President Joseph F. Smith, "we may find a difference between those things which are written in the books here and the things which are written in the books there" (CR, Apr. 1899, p. 68).

See also: Day of Judgment

Just

According to Webster, the word *just* can mean reasonable, proper, righteous, deserved, lawful, upright, or fair. When the Lord declared that justification is "just and true" (D&C 20:30), the word *just* could be interpreted as fair or correct. When we are told that Christ "suffered for sins, the just for the unjust" (D&C 138:7), it is a reminder that he who was righteous suffered for the unrighteous. To receive a just remuneration (D&C 42:72) is to receive a fair or deserved compensation. To declare that "we believe it just to preach the gospel to the nations of the earth" (D&C 134:12) is to suggest that it is lawful or proper.

See also: Just Men Made Perfect; Resurrection of the Just; Testimony of the Just

Just Men Made Perfect

Future inhabitants of the celestial kingdom will be "just men made perfect through Jesus" (D&C 76:69; see also Heb. 12:22-23). It is important to remember the role of the Savior in salvation, for "it is by grace that we are saved, *after* all we can do" (2 Ne. 25:23; italics added). According to Webster, to be "just" is to conform to the spiritual law, to be righteous before God.

Those who inherit the celestial kingdom will be those who have proven themselves capable of strictly obeying every law of God (GT 1:102-3). They will not immediately attain this celestial status, for perfection is a process.

Elder Bruce R. McConkie has said: "When the Saints of God chart a course of righteousness, when they gain sure testimonies of the truth and divinity of the Lord's work, when they keep the commandments, when they overcome the world, when they put first in their lives the things of God's kingdom: when they do all these things, and then depart this life—*though they have not yet become perfect—they shall nonetheless gain eternal life in our Father's kingdom; and eventually they shall be perfect as God their Father and Christ His Son are perfect*" (CR, Oct. 1976, p. 159; italics added).

In the meantime, the spirits of these "just men" continue to labor in the paradise of God (D&C 129:1-7; D&C 138:30).

See also: Perfect

Justice

"Justice continueth its course and claimeth its own," declared the Lord (D&C 88:40). According to Elder Bruce R. McConkie, "*Justice* deals with the unbending, invariable results that always and ever flow from the same causes. It carries a connotation of righteousness, fairness, impartiality. It embraces the principle and practice of just dealing, of conformity to a course of perfect rectitude, of adherence to a standard of complete integrity."

"According to the terms and conditions of the great plan of redemption, *justice demands that a penalty be paid for every violation of the Lord's laws.*" (MD, 405, 406.)

The penalty imposed by justice can be tempered by the mercy extended through the Atonement. Nevertheless, an ancient prophet announced that without repentance there would be no mercy, for "justice claimeth the creature and executeth the law, and the law inflicteth the punishment" (Alma 42:22). A modern-day prophet, Spencer W. Kimball, warned that "the Lord may temper justice with mercy, but he will never supplant it. Mercy can never replace justice. God is *merciful*, but he is also *just*." (MF, 358.)

An excellent discussion of the relationship between justice and mercy, and the role of Jesus Christ as Mediator can be found in a general conference address by Elder Boyd K. Packer (see En., May 1977, pp. 54–56).

See also: Anger, Atonement, Mercy

Justification

On the day the Church was organized, the Prophet Joseph declared "that justification through the grace of our Lord and Savior Jesus Christ is just and true" (D&C 20:30). Paul told the Romans that we are "justified by faith" (Rom. 5:1).

Smith and Sjodahl defined the doctrine of justification as "a judicial act, whereby God declares that the sinner who repents and by faith accepts the sacrifice of the Lamb of God, and who is baptized according to the Word of God, is acquitted and received into His Kingdom." (SS, 104.) Thus, one who is justified is declared righteous and pronounced innocent before God. This presupposes that the individual remains on the road of righteousness, doing all that is required for celestial salvation (2 Ne. 31:19–20).

Man is incapable of becoming justified through his own efforts alone. He must rely on the grace of Christ (2 Ne. 25:23; Alma 22:14).

K

Key to the Knowledge of God

The Melchizedek Priesthood "holdeth the key of the mysteries of the kingdom," declared the Lord, "even the key of the knowledge of God" (D&C 84:19). This key appears to be the power of divine revelation, for "one great privilege of the Priesthood," according to Joseph Smith, "is to obtain revelations of the mind and will of God" (HC 2:477).

Nevertheless, "the things of God are of deep import; and *time, and experience, and careful and ponderous and solemn thoughts can only find them out*" (HC 3:295; italics added). Thus, while the "key" is revelation from God, there are certain prerequisites that must be fulfilled in order for that knowledge to be divinely dispensed.

To possess "the knowledge of God," in the ultimate sense, is to possess that knowledge which God himself possesses, which is *all* knowledge (D&C 38:1–2; 2 Ne. 9:20). Additionally, however, "the knowledge of God" is to know Him and His Beloved Son. "This is eternal lives—to know the only wise and true God, and Jesus Christ, whom he hath sent" (D&C 132:24; John 17:3).

The discovery of Deity is described in the following words: "He is not to be discovered by an archaeologist's pick, a translator's interpretation of an ancient text, nor a theologian's imagination about how he was named and known by them of old. God is and can be known only by revelation" (PM, 100–101). Revelation can be found in the fulness of the holy scriptures, which Joseph Smith defined as "the key of knowledge" (JST, Luke 11:53).

Keys of Salvation

The Prophet Joseph declared that to Adam "was made known the plan of ordinances for the salvation of his posterity unto the end" (HC 4:207). Furthermore, "Jesus . . . set the ordinances to be the same forever and ever, and set Adam to watch over them, to reveal them from heaven to man, or to send angels to reveal them" (HC 4:208). Thus, whenever the true ordinances of salvation have been practiced among mankind, it has been through the direct authorization of Adam, who holds the keys of salvation (D&C 78:16), or the power to authorize the use of the saving ordinances.

These ordinances must be administered through the priesthood, which power was first given to Adam. Through him it has been given to authorized servants of God down through the ages. Joseph Smith stated that Adam held the keys of the priesthood and whenever they are revealed from heaven, "it is by Adam's authority" (HC 3:386).

Keys of the Church

The name of the true Church of Christ is frequently used synonymously with the term *kingdom of God*. Thus, the keys of the kingdom of God are the keys of the Church. (D&C 42:69.) These keys are the authorized power to preside over and administer the affairs of the Lord's church here upon the earth. Joseph Smith indicated that the parable of the mustard seed (Matt. 13:31–32; Mark 4:30–32; Luke 13:19–20) was given to represent the growth of the Church (kingdom) in the last days (TPJS, 98–99).

See also: Keys of the Kingdom of God

Keys of the Gathering of Israel

The authority whereby the dispersed of Israel are gathered is known as the "keys of the gathering of Israel." "Moses received the keys of the gathering of Israel at Sinai, when he was called and sent to lead Israel from Egypt to the promised land which the Lord had given to their father

Abraham. He gathered Israel, and while he was not privileged to place them in possession of the land, nevertheless the keys were in his hands for the gathering. He came to Peter, James, and John on the mount at the transfiguration and there bestowed upon them the same keys for the gathering of Israel in the days in which they lived. (Matt. 17:3.) He was sent to the Prophet Joseph Smith and Oliver Cowdery to bestow the keys for the gathering of Israel in the dispensation of the fulness of times." (DS 3:257; D&C 110:11.)

See also: Moses

Keys of the Kingdom of God

In a revelation given in October 1831, the Lord announced that "the keys of the kingdom of God are committed unto man on the earth, and from thence shall the gospel roll forth unto the ends of the earth" (D&C 65:2). President Joseph Fielding Smith declared, "We . . . hold the keys of the kingdom of God on earth, which kingdom is The Church of Jesus Christ of Latter-day Saints.

"These keys are the right of presidency; they are the power and authority to govern and direct all of the Lord's affairs on earth. Those who hold them have power to govern and control the manner in which all others may serve in the priesthood. . . . They have been given to each man who has been set apart as a member of the Council of the Twelve. But since they are

the right of presidency, they can only be exercised in full by the senior Apostle of God on earth, who is the President of the Church." (CR, Apr. 1972, pp. 98–99; italics added; see also D&C 81:2; 112:15, 30–32; 132:7; GD, 168.)

See also: Apostles; First Presidency of the Church; Keys of the Kingdom of Heaven; Kingdom of God; Kingdom of Heaven

Keys of the Kingdom of Heaven

" 'The keys of the kingdom are the power, right, and authority to preside over the kingdom of God on earth (which is the Church) and to direct all of its affairs' (*Mormon Doctrine*, pp. 377–379). These keys include the *sealing power*, that is, the power to bind and seal on earth, in the Lord's name and by his authorization, and to have the act ratified in heaven" (DNTC 1:389).

"When the ordinances of salvation and exaltation are performed by or at the direction of those holding these keys such rites and performances are of full force and validity in this life and in the life to come, that is, they are binding on earth and in heaven" (DNTC 1:424). The terms *kingdom of God* and *kingdom of Heaven* are often used interchangeably. However, Elder James E. Talmage drew a distinction between the two, stating that "the kingdom of God is a preparation for the kingdom of Heaven, which is yet to come" (CR, Apr. 1917, p. 65).

Thus, the keys of the *kingdom of heaven* appear to be vicariously vested in those mortal men (prophets and Apostles) who hold the keys of the *kingdom of God on earth*, enabling them to perform ordinances which are valid in the eternities of heaven. These keys were bestowed upon Peter and his presidency in the days of the Savior and restored to the Prophet Joseph Smith in our day (see Matt. 16:13–19; 17:1–7; 18:18; D&C 27:12–13; 128:20). They are held by those ordained Apostles who have been set apart as members of the Council of the Twelve (CR, Apr. 1972, p. 99).

See also: Keys of the Kingdom of God; Kingdom of God; Kingdom of Heaven

Keys of the Ministering of Angels

Both the Lord and John the Baptist declared that the "keys of the ministering of angels" are vested in the Aaronic Priesthood (D&C 13; 84:26–27). Nevertheless, in their fulness all priesthood keys are held by only one man on earth at a time, that man being the President and prophet of The Church of Jesus Christ of Latter-day Saints (D&C 132:7). However, "he may delegate any portion of this power to another, in which case that person holds the keys of that particular labor" (GD, 136). Thus, a bishop, as

president of the Aaronic Priesthood within his ward, holds the keys of the ministering of angels (D&C 107:87–88). These keys contain the right, when necessary, to receive instruction from "angels" sent to declare the word of God.

The ancient Nephite prophet Moroni taught that "it is by faith that angels appear and minister unto men; wherefore, if these things have ceased wo be unto the children of men, for it is because of unbelief, and all is vain" (Moro. 7:37). President George Q. Cannon defined an angel as "any being who acts as a messenger for our heavenly Father . . . , be he a God, a resurrected man, or the spirit of a just man" (JI 26:53). In a very real sense, therefore, those priesthood leaders who have been called by divine revelation to direct the affairs of the kingdom here upon the earth also act in the capacity of ministering angels as they impart the word of God. This is affirmed in this statement by Heber C. Kimball: "While in the act of ministering the Gospel, the servants of God may be considered angels" (JD 10:103).

Lee A. Palmer suggested the following categories of ministering angels: (1) Unembodied spirits —those who have not yet received a body of flesh and bones, but who belong to this earth and shall yet be born thereon; (2) Translated beings—those who have been granted a temporary stay of death to continue their mortal ministry, such as

John the Beloved (D&C 7; John 21:20–25); (3) Resurrected beings; (4) Departed spirits in paradise—those who have died and not yet been resurrected; (5) And those who will remain angels forever in the hereafter (D&C 131:1–4; 132:17; APTC, 300).

The ministering of angels is not restricted to priesthood bearers only, for the prophet Alma declared that God imparts "his word by angels unto men, yea, not only men but women also" (Alma 32:23). The Book of Mormon records a marvelous outpouring of the Spirit when angels ministered unto little children (3 Ne. 17:21–25).

Keys of the Mysteries of the Kingdom

The "keys of the mysteries" (D&C 28:7), or the "keys of the mysteries of the kingdom" (D&C 64:5), are the right to receive the mind and will of the Lord in behalf of the kingdom (Church) here on the earth (CHMR 1:235; D&C 43:1–6). The keys are the authority (SS, 390).

Only the senior Apostle on earth—the President of The Church of Jesus Christ of Latter-day Saints—may reveal the mysteries to the Church and the world. However, as an ancient prophet said, "It is given unto many to know the mysteries of God; nevertheless they are laid under a strict command that they shall not impart only according to

the portion of his word which he doth grant unto the children of men, according to the heed and diligence which they give unto him" (Alma 12:9). "Knowledge through our Lord and Savior Jesus Christ," said the Prophet Joseph, "is the grand key that unlocks the glories and mysteries of the kingdom of heaven" (HC 5:389).

See also: Mysteries of the Kingdom; Mysteries

Keys of This Dispensation

The "keys of this dispensation" (D&C 110:16) refer to the keys of the dispensation of the fulness of times. Joseph Smith received these keys and will hold them throughout eternity, under the direction of Adam, who, under the direction of the Savior, presides over all dispensations (CHMR 1:388; TPJS, 157–58).

See also: Dispensation of the Fulness of Times

Keys of This Ministry

According to President Joseph Fielding Smith, "the keys of this ministry" (D&C 7:7) "constituted the authority of Presidency of the Church" in the dispensation over which Peter, James, and John presided (HC 3:387; Matt. 17:1–9; D&C 81:1–2). "These keys were given at the transfiguration to these three Apostles, and they in turn gave them to Joseph Smith and Oliver Cowdery in this dispensation'' (CHMR 1:49; D&C 27:12–13; 128:20).

See also: Keys of the Kingdom of God; Mount, This

Keys Whereby He May Ask and Receive

Hyrum Smith was promised that he would receive the ''keys whereby he may ask and receive'' (D&C 124:95). Inasmuch as they were given as part of the keys belonging to the office of the Assistant President of the Church, they evidently refer to the keys of the kingdom, held by the Presidency of the Church. Oliver Cowdery had formerly held them in concert with Joseph Smith.

Speaking of Oliver's position, President Joseph Fielding Smith said: ''That which had been bestowed upon him was exceedingly great and had he been willing to humble himself, it was his privilege to stand with the Prophet Joseph Smith through all time and eternity, holding the keys of the Dispensation of the Fulness of Times'' (CHMR 1:121).

''Hyrum Smith received a double portion. He received the office of Patriarch which belonged to his father and came to him by right, and also received the keys to be 'Second President' and precede the counselors as Oliver Cowdery had done. So he would have remained as President of the Church had he not died a martyr.'' (DS 1:221.) The ''keys whereby he may ask and receive'' included the right to inquire after the mind and will of the Lord in behalf of the Church.

See also: Cowdery, Oliver; Keys of the Kingdom of God; Smith, Hyrum

Kick Against the Pricks

The Lord warned that those whose actions cause the withdrawal of his Spirit will be left unto themselves ''to kick against the pricks'' (D&C 121:38). This phrase was used by the Savior in referring to Saul's misguided mission of persecution against the ancient Saints (Acts 9:5).

A sharp instrument known as a ''goad'' was often used in earlier days to prod animals into activity. If the animal responded by kicking at the goad, it only injured itself by driving the point deeper into its body. Thus, the animal became the victim of self-inflicted pain. Those who ''kick'' against the ''goads'' of the gospel, find themselves the victims of their own misdirected actions.

Elder Harold B. Lee declared that when individuals ''fall away'' from the gospel, ''they first begin to 'kick against the pricks'. . . . These no doubt are the pricks of the gospel. I wonder, perhaps, if they are not those things President J. Reuben Clark . . . called 'restraints,' the restraints of the word of wisdom, the restraints imposed in keeping the Sabbath day holy, injunctions against card playing. . . . And so we might go on. These are the restraints against which some people seem to rebel and are kicking constantly against the —'pricks' of the gospel.'' (CR, Oct. 1947, pp. 65–66.)

More recently, President Spencer W. Kimball indicated that those who ''kick against the pricks'' are ''those who stifle and smother the convictions of the conscience, who rebel against God's truths and laws, who quarrel with his providence and who persecute and oppose his ministers.'' (CN, Nov. 4, 1978, p. 4.)

Kimball, Heber C.

One of the great names to grace the annals of history is that of Heber C. Kimball. His name appears but once in the Doctrine and Covenants, as a member of the Quorum of the Twelve (D&C 124:129), but the faithful history of his life is emblazoned on the records of the righteous. Elder Kimball was called as one of the original members of that august group of men in February 1835. Of these original twelve, Joseph Smith said only Brigham Young and Heber C. Kimball had failed to lift their heel against him (HC 5:412).

In 1847, Elder Kimball was called to serve as a counselor to Brigham Young in the First Presidency, which position he faithfully occupied until his death. His call to the Presidency was a fulfillment of a blessing bestowed on him by Patriarch Hyrum Smith on March 9, 1842: ''You shall be blest with a fullness and shall be not one whit behind the chiefest,'' said the Patriarch. ''As an Apostle you shall stand in the presence of God to judge the people; and as a Prophet you shall attain TO THE HONOR OF THE THREE!''

He was described by one biographer as ''broad and magnanimous in his ways, kind to the widow and the fatherless, beloved by his associates. . . . He was a loving, peaceful man, and was designated the 'Herald of Peace.' . . . His special gift of the Spirit was that of prophecy. His predictions and their fulfillment would make a long chapter of themselves, and full of thrilling interest. When the Saints were about to settle in Commerce, Ill., and though received with open arms by the good people of Illinois, Apostle Kimball looked upon the beautiful site and said sorrowfully, 'This is a beautiful place, but not a long resting place for the Saints.' . . . When hard times pressed the Saints in Salt Lake City, and a thousand miles separated them from commercial points, President Kimball stood up in the Tabernacle and prophesied that in less than six months clothing and other goods would be sold in the streets of Great Salt Lake City cheaper than they could be bought in New York. This astonished the people. One of his brethren said to him after the meeting that he did not believe it. 'Neither did I,' said Brother Kimball, 'but I said it. It will have to go.' No one saw the possibility of its verification. Six months, however, had not passed away when large companies of emigrants, burning with the gold fever from the East, came into the city, and becoming eager to reach the glittering gold fields of California, they sold their merchandise on the streets for a less price than the New York prices. . . . These are but examples of many like predictions uttered by this great Apostle of the Lord." (Jenson 1:34–37.)

A statement in the *Deseret News*, dated June 22, 1868, the day of his death, said of him: "A prince and a great man has this day passed from among us! . . . A faithful and unflinching servant of God, who had passed through the most severe ordeals with unyielding integrity."

Kimball, Spencer W.

On September 30, 1978, a momentous revelation on priesthood was presented for approval to the assembled Saints at the 148th Semiannual General Conference of The Church of Jesus Christ of Latter-day Saints. This revelation, known as Official Declaration — 2 (OD—2) in the Doctrine and Covenants, was received the previous June in a sacred meeting of the First Presidency and Council of the Twelve Apostles. Spencer W. Kimball, twelfth prophet, seer, and revelator of the Church in this dispensation, had his prayerful petition answered as the Lord manifested his will.

This prophet of God was born on March 28, 1895 to Andrew Kimball, then serving as president of the Indian Territory Mission, and Olive Wooley Kimball. That he was destined to become one of the Lord's anointed was evidenced early to those who were close to him and in touch with the Spirit. When Spencer was but ten years of age, his father said to a neighbor: "That boy, Spencer, is an exceptional boy. . . . I have dedicated him to be one of the mouthpieces of the Lord — the Lord willing. You will see him some day as a great leader." (IE, Nov. 1943, p. 702.) This inspired pronouncement was in keeping with the Prophet Joseph Smith's observation that "every man who has a calling to minister to the inhabitants of the world was ordained to that very purpose in the Grand Council in heaven before this world was" (HC 6:364).

Spencer's Aunt Mary Kimball was also moved by the spirit of inspiration when she said of the young boy, "That boy will some day be the prophet of the Lord" (En., May 1974, p. 60). Almost seven decades later, as the seventy-seven-year-old Apostle underwent open-heart surgery, that same spirit of inspiration whispered its warm message to the noble surgeon who performed this delicate operation. Dr. Russell M. Nelson, who himself would one day receive the Apostolic office, was inspired to know that the man lying on that operating table was the choice of

Providence to become one of his prophets and preside over his church (SWK, 8).

When Elder Kimball was called to the Apostleship in 1943, one of his acquaintances said of this new church leader, "Two of his outstanding characteristics are, first, his love for people, a love which begets love . . . , and second, his relentless attention to the duties of the day" (IE, Oct. 1943, p. 639). These two characteristics became trademarks of his ministry both as an Apostle and later as President of the Church.

He was set apart to the "highest office in the world" (CR, Oct. 73, p. 53) on December 30, 1973. From that day, the inspiration guiding his hand in the administration of Church affairs was evident. One of the most significant events of his ministry was the organization of the First Quorum of the Seventy, which included the calling of General Authorities from the international areas of the Church. Numerous innovations in Church procedure came under his inspired leadership. However, he should not be remembered for his genius in governing, but for his spiritual strengths.

One of his fellow Apostles said of him, "Above all his other talents, he developed the talent for spirituality—the talent to believe and accept the truth, the talent to desire righteousness" (En., May 1974, p. 73). Another of his Apostolic Brethren said, "When he prays we feel the Lord's power near. . . . To pray with President Kimball is a spiritual refreshment." (En., May 1974, pp. 36–37.)

This prophet is a prototype of spirituality for all to follow. His marvelous, mortal ministry came to a close when he passed away on November 5, 1985.

Kindled

See: Anger

Kindness

See: Bowels; Brotherly Kindness

Kindred

The term *kindred* appears several times in the Doctrine and Covenants, usually in connection with the phrase every kindred, tongue, and people (D&C 10:51; 77:8, 11; 124:58; 133:37). Webster defines *kindred* as "a group of persons interrelated by blood; a family, clan, race, or the like." Thus, the kindred of the earth are the multitudinous people of the earth, who are ultimately related to one another through their common parents —Adam and Eve.

King Benjamin

As a result of having lost 116 pages of precious manuscript

from the translation of the Book of Mormon, Joseph Smith was informed that he was not to retranslate the lost portion, which was contained on what are known as the large plates of Nephi, or the "other plates" (1 Ne. 9:4), but instead should translate the material found on the small plates of Nephi, or "these plates" (1 Ne. 9:3). These latter plates covered the same time period as the former plates and were, in a sense, a duplication. However, the Lord indicated the small plates were of greater worth in terms of the things he wanted to bring to the attention of his people.

These plates covered the time period from 600 B.C. down to "the reign of king Benjamin," whose record is contained in the book of Mosiah, the eighth book in the Book of Mormon (D&C 10:40–41). King Benjamin was a Book of Mormon prophet who served as king over the Nephite nation about 120 B.C. He succeeded his father, Mosiah, as the king over the land of Zarahemla. Under his stewardship, the record of the kings (large plates) and the record of the prophets (small plates) were combined into one record.

Thus, beginning with the book of Mosiah in the Book of Mormon, we have a unified record. Prior to this time a duplicate record was being kept. (See Omni 1:23–25; Words of Mormon 1:10.) He delivered one of the major sermons in the Book of Mormon, much of which was based upon things made known to him by an angel from God (see Mosiah 2, 3, 4).

See also: Manuscript (116 Pages)

King Immanuel

The only time the title "King Immanuel" appears in the Doctrine and Covenants is in section 128, verse 22. The name applies to the Lord Jesus Christ. The title of "King" represents the regal position occupied by the Savior as our Eternal King (D&C 128:23). "Immanuel" literally means "God with us." This is the name which Gabriel announced should be given to the Son of Mary in fulfillment of the prophecy of Isaiah (Matt. 1:23; Isa. 7:14).

See also: Jesus Christ

Kingdom of God (in Heaven)

President Joseph Fielding Smith stated: *"The celestial kingdom is the kingdom spoken of in the scriptures as the kingdom of God,* which men are commanded to seek first in preference to all else. [D&C 6:7; Matt. 6:33; Luke 12:31; 3 Ne. 13:33.] It is the place where those who enter receive eternal life, in addition to immortality. Immortality is the gift to live forever given to all men. Eternal life is life in the presence of the Father and the Son and is the *kind* of life which they possess." (DS 2:23–24.)

See also: Keys of the Kingdom of God; Keys of the Kingdom of Heaven; Kingdom of God (on Earth); Kingdom of Heaven

Kingdom of God (on Earth)

An 1834 revelation indicated the kingdoms of this world were to acknowledge the kingdom of Zion (the Church) as the "kingdom of our God and his Christ" (D&C 105:32). "The Kingdom of God is the Church established by divine authority upon the earth; this institution asserts no claim to temporal rule over nations; its sceptre of power is that of the Holy Priesthood, to be used in the preaching of the gospel and in administering its ordinances for the salvation of mankind living and dead" (Talmage, 788).

Joseph Smith authoritatively declared: "I say, in the name of the Lord, that the kingdom of God was set upon the earth from the days of Adam to the present time. Whenever there has been a righteous man on earth unto whom God revealed His word and gave power and authority to administer in His name, . . . in the ordinances of the gospel and officiate in the priesthood of God, there is the kingdom of God. . . .

"Where there is no kingdom of God there is no salvation. *What constitutes the kingdom of God? Where there is a prophet, a priest, or a righteous man unto whom God gives his oracles, there is the kingdom of God;* and where the oracles of God are not, there the kingdom of God is

not." (HC 5:256–257; italics added.)

"It has at times also been referred to as the kingdom of heaven, as in the parables of the Savior, see particularly the parable of the ten virgins," noted President Joseph Fielding Smith. "In the sense in which this term is used in these revelations . . . *the kingdom of God is the Church of Jesus Christ of Latter-day Saints.*" (CHMR 1:194; italics added.)

See also: Keys of the Kingdom of God; Kingdom of God (in Heaven); Kingdom of Heaven

Kingdom of Heaven

Two statements by Elder James E. Talmage clarify the term *kingdom of Heaven* (D&C 65:6). "The Kingdom of Heaven is *the divinely ordained system of government* and dominion in all matters, temporal and spiritual; *this will be established on earth only when its rightful Head, the King of kings, Jesus the Christ, comes to reign.* His administration will be one of order, operated through the agency of His commissioned representative invested with the Holy Priesthood. When Christ appears in His glory, and not before, will be realized a complete fulfillment of the supplication: 'Thy kingdom come. Thy will be done in earth, as it is in heaven.' " (Talmage, 788–89; italics added.)

"Do you believe that the kingdom of heaven has been already set up upon the earth?" queried Elder Talmage. "I do not. I know that *the kingdom of God is a preparation for the kingdom of heaven, which is yet to come.* The expressions 'Kingdom of God' and 'Kingdom of Heaven' are oft times used synonymously and interchangeably in our imperfect English translation of the Holy Bible, particularly in the Gospel according to Matthew, where the expression 'Kingdom of Heaven' is most commonly used. . . . The kingdom of God is the Church of Christ; the kingdom of heaven is that system of government and administration which is operative in heaven, and which we pray may some day prevail on earth. The kingdom of heaven will be established when the King shall come, as come He shall, in power and might and glory, to take dominion in and over and throughout the earth.'' (CR, Apr. 1917, p. 65; italics added.)

See also: Keys of the Kingdom of God; Keys of the Kingdom of Heaven; Kingdom of God

Kingdom of the Jews

The kingdom of the Jews (D&C 84:28), according to one source, was the political kingdom of the Jewish people extant at the time of John the Baptist's ministry. John ''had the authority to close the Mosaic dispensation, after a last call to the people for repentance. He exercised that authority, and the result was the overthrow of the Jewish polity, the destruction of Jerusalem, and the dispersion of the people.'' (SS,

503.) Sperry, however, suggested that the overthrow of the kingdom of the Jews had reference to the spiritual kingdom rather than the physical kingdom which was overthrown by the Romans in A.D. 70 (DCC, 392).

In light of John the Baptist's mission to act as a forerunner in preparing the way for the Savior's ministry, this makes sense. The Jews had spiritually trodden crooked paths, and the ministries of John and Jesus were to make those paths ''straight'' (see Matt. 3:3) by overthrowing false philosophies and establishing the true kingdom.

See also: Jews; John the Baptist

Kingdom of Zion

See: Church of Jesus Christ of Latter-day Saints, The; Kingdom of God (on Earth)

Kingdom Which Is Not a Kingdom of Glory

In section 88, the Lord manifest the principle whereon one obtains an inheritance in a celestial, terrestrial, or telestial kingdom — obedience to the laws which govern each respective kingdom (D&C 88:22–24). One who cannot abide the laws of a given kingdom will not inherit that kingdom. This is an irrevocable decree! (D&C 130:20–21.)

These three kingdoms are all kingdoms of ''glory,'' that is, they shall have varying degrees of that light which emanates from the presence of Deity. However, to those who are classified as "sons of perdition" or as "angels to the devil," there shall come no glory for their fate is to have all light taken from them. They must abide a kingdom which is not a kingdom of glory (D&C 88:24, 32).

These inhabitants of hell, as well as the future inhabitants of the telestial glory, will have already spent time in an *outer darkness*, or place devoid of the presence of God, prior to the last and final judgment. However, telestial beings will eventually be redeemed from the depths of darkness while the sons of perdition will have to "return again to their own place," a place of neither light nor glory (Alma 40:13; D&C 88:32; 101:90–91; 133:71–73; GT 1:85).

See also: Damnation of Hell; Hell; Lake of Fire and Brimstone; Outer Darkness; Sons of Perdition

Kingdoms of the World

The Prophet Joseph Smith taught that the beasts which Daniel saw in his vision (Daniel 7) represented the kingdoms of the world, or the inhabitants thereof. These inhabitants were "beastly and abominable characters; they were murderers, corrupt, carnivorous, and brutal in their dispositions" (TPJS, 289).

The kingdoms of the world represent all that is in opposition to the kingdom of God. There-fore, as one fails to keep the commandments—to stay on the Lord's side of the line—one forfeits citizenship with the Saints in the household of God and becomes a subject in the kingdoms of the world (D&C 103:8).

See also: Babylon; Idumea; World

Kings

The plural word *kings* appears eight times in the Doctrine and Covenants, with all but one of those occasions referring to men who hold positions of sovereignty over lands and peoples of the earth (e.g., 1:23; 109:55; 124:3). The exception is when the Lord applies the term *kings* to those who will be exalted within the celestial kingdom (D&C 76:56). These kings will be given divine dominion, through the power of the priesthood, to rule in their respective spheres and stewardships forever. They will be among the royal house of Christ, who is the King of kings (Rev. 17:14; 19:16).

"Those holding the fullness of the Melchizedek Priesthood are kings and priests of the Most High God," declared the Prophet Joseph, "holding the keys of power and blessings" (HC 5:555).

Kirtland, Ohio

It is hard to imagine that a town in which 47 of the canonized revelations contained in the

Doctrine and Covenants were received is so insignificant to the world that a recent edition of the *National Geographic Atlas* does not even acknowledge its existence. Such is the lot of Kirtland, Ohio; headquarters of the Church from 1831 until 1837. In this obscure village, located about six miles from the shores of Lake Erie in the northeastern part of Ohio, significant, sacred events took place.

It was in Kirtland that the first temple of modern times was erected and dedicated to the Lord on March 27, 1836 (D&C 109). Within its sacred walls, angels mingled with men on that holy occasion (HC 2:427–28). Less than one week later, the Prophet and Oliver Cowdery were visited by such heavenly beings as the Savior, Moses, Elijah, and Elias as keys of authority were restored to the earth (D&C 110).

The first high council and first stake of the Church were organized at Kirtland in February 1834 (D&C 102). One year later, the first Quorum of the Twelve Apostles and the First Quorum of the Seventy were organized. Two years prior to this, the primary quorum of the Church—the First Presidency—had been established. Thus, Kirtland was the spawning ground for the three basic quorums which preside over the Church today (D&C 107:22–26).

Even though the Lord had revealed that Missouri was to be the "land of Zion," or the Saints' inheritance (D&C 57:1–3), two months later, in September 1831,

he commanded that a "strong hold in the land of Kirtland" be maintained "for the space of five years" (D&C 64:21). The building of a temple and the restoration of keys from heaven might not have been possible under the conditions in which the Saints lived in Missouri.

Kirtland was to survive as a strong hold of Zion until she met the *measure of her creation.* She must first give birth to those wondrous events for which she was created. "After this glorious event," said Joseph Fielding Smith, "the members of the Church were at liberty to remove to Zion (Missouri). In fact there followed a few months later an apostasy, and many turned away from the Church, but some were saved and they were under the necessity of fleeing from the place." (CHMR 1:237.) The deserted temple stood sound in structure, yet barren of spirit.

See also: Kirtland Temple; Shinehah

Kirtland Temple

On December 27, 1832, the Saints were commanded to build a house of God (D&C 88:119). About six months later the Saints were reprimanded for not having commenced the work of the temple (D&C 95:3). Several days later the work of building the temple began (ECH, 128–29).

The Kirtland (Ohio) Temple was dedicated on March 27,

1836, the first temple in the dispensation of the fulness of times (D&C 109). A great outpouring of the Spirit occurred on this occasion (HC 2:427–28). Several days later, the resurrected Lord appeared to the Prophet Joseph Smith and Oliver Cowdery and other heavenly messengers bestowed keys of authority on these anointed leaders (D&C 110).

The temple was built for purposes of worship rather than for ordinance work relating to the redemption of the dead (LDS 1:151–52). Following the flight of the Saints from Kirtland because of apostasy and persecution, the temple was abandoned and became an ordinary building devoid of the Spirit.

Elder James E. Talmage has written: "The building is yet standing, and serves the purposes of an ordinary meeting-house for an obscure sect that manifest no visible activity in temple building, nor apparent belief in the sacred ordinances for which temples are erected. The people whose sacrifice and suffering reared the structure no longer assert claims of ownership. What was once the Temple of God, in which the Lord Jesus appeared in person, has become but a house, —a building whose sole claim to distinction among the innumerable structures built by man, lies in its wondrous past." (HL, 123.)

See also: Breastwork of the Pulpit; Kirtland, Ohio; Rods; Temple

Knight, Joseph, Sr.

The name of Joseph Knight appears in two places in the Doctrine and Covenants, once in the preface of section 12, a revelation directed to him personally, and once in section 23, verse 6. The first revelation was a direction to help "establish the cause of Zion," and the second revelation admonishes him to take up his "cross" and "pray vocally before the world as well as in secret." Knight was baptized shortly after this latter revelation was received.

This kindly "old gentleman" is first mentioned in the Prophet's history when he came to Joseph's assistance by bringing a quantity of provisions which enabled the work of the translation of the Book of Mormon to continue. This help was rendered on several occasions thereafter. (HC 1:47.) Knight also employed the Prophet and was at the Smith home when Joseph went to obtain the plates from the Hill Cumorah.

Under the date of August 22, 1842, the Prophet wrote the following tribute to Joseph Knight, Sr.: "I am now recording in the Book of the Law of the Lord, of such as have stood by me in every hour of peril, for these fifteen long years past, say, for instance, my aged and beloved brother, Joseph Knight, Sen., who was among the number of the first to administer to my necessities, while I was laboring in the commencement of the bringing forth of the work of the Lord, and of laying the foundation of the Church of Jesus Christ of Latter-day Saints. For fifteen years he has been faithful and true, and even-handed and exemplary, and virtuous and kind, never deviating to the right hand or to the left. Behold he is a righteous man, may God Almighty lengthen out the old man's days; and may his trembling, tortured, and broken body be renewed, and in the vigor of health turn upon him, if it be Thy will, consistently, O God; and it shall be said of him, by the sons of Zion, while there is one of them remaining, that this man was a faithful man in Israel; therefore his name shall never be forgotten." (HC 5:124–25.)

Joseph Knight, Sr., died a faithful member of the Church on February 3, 1847, at Mount Pisgah, Iowa, during the exodus.

Knight, Newel

"Having been born of goodly parents," Newel Knight was a strength and true friend to the Prophet Joseph. He is mentioned in four sections of the Doctrine and Covenants (D&C 52:32; 54:2; 56:6–7; 124:132). Section 124 refers to his participation on the Nauvoo high council. He also served in similar capacities in Missouri (HC 2:124, 523).

Knight's name occupies a unique position within the Church, for it was from him that the Prophet cast out a devil, performing what has been labeled the "first miracle of the Church." Knight saw the devil leave him and vanish from the room. "This was the first miracle which was done in the Church, or by any member of it," said the Prophet, "and it was done not by man, or by the power of man, but it was done by God, and by the power of godliness; therefore, let the honor and the praise, the dominion and the glory, be ascribed to the Father, Son, and Holy Spirit, for ever and ever" (HC 1:82–83).

He experienced a great spiritual manifestation June 9, 1830. During a great outpouring of the Spirit at the first conference of the Church, the Prophet recorded the following: "Brother Newel Knight, had to be placed on a bed, being unable to help himself. By his own account of the transaction, he could not understand why we should lay him on the bed, as he felt no sense of weakness. He felt his heart filled with love, with glory, and pleasure unspeakable, and could discern all that was going on in the room; when all of a sudden a vision of the future burst upon him. He saw there represented the great work which through my instrumentality was yet to be accomplished. He saw heaven opened, and beheld the Lord Jesus Christ, seated at the right hand of the majesty on high, and had it made plain to his understanding that the time would come when he would be admitted into His presence to enjoy His society for ever and ever." (HC 1:85.)

"Newel Knight . . . was a faithful and staunch member of the Church, continuing thus until the time of his death," which occurred on the winter plains of the Midwest, January 11, 1847 (Jenson 2:744).

Knight, Vinson

The name of Vinson Knight appears twice in section 124. In verse 74 the Lord admonishes him to buy stock in the Nauvoo House, and in verse 141 he is named as a bishop in Nauvoo. He had previously served as a counselor in the bishopric in Kirtland (HC 2:365, 509). On February 1, 1841, he was elected as one of the first councilors for the City of Nauvoo (HC 4:287).

On August 31, 1842, Joseph Smith penned the following: "In council with Bishops Miller and Whitney, Brigham Young, John Taylor, &c., concerning Bishop Vinson Knight's sickness. Brother Knight has been sick about a week, and this morning he began to sink very fast until twelve o'clock when death put a period to his sufferings." (HC 5:84.)

Knowledge

The Lord promised that those who faithfully sought him would receive "revelation upon revelation, knowledge upon knowledge, . . . that which bringeth joy, that which bringeth life eternal" (D&C 42:61; see also 1:28; 2 Ne. 28:30). Joseph Smith declared that "a man is saved no faster than he gets knowledge" (TPJS, 217). However, "the fact is, knowledge alone is not sufficient to save men. They must put their knowledge into practice and act up to that which they know." (GT 2:273.) Thus, when the Lord decreed that "it is impossible for a man to be saved in ignorance" (D&C 131:6), he had specific reference to the saving ordinances of the gospel and the proper application of knowledge to righteous ends. (DS 1:290.)

Elder Marion G. Romney taught, "the knowledge one must have to be saved is that which comes with a testimony of the truthfulness of the gospel of Jesus Christ, including all the principles that it teaches" (LTG, 45). Those who lack this knowledge because of their own "wilful and sinful neglect" will be accordingly condemned, while those who lacked *opportunity* to gain this knowledge will find this but a "temporary deficiency; for Eternal Justice provides means of education beyond the grave" (VM, 278).

There is, of course, other knowledge which should be sought. "As a people the Latter-day Saints are ardent friends of learning, true seekers after knowledge," declared President George Q. Cannon (GT 2:234). The Lord admonished Joseph Smith "to obtain a knowledge of history, and of countries, and of kingdoms, of laws of God and man, and all this for the salvation of Zion" (D&C 93:53). Similarly, the patrons of the School of the Prophets were likewise admonished to obtain a knowledge of temporal as well as spiritual things (D&C 88:77–80).

Ultimately one must acquire a knowledge of *all* things to become as omniscient as God is. However, knowledge alone will not be sufficient to give one the "fulness" which the Father hath (DS 1:291; D&C 93:26–27). President Spencer W. Kimball said, "It is my understanding that when we have learned all we need to *know* about creation of worlds, that we shall still need the power of the Priesthood to effect the creation" ("The New and Everlasting Covenant," Ten-Stake Fireside Address, BYU, September 30, 1973, manuscript copy, p. 6).

Satan's knowledge gives him temporary power, but he, and those who follow him, will never experience the joy that the power of the priesthood provides the righteous. And, regardless of the extent of his knowledge, he will always be subservient to the power of the Priesthood.

See also: Hidden Treasures of Knowledge; Treasures; Unfruitful in the Knowledge of the Lord; Word of Knowledge

L

Laban

The "sword of Laban" is one of the artifacts the Three Witnesses of the Book of Mormon were privileged to see (D&C 17:1; LJFS, 242). Laban was a descendant of Joseph, who was sold into Egypt. He lived in Jerusalem about 600 B.C. and possessed a genealogical record of Joseph's family (1 Ne. 3:3; 5:14, 16). This record, engraven upon plates of brass, also contained the first five books of the Old Testament, a record of the Jews down to the reign of King Zedekiah, and prophetic utterances from "the beginning" down to the time of Jeremiah (1 Ne. 3:3; 5:11–13).

Laban rejected the request to deliver up these plates of brass to the prophet Lehi and even sought to slay Lehi's sons after having stolen their wealth. His power was such that he could command and even slay fifty men (1 Ne. 3:31). Nevertheless, the power of the Lord was greater. The plates were delivered into Nephi's hands, and Laban's life was taken as a result of the Lord's dictum that "it is better that one man should perish than that a nation should dwindle and perish in unbelief" (1 Ne. 4:13).

See also: Sword of Laban

Laborers in the Vineyard

The Lord's mention of the "laborers in the vineyard" (D&C 33:3; 39:17) has direct reference to the New Testament parable of the same name (Matt. 20:1–16; see also Jacob 5:71–75). "In principle the *Parable of the Laborers in the Vineyard* applies to all who are called into the ministry of the Master" (DNTC 1:561).

Elder James E. Talmage suggested the parable "was delivered by the Master, as a rebuke of the bargaining spirit in the Lord's work. . . . Those who diligently labor, knowing that the Master will give to them whatever is right, and with thought for the work rather than for the wage, shall find themselves more bountifully enriched. A man may work for wages and yet not be a hireling. Between the worthy hired servant and the hireling there is the difference that distinguishes the shepherd from the sheep herder." (Talmage, 481–82.)

Lake of Fire and Brimstone

The reference to a "lake of fire and brimstone" appears twice in the Doctrine and Covenants (D&C 63:17; 76:36), ten times in the Book of Mormon (e.g., 2 Ne. 9:16, 19, 26), and twice in the New Testament (Rev. 19:20; 21:8). Additional references are made to "fire and brimstone" within the Bible (e.g., Gen. 19:24; Ps. 11:6; Rev. 14:10).

The wicked are warned that they shall be cast into such a lake unless they repent. Brimstone is a sulphurous substance found in great quantities on the shores of the Dead Sea. Peloubet indicates that it is "very inflammable, and when burning emits a peculiar suffocating odor" (Peloubet, 100). Thus, one who is *spiritually* cast into such a lake, would suffer great discomfort and anguish, literally *suffocating* the spirit by the stench of one's sins.

Just as one could not physically survive submersion in a literal lake of fire and brimstone, neither can one spiritually survive submersion in sin. The effects are similar, for one destroys the body and the other the spirit. This is the end state of the "devil and his angels," who shall be cast into such a lake of "everlasting fire" (D&C 29:28).

See also: Fire; Hell

Lamanites

The term *Lamanites* appears a dozen times in the Doctrine and Covenants (e.g., D&C 3:18, 20; 19:27; 49:24). In a specific sense, Lamanites are descendants of the rebellious, eldest son of the prophet Lehi (1 Ne. 2:5). However, throughout the Book of Mormon the term is normally applied to those individuals who, like the man after whom they were named, rebelled against the light of the gospel and the prophets who proclaimed it. They were those who sought to destroy the people of Nephi or who "revolted" against the Church and "wilfully rebelled" against the gospel (Jacob 1:14; 4 Ne. 1:20).

There were times throughout the one-thousand-year recorded history of the Lamanites when they accepted the gospel, became righteous, and were even assimilated among the Nephites (Alma 19:35; 23:7; 24:19; Hel. 6:1). From A.D. 34 until A.D. 194, for example, there was no separate Lamanite nation, but all were "children of Christ" (4 Ne. 1:1–20). Ultimately, the Lamanites were reestablished as a separate nation and totally destroyed the Nephite nation. They became the forefathers of what Joseph Smith identified as the western tribes of Indians. (TPJS, 17, 92–93.)

In 1976, President Spencer W. Kimball identified the Lamanites as the sixty million or more native inhabitants of the Americas and the islands of the South Pacific (CR, Oct. 1976, p. 9). According to Elder Wilford Woodruff, these people will "blossom as the rose," and "a nation will be born in a day" as they accept the gospel (JD 15:282).

A dark skin was originally placed upon the Lamanites to distinguish them from the Nephites and to keep the two people from mixing (2 Ne. 5:21; Alma 3:7–8). President Joseph Fielding Smith has written that "the dark skin was the sign of the curse. The curse," however, "was the withdrawal of the Spirit of the Lord." (AGQ 3:122.) Thus, when they or any other people accept the light of the gospel, "their scales of darkness shall begin to fall from their eyes" (2 Ne. 30:6).

In our day, "the dark skin of those who have come into the Church is no longer considered a sign of the curse" (AGQ 3:123).

See also: Jacob Shall Flourish in the Wilderness; Lemuelites; Line Running Between Jew and Gentile; Testimony of Their Fathers

Lamanites Shall Blossom as the Rose

See: Jacob Shall Flourish in the Wilderness

Lamb

The "Lamb" is Jesus Christ (D&C 76:21, 85, 119; 88:106, 115; 109:79). He was slain (D&C 76:39) and took upon himself our sins (Alma 7:14). The Lamb will soon stand upon Mount Zion (D&C 133:55–56) to usher in the Millennium and will invite the faithful to feast at his marriage supper (D&C 58:11; 65:3). To him will the "song of the Lamb" be eternally sung (D&C 133:56).

Just as sacrificial lambs had to be "without blemish and without spot," so did his life have to be unblemished in order to effect the

Atonement (1 Pet. 1:19; Heb. 9:14). It was most appropriate for John the Baptist to announce the Savior's ministry by declaring, "Behold the Lamb of God, which taketh away the sin of the world" (John 1:29). The appelation "Lamb of God" was used extensively by the ancient prophet Nephi when referring to the Savior (1 Ne. 10–14).

See also: Jesus Christ; Marriage of the Lamb

Lamb's Book of Life

See: Book of Life

Lamech

The Old Testament mentions a fifth lineal descendant from Cain named Lamech (Gen. 4:16–24). This man followed his forefather's wicked ways and entered into a secret covenant with Satan whereby "he became Master Mahan" (Moses 5:49). He, who was denied priesthood blessings, is *not* the same Lamech mentioned in the priesthood lineage of section 107 (D&C 107:51). This latter Lamech, the father of Noah (Gen. 5:25–31), was the first of the early patriarchs to receive the priesthood under the hands of someone other than Adam, being ordained by Seth at the age of thirty-two.

Lamps Trimmed and Burning

The Lord has counseled his people to "be faithful, praying always, having your lamps trimmed and burning, and oil with you, that you may be ready at the coming of the Bridegroom" (D&C 33:17). Commenting on the lamps and oil used in the parable of the wise and foolish virgins (Matt. 25:1–13), Elder James E. Talmage said: "The lighted lamp, which each of the maidens carried, is the outward profession of Christian belief and practice; and in the oil reserves of the wiser ones we may see the spiritual strength and abundance which diligence and devotion in God's service alone can insure" (Talmage, 578–79).

Land

See: Earth . . . Like It Was in the Days Before It Was Divided; Eastern Brethren/Countries/Lands; Good of the Land of Zion; Goodly Land, The; Holy Land; Islands of the Sea; Land Flowing with Milk and Honey; Land of Inheritance; Land of Kirtland; Land of Missouri; Land of Promise; Land of the Living; Land of Zion; Sickness of the Land; This Land

Land Flowing with Milk and Honey

At a conference of the Church in 1831, Jesus Christ spoke of giving his Saints "a land of promise, a land flowing with milk and honey, upon which there shall be no curse when the Lord cometh" (D&C 38:18). Such a land appears to be descriptive of the state of the terrestrial earth during the Millennium, when it will have returned to its paradisiacal glory, the state in which it existed before the Fall (Articles of Faith 1:10; AF, 375–77).

The reference to a land flowing with milk and honey is "a proverbial expression indicating fertility and abundance" (Dummelow, 51). It is found in the Old Testament and is descriptive of the land of promise into which Jehovah led the children of Israel (Ex. 3:8; Lev. 20:24; Jer. 11:5).

See also: Land of Inheritance; Land of Promise; Milk

Land of Inheritance

Reference to a land of inheritance may have reference to Missouri, the site of the future New Jerusalem (D&C 101:1), or it may have reference to the paradisiacal earth during the Millennium or even thereafter when it attains its celestial state (D&C 38:19; AF, 375–81; MD, 210–11).

See also: Land Flowing with Milk and Honey; Land of Promise

Land of Kirtland

See: Kirtland

Land of Missouri

See: Missouri

Land of Promise

Two revelations received in 1831 speak of a land of promise.

In the first instance, the land of promise is the future regenerated earth (D&C 38:18–19; AF, 375–81), and in the second instance it refers specifically to the land of Missouri (D&C 57:1–3).

Reference in the Old Testament to the land of promise is to the land of Canaan, which Jehovah promised to give the children of Israel (Josh. 23:5). The land of promise referred to in the Book of Mormon (1 Ne. 2:20; Ether 2:7) is the land of America.

See also: Land Flowing with Milk and Honey; Land of Inheritance

Land of the Living

The phrase "land of the living" is found three times in scripture (D&C 81:3; Ps. 27:13; 116:9). It is an expression referring to the state or value of mortal life as opposed to that of the dead or those who dwell in the spirit world (Dummelow, 340).

Land of Zion

"The whole of America is Zion itself from north to south," declared the Prophet Joseph Smith (TPJS, 362). There are over fifty references to the "land of Zion" in the Doctrine and Covenants, however, and these refer to the land of Missouri in which the Saints attempted to establish the *cause* and the *city* of Zion (e.g., D&C 57:14; 63:24–48; 78:3; 103).

President Joseph Fielding Smith said, "We accept the fact that the *center place* where the City New Jerusalem is to be built, is in Jackson County, Missouri. . . . But we do hold that Zion, when reference is made to the land, is as broad as America, both North and South—*all of it is Zion.*" (DS 3:72.) Thus, the references to building up Zion, found in prophetic utterances, has implications far beyond the borders of Missouri.

See also: Zion

Laneshine House

In order to maintain secrecy, a revelation given on April 3, 1834, referred to the building that housed the printing office in Kirtland as the "Laneshine house" (D&C 104:28, pre-1981 edition; HC 1:255). Perhaps the destruction of the Saints' press in Missouri the previous year was part of the reasoning for such secrecy. Oliver Cowdery, one of two called upon to manage the office, was assigned to occupy a lot adjacent to that which housed the printing establishment.

See also: Shinelah

Last Days

The singular *last day* and the plural *last days* are phrases appearing frequently in the Doctrine and Covenants (e.g., D&C 1:4; 4:2; 64:34; 136:22). One also finds the synonymous terms *last time* (D&C 24:19) and *last times* (D&C 121:27)

interspersed throughout the pages of the Doctrine and Covenants. When the Lord promises that the "faithful . . . shalt be lifted up at the last day" (D&C 5:35), reference is made to the glorious day when "time shall be no more" and the righteous shall inherit celestial crowns.

"The rise of the Church of Christ in these last days" (D&C 20:1), the committing of the keys of the priesthood "for the last times" (D&C 27:13), and the labors in the "vineyard for the last time" (D&C 43:28) all have reference to these final days before the Second Coming of Christ and the ushering in of the Millennium. Elder Joseph Fielding Smith said, "By the 'last time' the Lord meant the Dispensation of the Fulness of Times" (CR, Apr. 1946, p. 155).

See also: Dispensation of the Fulness of Times

Last Death

Speaking of those who are "spiritually dead," the Lord referred to this death as both the "first death" and the "last death" (D&C 29:41). This latter death has been described as "the final judgment passed upon the wicked . . . , *banishment from the presence of the Lord*" (DS 2:217).

The last death is not "the dissolution or annihilation of both spirit and body," for, once resurrected, they are never again to be divided (DS 2:222; Alma 11:45). The last death is reserved for "those who have sinned unto death'' (D&C 64:7), whose loathsome lives have branded them as ''sons of perdition'' (D&C 76:32–38). They shall die a ''second death, for they are cut off again as to things pertaining to righteousness'' (Hel. 14:16–18).

See also: Sons of Perdition; Spiritually Dead

Last Resurrection

When the trump sounds, announcing the Second Coming, the Saints will come forth in a glorious resurrection. However, the Lord will declare to the sinners, ''stay and sleep until I shall call again'' (D&C 43:18). These are those who ''are to be judged and are found under condemnation'' (D&C 88:100), who shall not come forth until the ''last resurrection'' (D&C 76:85).

This resurrection will include all beings of a telestial order and also those miserable creatures whose actions have designated them as ''sons of perdition'' (D&C 76:31–33, 81–85; 88:32). These are they who arise in the ''resurrection of the unjust'' (D&C 76:17).

See also: Resurrection; Resurrection of the Unjust

Latter Days

The latter days (D&C 138:44; 1 Ne. 15:13), latter times (Hel. 15:12), or last times (D&C 121:27) have reference to the period of time preceding the Second Coming.

Latter-day Saints

See: Saints

Laughter

If one were to rely strictly on the few references to laughter in the Doctrine and Covenants as a measure of the place of humor in life, superficial sobriety might abound. Therefore, it is important to understand the setting in which the statements regarding laughter were made. It is in connection with Sabbath activities that the Lord counsels us to have ''cheerful hearts and countenances,'' but to avoid ''much laughter'' (D&C 59:15).

To the participants in the school of the prophets the admonition was to cast away their ''excess of laughter,'' and to ''cease from all your light speeches, from all laughter, from all your lustful desires'' (D&C 88:69, 121). The purposes of this spiritual school made it inappropriate to mingle jest and joviality with the serious and sacred matters under consideration. In this particular setting, light-mindedness had no place.

In our day there are places where light-mindedness and loud laughter are inappropriate. Elder Joseph Fielding Smith counseled that ''amusement, laughter, [and] light-mindedness, are all out of place in the sacrament meetings of the Latter-day Saints'' (CR, Oct. 1929, p. 62). This same counsel was applied to general conference sessions when the Lord's spokesman, President Harold B. Lee, cautioned the speakers and congregation about "great crescendos" of laughter "that might be mistaken by those who are listening on the outside" (CR, Oct. 1972, p. 176).

The scriptures remind us that "to every thing there is a season, and a time to every purpose under the heaven," including "a time to laugh" (Eccl. 3:1–4). Elder Boyd K. Packer has observed that the Savior himself "would chuckle with approval when at times of recreation the music is comical or melodramatic or exciting. Or at times when a carnival air is in order that decorations be bright and flashy, even garish."

Nevertheless, Elder Packer cautioned, "I am sure He would be offended at immodesty and irreverence in music, in art, in poetry, in writing, in sculpture, in dance, or in drama" (DSY, 1976, p. 279).

There is a standard which governs the appropriateness of merriment. In this respect Elder Joseph Fielding Smith counseled: "I do not believe the Lord intends and desires that we should pull a long face and look sanctimonious and hypocritical. I think he expects us to be happy and of a cheerful countenance, but he does not expect of us the indulgence in boisterous and unseemly conduct and the seeking after the vain and foolish things which amuse and entertain the world." (CR, Oct. 1916, p. 70.) That which evokes our laughter must be celestially compatible with Christ's sense of humor.

Appropriate laughter and a smiling countenance should be part of a religion that espouses the doctrine that "men are, that they might have joy" (2 Ne. 2:25), and whose founding Prophet proclaimed, "Happiness is the object and design of our existence; and will be the end thereof, if we pursue the path that leads to it; and this path is virtue, uprightness, faithfulness, holiness, and keeping all the commandments of God" (TPJS, 255–56). Latter-day Saints must not be "pallbearer types," quipped Elder Paul H. Dunn; "you can be spiritual and have fun too" (CN, Apr. 15, 1978, p. 14).

See also: Light-Mindedness

Law and the Prophets

The Lord's reference to "the law and the prophets" (D&C 59:22) is one which he used anciently on both hemispheres (Matt. 5:17; 22:40; 3 Ne. 15: 2–10). The "law" generally referred to the Pentateuch, or first five books of the Bible, with particular emphasis on the Mosaic law. The "prophets" had reference to the other extant writings of the Old Testament, commencing with Joshua, which had been canonized as scripture at that time.

Thus, "the law and the prophets" was the accepted Hebrew scripture, indicating God's will as revealed through his prophets. To the Nephites, the resurrected Lord said: "Behold, I have given unto you the commandments; therefore keep my commandments. And this is the law and the prophets," he declared. (3 Ne. 15:10.)

See also: Law of Carnal Commandments; Law of Moses

Law of Carnal Commandments

The Lord speaks of "the law of carnal commandments" in a revelation on priesthood (D&C 84:27). Of this law, Elder Bruce R. McConkie has written: "To Moses the Lord first gave the higher priesthood and revealed the fulness of the gospel. But Israel rebelled and manifest such gross unworthiness that their God took from them the power whereby they could have become a kingdom of priests and of kings and gave them instead a lesser law, a law of carnal commandments, a preparatory gospel, a schoolmaster to bring them to Christ and the fulness of his gospel. He gave them instead the law of Moses." (MD, 434; D&C 84:17–28; Gal. 3; Heb. 4:2; JST, Ex. 34:1–2.)

See also: Law of Moses

Law of Christ

The Lord declared that those "who are not sanctified through the law which I have given unto you, even the law of Christ, must

inherit" kingdoms other than the celestial kingdom (D&C 88:21). The law of Christ encompasses all of the commandments, covenants, and ordinances in the gospel that set the requirements for receiving a fulness of the glory of the Father in his eternal presence.

Law of Circumcision

The Prophet Joseph's inspired rendition of Genesis 17 provided much insight regarding the law of circumcision. To Abraham, the Lord declared: "And I will establish a covenant of circumcision with thee, and it shall be my covenant between me and thee, and thy seed after thee. . . . This is my covenant . . . ; every man child among you shall be circumcised. And ye shall circumcise the flesh of your foreskin; and it shall be a token of the covenant betwixt me and you. And he that is eight days old shall be circumcised among you, every man child in your generations." (JST, Gen. 17:8–20.)

"One of the provisions of this law of circumcision was that it should be practiced by the chosen seed, to identify and distinguish them, until the day of the mortal ministry of Christ. From Abraham to the meridian of time, the gospel and such of the laws of salvation as were revealed in any period were reserved almost exclusively for the seed of Abraham in whose flesh the token of circumcision was found.

"But beginning in the meridian of time the Lord's eternal plans called for sending the gospel to all the world; the Gentile nations were to be invited to come to Christ and be heirs of salvation. The laws of salvation were to be offered to those in whose flesh the token of the everlasting covenant was not found. . . . Accordingly, the need for the special token in the flesh no longer existed, and so circumcision as a gospel ordinance was done away in Christ. . . .

"Paul, the Apostle to the Gentiles, of necessity had to write and teach much about circumcision so that his converts would understand that it was done away in Christ." (MD, 143–44; see also Rom. 2–4; 1 Cor. 7:19; Gal. 5:6; 6:15; Col. 2:11; 3:11.) It was, in fact, Paul's writings to the Corinthians on this issue that prompted the inspired explanation in Doctrine and Covenants 74.

Law of Moses

The "law of Moses" is mentioned by name in only two sections of the Doctrine and Covenants (D&C 22:2; 74:3–5), although it is also spoken of as "the law of carnal commandments" (D&C 84:27). Elder Bruce R. McConkie has succinctly described this law as follows: "Moses received by revelation many great gospel truths, as for instance the Ten Commandments recorded in the 20th chapter of Exodus. These gospel truths, being eternal in their nature, are part of the fulness of the everlasting gospel; they have always been in force in all dispensations. They are part of 'the law of Christ.' (D&C 88:21.) But the particular things spoken of in the scriptures as the law of Moses were the ordinances and performances that were 'added because of transgressions.' (Gal. 3:19.) They were the 'divers washings, and carnal ordinances, imposed on them until the time of reformation.' (Heb. 9:10.) They were 'the law of commandments contained in ordinances.' (Eph. 2:15.) In great detail they are recorded in Exodus, Leviticus, Numbers, and Deuteronomy, and were preserved on the brass plates which the Nephites took with them. (1 Ne. 4:15–16.)" (MD, 434–35.)

The Book of Mormon gives added insight to the nature of this law. Among the more important references are chapters 12 to 16 of Mosiah, wherein the prophet Abinadi said: "The law of Moses . . . is a shadow of those things which are to come — Teach . . . that redemption cometh through Christ the Lord" (Mosiah 16:14–15).

Of significance is the resurrected Lord's personal pronouncement that "the law is fulfilled that was given unto Moses. Behold, I am he that gave the law, . . . therefore, the law in me is fulfilled . . . ; therefore it hath an end" (3 Ne. 15:2–10).

See also: Law and the Prophets; Law of Carnal Commandments

Law of Sarah

"Sarah gave Hagar to Abraham in accordance with law. It is known that, according to the Code of Hammurabi, which, in many respects, resembles the later Mosaic law, if a man's wife was childless, he was allowed to take a concubine and bring her into his house, though he was not to place her upon an equal footing with his first wife. This was the law in the country from which Abraham came. A concubine was a wife of inferior social rank." (SS, 831.)

The "law of Sarah" seems to be the approval given by the first wife for the husband to take additional wives, in order to "raise up seed" unto the Lord (D&C 132:61, 64–65). Even though God commanded Abraham to take Hagar to wife, Sarah, as the first wife, gave her approval (D&C 132:34). It appears that if the first wife will not give her approval, however, after having been properly taught the priesthood propriety of such action, she is under condemnation and the husband is exempt from this "law of permission."

A caution should be issued in relation to this law. Currently this law and all principles pertaining to the practice of plural marriage have been officially suspended by The Church of Jesus Christ of Latter-day Saints. Since 1890, this has been the position proclaimed by the prophets of God.

For example, in recent years President Spencer W. Kimball declared: "We warn you against the so-called polygamy cults which would lead you astray. Remember the Lord brought an end to this program many decades ago through a prophet who proclaimed the revelation to the world. People are abroad who will deceive you and bring you much sorrow and remorse. Have nothing to do with those who would lead you astray. It is wrong and sinful to ignore the Lord when he speaks. He has spoken—strongly and conclusively." (En., Nov. 1975, p. 5.)

See also: Hagar; One Wife; Sarah; Uriah

Law, William

Unfortunately, infamy now claims the name of William Law, a man whose name is found among the latter verses of section 124. At that time, he was called to serve as second counselor in the First Presidency, which position he occupied for about three years (1841–1844).

Although "for a season considered a good and faithful man," he allowed the spirit of apostasy to enter his heart to the degree that he sought the death of Joseph the Prophet and was described as Joseph's "most bitter foe and maligner" (HC 7:57). He was excommunicated from the Church on April 18, 1844. A short time later, Law openly opposed the Prophet and was one of the instigators of the infamous *Nauvoo Expositor*, which Joseph called a "foul, noisome, filthy sheet" (HC 6:585).

The name of William Law "is classed in history with those . . . who were the instigators and abettors of the murder of Joseph and Hyrum Smith" (Jenson 1:53). Of him, well might the Psalmist have written: "Yea, mine own familiar friend, in whom I trusted, which did eat of my bread, hath lifted up his heel against me" (Psalm 41:9).

Lay It to Heart

The admonition to "lay it to heart" was included in instructions given some elders of the Church in 1831 (D&C 58:5). This is similar to the admonition to "treasure up in your heart" (D&C 11:26) or to "ponder it in your heart" (Moro. 10:3). All of these admonitions mean to seriously consider something. Jehovah told the ancient Israelites to "lay up [carefully consider and remember] these my words in your heart and in your soul" (Deut. 11:18).

Laying On of Hands

See: Gift of the Holy Ghost

Lee, Ann

Although she is not mentioned in the text of a revelation, Ann Lee is mentioned in the preface of section 49 in 1981 editions of the Doctrine and Covenants.

She is believed to have been born in Manchester, England, on February 29, 1736, and spent her early life as a member of the Anglican Church. She married Abraham Stanley, by whom she had four children, all of whom died in infancy. She converted to the "Shaking Quakers" in 1758, a sect headed in England by Jane and James Wardley, and later became a leader in that movement.

Lee believed that the deaths of her children were judgments upon her sexual desires, and she developed the doctrine that sexual expression is a source of sin. She also claimed to have seen a vision that showed Adam and Eve transgressed sexually. This led to the practice of celibacy among her followers.

The Shaking Quakers got their name from their practice of whirling, trembling, and shaking during religious services, which they believed helped rid them of their sins. Lee began exercising this practice in Anglican church services and finally was imprisoned for blasphemy. The Wardleys became convinced that Christ would come the second time in the form of a woman, and when Lee was released from prison she was declared the fulfillment of that role. She then became known as "Mother Ann" or "Ann of the Word."

She emigrated to the United States in 1774 and established a communal society in Watervliet, New York, near Albany. The Quakers, also known as the

United Society of Believers in Christ's Second Appearing, believed strongly in personal confession before two witnesses. Lee died on September 8, 1784, but others carried the work forward. Quakerism was at its peak between 1830–1850 but today is virtually extinct, due largely to the practice of celibacy. (See *Encyclopedia Americana*, vols. 17, 24, 1985 ed.)

See also: One Wife; Shakers; Son of Man Cometh Not in the Form of a Woman

Left Hand

The Savior warns the wicked, they who are found on his left hand, that they will be subject to woes and he will be ashamed of them before the Father (D&C 19:5; 29:27; Matt. 25:41). King Benjamin cautioned those who do not choose to take upon them the name of Christ that they will be found on the left hand of God (Mosiah 5:10, 12). The left hand is called the sinister, which "is associated with evil, rather than good. Sinister means *perverse*." (DS 3:108.)

It is significant that covenants with the Lord are associated with the right hand and the hand of friendship is generally extended with the right hand. Those who keep their covenants with Christ and seek to be his friend (D&C 93:45) will be found in the *favorable* position—on his right hand.

See also: Right Hand

Lehi

The man Lehi, spoken of in Doctrine and Covenants 17:1, is the patriarch-prophet whose posterity's history is contained in the Book of Mormon. He was one of the many prophets in Jerusalem around 600 B.C. and was a contemporary of the Old Testament prophet Jeremiah (1 Ne. 1:4; 5:13).

His was not only the voice of warning to the wicked but also the voice of Messianic hope as he testified of the Messiah's forthcoming mission (1 Ne. 1:18–19; 10:4–10). The people rejected his testimony and sought his life, but the Lord led him to safety and ultimately to a new and "promised" land (1 Ne. 1:20; 2:1–3, 20; 18:23).

He and his wife, Sariah, were the parents of six sons—Laman, Lemuel, Sam, Nephi, Jacob, and Joseph—and of at least two unnamed daughters (1 Ne. 1:1, 5; 18:7; 2 Ne. 5:6; JD 23:184). Many years after his death he was described as a man of good works (Hel. 5:6).

See also: Book of Mormon; Jacobites; Josephites; Lamanites; Lemuelites; Nephites

Lemuelites

The Lord indicated his desire to have the Book of Mormon come to the knowledge of the Lemuelites (D&C 3:18). Specifically, the Lemuelites were originally those people who descended from Lemuel, second oldest son of Lehi (1 Ne. 2:5). They were generally known as Lamanites throughout the Book of Mormon, in deference to their following the leadership of that group (Jacob 1:13–14; Alma 3:7–8; Alma 47:35; Morm. 1:9). Lemuelite blood is intermixed among the people known as Lamanites in our day.

See also: Lamanites

Lesser Priesthood

The Lord himself defined the meaning of "lesser priesthood." "Why it is called the lesser priesthood is because it is an appendage to the greater, or the Melchizedek Priesthood, and has power in administering outward ordinances" (D&C 107:13–14). Elder Boyd K. Packer reminds us that "the Melchizedek Priesthood *always* presides over the Aaronic, or the lesser Priesthood" (CR, Nov. 1981, p. 44). For example, when John the Baptist restored the lesser priesthood in our dispensation, he affirmed that he acted under the direction of those who held the keys of the higher priesthood (JS—H 1:68–72).

The term *lesser* must not be taken lightly, however, for "it is neither small nor insignificant" (AF, 204). President Wilford Woodruff proclaimed: "I desire to impress upon you the fact that it does not make any difference whether a man is a Priest or an Apostle, if he magnifies his calling. A Priest holds the keys of the ministering of angels. Never in my life, as an Apostle, as a Seventy, or as an Elder, have I ever had more of the protection of the Lord than while holding the office of a Priest. The Lord revealed to me by visions, by revelations, and by the Holy Spirit, many things that lay before me." (MS 53:629.)

See also: Aaronic Priesthood; First Priesthood; Levitical Priesthood; Priesthood

Letter of the Gospel

The *letter of the gospel* (D&C 107:20) encompasses all of the divinely mandated covenants, ordinances, and principles of the gospel. One must adhere to the letter of the gospel in order to qualify for the promised blessings (see D&C 130:30–31). However, there must be harmony between one's heart and one's actions. To mechanically go through the motions of compliance to prescribed procedures without the accompanying commitment in one's heart does not bring a fulness of blessings.

The Apostle Paul drew a distinction between those who were outwardly observing the law as opposed to those who had an inner conviction (Rom. 2:28–29). Moroni cautioned against doing things grudgingly, for without "real intent of heart . . . it profiteth him nothing, for God receiveth none such" (Moro. 7:6–11).

See also: Gospel; Full Purpose of Heart

Levi

The sons of Levi are referred to three times in the Doctrine and Covenants (D&C 13; 124:39; 128:24). Levi was the third son of Jacob and Leah (Gen. 29:34). Though there was at least one episode in his life which caused his father some heartache (Gen. 34; 49:5-7), Levi must have been judged sufficiently faithful to have been granted posterity such as Moses, Aaron, and all who would later minister in the ordinances of the lesser priesthood to the other tribes of Israel (Ex. 4:14; Num. 3; 4; 8).

See also: Levitical Priesthood; Priesthood; Sons of Levi

Levitical Priesthood

The Aaronic Priesthood is divided into two sections — Aaronic and Levitical — but it is *one* priesthood. The Aaronic Priesthood, as restored to the earth in this dispensation, includes the Levitical order. Elder James E. Talmage wrote that the Levitical Priesthood "is to be regarded as an appendage to the Priesthood of Aaron, not comprising the highest priestly powers" (AF, 205).

The tribe of Levi was chosen to assist Aaron in ministering the functions of the priesthood to the other tribes of Israel (Num. 3; 4; 8). "However, within the tribe, only Aaron and his sons could hold the office of priest. And, still further, from the firstborn of Aaron's sons (after Aaron) was selected the high priest (or president of the priests). Thus Aaron and his sons after him had greater offices in the Levitical Priesthood than did the other Levites." (BD, 599.)

"The sons of Aaron, who *presided* in the Aaronic order, were spoken of as holding the *Aaronic Priesthood;* and the sons of Levi, who were not sons of Aaron, were spoken of as the *Levites. They held the Aaronic Priesthood* but served under, or in a lesser capacity, than the sons of Aaron." (DS 3:86.)

See also: Aaronic Priesthood

Liars

Some of the most harsh pronouncements have been uttered against liars, "those who knowingly utter or act out falsehoods" (MD, 440). By the word of the Lord, liars will "be thrust down to hell" (2 Ne. 9:34), "not have part in the first resurrection" (D&C 63:17-18)—which means they will inherit the telestial kingdom—and "suffer the wrath of God." (D&C 76:102-6.)

God, as a being of total truth, cannot lie (D&C 62:6; 3 Ne. 27:18). On the other hand, Lucifer "is the father of all lies" (2 Ne. 2:18) and "was a liar from the beginning" (D&C 93:25). Those possessed with a lying spirit "put off the Spirit of God" that it has no place in them, giving the devil power over them (Alma 30:42).

See also: Feigned Words; Hypocrisy

Liberty

"Abide ye in the *liberty* wherewith ye are made free; *entangle not yourselves in sin,*" declared the Lord (D&C 88:86; italics added). Unfortunately, misguided and twisted thinking has caused many to equate liberty and freedom with a lack of constraints and a submersion in sin. According to the Lord, however, sin brings bondage (D&C 84:50).

Elder Rulon S. Wells observed, "We sometimes boast of being in the land of the free. . . . Nevertheless, we are not free until we have overcome evil —until we liberate ourselves from bondage of sin." (CR, Apr. 1930, p. 70.) The bondage of sin is to be shackled as slaves, in servitude to sin; it is to be fettered with chains of carnality and to be taken captive by the devil (Alma 12:11). Elder Charles H. Hart said that "sin is the barbed wire that cuts and scars, and sometimes leaves the poison of its rust within the wound, to destroy the body and to contaminate the soul" (CR, Oct. 1913, p. 43).

True liberty comes with making the right choices that lead to eternal life; horizons are expanded, opportunities are multiplied, and the realm of the righteous is to reign over dominions, kingdoms, and principalities, worlds without end (D&C 121:29; 132:19). The progress of the wicked, however, is restricted; sin will eternally limit their choices. They will be without true liberty. Truly they have sold an eternal inheritance for a mess of pottage (Gen. 25:29–34; for an excellent example of a story where one man mistook the meaning of liberty, see En., Nov. 1986, p. 12).

See also: Banner of Liberty

Liberty, Missouri

Located just a few miles directly north of Independence, Missouri, is the town of Liberty, in Clay County. Although it is not expressly mentioned in the Doctrine and Covenants, other than in three prefaces, it was the location where three significant revelations were received (D&C 121; 122; 123). The impassioned pleas of the imprisoned Prophet burst forth from the bowels of Liberty Jail, to be soothed by God's Spirit: "My son, peace be unto thy soul; thine adversity and thine afflictions shall be but a small moment" (D&C 121:7). The "small moment" was to last from the latter part of November 1838 until April 1839.

Joseph and Hyrum Smith, Sidney Rigdon, Lyman Wight, Alexander McRae, and Caleb Baldwin were confined in an unheated dungeon area with two small grilled windows. It was 14 feet square, 6½ feet high, and had no sanitary facilities. Their bed was the flat side of a hewn oak log that lay on the floor. "Here they suffered, during that time, many untold hardships.

Much of the time they were bound in chains. Their food was often not fit to eat, and never wholesome or prepared with the thought of proper nourishment. Several times poison was administered to them in their food, which made them sick nigh unto death, and only the promised blessings of the Lord saved them." (ECH, 210.)

Hyrum Smith was to later testify that they "were also subjected to the necessity of eating human flesh for the space of five days or go without food. . . . The latter I chose in preference to the former." (HC 3:420.) The guard boasted he had fed them on "Mormon beef."

Perhaps this total experience illustrates that even in dire conditions of physical and mental suffering, the spirit can soar beyond physical walls of confinement and depravity. One need not succumb and surrender to the environment.

See also: Clay County

License

The word *license* is used in two different contexts in the Doctrine and Covenants. In 1830, some priesthood bearers are told to obtain a license authorizing them to perform the duties of their callings (D&C 20:63–64). These were simply certificates attesting to the fact that the men claiming authority were in fact duly ordained to their respective priesthood offices. Today we would call these certificates of ordination.

When the Lord instructed Sidney Gilbert to establish a store and obtain a license (D&C 57:8–9), it had reference to government granted authorization to conduct his business affairs (DCC, 234).

Lift Up the Heel

To "lift up the heel against" someone (D&C 121:16) is to treat him treacherously, brutally, violently, or without feeling (Dummelow, 345). Judas lifted up his heel against the Savior when he betrayed the Master into the hands of wicked men (Ps. 41:9; John 13:18).

Lifted Up at the Last Day

Those who are faithful in keeping the commandments are promised that they shall be lifted up at the last day (D&C 5:35; 9:14; 17:8; 75:16). The words *raise up* (John 6:39; 3 Ne. 15:1) and *caught up* (D&C 17:18; 1 Thess. 4:17) are also found in scripture. To be *lifted, raised,* or *caught up* is to take part in the first resurrection (D&C 88:96–98). It is to meet and return with the Savior at his second coming and to "be saved in the everlasting kingdom of the Lamb" (1 Ne. 13:37; DNTC 3:51).

See also: First Fruits; Trump of the Angel of God

Light

See: Angel of Light; Children of Light; Clothed with Light for a Covering; Light and Life of the World; Light of Christ; Light to the World; Light unto the Gentiles

according to the plan of God the Father, Jesus Christ is the Creator, the source of the light and life of all things." (En., Nov. 1987, p. 63.)

See also: Children of Light; Jesus Christ

Light and Life of the World

"I am the light of the world," declared the Savior during his earthly ministry, and "he that followeth me shall not walk in darkness, but shall have the light of life" (John 8:12; D&C 45:7). Jesus is the light "which giveth life to all things" (D&C 88:13). He is the light who illuminates the path and points the way to safety in this life.

Those who faithfully follow that strait and narrow path will themselves be filled with celestial light and inherit eternal life in the hereafter. For, said the Lord, "he that receiveth light, and continueth in God, receiveth more light; and that light groweth brighter and brighter until the perfect day" (D&C 50:24).

All who turn from darkness and accept the fulness of Christ's gospel will find themselves awakening as from a deep sleep. They will "awake unto God," and their souls will be "illuminated" by the light of his everlasting word (Alma 5:7). Elder Dallin H. Oaks noted that "Jesus Christ is the light and life of the world because all things were made by him. Under the direction and

Light of Christ

The "light of Christ" (D&C 88:7) is synonymous with "the light of truth" (D&C 88:6), "the Spirit of Jesus Christ" (D&C 84:45–47), "the Spirit of the Lord" (D&C 121:37), and "the Spirit of Christ" (Moro. 7:16). It is that power which gives light to men's minds, as well as to the sun, moon, and stars, "which light proceedeth forth from the presence of God to fill the immensity of space—The light which is in all things, which giveth life to all things, which is the law by which all things are governed, even the power of God" (D&C 88:6–13).

President Joseph Fielding Smith said, "This Light of Christ is not a personage. It has no body. I do not know what it is as far as substance is concerned; but it fills the immensity of space and emanates from God. It is the light by which the worlds are controlled, by which they are made." Furthermore, it "is impersonal and has no size, nor dimension." It "is the active agency by which the great discoveries in these modern times have been accomplished. It is this

Spirit which the Lord declares he will withdraw from the world [D&C 63:32], and which he said to Noah would not always 'strive with man,' and not the Holy Ghost which they never had. [Moses 8:17; Gen. 6:3; D&C 1:33.] It is this Spirit which led Columbus in his discoveries.'' (DS 1:52–53.) The Light of Christ should not be confused with the Holy Ghost, who is ''a personage of Spirit.'' (D&C 130:22.) However, ''the person of the Holy Ghost can work through the Spirit of Christ that permeates everything, or he can work by personal contacts'' (DS 1:54).

An ancient prophet declared that ''the Spirit of Christ is given to every man, that he may know good from evil'' (Moro. 7:16). In other words, it acts as our conscience. A modern-day prophet said, ''Every soul who walks the earth, wherever he lives, in whatever nation he may have been born, no matter whether he be in riches or in poverty, had at birth an endowment of that first light which is called the Light of Christ, the Spirit of Truth, or the Spirit of God—that universal light of intelligence with which every soul is blessed'' (SHP, 115). It is this Spirit which touches one's heart, declaring the truthfulness of the gospel to the soul. Brigham Young proclaimed that this Spirit has ''enlightened, instructed, and taught by revelation'' every man or woman who has ever been upon the face of the earth (JD 2:139–40).

See also: Conscience

Light Speeches

See: Laughter; Light-Mindedness

Light to the World

As defined by the Lord, the ''light to the world'' is the everlasting covenant, or, in other words, the fulness of the gospel of Jesus Christ as revealed through his church (D&C 45:9, 28). Isaiah wrote of a ''standard'' that was to be set up to the people of this world (Isa. 49:22; 1 Ne. 21:22). Elder Marion G. Romney identified the Church as that standard of which Isaiah spoke (CR, Apr. 1961, p. 119).

To the Church the Lord declared: ''Arise and shine forth, that thy light may be a standard for the nations'' (D&C 115:5). The charge to the Saints in all ages has been to dispel darkness with the light of the gospel (Matt. 5:14–16; 3 Ne. 12:14–16; D&C 115:42–5). For example, Paul declared that his mission was to open the eyes of the people and ''to turn them from darkness to light, and from the power of Satan unto God'' (Acts 26:18).

See also: Children of Light; Church of Jesus Christ of Latter-day Saints, The; Light and Life of the World; Standard for My People

Light unto the Gentiles

See: Children of Light

Light-Mindedness

Among the admonitions given in the revelation known as the Olive Leaf is the counsel to cease from light-mindedness (D&C 88:121). To be light-minded is to be lacking in seriousness, which is contrary to the divine counsel to "let the solemnities of eternity rest upon your minds" (D&C 43:34). This does not mean that man should be without laughter and joy, but that he should shun that which is frivolous and inappropriate. We should avoid "seeking after the vain and foolish things which amuse and entertain the world," declared Elder Joseph Fielding Smith (CR, Oct. 1916, p. 70).

See also: Laughter

Line Running Between Jew and Gentile

The Lord used the expression "the line running directly between Jew and Gentile" to refer to a boundary of land he wished the Saints to purchase (D&C 57:4). "This expression," said President Joseph Fielding Smith, "has reference to the line separating the Lamanites from the settlers in Jackson County. At this time the United States Government had given to the Indians the lands west of the Missouri. . . . The Lamanites, who are Israelites, were referred to as Jews, and the Gentiles were the people, many of whom were the lawless element, living east of the river." (CHMR 1:188–89; DS 3:264.) In 1831, the Missouri River served as a very readily identified line that separated these two diverse societies.

See also: Borders by the Lamanites; Jacob Shall Flourish in the Wilderness; Lamanites

Lineage

The dictionary defines *lineage* as a direct descent from a common progenitor. The term as used in the Doctrine and Covenants refers to one's right to hold the priesthood or an office therein (D&C 68:21; 84:14–15; 86:8, 10; 107:41; 113:8). For example, section 68 speaks of the "literal descendants of Aaron" who have a right to the bishopric (D&C 68:21), while section 107 speaks of he who has a right to the office of Patriarch to the Church (D&C 107:41). These two offices are the only authorized "hereditary" offices (those passed from father to son, or inherited because of one's ancestry) in the Church. (DS 3:160.)

In a different vein, lineage refers to one's membership in one of the twelve tribes of Israel. This lineage is declared in the course of a personal patriarchal blessing, which makes the individual heir to the promised blessings of that particular tribe. Although one's lineage may be declared to be from a particular tribe, or blood line, it is undoubtedly a mixed lineage, for "no one can lay claim to a perfect descent from father to son through just one lineage" (AGQ 3:61). It is even possible for two individuals from the same family to be declared as belonging to two separate tribes (AGQ 5:167).

It should be remembered that all members of The Church of Jesus Christ of Latter-day Saints are of the lineage of Abraham, the great-grandfather of the twelve tribes (Abr. 2:9–11; Gal. 3:26–29).

See also: Bishop; Literal Descendant of Aaron; Order of This Priesthood; Patriarch; Patriarchal Blessings; Seed of Abraham

Literal Descendant of Aaron

A man who can trace his lineage directly back to Aaron would be a "literal descendant of Aaron." Aaron was a descendant of Levi, who was a son of Jacob (Ex. 6:16–20; Gen. 29:43). Inspired patriarchs have pronounced the lineage of Levi upon many men in the Church, but a descendant of Levi is not necessarily also of Aaron's lineage, for he may have come through a different line of Levi's posterity. President Joseph Fielding Smith has written, "There is evidently a great host of men who are descendants of Levi but not of Aaron" (DS 3:92).

By revelation, the Lord has designated these "literal descendants" as individuals who "have a legal right to the bishopric, if

they are the firstborn among the sons of Aaron" (D&C 68:16–18; 107:16). The "bishopric" mentioned "has no reference whatever to bishops of wards," said President Joseph Fielding Smith, but instead refers to one who has been designated to preside over the Aaronic Priesthood by the First Presidency of the Church (DS 3:92; D&C 68:21).

Presently, the First Presidency has designated that the youth programs of the Church be under the direction of the Quorum of the Twelve. This includes the Aaronic Priesthood. (CR, Apr. 1977, p. 51.)

See also: Aaron; Bishop; Firstborn; Lineage

Little Children

When the Lord declared that "little children are redeemed from the foundation of the world" (D&C 29:46), he was speaking of children who had not yet reached the age of accountability and were therefore innocent (see D&C 29:46–47; 68:27; JST, Gen. 17:11; Moro. 8:12, 20). We are commanded to become as little children (i.e., innocent) in order to merit God's kingdom (Matt. 18:3; Mosiah 3:19).

The title of "little children" can also be used figuratively in referring to those whose judgment is not mature on a given subject (see D&C 78:17; John 13:33).

See also: Accountable Before Me

Little One Become a Strong Nation

In speaking of the events preceding his second coming, the Lord spoke of "the day when the weak shall confound the wise, and the little one become a strong nation, and two shall put their tens of thousands to flight" (D&C 133:58). The latter part of this scripture refers to the two prophets to be raised up to the Jewish nation of Israel who will hold the armies of the earth at bay (D&C 77:15; Rev. 11:1–14).

The cross-reference to "the little one" who becomes "a strong nation" is found in Isaiah's words: "A little one shall become a thousand, and a small one a strong nation" (Isa. 60:22). This citation could refer specifically to the Jewish nation, Israel, which from a very small beginning has become a nation of prominence with proven military clout. She who was once considered "barren" and "desolate" has indeed brought forth considerable posterity. Her "husband," the Lord, the Holy One of Israel, has not forsaken her and has removed her reproach (Isa. 54; 3 Ne. 22).

On the other hand, the "little one" who was to "become a strong nation" may also refer to the Lord's people in general. This "nation of Israel," not confined to a geographical location, had its birth on April 6, 1830, when six men organized The Church of Jesus Christ of Latter-day Saints. This was the small stone destined to become a mountain and fill the earth (D&C 65:2; 109:72–73; Dan. 2:34–35, 44).

See also: Church of Jesus Christ of Latter-day Saints, The; Israel

Little Ones

The title "little ones" may have reference to children (D&C 31:2), particularly those who have not arrived at the age of accountability (JST, Matt. 18:11), or it may refer in general to those who hold membership in the kingdom of God on earth (D&C 121:19).

Little Season

See: Season

Littleness of Soul

The Lord chastised one of the early brethren for his littleness of soul on one occasion (D&C 117:11). This had reference to his smallness of spirit or his lack of spiritual strength at this particular time.

Loins

See: Fruit of Loins; Gird Up Your Loins

Long-Suffering

One of the characteristics of one possessing priesthood power is that of long-suffering (D&C 121:41). To be long-suffering is to be forbearing, patient, or enduring, particularly in the face of adversity. It is a characteristic of those holding membership in the presiding quorums of the Church (D&C 107:30).

Loosed in Heaven

See: Sealing and Binding Power

Lord

Regarding the name *Lord,* Elder Bruce R. McConkie has written: "Both the Father and the Son, as omnipotent and exalted personages, are commonly known by the name-title *Lord.* (Ps. 110:1; Matt. 22:41–46.) Embraced within this appellation is the concept that they are supreme in authority and sovereign over all, that they are the rulers and governors of all things. Since it is Christ in particular, however, through whom Deity operates where men and their affairs are concerned, it follows that most scriptural references to the Lord have reference to him. (D&C 76:1; Isa. 43:14; 49:26; Luke 2:11; Acts 10:36; Philip. 2:11.)" (MD, 450.)

See also: Father, The; God; Jesus Christ; Lord of Hosts; Lord of Sabaoth; Lord's Day; Lord's Errand

Lord of Hosts

Jesus Christ is the Lord of Hosts or the Leader and King of the hosts of heaven as well as the righteous hosts of Israel here upon the earth (1 Chron. 17:24; Isa. 6:5). "I am a great King, saith the Lord of hosts, and my name is dreadful among the heathen" (Mal. 1:14). Thus, to the righteous, the appearance of the Lord of Hosts is a joyful occasion, but the wicked tremble and seek to hide themselves when he manifests himself (Rev. 6:15–16).

The title appears to be used in instances in which a stern warning or reprimand is necessary. For example, of the twelve references in the Doctrine and Covenants that use the phrase *Lord of Hosts,* the majority of them are couched in the context of a warning or reprimand (see D&C 1:33; 29:9; 56:10; 64:24; 85:5; 121:63; 127:4; 133:64; 135:7).

Elder Bruce R. McConkie suggested that Lord of Hosts refers to the Lord as "a man of war (Ex. 15:3), a God of battles (Ps. 24:8), a leader of his saints in days of conflict and carnage" (MD, 451).

See also: Jesus Christ; Lord of Sabaoth

Lord of Sabaoth

The title "Lord of Sabaoth" was divinely defined to the Prophet Joseph in 1833: "The creator of the first day, the beginning and the end" (D&C 95:7).

Smith and Sjodahl suggested that " 'Sabaoth' is a Hebrew word meaning 'hosts.' It sometimes refers to the armies of Israel and other nations; sometimes to the priests officiating in the Sanctuary; sometimes to the people of God generally, and sometimes to the stars and planets in the sky. 'Lord of Hosts' is equivalent to the 'all-sovereign,' or 'omnipotent' Lord.'' (SS, 540.)

Thus, the Lord of Sabaoth is He who is Lord over the hosts or armies of Israel, as well as the creator of heaven and earth (Hel. 14:12; Mosiah 3:8). It is to him that the people of God should look for leadership, hope, encouragement, and direction.

See also: Jesus Christ; Lord of Hosts

Lord's Anointed

See: Anointed; Prophet

Lord's Business

See: Lord's Errand

Lord's Day

The term *Lord's day* (D&C 59:12) was defined by President George Q. Cannon as follows: " 'The Lord's Day' (Rev. 1:10) is the day on which He rose from the dead and on which His disciples at that period assembled to worship and break bread in His name. That was the 'first day of the week' (John 20:1; Acts 20:7), as they counted time. This custom was observed in the primitive Christian Church, and the Seventh Day was also observed by the Jewish disciples for a time. But Paul and other leading Elders of the Church set themselves against the observance of the rites and rules of the Mosaic law and proclaimed the liberty of the Gospel, the law having been fulfilled in Christ. He chided those who were sticklers for special days as required by the law but himself observed the *Lord's Day—the first day of the week.* It is the spirit of Sabbath observance that is acceptable to God rather than its letter. One day out of seven is to be a day of rest and worship. It would not matter which day of the week that was but for the sake of order and uniformity. So the Lord has designated for the Saints which day they should keep holy, and that is the 'Lord's Day,' commonly called 'the first day of the week.' '' (GT 2:143; italics added.)

The "Lord's day" (the Sabbath) should not be confused with the "day of the Lord," which has reference to Christ's second coming.

See also: Sabbath Day

Lord's Errand

To be on an "errand" is to be about the business of doing something that needs immediate attention. It is to have received a charge to accomplish a given objective, to act as an authorized agent. The Lord reminded several servants that they should "be in haste upon their errand and mission" (D&C 61:7). Again, he declared, "as ye are agents, ye are on the Lord's errand" (D&C 64:29).

President Harold B. Lee said, "When one becomes a holder of the priesthood, he becomes an agent of the Lord. He should think of his calling as though he were on the Lord's errand. That is what it means to magnify the priesthood." (SHP, 255.) Thus, whether as a holder of the priesthood or functioning within any divinely received calling, one is on the Lord's errand by duly acting in his behalf.

Lot of Tahhanes

In a revelation dealing with the United Order, the Lord specified the inheritance that each member of the order should receive. Sidney Rigdon was told to maintain the place where he then resided and "the lot of Tahhanes." (D&C 104:20, pre-1981 edition). This latter location was the tannery, which Rigdon was competent to manage and which would support him while in the ministry (DCC, 542). A tannery is a place where animal skins or hides are made into leather.

Love

One of the attributes necessary for success in the work of the Lord is love (D&C 4:5; 12:8). The Lord has commanded his Saints to "live together in love" (D&C 42:45) and to "let thy love abound unto all men" (D&C 112:11). The Father and Son are examples of perfect love, and the Atonement is a manifestation of that love (D&C 138:3; John 3:16).

Love is a word of beauty and hope that symbolizes strong feelings of attraction toward something or someone and concern for his or her well-being. True love lifts another. It is not confined to physical displays, although these can be an important element of love. Love's driving force has the power not only to create life but also to sustain and transform it for the better. To speak of love in the context of something contrary to that which is wholesome, uplifting, and in keeping with the will of God is to misuse its divine meaning, to prostitute and demean a word which should be held in the highest respect and reverence.

The Prophet Joseph Smith noted that "love is one of the chief characteristics of Deity, and ought to be manifested by those who aspire to be the sons of God. A man filled with the love of God, is not content with blessing his family alone, but ranges through the whole world, anxious to bless the whole human race." (TPJS, 174.) He further observed that "nothing is so much calculated to lead people to forsake sin as to take them by the hand and watch over them with tenderness. When people manifest the least kindness and love to me, oh, what power it has over my mind, while the opposite course has a tendency to harrow up all the harsh feelings and depress the human mind." (In., July 1964, p. 252.)

See also: Charity; Love of Men Shall Wax Cold; Love Unfeigned

Love of Men Shall Wax Cold

One of the signs of the last days is that "the love of men shall wax cold, and iniquity shall abound" (D&C 45:27; see also JS—M 1:10; Matt. 24:12). Elder Bruce R. McConkie suggests that this has reference to Saints who sin and lose their love of God, thereby apostatizing from the Church (DNTC 1:641).

See also: Love

Love Unfeigned

Among the qualities that give power to the priesthood, or the capacity to exercise a positive influence over another, is that of love unfeigned (D&C 121:41). Such love is genuine, sincere, without pretense or intent to deceive. In this sense we reflect on the words of the Apostle Paul and say that love unfeigned "doth not behave itself unseemly, seeketh not her own, . . . thinketh no evil" (1 Cor. 13:5). Unfeigned love does not seek a selfish advantage over another.

See also: Love

Lowliness of Heart

One of the attributes the righteous should possess is lowliness of heart (D&C 107:30; Eph. 4:2; 1 Ne. 2:19; Moro. 8:26). To be lowly in heart is to be meek and humble, submissive to God's will and not self-seeking.

Lucifer

The name *Lucifer* is found in each of the standard works except the Pearl of Great Price (D&C 76:25–27; 2 Ne. 2:17–18; Isa. 14:12–20; Luke 10:18). It is the name by which the devil was known in the premortal councils of heaven, before he was cast out and "the heavens wept over him" (D&C 76:26). According to Smith and Sjodahl, "The name means 'Light-bearer' and indicates the exalted position of him who was so called, for a 'light-bearer' is a sun in the firmament. But when he was cast out, he was called *Perdition*." (SS, 450.)

See also: Devil

Lust

Those who lust after another lose the Spirit, commit adultery in their hearts, and deny the faith (D&C 42:23; 63:16). In this context, to lust is to have unrighteous sexual desires toward another. Lustful desires (D&C 88:121) are carnal cravings. In a broad sense, to lust is to have an excessive desire to possess something thought to bring one great pleasure which is inherently sinful or which might lead to sin.

See also: Adultery; Covet; Sin; Uncleanness

Lyman, Amasa

The name of Amasa Lyman appears in two sections of the Doctrine and Covenants, once in conjunction with his position in the presidency of the quorum of high priests in Nauvoo (D&C 124:136) and once in connection with his service as one of the leaders of the pioneer camp (D&C 136:14).

He joined the Church as a young man, being baptized on April 27, 1832. His initial meeting with the Prophet Joseph was described as follows: "When he grasped my hand in that cordial way . . . I felt as one of old in the presence of the Lord; my strength seemed to be gone, so that it required an effort on my part to stand on my feet; but in all this there was no fear, but the serenity and peace of heaven pervaded my soul, and the still small voice of the spirit whispered its living testimony in the depths of my soul, where it has ever remained, that he was the Man of God."

Lyman served numerous missions during his early years in the Church, many in connection with his call as an Apostle. He joined that high quorum on August 20, 1842, but was replaced a few months later because of the reinstatement of Orson Pratt to the Twelve.

He was appointed a counselor to the First Presidency about February 4, 1843, and retired from that position with the death of the Prophet Joseph. He was placed in the Quorum of the Twelve on August 12, 1844, but because of difficulties with doctrine he was deprived of his Apostolic office on October 6, 1867, and was excommunicated on May 12, 1870. He died at Fillmore, Utah, on February 4, 1877. (Jenson 1:96–99; CA 1978, 104.)

M

Madison (Iowa)

William Law, second counselor in the First Presidency, was counseled by the Lord to "proclaim [the] everlasting gospel with a loud voice, and with great joy, as . . . moved upon by [the] Spirit, unto the inhabitants of Warsaw, . . . Carthage, . . . Burlington, and . . . Madison" (D&C 124:88). Although we are still uncertain regarding its exact location, it is assumed that the present site of Ft. Madison, Iowa, is the town of Madison spoken of in the revelation, for it is the only town of that name in the same general area as the other three towns mentioned in the revelation and is located just across the Mississippi River and northeast of Nauvoo, Illinois.

Magistrate

Latter-day Saints "believe in being subject to kings, presidents, rulers, and magistrates" (AF, 1:12). Magistrates are public officials charged or vested with the responsibility of administering the law (see D&C 134:4; Acts 16:19–21).

Magna Charta

In a broad sense, the "magna charta of the United States," as mentioned in the memorial written by John Taylor (D&C 135:7), refers to the constitution of our country, which guarantees the rights and privileges that were so flagrantly violated, leading to the martyrdoms of Joseph and Hyrum Smith.

The word comes from the magna charta, or Great Charter, to which the English barons forced King John to affix his seal June 15, 1215. It was based on an earlier charter but included rights and principles which later came into existence and laid the foundation for the security of English political and personal liberty.

Magnifying Their Calling

The Lord makes great promises to those who magnify their calling in the priesthood (D&C 84:33–38), including the promise of eternal life and all that God the Father himself possesses. To magnify one's calling is to literally enlarge upon it in the same sense in which a magnifying glass increases or broadens the borders of that which is being scrutinized.

President Joseph Fielding Smith observed that "priesthood offices or callings are ministerial assignments to perform specially assigned service in the priesthood. And the way to magnify these callings is to do the work designed to be performed by those who hold the particular office involved." (CR, Oct. 1970, 91.) To magnify one's calling is to keep "an eye single to the glory of God" and to "serve him with all your heart, might, mind and strength, that ye may stand blameless before God at the last day" (D&C 4).

See also: Oath and Covenant

Mahalaleel (#1)

The name *Mahalaleel* was found in previously published editions of the Doctrine and Covenants (D&C 82:11). At the time of this revelation, given April 26, 1832, it was not desirable that the world know who Mahalaleel was (see HC 1:255). Recent editions of the Doctrine and Covenants have identified Algernon Sidney Gilbert as the one referred to as Mahalaleel; thus Mahalaleel is no longer used in this scripture.

See also: Gilbert, Algernon Sidney

Mahalaleel (#2)

The second usage of the name *Mahalaleel* in the Doctrine and Covenants is really its primary use, for it refers to the ancient patriarch who was a great-great-grandson of father Adam (D&C 107:46; Gen. 5:4–12; Moses 6:10–19). He was one of the seven great high priests whom Adam called together in the valley of Adam-ondi-Ahman, three years before the latter's death

(D&C 107:53). Mahalaleel was 496 years of age at the time Adam ordained and blessed him, and he lived a total of 895 years (Gen. 5:17; Moses 6:20). His name is mentioned in the ancestral lineage of Joseph, husband of Mary (Luke 3:37). Mahalaleel begat Jared, who was also one of the great high priests of early times (Gen. 5:15–16; Moses 6:20; D&C 107:53).

Mahemson

Martin Harris was referred to by the name of "Mahemson" on two different occasions (D&C 82:11; 104:24, 26; pre-1981 edition). Occasionally the Lord preferred to hide the identity of those to whom he spoke in the early days of the Church, and this was the name he chose to apply to Harris in January 1832 and in April 1834 (HC 1:255). The name no longer is used in current editions of the Doctrine and Covenants.

See also: Harris, Martin

Majesty on High

The title "Majesty on high" is found in Doctrine and Covenants 20:16 and in the New Testament (Heb. 1:3; 8:1). In the latter instance the title is applied to God the Father, on whose right hand the Son stands (compare Heb. 12:2), while in the latter-day revelation it might be applied to either the Father or Son. The word *majesty* has reference to sovereign power, authority, and dignity. The Father and Son are the Sovereigns of salvation.

See also: Father, The; Jesus Christ

Maker

The title of "Maker" appears three times in the Doctrine and Covenants (D&C 30:2; 121:4; 134:6), and refers to Deity. In the ultimate sense, *the* Maker is our Father in Heaven, he who created our spirits (Heb. 12:9). However, inasmuch as the Son, Jesus Christ, shares the fulness of the Father (D&C 93:16–17), as well as being the Maker of the heavens and earth (John 1:1–14; D&C 38:1–3; 3 Ne. 9:15), the title appropriately applies to him as well.

See also: Creator; God

Malachi

The writings of the Old Testament prophet Malachi are thrice quoted in the Doctrine and Covenants (D&C 110:14; 128:17; 133:64). In addition, without mentioning his name, Moroni quotes his words in section 2. In each instance reference is made to the mission of Elijah and the events connected with that mission. Malachi wrote the last book of the Old Testament, which was of such importance that the resurrected Lord quoted portions of it to the ancient inhabitants of the Americas during his visit among them, having been "com-manded" of the Father to do so (3 Ne. 24:1–3; 25:1–6; 26:1–2).

The angel Moroni likewise quoted the writings of Malachi during his initial visit to the young prophet Joseph Smith on the night of September 21, 1823 (JS—H 1:36–39). Other than his legacy of great prophetic writings — which were probably written the latter half of the fifth century B.C.—little is known of Malachi. He was among the "great and mighty" seen in vision by President Joseph F. Smith (D&C 138:38–46).

Mammon of Unrighteousness

In the Sermon on the Mount the Savior explicitly cautioned against serving "mammon," which is the Aramaic word for riches (Matt. 6:24; 3 Ne. 14:24). Therefore, it may seem strange to some that in 1832 he would say, "Make unto yourselves friends with the mammon of unrigh-teousness, and they will not destroy you" (D&C 82:22).

President Joseph Fielding Smith offered the following explanation: "It is not intended that in making friends of the 'mammon of unrighteousness' that the brethren were to partake with them in their sins; to receive them to their bosoms, intermarry with them and otherwise come down to their level. They were to so live that peace with their enemies might be assured. They were to treat them kindly, be friendly with them as far as correct and virtuous principles would permit, but never to swear with them or drink and carouse with them. If they could allay prejudice and show a willingness to trade with and show a kindly spirit, it might help to turn them away from their bitterness." (CHMR 1:323.)

Man . . . Like as Moses

Elder John A. Widtsoe gave the following explanation of the "man . . . like as Moses": "In the early days of the Church, persecution raged against the Saints in Jackson County, Missouri. For the comfort of the people, the Lord gave several revelations. In one He promised: 'I will raise up unto my people a man, who shall lead them like as Moses led the children of Israel.' (D&C 103:16.)"

"In modern revelation the President of the Church is frequently compared to Moses. Soon after the organization of the Church, the Lord said, 'no one shall be appointed to receive commandments and revelations in this church excepting my servant Joseph Smith, Jun., for he receiveth them even as Moses.' (D&C 28:2.) In one of the great revelations upon Priesthood, this is more specifically expressed: 'the duty of the President of the office of the High Priesthood is to preside over the whole church, and to be like unto Moses.' (D&C 107:91.)

"The discussion of this question among the Saints, led to the following statement in the *Times and Seasons* (6:922) by Elder John Taylor, then the editor: 'The President (of the Church) stands in the Church as Moses did to the children of Israel, according to the revelations.'

"The man like unto Moses in the Church is the President of the Church." (ER, 248.)

See also: Chosen by the Body; President of the High Priesthood

Man of God

An 1833 revelation counseled Bishop Newel K. Whitney to search diligently for an agent to handle secular matters. One of his prime qualifications was that he be "a man of God, and of strong faith" (D&C 90:22). In a broad sense, a man of God is one who avoids that which is "foolish and hurtful" and "follow[s] after righteousness, godliness, faith, love, patience, meekness" (1 Tim. 6:5–12). He is full of good works (2 Tim. 3:17). In a more specific sense a man of God is an authorized minister or servant of God such as Moses (Deut. 33:1), Samuel (1 Sam. 9:6–10), or Nephi (Hel. 11:18).

Man Should [Not] Possess That Which Is Above Another

President Joseph F. Smith said: "It is written that 'It is not given that one man should possess that which is above another.' [D&C 49:20.] Of course, there is some allowance to be made for this expression. A man who had ability superior to another man, and is able to manage and control larger affairs than another, may possess far more than another who is not able to control and manage as much as he. But if they each had what they were capable of managing and of using wisely and prudently, they would each have alike." (CR, Oct. 1898, pp. 23–24.)

See also: Equal

Man That Sheddeth Blood or Wasteth Flesh

The Lord has indicated that one who forbids the use of meat "is not ordained of God." Nevertheless, he warns man that blood should not be shed nor flesh wasted (D&C 49:18–21). The Prophet Joseph Smith clarified the meaning of shedding blood in his inspired revision of Genesis 9: "Every moving thing that liveth shall be meat for you," declared the Lord to Noah. "But the blood of all flesh which I have given you for meat, shall be shed upon the ground, which taketh life thereof, and the blood ye shall not eat. And surely, blood shall not be shed, only for meat, to save your lives; and the blood of every beast will I require at your hands." (JST, Gen. 9:8–11.)

Further cautions have come from Church Presidents. President Joseph Fielding Smith said: "It is a grievous sin in the sight of God to kill merely for sport. Such a thing shows a weakness in the spiritual character of the individual. We cannot restore life when it is taken, and all creatures have the right to enjoy life and happiness on the earth where the Lord has placed them. Only for food, and then sparingly, should flesh be eaten, for all life is from God and is eternal." (CHMR 1:210; see also En., Nov. 1978, pp. 44–45 for President Spencer W. Kimball's feelings on this issue.)

Commenting on the Word of Wisdom, President Ezra Taft Benson said: "In this revelation the Lord counsels us to use meat sparingly. I have often felt that the Lord is further counseling us in this revelation against indiscriminately killing animals." (En., May 1983, p. 54.)

See also: Beasts; Flesh; Word of Wisdom (#2)

Manchester, New York

On a recognition test, many Latter-day Saints would score well on the name of "Palmyra, Ontario County, New York" but would probably not do too well with "Manchester, New York." Yet, it is in Manchester that the Prophet Joseph received his first heavenly manifestations. Located just west of Palmyra in the same county of Ontario, the town of Manchester became the residence of the Smith family during Joseph's fourteenth year (JS—H 1:3; SLS, 24–25). Shortly thereafter, in a grove adjacent to the family farm, celestial light burst through the abyss of spiritual darkness which had long encompassed the earth; revelatory rays illuminated the mind of a young boy who communed personally with the Father and Son. Though no temple has been built upon its land, Manchester stands as a sacred spot where Deity once visited. (JS—H 1:5–20.) During the next few years in which he resided at Manchester, the young Prophet was to receive visits from other heavenly messengers (JS—H 1:27–54; JD 15:185; 17:374; 21:161). From the bosom of the Hill Cumorah, located "convenient to the village of Manchester," Joseph received the sacred plates from which the Book of Mormon was translated. It was in a wooded area adjacent to the Smith residence in Manchester that Joseph showed the plates to the Eight Witnesses (HC 1:57). This town was one of the three centers of Church activity in New York during its first year of existence (D&C 24:3), and four sections of the Doctrine and Covenants originated within its borders (D&C 2; 19; 22; 23).

See also: New York State

Manifestations of the Spirit

The Lord promised that those who believe will be visited by "manifestations of the Spirit" (D&C 5:16). According to scripture, it is the Holy Ghost "which manifesteth all things which are expedient unto the children of men" (D&C 18:18). As a revelator, the Holy Ghost's presence is felt in the warm whispers, or burning spiritual sensations, one feels deep within the soul.

The Spirit's purifying power also enables one to endure the presence of Deity (D&C 67:11–13; 76:118), for all who hearken to the promptings of the Spirit will come to the Father (D&C 84:46–47).

The Prophet Joseph Smith noted that "the Lord cannot always be known by the thunder of His voice, by the display of His glory or by the manifestations of His power" (HC 5:30–31). The Apostle Paul observed that "the things of God knoweth no man, *except he has the Spirit of God*" (JST, 1 Cor. 2:11; italics added).

Manifestations from the Spirit of God are directed to the spirit of man. Joseph Smith taught that "all things whatsoever God in his infinite wisdom has seen fit and proper to reveal to us, while we are dwelling in mortality, in regard to our mortal bodies, are revealed to us in the abstract, and independent of affinity of this mortal tabernacle, but are *revealed to our spirits precisely as though we had no bodies at all*; and those revelations which will save our spirits will save our bodies" (HC 6:313; italics added).

See also: Holy Ghost; Revelation

Manifesto

The declaration ending the practice of plural marriage (OD—1) is popularly referred to as the Manifesto. It is identified as such in the 1981 edition of the Doctrine and Covenants, which includes excerpts from three addresses on the subject by Wilford Woodruff. As shown in these excerpts, the Manifesto is the result of revelation from God to his prophet, who said, "I wrote what the Lord told me to write."

See also: Law of Sarah; One Wife; Utah Commission

Man's Time

Man's time is reckoned according to the planet whereon he resides (D&C 130:4–5). Here on earth, 24 hours equal one day and 365 days equal one year. A year on the planet Mercury is equal to 88 of our days, while Saturn's year is equal to 10,767 of our days, or 29½ of our years.

This is still a diminutive figure, however, when one considers that God's residence, the celestial sphere Kolob, passes but one day's time at the same time our earth has passed through one thousand years (Abr. 3:1–9; 2 Pet. 3:8).

Mansions of My Father

The Savior declared, "In my Father's house are many mansions" (D&C 98:18; John 14:2). The promise of a "crown" in those mansions is restricted to those who merit eternal life because of their unwavering righ-teousness, being "faithful in all things" (D&C 20:14; 59:2; 66:12; 106:8; 124:5).

The Prophet Joseph Smith announced, "There are mansions for those who obey a celestial law, and there are other mansions for those who come short of the law every man in his own order" (TPJS, 366). Thus, the phrase "In my Father's house are many mansions" should be rendered "In my Father's kingdom are many kingdoms" (TPJS, 366).

Latter-day revelation outlines the three major kingdoms (mansions) which God has prepared (D&C 76; 88). However, "the three kingdoms of widely differing glories are severally organized on a plan of graduation. The Telestial kingdom comprises subdivisions; this also is the case . . . with the Celestial; and, by analogy, we conclude that a similar condition prevails in the Terrestrial. Thus the innumerable degrees of merit amongst mankind are provided for in an infinity of graded glories. . . . We may conclude that degrees and grades will ever characterize the kingdoms of our God." (AF, 409; D&C 76:98; 131:1.)

See also: Celestial; Crown of Righteousness; Glory; Telestial; Terrestrial

Mantle

The Lord has counseled to "clothe yourselves with the bond of charity, as with a mantle, which is the bond of perfectness and peace" (D&C 88:125). A mantle is a robe or a cloak and the term is often used symbolically to express a covering that characterizes a trait or the authority which an individual possesses. For example, when Elijah cast his mantle upon Elisha, this was symbolic of the authority being transferred from the one to the other (1 Kgs. 19:19). Elisha later used both the mantle of cloth and the mantle of authority to perform miracles (2 Kgs. 2:13–14).

Manuscript, 116 Lost Pages of

The 116 manuscript pages referred to in the prefaces of sections 3 and 10 represented the book of Lehi. Joseph Smith gave it this name in his preface to the first edition of the Book of Mormon. This book was part of an abridged record the ancient prophet Mormon had placed in the safekeeping of his son, Moroni (Words of Mormon; Morm. 6:6). Moroni, in turn, gave the sacred record into the hands of a young prophet who translated the writings and published them as the Book of Mormon. The book of Lehi is not contained in this sacred volume and its loss is explained by Joseph Smith in the following words:

"Some time after Mr. [Martin] Harris had begun to write for me, he began to importune me to give him liberty to carry the writings home and show them; and desired of me that I would inquire of the Lord, through the Urim and Thummim, if he might not do so. I did inquire and the answer was that he must not. However, he was not satisfied with this answer, and desired that I should inquire again. I did so and the answer was as before. Still he could not be contented, but insisted that I should inquire once more. After much solicitation, I again inquired of the Lord, and permission was granted him to have the writings on certain conditions; which were that he show them only to his brother Preserved Harris, his own wife, his father and his mother, and a Mrs. Cobb, a sister to his wife. In accordance with this last answer, I required of him that he should bind himself in a covenant to me in the most solemn manner that he would not do otherwise than had been directed. He did so. He bound himself as I required of him, took the writings, and went his way. Notwithstanding, however, the great restrictions which he had been laid under, and the solemnity of the covenant which he had made with me, he did show them to others, and by strategem they got them away from him, and they have never been recovered." (HC 1:21.)

In the preface of the first edition of the Book of Mormon, the Prophet Joseph added the following information: "As many false reports have been circulated respecting the following work, and also many unlawful measures taken by evil designing persons to destroy me, and also the work, I would inform you that I translated, by the gift and power of God, and caused to be written, one hundred and sixteen pages, the which I took from the Book of Lehi, which was an account abridged from the plates of Lehi, by the hand of Mormon; which said account, some person or persons have stolen and kept from me, notwithstanding my utmost exertions to recover it again—and being commanded of the Lord that I should not translate the same over again, for Satan had put it into their hearts to tempt the Lord their God, by altering the words, that they did read contrary from that which I translated and caused to be written: and if I should bring forth the same words again, or, in other words, if I should translate the same over again, they would publish that which they had stolen, and Satan would stir up the hearts of this generation, that they might not receive this work" (see D&C 10:10–46).

The chronological period covered by the book of Lehi is covered in the first six books of our present edition of the Book of Mormon. These writings were taken from the plates known as the "small plates," while the lost manuscript was taken from the "large plates" of Nephi (see 1 Ne. 9; Words of Mormon).

See also: Book of Mormon; Harris, Martin; Plates of Nephi; Wicked Man, A

Marks, William

In July 1838, William Marks was called to preside in Far West, Missouri, and promised that if he proved "faithful over a few things . . . he shall be a ruler over many" (D&C 117:10). In a previous revelation to the Prophet Joseph, Marks had been portrayed as a great man whom the Lord would raise up "for a blessing unto many people" (Jenson 1:284).

Although he commenced in the course outlined for him by the Lord, presiding over the Nauvoo Stake from 1839 until 1844, Marks lost his grip on the "iron rod" and wandered along "forbidden paths" (see 1 Ne. 8:19–28). Following the martyrdoms of Joseph and Hyrum Smith, Marks initially supported the claims of Sidney Rigdon to the Presidency of the Church. Consequently, the Saints rejected Marks as their stake president in October 1844.

He appeared to experience a change of heart, for on December 9, 1844, he published the following notice in the Times and Seasons: "After mature and candid deliberation, I am fully and satisfactorily convinced that Mr. Sidney Rigdon's claims to the Presidency of The Church of Jesus Christ of Latter-day Saints are not found in truth. I have been deceived by his specious pretenses and now feel to warn every one over whom I may have any influence to beware of him, and his pretended visions and revelations. The Twelve are the proper persons to lead the Church."

Unfortunately, those "forbidden paths" beckoned him once more, and he was excommunicated. He later affiliated with the apostate cults of James J. Strang, in which Marks served in the first presidency; in the organizations of Charles B. Thompson and John E. Page, both apostates; and, finally, Marks helped "ordain" Joseph Smith, III, as president of what is now the Reorganized Church, later becoming a counselor in that organization's first presidency. (DS 1:253.)

Marriage

See: Marriage of the Lamb; New and Everlasting Covenant of Marriage; Plural Marriage

Marriage of the Lamb

The "Lamb" spoken of in the scriptures is Christ (D&C 76:85; John 1:29, 36). The following explanation has been rendered regarding the "marriage supper of the lamb" (D&C 58:6–11; 65:3). "In this dispensation the Bridegroom, who is the Lamb of God, shall come to claim his bride, which is the Church composed of the faithful saints who have watched for his return. As he taught in the parable of the marriage of the king's son, the great marriage supper of the Lamb shall then be celebrated. (Matt. 22:1–14.)" (MD, 469.)

"The elders of Israel are now issuing the invitations to the marriage supper of the Lord; those who believe and obey the gospel thereby accept the invitation and shall sit in due course with the King's Son at the marriage feast" (DNTC 3:563–64). "Many are called to the marriage supper of the Lamb, to the Church and kingdom of God on earth, but few are chosen for salvation in the kingdom of God in heaven, because they do not keep the commandments" (DNTC 1:599).

The Prophet Joseph penned this inspired phrase: "For many are called, but few chosen; *wherefore all do not have on the wedding garment*" (JST, Matt. 22:14; italics added). The Old Testament speaks of the plight of those who do not possess this garment: "The day of the Lord is at hand. . . . And it shall come to pass . . . that I will punish . . . all such as are clothed with *strange apparel.*" (Zeph. 1:7–8; italics added.)

John the Revelator added this witness: "The marriage of the Lamb is come, and his wife hath made herself ready. And to her was granted that she should be arrayed in fine linen, clean and white: for the fine linen is the righteousness of saints. And he saith unto me . . . , Blessed are they which are called unto the marriage supper of the Lamb." (Rev. 19:7–9.)

See also: Lamb; Jesus Christ

Marrow

The word *marrow* is found six times in the Doctrine and Covenants and refers to the soft substance that fills bone cavities but is often used to represent vitality and strength (D&C 6:2; 11:2; 12:2; 14:2; 33:1; see also Heb. 4:12). Those who keep the Word of Wisdom are promised that they "shall receive health in their navel and marrow to their bones" (D&C 89:18).

See also: Health in Their Navel; Word of Wisdom

Marsh, Thomas B.

Thomas B. Marsh is mentioned in several revelations in the Doctrine and Covenants (D&C 31; 52:22; 56:5; 75:31; 112). Marsh was very prominent in the early affairs of the Church and had the distinction of being called as the first President of the Quorum of the Twelve Apostles. Prior to joining the Church in 1830, he was described as one upon whom "the spirit of prophecy . . . rested . . . in some degree." He became acquainted with the Church through a newspaper description of the "golden Bible." He journeyed to Palmyra, arriving just in time to see the first sixteen pages of the Book of Mormon come off the printing press. He secured a copy of this, in which both he and his wife expressed their belief. (Jenson 1:79.)

His ordination as an Apostle on April 26, 1835, placed him constantly in the ministry. He experienced the persecution in Missouri and at one point spoke so movingly on the suffering of the Saints that even his tormentors shed tears. However, in the fall of 1838, disaffection settled into his life and he took offense at "a trivial matter," which led him to publish false accusations against the Saints (HC 3:166–67; see also JD 3:283–84). George A. Smith later stated that this affidavit was responsible for the "extermination order" signed against the Mormons by the governor of Missouri, Lilburn W. Boggs (JD 3:284).

He was excommunicated March 17, 1839. He rejoined the Church in July 1857, and spoke the following words at a Sunday service in Salt Lake City, on September 6, 1857: "Many have said to me, 'How is it that a man like you, who understood so much of the revelations of God as recorded in the Book of Doctrine and Covenants, should fall away?' I told them not to feel too secure, but to take heed lest they also should fall; for I had no scruples in my mind as to the possibility of men falling away.

"I can say, in reference to the Quorum of the Twelve, to which I belonged, that I did not consider myself a whit behind any of them, and I suppose that others had the same opinion: but, let no one feel too secure; for, before you think of it, your steps will slide. You will not then think nor feel for a moment as you did before you lost the Spirit of Christ; for when men apostatize, they are left to grovel in the dark. . . .

"I have frequently wanted to know how my apostasy began, and I have come to the conclusion that I must have lost the Spirit of the Lord out of my heart.

"The next question is, 'How and when did you lose the Spirit?' I became jealous of the Prophet, and then I saw double, and overlooked everything that was right, and spent all my time in looking for the evil; and then, when the Devil began to lead me, it was easy for the carnal mind to rise up, which is anger, jealousy, and wrath. I could feel it within me; I felt angry and wrathful; and the Spirit of the Lord being gone, as the Scriptures say, I was blinded, and I thought I saw a beam in brother Joseph's eye, but it was nothing but a mote, and my own eye was filled with the beam." (JD 5:206–7.)

Marsh died in January 1866 at Ogden, Utah.

See also: Thomas

Martyrdom

Section 135 is an account of the martyrdom of two of God's noble sons, Joseph and Hyrum Smith. "In the gospel sense, martyrdom is the voluntary acceptance of death at the hands of wicked men rather than to forsake Christ and his holy gospel. It is the supreme earthly sacrifice in which a man certifies to his absolute faith and to the desires for righteousness and for eternal life which are in his heart." (MD, 426.)

Andrew Jenson cited three categories of martyrs: (1) those who are put to death violently, such as the Smith brothers and David W. Patten; (2) those who have died in the mission field; and (3) those who died of deprivation inflicted by mobocracy. (CR, Oct. 1925, p. 54.) Martyrdom is a supreme sacrifice, the complete consecration of oneself to the Lord.

The selfless sacrifice of one's life is, perhaps, merely symbolic of a lifetime of selfless service and complete commitment to the cause of Christ and Kingdom. In the words of Elder Robert D. Hales, "It is not in death or in one event that we give our lives, but in every day as we are asked to do it." (En., May 1975, p. 44.)

See also: Broad; Carthage; Carthage Jail; Escutcheon; Illinois; Innocent Blood; Murdered in Cold Blood; Sealed His Mission with His Blood; Smith, Hyrum; Smith, Joseph

Marvelous Work

A half dozen times in the Doctrine and Covenants the Lord speaks of a "marvelous" or a "great and marvelous work and a wonder" (D&C 4:1; 6:1; 11:1; 12:1; 14:1; 18:44). President Joseph

Fielding Smith provided the following commentary: "More than seven hundred years before the birth of Jesus Christ the Lord spoke through Isaiah of the coming forth of the Book of Mormon and the restoration of the Gospel. Isaiah, by prophecy, spoke of the restoration of the new and everlasting covenant, and the Lord performing a 'marvelous work and a wonder,' which should cause 'the wisdom of their wise men' to perish, and 'the understanding of their prudent men' to be hid. . . . *This marvelous work is the restoration of the Church and the Gospel* with all the power and authority, keys and blessings which pertain to this great work for the salvation of the children of men." (CHMR 1:35; italics added; Isa. 29:11–14; 2 Ne. 27:6–26.)

See also: Restoration, The; Restoration of All Things; Restoration of the Priesthood

Massachusetts

The state of Massachusetts is one of eight states of the Union in which revelations have been received and recorded in the Doctrine and Covenants. The Prophet Joseph Smith received a revelation in Salem, Massachusetts, on August 6, 1836 (D&C 111). Massachusetts was one of the original thirteen colonies that banded together in 1776 to declare their independence from the British empire and form the United States of America. It is of interest that Massachusetts was founded in part by men who were seeking freedom of religious expression.

See also: Northern States; Salem, Massachusetts

Matthew

The Gospel of Matthew is referred to once in the Doctrine and Covenants (D&C 128:10). The Prophet Joseph quoted the words of the Savior regarding the rock of revelation and the sealing powers which the president of Christ's church possesses (Matt. 16:18–19). Matthew, also known as Levi, son of Alphaeus, was called as one of the Twelve Apostles to serve in the earthly ministry of the Savior (Mark 2:14; Matt. 9:9; 10:2–3).

Prior to his call he had been a tax collector. "His Gospel was written for the use of Jewish converts in Palestine. It is full of quotations from the [Old Testament]. His chief object is to show that Jesus is the Messiah of whom the prophets spoke. He also emphasizes the truth that Jesus is the King and Judge of men. . . . A tradition of the Western Church asserts that he died a martyr's death." (BD, 102.)

McIlwaine's Bend, Missouri

In the Prophet's history, he states that he and ten elders left Independence, Missouri, on August 9, 1831, to return to Kirtland, Ohio (HC 1:202–3). They traveled by canoe down the Missouri River. On their third day of travel, they experienced "many of the dangers so common upon the western waters." While camping on the bank of the river at a place called McIlwaine's Bend, W.W. Phelps "in open vision by daylight, saw the destroyer in his most horrible power, ride upon the face of the waters; others heard the noise, but saw not the vision." The following morning, after supplicating the Lord, Joseph received the revelation found in section 61.

The geographical location of McIlwaine's Bend can be seen on "The Missouri-Illinois Area" map found on page 297 of editions of the Doctrine and Covenants published since 1981.

See also: Missouri

McLellin, William E.

One of the sad stories of early Church history is that of William E. McLellin (occassionally spelled M'Lellin). In October 1831, section 66 was directed to him personally wherein he was promised by the Savior that if he proved faithful he would "have a crown of eternal life at the right hand of my Father" (D&C 66:12). Just a month later, however, the first intimations of rebellion were displayed by him when he joined with those who criticized the language of some revelations received by the Prophet Joseph. The Lord challenged them to "appoint him that is the most wise among you" to try to write a revelation that was as good as "the least that is among" those that comprised the Book of Commandments (D&C 67:6).

Of this event, the Prophet wrote that McLellin, "as the wisest man in his own estimation, *having more learning than sense,* endeavored to write a commandment like unto one of the least of the Lord's, but failed. . . . All present that witnessed this vain attempt of a man to imitate the language of Jesus Christ, renewed their faith in the fulness of the gospel, and in the truth of the commandments and revelations which the Lord had given to the Church through my instrumentality." (Jenson 1:82; italics added.) Again in January 1832, the Lord had to chasten him "for the murmurings of his heart," but forgave him and sent him forth in the ministry (D&C 75:6–8). Two years later, the Lord again publicly reprimanded McLellin (D&C 90:35).

That this man had potential for doing good is illustrated in the service he did render. He served on the high council in Clay County, Missouri; was chosen an "assistant teacher" in the School of the Elders in Kirtland; and was finally called in February 1835 as one of the original Twelve Apostles of this dispensation. Though he rendered some valuable service, eventually the spirit of faultfinding entered into his heart once more, and on May 11, 1838, he was excommunicated from the Church for his lack of confidence in the presidency of the Church, his lack of praying, and "sinful lusts." The cancer of contention continued to spread throughout his system, dispelling any semblance of spirituality. He participated in the mobbing of the Saints in Missouri and once even sought to personally harm the Prophet: "While Joseph was in prison at Richmond, Mo., Mr. McLellin, who was a large and active man, went to the sheriff and asked for the privilege of flogging the Prophet; permission was granted, on condition that Joseph would fight. The sheriff made McLellin's earnest request known to Joseph, who consented to fight, if his irons were taken off. McLellin then refused to fight, unless he could have a club, to which Joseph was perfectly willing; but the sheriff would not allow them to fight on such unequal terms." (Jenson 1:83.)

The tragedy of William E. McLellin's demise illustrates one of the "keys" which the Prophet Joseph gave to the Church: "That man who rises up to condemn others, finding fault with the Church, saying that they are out of the way, while he himself is righteous, then know assuredly, that that man is in the high road to apostasy; and if he does not repent, will apostatize, as God lives" (TPJS, 156–57). Thus having removed the promised "crown," McLellin died devoid of his promised inheritance on April 24, 1883, at Independence, Missouri.

See also: Those Who Have Fallen

Measure of Its Creation

The Lord speaks of the earth filling the "measure of its creation" (D&C 88:19, 25). Similarly, he has spoken of its answering "the end of its creation" (D&C 49:16). For what purpose was the earth created? To the end that it might serve as a place whereon God's children may dwell and prove themselves (see Abr. 3:22–26).

The earth fulfills the measure of its creation not only as a home and testing ground for mankind but also as a place of habitation for all creations which God has designated should inhabit and give life and beauty to this planet.

The ultimate measure of the earth's creation is to become a celestialized orb on which glorified, sanctified, and celestialized sons and daughters of God will dwell in future eternities (see D&C 77:12; 88:17, 20).

See also: Measure of Man

Measure of Man

The phrase *measure of man* appears only in Doctrine and Covenants 49:17 and relates to the sacred command of man and woman to "be fruitful, and multiply, and replenish the earth" (Gen. 1:27–28; Moses 2:28).

There are a designated number (measure) of God's spirit

children who are assigned to inhabit the earth. President Joseph Fielding Smith said: "The people who inhabit this earth were all living in the spirit life before they came to this earth. The Lord informs us that this earth was designed, before its foundations were formed, for the abode of the spirits who kept their first estate, and all such must come here and receive their tabernacles of flesh and bones, and this is according to the number, or measure of man according to his creation before the world was." (CHMR 1:209.)

See also: Measure of Its Creation

Meat

The word *meat* normally refers to the flesh of creatures created by God for food (D&C 49:18; 1 Ne. 17:2) but can also refer to food in general (D&C 51:13; 3 Ne. 13:25). The word can also be symbolic of something with more substance, i.e., a more advanced teaching, principle, or concept (D&C 19:22). Just as the ingestion of physical meat requires an advanced digestive system, so the ingestion of spiritual or intellectual meat requires proper preparation (see 1 Cor. 3:2).

See also: Milk

Mediator

Jesus Christ is "the mediator of the new covenant who wrought out [the] perfect atonement through the shedding of his own blood" (D&C 76:69; 107:19; Heb. 12:24). "As Moses was the mediator of the old covenant or testament, so Jesus is the Mediator of the new covenant or testament. . . . 'Our Lord's mission was to bring to pass "the great mediation of all men," meaning that in his capacity as Mediator he had power to intervene between God and man and effect a reconciliation. This mediation or reconciliation was affected through his atoning sacrifice, a sacrifice by means of which sinful men—by the proper use of agency—can wash away their guilt and place themselves in harmony with God. Men "are free to choose liberty and eternal life, through the great Mediator of all men, or to choose captivity and death, according to the captivity and power of the devil." (2 Ne. 2:27.)' " (DNTC 3:78.)

The Apostle Paul reminds us that "there is one mediator between God and men, the man Christ Jesus" (1 Tim. 2:5).

See also: Jesus Christ

Meek

Reiterating a previously announced decree, the Lord stated that the "meek" shall inherit the earth (D&C 88:17). This principle had been spoken of in sermons on both the eastern and western hemispheres (Matt. 5:5; 3 Ne. 12:5). Elder Alvin R. Dyer once stated that "meekness is a condition of voluntary humility" (CR, Oct. 1970, p. 151).

Some years prior to this, Elder Orson Pratt proclaimed: "The law of meekness includes all the laws of the Gospel, with its ordinances and blessings, Priesthood and powers, through obedience to which mankind become justified, sanctified, purified, and glorified. Such are the meek of the earth." (JD 1:332.)

Thus, those who are obedient and humble, who do *all* that is required of them, are the meek who will inherit the celestialized earth (JD 17:117).

Meet

According to Webster, an older usage of the word *meet* is to signify that which is suitable, acceptable, appropriate, proper, or fit. By substituting these words for the word *meet* as it appears in the Doctrine and Covenants, one gains a better understanding of the intended meaning.

In the following examples from the Doctrine and Covenants, *meet* has been replaced to illustrate this point: "it is [appropriate for] you to know" (D&C 19:8); "it is not [appropriate] that the things which belong to the children of the kingdom should be given to them that are not worthy" (D&C 41:6); "it is [proper] that . . . Joseph . . . should have a house" (D&C 41:7); "it is [acceptable] that . . . Sidney . . . should live as seemeth him good"

(D&C 41:8); "it is not [suitable or necessary] that I should command in all things" (D&C 58:26); "it is not [proper] that my servants . . . should sell their store" (D&C 64:26); "bring forth fruit [suitable] for their Father's kingdom" (D&C 84:58); "he is not [fit] for a kingdom of glory" (D&C 88:24); "it is not good, neither [acceptable] in the sight of your Father" (D&C 89:5); "it is [suitable] in mine eyes that she should go" (D&C 90:30).

Melchizedek

The Lord informs us that "Melchizedek was such a great high priest," that the priesthood of God was named in his honor (D&C 107:1–4). The Old Testament mentions his name only twice (Gen. 14:28; Psalm 110:4), and Paul's epistle to the Hebrews makes some additional references to him or the order of the priesthood which bears his name (Heb. 5–7).

To the Prophet Joseph Smith goes the credit for obtaining additional information on this great high priest. We are informed that "Melchizedek was a man of faith, who wrought righteousness; and when a child he feared God, and stopped the mouths of lions, and quenched the violence of fire" (JST, Gen. 14:26). He was a king over the land of Salem, and was a man of such "mighty faith" that he brought a people who "had all gone astray" and "were full of all manner of wickedness" to such a state of repentance that the whole city was taken up to heaven (Alma 13:17–18; JST, Gen. 14:33–34). Therefore, he earned the title "prince of peace." Paul renders this title as "King of peace," or "King of righteousness" (Heb. 7:2).

It was from Melchizedek that Abraham received his priesthood and to whom he paid his tithes (TPJS, 322–23; Gen. 14:20; Alma 13:15). A fitting tribute to Melchizedek is rendered by the ancient prophet Alma, who said: "Now, there were many before him, and also there were many afterwards, but none were greater" (Alma 13:19).

See also: Melchizedek Priesthood

Melchizedek Priesthood

In the Doctrine and Covenants, God's priesthood is referred to as the Melchizedek Priesthood (D&C 68; 84; 107), the "greater priesthood" (D&C 84:19), the "priesthood which is after the holiest order of God" (D&C 84:18), the "high priesthood" (D&C 84:29), and the "Holy Priesthood, after the Order of the Son of God" (D&C 107:3). The Prophet Joseph Smith gives the following explanation of Priesthood: "There are two Priesthoods spoken of in the Scriptures, viz., the Melchizedek and the Aaronic or Levitical. Although there are two Priesthoods, yet the Melchizedek

Priesthood comprehends the Aaronic or Levitical Priesthood, and is the grand head, and holds the highest authority which pertains to the priesthood, and the keys of the Kingdom of God in all ages of the world to the latest posterity on the earth; and is the channel through which all knowledge, doctrine, the plan of salvation and every important matter is revealed from heaven.

"Its institution was prior to 'the foundation of this earth' . . . and is the highest and holiest Priesthood, and is after the order of the Son of God, and all other Priesthoods are only parts, ramifications, powers and blessings belonging to the same, and are held, controlled, and directed by it. It is the channel through which the Almighty commenced revealing His glory at the beginning of the creation of this earth, and through which He has continued to reveal Himself to the children of men to the present time, and through which He will make known His purposes to the end of time." (TPJS, 166–67.)

In a further discourse on priesthood, Joseph stated that "those holding the fulness of the Melchizedek Priesthood are kings and priests of the Most High God, holding the keys of power and blessings. In fact, that Priesthood is a perfect law of theocracy, and stands as God to give laws to the people administering endless lives to the sons and daughters of Adam." (TPJS, 322.)

The Melchizedek Priesthood is "without father, without

mother, . . . having neither beginning of days, nor end of life," for it is eternal, having coexisted with God forever (JST, Heb. 7:3). It is bestowed by right of God upon his worthy sons rather than being an inherited right with "descent from father and mother" (TPJS, 323).

The various administrative callings within the Melchizedek Priesthood include the offices of elder (D&C 107:89), seventy (D&C 107:90), high priest (D&C 68:19), patriarch or evangelist (D&C 107:39), and Apostle (D&C 20:38).

Regarding offices in the Melchizedek Priesthood, the words of President Joseph F. Smith are worth remembering: "There is no office growing out of this Priesthood that is or can be greater then the Priesthood itself. It is from the Priesthood that the office derives its authority and power. No office gives authority to the Priesthood. No office adds to the power of the Priesthood." (GD, 148.) He further stated that "every man holding the Holy Melchizedek Priesthood may act in any capacity and do all things that such Priesthood holds, provided he is called upon by proper authority to so officiate" (GD, 175).

See also: First Priesthood; Holy Priesthood After the Order of the Son of God; Order of Melchizedek; Order of the Only Begotten Son; Order of the Priesthood; Priesthood; Sons of Aaron; Sons of Moses

Memorial

The Lord told Thomas B. Marsh that his alms had "come up as a memorial before me" (D&C 112:1). Memorial, in this sense, means a reminder or evidence of Marsh's good deeds.

See also: Marsh, Thomas B.; Memorials for Your Sacrifices

Memorials for Your Sacrifices

The Lord revealed that one of the purposes for a future temple was for "your memorials for your sacrifices by the sons of Levi" (D&C 124:39). "The Hebrew word translated as *memorial* in our Old Testament (cf. Lev. 2:2, 9, 16; 5:12; 6:8; Num. 5:26) is that part of the meal offering which is burnt" (DCC, 654).

The following explanation was issued by Joseph Smith: "It is a very prevalent opinion that the sacrifices which were offered were entirely consumed. This was not the case; if you read Leviticus, second chap., second and third verses, you will observe that the priests took a part as a *memorial* and offered it up before the Lord, while the remainder was kept for the maintenance of the priests; so that the offerings and sacrifices are not all consumed upon the altar—but the blood is sprinkled, and the fat and certain other portions are consumed.

"These sacrifices, as well as every ordinance belonging to the

Priesthood, will, when the Temple of the Lord shall be built, and the sons of Levi be purified, be fully restored and attended to in all their powers, ramifications, and blessings." (HC 4:211; italics added.)

See also: Offering unto the Lord in Righteousness; Sacrifice; Sons of Levi

Mercy

In order to satisfy the demands of justice, which require a penalty from all who have broken the laws of God, mercy must intervene. "And, by eternal law," said Elder Boyd K. Packer, "mercy cannot be extended save there be one who is both willing and able to assume our debt and pay the price and arrange the terms for our redemption" (CR, Apr. 1977, p. 80; Alma 42:15).

The One who was both willing, able, and chosen to extend such mercy was the Lord Jesus Christ. In a revelatory proclamation issued in 1830, he said: "Listen to the voice of Jesus Christ, your Redeemer, the Great I Am, whose *arm of mercy hath atoned for your sins*" (D&C 29:1; italics added). The arm of mercy is symbolic of the power of mercy which Christ offers to mankind. However, the mercy of the Savior's atonement "claimeth [only] the penitent" (Alma 42:23). The law of mercy "consists in our Lord's forbearance, on certain specified conditions, from impos-

ing punishments that, except for his grace and goodness, would be the just reward of man" (MD, 483).

President Spencer W. Kimball declared: "Many have greatly misunderstood the place of mercy in the forgiveness program. Its role is not to give great blessings without effort." (MF, 358.) The Lord warned that all who will not repent must pay the price which justice demands (D&C 19:15–20), for mercy cannot rob justice (Alma 42:13–26).

The Prophet Joseph Smith added this thought: "There is never a time when the spirit is too old to approach God. All are within the reach of pardoning mercy, who have not committed the unpardonable sin." (TPJS, 191.) "Sow to yourselves in righteousness, reap in mercy," proclaimed the prophet Hosea (Hosea 10:12).

See also: Atonement; Justice

Meridian of Time

The distinctive phrase *meridian of time* is found only in the Doctrine and Covenants (D&C 20:26; 39:3) and the Pearl of Great Price (Moses 5:57; 6:57, 62; 7:46) and refers to the time period in which our Savior lived upon the earth.

President Joseph Fielding Smith said: "This means that it was about half way from the *beginning of 'time' to the end of 'time.'* Anyone who desires can figure it for himself that our Lord came about 4,000 years from the time of the fall. The millennium is to come some time following the 2,000 years after his coming. Then there is to be the millennium for 1,000 years, and following that a *'little season,'* the length of which is not revealed, but which may *bring 'time'* to its end about 8,000 years from the beginning." (DS 1:81.)

Messenger of Salvation

The only place in holy writ where the title "messenger of salvation" occurs is in the Doctrine and Covenants (D&C 93:8). It is, of course, one of the many titles applied to Jesus Christ and is descriptive of his message and mission of salvation. A messenger is one who bears a message or does an errand. Christ both bore the message of salvation and performed the acts whereby mankind can reap the rewards thereof.

See also: Jesus Christ

Messiah

The term *Messiah* comes from the Hebrew and means Anointed One. In the New Testament the Apostle John equates *Messiah* with *Christ* (John 1:41; 4:25). When one testifies that Jesus is the Christ, therefore, record is born of the Messianic mission which he has fulfilled and which he will continue to fulfill. Jesus himself bore such a record when speaking to the woman at the

well in Samaria: "I who speak unto thee am the Messias" (JST, John 4:28).

The term *Messias* is the Greek equivalent of the Hebrew *Messiah*. This term, as a title or office of Jesus, is used liberally throughout the Book of Mormon; appropriately so, inasmuch as this sacred volume's major message is to convince both Jew and Gentile that Jesus is the Christ (see Title Page; 1 Ne. 6:4; Morm. 3:20–22).

An ancient Book of Mormon prophet defined Messiah as the anointed "Savior of the world" (1 Ne. 10:4).

See also: Jesus Christ

Mete

There are two occasions in the Doctrine and Covenants where the term *mete* is used. Those who go forth in the ministry are promised divine guidance in that which they shall mete (allot) to every man (D&C 84:85). God will mete out (allot or assign a measure of) just recompense to those who oppress his Saints (D&C 127:3).

Methuselah

The name of *Methuselah* rings a bell of familiarity among most people, for he is reported to have been the oldest man who ever lived. His years are numbered at 969, seven years longer than his grandfather, Jared (Gen. 5:20–27; Moses 8:7). His name appears in the Doctrine and Covenants in connection with the great revelation on priesthood, received March 28, 1835 (D&C 107:50–53).

Methuselah was one hundred years of age when "he was ordained under the hand of Adam," and he in turn ordained Noah when the latter was only ten years old. The Pearl of Great Price informs us that Methuselah was not taken to heaven along with Enoch and his people in order that "Noah should be of the fruit of his loins" and "that from his loins should spring all the kingdoms of the earth" (Moses 8:2–3).

Noah was the son of Lamech, who was the son of Methuselah (Gen. 5:25–29; Moses 8:7–9).

Michael

Michael is the noble pre-earthly spirit who came to earth to become the "father of all flesh" and is known in the annals of history as Adam—the first mortal man to walk this planet (HC 4:207–8; Moses 1:34; 3:7; Abr. 1:3; 1 Ne. 5:11; D&C 27:11). His name means "Who is as God" (SS, 136).

In pre-earth life, Michael stood as *the archangel*, or the prince who presided over all other angels (D&C 27:11), but always under the direction of the Father and the Son (D&C 107:54; HC 4:208). Under their direction, he helped to organize this earth (JD 1:51).

He successfully led the armies of the Lord in battle against the forces of evil in our pre-earth experience (Rev. 12:7–9) and shall be called upon to perform the same role in the great and last battle with the devil and all who dwell in his demented domain (D&C 88:110–15).

See also: Adam; Ancient of Days; Archangel; Dispensation of the Fulness of Times; Father of All; Keys of Salvation; Seventh Angel

Michigan

Although the state of Michigan is not directly mentioned in the Doctrine and Covenants, one of her cities is. An 1831 revelation instructed several missionaries to journey to Detroit (D&C 52:8). At this time Michigan was a territory and did not become the twenty-sixth state of the Union until 1837, about the time that the Saints fled from the adjoining state of Ohio. According to the *Encyclopedia Britannica*, "the state's name is derived from a Chippewa Indian word meaning, approximately, 'large lake' " (15th ed., 12:104).

See also: Detroit, Michigan; Northern States

Mighty God of Jacob

The title "Mighty God of Jacob" appears but once in latter-day scripture, that being in the dedicatory prayer of the Kirtland Temple (D&C 109:68). The title applies to Jehovah, God of the Old Testament, who is Jesus

Christ. The term "God of Jacob" (1 Ne. 19:10; Alma 29:11; 3 Ne. 4:30; Morm. 9:11), "Mighty One of Jacob" (1 Ne. 21:26; 2 Ne. 6:18), "Holy One of Jacob" (2 Ne. 27:34), and "Mighty One of Israel" (D&C 36:1; 1 Ne. 22:12) are variations of the title and appear elsewhere. Jacob, or Israel, was the father of the twelve tribes bearing his name and who were called upon to worship the true and living God, the Mighty Jehovah.

See also: Israel's God; Jesus Christ

Mighty One of Israel

See: Israel's God; Mighty God of Jacob

Miles, Daniel

The name of Daniel Miles appears but once in the Doctrine and Covenants, when he is mentioned as one of the Seven Presidents of the Seventies (D&C 124:138). He was called to this position on April 6, 1837. He suffered the persecution heaped upon the Saints in Missouri and was one of the first settlers at the site later known as Nauvoo, Illinois. Not much is known of his life or service. "Elder Miles died as a faithful member of the Church in the early part of 1845" and was described as "a man of good faith, constant in his attendance at the meetings of the council, until the time of his death, which occurred at quite an advanced stage of his life" (Jenson 1:192).

Milk

The word *milk* appears twice in the Doctrine and Covenants, both times in a symbolic sense. In reference to gospel concepts, the Lord declared that milk must be dispensed before meat (D&C 19:22). In other words, one must digest the basic, elementary principles of the gospel before attempting to swallow the meatier matters (see 1 Cor. 3:2; Heb 5:12). The reference to a "land flowing with milk and honey" (D&C 38:18) is symbolic of a land of great abundance.

See also: Land Flowing with Milk and Honey; Meat

Millennium

One of the most anxiously awaited ages of this planet earth is that thousand-year period known as the great Millennium. Interestingly enough, this word is unique in all of scripture to the Doctrine and Covenants, where it appears in two sections, plus the preface of section 29 (D&C 43:30; 130:16). The synonymous term *thousand years* appears in three other sections of the Doctrine and Covenants (D&C 29:11, 22; 77:12; 88:101, 110). This latter term is also used in other scripture (Rev. 20:2, 4, 7; Moses 7:64–65).

"Just as *century* means a period of 100 years so *millennium* means a period of 1000 years. This earth, according to the divine plan, is passing through a mortal or temporal existence of seven millenniums or 7000 years. (D&C 77:6–7.) During the first six of these (covering a total period of 6000 years from the time of the fall of Adam) conditions of carnality, corruption, evil, and wickedness of every sort have prevailed upon the earth. Wars, death, destruction and everything incident to the present *telestial state* of existence have held sway over the earth and all life on its face.

"When the 7th thousand years commence, however, radical changes will take place both in the earth itself and in the nature and type of existence enjoyed by all forms of life on its face. This will be the long hoped for age of peace when Christ will reign personally upon the earth: when the earth will be renewed and receive its paradisiacal glory; when corruption, death, and disease will cease; and when the kingdom of God on earth will be fully established in all its glory, beauty, and perfection. (Tenth Article of Faith.) This is the period known to the saints of all ages as the *millennium*." (MD, 492.)

"Some members of the Church have an erroneous idea that when the millennium comes all of the people are going to be swept off the earth except righteous members of the Church. That is not so. There will be millions of people, Catholics, Protestants, agnostics, Mohammedans, people of all classes, and of all beliefs, still permitted to remain upon the face of the earth, but they will be those who have lived clean lives, those who have been free from wickedness and corruption. All who belong, by virtue of their good lives, to the terrestrial order, as well as those who have kept the celestial law, will remain upon the face of the earth during the millennium." (DS 1:86.)

"When our Savior comes to rule in the millennium, all governments will become subject unto his government, and this has been referred to as the kingdom of God, which it is; but this is the *political kingdom* which *will embrace all people whether they are in the Church or not.* . . . When the Savior prayed, 'Thy kingdom come,' he had reference to the kingdom in heaven which is to come when the millennial reign starts." (DS 1:229–30.)

At the end of this period of peace, men will once again begin to deny their Creator, Satan will be loosed "for a little season," and the last battle will take place between the forces of good and evil (D&C 29:22; 43:31; 88:110–16). Then shall the earth be celestialized and become the "new earth" of which the scriptures speak (D&C 29:23; DS 1:87–89).

See also: Little Season; Michael; New Heaven and Earth; Paradisiacal; Thousand Years

Miller, George

A life which illustrates the necessity of constant vigilance, never resting on today's laurels at the expense of tomorrow's salvation, is that of George Miller. In 1841, the Lord said that Miller was "without guile; he may be trusted because of the integrity of his heart; and for the love which he has to my testimony I, the Lord, love him" (D&C 124:20).

Unfortunately, that love of testimony and truth did not endure. Appointed to the bishopric by revelation, Miller is listed among the Presiding Bishops of the Church, where he served as "Second Bishop" from 1844 to about 1847 (CA 1978:123). His name appears frequently in the Prophet's journals. He was appointed to act as one of two trustees-in-trust of the Church following the death of Joseph Smith and later officiated in the Nauvoo Temple (HC 7:247, 547).

He led a company of pioneers in the westward movement, but began to take exception to the directions issued by the Twelve Apostles and soon found himself in open opposition to them. He declared that he had "a special appointment from the Prophet Joseph Smith" and stated that the Church should move to the southern part of Texas rather than to the Rocky Mountains. He moved there to join with Lyman Wight, but soon left to affiliate himself with the apostate movement of James J. Strang.

"Of his later movements and death our annals give no information but his career illustrates the truth of President [Brigham] Young's remarkable prophecy, delivered on the 8th of August, 1844: '*All that want to draw away a party from the church after them, let them do it, if they can, but they will not prosper.*' " (CHC 3:157–59.)

Miller was disfellowshipped December 12, 1848. President Joseph Fielding Smith observed that when the Saints came west, "there were a few among them who lacked the faith to continue the journey and fell by the wayside, among them Bishop George Miller" (DS 3:343).

Millstone

According to Webster a millstone can be either a circular stone used for grinding or a heavy burden. To those who swear falsely against God's servants or who lead his children astray through lying and treacherous teachings, the Lord declared that "it had been better for them that a millstone had been hanged about their necks, and they drowned in the depth of the sea" (D&C 121:22; Matt. 18:6). It would be better for a false teacher or accuser to be drowned and denied mortality than to continue in life to lead souls astray and to suffer eternal death.

Mind

See: Carnal Desires/Mind; High-Mindedness; Light-Mindedness; Mind Became Darkened; Mind of the Lord; Speak Peace to Your Mind; Weary in Mind; Willing Mind

Mind Became Darkened

When the Prophet Joseph lost the 116 pages of manuscript known as the book of Lehi, the Lord took away his translating privileges and said: "And you also lost your gift at the same time, and your mind became darkened" (D&C 10:2). By doing something contrary to the Redeemer's will, Joseph turned from light to darkness.

The Savior declared, "I am the light of the world: he that followeth me shall not [or even can not] walk in darkness" (John 8:12). The Lord has promised "if your eye be single to my glory, your whole bodies shall be filled with light" (D&C 88:67).

When the Lord's ways are followed, men will be filled with light and the whisperings of the Spirit will penetrate their inner center of perception, understanding, thinking and feeling—their minds. It will be as if the voice of the Lord came into their minds speaking peace and understanding (see Enos 1:1–10; D&C 6:23; Gen. 41:16).

Darkened minds are those not capable of understanding things of light (see TPJS, 91).

See also: Darkness

Mind of the Lord

When the scriptures speak of obtaining the mind or will of the Lord on a matter it means to come to know his views and desires on a given subject (D&C 68:4; 95:13; 102:23; 133:61; Lev. 24:12; Rom. 11:34). Such knowledge can only come through revelation from the Lord (Jacob 4:8). Satan, who is an enemy to all righteousness (Mosiah 4:14), does not know the mind of God and consequently his evil efforts to thwart God's plans will come to naught (Moses 4:6).

To have the mind of Christ (1 Cor. 2:16) is to "think what he thinks, know what he knows, say what he would say, and do what he would do in every situation—all by revelation from the Spirit" (DNTC 2:322). The Prophet Joseph Smith taught that God and Christ possess "the same mind" and that "all those who keep [the] commandments shall grow up from grace to grace, and become heirs of the heavenly kingdom . . . possessing the same mind . . . and become one . . . even as the Father, Son and Holy Spirit are one" (LF, 50–51).

Ministering Angel

The specific use of the term *ministering angel* in Doctrine and Covenants 7:6 refers to the mission which the Apostle John was to perform as a translated being —a man who has not yet tasted of death and is consequently not yet a resurrected being. The Prophet Joseph Smith declared that one who is translated "obtains deliverance from the tortures and sufferings of the body, but their existence will prolong as to the labors and toils of the ministry" (TPJS, 171). On another occasion he said: "Translated bodies cannot enter into rest until they have undergone a change equivalent to death. Translated bodies are designed for future missions." (TPJS, 191.)

John's mission was to continue as a "ministering angel" to the inhabitants of this earth until such time as he would be called upon to lay down his terrestrial (translated) body and take up a celestial body. At least a portion of this continuing ministry has been spent with the Ten Lost Tribes, for such was prophetically proclaimed in June 1831. (HC 1:176.)

See also: John the Apostle; Keys of the Ministering of Angels; Ministers

Ministering of Angels

See: Keys of the Ministering of Angels

Ministering Servants

The title of "ministering servants" is used twice in the Doctrine and Covenants, with two different meanings. In D&C 136:37 those angels who have ministered to the prophets of God are referred to as "ministering servants." These are they who have functioned under the "ministering of angels," as defined elsewhere in this volume.

On the other hand, the "ministering servants" spoken of in the revelation on celestial marriage (D&C 132:16) are resurrected beings who fall short of exaltation, remaining "separately and singly, without exaltation, in their saved condition to all eternity; and from henceforth are not gods, but are angels of God forever and ever." These "saved" souls shall serve "those who are worthy of a far more, and an exceeding, and an eternal weight of glory." (D&C 132:15–17.)

See also: Ministers

Ministering Spirits

The term *ministering spirits* is used but once in the Doctrine and Covenants (D&C 76:88) and should not be confused with the "ministering spirits" of whom the Prophet Joseph spoke when explaining the difference between these disembodied spirits and angels (TPJS, 191; see also D&C 129). As used in the Doctrine and Covenants, a "ministering spirit" is one who has a resurrected body and is assigned to minister to other resurrected beings of a lower order, such as terrestrial beings ministering to those of a telestial world (see also Heb. 1:14).

See also: Ministers

Ministers

Those who serve as authorized agents of the Lord in seeing to the needs of others and carrying out the work of God are ministers (see D&C 84:111; 107:97;

124:137). They do not need academic credentials but rather a divine commission from Deity (Articles of Faith 1:5; Heb. 5:4).

See also: Evangelical Ministers; Ministering Angel; Ministering Servants; Ministering Spirits; Standing Ministers; Traveling Ministers

Miracles

In spite of its frequent use in religious parlance, the word *miracles* appears but five times in the Doctrine and Covenants (D&C 24:13; 35:8; 45:8; 46:21; 138.26). Parley P. Pratt offers the following explanation of miracles: "Among the popular errors of modern times, an opinion prevails that miracles are contrary to the laws of nature, that they are effects without a cause. If such is the fact, then, there never has been a miracle, and there never will be one. The laws of nature are the laws of *truth*. Truth is unchangeable, and independent in its own sphere. That which, at first sight, appears to be contrary to the known laws of nature, will always by found, on investigation, to be in perfect accordance with those laws." (KT, 103.)

Much of what we take for granted in our world today, such as television and space travel, would have been considered miracles by our forefathers. As Orson F. Whitney succinctly said, "Miracles are not contrary to law; they are simply extraordinary results flowing from superior means and methods of doing things" (CR, Oct. 1928, pp. 64–65). One of the signs of the true Church will be the presence of miracles, for the Lord is a "God of miracles" and "he changeth not" (Morm. 9:19).

See also: Healing

Miraculous Directors

Following a night in which the Lord spoke to him and commanded him to journey into the wilderness, the Book of Mormon prophet Lehi found a "round ball of curious workmanship" outside his tent (1 Ne. 16:9–10). This ball, made of fine brass, contained two spindles, one of which pointed the way Lehi and his party should travel in the wilderness by the borders of the Red Sea. The ball worked according to the faith and righteous diligence of Lehi and his followers. Writings appeared on its surface which changed from time to time and gave the people "understanding concerning the ways of the Lord" (1 Ne. 16:26–30; 18:12, 21). It was variously referred to as a "ball or compass" (2 Ne. 5:12), a "director" (Mosiah 1:16), or a "Liahona" (Alma 37:38).

Smith and Sjodahl have written: "When Lehi perceived the wonderful qualities of this instrument, he exclaimed, in ecstasy, *Liahona!* and that became its name. . . . Liahona is a Hebrew word with, possibly, a Nephite termination, added later. *L* means 'to'; *Jah* is an abbriviated form of the sacred name, 'Jehovah,' and *on* means 'light.' The meaning, then, is, 'To Jehovah is light'; that is, 'God has light; light comes from God,' for He had answered his prayers for light and guidance." (SS, 78.)

David Whitmer testified that he—along with Oliver Cowdery, Martin Harris, and Joseph Smith —saw this instrument as promised by the Lord (LJFS, 242; D&C 17:1).

Missouri

On June 7, 1831, the Lord revealed that the next conference of the Saints was to convene "in Missouri, upon the land which I will consecrate unto my people, . . . the land of your inheritance, which is now the land of your enemies" (D&C 52:2–3, 42). Other revelations followed wherein elders were urged to go to the "land of Missouri" (D&C 54:8; 56:5, 9). In July 1831, the Lord revealed that the "place for the city of Zion" was to be in this "land of Missouri," specifically at Independence, Jackson County. Here a great temple was to be built and the New Jerusalem established (D&C 57:1–4; Ether 13:2–10; DS 3:67–79).

Later revelation announced the "land of Missouri" as the location of the Garden of Eden, and Adam-ondi-Ahman as a place where Adam dwelt following his expulsion from the Garden (D&C 116; JD 16:48; 18:343; MA, 69–70). It is here that Adam will receive an accounting from

all dispensations and in turn report his stewardship to the Savior (TPJS, 122; 157–58). Other names by which the Lord refered to this land in the Doctrine and Covenants were "land of Zion" (D&C 59:3), "land of promise" (D&C 57:2), and "land of inheritance" (D&C 101:1).

Thus, to the Latter-day Saints, Missouri provided a paradox of extremes: to the dreamer it was a vision of hope and heritage; yet, it became a nightmare of darkness, destruction, and despair. To those who initially entered its borders it was the divinely designated land of Zion; the cradle, Eden, from whence the human race sprang; holy ground where ancient prophets had met and would once again gather; and the land where the New Jerusalem was to be established. These dreams encased the thinking of those who came to "possess" the promised land.

It is likely that Satan took a keen interest in the efforts of the Saints to establish Zion upon land where he had once won a minor skirmish with Adam and Eve yet had lost a major battle with God. Thus, his insidious influence was evident in the ill treatment the Saints received from the hands of their Missouri persecutors. Perhaps the zeal of the Saints in endeavoring to establish their Zion was a major factor in their rejection by the citizens of that state. That the Saints also had a degree of culpability for their expulsion is evidenced by the reprimands received from the Lord (D&C 101:1–2; 103:1–4). From their peaceful entry in 1831 to their bloody exit in 1838, Missouri had left its indelible stamp upon the Saints.

The official seal of expulsion was placed upon the Saints by the infamous chief executive of the state of Missouri, Lilburn W. Boggs, who ordered the Mormons "exterminated or driven from the state." This executive order of October 27, 1838, was repealed on June 25, 1976, by Governor Christopher S. Bond, who expressed the "deep regret" of all Missourians for the "injustice and undue suffering" which had been inflicted upon these early Saints (CR, Oct. 1976, p. 5).

The day is not far distant when the promised return to the "land of Zion" shall occur, for such is the promise of the Lord (D&C 101:3, 16–20). "Is the State of Utah the proper monument of the Mormon people?" asked Orson F. Whitney. "No . . . the monument to Mormonism will stand in Jackson County, Missouri." (SS, 147.) However, only a "portion of the Priesthood will go and redeem and build up the Center Stake of Zion," said Brigham Young (JD 11:16; 18:355–56). Inasmuch as the whole of America—North and South—is Zion, members will continue to live in other locations as well, as Zion continues to flourish and establish her stakes (TPJS, 362; DS 3:72).

See also: Adam-ondi-Ahman; Boggs, Lilburn W.; Clay County; Daviess County; Far West; Fishing River; Garden of Eden; Goodly Land, The; Independence; Jackson County; Land of Promise; Liberty; McIlwaine's Bend; Missouri River; New Jerusalem; Southern States; Spring Hill; St. Louis; Van Buren County; Wight's Ferry; Zion

Missouri River

In discussing the improbability of any power preventing the heavens from dispensing knowledge to the Latter-day Saints, Joseph Smith compared such efforts to an attempt to stop the Missouri River from following its decreed course (D&C 121:33). Reference to such a river was logical inasmuch as its course ran just south of Liberty Jail, in which the Prophet was then incarcerated. The river is mentioned again in the preface of section 136, at which time its west bank served as the site for Winter Quarters, Nebraska.

According to the *Encyclopedia Britannica*, the Missouri River is the longest tributary of the Mississippi River. Its flow originates in the Rocky Mountains from whence it meanders in a southeastern direction to ultimately form a portion of the dividing line of the Nebraska-Iowa, Nebraska-Missouri, and Kansas-Missouri state boundaries.

Moon

See: Army with Banners; Fair as the Moon/Sun; Moon Shall Be Turned into Blood

Moon Shall Be Turned into Blood

"The sun shall be turned into darkness, and the moon into blood, before the great and the terrible day of the Lord come," proclaimed the prophet Joel (Joel 2:31; JS—H 1:41). This phenomenal event has also been prophesied on other occasions (Matt. 24:29; Rev. 6:12; D&C 29:14; 34:9; 45:42; 88:87; 133:49). In a similar vein, Isaiah declared "the moon shall not cause her light to shine" (Isa. 13:10).

It is conceivable that this event could occur when the earth is "rolled back" into its paradisiacal planetary orbit where its light is received from the presence of God rather than the direct solar rays of the sun or reflected rays of the moon (TPJS, 181; JD 17:143).

The "blood" color of the moon may be descriptive in the same sense in which we view the distant planet Mars as being red in color.

See also: Stars Shall Fall from Heaven; Sun Shall Be Darkened

Morley, Isaac

The name of Isaac Morley first appears in a revelation received in June 1831 when he was called on a mission to Missouri (D&C 52:23). His farm is indirectly referred to in a later revelation (D&C 63:38), and thereafter he is chastised for faultfinding and not selling his farm as commanded (D&C 64:15–16, 20). His later faithfulness, however, is evidenced in the supreme sacrifice he was willing to make, along with six other men, when they offered their lives as a ransom of sacrifice for the safety of the Saints in Missouri.

In 1835, Morley and Bishop Edward Partridge were vindicated from their earlier rebuke (D&C 64:15–17) when the Prophet Joseph announced this revelation from the Lord: "Behold I am well pleased with my servant Isaac Morley and my servant Edward Partridge, because of the integrity of their hearts in laboring in my vineyard, for the salvation of the souls of men." He served as First Counselor in the Presiding Bishopric from 1831 until 1840 and was ordained as a patriarch for the community of Far West, Missouri, in which capacity he continued to function later in Utah.

His home, cooper's shop, and fields in Illinois were burned by a mob in 1845, but he remained faithful and optimistic. He was largely responsible for maintaining the survival hopes of those who later settled in Sanpete County, Utah, where he died on June 24, 1865.

"Isaac Morley was of a kind and gentle disposition, unassuming in his manner; and his public preaching and that of his fellow-laborer, Bishop Partridge, was spoken of by the Prophet Joseph, in the following characteristic terms: 'Their discourses were all adapted to the times in which we live and the circumstances under which we are placed. Their words are words of wisdom, like apples of gold in pictures of silver, spoken in the simple accents of a child, yet sublime as the voice of an angel.' " (Jenson 1:235–36.)

See also: Farm, This

Mormon

Although the prophet Mormon is not mentioned in the Doctrine and Covenants, the book bearing his name and the pseudonym of the Church which accepts that book as scripture do appear (e.g., D&C 1:29; 33:16; 135:7). Mormon stepped into the spiritual spotlight when but a boy. At the age of ten he was given charge of the sacred records which would someday be translated as the Book of Mormon (Morm. 1:2–4). In his sixteenth year he displayed great capacity in both spiritual and temporal affairs: he saw the Savior (Morm. 1:15) and was chosen to lead an army of Nephite warriors (Morm. 2:2).

In spite of living in one of the most degenerate of societies, Mormon exercised his agency by following God's ways. He remained unsullied from sin, a powerful example of righteous resistance to wrong. He proved that it is possible to live in the world and yet not be of the world (1 John 2:15). His commitment to the cause of righteousness was unsurpassed. Elder Sterling W. Sill observed that "most of us have to be coaxed and begged

and reminded to do our duty. Mormon had to be held back." (UR, 248; Morm. 1:16–17.)

Under the direction of the Spirit of God, Mormon undertook the mammoth task of abridging all of the Nephite records which had been handed down from 600 B.C. to his day, which was around A.D. 385. His abridgment consists of the books of Mosiah, Alma, Helaman, 3 Nephi, and 4 Nephi in the Book of Mormon. In addition to these writings, he wrote the Words of Mormon, the first seven chapters of Mormon, and contributed teachings or epistles found in chapters 7, 8, and 9 of his son Moroni's book.

This great prophet-general was still leading the Nephite armies some fifty-eight years after he had first stood at their helm, and died with most of his people at the great battle of Cumorah (see Morm. 1–7; 8:3; Words of Mormon; Moro. 7–9).

See also: Book of Mormon; Mormonism

Mormonism

In eulogizing Joseph and Hyrum Smith as martyrs, Elder John Taylor said "their *innocent blood* on the floor of Carthage jail is a broad seal affixed to 'Mormonism' that cannot be rejected by any court on earth" (D&C 135:7). In the words of Orson F. Whitney, "Mormonism is no mere nineteenth century religion; it is not merely a religion of time. It is the religion of the eternities, and has come down from the presence of Jehovah, as the preordained plan for the salvation of the children of men." (CR, Apr. 1908, p. 89.)

The word *Mormonism* represents a way of life for those who wish to affiliate with The Church of Jesus Christ of Latter-day Saints and abide by the precepts and ordinances taught therein. This was attested to by Elder Hugh B. Brown, who noted that "Mormonism is not just a code of ethics; it is not merely a set of inhibitive injunctions; it is not just a theoretical system of doctrine and philosophy. It is rather a way of life." (CR, Apr. 1956, p. 103.)

Many years ago, Count Leo Tolstoi, the great Russian author, statesman, and philosopher, said the following of the Latter-day Saints: "If the people follow the teachings of this Church, nothing can stop their progress—it will be limitless. There have been great movements started in the past but they have died or been modified, before they reached maturity. If Mormonism is able to endure, unmodified, until it reaches the third or fourth generation, it is destined to become the greatest power the world has ever known." (IE, Feb. 1939, p. 94.)

President George Q. Cannon declared, "That which the world call 'Mormonism' embraces within its scope every good thing upon the face of the earth, leaving nothing outside" (JD 24:58). President David O. McKay added that "Mormonism has everything of which to be humbly proud" (IE, Sep. 1965, p. 756). A simple

definition of the term was given by President Joseph F. Smith: "I desire to say that 'Mormonism,' as it is called, is still, as always, nothing more and nothing less than the power of God unto salvation, unto every soul that will receive it honestly and will obey it." (GD, 72.) More recently, Elder Bruce R. McConkie noted that "what men call Mormonism is the very system of laws and truths which will make of earth a heaven and of man a god" (CR, Oct. 1979, p. 82).

The origin of the name *Mormon*, from whence "Mormonism" is derived, is found in a letter Joseph Smith wrote to the *Times and Seasons*, dated May 15, 1843. The Prophet explained that the word did not have its origin in the Greek language, but rather came from the "reformed Egyptian" language as used in the Book of Mormon. (Morm. 9:32.) "I may safely say," declared the Prophet, "that the word Mormon stands independent of the learning and wisdom of this generation. . . . We say from the Saxon 'good'; the Dane, 'god'; the Goth, 'goda'; the German, 'gut'; the Dutch, 'goed'; the Latin, 'bonus'; the Greek, 'kalos'; the Hebrew, 'tob'; and the Egyptian, 'mon.' Hence, with the addition of 'more,' or the contraction 'mor,' we have the word 'mormon': which means, literally, 'more good.' " (TPJS, 299–300.)

Originally, the term *Mormon* was applied to members of the Church by those who sought to ridicule the religion of the Saints and the book which bore the name of *Mormon*. However, President Joseph Fielding Smith explained: "As time advanced the expression became softened and began to be used by friend and foe alike in reference to the name of the Church and its members." Nevertheless, he cautioned that "while there can be no disgrace nor condemnation in being called 'Mormons,' and the Church, the 'Mormon Church,' the fact remains, and this we should all emphasize, that we belong to The Church of Jesus Christ of Latter-day Saints, the name the Lord has given by which we are to be known and called." (AGQ 4:174–75; D&C 115:4.)

See also: Church of Jesus Christ of Latter-day Saints, The

Moroni

On a recognition test, among Latter-day Saints, the name of Moroni would undoubtedly score very high. This angel of the restoration who held the keys of the "stick of Ephraim" (D&C 27:5) was envisioned anciently by John the Revelator (Rev. 14:6–7). It should be noted that "Moroni brought the message, that is, the word; . . . other angels brought the keys and priesthood, the power." Thus the angel John saw "fly in the midst of heaven, having the everlasting gospel," was probably a composite being representing several angels of the restoration, among whom was Moroni (DNTC 3:529–31). This faithful Nephite prophet received the sacred Book of Mormon records from his father, Mormon, and continued the task commenced by his father.

To Mormon's literary contributions, Moroni added the following writings: the abridgment of the Jaredite record, or book of Ether; chapters 8 and 9 of Mormon; the book of Moroni; and the title page to the Book of Mormon. It is from Moroni, therefore, that the book derives its name. (HC 1:71.) Like his father, Moroni was true to his covenants, standing firm amidst the whirlwinds of wickedness that prevailed in the Nephite world. His faithfulness was attested to by Mormon, who said: "Behold, my son, I recommend thee unto God, and I trust in Christ that thou wilt be saved." (Moro. 9:22.) Moroni buried the sacred plates around A.D. 421, and next appeared as a resurrected angel to Joseph Smith in 1823.

Moroni's close personal association with the youthful prophet evidently came to a close upon the completion of the work (JS—H 1:28–60). The publication in 1830 of the "stick of Ephraim" as the Book of Mormon was the day for which Moroni and the other Nephite prophets had long prayed. His next appearance may well be when he will "drink of the fruit of the vine" with the Savior, upon the latter's return to the earth (D&C 27:5).

See also: Angel Flying Through the Midst of Heaven; Book of Mormon; Elias; Fifth Angel or Trump; Holy Angel

Morrow

Authorized ministers who go forth to preach the gospel are counseled to "take no thought for the morrow" (D&C 84:81; Matt. 6:34; 3 Ne. 13:34). According to Webster, *morrow* could mean one of three things: (1) morning, (2) the next day, or (3) the time immediately after a specified event.

Moses

A modern-day Apostle has declared: "The prophet Moses was a reality. He was one of the mightiest men who ever lived. He was a prophet of God without parallel, a man whose work had both ancient and modern significance. With the possible exception of the Prophet Joseph Smith, Abraham, Enoch, and the brother of Jared, Moses appears to have had a closer personal relationship with the Almighty than any other man of whom we know." (MMM, 13.)

The following is a scriptural prophetic profile of Moses: "He was called to the work by the personal visitation and direct voice of the Lord. (Ex. 3:4.) At one time heavenly glory came upon him and he was able to endure it. (Moses 1:1–31.) He walked and talked with God as did Enoch. (Moses 1:1–42.) He was described by the Deity as being 'in the similitude of the Only Begotten.' (Moses 1:6.) He beheld in vision the creations of God. (Moses 1:4, 8; 2:1.) He beheld this entire world and all of its inhabitants. . . . (Moses 1:28.) He battled Satan face to face—and won! (Moses 1:12–22.) He saw in vision the bitterness of hell. (Moses 1:20.) He delivered Israel from bondage. (Ex. 12–14.) He received the tablets of the Decalogue from the Lord (Deut. 10), and . . . gave . . . the law . . . to Israel. (3 Ne. 15.) He wrote Genesis and other books of the Bible. (1 Ne. 5:11–14.) He ministered to the Lord Jesus Christ on the Mount of Transfiguration. . . . (Matt. 17:1–3.) He played an important part in the modern restoration of the gospel by coming to Joseph Smith in the Kirtland Temple. There he delivered . . . the keys of the gathering of Israel. . . . (D&C 110.)" (MMM, 13–14.)

Though the Bible seems to indicate that Moses died a natural death (Deut. 34:1–8; Josh. 1:1–2), modern-day revelation has clarified this "death" as a "translation," whereby he was enabled to retain an earthly body for a yet-to-be performed earthly mission on the Mount of Transfiguration (Alma 45:18–19; DS 2:110–11). Following the resurrection of the Savior, Moses went through an instantaneous death and resurrection; it was in this form that he appeared in 1836 to Joseph Smith and Oliver Cowdery.

See also: Keys of the Gathering of Israel

Most High

The title "Most High" or "Most High God" appears more than a dozen times in the Doctrine and Covenants (e.g., D&C 39:19; 59:10, 12; 76:112) and refers to the exalted and lofty positions occupied by both the Father and the Son. "This designation connotes a state of supreme exaltation in rank, power and dignity; it indicates that each of these Gods is God above all" (MD, 516).

See also: God; Jesus Christ; Servants of the Most High

Mote

The only appearance of the word *mote* in the Doctrine and Covenants appears in the Lord's promise that "not one hair, neither mote, shall be lost, for it is the workmanship of mine hand" (D&C 29:25). Mote means a small particle or anything minute. Thus, in the resurrection of man, earth, and beast, the Lord will not overlook even the most insignificant speck of dust. His work is all encompassing.

Mother of Abominations

See: Church of the Devil; Great and Abominable Church

Mount, The

In section 63, verse 21, the Lord refers to "the mount" upon which his three chief Apostles— Peter, James, and John—were shown thngs of which we do not yet have the full record. This "mount" is an unnamed mountain whose only description is that it is "an high mountain" where they could be "apart by themselves" (Mark 9:2). It is commonly referred to as the Mount of Transfiguration (D&C 138:45).

Elder James E. Talmage indicated that Mt. Tabor in Galilee has been one traditional location for this special event. However, Mt. Hermon, located "near the northcrly limits of Palestine, just beyond Caesarea Philippi, where Jesus is known to have been a week before the Transfiguration," is now generally favored, "though nothing that may be called decisive is known in the matter." (Talmage, 376; see also LDSBD, 786.)

Important keys of authority were bestowed upon the three chief Apostles of the Lord on this mount and the experience is recognized as one of the most important events recorded in scripture. However, there is much yet to be revealed about this significant event.

Elder Bruce R. McConkie has observed, "Until men attain a higher status of spiritual understanding than they now enjoy, they can learn only in part what took place upon the Mount of Transfiguration" (DNTC 1:399).

Mount, This

Some of the conditions surrounding the Second Coming are reviewed in section 45. One of these is the statement that the Lord shall "set his foot upon this mount, and it shall cleave in twain" (D&C 45:48). This has specific reference to Christ's appearance on the mount of Olives, or Olivet, for this is the "mount" that will part asunder to provide a valley wherein the Jews may escape their enemies (Zech. 14:1–7; ST, 170).

See also: Mount of Olivet

Mount of Olivet

One of the places the Savior will appear at his Second Coming will be the "mount of Olivet," which literally means "olive yard" (D&C 133:20). This title is found in both the Old and New Testaments (2 Sam. 15:30; Acts 1:12) but is also rendered as "the mount of Olives" (Zech. 14:4; Mark 14:26; Luke 21:37). At the base of this mount is Gethsemane, that sacred, sacrificial spot where Christ suffered for our sins (Luke 22:39–44; Matt. 26:36–44; D&C 19:15–20). This is also the place from whence the resurrected Lord ascended to heaven (Acts 1:1–12) and to which he shall make a return visit.

At the time Christ will appear upon "the mount of Olivet," the Jews will be under siege of a massive army. Of this event, Elder Charles W. Penrose has written: "At the crisis of their fate, when the hostile troops of several nations are ravaging the city and all the horrors of war are overwhelming the people of Jerusalem, he [Christ] will set his feet upon the Mount of Olives, which will cleave and part asunder at his touch. Attended by a host from heaven, he will overthrow and destroy the combined armies of the Gentiles, and appear to the worshipping Jews as the mighty Deliverer and Conquerer so long expected by their race; and while love, gratitude, awe, and admiration swell their bosoms, the Deliverer will show them the tokens of his crucifixion and disclose himself as Jesus of Nazareth whom they had reviled and whom their fathers put to death. Then will unbelief depart from their souls, and 'the blindness in part which has happened unto Israel' be removed." (MS 21:582–83, Sep. 10, 1859; see also Zech. 14:1–7.)

See also: Mount, This

Mount of Transfiguration

See: Mount, The

Mount Sinai

There is a single reference in the Doctrine and Covenants to Mount Sinai (D&C 29:13). The wilderness of Sinai is the place where the children of Israel arrived three months after leaving the land of Egypt (Ex. 19:1). It was here, on the sacred slopes of the mountain, that the Lord revealed divine manifestations to Moses, including the Ten Commandments.

Several millennia later, the Savior revealed some signs of his second coming to Joseph Smith. Among these was the commandment that a "trump shall sound both long and loud, even as upon Mount Sinai . . . , and they shall come forth—yea, even the dead which died in me, to receive a crown of righteousness" (D&C 29:13).

Of this event, Smith and Sjodahl have written: "The resurrection will be accompanied by divine manifestations similar to those that accompanied the giving of the Law on Sinai. The dead will hear and answer the summons." (SS, 150.) Thus, the Lord used an ancient symbol of sacred manifestations—Mt. Sinai—to illustrate a forthcoming divine display by Deity.

Mount Zion

There are a number of references to the Second Coming which indicate that Christ will stand upon "mount Zion" with some of his select Saints (D&C 76:66; 84:2, 32; 133:18, 56; Rev. 14:1). Elder Bruce R. McConkie has discussed "mount Zion" in the following words: "There are two Jerusalems and two Mount Zions. The old city and mount are in Canaan, the holy land of an-

cient times; the new city and mount are in America, the Zion and choice land of latter-days.

"Mount Zion of old, adjacent to Jerusalem, was a sacred site in ancient Israel (Ps. 48:1–3; 74:2; 78:68; 125:1; Isa. 8:18), and the new Mount Zion, which shall yet flourish on the American continent in heaven-borne splendor, shall stand as a holy place in the worship of modern Israel. (Ps. 48:1–3; Isa. 4:5; 18:7; 24:23; 29:8; 31:4; Joel 2:32; Obad. 17, 21; Mic. 4:7.)"

"All of the references to Mount Zion which talk of the Second Coming and related latter-day events appear to have in mind *the new Mount Zion in Jackson County, Missouri*. . . . It seems clear that the Lord and his exalted associates shall stand in glory upon the American Mount Zion, although it may well be that in his numerous other appearances, including that on the Mount of Olivet, which is itself but a few stones' throw from old Mount Zion, he shall also be accompanied by the 144,000 high priests, 'for they follow the Lamb whithersoever he goeth.' " (DNTC 3:525–26; italics added; see also D&C 57:1–3; AF, 345–55; JD 18:69; italics added.)

Mountains Flow Down

In his dedicatory prayer for the Kirtland Temple, Joseph Smith quoted Isaiah, who spoke of the coming of the Lord causing "the mountains to flow down at

[his] presence'' (D&C 109:74; Isa. 64:1–3). This same passage of Isaiah is included in Doctrine and Covenants 133:40, 44.

Elder Parley P. Pratt said: ''In the resurrection which now approaches, and in connection with the glorious coming of Jesus Christ, the earth will undergo a change in its physical features. . . . Its mountains will be levelled, its valleys exalted, its swamps and sickly places will be drained and become healthy, while its burning deserts and its frigid polar regions will be redeemed and become temperate and fruitful.'' (KT, 132.)

To one who has observed the flow of mountains during volcanic disruptions, it is not inconceivable to think that this force of nature may play some role in fulfilling this prophecy, especially considering that the Lord's presence is spoken of as ''the melting fire that burneth, and . . . causeth the waters to boil'' (D&C 133:41).

See also: Presence of the Lord Shall Be As the Melting Fire

Mountains of the Lord's House

Isaiah spoke of ''the mountain of the Lord's house [being] established in the top of the mountains'' in the last days (Isa. 2:2–3; 2 Ne. 12:2–3). Speaking of the Salt Lake Temple during general conference, Elder LeGrand Richards said: ''This temple on this temple block is that house of the God of Jacob'' (CR, Oct. 1975, p.

77). However, in the Doctrine and Covenants *Judah* is warned to ''flee unto Jerusalem, unto the mountains of the Lord's house.'' This latter reference evidently has reference to another temple to be constructed in Jerusalem, of which the prophets have testified (D&C 133:13; BMC, 174; HC 5:337; JD 18:111).

An extended meaning of ''mountains of the Lord's house'' was suggested in the *Old Testament, Part Two: Gospel Doctrine Teacher's Supplement*, published in 1980: ''The word *mountain* as it appears in the scriptures . . . is a place on earth where God meets his servants to instruct them and direct their activity. . . . When an earthly place has been sanctified to the Lord where he may commune with his servants (Exodus 25:21–22; 29:42–46), then such a place may be called 'the mountain of the Lord.' . . . Thus, the mountain of the Lord is the Lord's administrative center where he is at work directing the affairs of his kingdom until the kingdom of heaven comes to earth. The entire earth will then be a 'mountain.' '' (P, 182; see also TPJS, 332–33.)

See also: Salt Lake Temple

Mountains Shout for Joy

In a poetic outburst, the Prophet invited the mountains to shout for joy (D&C 128:23). This expression is related to others which refer to the mountains or hills singing (Isa. 42:11; 44:23;

55:12; 1 Ne. 21:13). This appears to be an expression of the rejoicing of nature on occasions when God is praised by his creations or when he is particularly pleased because of the rolling forth of the work of righteousness and redemption.

Municipals

The only mention of the "municipals" of Zion occurs in Doctrine and Covenants 124:39. The word *municipals*, as used in this sense, is probably akin to *municipalities*, which Webster defines as administrative areas having powers of local self-government. Therefore, municipals in this case undoubtedly has reference to the far-flung ecclesiastical units of the Church—branches, wards, districts, and stakes—which, while operating under the jurisdiction of the General Authorities, must function on a local basis.

Murdered in Cold Blood

The martyrdom of the Prophet Joseph Smith fulfilled his prophecy that he would be "murdered in cold blood" (D&C 135:4). Those who wantonly kill in cold blood do so without pity or mercy and with the clear intent to take a life.

See also: Innocent Blood; Martyrdom; Sealed His Mission with His Blood; Smith, Joseph

Murdock, John

The name of John Murdock surfaces in two revelations, once in section 52 when he is called to accompany Hyrum Smith to Missouri by way of Detroit (D&C 52:8), and again in section 99, which is given in total to Murdock. This latter revelation called him on a mission to the east.

Murdock's name is tragically intertwined with that of Joseph Smith, for it was his two motherless twins who were adopted by the Prophet and his wife Emma. The twins, Joseph S. and Julia, were born the same day that Emma gave birth to twins who lived but three hours, dying the same day that Sister Murdock passed away. The infant Joseph S. died some eleven months later as a result of the exposure he suffered the night his adopted father—the Prophet—was dragged from his home and brutally beaten, tarred, and feathered. As a result of this death in March 1832, the *Millennial Star* of March 18, 1889, referred to the toddler as "the first martyr of this dispensation" (p. 161).

Brother Murdock joined the Church in November 1830, being baptized by Parley P. Pratt. He was a member of Zion's Camp and served on the high council in both Far West, Missouri, and the Salt Lake Valley. He was ordained a bishop in Nauvoo in 1842 and served in that capacity both in Illinois and in Utah.

Under the direction of Parley P. Pratt, he opened the mission in

Australia and was later ordained a patriarch. His first three wives preceded him to the grave, and he joined them on December 23, 1871, at the age of seventy-nine. (Jenson 2:362–64.)

Murmurings of His Heart

One of the early leaders of the Church was chastened because of "the murmurings of his heart" (D&C 75:7). To murmur is to complain or express grumbling discontent. "Murmur not among yourselves," declared Jesus to a crowd of his critics" (John 6:43). The Lord's counsel to Emma Smith should be taken to heart by all who are prone to criticize: "Murmur not because of the things which thou hast not seen [or understood]" (D&C 25:4; see also 1 Ne. 2:12).

My Mother

See: Smith, Lucy Mack

Mysteries

The Doctrine and Covenants speaks of the "mysteries," "mysteries of God," "mysteries of godliness," "mysteries of my kingdom," "hidden mysteries," and "mysteries of the kingdom of heaven" (D&C 6:11; 11:7; 19:10; 63:23; 76:7; 107:19). According to President Joseph Fielding Smith, "There are no mysteries pertaining to the Gospel truth. Without question, there are principles which in this life we cannot understand, but when the fulness comes we will see that all is plain and reasonable and within our comprehension. The 'simple' principles of the Gospel, such as baptism, the atonement, are mysteries to those who do not have the guidance of the Spirit of the Lord." (CHMR 1:43.)

There are, however, certain "mysteries" that are held in reserve for those whose hearts are right and whose faith is full (3 Ne. 26:9–11; Ether 4:7). The Prophet Joseph Smith taught that the mysteries can only be revealed to men of faith, for the moment you teach these sacred secrets to those of fallible faith, "they will be the first to stone you and put you to death" (TPJS, 309).

President Harold B. Lee noted that the "mysteries of Godliness [D&C 19:10] are reserved for and taught only to the faithful Church members in sacred temples. . . . The Lord said He had given to Joseph 'the keys of the mysteries, yea, all the hidden mysteries of my kingdom from days of old. . . .' (D&C 76:7.) In this sense, then, a mystery may be defined as a truth which cannot be known except by revelation." (YLW, 210–11.)

See also: Keys of the Mysteries of the Kingdom

N

Nashville, Iowa

In discussing places where the Saints could settle, the Lord referred to a place called Nashville (D&C 125:4). This was "a little town, pleasantly situated on the Mississippi River, at the head of Des Moines Rapids, in Lee County, Iowa, three miles by rail southeast of Montrose, and eight miles north of Keokuk, [which] was purchased by the Church together with 20,000 acres of land adjoining it, June 24th, 1839. . . . It continued to exist as a 'Mormon' town until the general exodus in 1846." (Historical Record, p. 983; SS, 796.)

Nathan

Speaking of King David, the Lord makes reference to those wives who were given the king by "Nathan, my servant" (D&C 132:39). This Old Testament prophet is first mentioned in connection with the building of the ancient temple which David contemplated erecting (2 Sam. 7).

Nathan is best remembered, however, for his stern and prophetic rebuke of the king's clandestine relationship with Bathsheeba, the wife of another man. The prophet portrayed David's sin in a parable, having the king pronounce the penalty upon himself (2 Sam. 12).

Nathanael

The name of one of Christ's fellow travelers in his earthly ministry, the Apostle Nathanael, is noted in a revelation given February 4, 1831 (D&C 41.11). Edward Partridge is compared with this ancient Apostle and informed that the two are similar in that they are "pure" and "without guile." To be without guile is to be free from deceitful cunningness.

The origin of this comparison dates back to a statement found in the Gospel of John: "Jesus saw Nathanael coming to him and saith of him, Behold an Israelite indeed, in whom is no guile" (John 1:47).

He is also known as Bartholomew (Matt. 10:3). Of this double identity, Elder James E. Talmage has written: "The reasons for assuming that Bartholomew and Nathanael are the same person are these: Bartholomew is named in each of the three synoptic Gospels as an apostle, but Nathanael is not mentioned. Nathanael is named twice in John's Gospel, and Bartholomew not at all; Bartholomew and Philip, or Nathanael and Philip are mentioned together." (Talmage, 222.)

See also: Guile

Natural

Whether referring to death (D&C 29:43), eyes (D&C 58:3), mind (D&C 67:10), man (D&C 67:12), or body (D&C 88:28), the Doctrine and Covenants clearly delineates between the natural, fleshy, physical aspect of being and the spiritual. The scriptures stress repeatedly that the natural man cannot see, know of, and understand the things of God, for "the things of God knoweth no man, except he has the Spirit of God" (JST, 1 Cor. 2:11).

Paul warned the Corinthians that "the natural man receiveth not the things of the Spirit of God: for they are foolishness unto him; neither can he know them because they are spiritually discerned. But he that is spiritual judgeth all things." (1 Cor. 2:14–15.) Smith and Sjodahl described this concept in these terms: "Visions of our Lord are not perceived with the outward eye, or reflected in the natural mind, but with the spiritual eye. There is a spirit within, whose range of vision is limited by the capacity of physical organs, so that it can neither see nor hear that which lies beyond the boundaries of what we call 'matter,' but when the veil is lifted, the spirit can perceive the spiritual world." (SS, 407.) The con-

stant challenge of man is to live in such a way that he can subdue the flesh and allow the spirit to rise to the forefront so that he will be worthy of penetrating the "veil" when necessary.

Elder Marion G. Romney has said, "I know the scriptures say that 'the natural man is an enemy of God.' . . . (Mosiah 3:19.) And so he is when he rejects the promptings of the Spirit and follows the lusts of the flesh. But he is not an enemy of God when he follows the promptings of the Spirit.

"I firmly believe that notwithstanding the fact that men, as an incident to mortality, are cast out from the presence of God and deprived of past memories, there still persists in the spirit of every human soul a residuum from his pre-existent spiritual life which instinctively responds to the voice of the Spirit of Christ until and unless inhibited by the free agency of the individual." (IE, June 1964, p. 506.)

Natural Death

See: Temporal Death

Naught

When "men set at naught the counsels of God" (D&C 3:7), they disregard, despise, or scorn his words. To say that something will come to naught means it will amount to nothing (D&C 3:1; 1 Ne. 17:48).

Nauvoo House

Throughout section 124, instructions are given for the building of a boarding house to be known as the "Nauvoo House." The Lord commanded certain individuals to buy stock in the project, and a building committee was appointed. On February 23, 1841, the state of Illinois approved "An Act to Incorporate the Nauvoo House Association" (HC 4:301–3).

Sperry described the name of the building as "a delightful habitation" because "Nauvoo is taken from a Hebrew word meaning 'comely', 'lovely', 'beautiful', (Isa. 52:7) and a resting-place for the weary traveler, that he may contemplate the glory of Zion (D&C 124:23–24) and the glory of this, the cornerstone, thereof (i.e., Nauvoo Stake; cf. vs. 2). Here the traveler may also receive counsel and teaching from the Lord's servants, 'plants of renown,' who have been set as 'watchmen' upon the walls . . . of Nauvoo (vs. 61)." (DCC, 656.)

Brooks described the history of this building as follows: "They began construction of the building in 1841, and when the Saints were being driven from Nauvoo, in 1846, the workmen who were still attempting to finish the edifice had completed above two stories. The Nauvoo House was shaped like an 'L,' and was located on the bank of the Mississippi River."

"When the Saints left Nauvoo, the building, unfinished as it was, became the property of Emma Smith, widow of Joseph the Prophet. It later became the property of her second husband, Major Lewis C. Bidamon. He put part of it under roof and used it for a hotel. He called it 'The Bidamon House.' " (LDS 1:322–23.)

See also: Quorum of the Nauvoo House

Nauvoo, Illinois

The city of Nauvoo "is situated on the east bank of the Mississippi River, at the head of the Des Moines Rapids, in Hancock County, bounded on the east by an extensive prairie of surpassing beauty, and on the north, west and south by the Mississippi. Nauvoo is about one hundred and ninety miles up the river from St. Louis, and nearly the same distance from Chicago, towards the west." (ECH, 221.)

Its turbulent history began with a peaceful notation penned by the Prophet Joseph on Friday, May 10, 1839: "I arrived with my family . . . and took up my residence in a small log house on the bank of the river, about one mile south of Commerce City, hoping that I and my friends may here find a resting place for a little season at least" (HC 3:349). Unfortunately, the "season" was to be short, for within five years the Prophet and his brother would be slain, and two years later the Saints would be relentlessly driven from their newfound "resting place." Of this site, Elder Heber C. Kimball had prophetically said: "It is a very pretty place, but not a long abiding home for the Saints" (LHCK, 256–57).

Commerce, Illinois, the malarial swamp jutting into the mighty Mississippi, had few inhabitants prior to the arrival of the Saints. Trappers, traders, and mosquitos had shared this unwelcome terrain that was to become the home of Nauvoo, the "City Beautiful." The vision of the Prophet and the obedience and diligence of God's people were to change this undesirable swamp into a beautiful "Mormon Mecca" that was to become thrice the size of Chicago before the Saints would once again be forced to seek sanctuary elsewhere.

Upon their arrival, the Saints found a wilderness. "The land was covered with trees and bushes, and much of it, in the lower parts near the river, was so wet that travel by team was impossible, and on foot, most difficult. Notwithstanding the unhealthful condition, the Prophet felt that by draining the land, and through the blessing of the Lord, the place could be made a pleasant habitation for the Saints." (ECH, 221.)

As the work of building commenced, not only was the land healed of its malarial malady, but physical bodies were healed as well. On the morning of July 22, 1839, Joseph arose from a sick bed and began the process of rebuking the destroyer and disease. Commencing within his own household and continuing throughout the sick-laden land, the Prophet commanded the sick, in the name of the Lord Jesus Christ, to arise and be made whole—"and the sick were healed upon every side of him." As he spoke, "his voice was like the voice of God, and not of man." (HC 4:3–5.)

The "voice of God" continued to be heard in Nauvoo. Nine public revelations were to be received within her borders (D&C 124–129; 132; 135) in addition to the countless private manifestations to the Prophet and Church members alike. Joseph declared that the name *Nauvoo* was of Hebrew origin and signifies a beautiful situation, or place, carrying with it also the idea of rest (ECH, 221). For a "season," the Lord's people found rest upon this redeemed land.

A temple was reared on this site, and on March 17, 1842, the "key" was turned in behalf of the sisters of the Church as the "Female Relief Society" was organized. Though the wicked soon wrested the Saints from their land, and desecrated the temple, the Relief Society still stands as a living monument to the women of the Church, a constant reminder of the eternal partnership they share with the priesthood bearers of God. Metal monuments have recently been added to Nauvoo's terrain to emphasize the vital role of women in our society.

Although a temporary lull occurred following the deaths of

Joseph and Hyrum Smith, it proved to be but the "eye of the storm," for soon the full fury of mobocracy once again burst upon the storm-tossed Saints. In January 1845, the Illinois state legislature repealed the Nauvoo Charter, which Joseph had "concocted . . . for the salvation of the Church, and on principles so broad, that every honest man might dwell secure under its protective influence without distinction of sect or party" (HC 4:249). One year later, the Saints began their forced exit from the site they had since renamed the "City of Joseph" (HC 7:394).

Commencing in July 1846, all-out warfare was waged against this once sacred sanctuary of Saints, and on September 17, mob forces "captured" the city. The victory was "hollow," however, for although sound structures still stood where Saints once dwelt, they were mere shells without spirit. Just as the flight of Joseph's spirit had left his clay tabernacle lifeless, so had the flight of the Saints left Nauvoo without the spirit and life she once knew.

See also: City of Enoch (Joseph); Nauvoo House; Nauvoo Temple; Quorum of the Nauvoo House

Nauvoo Temple

In January 1841, the Lord revealed his will regarding the building of a temple in Nauvoo, Illinois (D&C 124:40–43). One

month later the digging of the cellar commenced and on April 6, 1841, the cornerstone for the temple was laid. The first baptisms for the dead were performed on November 21 of that year. Sacred endowments for the living were performed in the temple from December 10, 1845, to February 7, 1846.

Under the direction of the Quorum of the Twelve Apostles the completed structure was dedicated in a private ceremony on April 30, 1846. A public dedication was held May 1–3, with Elder Orson Hyde of the Quorum of the Twelve offering the dedicatory prayer (CA 1978, 265).

Following the Saints' departure from the City of Joseph (Nauvoo), the temple fell into the hands of wicked men. It was set on fire on November 18, 1848, leaving only the walls standing— these fell during a tornado on May 27, 1850. The building was gone but the purposes for which it had been built would remain eternally.

See also: Nauvoo; Temple

Navel, The

See: Health in the Navel

Nebraska

"The name Nebraska is derived from an Indian word meaning 'flat water,' a reference to the Platte River" (*Encyclopedia Britannica*, 15th ed., 12:922). The Oregon Trail followed the south side of the Platte River and the Mormon pioneers followed a new route on the north side of the river from their settlement in Winter Quarters (now Florence, Nebraska) to Fort Laramie in Wyoming (SLS, 242–43).

The thirty-seventh state of the Union did not achieve statehood until 1867, over two decades after the Saints had first trodden across the soil that was, at the time of their trek, Indian territory. (See map no. 4 on page 298 of the 1981 edition of the D&C.)

The Chronological Order of Contents of the Doctrine and Covenants indicates that Brigham Young received the revelation found in Doctrine and Covenants 136 at Winter Quarters located on land that is now part of Nebraska.

See also: Winter Quarters

Neck

See: Stiffneckedness

Nefarious and Murderous Impositions

See: Concatenation

Neighbor

Throughout scripture we are counseled to treat our neighbors with consideration, kindness, and respect (Ex. 20:16–17; Lev. 19:13; Prov. 3:29; Matt. 5:43; Eph. 4:25; Mosiah 27:4; D&C 42:27; 82:19). The Savior gave the parable of the good Samaritan in response to the query, ''Who is my neighbour?'' (Luke 10:29–37.) A neighbor, therefore, is not simply one who lives nearby, but is one's fellowman or anyone who has needs. In the context of salvation, all who do not presently have a knowledge and witness of the restored gospel of Jesus Christ with all its saving ordinances are in spiritual need and are the neighbors with whom Latter-day Saints should share such a message (D&C 88:81).

Nephi of Old

There are at least four great prophets named Nephi who presided among the people of the Book of Mormon: the original Nephi, son of Lehi, who lived about 600 B.C. (1 Ne. 1:1); Nephi, the eldest son of Helaman, who lived about 45 B.C. (Hel. 3:21); Nephi, chief disciple of the resurrected Lord (3 Ne.12:1), eldest son of Nephi, who was the son of Helaman; and Nephi, the record keeper, who lived about A.D. 36-110 (4 Nephi 1:19). These last two might have been the same person.

While all of these were men of great faith, the Nephi who is spoken of twice in the Doctrine and Covenants (D&C 33:8; 98:32) is Nephi, the son of Lehi, who was the founder-father of the Nephite civilization. His history is replete with examples of great faith and devotion to the cause of righteousness, often in the face of great adversity. Said this great prophet of faith, "If God had commanded me to do all things I could do them" (1 Ne. 17:50).

Whether it was taming the physical elements or the rebellious spirits of men, Nephi exhibited his unfaltering faith (1 Ne. 18:21; 17:45–55). His was the privilege of seeing great visions and of personally seeing the Savior (1 Ne. 10–14; 2 Ne. 11:2–3). He loved the scriptures, likening them to his life and people and learning therefrom (1 Ne. 19:23–24; 2 Ne. 25:5). His life could be summed up in his statement that his whole purpose was "to persuade men to come unto the God of Abraham, and the God of Isaac, and the God of Jacob, and be saved" (1 Ne. 6:4).

See also: Nephites

Nephites

Two major groups of people occupy most of the recorded pages of history in the Book of Mormon: the Nephites and the Lamanites. Both of these groups are mentioned in an 1828 revelation (D&C 3:17). The Nephites were originally those people who followed their prophet-leader Nephi in preference to his elder brothers, Laman and Lamuel, and took upon them the name of "the people of Nephi" (2 Nephi 5:5–9). Nephi's younger brother later designated those who were "friendly" to Nephi as Nephites, and those who "sought to destroy" the people of Nephi as Lamanites (Jacob 1:14).

Throughout the Book of Mormon the Nephites are those people from whom the record keepers are selected and from whom the prophets were generally called. During the golden era of peace following the visit of the resurrected Savior to the American continent, there were no categories of people and all were called the "children of Christ" (4 Nephi 1:17).

In A.D. 231, however, because of the previous revolt of some of the Church who took upon themselves the name of Lamanites, the "true believers in Christ" were called Nephites, regardless of their original ancestry (4 Nephi 1:20–36). Their descendants were ultimately destroyed by the Lamanites. Mormon, one of the last surviving Nephites, "hid up" many of the sacred records of their history about A.D. 385, and entrusted the records to his son Moroni (Morm. 6). Moroni finished the record and was among the last of his civilization to survive (Morm. 8:1–7). Nephite blood has been preserved through the lineage of the Lamanites and is sprinkled among them today.

See also: Book of Mormon; Fallen People; Mormon; Moroni; Nephi of Old

New and Everlasting Covenant

There is a difference between *the* new and everlasting covenant and *a* new and everlasting covenant. The former comprehends the "fulness of the gospel," with all of its "covenants, contracts, bonds, obligations, oaths, vows, performances, connections, associations, or expectations" (D&C 132:7). A new and everlasting covenant is only a portion of the fulness of the gospel.

President Joseph Fielding Smith has written: "Marriage for eternity is *a* new and everlasting covenant. Baptism is also *a* new and everlasting covenant, and likewise ordination to the priesthood, and every other covenant is everlasting and a part of *the* new and everlasting covenant which embraces all things." (AGQ 1:65; see also D&C 22, 132.)

See also: Everlasting Covenant

New and Everlasting Covenant of Marriage

The new and everlasting covenant of marriage is a portion of *the* new and everlasting covenant, which is the fulness of the gospel. It is a sacred marriage, solemnized between husband and wife in one of the holy temples of the Lord and performed by one authorized of the Lord through His earthly prophet. It is an everlasting marriage which transcends time and endures throughout eternity.

President George Q. Cannon has written: "We believe that when a man and woman are united as husband and wife, and they love each other, their hearts and feelings are one, that that love is as enduring as eternity itself, and that when death overtakes them it will neither extinguish nor cool that love, but that it will brighten and kindle it to a purer flame, and that it will endure through eternity" (JD 14:320–21).

Only those who enter into this order of marriage, and through their life-long righteousness have this relationship ratified, will receive the blessings of exaltation and eternal increase, as husband and wife together, throughout the eternities (D&C 131:1–4; 132:4, 7, 18–20).

See also: Everlasting Covenant; New and Everlasting Covenant; Time

New Covenant

On three occasions in the Doctrine and Covenants the Lord speaks of the "new covenant." Two of these citations refer to Jesus as "the mediator of the new covenant," which has specific reference to his redeeming role in the plan of salvation as our Mediator with the Father (D&C 76:69; 107:19). In this sense, the new covenant is the gospel of Jesus Christ.

The Prophet Joseph Smith spoke of the first principles of the gospel as being "the requirements of the new covenant," and then quoted Peter in admonishing the Saints to add to these basic principles the virtues of godliness which would assure the Saints of exaltation (HC 1:314–15; 2 Pet. 1:4–10).

The third reference to the "new covenant" is found in section 84 where the Lord admonishes his people to "remember the new covenant, even the Book of Mormon and the former commandments [i.e., previously issued scriptures, the Old and New Testaments] which I have given" (D&C 84:57).

President Ezra Taft Benson explained, "In the Bible we have the Old Testament and the New Testament. The word *testament* is the English rendering of a Greek word that can also be translated as *covenant*. Is this what the Lord meant when He called the Book of Mormon the 'new covenant'? It is indeed another testament or witness of Jesus. This is one of the reasons why we have recently added the words 'Another Testament of Jesus Christ' to the title of the Book of Mormon." (En., Nov. 1986, p. 4.)

See also: New and Everlasting Covenant; People of the Lord

New Heaven and a New Earth

"The new heaven and new earth . . . is the final change, or resurrection, of the earth, after the 'little season' *which shall follow the Millennium*. When this time comes all things are to be restored by and through the resurrection." (CHMR 1:143; italics added; D&C 29:22–25; Rev. 21.) This earth, and the heavens surrounding and belonging to it, are to be celestialized and become the abode of Deity. The earth "shall be crowned with glory, even with the presence of God the Father" (D&C 88:19). It shall be a "sea of glass" in its "sanctified, immortal, and eternal state" (D&C 77:1–2; Rev. 4:6).

The "new heaven and earth" spoken of by Isaiah in his writings (Isa. 65:17–25; 66:22–24), and described in Doctrine and Covenants 101:23–31, is not the same as that previously described. Isaiah's writings have "reference to the change which shall come to the earth and all upon it, at the *beginning of the Millennial reign*, as we declare in the tenth article of the Articles of Faith. This is the renewed earth when it shall receive its paradisiacal glory, or be restored as it was before the fall of man." (CHMR 143; italics added; AF, 375–81.)

See also: Day of Transfiguration; Earth Shall Tremble and Reel To and Fro; End of the World; Paradisiacal

New Jerusalem

"I shall say with brevity," declared Joseph Smith, "that there is a New Jerusalem to be established on this continent, and also Jerusalem shall be rebuilt on the eastern continent" (TPJS, 86). An ancient Book of Mormon prophet had earlier taught this same distinction. Speaking of the eastern continental city from whence his ancestors came, Moroni said, "Wherefore, it could not be a new Jerusalem for it had been in a time of old; but it should be built up again, and become a holy city of the Lord" (Ether 13:5). Furthermore, "a New Jerusalem should be built upon *this* land unto the remnant of the seed of Joseph" (Ether 13:6; italics added). Thus, the New Jerusalem is to be built upon the American continent.

In 1831, the Lord revealed the location of this city as being at Independence, Missouri (D&C 57:1–3). The terms *City of Zion* and *Zion* are frequently used synonymously with the New Jerusalem. According to President Joseph Fielding Smith, the terms *City of Zion* and *New Jerusalem* "have reference to the same sanctified place" (DS 3:67). This will be a millennial city "from whence the law and the word of the Lord shall go forth to all people" (DS 3:68–69). It will be one of two world capitals, the other being the old Jerusalem (Isa. 2:2–5; Micah 4:1–7; 2 Ne. 12:2–5). The inhabitants of these holy cities will be "they whose garments are white through the blood of the Lamb" (Ether 13:10–11).

See also: Center Place; City of the Heritage of God; City of the Living God; City of Zion; Garden of Eden; Holy City

New Testament

On March 7, 1831, the Prophet Joseph was instructed to pursue the inspired revision of the New Testament, which he commenced the very next day (D&C 45:60). This project was intended to restore many of the "plain and most precious" truths which had been lost from this sacred volume of holy writ (1 Ne. 13:24–29). Two years later, the Prophet penned these words: "I completed the translation and review of the New Testament, on the 2nd of February, 1833, and sealed it up, no more to be opened till it arrived in Zion" (HC 1:324).

Elder B. H. Roberts makes the following comments regarding that statement: "It was the intention of the Prophet to have this revised version of the Scriptures, which he had made with such laborious care, published in Zion, at the printing establishment of the Church in that place, (New Testament and Book of Mormon to be published together; see [HC 1:341]), but before the work could even be commenced, the persecution arose which made the undertaking impracticable. And such was the unsettled state of the Church throughout the remaining years of the Prophet's life that he found no opportunity to publish the revised Scriptures." Elder Roberts further quotes President George Q. Cannon, who said, "We have heard President Brigham Young state that the Prophet, before his death, had spoken to him about going through the translation of the Scriptures again and perfecting it upon points of doctrine which the Lord had restrained him from giving in plainness and fulness at the time of which we write [2nd Feb., 1833].' " (HC 1:324, footnote.)

The New Testament is a compilation of some twenty-seven books. Latter-day Saints accept this along with the Old Testament as valid scripture from God, "as far as it is translated correctly" (see Articles of Faith 1:8; AF, 245-53).

See also: New Translation

New Translation

The "new translation" (D&C 124:89) is Joseph Smith's inspired translation of the Bible. Joseph Fielding Smith provided the following information regarding this work: "It has been thought by some, that the Prophet went through the Bible beginning with the first chapter of Genesis and continued through to the Book of Revelation, but this was not the case. He went through the Bible topic by topic, and revising as the Spirit of the Lord indicated to him where changes and additions should be made. There are many parts of the Bible that the Prophet did not touch, because the Lord did not direct him to do so. Therefore, there are many places in the Scriptures where errors still are found. This work was never fully completed, but the Prophet did as much as the Lord commanded him to do before the days of Nauvoo. February 2, 1833, he finished the revision of the New Testament, and on the second day of July that same year, he finished the Scriptures, as far as the Lord permitted him to go at that time." (HC 1:324-68.) It was his intention to make other corrections in Nauvoo, but it seems that the Lord did not permit him to do so. Perhaps the reason for this is given in 3 Nephi, wherein the Lord forbade Mormon to write more than he has given us, because the people are not prepared to receive it. (3 Ne. 26:6-9.)

"The purpose for this revision is explained by Nephi in writing of the coming forth of the record of the Nephites, (1 Nephi 13), and by the Lord to Moses, as given in the Book of Moses in the Pearl of Great Price. (Moses 1:40-41.) The Book of Moses in the Pearl of Great Price is a part of this revision revealed to the Prophet." (CHMR 1:242.)

Sidney Rigdon was called as a scribe to Joseph Smith in this project (D&C 35:18-20).

See also: New Testament; Translation of My Scriptures; Translation of the Prophets; Work of Translation

New York City

A major port of entry to the United States, known to millions throughout the world, is the city of New York. As recorded in Doctrine and Covenants 104:81, the Lord refers to creditors residing in New York to whom the Church owed money in 1834; it is unclear whether the city or the state is intended. However, New York City is referred to in an 1832 revelation (D&C 84:114–15). At this time, Bishop Newel K. Whitney was commanded to go to the cities of New York, Albany, and Boston, "and warn the people of those cities with the sound of the gospel." He was accompanied on his visit by the Prophet Joseph in the fall of 1832. (HC 1:295.)

The Lord warned that "desolation" awaited the inhabitants of these cities unless they repented. In 1866, Elder Orson Pratt repeated this warning to this triad of cities, promising that they would yet be left "desolate" (MS 28:633–34). On another occasion he said, "The great and populous city of New York, that may be considered one of the greatest cities of the world, will . . . become a mess of ruins. The people will wonder while gazing on the ruins that cost hundreds of millions to build, what has become of its inhabitants." (JD 12:344.)

How or when such an event will occur is not known. However, stakes of Zion will be established in New York, declared Joseph Smith (JD 8:205), and "the righteous need not fear" (1 Ne. 22:17–22).

See also: Cainhannoch

New York State

From that marvelous moment in the spring of 1820, when the veil was rent and the breath of heaven bathed the soul of a young prophet, until the removal of Joseph Smith to Ohio in January 1831, the state of New York was the focal point of early Church activity. Its soil held the records that were to become the Book of Mormon (JS—H 1:28–60).

Within the borders of this state, six of the revelations contained in the Doctrine and Covenants were received, as well as numerous other manifestations from heaven, including a personal visit by the Father and Son themselves (JS—H 1:10–20). The "stone cut out of the mountain without hands" originated in New York and has commenced its rolling throughout the world (D&C 65:2; 109:72–73; Dan. 2:34–35, 44).

See also: Albany; Cainhannoch; Colesville; Fayette; Freedom; Manchester; New York City; Northern States; Perrysburg; Seneca County; Stone Cut Out of the Mountain; Susquehanna River; Wilderness of Fayette

Nicolaitane Band

In July 1838, the Lord warned Bishop Newel K. Whitney to "be ashamed of the Nicolaitane band and of all their secret abominations" (D&C 117:11). Joseph Fielding Smith said this phrase applied to those in Kirtland who had participated in "abominations" (CHMR 2:98). The name appears in the book of Revelation (Rev. 2:6, 15) and has been defined as "members of the Church who were trying to maintain their church standing while continuing to live after the manner of the world.

"Whatever their particular deeds and doctrines were, the designation has come to be used to identify those who want their names on the records of the Church but do not want to devote themselves to the gospel cause with full purpose of heart" (DNTC 3:446).

Nigh at Hand

The phrase *nigh at hand* is used throughout the Doctrine and Covenants to express the close proximity of the coming of the Lord (D&C 1:35; 29:9; 43:17; 106:4). According to Webster, *nigh* means near in place, time, or relationship; close, nearly, or almost. The word *nigh* is found frequently in the Book of Mormon in phrases such as "nigh unto [closely resembling] an angel of light" (2 Ne. 9:9); "repenting nigh [almost] unto death" (Mosiah 27:28); and "the day of salvation draweth nigh [near]" (Alma 13:21). The Pearl of Great Price tells us that "Kolob is set nigh [near in place] unto the throne of God" (Abr. 3:9).

Noah

The great prophet Noah was a grandson of Methuselah and received the priesthood under his hands at the age of ten (Gen. 5:25–29; D&C 107:52). He was ordained after the order of the Lord and was sent forth to declare the gospel to the inhabitants of the earth, some of whom had sought his life (Moses 8:18–19). According to Joseph Smith, "Noah was born to save seed of everything, when the earth was washed of its wickedness by the flood" (TPJS, 12). The history of that flood is found in the Old Testament (Gen. 6, 7, 8), with some additional information appearing in the Pearl of Great Price (Moses 8).

As a result of this "baptism" of the earth, all mankind are descendants of Noah, through his sons, Japheth, Shem, and Ham (Gen. 8:13). The Prophet Joseph declared that Noah "stands next in authority to Adam in the Priesthood" and is the angel Gabriel who was privileged to announce the forthcoming births and missions of John the Baptist and Jesus the Christ (TPJS, 157; Luke 1:5–38). He was scripturally described as "a just man, and perfect in his generation; and he walked with God" (Moses 8:27).

He is also known as Elias, in which capacity, according to Joseph Fielding Smith, he appeared in the Kirtland Temple on April 3, 1836, restoring the keys of the dispensation of Abraham to Joseph Smith and Oliver Cowdery (AGQ 3:138–41; D&C 110:12). He was among the "congregation of the righteous" whom the Savior visited in the spirit world following his death on Calvary (D&C 138:38, 41).

See also: Elias; Gabriel

Nobleman

A parable about the redemption of Zion speaks of a nobleman (D&C 101:44–68; see also 103:21). This term is also found in a parable in the New Testament (Luke 19:12) and in reference to a man whose son was sick (John 4:46). A nobleman is a man of high station in society or one of nobility. In the two parables cited, the nobleman refers to the Lord.

North Countries

See: Ice Shall Flow Down at Their Presence; They Who Are in the North Countries

Northern States

A remarkable prophecy by Joseph Smith in December 1832 foretold of the coming conflict between the southern and northern states in America (D&C 87:3). The fulfillment of his prophecy commenced some twenty-nine years later, when eleven states from the South seceeded from the remaining twenty-three states in the North. The northern states consisted of: California, Connecticut, Delaware, Illinois, Indiana, Iowa, Kansas, Kentucky, Maine, Maryland, Massachusetts, Michigan, Minnesota, Missouri, New Hampshire, New Jersey, New York, Ohio, Oregon, Pennsylvania, Rhode Island, Vermont, and Wisconsin.

Nowise

The word *nowise* occurs occasionally in scripture (D&C 33:12; 58:28; 84:90; Matt. 5:18; Mosiah 27:26; Moses 6:57). It simply means "no way," or, if preceded by the word *in*, it means "in no way."

O

O Lord My God!

In recounting the events of the marytrdom, Elder John Taylor related that the Prophet Joseph's dying words were, "O Lord my God!" (D&C 135:1; see also Ps. 38:21.) Elder B. H. Roberts has discussed the meaning of this phrase in the following words: "Were Joseph Smith's last words — '*O Lord My God*' — an interrupted Masonic cry of distress? The question has been somewhat widely debated. Of it the author of this *History* can form no adequate or positive opinion. In an editorial of the *Times and Seasons,* published soon after the murder (July 15th, 1844), the following passage occurs; referring to Joseph and Hyrum Smith:

'They were both Masons in good standing. Ye brethren of "the mystic tie," what think ye! Where is our good Master Joseph and Hyrum? Is there a pagan, heathen, or savage nation on the globe that would not be moved on this great occasion, as the trees of the forest are moved by a mighty wind? Joseph's last exclamation was, "*O Lord My God!*" If one of these murderers, their abettors or accessories before or after the fact, are suffered to cumber the earth, without being dealt with according to law, what is life worth, and what is the benefit of laws? And more than all, what is the use of institutions which savages would honor, where civilized beings murder without cause or provocation? In the same editorial it is said: 'With *uplifted hands* they gave such signs of distress as would have commanded the interposition and benevolence of savages or pagans.'

"Against this evident belief of his associates and companions in prison—the editorial was most likely written by John Taylor, W. W. Phelps, or Willard Richards, and may have been the result of consultation among them—there is nothing but the strange fact in human experience that when men are overtaken by sudden death, they so frequently die with some appeal to God upon their lips, especially if thoughts upon God have largely entered into their lives; and for one I can readily believe that not thoughts of deliverance from men and their violence [were] in the Prophet's mind, but thoughts of God and sacrifice blended in his *martyr-cry—'O Lord My God!'*" (CHC 2:287.)

Oath and Covenant

One of the most solemn and sacred oaths available to man is the celestial contract known as "the oath and covenant of the priesthood" (D&C 84:33–42.) Joseph Fielding Smith explained: "There is no exaltation in the kingdom of God without the fullness of the priesthood, and every man who receives the Melchizedek Priesthood does so with an oath and a covenant that he shall be exalted.

"The covenant on man's part is that he will magnify his calling in the priesthood and that he will live by every word that proceedeth forth from the mouth of God, and that he will keep the commandments.

"The covenant on the Lord's part is that if man does as he promises, then all that the Father hath shall be given unto him; and this is such a solemn and important promise that the Lord swears with an oath that it shall come to pass." (CR, Apr. 1970, pp. 58–59.)

To receive "all that the Father hath" is "to inherit the same power, the same glory and the same exaltation, until you arrive at the station of a God, and ascend the throne of eternal power, the same as those who have gone before" (TPJS, 347).

Marion G. Romney observed that "it seems perfectly clear to me that to receive the holy priesthood and not magnify my calling in it, I will fall short of eternal life; and that if I fail to receive the holy priesthood, I will likewise fall short. There is but one safe course, and that is to receive it and magnify my calling in it." (CR, Oct. 1975, p. 110.)

Obedience

The scriptures are replete with divine injunctions to obey God's laws and walk in his ways (Deut. 30:19–20; Jer. 11:3–4; Matt. 7:21; Mosiah 5:8; D&C 56:3; 59:21; Abr. 3:24–26; AF 1:3). To render obedience is simply to do as requested, thereby reaping resultant blessings associated with God's laws (D&C 130:20–21).

Elder Francis M. Lyman noted that "Obedience is the first law of God" (CR, Oct. 1899, p. 35). "The Church does not desire blind obedience," observed Elder Neal A. Maxwell, "rather, that we see things with the eye of faith" (WWPTH, 21). President N. Eldon Tanner further commented, "We do not suggest blind obedience, but obedience by *faith in those things which may not be fully understood by man's limited comprehension, but which in the infinite wisdom of God are for man's benefit and blessing*" (CR, Oct. 1977, p. 67).

Two classic statements regarding obedience that are worthy of following can be found in the words of two noble prophets. At the beginning of man's history, in response to a query by an angel as to why he was offering a sacrifice to the Lord, Adam said, "I know not, save the Lord commanded me" (Moses 5:6). Centuries later, the Prophet of the restoration declared, "I made this my rule: When the Lord commands, do it" (HC 2:170).

Oblations

We are commanded to offer "oblations" to the Lord on his holy day (D&C 59:12). "In the Mosaic dispensation, an oblation, or offering, was anything presented to God to atone for sins, to merit favors, or to express gratitude for favors received. The firstlings of the flock, first fruits, tithes, incense, the shewbread, all these were oblations or offerings; some prescribed by law, some entirely voluntary. In the New and Everlasting Covenant the Lord graciously accepts tithes and offerings, donations and gifts; and the Lord's day is a very proper day upon which to remember such obligations." (SS, 352.)

Obviate

An epistle from Joseph Smith uses the phrase "to obviate this difficulty" (D&C 128:3), which simply means "to prevent or preclude this difficulty."

Offering unto the Lord in Righteousness

"What kind of offering will the sons of Levi make to fulfil the words of Malachi and John? [Mal. 3:1–4; D&C 13; 124:39; 128:24.] Logically such a sacrifice as they were authorized to make in the days of their former ministry when they were first called. [Ezek. 43:18–27; 44:9–27.] Will such a sacrifice be offered in the temple? Evidently not in any temple as they are constructed for work of salvation and exaltation today. It should be remembered that the great temple, which is yet to be built in the City Zion, will not be one edifice, but twelve. Some of these temples will be for the lesser priesthood." (DS 3:93.)

The Prophet Joseph Smith proclaimed: "The offering of sacrifice has ever been connected and forms a part of the duties of the Priesthood. . . . Sacrifices, as well as every ordinance belonging to the Priesthood, will, when the Temple of the Lord shall be built, and the sons of Levi be purified, be fully restored and attended to in all their powers, ramifications, and blessings. This ever did and ever will exist when the powers of the Melchizedek Priesthood are sufficiently mani-

fest; else how can the restitution of all things spoken of by the Holy Prophets be brought to pass. It is not to be understood that the law of Moses will be established again with all its rites and variety of ceremonies; this has never been spoken of by the prophets; but those things which existed prior to Moses' day, namely, sacrifice, will be continued." (TPJS, 172–73.)

Until the future day of sacrifice is restored, the present-day "Offering unto the Lord in righteousness" may well be manifest in the faithful observance of priesthood responsibilities by those who presently hold offices within the priesthood.

See also: Memorials for Your Sacrifices; Sacrifice; Sons of Levi

Offerings of Cain

In an 1841 revelation, the Lord made reference to "the offerings of Cain" (D&C 124:75). The meaning thereof was described by the Prophet Joseph: "By faith in [the] atonement or plan of redemption, Abel offered to God a sacrifice that was accepted, which was the firstlings of the flock. Cain offered of the fruit of the ground, and was not accepted, because he could not do it in faith, he could have no faith, or could not exercise faith contrary to the plan of heaven. It must be shedding the blood of the Only Begotten to atone for man; for this was the plan of redemption; and without the shedding of blood was no remission; and as the sacrifice was instituted for a type, by which man was to discern the great Sacrifice which God had prepared; to offer a sacrifice contrary to that, no faith could be exercised, because redemption was not purchased in that way, nor the power of atonement instituted after that order; consequently Cain could have no faith; and *whatsoever is not of faith is sin.''* (TPJS, 58; italics added.)

"The mere shedding of the blood of beasts or offering anything else in sacrifice, could not procure a remission of sins, except it were performed in faith of something to come; if it could, Cain's offering must have been as good as Abel's." (TPJS, 59.)

Moses tells us that Cain loved Satan more than God and offered his sacrifice unto the Lord as a result of Satan's commanding him to do so. The devil knew it would not be respected by the Lord and thereby Cain would become angry. (Moses 5:18, 21.) The tragedy of Cain's offering might be summed up in these words: "He rejected the greater counsel which was had from God; and this is a cursing" (Moses 5:25; see also WTP, 99–100).

Thus, an *"offering of Cain"* *might well be any offering made to the Lord that is done without full purpose of heart—without faith* (see Moro. 7:6–8). Any such offerings will be rejected by God. Elder Bruce R. McConkie wrote, "If faith is not present in religious rites, can we reach any other conclusion, with reference to them, than that whatsoever is not of faith is sin?" (DNTC 3:198.)

Office of Priesthood and Patriarch

On January 19, 1841, the Lord revealed that Hyrum Smith was to be released from his position as a counselor in the First Presidency in order to assume his rightful place as the Patriarch to the Church (D&C 124:91–92). This followed the death of his father, Joseph Smith, Sr. Simultaneously, Hyrum was elevated to the position of Associate President of the Church, holding the keys of the kingdom jointly with the Prophet Joseph. (See D&C 124:94–95; DS 1:216–22.) Perhaps it was in this latter capacity that "the office of Priesthood . . . which came by blessing" was more readily manifest, for it did not come "by right" of inheritance.

Hyrum's "inheritance" was his patriarchal position. Richards and Little explained this "right" as follows: "Joseph Smith, Sen., inherited the Patriarchal Priesthood, by right from the father over the house of Israel in this dispensation. For this right to have descended to him, by lineage, he must of necessity be an Ephraimite, for Ephraim, by right of appointment and ordination by his father Jacob, is the head of Israel." (1 Chron. 5:1; Gen. 48:16, 20; Jer. 31:9.) "By virtue of this adoption of Ephraim, as the head of the house of Israel, and Joseph Smith, Sen., being the oldest son of Ephraim, holding the Priesthood in this dispensation, he is Patriarch of the whole church by right. This right should be perpetuated in his family, as the oldest branch of the tribe of Ephraim. If, from any cause, there should be failure of a son to exercise this right, then the office would be filled from the next eldest branch of the family." (RL, 74–75.)

See also: Evangelical Minister; Gifts . . . Once Put upon Oliver Cowdery; Patriarch; Smith, Hyrum

Offspring

The reference to offspring in Doctrine and Covenants 122:6 has particular reference to Joseph Smith's children, and speaks of him being torn from their presence by his enemies.

See also: Fruit of . . . Loins; Seed

Ohio

In December 1830, the Prophet Joseph was told to "go to the Ohio" (D&C 37:1). It was here that he was to receive the "law" of the Lord and "be endowed with power from on high" (D&C 38:32). The headquarters of the Church were moved from New York to Ohio in January 1831, when Joseph settled within her borders. As promised, the "law" was revealed the following month (D&C 42), and the promised "endowment of power" came on April 3, 1836, in the newly dedicated Kirtland Temple (D&C 110).

From within her borders, Ohio was to give birth to the fun-damental organization that exists within the Church today. The First Presidency of the Church was established in Ohio, as well as the Quorum of the Twelve Apostles, First Quorum of the Seventy, and the first stake of the Church, with its attendant high council. Between February 1831, and April 1836, sixty-four of the revelations recorded in the Doctrine and Covenants were received in Ohio. The towns of Kirtland, Thompson, Hiram, Orange, and Amherst were the host grounds for the revelatory information received.

The reference to "Ohio" in the revelations, in general, refers to those areas where the Saints gathered, mostly in the northeastern part of the state. Kirtland served as the major headquarters of the Church until shortly after the dedication of the temple, when the Prophet moved to Missouri.

See also: Amherst, Ohio; Cincinatti, Ohio; French Farm; Hiram, Ohio; Kirtland, Ohio; Kirtland Temple; Orange, Ohio; Plains of Olah Shinehah; Northern States; Shinehah; Thompson, Ohio

Oil

See: Lamps Trimmed and Burning

Old Father Whitmer

The reference to "old Father Whitmer" in Doctrine and Covenants 128:21 means Peter Whitmer, Sr., in whose home the Prophet Joseph found hospitality and experienced great outpourings of the Spirit of God (see HC 1:60). At the time of this revelation, the elder Whitmer was sixty-nine years of age, which in 1842 was considered to be rather "old."

See also: Chamber of Old Father Whitmer; Peter Whitmer, Sr.

Olihah

The name *Olihah* appeared four times in pre-1981 editions of the Doctrine and Covenants, each time as a pseudonym for Oliver Cowdery (D&C 82:11; 104:28, 29, 34). The use of this name in revelation covered a two-year period, with the first revelation being given in April 1832, and the second one in April 1834.

The Lord did not always want the names of individuals to whom he was speaking to be recognized by the general public, so a system of code names was utilized (HC 1:255). It is interesting to note that the Saints reverted to this same idea at the time of great persecution when polygamy was being opposed by the government (see Gustive O. Larsen, *The "Americanization" of Utah for Statehood*, San Marino, Ca.: Huntington Library, 1971, p. 120).

In current editions of the Doctrine and Covenants, the name Olihah is no longer used.

See also: Cowdery, Oliver

Olive Leaf

In a letter sent from Kirtland, Ohio, dated January 14, 1833, the Prophet Joseph Smith said to W. W. Phelps, one of the presiding brethren in Missouri, "I send you the 'olive leaf' which we have plucked from the Tree of Paradise, the Lord's message of peace to us; for though our brethren in Zion [Missouri] indulge in feelings toward us, which are not according to the requirements of the new covenant, yet, we have the satisfaction of knowing that the Lord approves of us, and has accepted us, and established His name in Kirtland for the salvation of the nations" (HC 1:316).

There appeared to have been some antagonisms on the part of some of the brethren in Missouri, and so the Prophet sent to them a sublime symbol of peace, the "olive leaf" containing the revelation now found in section 88 (D&C 88:preface). The olive leaf has traditionally been a symbol of peace between men. It is not unlikely that the Prophet hoped the sublime truths of this revelation would bring peace and solace to the troubled souls in Zion.

Perhaps the "olive leaf" sent by the Prophet served as a sign to them of the spiritual safety to be found in the gospel in the same sense that the olive leaf in the beak of the dove was a sign to Noah that it was once again safe to walk upon the earth (see Gen. 8:10–11).

Olive Trees

It is appropriate that the olive tree should be used as a symbol in parables. The trees are extensively cultivated in the land where Jesus lived. During troubled times in Missouri, the Lord gave the "parable of the nobleman and the olive trees signifying the troubles and eventual redemption of Zion" (D&C 101:43–62). The olive tree is used several times in scripture as a symbol of a truth being revealed. The Apostle Paul referred to the grafting of the Gentiles into the olive tree (Rom. 11:17–24). The classic allegory of Zenos, which has been described as "one of the greatest parables ever recorded," describes the history of the house of Israel (Jacob 5; AGQ 4:141–42).

Omaha Nation

The pressures and outrages of mob actions against the Saints caused them to leave Nauvoo as early as February 1846. Almost a year later, "the word and will of the Lord" came to Brigham Young instructing him how to organize the pioneer companies in their trek to the west. The revelation contained in section 136 was received at a place designated as Winter Quarters, on land belonging to the Omaha Nation, on the west bank of the Missouri River (D&C 136:preface).

The Omaha Nation was a tribe of American Indians for whom that particular plot of ground had been set aside by the federal government. The Indians had given permission for the Saints to locate on the land.

See also: Winter Quarters

Omegus

The word *Omegus* is cited in Doctrine and Covenants 95:17. The word refers to the Lord and is a derivative of the Greek word *Omega*, which is the last letter of that alphabet. It denotes "the end." *Omegus* is the Greek word *Omega* with a Latin ending.

See also: Alpha and Omega; Jesus Christ; The Beginning and the End

One Eternal Round

The description of the Lord's course as being "one eternal round" is found twice in the Doctrine and Covenants (D&C 3:2; 35:1) and three times in the Book of Mormon (1 Ne. 10:19; Alma 7:20; 37:12). God's work—"to bring to pass the immortality and eternal life of man"—is a fixed, constant course from which he does not deviate (Moses 1:39). God follows "one [singular or unified] eternal [recurring] round [course], the same today as yesterday, and forever," of providing the means whereby his children might receive a fulness of his glory (D&C 35:1; 93:20).

Just as a ring has no beginning or ending, and as his priesthood has neither "beginning of days or end of years" (Alma 13:7), so is the course of God one eternal round.

See also: Beginning and End; Walk in Crooked Paths

One Flesh

The command that husband and wife should be one flesh is one of the longest standing commandments of the Lord (Gen. 2:24; Matt. 19:5–6; Eph. 5:31; Moses 3:24; D&C 49:16). One flesh is *not* confined to the physical or affectional aspects of a marital relationship, it is symbolic of the total unity in which the marriage should function.

President Marion G. Romney provided the following commentary on the meaning of one flesh: "They [husband and wife] should be one in harmony, respect, mutual consideration. Neither should plan or follow an independent course of action. They should consult, plan and decide together." (En., Dec. 1978, p. 2.)

One God

In contrast to the general Christian world which professes a belief in one God who manifests himself as Father, Son, and Holy Ghost, "a most pure spirit, invis-

ible, without body, parts, or passions," the Latter-day Saints proclaim, "We believe in God, the Eternal Father, and in His Son, Jesus Christ, and in the Holy Ghost" (Articles of Faith 1:1). Indeed, revelation teaches not only the separate nature of each member of the Godhead but also that the Father and Son possess celestial, tangible, bodies of flesh and bone which each house an eternal spirit (D&C 130:22).

Why then, do latter-day scriptures speak of Father, Son, and Holy Ghost as "one God?" (See D&C 20:28; Testimony of the Three Witnesses; 2 Ne. 31:21.) President Charles W. Penrose offered the following explanation: "There is the oneness of Deity, the three in one; not as some preachers try to expound it, in the doctrines of the outside world . . . making them one immaterial spirit—no body, no real personage, no substance. On the contrary, they are three individuals, one in spirit, one in mind, one in intelligence, united in all things that they do, and it takes the Father, and the Son, and the Holy Ghost, to make the perfect Trinity in one, three persons and one God or Deity, one Godhead." (CR, Apr. 1921, pp. 13–14.)

The Savior himself spoke of the "oneness" which he and the Father and the Holy Ghost enjoy, and he prayed that his disciples would join that unity (John 17:20–23; see also D&C 35:2; 3 Ne. 11:27, 31–36; 19:20–23).

See also: Elohim; God; Father, The; Father, Jesus; Holy Ghost; Jehovah; Jesus Christ

One Mighty and Strong

On November 27, 1832, Joseph Smith wrote a memorable letter from Kirtland to W. W. Phelps in Missouri, part of which has since been canonized as section 85 of the Doctrine and Covenants (HC 1:297–99). In the context of the letter, Joseph, speaking in behalf of the Lord, criticized the manner in which Bishop Edward Partridge had been conducting the affairs of the Church, and threatened to "send one mighty and strong . . . to set in order the house of God" (D&C 85:7). President Joseph Fielding Smith has said that verses 6, 7, and 8 of this section "have caused no end of needless speculation due to a misunderstanding of what is written. . . .

"There have arisen from time to time men of doubtful intelligence who have laid claim to being the 'one mighty and strong.' Some of these, notwithstanding their limitations of intellect and power of understanding, have succeeded in gathering around them a few followers of like spirit and lack of understanding." (CHMR 1:350.)

On November 13, 1905, the *Deseret News* carried an official proclamation from the First Presidency regarding the nature of "the one mighty and strong." A portion of that explanation follows: "This whole letter . . . related to the affairs of the Church in Zion, Independence, Jackson county, Missouri. And inasmuch as through his repentance and sacrifices and suffering, Bishop Edward Partridge undoubtedly obtained a mitigation of the threatened judgment against him of falling 'by the shaft of death, like as a tree that is smitten by the vivid shaft of lightning,' so the occasion for sending another to fill his station—'one mighty and strong to set in order the house of God, and to arrange by lot the inheritances of the Saints'—may also be considered as having passed away and the whole incident of the prophecy closed.

"If, however, there are those who still insist that the prophecy concerning the coming of 'one mighty and strong' is still to be regarded as relating to the future, let the Latter-day Saints know that he will be a future bishop of the Church who will be with the Saints in Zion, Jackson county, Missouri, when the Lord shall establish them in that land. . . . He will hold the same high exalted station that Edward Partridge held; for the latter was called to do just this kind of work—that is, to set in order the house of God as pertaining to settling the Saints upon their inheritances. . . . This future bishop will also be called and appointed of God as Aaron of old, and as Edward Partridge was. He will be designated by the inspiration of the Lord, and will be accepted and sustained by the whole Church as the law of God provides. His coming will not be the result of a wild, erratic movement, or the assumption of authority by a self-appointed egotist seeking power that he may lord it over the people; God's house is one of order, and admits of no such irregular procedure." (MFP 4:109–20.)

See also: Ark of God, Steady the; Man . . . Like as Moses; Partridge, Edward; President of the High Priesthood; That Man

One Wife

In March 1831, the Lord reaffirmed the divine nature of marriage and added that a man should have but one wife (D&C 49:15–16; HC 1:167). "The statement in relation to marriage . . . was given to the Church several years before the revelation known as Section 132 was revealed. Hence, it is worded as we find it here *according to the law of the Church in 1831*. This statement in relation to marriage was given to correct the false doctrine of the Shakers that marriage was impure and that a true follower of Jesus Christ must remain in the condition of celibacy to be free from sin and in full fellowship with Christ." (CHMR 1:209; italics added.)

Section 132, recorded in 1843, authorized the practice of plural marriage. The keys to this practice however, are vested only in the Lord's prophet and used only with divine approbation (D&C 132:7; Jacob 2:30; HC 6:46). Because a Prophet of God, holding these keys, revoked the law of plural marriage in 1890 (see OD—1), the law of the Church at the present time is the same as when section 49 was revealed:

"Wherefore, it is lawful that [a man] should have one wife" (D&C 49:16).

See also: Law of Sarah; Lee, Ann; Manifesto; Whitney, Newel K.

Only Begotten of the Father

See: Jesus Christ; Only Begotten Son

Only Begotten Son

Jesus Christ is identified in all standard works of scripture used by Latter-day Saints as the Only Begotten Son of God (Jacob 4:11; D&C 49:5; Moses 1:6; John 3:16). In a classic sermon delivered by President Joseph F. Smith at the Box Elder Stake conference of December 20, 1914, as recorded in the *Box Elder News* of January 28, 1915, the following inspired insights were given: "How are children begotten? I answer just as Jesus Christ was begotten of his Father. . . . Just as the infidel was begotten and born, so was Christ begotten by his Father. . . . We want to try to make it appear that God does not do things in the right way, or that he has another way of doing things than what we know; we must come down to the simple fact that God Almighty was the Father of His Son Jesus Christ. Mary, the virgin girl, who had never known mortal man, was his mother. God by her begot His son Jesus Christ, and He was born into the world with power and intelligence like that of His Father."

Elder James E. Talmage has written: "That Child . . . born of Mary was begotten of Elohim, the Eternal Father, not in violation of natural law but in accordance with a higher manifestation thereof; and the offspring from that association of supreme sanctity, celestial Sireship, and pure though mortal maternity, was of right to be called the 'Son of the Highest' " (Talmage, 81).

According to President Smith, "Mary was married to Joseph for time. No man could take her for eternity because she belonged to the Father of her divine Son." (*Box Elder News*, Jan. 28, 1915.)

The term *only begotten* means exactly what it says. Though God the Father is the pre-earth father of all His children conceived and born in the spirit world—of whom Jesus was the first—only this Son, Jesus the Christ, also had a Heavenly Father of the flesh.

See also: Jesus Christ; Son of God

Open Your Hearts

Occasionally the Lord will admonish us to open our hearts (D&C 31:7; 63:1). According to Smith and Sjodahl, "To 'open' one's 'heart' is to listen to the Word of God with love and affection, and with an eager desire to understand it and to do the will of God" (SS, 373).

In opening your heart you allow the free-flowing circulation of the eternal life-giving substance of the Spirit, which is the opposite of hardening your heart.

See also: Harden Their Hearts

Oracles

The term *oracles* is found in Doctrine and Covenants 90 and 124. In the first instance, the Lord reveals that the "oracles" should be given unto the Church by the Prophet Joseph (D&C 90:4–5). "The interpretation of the term 'oracles' as used in this revelation is given in the dictionary to be 'an infallible authority.' " (CHMR 1:388). Thus, the Church was assured that an "infallible authority" would be left even if something should befall the Prophet Joseph. When the powers of darkness succeeded in snuffing out the light of Joseph's mortal life, those oracles remained ever bright upon the earth with the Twelve Apostles.

In a later revelation, the Lord spoke of the "oracles in your most holy places" (D&C 124:39). Of this meaning, Smith and Sjodahl wrote: " 'Oracles' means the place in which the divine revelations are received. The name is applied to the sacred Scriptures, which contain the Word of God, and also to the part of the Temple called the Holy of

Holies, where the presence of God was manifested (1 Kgs. 8:6; 2 Chron. 4:20; Ps. 28:2)." (SS, 778.)

In Doctrine and Covenants 124:126, the Lord indicated that the First Presidency was "to receive the oracles for the whole church." In other words, they are the designated body to receive *revelations* — the oracles of God — for the Church, and in that sense they are the *living oracles*.

See also: Apostle; First Presidency of the Church

Orange, Ohio

During the month of October 1831, three conferences of the Church were held in northeastern Ohio. The first was at the home of John Johnson in Hiram, Portage County, where the Prophet was staying. The second was held in Kirtland, Geauga County, and the third was held on October 25 and 26, at Orange, Cuyahoga County, Ohio. The conference convened at the home of Irenus Burnett and was described as "very important."

Elder B. H. Roberts said: "Very many of the brethren holding the Priesthood addressed the conference, and each one expressed his willingness to consecrate all he possessed to God and His cause. The minutes of the Prophet's remarks . . . stand as follows: 'Brother Joseph Smith, Jun., said that he had nothing to consecrate to the Lord of the things of the earth, yet he felt to consecrate himself and family.' . . .

" 'Brother Hyrum Smith said that he thought best that the information of the coming forth of the Book of Mormon be related by Joseph himself to the Elders present, that all might know for themselves.'

" 'Brother Joseph Smith, Jun., said that it was not intended to tell the world all the particulars of the coming forth of the Book of Mormon; and also said that it was not expedient for him to relate these things.' " (HC 1:219–20, footnote.)

At this conference, the revelation contained in section 66 was received. Orange was located about twelve miles south of Kirtland, near the Chagrin River.

See also: Book of Mormon; Translation; Urim and Thummim

Ordain

The words *ordain* and *ordained* are used a number of times with various meanings in the Doctrine and Covenants. A divine decree for example, is represented in a statement such as "King Immanuel . . . hath ordained, before the world was, that which would enable us to redeem them out of their prison" (D&C 128:22).

The calling of one to a position, though not a priesthood office, is illustrated with Newel K. Whitney's appointment to be ordained the "agent" in Kirtland (D&C 63:45) or the calling of six brethren to be ordained stewards over the revelations which would comprise the forthcoming Book of Commandments (D&C 70:3). Certain foods are described as being "ordained [set apart or made available] for the use of man" (D&C 89:10, 12, 14). Presiding officers of both the Aaronic and Melchizedek priesthoods are spoken of as being ordained (permanently set apart) to their callings (D&C 107:21).

Certain ordinances are referred to as being ordained of God (D&C 124:39). Joseph Smith spoke of his being "ordained from before the foundation of the world" (D&C 127:2), and the Lord speaks of those "who have been ordained among you, whom I have called but few of them are chosen," which further illustrates the principle of foreordination. Offices in the priesthood are to be conferred through ordination (D&C 20:39; 41:9; 107:39).

Six months after he was set apart as the First Counselor in the Presidency of the Church, Sidney Rigdon was called to be the "spokesman" for Joseph Smith with the promise that he would be ordained (set apart) to this calling (D&C 100:9). In March 1829, the Lord promised the Prophet Joseph that three witnesses were to be called and ordained (set apart) to bear testimony of the Book of Mormon (D&C 5:11). These witnesses were later charged to seek out the Twelve Apostles (D&C 18:37) and were responsible for laying hands

upon the Twelve and conferring their apostolic blessings upon them. It was not until 1843 that the Prophet Joseph bestowed the fulness of the keys of authority upon the Twelve (TS 5:650, 651, 698; DS 1:259).

President Joseph Fielding Smith commented on the use of the term *ordained* in the early history of the Church. "When the Prophet received the Presidency of the High Priesthood, the history says that he was *ordained*. [See D&C 107:22.] Today we would say *set apart*. They used the term *ordain* in the early days of the Church for everything, even when sisters were *set apart* to preside in the Relief Society." (DS 3:106; CHMR 1:61, 126.) Thus, in grasping the full meaning of the word *ordain*, one must look at the context in which it was used and relate this to its *present* usage in the Church.

At the present time, men are *ordained* to the offices of deacon, teacher, priest, elder, seventy, high priest, bishop, patriarch, and Apostle. In addition, at the present time when the senior Apostle has been set apart to his office as the prophet, seer, revelator, and President of The Church of Jesus Christ of Latter-day Saints, the term *ordain* is used in this priesthood ordinance (see En., Dec. 1985, pp. 2–7).

The difference between being ordained and being set apart is that to be ordained is to receive an office that one holds forever even though additional offices or calls may come. For example, though he stood as the senior Apostle in the Church, President Spencer W. Kimball once declared to an assembled priesthood body, "I am a deacon. . . . and a teacher, and a priest" (CR, Apr. 1975, p. 117). In being "set apart," one receives no permanent office or title. Nevertheless, whether one is ordained or set apart to an office, his stewardship extends only to the day of his release. Thus, for example, if a man is released from presiding over a ward as a bishop, he retains his ordination but not his *office*. If, at any future date, he were once again called to serve as an active bishop, he would merely be *set apart* to his office for he had previously received his *ordination*.

Ordained unto this Condemnation

The only ones who will ever know the miserable consequences of becoming a son of perdition will be "those who are ordained [sentenced or consigned] unto this condemnation" (D&C 76:48). These unhallowed "angels of the devil," were not foreordained to this fate, but by their own actions have chosen the calamitous consequences of rebelling against righteousness. Their fate is "ordained" because it is a divine decree.

Smith and Sjodahl have written: "God has ordained that rebellion against Him shall result, if persisted in to the end, in misery,

but He has not foreordained anyone to that fate. A legislature may ordain that thieves must be imprisoned and murderers killed, but that does not mean that it has foreordained any individual, or any number of individuals, to do that which ends in imprisonment, or death. The sons of Perdition pursue their course according to their own choice, and not as victims of inexorable destiny." (SS, 455.)

See also: Sons of Perdition

Order of Enoch

A single reference to "the order of Enoch" appears in the revelation on the three degrees of glory (D&C 76:57). Speaking of those who inherit the celestial glory, the Lord declared them to be "priests of the Most High, after the order of Melchizedek, which was after the order of Enoch, which was after the order of the Only Begotten Son."

Smith and Sjodahl indicate that "the order of Melchizedek" meant that they held the priesthood of that name (SS, 457). The Doctrine and Covenants explains that this priesthood used to be called "the Holy Priesthood, after the Order of the Son of God" (D&C 107:2–4).

Elder Bruce R. McConkie equates the order of Enoch with the United Order, which he defined as follows: "*The United Order is not a communal system; it is not one under which all things are held in com-*

mon. Rather, after a person has made his consecration, the Lord's agent forthwith reconveys to the donor 'as much as is sufficient for himself and family' (D&C 42:32), each 'according to his family, according to his circumstances and his wants and needs' (D&C 51:3), 'inasmuch as his wants are just.' (D&C 82:17.)'' (MD, 548, 813.)

This order, which the people of Enoch lived, created a Zion amongst them ''because they were of one heart and one mind, and dwelt in righteousness; and there was no poor among them'' (Moses 7:18).

See also: Order of Melchizedek; United Order

Order of Melchizedek

Those men who obtain the celestial kingdom must be ''priests after the order of Melchizedek'' (D&C 76:57). This ''order'' is the order of the holy Melchizedek Priesthood, which encompasses all who have been ordained unto this priesthood and who by their ''fruits'' have proven themselves worthy of holding it eternally (D&C 84:33–42; 107:1–12).

See also: Melchizedek Priesthood; Order of Enoch

Order of the Only Begotten Son

''The order of the Only Begotten Son'' spoken of in Doctrine and Covenants 76:57 is the same as ''the Holy Priesthood, after the Order of the Son of God,'' which we presently call the Melchizedek Priesthood (D&C 107:1–4).

See also: Holy Priesthood After the Order of the Son of God; Melchizedek Priesthood

Order of This Priesthood

The meaning of ''the order of this priesthood'' (D&C 107:40), according to Smith and Sjodahl, is ''the priesthood of a patriarch'' (SS, 705). President Joseph Fielding Smith wrote that ''the priesthood which prevailed from Adam to Moses was *the Patriarchal Order*, yet it was only a part of the Melchizedek Priesthood. *All of the ancient patriarchs were high priests, but the direction of the Church in those days was by patriarchs.* After the time of Moses, when the Melchizedek Priesthood was withdrawn from Israel, this *order* as it is called, of *Patriarchal Priesthood*, did not continue. There came, then, the Aaronic Priesthood, with the prophets holding the Melchizedek Priesthood as high priests. The bestowal of the higher authority, however, had to come by special designation.'' (DS 3:104.)

Thus, while the prophets from Adam to Moses acted in administrative and presiding positions while holding the patriarchal priesthood, the patriarchal office today is one of blessing, not one of administration, for, in all such callings, the patriarch serves under the direction of a presiding high priest. On a stake level this is a stake president, and on a general Church level this is the President of the Church.

This doctrine was emphasized in an editorial by Elder John Taylor, who said: "The president of the church presides over all patriarchs . . . , and this presidency does not depend so much upon genealogy as upon calling, order, and seniority" (TS 6:921, June 1, 1845).

It should be remembered that a patriarch is an office of calling within the Melchizedek Priesthood and does not constitute a separate priesthood. "All priesthood is divine authority, but it is divided into the two grand heads, Melchizedek and Aaronic, although we speak of the order of the evangelist, or patriarch, and the order of the Levites. We could also speak of the order of high priests, or the order of seventies, or of elders, meaning the calling of those who hold these offices." (DS 3:104.)

See also: Office of Priesthood and Patriarch; Patriarch

Ordinance

Elder John A. Widtsoe said, "An ordinance is an earthly symbol of a spiritual reality. It is usually also an act symbolizing a covenant or agreement with the Lord. Finally, it is nearly always an act in anticipation of a blessing from heaven. An ordinance, then, is distinctly an act that connects heaven and earth, the spiritual and the temporal." (PC, 107.)

Elder Bruce R. McConkie has distinguished between two kinds of ordinances: (1) "*Ordinance-commandments,*" which include all God's decrees, laws, commandments, statutes, and judgments; and (2) "*Ordinance-rites.*" This latter group of rites and ceremonies could "be pictured as a smaller circle within the larger circle of ordinance-commandments." Examples of these rites would be baptism and celestial marriage. In "ordinance-rites," a prayer is offered and a specified action takes place. (MD, 548–49.)

It is because men have strayed from God's ordinances and broken their covenants that darkness rules the minds of many (D&C 1:15). The covenant of the Saints of God is "that we will walk in all the ordinances of the Lord" (D&C 136:2–4). Joseph Fielding Smith has emphatically stated that "*all of the ordinances of the gospel pertain to the celestial kingdom of God.*

"We are not preaching the gospel with the idea of trying to save people in the terrestrial world. *Ours is the salvation of exaltation.*" (DS 2:190.)

See also: Baptism; Endowment; Gift of the Holy Ghost; Ordinance of the Washing of Feet; Outward Ordinances

Ordinance of the Washing of Feet

At the time the School of the Prophets was established, one of the criteria given by the Lord for entrance into that establishment was that members be "received by the ordinance of the washing of feet" (D&C 88:139–41). This ordinance was originally "the custom of the Jews under their law," said the Apostle John (JST, John 13:10). Additionally, however, the Lord instituted it as a sacred ordinance among his chosen disciples at the Last Supper (John 13:4–17).

It was reinstituted on December 27, 1832, by revelation to Joseph Smith. The Prophet administered the ordinance to a group of brethren gathered in conference on January 23, 1828 (HC 1:323–24).

Later, in remarks delivered to the Twelve Apostles on November 12, 1835, Joseph said: "The item to which I wish the more particularly to call your attention tonight is the ordinance of the washing of feet. This we have not done as yet, but it is necessary now, as much as it was in the days of the Savior; and we must have a place prepared, that we may attend to this ordinance aside from the world. . . .

"It was never intended for any but official members. It is calculated to unite our hearts, that we may be one in feeling and sentiment, and that our faith may be strong, so that Satan cannot overthrow us, nor have any power over us here!" (HC 2:307–9.)

During the dedication of the Kirtland Temple, the choir sang a verse from the hymn, "The Spirit of God Like a Fire Is Burning," which said: "We'll wash and be washed, and with oil be anointed, Withal not omitting the washing of feet." Two days later, the ordinance was commenced among the leaders of the Church. (HC 2:426, 430–31.)

Other Sheep

See: Branch of the House of Jacob

Other Wise Documents and Instructions

In eulogizing Joseph Smith, John Taylor spoke of the Book of Mormon, the Doctrine and Covenants, "and many other wise documents and instructions for the benefit of the children of men" which the Prophet had brought to light (D&C 135:3). Those "other documents and instructions" are found in additional publications such as the books of Moses, Abraham, Joseph Smith, and the Articles of Faith, which are all located in the Pearl of Great Price. The numerous corrections and clarifications of the Bible found in the Joseph Smith Translation are additional "wise documents and instructions."

Furthermore, Joseph's prophetic pronouncements as found in such publications as the six volumes of Church History, which he penned, the *Teachings of the Prophet Joseph Smith* — a classic in Mormon literature — and the numerous other sources in which his inspired utterances may be found, could all be classified as part of the "many other wise documents and instructions" spoken of by Elder Taylor.

The extent of Joseph's contribution to sacred writ is described by Elder Bruce R. McConkie: "Here is a man who has given to our present world more holy scripture than any single prophet who ever lived; indeed, he has preserved for us more of the mind and will and voice of the Lord than the total of the dozen most prolific prophetic penmen of the past" (En., May 1976, p. 95).

Outer Darkness

The concept of outer darkness is mentioned twice in the Doctrine and Covenants (D&C 101:91; 133:73). This place is described by an ancient prophet who said, "The spirits of the wicked, yea, who are evil—for behold, *they have no part nor portion of the Spirit of the Lord*; for behold, they chose evil works rather than good; therefore the spirit of the devil did enter into them, and take possession of their house . . . ; these shall be cast out into *outer darkness*; there shall be weeping, and wailing, and gnashing of teeth, and this because of their own iniquity, being led captive by the will of the devil" (Alma 40:13; italics added).

Those individuals who have committed sins that require redemption through hell, who will become inhabitants of the teles-tial kingdom, will be in "outer darkness" until their day of redemption, which will be the final resurrection at the end of the Millennium (GT 1:85; see also D&C 76:81–85; AF, 92; DS 2:22–23).

Those designated as sons of perdition will receive a resurrected body without glory. Following the final conflict between good and evil, heaven and hell, these dreadful beings will be eternally confined to "a kingdom which is not a kingdom of glory" for "they were not willing to enjoy that which they might have received" (D&C 88:24, 32). They will join the devil and his hellish host of fallen angels in a banishment to an outer darkness where the tiniest rays of the Light of Christ will be unavailable.

See also: Hell; Kingdom Which Is Not a Kingdom of Glory; Sons of Perdition; Telestial Kingdom

Outward Ordinances

A great revelation on priesthood revealed that the lesser or Aaronic Priesthood "has power in administering outward ordinances" (D&C 107:14, 20). The nature of these ordinances was discussed by Elder Orson Pratt, who said: "The Priesthood of Aaron, being an appendage to the higher Priesthood, has power to administer in *temporal* [or outward] *ordinances*, such as that of baptism for remission of sins, the administration of the Lord's Supper, and in attending to temporal things for the benefit of the people of God'' (JD 18:363–64; italics added).

President Joseph Fielding Smith taught: "We may be sure that the Aaronic Priesthood will never be taken from the earth while mortality endures, for there will always be need for *temporal direction* and the performance of *ordinances pertaining to the preparatory Gospel*'' (CHMR 1:62; italics added).

A further understanding of the outward (temporal) ordinances of the preparatory gospel is provided by Elder John A. Widtsoe: "Baptism is a logical sequence of faith," he said. "Every ordinance becomes . . . a necessary *tangible outward evidence* of some phase of that inward conviction called faith." (ER, 196–97; italics added.) Less tangible ordinances, such as the laying on of hands—whereby the

gift of the Holy Ghost is received —and the sealing blessings of the temple, pertain to the higher priesthood, which is Melchizedek.

See also: Ordinances; Preparatory Gospel

Ozondah

In April 1832, the Lord instructed Newel K. Whitney to retain responsibility for the "Ozondah," which was the *mercantile establishment in Kirtland* (D&C 104:39–41; pre-1981 edition). The use of the word *Ozondah* was a precautionary measure which the Lord occasionally employed to prevent enemies of the Church from knowing what his purposes were (HC 1:255). The term *Ozondah* is found only within this revelation.

P

Packard, Noah

In 1841, Noah Packard was called as a counselor to Don Carlos Smith, who presided over the high priests quorum in Nauvoo (D&C 124:136). He was born May 7, 1796, at Plainfield,

Hampshire County, Massachusetts, and joined the Church on June 1, 1832.

Within a year after joining the Church he served a short mission to the east and on May 6, 1833, was ordained an elder. He presided over a branch in Parkman,

Ohio, and served on the high council in Kirtland. Packard performed several missions, without purse or scrip, between 1841 and 1845. It is said that during this time he traveled about 15,000 miles on foot, preached 480 discourses, and baptized 53 people.

He migrated to Utah in 1850, eventually settling in Springville, where he served as a counselor in a branch presidency. The following statement by Andrew Jenson is a fitting tribute to Packard's life: "His death took place Feb. 17, 1860, at Springville. He died as he had lived firm and unshaken in the gospel of Christ, being in fellowship with his brethren and leaving many friends to lament his loss." (Jenson 2:685.)

Page, Hiram

In September 1830, the Lord gave a revelation in which he stressed that the right to receive revelation for the Church rested only with its President (D&C 28:2). The revelation was necessitated by the claims of Hiram Page, a brother-in-law of the Whitmer boys, that he was receiving revelation for the Church via a so-called seer stone in his possession. Oliver Cowdery was specifically counseled by the Lord to tell Page that Satan had deceived him, for that which had come from the stone was not from God (D&C 28:11).

Prior to this foray in false revelation, Page had been privileged to stand along with seven other men and view the reality of the gold plates from which the Book of Mormon was translated. His signature at the beginning of that sacred publication bears record of this unique experience. Although he endured the persecutions of mobs in Jackson County and helped to found the city of Far West, Missouri, as a home for the Saints, he severed his connection with the Church in 1838.

In spite of his remaining outside the faith fostered by the Book of Mormon until his dying day, his knowledge of the truthfulness of the book never waned. Some years after the death of Page, one of his children wrote the following: "I knew my father to be true and faithful to his testimony of the divinity of the Book of Mormon until the very last. Whenever he had an opportunity to bear his testimony to this effect, he would always do so, and seemed to rejoice exceedingly in having been privileged to see the plates and thus become one of the Eight Witnesses." (Jenson 1:278.)

See also: Book of Mormon; Stone, That

Page, John E.

The call of John E. Page to fill a vacancy in the Quorum of the Twelve Apostles is recorded in a revelation received July 8, 1838 (D&C 118:6). His position within that quorum is again mentioned in a later revelation (D&C 124:129). Page was baptized by Martin Harris's brother Emer on August 18, 1833.

"In May, 1836, he was called to go on a mission to Canada, to which he objected for the reason that he was destitute of clothing. The Prophet Joseph took off his coat and gave it to him, telling him to go, and the Lord would bless him." (Jenson 1:92.) During the two years in which he labored, he baptized over six hundred people. During the persecutions in Missouri, he lost his wife and two children, "who died as martyrs for their religion, through extreme suffering, for the want of the common comforts of life."

He had a tendency to disobey counsel and occasionally found himself at odds with the Prophet and other members of the Twelve. For example, though called to accompany Orson Hyde on a mission to Jerusalem, Page failed to leave American soil. On another occasion he reversed the actions of three members of the Twelve, following their departure from the branch at Cincinnati. His spiritual demise is written in the following words by Andrew Jenson: "Soon after Pres. [Joseph] Smith's death, an advertisement appeared in the Beaver (Penn.) 'Argus,' that Elder John E. Page was out of employment and would preach for anybody that would sustain his family."

Elder Page was disfellowshipped from the Quorum of the Twelve on Feb. 9, 1846, after which he became very bitter against his former associates and advised the Saints to accept the apostate James J. Strang as their leader. Soon afterwards he left Nauvoo, and after traveling about 120 miles he met a company of Saints coming from Canada. These were advised by Page to accompany him to Voree, Wisconsin, the site designated by Strang as the gathering place. A few were deceived, but the majority continued on to Nauvoo. Page was excommunicated from the Church on June 26, 1846, and died in obscurity near Sycamore, Illinois, in the fall of 1867. (Jenson 1:93.)

Palms in Our Hands

The Prophet petitioned the Lord to remember the Saints, that on the day of resurrection they might come forth with "palms in [their] hands" (D&C 109:76). John the Revelator saw "a great multitude, which . . . stood before the Lamb, clothed with white robes, and palms in their hands" (Rev. 7:9). The palms in the hands of these celestial Saints are "the antitype to Christ's entry into Jerusalem amidst the palm-bearing multitude. . . . The palm branch is the symbol of joy and triumph." (DNTC 3:495.) Surely, the joy of being in the eternal presence of the Father and Son is the ultimate triumph.

Parable

Consistent with his style of teaching in the New Testament, our Lord used parables to illustrate his messages in the Doctrine and Covenants. In several instances, an explanation is given of New Testament parables (D&C 45:56; 86). The parable of the fig tree is referred to twice (D&C 35:16; 45:34–39); the wheat and the tares twice (D&C 86; 101:65–66); and the parable of the redemption of Zion also twice (D&C 101:43–62; 103:21).

Three unique parables are found in the Doctrine and Covenants: the man with the twelve sons (D&C 38:24–27); the degrees of glory (D&C 88:51–61); and the woman and the unjust judge (D&C 101:81–95).

Elder James E. Talmage gave the following definition of a parable: "The essential feature of a parable is that of comparison or similitude, by which some ordinary, well-understood incident is used to illustrate a fact or principle not directly expressed in the story. The popular thought that a parable necessarily rests on a fictitious incident is incorrect; for, inasmuch as the story or circumstance of the parable must be simple and indeed commonplace, it may be real. . . . The narrative or incident upon which a parable is constructed may be an actual occurence or fiction; but, if fictitious, the story must be consistent and probable, with no admixture of the unusual or miraculous. . . . The parable is designed to convey some great spiritual truth." (Talmage, 298.)

Paradise of God

The term *paradise* is sparingly scattered through the scriptures, being used a total of ten times. Its specific usage in the Doctrine and Covenants is confined to section 77, verses 2 and 5, in which "the paradise of God" is mentioned. This heavenly habitation has been described as follows: "Paradise is the abode of the spirits of the just pending the day of their resurrection. (Alma 40:11–14.) Paradise is not heaven; it is not the ultimate home of the saints; it is not the abode of saved beings. See Luke 16:19–31." (DNTC 1:824; see also 2:447; 3:447.)

When the Savior spoke to the thief on the cross, he did not promise him salvation based upon "deathbed repentance," but rather said: "This day thou shalt be with me in the world of spirits: then I will teach you . . . and answer your inquiries" (TPJS, 309; Luke 23:43). This declaration was in keeping with a previous promise that the "dead" would soon hear the voice of the Son of God (John 5:25).

That there is a paradise of happiness for the righteous and prison for the wicked is made clear in the scriptures (D&C 138; see especially verses 12, 20–22, 28–31; DS 2:228–30). Joseph Smith taught that "the spirits of the just are exalted to a greater and more glorious work; hence they are blessed in their departure to the world of spirits. Enveloped in flaming fire, they are not far from us, and know and understand our thoughts, feelings, and motions, and are often pained therewith." (TPJS, 326.)

Paradisiacal Glory

Although the term *paradisiacal glory* is not found in the Doctrine and Covenants, it is defined in this volume in order that the concept of a "new heaven and new earth" might be more readily understood. The tenth article of faith states, "We believe . . . that Christ will reign personally upon the earth; and, that the earth will be renewed and receive its paradisiacal glory."

President Joseph Fielding Smith stated: "Too many have the idea that this has reference to the celestialized earth, but this is *not* the case. It refers to the *restored earth* as it will be when Christ comes to reign. This is taught in Isaiah 65:17–25, and in the Doctrine and Covenants, section 101:23–31. . . .

. . . Now in time past this earth had a paradisiacal glory, and then came the fall, bringing a change, and that change has been upon the earth in the neighborhood of 6,000 years.

"*This earth is to be renewed and brought back to the condition in which it was before it was cursed through the fall of Adam.* When Adam passed out of the Garden of Eden, then the earth became a telestial world, and it is of that order today. I do not mean a telestial glory such as will be found in telestial worlds after the resurrec-

tion, but a telestial condition which has been from the days of Adam until now and will continue until Christ comes. . . .

"It will become a terrestrial world then and will so remain for 1,000 years. . . . At the end of the world *the earth will die; it will be dissolved, pass away, and then it will be renewed, or raised with a resurrection.* It will receive its resurrection to become a celestial body." (DS 1:84–88.)

See also: Day of Transfiguration; End of the World; Millennium; New Heaven and a New Earth; Terrestrial

Partridge, Edward

The name of Edward Partridge appears in the following sections of the Doctrine and Covenants: 41, 42, 50, 51, 52, 57, 58, 60, 64, 115, and 124. He served as the first bishop of the Church, being called by revelation to that position on February 4, 1831 (D&C 41:9). As a young boy "he remembers that the Spirit of the Lord strove with him a number of times, insomuch that his heart was made tender and he went and wept; and that sometimes he went silently and poured the effusions of his soul to God in prayer."

Bishop Partridge was one of the early converts from the Campbellite movement, being baptized on December 11, 1830. Joseph Smith described this new convert as "a pattern of piety, and one of the Lord's great men, known by his steadfastness and patient endurance to the end." The Lord himself issued this compliment of Bishop Partridge: "His heart is pure before me, for he is like unto Nathanael of old, in whom there is no guile" (D&C 41:11).

He was present at the dedication of the site for the yet-to-be-built temple at Independence, Missouri, and was also in attendance at the dedication of the Kirtland Temple. During the persecutions in Missouri, he was taken from his home and publicly tarred and feathered, having rejected their offer of clemency if he would renounce his faith. To this request he replied: "I told them that the Saints had suffered persecution in all ages of the world; that I had done nothing which ought to offend anyone; that if they abused me they would abuse an innocent person; that I was willing to suffer for the sake of Christ. . . .

"I bore my abuse with so much resignation and meekness, that it appeared to astound the multitude, who permitted me to retire in silence, many looking very solemn, their sympathies having been touched as I thought; and as to myself, I was so filled with the Spirit and love of God, that I had no hatred toward my persecutors or anyone else." (HC 1:390–91.)

As a result of the many persecutions he endured, his health was broken and he died on May 27, 1840, at the age of forty-seven. Of his demise, the Prophet wrote: "He lost his life in conse-

quence of the Missouri persecutions, and he is one of that number whose blood will be required at their hands." This was not to be his final epitaph, however, for the Lord pronounced in a revelation in January 1841 that Edward Partridge "is with me at this time" (D&C 124:19; Jenson 1:218–22).

See also: Alam; Ark of God, Steady the; One Mighty and Strong; That Man

Patience

One of the cardinal virtues for effectively serving others is patience (D&C 4:6). The Lord has instructed us to be patient in afflictions (D&C 24:8; Alma 34:40–41), to wait patiently for answers to prayers (D&C 98:1–2; see also Mosiah 23:21), and to "continue in patience until ye are perfected" (D&C 67:13; see also Heb. 12:1). "In patience ye may possess your souls, and ye shall have eternal life," declared the Savior (D&C 101:38; Luke 21:19).

Patience is the ability to persist, to calmly, perhaps even happily, endure some temporary inconvenience for a higher reward or condition at a later time. Elder Neal A. Maxwell noted: "Patience is not indifference. Actually, it means caring very much but being willing, nevertheless, to submit to the Lord and to what the scriptures call the 'process of time.'

"Patience is tied very closely to faith in our Heavenly Father. Actually, when we are unduly impatient we are suggesting that we know what is best—better than does God. Or, at least, we are asserting that our timetable is better than His." (DSY, 1979, p. 215.)

Patriarch

The term *Patriarch* appears three times in the Doctrine and Covenants, each time referring to the office which Hyrum Smith held (D&C 124:91, 124; 135:1). The office of Patriarch to the Church is a hereditary office bestowed upon the worthy descendants of Joseph Smith, Sr., through his son Hyrum (D&C 124:91–92; see also 23:3; TPJS, 38–39; DS 3:160–65). This office should not be confused with Hyrum's additional calling as an Assistant President of the Church, in which capacity he held the keys of the kingdom jointly with his prophet-brother, Joseph (D&C 124:94–95; DS 3:165–66; 1:216–22).

Those who have succeeded Hyrum as Patriarch to the Church were called by revelation through the President of the Church and served under his direction. They hold no keys of administrative responsibility but only those keys pertaining to the bestowing of patriarchal blessings. The Patriarch to the Church is sustained as a prophet, seer, and revelator (PCG, 248).

At the October general conference in 1979, the First Presidency announced the release of the Patriarch to the Church with the following explanation: "Because of the large increase in the number of stake patriarchs and the availability of patriarchal services throughout the world, we now designate Elder Eldred G. Smith [who had been serving as Patriarch since 1947] as a Patriarch Emeritus, which means that he is relieved of all duties and responsibilities pertaining to the office of Patriarch of the Church" (CR, Oct. 1979, p. 25).

See also: Evangelical Ministers; Order of This Priesthood; Office of Priesthood and Patriarch; Patriarchal Blessings; Sealing Blessings of My Church; Smith, Hyrum

Patriarchal Blessings

In 1841 Hyrum Smith was given the "keys of the patriarchal blessings" (D&C 124:92). These blessings, given under the hands of ordained patriarchs and worthy fathers, are inspired declarations (DS 3:169–72). Each is a revelation to the recipient. One's lineage in one of the tribes of Israel is generally pronounced in such blessings, along with inspired counsel. Karl G. Maeser described these blessings as "paragraphs from the book of your possibilities" (SHP, 117).

"Since all men differ, their blessings may differ; but a patriarchal blessing always confers promises upon us, becomes a warning against failure in life, and a means of guidance in attaining the blessings of the Lord," said Elder John A. Widtsoe.

"These blessings are possibilities predicated upon faithful devotion to the cause of truth. They must be earned. Otherwise they are but empty words."

"It should always be kept in mind that the realization of the promises made may come in this or the future life. Men have stumbled at times because promised blessings have not occurred in this life. They have failed to remember that, in the gospel, life with all its activities continues forever and that the labors of the earth may be continued in heaven. Besides, the Giver of the blessings, the Lord, reserves the right to have them become active in our lives, as suits His divine purpose." (ER, 322–23.)

"Patriarchal blessings are individual blessings, sacred to those who receive them. It is not intended that patriarchal blessings should become public property," said President Joseph Fielding Smith. (DS 3:172.) This counsel was reiterated by President Harold B. Lee: "A patriarchal blessing is a sacred document to the person who has received it and is never given for publication and . . . should be kept as a private possession to the one who has received it" (CR, Oct. 1972, p. 125).

See also: Evangelical Ministers; Patriarch; Sealing Blessings of My Church

Patten, David W.

A short revelation given in April 1838 deals with a spiritual giant of great faith and courage, David W. Patten (D&C 114). Patten had been sustained a member of the Quorum of the Twelve Apostles in February 1835. His great spiritual capacity had been earlier attested to in a letter written by Joseph Smith in September 1833. Said the Prophet: "Many were healed through his instrumentality, several cripples were restored. As many as twelve that were afflicted came at a time from a distance to be healed; he and others administered in the name of Jesus, and they were made whole." (HC 1:408–9.) Jenson reported that "a woman who had suffered from an infirmity for nearly twenty years was instantly healed" by Elder Patten (Jenson 1:76).

He had many dreams and visions of future events and on at least one occasion was visited by an angelic messenger. Several times his life was threatened by mobocrats, but he courageously withstood their advances and they backed down. He bodily removed one disturber from a meeting of the Saints, prompting the saying that "David Patten had cast out one devil, soul and body."

His total commitment to consecration was evident in every facet of his life—and in his death. In the infamous battle of Crooked River, where three Saints lost their lives in attempting to defend their brethren, the shades of time were drawn for David W. Patten. To the last breath he bore a strong witness of the divinity of the work in which he had immersed himself from the day of his baptism in June 1832. In his final moments he pleaded with his wife: "Whatever you do else, do not deny the faith!"

Pointing to the lifeless body of this latter-day martyr, the Prophet Joseph declared: "There lies a man who has done just as he said he would: he has laid down his life for his friends" (Jenson 1:76–80). The Lord's pleasure with Elder Patten's life was revealed in a revelation received in January 1841: "David Patten . . . is with me at this time," proclaimed the Lord. "I have taken [him] unto myself; behold, his priesthood no man taketh from him." (D&C 124:19, 130.)

Paul

One of the great disciples of the Lord to walk this earth was the Apostle Paul. He is mentioned six times in the Doctrine and Covenants, and the authenticity of his apostolic calling is verified by the Savior (D&C 18:9). In spite of Paul's greatness, the Lord warned against those who claim celestial kinship on the basis of their devotion to specific disciples—including Paul—rather than to the Master (D&C 76:98–101).

The Prophet Joseph compared himself to Paul on several occasions in the scriptures, especially in relation to his commitment to his course in spite of persecution (D&C 127:2; JS—H 1:24). Paul's name even appears in the thirteenth article of faith, as we are reminded of those things to which we ought to cling or after which we ought to seek (Articles of Faith 1:13; Philip. 4:8).

This devoted disciple of the Master is honored for his zealous service to the truth and for his unflinching courage in the face of adversity. His consistent approach was to "straightway preach Christ," the name which he had been chosen to proclaim "before the Gentiles, and kings, and the children of Israel" (Acts 9:15, 20). His writings occupy thirteen of the twenty-seven books of the New Testament, and much of his ministry is found recorded in a fourteenth, the book of Acts. Paul sheds sublime light on divine concepts which are spoken of in the Doctrine and Covenants, such as the degrees of glory (1 Cor. 15:40–44; D&C 76; 88:28–32), salvation for the dead (1 Cor. 15:29; D&C 128), and the Fatherhood of God and man's ultimate destiny to become as God (Acts 17:28–29; 1 Cor. 8:5; Philip. 2:5, 6; D&C 132:20, 37).

The Prophet Joseph gave us a description of Paul, with whom he had evidently conversed, or at least seen and heard in vision: "He is about five feet high; very dark hair; dark complexion; dark skin; large Roman nose; short face; small black eyes, penetrating as eternity; round shoulders; a shining voice, except when elevated, and then it almost resembled the roaring of a lion. He was a good orator, active and diligent, always employing himself in doing good to his fellow man." (TPJS, 180.)

Paul's life is summarized in a statement he made near the end of his mortal sojourn: "I have fought a good fight, I have finished my course, I have kept the faith. Henceforth there is laid up for me a crown of righteousness, which the Lord, the righteous judge, shall give me at that day: and not to me only, but unto all them also that love his appearing." (2 Tim. 4:7–8.) Tradition has Paul being beheaded at Rome, placing him among the martyrs who have given their lives for the sake of Christ.

Pavilion

According to Webster, a pavilion is a covering, canopy, or tent. God's pavilion is a celestial canopy covering his presence. It is a veil that can only be rent by righteousness. In a moment of deep distress, Joseph Smith pleaded with the Lord to part his pavilion and let himself be heard (D&C 121:1, 4).

Peace

See: Ensign of Peace; Feet Shod with the Preparation of the Gospel of Peace; Peaceable Things of the Kingdom; Speak Peace to Your Mind; Standard of Peace

Peaceable Things of the Kingdom

The Lord has promised that the Comforter, who is the Holy Ghost, shall teach "the peaceable things of the kingdom" (D&C 36:2; 39:6). The Savior declared to his disciples, "Peace I leave with you. My peace I give unto you; not as the world giveth, give I unto you." (John 14:27.) Christ is the "Prince of Peace" (Isa. 9:6), and those who proclaim his gospel are the "peacemakers" who "shall be called the children of God" (3 Ne. 12:9; Matt. 5:9; DNTC 1:216).

As the Comforter testifies of the truthfulness of the gospel, and sorrow for sin takes effect, one receives the reward of peace of mind (D&C 59:23). President David O. McKay said: "No man is at peace with himself or his God who is untrue to his better self, who transgresses the law of right either in dealing with himself by indulging in passion, in appetite, yielding to temptation against his accusing conscience, or in dealing with his fellow men, being untrue to their trust. Peace does not come to the transgressor of law; peace comes by obedience to law, and it is that message which Jesus would have us proclaim among men." (CR, Oct. 1938, p. 133.)

Thus, the "peaceable things of the kingdom" are those principles of righteous living which, if lived, engender peace in one's own life as well as in the lives of those with whom one makes contact. Ultimate peace can only come by heeding the promptings of the Comforter and following the strait and narrow path which leads to a fulness of joy, even eternal life (D&C 42:61). This is that peace which the Savior promised his disciples.

Pearls . . . Cast Before Swine

On three occasions, the Lord counseled against casting pearls before swine (Matt. 7:6; 3 Ne. 14:6; D&C 41:6). The pearls of which the Savior spoke are the sacred truths and precepts of the gospel; his disciples are counseled against being indiscreet in conveying these to others (Talmage, 244). The swine—whose flesh was an abhorrence to the Israelites (Lev. 11:7; Deut. 14:8; Isa. 65:4)—are symbolic of the unbelievers, those who might treat lightly or trample upon the precious pearls of the gospel.

See also: Dogs

Pelagoram

On three different occasions, the Lord referred to Sidney Rigdon as *Pelagoram* (D&C 78:9; 82:11; 104:20, 22; pre-1981 edition). Each of these instances was in conjunction with Rigdon's participation in the Order of Enoch, or the United Order. At that particular time it was felt necessary to hide the identity of those in-

dividuals to whom the revelations were given, thus the use of pseudonyms (HC 1:255). In current editions of the Doctrine and Covenants, Rigdon's real name rather than the pseudonym is used.

See also: Rigdon, Sidney

Pennsylvania

One of the original thirteen American colonies, founded in 1681, Pennsylvania played a small but important part in the restoration of the gospel. It was from within her borders that the Prophet Joseph found his wife Emma, where much of the work of translating the Book of Mormon took place, and where the Aaronic Priesthood was restored (JS—H 1:56–75; D&C 13).

Pennsylvania also played a vital role in the founding of the United States and in its continuing history as a nation. The first and second continental congresses met within her borders, and it was here that the Declaration of Independence was signed. Later Pennsylvania's southern border became the Mason and Dixon Line, which was the dividing line between the slave and free states during the Civil War. The decisive battle of Gettysburg was fought on her soil.

See also: Harmony, Pennsylvania; Northern States; Susquehanna County; Susquehanna River

Pentecost

During the dedication of the Kirtland Temple, the Prophet Joseph petitioned the Lord to let the "anointing" of his ministers "be fulfilled upon them, as upon those on the day of Pentecost" (D&C 109:35–37). The day to which he referred was one upon which many marvelous manifestations of the Spirit occurred to the ancient Saints (Acts 2:1–17).

Joseph's request of Deity was granted, for he later recorded these words in his journal: "The Savior made His appearance to some while angels ministered to others, and it was a Pentecost and an endowment indeed, long to be remembered, for the sound shall go forth from this place into all the world, and the occurrences of this day shall be handed down upon the pages of sacred history, to all generations; *as the day of Pentecost, so shall this day be numbered and celebrated* as a year of jubilee, and time of rejoicing to the Saints of the Most High God." (HC 2:432–33; italics added.)

The meaning of Pentecost has been thus described: "In ancient Israel 'the feast of weeks' (Ex. 34:22; Deut. 16:10), or 'the feast of harvest' (Ex. 23:16), or 'the day of the firstfruits' (Num. 28:26), was celebrated 50 days after the Passover. This occasion, from the Greek word *Pentekoste* (meaning 50th) was known as the *day of Pentecost*. It was on this day of Jewish celebration, in the year our Lord was resurrected, that the promised endowment of the Holy Spirit was first enjoyed in the Christian Era." (MD, 181.)

People of the Lord

In August 1831, the Lord counseled with those who "call yourselves the people of the Lord" (D&C 63:1). According to the Prophet Joseph, "The people of the Lord [are] those who have complied with the requirements of the new covenant" (TPJS, 17). The "new covenant" includes the fulness of the gospel, with every ordinance, covenant, and commandment belonging thereto. Those who comply therewith are they who have fully taken upon themselves the name of Christ with a determination to "always remember him and keep his commandments" (D&C 20:77).

See also: New Covenant

Perdition

The term *perdition* appears only in section 76 and is used to describe both an individual—Lucifer—and a group of people—sons of perdition—all of whom will suffer an indescribable fate known only "to those who are made partakers thereof" (HC 1:366; D&C 76:25–43).

Elder Bruce R. McConkie has written: "Two persons, Cain and Satan, have received the awesome name-title *Perdition*. The name signifies that they have no hope whatever of any degree of salvation, that they have wholly given themselves up to iniquity, and that any feeling of righteousness whatever has been destroyed in their breasts. Both had great administrative ability and persuasive power in pre-existence, but both were rebellious and iniquitious from eternity. (D&C 76:25–27; 2 Ne. 2:17–18.) Both came out in open rebellion against God having a perfect knowledge that their course was contrary to all righteousness." (MD, 566; see also Moses 5:24.)

See also: Cain; Satan; Sons of Perdition

Perfect

On two continents Jesus Christ exhorted his followers to seek to be perfect (Matt. 5:48; 3 Ne. 12:48). In his sermon to the Jews the Savior only referred to his Father as being perfect but in his sermon to the Nephites, following his resurrection when he had received "all power . . . in heaven and in earth" (Matt. 28:18), he included himself as an example of perfection.

Striving to become perfect can be a frustrating experience if one expects immediate results. It requires patience (D&C 67:13) and a perspective of the larger picture of eternity. "Working toward perfection is not a one-time decision," said President Spencer W. Kimball, "but a process to be pursued throughout one's lifetime" (CR, Oct. 1978, p. 6). President Joseph Fielding Smith noted that "mortal man cannot be perfect, but the immortal man can. To reach that condition will take time and we have eternity for it." (CN, March 5, 1966, C–16; see also DS 2:18.)

President Joseph F. Smith noted, "We do not look for absolute perfection in man. Mortal man is not capable of being absolutely perfect. Nevertheless, it is given to us to be as perfect in the sphere in which we are called to be and to act, as it is for the Father in heaven to be pure and righteous in the more exalted sphere in which he acts." (GD, 132.)

Elder Bruce R. McConkie offered the following insights about seeking perfection: "If we keep two principles in mind we will thereby know that good and faithful members of the Church will be saved even though they are far from perfect in this life.

"These two principles are: (1) that this life is the appointed time for men to prepare to meet God—this life is the day of our probation; and (2) that the same spirit which possesses our bodies at the time we go out of this mortal life shall have power to possess our bodies in that eternal world.

"What we are doing as members of the Church is charting a course leading to eternal life. There was only one perfect being, the Lord Jesus. If men had to be perfect and live all of the law strictly, wholly, and completely,

420 / Perfect Day

there would be only one saved person in eternity." (DSY, 1980, pp. 78–9.)

As one strives to be perfect it would be helpful to keep the words of two modern-day Apostles in mind. Elder Neal A. Maxwell noted, "Obviously, our imperfections make God's full and final approval of our lives impossible now, but the basic course of our life can be approved" (En., Aug. 1981, p. 13). Elder Marvin J. Ashton observed, "It is a fact of life that the direction in which we are moving is more important than where we are" (En., May 1987, p. 67).

See also: Just Men Made Perfect; Perfect Day; Perfect Frame; Perfect Man; Walked with God

Perfect Day

Almost hidden in the context of an 1831 revelation is the truth that the righteous will grow brighter and brighter in light as they continue to follow God until they reach "the perfect day" (D&C 50:24). Sperry indicates this will occur when we fulfill the admonition to be as perfect as our Father and his Beloved Son are (DCC, 213; 3 Ne. 12:48).

Perfect Frame

In his vision of the redemption of the dead, President Joseph F. Smith saw that the process of the resurrection will restore one's body to its perfect frame (D&C 138:17). The missionary Amulek also taught that in the resurrection "the spirit and the body shall be reunited again in its perfect form . . . ; every thing shall be restored to its perfect frame . . . , the whole becoming spiritual and immortal, that they can no more see corruption" (Alma 11:42–45). These perfected, resurrected bodies "will no longer be quickened by blood but quickened by the spirit which is eternal and they shall become immortal and shall never die" (CR, Apr. 1917, p. 63).

Speaking of this perfected state, President Joseph Fielding Smith said: "We have reason to believe that the appearance of old age will disappear and the body will be restored with the full vigor of manhood and womanhood. Children will arise as children, for there is no growth in the grave. Children will continue to grow until they reach the full stature of their spirits. Anything contrary to this would be inconsistent. When our bodies are restored, they will appear to be in the full vigor of manhood and womanhood, for the condition of physical weakness will all be left behind in the grave." (AGQ 4:185.)

President Joseph F. Smith taught that in the resurrection "deformity will be removed; defects will be eliminated, and men and women shall attain to the perfection of their spirits, to the perfection that God designed in the beginning. It is his purpose that men and women, his children, born to become heirs of God, and joint heirs with Jesus Christ, shall be made perfect, physically as well as spiritually, through obedience to the law by which he has provided the means that perfection shall come to all his children." (GD, 23.)

See also: Resurrection

Perfect Man

The Lord speaks of Seth, son of Adam, as being "a perfect man, and his likeness was the express likeness of his father" (D&C 107:43). The Old Testament identifies Noah as a "just man and perfect in his generations" (Gen. 6:9) and Job as a man that "was perfect and upright" (Job 1:1). The footnote reference to *perfect* in the Genesis citation indicates the word comes from Hebrew, meaning "complete, whole, having integrity." While there have been many righteous men and women who have walked the "path of perfect righteousness," there has been only *One* who was perfect in the "supreme sense," the Lord Jesus Christ (MD, 567–68; Alma 13:10–12).

See also: Perfect; Seth (Son of Adam)

Perrysburg, New York

On October 5, 1833, Joseph Smith, Sidney Rigdon, and Freeman Nickerson left Kirtland for a missionary journey to Canada. They arrived in Perrysburg, Cattaraugus County, New York, on October 12, where Joseph received the revelation contained in section 100. This town was the residence of Joseph's traveling companion, "Father" Nickerson, as Joseph called him. The following day Joseph recorded: "Elder Rigdon preached to a large congregation, at Freeman Nickerson's, and I bore record while the Lord gave His Spirit in a remarkable manner" (HC 1:416–21). The town is located near the northeast boundary of Lake Erie (see map on page 296 of the 1981 edition of the D&C).

Perverse

See: Crooked

Peter

This ancient Apostle of Jesus is mentioned in five sections of the Doctrine and Covenants (D&C 7:4, 5; 13:Preface; 27:12; 49:11; and 128:10, 20). However, there are over 180 references to him in the New Testament, where his rise from the role of a humble fisherman to "the number one man in all the world" is recorded (FPM, 244).

Peter and his brother, Andrew, were "fishers" who responded to the Savior's call to become "fishers of men" by "straightway" forsaking their nets and following him (Mark 1:16–18). His given name was Simon, but this was changed to

Peter or Cephas by divine decree (Matt. 10:2; Mark 3:16; Luke 6:14; John 1:42). "Thou art Simon," said Jesus to this devoted disciple, "thou shalt be called Cephas, which is, by interpretation, a seer, or a stone" (JST, John 1:42). Thus, in the Savior's often misunderstood declaration to Peter, found in Matthew 16:15-19, He might well have said: "Thou art a seer; and upon this rock (principle of seership) I will build my church" (TRG, 137).

There is no question about Peter's preeminence among the Twelve Apostles, for his role as chief spokesman is readily seen (Matt. 15:15; 16:15-16; Mark 8:29; 9:5; 10:28; Luke 8:45; 12:41; John 6:68). Elder David O. McKay wrote that Peter "was undoubtedly appointed and set apart as the President of the Council of Twelve" (AA, 20). He, along with James and John, served as the First Presidency of the Church anciently and brought those keys of authority to the Prophet Joseph (D&C 7:7; Matt. 16:19; D&C 27:12; 128:20; TPJS, 158).

Evidently these three Apostles served in a dual capacity as members of the Quorum of the Twelve and as the First Presidency, for "there is no evidence in any scripture or prophecy declaring that these three men acted independently, or apart from the Council of the Twelve Apostles" (DS 3:152).

Of this great man, President Spencer W. Kimball said: "When Christ chose this fisherman for his first and chief apostle, he was taking no chances. He picked a diamond in the rough—a diamond that would need to be cut, trimmed, and polished by correction, chastisement, and trials—but nevertheless a diamond of real quality. The Savior knew this apostle could be trusted to receive the keys of the kingdom, the sealing and the loosing power. Like other humans, Peter might make some errors in his developing process, but he would be solid, trustworthy, and dependable as a leader of the kingdom of God." ("Peter, My Brother," SY:1971, p. 2.)

Peterson, Ziba

In October 1830, four missionaries were called to labor among the Lamanites. Among the four was a little-known man called Ziba Peterson (D&C 32:3). It appears that he was baptized on April 18, 1830, but there is some discrepancy here. In the *History of the Church*, there is record of a Richard B. Peterson baptized on that date. However, in the *Historical Record* the name appears as Richard Z. Peterson. In the Doctrine and Covenants he is referred to as Ziba Peterson. All three appear to be the same individual (HC 1:81; SS, 169).

Peterson is publicly chastised in a revelation received in August 1831 for not confessing his sins and for attempting to hide them (D&C 58:60). He was subsequently mentioned in a letter signed by the First Presidency of the Church in June 1833, wherein they said: "We deliver Brother Ziba Peterson over to the buffetings of Satan, in the name of the Lord, that he may learn not to transgress the commandments of God" (HC 1:367.) He did not return to fellowship in the faith that could have brought him the blessings of eternal life.

Pharaoh

At a time when the threat of mob action was at a high point, the Lord promised the Prophet Joseph that he would "soften the hearts of the people, as I did the heart of Pharaoh, from time to time" (D&C 105:27). The title "Pharaoh" was given anciently to the Egyptian kings. The Pharaoh to whom the Lord refers here is he who reigned in Egypt at the time of the exodus of the children of Israel (Ex. 5–15). There is no unanimity among biblical scholars as to this man's exact identity, but most believe him to be either Ramses II or his son, Menephthah (Peloubet, 506; LDSBD, 750).

Phelps, W. W.

Among those who played a dominant role in the early history of the Church was William W. (W.W.) Phelps. In fact, the fruits of his labors are still being enjoyed on a worldwide basis; for

each Sunday morning, as the Mormon Tabernacle Choir commences their theme song, "Gently Raise the Sacred Strain" (Hymns, no. 146), the words penned by Phelps decades ago are heard by countless listeners throughout the world. Other favorites such as "Praise to the Man" (Hymns, no 27) and "Now Let Us Rejoice" (Hymns, no 3) were also written by Phelps.

The name of W. W. Phelps initially appears in the Doctrine and Covenants in section 55, which is directed to him and in which he is called upon to assist Oliver Cowdery in "the work of printing, and of selecting and writing books for schools in this church" (D&C 55:4). In a later revelation he is specifically called to be a printer for the Church in the land of Zion—Jackson County, Missouri (D&C 57:11; 58:40).

Later yet he was appointed one of the "stewards" over the revelations which were to make up the Book of Commandments, the forerunner to the Doctrine and Covenants (D&C 70:1). On July 20, 1833, his house was attacked by a mob and the printing office destroyed along with the initial copies of the Book of Commandments.

Phelps took an active part in the Church in Missouri, being present when the temple lot at Independence, Missouri, was dedicated by the Prophet. He also took part in the proceedings during the excavation of the Far West temple site. He offered his life as a ransom for the Saints on one occasion and served in a stake presidency along with David and John Whitmer.

This presidency was rejected by the Saints on February 6, 1838, after which Phelps became embroiled in bitterness against the Church. His actions led to his being excommunicated on March 17, 1839. On June 29, 1840, he wrote to the Prophet Joseph and asked for forgiveness and fellowship (HC 4:141–42). In Joseph's reply, he expressed his frank forgiveness in these poetic lines: "Come on, dear brother, since the war is past, for friends at first, are friends again at last" (HC 4:162–64).

Following his return, Phelps was ever loyal and active in the cause of truth. He served on the Nauvoo city council at the time of the martyrdom and was involved in the subsequent legal entanglements. He and his wife were among the first to receive their endowments in the Nauvoo temple, and he later served as an ordinance worker there as well as in the Salt Lake Valley. He labored in various civic and governmental positions in the territory and died a faithful member of the Church on March 7, 1872. (Jenson 3:692–97.)

See also: Shalemanasseh

Pierceth all Things

See: Sharper Than a Two-Edged Sword; Still Small Voice

Pilgrims

See: Strangers and Pilgrims on Earth

Pillar of Fire

One of the great events of the Second Coming of Christ will be his appearance with his Twelve Apostles, who will stand at his right hand "in a pillar of fire, being clothed with robes of righteousness" (D&C 29:12). The descriptive term *pillar of fire* has been used on other occasions to describe great spiritual outpourings, accompanied by physical manifestations.

Father Lehi was shown marvelous truths while observing a pillar of fire resting upon a rock (1 Ne. 1:6). Two of his descendants, one of whom bore his name, were protected by a pillar of fire which later surrounded an entire body of people (Hel. 5:24, 43). The children of Israel were led from bondage by a pillar of fire (Ex. 13:21).

Inasmuch as "God dwells in everlasting burnings" (TPJS, 361), it appears that this fire, through which he occasionally manifests himself (Ex. 3:2), is a *form of celestial light*, a light so exquisite that it may appear as fire. The angel Moroni, for example, was described as having a "countenance truly like lightning" (JS—H 1:32), and the Savior's eyes have been described "as a flame of fire" (D&C 110:3).

The righteous receive a "baptism of fire," whereby they are purified to enter God's presence (D&C 20:41).

See also: Fire

Pillar of Heaven

At the Second Coming the righteous shall be "caught up to meet [Christ] in the midst of the pillar of heaven" (D&C 88:97). A pillar is a support. This phrase is possibly symbolic of the support which the righteous receive from the Savior, who is the central support of the plan of salvation. In this sense, the Redeemer, who made the resurrection possible, is a Pillar of heaven himself.

See also: Jesus Christ

Pit

In the agony of his soul, Joseph Smith cried from the confines of prison for relief, only to have the Lord indicate that yet further trials awaited him. Among those trials was the possibility of being "cast into the pit, or into the hands of murderers" (D&C 122:7). The Prophet Joseph's experience was not unlike the unjust confinement which the ancient seer after whom he was named (2 Ne. 3:14–15) experienced when he was cast into a pit and ultimately into prison (Gen. 37:24; 39).

To Joseph Smith, the pit may have symbolized the clutches of the enemies of righteousness—the murderers—who would seek and ultimately take his life. From this pit, however, there would be an escape from his enemies, for at the moment of death, the martyr's spirit soared beyond their grasp.

As the Prophet's bereaved mother looked upon the lifeless bodies of her slain sons she said: "I seemed almost to hear them say, 'Mother, weep not for us, we have overcome the world by love; we carried to them the gospel, that their souls might be saved; they slew us for our testimony, and thus placed us beyond their power; their ascendancy is for a moment, ours is an eternal triumph!' " (LMS, 325.)

Plains of Olaha Shinehah

In July 1838, the Lord spoke of "the plains of Olaha Shinehah, or the land where Adam dwelt" (D&C 117:8). President Joseph Fielding Smith said that this area "must be a part of, or in the vicinity of Adam-Ondi-Ahman. The name Olaha Shinehah may be, and in all probability is, from the language of Adam. We may without great controversy believe that this is the name which Adam gave this place, at least we may venture this as a probable guess. Shinehah, according to the Book of Abraham, is the name given to the sun. (Abraham 3:13.) It is the name applied to Kirtland when the Lord desired in a revelation to hide its identity. (Sec. 82.) Elder Janne M. Sjodahl commenting on the name, Olaha Shinehah, has said: 'Shinehah means sun, and Olaha is possible a variant of the word Olea, which is "the moon." (Abraham 3:13.) If so the plains of Olaha Shinehah would be the Plains of the Moon and the Sun, so called, perhaps because of astronomical observations there made.' We learn from the writings of Moses that the Lord revealed to the ancients great knowledge concerning the stars, and Abraham by revelations and through the Urim and Thummim received wonderful information concerning the heavens and the governing planets, or stars. It was also revealed by the Prophet Joseph Smith that Methuselah was acquainted with the stars as were others of the antediluvian prophets including Adam. So it may be reasonable that here in this valley important information was made known anciently in relation to the stars of our universe." (CHMR 2:97–98.)

Plates

Other than specific reference to "the plates of Nephi," which are discussed elsewhere in this volume, the Lord speaks several times in a general sense of "the plates" (D&C 3:19; 5:1, 4; 17:1). These "plates" are the gold plates given to the Prophet Joseph Smith and from which he translated the Book of Mormon (see JS—H 1:27–59).

See also: Book of Mormon; Plates of Nephi

Plates of Nephi

The "plates of Nephi" are spoken of in Doctrine and Covenants 10:38–45. By June 1828, Joseph Smith had completed 116 pages of translation on the Book of Mormon. Bending to pressure, he importuned the Lord to allow Martin Harris to take that translation and show it to designated individuals. Harris broke his solemn promise not to display the sheets to others than the designated few, and the translation was lost.

Besides being severely rebuked for his negligence, the Prophet Joseph was informed that he was not to retranslate what had been lost, for enemies of the Church had planned to alter the original translation and claim his seership to be spurious (HC 1:21–23). The 116 pages had been translated from the portion of the large plates of Nephi known as the book of Lehi, which contained a history of the colony of Lehi from 600 B.C. down to the reign of king Benjamin, about 120 B.C. There was a parallel set of records being kept at this same time known as the small plates of Nephi, which contained "the more part of the ministry" of those ancient people while the large plates contained "the more part of the reign of kings and the wars and contentions" of those people (1 Ne. 9:4).

Thus, the Lord in his all-knowing wisdom prepared for the eventual loss of the 116 pages of manuscript centuries before it occurred. As one of the ancient record keepers stated, "The Lord hath commanded me to make these plates for a wise purpose in him. . . . The Lord knoweth all things from the beginning." (1 Ne. 9:5–6.) The small plates of Nephi consisted of what is now the first six books in the Book of Mormon. They were attached in their original form—unabridged —to the abridged record which the ancient prophets Mormon and Moroni had prepared and which Joseph Smith would "translate by the gift and power of God" to become the Book of Mormon. They are referred to as "these plates" in the Book of Mormon, while the large plates of Nephi are referred to as the "other Plates" (1 Ne. 9; Words of Mormon).

See also: Book of Mormon; King Benjamin; Manuscript, 116 Lost Pages of

Plural Marriages

See: Concubines; Hagar; Law of Sarah; Manifesto; One Wife; Utah Commission; Whitney, Newel K.; Woodruff, Wilford

Pollute

The Lord has warned that we should not pollute holy places or ordinances (D&C 84:59; 88:134;

101:97; 105:15; 110:8; 124:46). The verb *pollute* means to defile; to make something unclean or impure; to introduce elements into something that are foreign to its nature. For example, man's body is a temple for his spirit which is the offspring of Deity (1 Cor. 3:16–17; Heb. 12:9). When man allows that body to become polluted through sin, God's Spirit "has no place in him, for he dwelleth not in unholy temples" (Mosiah 2:36–7).

Moroni warned of a day when there would be "great pollutions upon the face of the earth" (Morm. 8:31). Although this may have some reference to our modern-day ecological problems (En., Nov. 1978, p. 58), it is likely that these pollutions also referred to the filthy wave of profanity, vulgarity, and pornography that is presently engulfing the earth (En., May 1986, p. 49).

Polygamy

See: Plural Marriages

Ponder

On three occasions in the Doctrine and Covenants the Lord invites us to *ponder* His words or ways (D&C 30:3; 88:62, 71). The mother of our Savior "pondered" the experiences of that sacred night when her holy Son came into mortality as the Babe of Bethlehem (Luke 2:19). And the ancient prophet Moroni admonished futuie readers of the sacred record entrusted to his care to "ponder it in your hearts" (Moro. 10:3). The revelation in Doctrine and Covenants 138 came as a result of Joseph F. Smith's "pondering over the scriptures" (D&C 138:1).

The meaning and power of this word have been described by President Marion G. Romney: "As I have read the scriptures, I have been challenged by the word *ponder*. . . . The dictionary says that *ponder* means 'to weigh mentally, think deeply about, deliberate, meditate.' . . . Pondering is, in my feeling, a form of prayer. . . . Desiring, searching, and pondering over 'the words of eternal life,' all three of them together, as important as they are, would be inadequate without prayer." (CR, Apr. 1973, pp. 117–18.)

Pontus

In a 1918 vision, President Joseph F. Smith pondered on the "primitive [former-day] saints scattered abroad throughout Pontus, Galatia, Cappadocia, and other parts of Asia" (D&C 138:5). "Pontus [was] a large district in the north of Asia Minor, extending along the coast of the Pontus Euxinus or Black Sea, from which the name was derived. It corresponds nearly to the modern Trebizond." (Peloubet, 524.) It is mentioned three times in the New Testament (Acts 2:9; 18:2; 1 Pet. 1:1). It can be found in section E3 of map 13 in the LDS Edition of the King James Version of the Bible (see also maps 20, 21, 22).

Poor

The term *poor* is used basically in two senses in the Doctrine and Covenants. In most cases it refers to those who are needy or destitute, and the Saints are consistently commanded to help alleviate the suffering of such souls (D&C 38:35; 42:30; 56:16; 136:8). These individuals are not exempt from keeping the commandments, for strict compliance to God's laws is required of them as of others (D&C 56:17–18; 58:47).

There is another group of "poor" spoken of in scripture, usually in association with the "meek" (D&C 35:15; 88:17). These are "the poor in spirit who come unto me," declared the Savior. They are "the meek [who] shall inherit the earth" (3 Ne. 12:3, 5; D&C 56:18; 88:17, 26).

This latter category consists of "those who are humble and contrite, who have a broken heart and a contrite spirit, who are devoid of pride, self-righteousness, and self-conceit . . . , who accept Christ by accepting his gospel. They gain entrance to the Church or kingdom on earth and become heirs of the kingdom or celestial world in the realms of immortality" (DNTC 1:215.)

Power of Godliness

In 1832, the Lord emphatically declared that without the

authority and ordinances of the priesthood, "the power of godliness is not manifest unto men in the flesh" (D&C 84:19–21). President Charles W. Nibley stated that "in the administration of it [the priesthood] we have seen and do see the power of godliness. . . . We see it in the temples of the Lord; we see it in the sick rooms; we see it manifested in presidencies of stakes, bishoprics of wards. In all the leadership of the priesthood you see that same power of godliness. . . . It is the power of godliness, of godly lives. *It is the power of godly men and godly women, through the ordinances of the priesthood made manifest*; and everyone shares in it." (CR, Apr. 1927, pp. 26–27; italics added.)

The power of godliness, or *the power to become like unto God*, is particularly manifest in the higher ordinances administered in the temples (DS 2:143). These saving ordinances provide the keys whereby one may ultimately receive a fulness of the glory of the Father (see D&C 93:11–20).

See also: Fulness of the Glory of the Father

Power of Heaven

See: Power of the Priesthood

Power of the Priesthood

When the prophet Isaiah admonished Israel to put on her strength, he envisioned her putting on the authority and power of the priesthood (Isa. 52:1; D&C 113:7–9; 2 Ne. 8:24; 3 Ne. 20:36). The "powers of heaven" (D&C 121:34–36) are synonymous with the "power of the priesthood." However, as Bishop H. Burke Peterson declared, "Power and authority in the priesthood are not necessarily synonymous. All of us who hold the priesthood have the authority to act for the Lord, but the effectiveness of our authority—or if you please, the power that comes through that authority—depends on the pattern of our lives; it depends on our rightousness." (CR, Apr. 1976, p. 50.)

Thus, to have received authority is not sufficient to guarantee the exercise of power. Just as the amount of light emanating from a given source will depend upon the power which is supplied to that source, so will the effectiveness of the priesthood be determined by its power source. Celestial conduct brings forth priesthood power, and conduct which is terrestrial or telestial tarnishes and corrodes the conduits of priesthood power.

President John Taylor observed that "it is the intercourse and communication of the priesthood in heaven that gives power, life and efficacy to the living priesthood on earth" (GK, 130). Celestial channels of communication are maintained, as the Lord observed, "only upon the principles of righteousness" (D&C 121:36).

Bishop H. Burke Peterson summarized: "Success in the priesthood depends on the pattern of our life. When we learn to be led by the Spirit, then the priesthood authority we have will become priesthood power, the power to change lives for the better, to cause miracles to happen in the lives of boys and girls and fathers and mothers." (CR, Oct. 1974, p. 99.)

See also: Rights of the Priesthood

Powers of Darkness

One spring morning in 1820, Joseph Smith first experienced in its fullest fury the impact of "the powers of darkness." These powers, he later recalled, had from his "infancy" combined against him in an effort to destroy him. (JS—H 1:15, 16, 20.) Such powers are exercised by the devil and those who share his demented domain (D&C 21:6; 24:1; 38:11). These powers are willingly accepted by those who reject the light of God and are often vainly employed against those whom God has chosen to lead his Church.

Elder Bruce R. McConkie has said: "Such are the ways of Satan that when the God of heaven seeks to send the greatest light of the ages into the world, the forces of evil oppose it with the deepest darkness and iniquity of their benighted realm" (En., Nov. 1975, p. 18). The "powers of darkness" may rage relentlessly, but they are limited by, and subject to, the power of light—the power of the holy priesthood as it is administered in righteousness.

See also: Darkness; Devil

Praise of the World

See: Honors of Men

Pratt, Orson

The earliest mention of Orson Pratt in the Doctrine and Covenants came only six weeks after he was baptized a member of the Church by his brother, Parley. In this revelation the Lord said, "You are my son" and are "called of me to preach my gospel" (D&C 34:3, 5). He was called as one of the original members of the Quorum of the Twelve Apostles and is later mentioned as a member of this body (D&C 124:129). His name appears in the final section of the Doctrine and Covenants as one who is called upon to organize a pioneer company (D&C 136:13).

A full listing of his missionary journeys would occupy much space, for he was constantly responding to the charge given him by the Lord in 1830 to "preach my gospel." He crossed the Atlantic Ocean sixteen times in his missionary labors. He had a keen intellect, being much interested in mathematics and astronomy. While crossing the plains with the pioneers, Orson took astronomical and other scientific observations to determine the latitude and longitude of the most prominent places. He published several scientific books and pamphlets, including "Cubic and Biquadratic Equations," and at the time of his death was working on a manuscript titled "On the Differential

Calculus, Containing Original Principles."

He was no less a writer in the realm of religion; his prolific pen produced numerous tracts, articles, and books which explained and defended the principles of the kingdom of God. He served as the Church Recorder and Historian from 1874 until his death on October 3, 1881. His service in the Quorum of the Twelve ran from his ordination in the spring of 1835 until his death on October 3, 1881. However, there was an almost six-month period in which he did not serve, which caused a reordering of his status in Apostolic seniority. (CA 1978:106.)

The *Deseret News* eulogized him as follows: "Orson Pratt was truly an Apostle of the Lord. Full of integrity, firm as a rock to his convictions, true to his brethren and to his God, earnest and zealous in defense and proclamation of the truth, ever ready to bear testimony to the latter-day work, he had a mind stored with scripture, ancient and modern, was an eloquent speaker, a powerful minister, a logical and convincing writer, an honest man and a great soul who reached out after eternal things, grasped them with the gift of inspiration, and brought them down to the level and comprehension of the common mind. Thousands have been brought into the Church through his preaching in many lands, thousands more by his writings. He set but little store on the wealth of this world, but he has laid up treasures in heaven which will make him eternally rich." (Jenson 1:87–91.)

Pratt, Parley P.

The elder of the two famous brothers, Parley P. Pratt is mentioned in seven revelations in the Doctrine and Covenants. In 1830, the Lord declared of Elder Pratt: "I will that he shall declare my gospel and learn of me and be meek and lowly of heart" (D&C 32:1). Three years later the Lord expressed pleasure with Parley's labors (D&C 97:3). His missionary labors are mentioned in four sections (D&C 49:1, 3; 50:37; 52:26; 103:30, 37), and his membership in the Quorum of the Twelve Apostles is cited in another (124:129). Parley received his apostolic calling in February 1835 as one of the original members of the Twelve.

His testimony of the restored gospel came after he followed the promptings of the Spirit, which led him to discover the Book of Mormon. His reaction to "that book of books" is recorded in his autobiography: "I opened it with eagerness. . . . I read all day; eating was a burden, I had no desire for food; sleep was a burden when the night came, for I preferred reading to sleep. As I read the spirit of the Lord was upon me, and I knew and comprehended that the book was true, as plainly and manifestly as a man comprehends and knows that he exists. My joy was now full, as it were, and I rejoiced." (APP, 36–37.)

Elder Pratt became known for sermons and poetry; some of the latter have become well-known hymns to Latter-day Saints. Among them are such favorites as "The Morning Breaks; The Shadows Flee," "An Angel from on High," and "Come, O Thou King of Kings" (Hymns, 1, 13, 59). He was the founding editor of *The Millennial Star* and wrote the famous Mormon publications, *Voice of Warning* and *Key to Theology*.

During the Missouri persecutions, he was confined to prison without benefit of trial for about eight months, from which he finally escaped on July 4, 1839—an appropriate day on which to receive liberty. Elder Pratt became one of the Church's martyrs to die a violent death when he was murdered on May 13, 1857, while performing his duties as an Apostolic missionary near the Arkansas border. His dying words to his bereaved wife, Eleanor, were: "I die a firm believer in the Gospel of Jesus Christ as revealed through the Prophet Joseph Smith, and I wish you to carry this my dying testimony. I know that the Gospel is true and that Joseph Smith was a prophet of the living God, I am dying a martyr to the faith." (BYUS 15:248.)

Prayer

One of the earliest admonitions in the Doctrine and Covenants was to "pray always, that you may come off conqueror" (D&C 10:5). Prayerful petitioning of the Lord is mentioned over ninety times in the Doctrine and Covenants and is one of the basic requirements for remaining in touch with spiritual matters. "Prayer is the passport to spiritual power," said President Spencer W. Kimball (CR, Apr. 1973, p. 153). It is a spiritually refreshing pause amidst the pressures of day-to-day living. The Lord taught that we "receive the Spirit through prayer" (D&C 63:64). Prayer is to be part of one's public and private experiences: an audible expression from the lips as well as a silent plea from the depths of one's soul (D&C 19:28; 23:6).

Elder Neal A. Maxwell made the following observations regarding prayer: "Petitioning in prayer has taught me that the vault of heaven, with all its blessings, is to be opened only by a combination lock: one tumbler falls when there is faith, a second when there is personal righteousness, and the third and final tumbler falls only when what is sought is (in God's judgment, not ours) 'right' for us. Sometimes we pound on the vault door for something we want very much in faith, in reasonable righteousness, and wonder why the door does not open. We would be very spoiled children if that vault door opened any more easily than it does now. I can tell, looking back, God truly loves me by the petitions that, in his perfect wisdom and love, he has refused to grant me. Our rejected petitions tell us not only much about ourselves, but also much about our flawless Father." (DSY, 1976, p. 200; see also 3 Ne. 18:20; D&C 109:44.)

Among the ingredients necessary for powerful, prayerful experiences should be the following: (1) *Preparation*: making sure that one has prepared both the physical setting and one's own mind and spirit for proper petitioning. (2) *Personal relationship*: endeavoring to visualize the Father with whom one is speaking; establishing a righteous rapport and friendly, yet respectful, relationship with Deity. (3) *Pleading*: Alma's spiritual success was due to his "wrestling with God in mighty prayer" (Alma 8:10). President Ezra Taft Benson cautioned that "each of us would become disturbed if a friend said the same few words to us each day, treated the conversation as a chore, and could hardly wait to finish it in order to turn on the TV and forget us" (En., May 1977, p. 33). No man should endeavor to either enter nor depart God's presence in haste. (4) *Pause*: "Part of our worthwhile, urgency prayers today can be a reverent, quiet, listening period," said Elder Marvin J. Ashton (En., May 1974, p. 37). In a celestial conversation, one must listen as well as talk. (5) *Proceed*: "After making a request through prayer, we have a responsibility to assist in its being granted," admonished President Benson (En., May 1977, p. 33).

If one is to spiritually survive in a world of wickedness, he must be fortified with celestial sustenance. Prayer is one of the basic sources of such eternal nourishment.

See also: House of Prayer; In the Season Thereof

Precepts of Men

The Lord indicated that when the light of the gospel comes to dispel the darkness of sin and ignorance, many will not receive it "because of the precepts of men" (D&C 45:28-29). Their minds will have become too clouded by false philosophies to see the light of the gospel.

A precept, according to the dictionary, is "a principle intended as a general rule of conduct." "Precepts of men" are principles of conduct, or expressions of belief, which are "empty forms without spirituality" (CBM 1:407). That is, these precepts are not based upon the "living water" of gospel truths but rather leave men either thirsting or spiritually poisoned from their ill effects (John 4:10-14). These "precepts of men" are false doctrines which cause men to err and deny the power of God (2 Ne. 28:14-15, 26; JS—H 1:19).

Some of the "precepts of men" which were denounced in an address by Elder Ezra Taft Benson in 1969 included birth control, subversive educational theories, misuse of the arts and social sciences in promoting profane philosophies, and amoral or immoral teachings (CR, Apr. 1969, pp. 10-15).

President Harold B. Lee counseled: "If we find in school texts claims that contradict the word of the Lord as pertaining to the creation of the world, the origin of man, or the determination of what is right or wrong in the conduct of human souls, we may be certain that such teachings are but the theories of men; and as men improve their learning and experimentation, the nearer will their theories coincide with the truths that God has given to His church" (SHP, 73).

The Lord has commanded parents to fortify their chidren against the "precepts of men" by bringing them up "in light and truth" (D&C 93:40; see also 68:25). In summary, the Apostle Paul's words could well be reviewed: "Beware, lest any man spoil you through philosophy and vain deceit, after the tradition of men, after the rudiments of the world, and not after Christ" (Col. 2:8).

See also: Commandments of Men

Predicated

An 1843 instruction from the Prophet Joseph Smith indicates that all blessings are predicated upon obedience to laws (D&C 130:20–21). This simply means that blessings are contingent upon obedience to the laws upon which they are based.

Preparatory Gospel

Elder Bruce R. McConkie defined the preparatory gospel as "a lesser portion of the Lord's saving truths, a portion which prepares and schools men for a future day when the fulness of the gospel may be received, a portion which of itself is not sufficient to seal men up unto eternal life or assure them an inheritance in the celestial world. . . . It is a gospel system administered by the lesser or Aaronic Priesthood. When the power to bestow the Holy Ghost is enjoyed, which power is reserved for holders of the Melchizedek Priesthood, then the fulness of the gospel is manifest." (MD, 333.)

The Lord indicated that the preparatory gospel included "the gospel of repentance and of baptism, and the remission of sins, and the law of carnal commandments" (D&C 84:27). Because of transgression and unwillingness to hearken to the prophet Moses, the fulness of the gospel was taken from ancient Israel (D&C 84:19–27).

"If Israel had remained faithful, they would have received all the blessings and privileges of the Melchizedek Priesthood, but instead they were confined to the scope of the blessings of the Aaronic Priesthood and also became subject to the measures of the Law of Moses, which contained many temporal laws, some of which were severe and drastic in their nature. This condition continued until the resurrection of Jesus Christ, when this carnal law was fulfilled and was replaced by the fulness of the gospel." (DS 3:84; Gal. 3:19–24; 3 Ne. 9:15–22; 12:18; 15:1–10.)

Presence of God the Father

The Lord revealed that once the earth "hath filled the measure of its creation, it shall be crowned with glory, even with the presence of God the Father" (D&C 88:19). The destiny of this globe is to become celestialized and serve as the habitat of celestial beings.

"What will be the condition of the people who dwell upon that glorious celestial world?" asked Elder Orson Pratt. "They will have the presence of God the Father with them. They will be permitted to dwell where he is. He will light up that world; they will have no need of the rays of the sun, as we now have, neither of the moon, nor stars, so far as light is concerned, for the Lord God will be their light and their glory from that time henceforth and forever." (JD 21:205.)

Only those who inhabit this celestial sphere will enjoy "the presence of God the Father," for the inhabitants of other kingdoms will not enjoy, nor partake of, "the fulness of the Father" (D&C 76:50-86).

See also: Celestial; Presence of the Son

Presence of the Lord Shall Be as the Melting Fire

The statement in Doctrine and Covenants 133:41 that "the presence of the Lord shall be as the melting fire that burneth" is similar to Paul's proclamation that "our God is a consuming fire"

(Heb. 12:29). Explaining this latter scripture, Elder Bruce R. McConkie has said: "Joseph Smith taught that those who gain exaltation shall 'Dwell in everlasting burnings in immortal glory!' (TPJS, 347), and that 'God Almighty himself dwells in eternal fire; flesh and blood cannot go there, for all corruption is devoured by the fire. . . . When our flesh is quickened by the Spirit, there will be no blood in this tabernacle.' (TPJS, 367.)

"And Paul applies the truth here involved to the Second Coming when the Lord's earthly vineyard shall be burned, when 'the elements shall melt with fervent heat' (2 Pet. 3:10), when the earth itself shall 'burn as an oven; and all the proud, yea, and all that do wickedly, shall be stubble.' (Mal. 4:1.)" (DNTC 3:233-34.)

Thus, the presence of this Holy Being—the Promised Messiah—will consume, as if by fire, all who are not worthy to abide his presence. It is also possible that the "melting fire" may have reference to volcanic activity with its accompanying flow of liquid lava. Another possibility for the "fervent heat" (D&C 101:25) that will accompany the Lord's coming could be the result of the terrible heat and destruction caused by nuclear weapons.

See also: Mountains Flow Down

Presence of the Son

Speaking of the ultimate destinies of men, the Lord revealed that three kingdoms of glory exist —celestial, terrestrial, and telestial (D&C 76:88). Only those who abide a celestial law will enjoy "the presence of God and his Christ forever and ever", while those who earn a terrestrial glory only merit "the presence of the Son, but not of the fulness of the Father" (D&C 76:62, 77).

To enjoy "the presence of the Son" is to have this celestial being, Jesus the Christ, visit a terrestrial sphere on occasion. "Because they were honorable men, free from lying, adultery and kindred sins, they will receive of the Savior's glory. In other words, they will be entitled to visits from the Son, but not from the Father. They do not 'obtain the crown over the kingdom of our God.' " (SS, 462.)

See also: Presence of God the Father

Presidency of the Church

See: First Presidency of the Church

Presidency of the High Priesthood

President Joseph Fielding Smith has written: "The Melchizedek Priesthood 'holds the right of presidency, and has power and authority over all the offices in the church in all ages of the world, to administer in spiritual things.' The First Presidency of the Church are also known as 'the Presidency of the High Priesthood,' and they 'have a right to officiate in all the offices,' and they 'hold the keys of all the spiritual blessings of the Church.' " (DS 3:104–5.)

Thus, the three presiding high priests of the Church (D&C 107:22) serve as the Presidency of the High Priesthood of the Church, which priesthood is Melchizedek and "is the greatest of all" (D&C 107:64). With these three men, with one presiding over the other two, are always vested the "keys of the kingdom" (D&C 81:2).

See also: Chosen by the Body; First Presidency of the Church

Presidency of the Melchizedek Priesthood

See: First Presidency of the Church; Presidency of the High Priesthood

Presidency of the School of the Prophets

In section 88, the Lord outlined the responsibilities of the "presidency of the school of the prophets" (D&C 88:127). Several months later, the First Presidency of the Church was organized and by revelation was designated as the presidency of the School of the Prophets (D&C 90:1–7). This presidency consisted of Joseph Smith, Sidney Rigdon, and Frederick G. Williams.

See also: First Presidency of the Church; School of the Prophets

President of the High Priesthood (President of the Church)

"The President of the Church . . . is president of the High Priesthood," which priesthood is Melchizedek and embodies all other priesthoods and offices within those priesthoods (DS 3:135; D&C 20:67; 107:65). It is a title to which Joseph Smith was sustained on January 25, 1832, at a conference of the Church at Amherst, Ohio. He had previously been called by the Lord as an "Apostle" and "First Elder" of the Church at the time of its organization on April 6, 1830 (D&C 20:2; HC, 1:176–78; DS 3:155–56). Within the Doctrine and Covenants, several different titles have been applied to the individual who occupies the presiding position in the Church. He is referred to as the "presiding elder" (D&C 20:67; 88:140; 124:125), the "Presiding High Priest" (D&C 107:65–66), and a "translator, a revelator, a seer, and prophet" (D&C 107:92; 124:125).

The President of The Church of Jesus Christ of Latter-day Saints is "the highest office in the world," said President Ezra Taft Benson, a man who himself served for eight years in a United States Presidential cabinet and who in 1985 was set apart to that "highest office" (CR, Oct. 1972, p. 73).

"The President of the Church holds the keys over all the church. In him is concentrated the power of the priesthood. He holds all the keys of every nature, pertaining to the dispensation of the fulness of times. All the keys of former dispensations which have been revealed are vested in him." (DS 3:135.) He may delegate portions of this power to others, in which case they are authorized to act in a particular calling. However, this *delegated authority may be withdrawn* by the same person who authorized it, or his rightful successor, whenever they feel so inspired (GD, 168; DS 3:135).

The keys of authority are vested, in their fulness, in each man called and ordained to serve as a member of the Quorum of the Twelve Apostles (DS 3:155–56; GT 1:265–66). President Harold B. Lee, eleventh President of the Church, declared: "The beginning of the call of one to be President of the Church actually begins when he is called, ordained, and set apart to become a member of the Quorum of the Twelve Apostles. Each apostle so ordained under the hand of the President of the Church, who holds the keys of the kingdom of God in concert with all other ordained apostles, has given to him the priesthood authority necessary to hold every position in the Church, even to a position of presidency over the Church if he were called by the presiding authority and sustained by a vote of a constituent assembly of the membership of the Church." (CR, Apr. 1970, p. 123.)

Thus, when one from the Quorum of the Twelve Apostles is called to the presiding position of President, he receives no additional authority or keys for he already holds them. However, these keys are held dormant by each man receiving them "until, if the occasion arises, he is called to be the presiding officer of the Church." Until that time, each must acquiesce to the senior Apostle, who presides.

"Death and life become the controlling factors" in this selection process. Nevertheless, as President Spencer W. Kimball has observed, "since the death of his servants is in the power and control of the Lord, he permits to come to the first place [position of president] only the one who is destined to take that leadership" (CR, Oct. 1972, p. 29). "The pattern divine allows for no errors, no conflicts, no ambitions, no ulterior motives. The Lord has reserved for himself the calling of his leaders over his Church." (CR, Oct. 1972, p. 28.) It should be further noted, as cautioned by President Harold B. Lee, that "only the Lord has the time table . . . , and for us to speculate or to presume is not pleasing in the sight of the Lord" (CR, Oct. 1972, p. 129).

The President of the High Priesthood is the only one authorized to declare "new doctrine" for the Church (SHP, 109–10). This may be declared in concert with his two associate Apostles in the First Presidency, for "revela-tions of the mind and will of God to the Church are to come through the Presidency" (TPJS, 111). "What they say as a presidency," declared Elder Marion G. Romney, "is what the Lord would say if he were here in person" (CR, Apr. 1945, p. 90). "What I the lord have spoken, I have spoken, and I excuse not myself . . . ; whether by mine own voice, or by the voice of my servants, it is the same" (D&C 1:38; see also 68:1–5).

Each prophet called to this presiding position is there for a "special mission for his day and time," and, in the words of President Harold B. Lee, "It is folly to compare one . . . with another. No one takes the place of another President of the Church. Each President has his own place." (CR, Oct. 1972, pp. 19, 129.)

See also: Amherst, Ohio; Apostle; Chosen by the Body; First Presidency of the Church; Man . . . Like as Moses; One Mighty and Strong; Presidency of the High Priesthood; Presiding Elder; Presiding High Priest; Smith, Joseph, Jr.

President-Elect

Among those of high station to whom the Prophet Joseph was told to send a "solemn proclamation" in 1841 was "the honorable president-elect" (D&C 124:3). This had specific reference to William Henry Harrison who had been elected as the president of the United States but was not yet formally sworn into office. This revelation was received on January 19, 1841, and Harrison was sworn in as president on March 4, 1841. It is of interest to note that Harrison only served one month in office, dying on April 4, 1841.

Presiding Elder

The title "presiding elder" is used in two instances in the Doctrine and Covenants. First, it refers to the President of the high Priesthood of the Church, or the President of the Church, who at the time was Joseph Smith (D&C 20:66–67; 88:140; 124:125). It should be noted that Oliver Cowdery, as the "second elder of the Church," was a presiding elder, but always subservient to the Prophet Joseph Smith (D&C 20:3; DS 1:212; 3:165; GT 1:155). In a more general sense, "presiding elder" refers to one who occupies a presiding position over a body of the Church or quorum of the priesthood. "Of necessity there are presidents, or presiding officers," said the Lord (D&C 107:21). For example, "there must needs be presiding elders to preside over those who are of the office of an elder" (D&C 107:60).

See also: President of the High Priesthood

Presiding High Priest

A bishop is the presiding high priest of his ward and the stake president is the presiding high priest of his stake. As used in the Doctrine and Covenants, the title presiding high priest refers to the President of the Church (D&C 107:65– 66).

See also: President of the High Priesthood

Pride

"Beware of pride," cautioned the Lord, "lest thou shouldst enter into temptation" (D&C 23:1). Pride is one of the major character flaws against which the Lord has always cautioned his children. It was one of the major factors in the downfall of the ancient Nephite civilization (Moro. 8:27; see also D&C 38:39). The great and spacious building seen in the dream of Lehi was symbolic of "the pride of the world" (1 Ne. 11:36). Into this building flock those foolish ones who forsake the strait and narrow path leading to God (1 Ne. 8; 11–12; 15).

A modern-day prophet of God made the following observations regarding pride: "In the scriptures there is no such thing as righteous pride. It is always considered as a sin. We are not speaking of a wholesome view of self-worth, which is best established by a close relationship with God. But we are speaking of pride as the universal sin."

"Essentially, pride is a 'my will' rather than 'thy will' approach to life," said President

Ezra Taft Benson. (En., May 1986, p. 6.)

Priest

Although the term *priest* is sometimes used in other scripture to denote a general calling or ministry (2 Ne. 5:26; AGQ 1:114), it has two specific meanings in the Doctrine and Covenants. First, it refers to the third office in the Aaronic Priesthood (D&C 18:32; 20:38–68, 82–84; 38:40; 42:12, 70; 52:38; 84:111; 102:5; 107:10, 61–63, 87; 124:142). The scripturally given duties of this office are to preach, teach, expound, exhort, baptize, administer the sacrament, visit the members, ordain others to offices in the Aaronic Priesthood, assist the elders, and take the lead of meetings in the absence of an elder (D&C 20:46–52; 42:12).

In spite of those who hold this office being designated as "lesser priests" (D&C 84:111), it is a calling with potentially powerful experiences. President Wilford Woodruff, said: "I desire to impress upon you the fact that it does not make any difference whether a man is a Priest or an Apostle, if he magnifies his calling. A Priest holds the keys of the ministering of angels. Never in my life, as an Apostle, as a Seventy, or as an Elder, have I ever had more of the protection of the Lord than while holding the office of a Priest. The Lord revealed to me by visions, by revelations, and by the Holy Spirit, many things that lay before me." (MS 53:629, 1891.)

The second way in which the term *priest* is used is to describe those individuals who "come forth in the resurrection of the just," having overcome the wiles of the world, being sealed by the Holy Spirit of promise, and qualifying themselves for exaltation in the celestial kingdom to become "priests and kings" and "gods" (D&C 76:50–70; Rev. 1:6; 5:10).

See also: Aaronic Priesthood; Priest, The; Priests of the Most High

Priest, The

The priest referred to in Doctrine and Covenants 85:12 is Barzillai, who took his name from his father-in-law, Barzillai, the Gileadite who befriended King David in an hour of need (2 Sam. 17:27–29; Ezra 2:61–62; Neh. 7:63–64). For some reason, his children were "polluted" and "put from the priesthood." The Prophet Joseph declared that all who apostatize and whose names are not found written in "the book of the law" will likewise find themselves "polluted" and "shall not find an inheritance among the saints of the Most High" (D&C 85:11).

Priestcrafts

The Lord said that people erred "in many instances because

of priestcrafts'' (D&C 33:4). Priestcrafts are those activities practiced by religious leaders which seek selfish ends rather than the welfare of the people they are supposed to be serving. The Book of Mormon states that "priestcrafts are that men preach and set themselves up for a light unto the world, that they may get gain and praise of the world; but they seek not the welfare of Zion" (2 Ne. 26:29).

See also: Honors of Men; Praise of the World

Priesthood (#1)

The word *priesthood* appears well over one hundred times in the Doctrine and Covenants, and in each case one must look at the context in which it appears to identify its intended meaning. In most instances it refers to a specific priesthood—Aaronic (D&C 27:8), Levitical (D&C 107:1), or Melchizedek (D&C 84:6). Occasionally, one must be aware of historical circumstances to understand the meaning. For example, when the Lord speaks of those "ordained unto *this priesthood*, whose mission is appointed unto them to go forth," (D&C 68:2; italics added), he has reference to the priesthood possessed by Orson Hyde, who at that time held the Melchizedek Priesthood (D&C 68:1; SS, 409).

Brigham Young referred to the priesthood as "a perfect order and system of government" (DBY, 130). In an official explanation on the nature of priesthood, the following two aspects were defined: *"As pertaining to eternity,* priesthood is the eternal power and authority of Deity by which all things exist; by which they are created, governed, and controlled; by which the universe and worlds without number have come rolling into existence; by which the great plan of creation, redemption, and exaltation operates throughout immensity. It is the power of God.

"As pertaining to man's existence on this earth, priesthood is the power and authority of God delegated to man on earth to act in all things for the salvation of men." (IE 64:186.)

See also: Aaronic Priesthood; Authority of the Priesthood; Beautiful Garments; Dispensation of the Priesthood; Doctrine of the Priesthood; First Priesthood; First Presidency of the Melchizedek Priesthood; Fulness of the Priesthood; Greater Priesthood; High Priesthood; Holy Priesthood; Holy Priesthood After the Order of the Son of God; Lesser Priesthood; Levitical Priesthood; Melchizedek Priesthood; Office of Priesthood and Patriarch; Order of the Only Begotten Son; Order of the Priesthood; Power of the Priesthood; Powers of Heaven; Presidency of the High Priesthood; President of the High Priesthood; Priesthood After the Holiest Order; Restoration of the Priesthood; Rights of the Priesthood; Second Priesthood

Priesthood (#2)

When the heavenly messenger Moroni appeared to Joseph Smith in 1823, he quoted passages from Malachi. Among these was the promise that "the Priesthood" would be revealed "by the hand of Elijah the prophet" (D&C 2:1; see also Mal. 4:5–6).

Of this priesthood Joseph Smith said: "Elijah was the last prophet that held the keys of the priesthood, and who will, before the last dispensation, restore the authority and deliver the keys of the priesthood, in order that all the ordinances may be attended to in righteousness. . . . Why send Elijah? Because he holds the keys of authority to administer in all the ordinances of the priesthood; and without the authority is given, the ordinances could not be administered in righteousness." (TPJS, 172; 323.)

Although the Melchizedek Priesthood had been conferred upon Joseph Smith and Oliver Cowdery in 1829, under the hands of Peter, James, and John (D&C 27:12; 128:20), the "sealing power" was not yet restored. According to Joseph Fielding Smith, "That sealing power puts the stamp of approval upon *every ordinance* that is done in this Church and *more particularly those that are performed in the temples of the Lord*" (DS 3:129). That priesthood power was restored on April 3, 1836, when Elijah conferred the keys thereof upon Joseph and Oliver in the Kirtland Temple (D&C 110:13–16).

See also: Elijah

Priesthood . . . After the Holiest Order of God

The "priesthood which is after the holiest order of God" (D&C 84:18) is the same which is now called the Melchizedek Priesthood and which was previously known as "the Holy Priesthood, after the Order of the Son of God" (D&C 107:2–3).

See also: Melchizedek Priesthood

Priesthood of Aaron

See: Aaronic Priesthood

Priests of the Most High

Among the titles accorded those who merit exaltation in the celestial kingdom will be that of "priests of the Most High" (D&C 76:57). The "Most High" refers to both the Father and Son and identifies the exalted and lofty positions which they occupy. "Priests of the Most High" are those exalted holders of the Melchizedek Priesthood who "shall reign on earth" in its celestialized state throughout the eternities (Rev. 5:10). This is a position to which they will have been consecrated because of their worthiness.

See also: Most High; Priest

Prince of All

See: Michael

Prince of this World

Just as Christ is the "Prince of Peace" (2 Ne. 19:6; Isa. 9:6), so is Satan the "prince of this world" (D&C 127:11), or, rather, "the prince of darkness, who is *of* this world" (JST, John 14:30; italics added). He reigns in the benighted domain of the world of contention, carnality, and corruption—the world which the Apostle John warned us to avoid (1 John 2:15-17). This "prince" shall lose his satanical sceptre of power when evil is rejected for righteousness, "for he hath no power over the hearts of the people [who] dwell in righteousness" (1 Ne. 22:26).

See also: Devil; World

Principalities

One of the promises to the faithful is that they shall "inherit thrones, kingdoms, principalities, and powers, dominions, all heights and depths" (D&C 132:19). Webster says that a principality is "the state, office, or authority of a prince" or "the territory or jurisdiction of a prince." Those who qualify for a "fulness of the glory of the Father" (D&C 93:16-20) shall have royal reign over eternal principalities.

Prints of the Nails

On Golgotha's ground, the sinless Son of God was cruelly confined to a cross with nails driven through his hands, wrists,

and feet (MM 4:211, 215, 216; Isa. 22:23; En., May 1985, p. 10). In order to confirm his death, a soldier's spear was thrust into the side of his lifeless body (John 19:33-34). On occasion, the Savior has invited his followers to observe "the wounds which pierced my side, and also the prints of the nails in my hands and feet" (D&C 6:37; see also Luke 24:36-39; John 20:24-28; 3 Ne. 11:12-15).

Just days before his own death, one of the Savior's Apostles of our day declared: "I am one of his witnesses, and in a coming day I shall feel the nail marks in his hands and in his feet and shall wet his feet with my tears.

"But I shall not know any better then than I know now that he he is God's Almighty Son, that he is our Savior and Redeemer, and that salvation comes in and through his atoning blood and in no other way." (Bruce R. McConkie, En., May 1985, p. 11.)

At some future point, the unbelieving will look upon the Messiah and exclaim, "What are these wounds in thine hands? Then he shall answer, Those with which I was wounded in the house of my friends." (Zech. 13:6.) He shall declare himself to be "Jesus that was crucified . . . the Son of God" (D&C 45:52).

Prison

The word *prison* is used several different ways in the Doctrine and Covenants. One usage refers to an earthly incarceration (D&C

122:6). Other citations refer to the spiritual confinement of the unbelieving *or* to the condition experienced when the spirit is separated from the body (D&C 76:73; 128:22; 138:8–10, 18–21, 28–37, 42).

The unbelieving prisoners are released from their captivity in the darkness of their spiritual prison and brought forth into the light first through the preaching of the gospel by the faithful who also inhabit the spirit world, and next through the performance of sacred, saving ordinances by the living in behalf of those who have departed mortality. In addition, all are released from a prison, or state of bondage, when their spirits are reunited with their bodies in the glory of the resurrection, made possible by Him who holds the keys to those prison doors.

Promises Made to the Fathers

The prophet Malachi prophesied that part of the restoration of the keys of Elijah would be to "plant in the hearts of the children the promises made to the fathers, and the hearts of the children shall turn to their fathers" (Mal. 4:5–6; D&C 2:2). Elder Theodore M. Burton explained those promises as follows: "A promise was given to the early fathers on earth that those who died without a knowledge of the gospel and without an opportunity to receive the sealing ordinances of the priesthood would

be provided with such an opportunity in the future. The promise was given them that their righteous descendants in the latter days would perform vicariously such ordinances for them as could make possible their exaltation. They would be given an opportunity either on earth or in the spirit world to hear the gospel and to accept gospel truths, as well as to accept the saving ordinance work done in their behalf that would make that exaltation possible." (GGG, 77–79.)

Joseph Smith made this clear in his Vision of the Celestial Kingdom: "All who have died without a knowledge of this gospel, who would have received it if they had been permitted to tarry, shall be heirs of the celestial kingdom of God; also all who die henceforth without a knowledge of it, who would have received it with all their hearts, shall be heirs of that kingdom, for I, the Lord, will judge all men according to their works, according to the desire of their hearts. And I also behold that all children who die before they arrive at the years of accountability are saved in the celestial kingdom of heaven." (D&C 137:7–10.)

See also: Elijah; Hearts Shall Turn to Fathers

Promulgate

The verb *promulgate* is found once in the Doctrine and Covenants (D&C 118:4). It means to proclaim, declare, or make known. The gospel is to be promulgated. It is interesting to note that Joseph Smith's grandfather, Asael Smith, used the word *promulgate* in a prophecy he made about his prophet-grandson, Joseph: "It has been borne in upon my soul that one of my descendants will promulgate a work to revolutionize the world of religious faith" (ECH, 25).

Prophecy

See: Prophesy; Spirit of Prophecy

Prophesy

Among the gifts of the Spirit is the ability to prophesy (D&C 46:22). One possessing this gift speaks under the influence of divine inspiration and proclaims some future event that God has decreed shall come to pass. Such pronouncements may be conditional. For example, when Jonah prophesied that the citizens of Ninevah would be destroyed it was based upon their continuing in their wicked ways. Their repentance changed the course of events. (Jonah 3; see also D&C 130:20– 21; ER, 92–96.)

Note that the word *prophesy* is a verb (the action) whereas the word *prophecy* is a noun (the subject).

See also: Spirit of Prophecy

Prophets

The standard for determining a prophet was set long ago by one who understood the principle he proclaimed: "The testimony of Jesus is the spirit of prophecy," declared John the Revelator (Rev. 19:10). The Prophet Joseph Smith, in like fashion, declared that every man "who has the testimony of Jesus" is a prophet (TPJS, 119, 269). Elder Wilford Woodruff taught that "anybody is a prophet who has a testimony of Jesus Christ, for that is the spirit of prophecy" (JD 13:165).

In this respect, anyone is a prophet who has had the witness of the Spirit that Jesus is the Christ (1 Cor. 12:3; Moro. 10:6– 7; D&C 46:13). Thus, if those who profess to be the Saints of God are worthy of such a witness, there should be one prophet for every member of record in The Church of Jesus Christ of Latter-day Saints. What a strength there would be if the prayer of Moses were granted: "Would God that all the Lord's people were prophets, and that the Lord would put his spirit upon them!" (Num. 11:29.)

Elder John A. Widtsoe wrote that "a prophet is a *teacher*. That is the essential meaning of the word. He teaches the body of truth, the gospel, revealed by the Lord to man; and under inspiration explains it to the understanding of the people. He is an expounder of truth. Moreover, he shows that the way to human happiness is through obedience to God's law." (ER, 257; italics added.)

All who teach in the Church, which includes virtually everyone—home and visiting teachers, parents, officers, and classroom teachers—are *ministers* and should teach with the testimony of Jesus. Joseph Smith proclaimed that "salvation cannot come without revelation; it is vain for anyone to minister without it. No man is a minister of Jesus Christ without being a Prophet." (TPJS, 160.)

In terms of official *ecclesiastical calling*, however, there are only a few select men sustained to the office and calling of a prophet. These are the members of the First Presidency, Council of the Twelve Apostles, and, for periods of time, the Patriarch to the Church. Their principal business is not to foretell future events but to warn the world about the consequences of their wicked ways, to preach salvation through repentance and the saving ordinances of the gospel, and to "perfect the saints" (Eph. 4:11–14). Their major mission is to bear witness of the divinity of Jesus the Christ.

When a Latter-day Saint speaks of *the* prophet, he has reference to the one who holds the presiding position of senior Apostle and President of the Church (SHP, 153). He alone has the right to receive revelation for the Church, for in him is vested all authority and keys (D&C 132:7; DS 3:157). Though he is

sustained by the voice of the people as the President of the Church, he holds "the keys of the Priesthood," his prophetic power, "independent of their voice" (JD 1:133; DBY, 138). In addition to the living prophet, Joseph Smith is respectfully referred to as "the Prophet" or the Prophet Joseph."

Most of the references to the term *prophet* in the Doctrine and Covenants refer to a specific prophet by name. For example, Hyrum Smith, the Assistant President of the Church, was given the title by the Lord (D&C 124:94), and President Spencer W. Kimball was recognized as the prophet in general conference (OD—2). Joseph Smith is referred to as "the Prophet" in most section headings of the Doctrine and Covenants as well as in specific references (e.g., D&C 21:1; 107:92; 124:125; 127:12; 135:1, 3).

See also: President of the High Priesthood; School of the Prophets; Translation of the Prophets; Two Prophets

Prophet's Time

Joseph Smith stated that prophets reckon time according to the planet whereupon they reside (D&C 130:4–5). "The prophets count days and years as the people among whom they live and to whom they speak, or write. The people of Bible times and lands, it is thought, measured the years according to the phases of the moon and counted 354 days in a year, instead of 365, as now, and the prophets, of course, used the same time measure." (SS, 814.)

Propria Persona

The Prophet Joseph employed a unique Latin phrase in speaking of the work which must be done before one can be saved. Said he, "For out of the books shall your dead be judged according to their own works, whether they themselves have attended to the ordinances in their own *propria persona*, or by the means of their own agents" (D&C 128:8). According to Lewis and Short's *Latin Dictionary*, the word *proprie* means "in the strict sense; strictly for oneself; personally." The term *persona* denotes "a mask, character, or person." Therefore, the phrase *propria persona* implies that one is acting in person, strictly for oneself, as opposed to having a proxy (agent) perform an act in his behalf.

Proscribed

A declaration of belief warned against governments that foster one religious society while "another is proscribed in its spiritual privileges" (D&C 134:19). To be proscribed is to be hindered in the practice of one's beliefs by another's use of civil authority. Anciently, Daniel and his friends were proscribed from practicing their religious beliefs (Dan. 3; 6).

Prudent

In the same manner in which *wise* can be applied both negatively and positively (1 Cor. 3:19; Proverbs 12:15), the term *prudent* can also be seen both ways. The Lord declared himself to be *prudent* (2 Ne. 20:13; Isa. 10:13); yet, he speaks harshly against those who are "prudent in their own sight," for the things of God shall be hid from them (2 Ne. 15:21; Isa. 5:21; D&C 76:9; 128:18). Webster states that one who is prudent is capable of directing or conducting oneself wisely and judiciously — cautious, circumspect, and discreet in conduct. The "prudent" against whom the Lord speaks, are those who feign prudence or who appear to be "prudent in their own sight" but are blind and "looking beyond the mark," which is the "stone of Israel," even Jesus the Christ (Jacob 4:14–16; D&C 50:44).

To exercise prudence (D&C 89:11; Abr. 3:21) is to use discretion or to take the best course of action.

See also: Babes and Sucklings; Understanding of the Prudent; Wisdom of the Wise; Wise

Prune My Vineyard

The Lord told his early leaders of the Church and all who would be called to the ministry that they were "called to prune my vineyard with a mighty pruning" (D&C 24:19; D&C 39:17; 95:4). The process of pruning involves the cutting or trimming away of branches on a fruit tree to increase the yield.

An allegorical explanation of the pruning of the Lord's vineyard in the last days was described by the ancient prophet Zenos (Jacob 5:61–74). Pruning accomplishes two purposes: (1) the corrupt branches are cast off, and (2) the tree is strengthened with new, vigorous fruit.

See also: Vineyard

Pulsipher, Zera

The name of Zera Pulsipher appears but once in the Doctrine and Covenants, that being in a list of those who served as Presidents of the Seventies (D&C 124:138). He was ordained and set apart to this position on March 6, 1838, and functioned therein until April 12, 1862, when he was released for having "transcended the bounds of the Priesthood." He acknowledged his error and was subsequently ordained a high priest and a patriarch in the Church.

On January 1, 1872, "he died as a member in full fellowship in the Church." One of his most memorable experiences was baptizing Wilford Woodruff, one of the future Presidents of the Church. (Jenson 1:194.)

Pure

To be pure is to be clean, unsullied, without spot or taint. God has declared, "I will raise up unto myself a pure people" (D&C 100:16; see also 43:14). His people are to purify their hearts (D&C 112:28), to be examples in purity (1 Tim. 4:12), and to think on things that are pure (Philip. 4:8).

See also: Garments Pure and White; Holiness; Pure in Heart; Unspotted

Pure in Heart

It is significant that the Lord, with great emphasis, said, "for this is Zion—the pure in heart" (D&C 97:21). The phrase *pure in heart* is used several times in the Doctrine and Covenants (D&C 56:18; 97:16, 21; 101:18; 122:2; 124:54; 136:11) and is reminiscent of the famous phrase employed in sermons on two continents, "Blessed are the pure in heart: for they shall see God" (Matt. 5:8; 3 Ne. 12:8).

Smith and Sjodahl have defined this term as follows: "Pure in heart means pure in affections, unselfish in one's love of fellowmen" (SS, 325). One who obtains this state stands unpolluted and spotless before God, his garments have been washed in the blood of the Savior; i.e., the atonement of Christ has been accepted through the faith, repentance, and righteousness of the individual (Alma 5:21–27; 13:11–12).

In commenting on Psalm 24:3–4 and Alma 5:19, Elder Dallin H. Oaks said: "If we refrain from evil acts, we have clean hands. If we refrain from forbidden thoughts we have pure hearts. Those who would ascend and stand in the ultimate holy place must have both." (1985–1986 DFS, 29.)

See also: Zion

Pure Wine

In the section known as the Word of Wisdom, the Lord revealed the advisability of using only "pure wine" (D&C 89:6; see also 27:3). Smith and Sjodahl have rendered the following explanation of this term: "But what is 'pure wine' if not the *pure juice of the grape, before it has been adulterated by the process of fermentation?* No fewer than thirteen Hebrew and Greek terms are rendered in our Bible by the word 'wine.' There is the pure grape juice, and a kind of grape syrup, the thickness of which made it necessary to mingle water with it previ-ously to drinking (Prov. 9:2, 5). There was a wine made strong and inebriating by the addition of drugs, such as myrrh, mandragora, and opiates (Prov. 23:30; Isa. 5:22). Of the pure wine which was diluted with water, or milk, Wisdom invites her friends to drink freely (Prov. 9:2, 5). There was also 'wine on the lees,' which is supposed to have been 'preserves' or 'jellies' (Isa. 25:6). The *'pure wine' is not an intoxicating, but a harmless liquid."* (SS, 572; italics added.)

See also: Wine; Word of Wisdom (#2)

Purse

When servants of God are counseled not to take purse with them on their journeys, it means a moneybag or money (D&C 24:18; 84:78; Matt. 10:9).

See also: Scrip

Q

Quake

One of the common commotions of the earth is a trembling, shaking motion of the ground known as a quake, caused by a tremor beneath the earth's surface. Earthquakes were experienced at the time of Christ's crucifixion (Matt. 27:51; 3 Ne. 8:5–19) and will precede his second coming (D&C 29:13; JS—M 1:29).

There is another type of quaking with far more significant consequences than that of the earth; this occurs within men's bodies. We are told that the wicked will quake (shudder and shake because of fear) as they contemplate or experience the wrath of divine justice (1 Ne. 22:23; Mosiah 27:31).

On the other hand, the Spirit of God has caused the righteous to experience a shuddering of their bodies and a trembling of their bones. Joseph Smith said the still small voice of the Spirit often made his bones quake (D&C 85:6) and the Nephites felt every part of their frame quake when the small voice pierced them to the core (3 Ne. 11:3). Just as there are degrees of intensity of earthquakes, so are there differences of intensity in spiritual quakes.

See also: Still Small Voice

Quick and Powerful

The Lord refers to his word as "quick and powerful" (D&C 6:2; 11:2; 12:2; 14:2; 27:1; 33:1). The Bible Dictionary defines the word *quick* as "living, alive." Thus, the word of the Lord is not inert but is a source of life and a moving force of action.

Quicken

There appear to be several meanings to the term *quickened by the Spirit of God.* One is the special process whereby the Holy Ghost "quickens" (makes alive or awakens a sensitivity to) one's spiritual mind, eyes, and ears in order to see and understand the things of God and prepare the physical body for the presence of Deity (D&C 67:11). Another "quickening" is when the spirit reinhabits the body, creating a resurrected animation of the once lifeless limbs (Rom. 4:17). In this latter category are the living who pass through instantaneous death and resurrection and are "quickened and caught up to meet Christ at his coming" (D&C 88:96).

To be "quickened" is also to be converted. Paul wrote, "Even when we were dead in sins, hath [God] quickened us together with Christ" (Eph. 2:1–5). This "quickening" makes us "new creatures of the Holy Ghost, so that we are . . . born again and have become alive in Christ" (DNTC 2:499). It is the obedient whom the son quickeneth (John 5:21).

Quorum

The term *quorum* has been defined by Elder John A. Widtsoe as follows: "A quorum of the Priesthood consists of a specified group of men, holding the same office in the Priesthood, organized for the more efficient advancement of the work for which the Priesthood in the Church is responsible" (PCG, 134).

At the present time, the following quorums exist in the

Church: First Presidency (D&C 107:22); Twelve Apostles (D&C 107:23–24); Seventies (D&C 107:24–26; 93–96; En., Nov. 1974, p. 118; En., Nov. 1986, p. 48); high priests (PCG, 134); elders (D&C 107:89; CR, Apr. 1974, p. 124); priests (D&C 107:87); teachers (D&C 107:86); and deacons (D&C 107:85). When we speak of a quorum of the high council, or any of the above-mentioned priesthood bodies, we mean a simple majority of the membership thereof (D&C 107:28).

See also: Apostle; First Presidency of the Church; Quorum of the Nauvoo House; Seventy

Quorum of the Nauvoo House

The "quorum of the Nauvoo House" mentioned in Doctrine and Covenants 124:119 has reference to the building committee assigned to see that this special house was built according to the Lord's specifications. Members of this "quorum" were George Miller, Lyman Wight, John Smith, and Peter Haws (D&C 124:62). Although it was to be a boarding house for strangers, the house was to be built "unto" the name of the Lord—holy, an abode where weary travelers could "contemplate the glory of Zion" (D&C 124:23, 24, 60).

Because of these high objectives, the Lord declared that all who held stock in the Nauvoo House must be believers in the Book of Mormon and the other revelations given through Joseph the Prophet (D&C 124:118). This was no ordinary business enterprise, but a sacred religious project. Those mentioned as worthy to hold stock therein were Joseph Smith, Vinson Knight, Hyrum Smith, Isaac Galland, William Marks, Henry Sherwood, and William Law (D&C 124:56, 74, 77, 78, 80, 81, 82).

See also: Nauvoo House

Quorum of the Presidency of the Church

See: First Presidency of the Church

R

Railing

To rail is to revile or scold in harsh or abusive language. In ancient America, the faithful disciples of Christ received railings and unjust persecutions from others but did not respond in kind (3 Ne. 6:13). In latter days, the Lord counseled against using railing accusations (D&C 50:33).

Raiment

The word *raiment* is occasionally found in scripture and refers to clothing or that with which one is attired (D&C 43:13; 133:51; Mosiah 4:19).

Ramus, Illinois

The only mention of Ramus, Illinois, is in the preface of section 130. Although Nauvoo became the focal point of activity when the Saints settled in Illinois, satellite communities were established in the periphery thereof. Ramus was one of these and was located twenty-two miles southeast of Nauvoo at what was known as the Crooked Creek settlement (SLS, 162).

The Ramus stake was established in July 1840, but was discontinued in December 1841 (HC 4:467–68). Joseph Smith, as Trustee-in-Trust for the Church, received the town plat of Ramus in January 1842. Church members continued to occupy the area, and, in April 1843, the revelatory material of section 130 was received at Ramus (HC 5:323–25). The location of the town is shown on page 297 of the 1981 edition of the Doctrine and Covenants.

Raphael

In a review of the various heavenly messengers who had visited him, the Prophet Joseph mentioned the coming of Raphael (D&C 128:21). No biblical mention is made of this being; however, in the apocryphal book of Tobit, the following statement is made: "I am Raphael, one of the seven holy angels, which present the prayers of the saints, and which go in and out before the glory of the Holy One" (Tobit 15:12).

"As to Raphael's mortal identity we can only speculate. We do know the personages, however, who restored the keys exercised in the various great dispensations mentioned in the Bible, with the exception of the dispensation of Enoch. An inference thus arises that Raphael may be Enoch or some other great prophet from his dispensation. If this assumption is correct, then the keys restored by Raphael would be those enjoyed by the Saints in Enoch's day including, perhaps, the power whereby men may be translated." (MD, 618.)

Rearward

The promise of the Lord to be Israel's rearward is found in the Doctrine and Covenants (D&C 49:27), Book of Mormon (3 Ne. 20:42; 21:29), and Old Testament (Isa. 52:12). In the latter instance, "rearward" is rendered as "rereward." Not only will the Lord be the "rearward" of his people but he will also go before them. Thus, he will be the vanguard of protection on the front, as well as the rearguard (rearward). In addition, he will be in their midst, thus protecting both flanks from attack.

Records

"The matter of record keeping is one of the most important duties devolving on the Church," said President Joseph Fielding Smith (CHMR 1:103). At the time the Church was organized, the Lord's admonition was that "there shall be a record kept among you" (D&C 21:1). Unfortunately this was not strictly adhered to, and Joseph Smith himself was to ruefully say, "We have neglected to take minutes of

such things, thinking, perhaps, that they would never benefit us afterwards; which, if we had them now, would decide almost every point of doctrine which might be agitated. But this has been neglected, and now we cannot bear record to the Church and to the world, of the great and glorious manifestations which have been made to us with that degree of power and authority we otherwise could." (HC 2:198–99.)

President Spencer W. Kimball has counseled: "All members should write a personal history. . . . I urge all of the people of this church to give serious attention to their family histories, to encourage their parents and grandparents to write their journals, and let no family go into eternity without having left their memories for their children, their grandchildren, and their posterity. This is a duty and a responsibility, and I urge every person to start the children out writing a personal history and journal." (En., May 1978, p. 4; see also NE, Oct. 1975, pp. 4–5; CR, Oct. 1977, p. 4.)

An important aspect of record keeping relates to the saving ordinances of the temple. "And again, let all the records be had in order, that they may be put in the archives of my holy temple, to be held in remembrance from generation to generation, saith the Lord of hosts" (D&C 127:9).

In 1987 the Church changed the name of the Genealogy Department to the Family History Department. Elder Dallin H. Oaks declared: "When genealogy work leads on to temple work, and when ordinances are received and covenants are kept, the family history we call genealogy becomes [a] means by which we are sealed into our eternal family and receive exaltation" (Regional Representative Seminar, April 3, 1987).

See also: Temple

Records Which . . . Have Been Kept Back

In April 1829, the Lord revealed that "there are records which contain much of my gospel, which have been kept back because of the wickedness of the people" (D&C 6:26). Some of these records have since been revealed, such as the book of Moses, which was revealed to Joseph Smith in June and December of 1830, and the book of Abraham, which came into the Prophet's possession several years later; both have since been published in the Pearl of Great Price.

There is evidence in the Book of Mormon that the Lord does not allow the prophets to record all they know. For example, Nephi said that he was "forbidden [to] write the remainder of the things which [he] saw and heard" (1 Ne. 14:28). Years later, Moroni recorded these words: "And I was about to write more, but I am forbidden" (Ether 13:13). Furthermore, there were some things which were written but sealed up, to be shown in the "due time" of the Lord (Ether 3:27; 4:5). Joseph Smith was specifically told not to touch the sealed portion of the gold plates (Ether 5:1; JS—H 1:65).

In modern times, some of the Lord's special witnesses have commented on revelatory records which have not been made public. President Joseph Fielding Smith said: "*Many revelations have been given to the Church since the death of Joseph Smith. Some of these have been published; some have not.* It has been my privilege to read and handle a number of them that are still in the manuscript and have not as yet been given to the world for a wise purpose in the Lord. But they are on file and will be preserved." (DS 1:280.)

President Spencer W. Kimball recently stated that "revelation continues and that the vaults and files of the Church contain these revelations which come month to month and day to day" (CR, May 1977, p. 115). Again, Elder Boyd K. Packer declared: "Many revelations have been received and are found in evidence in the on-rolling work of the Lord. Perhaps one day other revelations which have been received and have been recorded will be published, and we stand in expectation that '. . . He will yet reveal many great and important things pertaining to the Kingdom of God.' [Articles of Faith 1:9.]" (CR, Apr. 1974, p. 139.)

Red in His Apparel

The Doctrine and Covenants contains the only reference to the red apparel or dyed garments with which the Savior will be clothed at his second coming (D&C 133:46–48). President Joseph Fielding Smith said, "This great day when the Lord shall come with his garments, or apparel, red and glorious . . . will be a day of mourning to the wicked, but a day of gladness to all who have kept his commandments. Do not let anyone think that this is merely figurative language, it is literal." (CHMR 1:191.)

The coloring of his garments may be symbolic of his having "trodden the wine-press alone" (D&C 76:107; 88:106; 133:50). The Jewish wine press consisted of two receptacles placed at different elevations, with the fruit being placed in the top one where it was trodden, squeezing the juice into the lower vat or tub. The garments of the one treading the fruit would obviously be stained by his labors. In similar fashion, the Savior's garments have been stained with the blood he shed in behalf of our sins (D&C 19:18; Luke 22:44). The wicked will ultimately be destroyed as if they were grapes being crushed in a wine press (D&C 88:106; 1 Cor. 15:25).

Elder Neal A. Maxwell noted the following regarding the Savior's red garments: "Having bled at every pore, how red His raiment must have been in Gethsemane, how crimson that cloak!

"No wonder, when Christ comes in power and glory, that He will come in reminding red attire (D&C 133:48), signifying not only the winepress of wrath, but also to bring to our remembrance how He suffered for each of us in Gethsemane and on Calvary!" (En., May 1987, p. 72.)

See also: Jesus Christ; Trodden

Red Sea

One of the most famous miracles of the Old Testament was Moses' parting of the waters of the Red Sea (Ex. 14:21–30). Although this manifestation of Godly power has been debunked by those who "are learned" and "think they are wise" (see 2 Ne. 9:28–29), the reality of this miraculous event has been attested to in two other scriptural records (D&C 8:3; 1 Ne. 17:27; Mosiah 7:19; Alma 36:28; Hel. 8:11). This sea is mentioned a second time in the Doctrine and Covenants when the Lord indicates that near its borders the prophet Lehi received the "miraculous directors" known as the "Liahona" (D&C 17:1; 1 Ne. 16:10; Alma 37:38).

The Red Sea is presently about 1450 miles long and 205 miles wide at its widest point. It separates Egypt and Arabia and "was probably crossed by the Israelites at a point north of the Gulf of Suez, now dry land, where at very high tides the Red Sea joined the waters of the Bitter Lakes." (BD, 130.)

Redeemer

"Hearken . . . and listen to the words of Jesus Christ, your

Lord and your Redeemer," declared the Lord in June 1829 (D&C 15:1; 16:1). The title of Redeemer is affixed to the Savior on numerous occasions in the Doctrine and Covenants and is also found in both the Old Testament and the Book of Mormon. Curiously, it is not used in either the New Testament or the Pearl of Great Price.

Christ is the Redeemer because he redeems mankind from the effects of death and personal transgression (D&C 29:40–46; 93:38; 2 Ne. 2:26–27). All will be redeemed from death (1 Cor. 15: 22), but only those whose garments are "purified" and "cleansed from all stain" (Alma 5:21) will be redeemed from the effects of personal transgression, for they cannot be redeemed "in their sins" (Hel. 5:10–11; D&C 19:15–20).

See also: Atonement; Jesus Christ; Redemption; Savior

Redemption

The words *redemption* (D&C 29:42), *redeem* (D&C 77:12), *redeemed* (D&C 29:44), and *Redeemer* (D&C 15:1) appear a number of times throughout the Doctrine and Covenants. To be redeemed is to nullify the effects of both the fall of Adam and one's own personal failings, through the intercession of Jesus Christ—the Redeemer—and one's own personal efforts. Elder Orson Pratt explained:

"Universal redemption from the effects of *original sin*, has nothing to do with redemption from our *personal sins*; for the original sin of Adam and the personal sins of his children, are two different things. The first was committed by man in his immortal state; the second was committed by man in a mortal state; the former was committed in a state of ignorance of good and evil; the latter was committed by man, having a knowledge of both good and evil.

"The children of Adam had no agency in the transgression of their first parents, and therefore, they are not required to exercise any agency in their redemption from its penalty. They are redeemed from it without faith, repentance, baptism, or any other act, either of the mind or body.

"*Conditional redemption* is also universal in its nature; it is offered to all but not received by all; it is a universal gift, though not universally accepted; its benefits can be obtained only through faith, repentance, baptism, the laying on of hands, and obedience to all other requirements of the gospel.

"*Unconditional redemption* is a gift forced upon mankind which they cannot reject though they were disposed. Not so with conditional redemption; it can be received or rejected according to the will of the creature.

"Redemption from the original sin is without faith or works; redemption from our own sins is given through faith and works.

Both are the gifts of free grace; but while one is a *gift forced* upon us unconditionally, the other is a gift merely *offered* to us conditionally. The redemption of the one is *compulsory;* the reception of the other is *voluntary.''* (MS 12:69; see also DS 2:9-10.)

Thus, the two phases of redemption are (1) the unconditional redemption from the dead, whereby *all* will be resurrected—a universal gift that cannot be rejected (D&C 88:14-17; Alma 12:25; 1 Cor. 15:19-23); and (2) the conditional redemption from one's personal sins which comes "through faith on the name of mine Only Begotten Son" (D&C 29:42-44) to those who manifest "a broken heart and a contrite spirit" (2 Ne. 2:6-7), are "baptized unto repentance" (Alma 9:27), and who "press forward with a steadfastness in Christ." (2 Ne. 31:19-20.) Even so, "it is by grace that we are saved, *after* all we can do'' (2 Ne. 25:23; italics added).

See also: Atonement; Day of Redemption; Redeemer; Redemption of Zion; Resurrection

Redemption of Zion

The "redemption of Zion" or the "redemption of your brethren" is spoken of in three sections of the Doctrine and Covenants (101, 103, 105). When the first of these revelations was given in December 1833, the Saints in Missouri were suffering great persecution. They had been driven by mob action from Jackson County—the site of their future city of Zion and her glorious temple (D&C 57:1-4)—and were now suffering similar persecutions in neighboring counties (HC 1:456-64).

W. W. Phelps wrote the Prophet Joseph and lamentingly said: "I know it was right that we should be driven out of the land of Zion, that the rebellious might be sent away. But, brethren, if the Lord will, I should like to know what the honest in heart shall do?" (HC 1:457.) In response to this query, the Lord provided a parable for the redemption of Zion (D&C 101). God later indicated that Zion would be redeemed by "power," under the leadership of a man "like as Moses" (D&C 103). As a result, Zion's Camp was organized and Joseph Smith, as commander-in-chief, led a body of men to Missouri (HC 2:61-134).

Upon arriving in Missouri, the Lord revealed that "in consequence of the transgressions of my people, it is expedient in me that mine elders should wait for a little season for the redemption of Zion" (D&C 105:1-10). He specified the conditions upon which Zion would be redeemed, "otherwise" said he, "I cannot receive her unto myself."

We are still awaiting the redemption of Zion, which, according to Elder Orson F. Whitney, "is more than the purchase or recovery of lands, the building of cities, or even the founding of nations. It is the conquest of the heart, the subjugation of the soul, the sanctifying of the flesh, the purifying and ennobling of the passions." (LHCK, 65.)

See also: Zion; Zion's Camp

Redound

The Lord promised William Law that if he put his trust in Him, "the sickness of the land shall redound to your glory" (D&C 124:87). The footnotes to the word *redound* refer to several promises given the Prophet Joseph whereby he is to receive recompense or a later advantage or reward because of his enduring well under current difficulties (D&C 121:8; 122:7). Thus, that which redounds ultimately turns to one's advantage.

Refiner's Fire

The phrase "he is like a refiner's fire, and like fullers' soap" is employed three times in holy writ: first in the Old Testament (Mal. 3:2), then again in the Book of Mormon (3 Ne. 24:2) and finally in the Doctrine and Covenants (D&C 128:24). Webster states that to refine is "to free from impurities to a pure state . . . , to perfect." A refiner is one charged with the responsibility of perfecting the good while discarding the dross. This is usually done through a process employing heat and fire. Christ's

second coming will be as a "refiner's fire," for the impure and coarse shall be separated from among the righteous as if by fire and cast off as dross. Those who remain in his presence will be refined, cleansed, and purified (3 Ne. 27:19).

Region and Shadow of Death

The reference to taking the gospel "unto those who sit in darkness and in the region and shadow of death" (D&C 57:10) is similar to Isaiah's Messianic prophecy (Isa. 9:2; Matt. 4:16; 2 Ne. 19:2). The darkness referred to is that which covers the minds of those not exposed to the illuminating light of the gospel (D&C 112:23; 2 Cor. 4:4). In a sense, they sit in the "region and shadow of [that] death" which is spiritual and which shall be pronounced upon the wicked (D&C 29:41).

The gospel is the call to light and life, for Jesus is "the life and light of the world" (D&C 10:70; 88:6–13; Mosiah 16:9; John 8:12). This principle applies to both the living and the dead, for the illuminating light of the gospel penetrates the darkness and shadows that exist in both spheres (D&C 138:30).

See also: Darkness

Remission of Their Sins

The phrase *remission of sins* occurs a number of times in the

Doctrine and Covenants (e.g., 19:31; 84:64) and is a promise to all who truly repent and are received into the waters of baptism. To have one's sins remitted is to receive a full pardon from the Eternal Judge for past mistakes. Initially, this pardon is received through the waters of baptism, whereby one witnesses the washing away of former sins and pledges a willingness to henceforth walk in paths of righteousness. This remission is renewed through the partaking of the sacrament. (DS 2:338–50; DNTC 3:275.)

Additonally, through an administration from the priesthood one may receive a remission of sins (James 5:15). "It is not the elder who remits or forgives the sick man's sins, but the Lord. *If by the power of faith and through the administration by the elders the man is healed, it is evidence that his sins have been forgiven.*" (DS 3:177.)

See also: Baptism; Forgiveness

Remnant of Jacob

The term *remnant of Jacob* is synonymous with *remnant of Israel,* referring to all the scattered people of the twelve tribes. However, a particular passage of scripture may refer to a specific branch of Jacob's posterity. For example, the footnote references associated with its use in Doctrine and Covenants 52:2 refer to the Lamanites (D&C 19:27; 49:24; 109:65; see also 2 Ne. 30:3; Alma 46:23). Moroni, on the title page of the Book of Mormon, calls the Lamanites "a remnant of the house of Israel." And the Lord himself identifies the Lamanites — the seed of father Lehi — as the "remnant" of whom he spoke in Nephi's writings (1 Ne. 13:34). During his visit among the people of the American continent, the resurrected Savior specifically spoke of that people being a "remnant of the house of Jacob" and of their posterity participating in the building of the New Jerusalem (3 Ne. 21:2, 22–23).

Referring to a broader application of the term, President Joseph Fielding Smith stated that the "remnant of the house of Israel . . . does not have reference only to the descendants of Lehi, but to all the house of Israel, the children of Jacob, those upon *this land* [America] and *those in other lands*" (DS 2:248).

It is interesting to note that Sidney Sperry identified the name of the prophet Isaiah's son Shearjashub as meaning a "remnant will return," which was a familiar theme of Isaiah's writings (DCC, 217; see Isa. 10:20–23).

See also: Branch of the House of Jacob; Heirs According to the Covenant

Remnants

According to the footnote reference (D&C 109:65), the term *remnants,* as used in the prophecy on war (D&C 87:5), refers to the Lamanites. In 1865, President Daniel H. Wells, Second Counselor in the First Presidency of the Church, suggested that at some future point in the history of the American nation, its inhabitants will "be greatly distressed" by the Lamanites, in fulfillment of this prophecy (MS 27:186–87). It does not appear likely that this vexation will come from those who have clothed themselves with the gospel of Christ, but rather from those who have not yet been spiritually subdued and converted.

See also: Lamanites; Remnant of Jacob; Remnants of Israel

Remnants of Israel

See: Remnant of Jacob

Renewing of Their Bodies

The Lord promises that those who receive the priesthood of God and magnify it will be "sanctified by the Spirit unto the renewing of their bodies" (D&C 84:33). Just as this "earth will be renewed and receive its paradisiacal glory" (Articles of Faith 1:10), so will the faithful men and women of this earth be renewed with celestial bodies.

Webster states that to renew is "to make new again; to restore to freshness, perfection." The sanctified Saints of the celestial kingdom will exhibit a wholesome freshness that will truly manifest their perfection, both physical and spiritual. The renewal of their bodies will allow them to

once again enter their Father's familiar mansions and inhabit divine dwellings eternally.

There are those who receive the benefits of renewed bodies here in mortality to some degree. Speaking at the April 1963 general conference, President Hugh B. Brown said: "I bear testimony to the fact that that promise [D&C 84:33] has been realized in the lives of many of us. I know that it has been realized in the life of President David O. McKay, that he has been sanctified by the Spirit unto the renewing of his body, and some of the rest of us are better off today than we were many years ago so far as physical health is concerned—and we attribute that fact to his blessing." (IE, June 1963, p. 507.)

Repentance

One of the most frequently mentioned concepts in all scripture is that of repentance. This is not surprising, for as early as April 1829, the Lord said: "Say nothing but repentance unto this generation" (D&C 6:9). Commenting on this imperative, Joseph Fielding Smith said: "We must not infer from this expression that those who went forth to preach were limited in their teachings so that all they could say was 'repent from your sins,' but in teaching the principles of the Gospel they should do so with the desire to teach repentance to the people and bring them in humility to a realization of the need for remission of sins. Even today, in all of our preaching it should be with the desire to bring people to repentance and faith in God." (CHMR 1:42.)

Elder Marion G. Romney offered this definition of repentance: "Repentance is the process by which every person must himself put into operation the plan of mercy on his own behalf if he would be redeemed from spiritual death. In other words, repentance consummates for an individual, with respect to his own sins, what the atonement of Jesus Christ did conditionally for the sins of all. Such is the place of repentance in the plan of redemption." (LTG, 101–2.)

Repentance is to alter one's course, to turn from darkness to light. The criteria whereby one may repent of his sins is outlined by the Lord: "By this ye may know if a man repenteth of his sins—behold, he will confess them and forsake them" (D&C 58:43). A very thorough discussion of the principle of repentance may be found in the classic work *The Miracle of Forgiveness* by Spencer W. Kimball (Salt Lake City: Bookcraft, 1969).

Reproving Betimes with Sharpness

An oft-quoted scripture is the admonition to "reprove . . . with sharpness, when moved upon by the Holy Ghost; and then showing forth afterwards an increase of love toward him whom thou hast reproved" (D&C 121:43). Perhaps the term *sharpness* could be interpreted as "clarity"; that is, reprove in such a way that the reproved person clearly knows wherein he has erred. Sharpness does not necessarily relate to one's tone of voice. To be moved upon by the Holy Ghost, rather than in the passion of anger, is an important criterion which the Savior himself utilized in cleansing the temple (John 2:13–16).

Joseph Smith said, "I frequently rebuke and admonish my brethren, and that because I love them, not because I wish to incur their displeasure, or mar their happiness" (HC 2:478).

In recent years, President Stephen L Richards remarked that "it is an unkindness to mitigate the gravity of offenses in those for whose guidance and direction we have responsibility" (CR, Apr. 1957, p. 97). "To withhold deserved reproof, and the reasons therefore, may be to withhold a warning that is urgently needed," said Elder Neal A. Maxwell. "Reproof is often a last railing before an erring individual goes over the edge of the cliff." (DSY 1976:192.)

See also: Betimes

Republic

The word *republic* is found in a declaration of belief regarding governments and laws (D&C 134:3). A republic is simply a government having a chief of state who is not a monarch (king or absolute ruler with unlimited authority) but who is subject to the will of the people. Supreme power in this form of government rests with the people rather than with a single sovereign.

Rest

The word *rest*, outside of its obvious uses, has several different connotations in the Doctrine and Covenants. "Entering into God's rest," (D&C 19:9) according to Joseph Fielding Smith, "means entering into the knowledge and love of God, having faith in his purposes and in his plans to such an extent that we know we are right, and that we are not hunting for something else; we are not disturbed by every wind of doctrine or by the cunning and craftiness of men who lay in wait to deceive" (CR, Oct. 1919, p. 8). To rest in his kingdom is to feel the peace and joy that comes from continuing to serve him (D&C 15:6; 16:6; 101:31; 121:32; 124:86).

"Sometimes we have thought of rest as being a place where we get on the chaise lounge, or in our sneakers, or we get outside and lie on the grass, something where we are at rest. That isn't the kind of rest that the Lord is speaking about," noted President Spencer W. Kimball. "It is he who is dynamic, the one who works the hardest, puts in the longest hours, and lives the closest to his Heavenly Father who is rested—rested from his labors, but not put away from his work." (CR, Oct. 1975, p. 121.)

Referring to the "rest of the Lord" President Joseph F. Smith said: "The rest here referred to is not physical rest, for there is no such thing as physical rest in the Church of Jesus Christ. Reference is made to the spiritual rest and peace which are born from a settled conviction of the truth in the minds of men. We may thus enter into the rest of the Lord today, by coming to an understanding of the truths of the gospel." (GD, 126.)

See also: Rest, His

Rest, His

Doctrine and Covenants 84 tells us the Lord decreed that Israel "should not enter into his rest while in the wilderness, which rest is the fulness of his glory" (D&C 84:24). Elder George Teasdale said: "What is meant by that rest? It means fulness of everything; to enjoy a fulness of love, a fulness of light, a fulness of intelligence, a fulness of power; to sit down with Christ upon His throne, as He has overcome and sits upon the throne of the Father—the promise that was given unto the Israel of God—the promise that was given to the sons of the Most High." (CR, Apr. 1899, p. 32.) This is the rest for which all should strive.

See also: Fulness of the Glory of the Father

Restoration, The

"The time of the restoration," mentioned in the explanation of some of John the Revelator's writings, could have several meanings (D&C 77:15). For example, the context of the verse in which the phrase is found speaks of "two prophets . . . to be raised up to the Jewish nation . . . after they [the Jews] are gathered and have built the city of Jerusalem in the land of their fathers." Thus, this phrase might specifically refer to the restoration of the Jews to their homeland (see D&C 109:61–64).

More generally, however, "the time of the restoration" could apply to that time period which commenced in 1820 when Deity dispersed darkness in a sacred grove and light once again radiated from heaven. This period, known as the dispensation of the fulness of times (Eph. 1:10), will continue until Christ ushers in the Millennium.

Since that spring morning in 1820 when a young prophet's mind was illuminated with revelatory rays of heavenly light, the radiation of restoration has been continuously felt. This restoration has included visitations by numerous heavenly messengers restoring lost keys and knowledge and the reestablishing of Christ's church upon this earth (D&C 13; 20:1; 27:5–13; 110; 128:20–21; JS—H 1).

In the words of President Spencer W. Kimball, "Never again will the sun go down. . . . Revelation is here to remain." (CR, Apr. 1977, p. 115.)

See also: Dispensation of Fulness of times; Marvelous Work; Restoration of All Things; Restoration of Scattered Israel

Restoration of All Things

The Lord informed the Prophet Joseph Smith that he had received an "appointment" and "the keys and power of the priesthood, wherein I [the Lord] restore all things" which had been "spoken by the mouths of all the holy prophets since the world began" (D&C 27:6; 86:10).

Peter spoke of this time period as being "the times of restitution of all things" (Acts 3:19–21). Commenting on Peter's statement, Bruce R. McConkie said: "It should be noted that Peter does not say that all things must be restored before Christ comes, but that the age, era, period, or times in the earth's history in which restoration is to take place must itself commence. That era did begin in the spring of 1820, but all things will not be revealed until after Christ comes." (DNTC 2:49; D&C 101:32–34.)

The "restoration of all things" must include the restoring of *all* keys, covenants, and powers held by prophets in previous ages. A successive string of visitations by heavenly messengers has already restored much (D&C 13; 20:1; 27:5–13; 110; 128:20–21;

JS—H 1), but there are things yet to be restored (D&C 101:32–34; Articles of Faith 1:9; DS 3:94).

One particular "restoration" which is yet to take place is the restoration of the earth to its "paradisiacal glory," wherein it will return to the perfect state prevailing before the Fall and also its condition prior to its being divided (Articles of Faith 1:10; AF, 375–81; D&C 133:24; Gen. 10:25).

See also: Dispensation of the Fulness of Times; Marvelous Work; Restoration; Restoration of Scattered Israel

Restoration of the Priesthood

In discussing the work of salvation for the dead, Joseph Smith referred to the promise of Malachi regarding Elijah's special mission (Mal. 4:5–6) and spoke of Malachi's eyes being "fixed on the restoration of the priesthood" (D&C 128:17). The Prophet Joseph also indicated that he could "have rendered a plainer translation" of Malachi's words, which may have reference to section 2 of the Doctrine and Covenants, wherein Malachi's words indicate that "the Priesthood" would be revealed by the hand of Elijah (D&C 2:1).

This latter scripture has reference to the "sealing power" which Elijah restored, whereby every ordinance performed by the power of priesthood authority is made valid. Thus, by this "sealing," earthly ordinances become validated and recognized in heaven as well as on earth (DS 3:129; TPJS, 172, 323). This power was restored on April 3, 1836, in the Kirtland Temple (D&C 110:13–16).

Earlier phases of "priesthood restoration" occurred in 1829 when both the Aaronic and Melchizedek priesthoods were restored to earth by heavenly messengers. John the Baptist conferred the "lesser" priesthood upon Joseph Smith and Oliver Cowdery on May 15, 1829 (D&C 13; 27:7–8; Pearl of Great Price, pp. 58–59, footnote, 1981 ed.). About a month later, Peter, James, and John were sent by the Lord to confer the "greater priesthood" upon Joseph and Oliver (D&C 27:12; 128:20).

See also: Aaronic Priesthood; Marvelous Work; Melchizedek Priesthood; Priesthood; Restoration of All Things

Restoration of the Scattered Israel

The "restoration of the scattered Israel" (D&C 45:17) is a theme frequently spoken of by the prophets. The blood of Israel has been sprinkled through the nations of the earth, and one of the major goals of our gospel dispensation is to gather Israel from the four corners of the earth, as well as in the spirit world. Israel is represented by those who accept the gospel and are adopted into Jacob's lineage (Gal. 3:27–29).

Scattered Israel is being restored in the following ways: (1) Through missionary work: "And he that will hear my voice shall be my sheep; and him shall ye receive into the church, and him will I also receive" (Mosiah 26:21; see also D&C 1:4–5). (2) The return of the Jewish people to their original homeland (Isa. 11:12; D&C 109:61–64). (3) Performing vicarious ordinance work for the salvation of those who died without opportunity to do the work themselves, "for their salvation is necessary and essential to our salvation" (D&C 128:15). When such work is performed, our dead ancestors "are considered to have been brought back into the presence of God" (CHMR 2:332). (4) The return of the ten lost tribes of Israel. These tribes are lost to the knowledge of mankind but are not lost to God and shall yet return from the north countries to claim their rightful place with the rest of Israel (1 Ne. 22:4; 3 Ne. 17:4; 3 Ne. 21:26; D&C 110:11; 133:26–34).

See also: Children of Israel; Gathering; Israel; Keys of the Gathering of Israel; Restoration; Restoration of All Things; Seed of Abraham; They Who Are in the North Countries

Resurrection

The gift of God for which no man pays a price is the universal resurrection. This doctrine is spoken of throughout the Doctrine and Covenants, especially in sections 76, 88, 132, and 138. This is the process whereby spirits will be reunited with their physical bodies, never again to be separated (Alma 11:44–45). This gift of immortality is the result of the freewill offering of the Savior, who voluntarily suffered his life to be taken in order that all men might be redeemed from death (2 Ne. 9:6–11).

Of the Savior's freewill sacrifice, Joseph Fielding Smith has said: "Of all who have dwelt upon this earth, *the Son of God stands out alone as the only one who possessed life in himself and power over death inherently.* Christ was never subject unto death, even on the cross, but death was ever subject unto him. 'As the Father hath *life in himself,*' the Savior said, 'so hath he given to the Son to have life in himself.' (John 5:26.) Again, he said: 'Therefore doth my Father love me, because I lay down my life, *that I might take it again.* No man taketh it from me, but I lay it down of myself. I have power to lay it down, *and I have power to take it again.* This commandment have I received of my Father.' [John 10:17–18.]" (DS 1:31.)

The Prophet Joseph taught that every man will rise in the resurrection just as he had been laid down. That is, a child will be resurrected as a child and will then grow to the full stature that it would have received had it been permitted to tarry during mortality. (TPJS, 199–200; DS 2:54; AGQ 4:185.)

These resurrected bodies will reflect the glory of that kingdom which they will inhabit throughout the eternities (D&C 88:28–32; 1 Cor. 15:20–23). The nature of this glorious resurrected body is indescribable, for, said the Prophet, "No man can describe it to you—no man can write it" (TPJS, 368).

Commenting on the process and miracle of resurrection, Elder Russel M. Nelson said: "Our bodies undergo constant rebuilding according to genetic recipes that are uniquely ours. Each time we take a bath, we lose not only dirt, but cells dead and dying, as they are replaced by a newer crop. This process of regeneration and renewal is but prelude to the promised phenomenon and future fact of our resurrection." (En., May 1987, p. 10.)

See also: Atonement; First Resurrection; Grace; Immortality; Last Resurrection; Perfect Frame; Redemption; Resurrection of the Just; Resurrection of the Unjust; Second Man; Second Resurrection; Twinkling of an Eye

Resurrection of the Just

The term *resurrection of the just* appears in the Doctrine and Covenants only in the revelation known as "a vision" (D&C 76:17, 50, 65), although it is also found in the New Testament (Luke 14:14; Acts 24:15; JST, John 5:29). This phrase has been defined by Smith and Sjodahl as follows: "This is also called the *first resurrection*, but the truth is here taught that only those who are just will have part in it. To be *just* is to be upright and sincere in one's actions and dealings with others. It is to be like Christ, who suffered, the just for the unjust (1 Peter 3:18). To be just is also to be justified. That is to say, *one who is just is, by God Himself, declared to be as he ought to be.* Such are they who have part in the first resurrection." (SS, 459; italics added.)

The resurrection of the just includes both celestial and terrestrial beings, the latter being the "honorable men of the earth." (D&C 76:75.)

See also: First Resurrection; Resurrection

Resurrection of the Unjust

The Lord declared that "they who have done evil" shall rise "in the resurrection of the unjust" (D&C 76:17). The phrase also appears once in the King James Bible (Acts 24:15) and also in the Joseph Smith Translation of the Bible (JST, John 5:29).

This resurrection has been defined as the "resurrection of damnation, the second resurrection. . . . At the end of the millennium, and in the morning of this second resurrection, those shall come forth who merit *telestial bodies,* and they shall be rewarded accordingly. Finally, in the afternoon of the second resurrection, those who 'remain filthy still,' those who having been raised in immortality are judged and found wholly wanting, those whom we call *sons of perdition*, shall be cast out with Lucifer and his angels." (DNTC 1:196–97; italics added.)

This resurrection is also referred to as the "last" one (D&C 76:85).

See also: Last Resurrection; Resurrection; Second Death; Sons of Perdition; Telestial

Revelation

The Doctrine and Covenants is a compilation of revelations; therefore, the terms *revelation* and *revelations* appear numerous times in that volume of sacred writ. Elder James E. Talmage defined *revelation* as follows: "In a theological sense the term *revelation* signifies the making known of divine truth by communication from the heavens . . . , a disclosure of that which had been wholly or in part hidden—the drawing aside of a veil" (AF, 296).

In like fashion, President Hugh B. Brown said: "Revelation is unfolding truth whether in the test tube, the human mind or a message from the Creator. It is the infinite becoming known." (CN, June 10, 1967, C–2.)

Revelation is a "rock" upon which the true Church of Christ is founded (TPJS, 274; SHP, 45; HC 5:258; Matt. 16:15–18; DNTC 1:385–87). Since that spring

morning in 1820 when the veil was parted and a young prophet communed with Deity, revelation has flowed "in a never-ending stream from God to his prophets in the earth." The testimony of one of those prophets, President Spencer W. Kimball, illustrates this principle: "I say in the deepest of humility, but also by the power and force of a burning testimony in my soul, that from the prophet of the Restoration to the prophet of our own year, the communication line is unbroken, the authority is continuous, and light, brilliant and penetrating, continues to shine. The sound of the voice of the Lord is a continuous melody and a thunderous appeal. For nearly a century and a half there has been no interruption." (CR, Apr. 1977, p. 115.)

George Albert Smith said: "The distinction between this great Church and that of all other churches from the beginning has been that we believe in direct revelation; we believe that our Father speaks to man today as He has done from the time of Adam." (CN, October 12, 1963, C–2.) Although in recent years, printed revelations, such as those found in the Doctrine and Covenants, have not been published as they were in the early days of the Church, yet revelations are still received on a regular basis by the prophets of God. President Spencer W. Kimball declared, "The vaults and files of the Church contain these revelations which come month to month and day to day'' (CR, Apr. 1977, p. 115; see also DS 1:280).

Revelations for the Church will *only* come through authorized channels. For the Church as a whole, they will come through the Presidency, and for individual units of the Church, they will come through those who preside over those units (TPJS, 111). ''Revelation continues in the Church,'' said Elder Boyd K. Packer, ''the prophet receiving it for the Church; the president for the stake, his mission, or his quorum; the bishop for his ward; the father for his family; the individual for himself'' (CR, Apr. 1974, p. 139). President Joseph F. Smith warned, ''Whenever you see a man rise up claiming to have received direct revelation from the Lord to the Church, independent of the order and channel of the Priesthood, you may set him down as an imposter.'' (JD 24:190.)

''Revelation comes to men in an unlimited number of ways,'' said Elder Marion G. Romney. Among the means whereby God has communed with man are the spoken word, visitation of angels, the power of the Holy Ghost through unspoken words that come into one's mind, impelling impulses to do a certain thing, dreams, visions, and flashes of ideas or inspiration that come to one's mind'' (LTG, 67–69).

The significance of the ''feeling'' type of revelation was expressed by President Spencer W. Kimball: ''In our day, as in times past, many people expect that if there be revelation it will come with awe-inspiring, earth-shaking display. For many it is hard to accept as revelation those numerous ones in Moses' time, in Joseph's time, and in our own year—those revelations which come to prophets as deep unassailable impressions settling down on the prophet's mind and heart as dew from heaven or as the dawn dissipates the darkness of night.

''Expecting the spectacular, one may not be fully alerted to the constant flow of revealed communication.'' (CR, Apr. 1977, p. 115.)

See also: Bosom Shall Burn; Feel; Holy Ghost; Manifestations of the Spirit; Prayer; Records Which . . . Have Been Kept Back; Revelations of John; Revelator; Spirit of Revelation; Still, Small Voice; Testimony

Revelations of John

The revelations of John spoken of in Doctrine and Covenants 20:35 refers to the last book of our present New Testament, the book of Revelation. This inspired book was authored by the Apostle John and contains great truths which have been hidden from the world but revealed to prophets and others who spiritually qualify (1 Ne. 14:18–28; TPJS, 287–94).

Elder Bruce R. McConkie has described this book as one which ''is not . . . for the theological novice, nor for the uninspired theological speculators of the world. It is written to the saints who already have a knowledge of the plan of salvation, to say nothing of the interpreting power of the Holy Spirit in their hearts." (DNTC 3:432.)

See also: John; John the Ancient Apostle; Ministering Angel

Revelator

With the exception of two references to the Apostle John (D&C 77:2; 128:6), the term *revelator*, as used in the Doctrine and Covenants, refers to one holding the presiding position of the Church, which initially included the office of Assistant President, that held by Hyrum Smith (D&C 100:11; 107:91–92; 124:94, 125). "A revelator makes known, with the Lord's help, something before unknown. It may be new or forgotten truth, or a new or forgotten application of known truth to man's need. Always the revelator deals with truth, certain truth (D&C 100:11) and always it comes with the divine stamp of approval." (ER, 258.)

"Each of the apostles when he is ordained has conferred upon him all the keys and authorities which were given by Joseph Smith to the apostles before his death. These brethren, however, cannot exercise these authorities except when the occasion arises that they come to the presidency. Before that time the powers lie dormant. This is one reason why they are sustained as prophets, seers and revelators in the Church, but there can be but one revelator for the Church at a time." (CHMR 1:389.)

In addition to the President of the Church, the Twelve Apostles and the counselors in the First Presidency are sustained as prophets, seers, and revelators. When the Church has had a Patriarch to the Church, he has also been sustained as a prophet, seer, and revelator.

See also: Apostle; First Presidency; John the Revelator; Patriarch; President of the High Priesthood; Smith, Hyrum; Smith, Joseph, Jr.

Reverence

To give reverence to laws or things pertaining to men is to give deference, respect, or obeisance within established guidelines (D&C 134:7; Cruden, 545). Reverence of Deity should have no limits. It is to experience godly fear, to be in awe of and have the deepest respect for each member of the Godhead. It is to sense the sacred soil upon which we kneel or stand when we approach our Father in prayer or enter into holy places and to feel, perhaps, as did Moses, the need to remove the shoes from our feet when in Deity's presence (Ex. 3:5). It is to speak of holy names with great care (Ex. 20:7; Mosiah 13:15; D&C 63:61–62; 107:1–4; 136:21).

To reverence God is also to cherish and respect the sacred ordinances, powers, and authorities he has bestowed upon us and to use them appropriately. It is to sustain his chosen servants and keep his commandments. To act reverently is to act godly, to speak, think, and conduct our lives in accordance with God's will.

See also: Worship

Reviling Not Against Revilers

To those called to "declare glad tidings"—the gospel of Jesus Christ—the admonition to "revile not against revilers" must not go unheeded (D&C 19:29–30). To revile is to abuse verbally. Though our enemies may rant, rave, and revile against us, our charge is to return such ill-treatment with the gospel of love, as is befitting the children of our Father (Matt. 5:44–45; 3 Ne. 12:44–45). In a classic commentary on this subject. Elder Marvin J. Ashton said: "We must not be manipulated or enraged by those who subtly foster contention. . . .

"When others disagree with our stand we should not argue, retaliate in kind, or contend with them. . . .

"Ours is to conscientiously avoid being abrasive in our presentations and declarations. . . .

"Our principles or standards will not be less than they are because of the statements of the contentious. Ours is to explain our position through reason, friendly persuasion, and accurate facts. Ours is to stand firm and unyielding on the moral issues of the day and the eternal principles of the gospel, but to contend with no man or organization. Contention builds walls and puts up barriers. Love opens doors. Ours is to be heard and teach." (En., May 1978, pp. 7–9.)

See also: Contention; Stir Up the Hearts

Rich, Charles C.

Though mentioned but once in the Doctrine and Covenants (D&C 124:132), the name of Charles C. Rich holds a place of honor in the annals of Church history. Active in ecclesiastical and political affairs, Elder Rich exhibited both physical and moral courage. He served as a member of the Nauvoo City council and as a major-general in the Nauvoo Legion.

"General Rich," as he was affectionately called, rode at the head of a group of men who rescued the Prophet Joseph from abductors who tried to imprison him in Missouri. He served on the Nauvoo high council, presided over the Mt. Pisgah settlement, and served as a counselor to John Smith, who presided in the Salt Lake Valley shortly after the arrival of the pioneers.

Elder Rich was ordained an Apostle on February 12, 1849, in which position he served until his death on November 17, 1883. "Throughout his lifetime he was less noted for his brilliant talents than for his real goodness. He was a man of generous impulses, and seemed to live for the happiness of others rather than his own. Cheerful, honest, industrious, benevolent, extending substantial sympathy to those in need, and giving fatherly counsel to and setting a worthy example before all around him, he moved on through life, honored and beloved by all who knew him." (Jenson 1:102–3.)

Richards, Willard

A name of celestial lustre in the Church is that of Willard Richards. Thrice mentioned in the Doctrine and Covenants, twice as an Apostle and once as a witness to the martyrdom of God's prophets, he played an important role in early Church history (D&C 118:6; 124:129; 135:2). Dr. Richards, a medical man by profession, was also handy with a pen and served as the private secretary to Joseph Smith. He kept the Prophet's private journals and later served as Church Historian and Recorder. In the Salt Lake Valley he edited the *Deseret News*.

His first contact with the Church came through a Book of Mormon which his cousin Brigham Young had left with another cousin. Opening the book at random, he read half a page and declared: "God or the devil has had a hand in that book, for man never wrote it." In the next ten days he read it twice, convinced of its truthfulness.

Although stricken with palsy shortly after this initial contact with the gospel, Elder Richards was not deterred from pursuing the course he knew to be correct and eventually found his way to Kirtland, where he was baptized on December 31, 1836. He served a mission to England with members of the Twelve Apostles, and on July 8, 1838, was himself called to serve in that quorum of special witnesses. Due to his travels, he was not ordained until April 14, 1840.

He was one of the two survivors of the tragedy at Carthage, and the only one who was left physically unmarred from the attack. His bravery and love of the Prophet were exemplified when, minutes before the martyrdom took place, Joseph asked him if he would accompany the Prophet to the inner cell area of the jail, as suggested by the jailer. Dr. Richards promptly replied: "Brother Joseph you did not ask me to cross the river with you — you did not ask me to come to Carthage — you did not ask me to come to jail with you — and do you think I would forsake you now? But I will tell you what I will do; if you are condemned to be hung for treason, I will be hung in your stead, and you shall go free." (HC 6:616.)

It was the calm, steady approach of Willard Richards that took charge of the affairs of the Church in the hours that followed the martyrdom, for Brigham Young and all of the Twelve but John Taylor — who was seriously wounded—were away from Nauvoo at the time. On September 27, 1847, he was sustained as Second Counselor in the First Presidency, where he served faithfully until his death on March 11, 1854. (Jenson 1:53–56.)

See also: Carthage Jail; Martyrdom

Riches of Eternity

"The riches of this earth are not the choicest the Lord has to bestow," said Elder Matthias F. Cowley (CR, Oct. 1899, p. 63). In January 1831, the Lord decreed: "And if ye seek the riches which it is the will of the Father to give unto you, ye shall be the richest of all people, for ye shall have the riches of eternity" (D&C 38:39).

These "riches of eternity" are spoken of elsewhere in the Doctrine and Covenants (D&C 67:2; 68:31; 78:18) and refer to those things upon which no tangible, earthly price can be set. Such riches as eternal life—God's greatest gift (D&C 14:7)—peace, joy, ever-expanding knowledge, and the promise to share the fulness of the Father's everlasting dominion, are treasures of an eternal nature.

The following observation by President George Q. Cannon should be contemplated: "The man who seeks after the perishable things of this life and allows his mind to dwell upon them, to the exclusion of the things of God which pertain to his eternal salva-

tion, has failed to comprehend the mission God has assigned him" (JD 10:348).

See also: Eternal Life; Fulness of the Glory of the Father; Hidden Treasures; Joy; Treasures

Rid Their Garments

The Lord promises that missionaries who "declare the word among the congregations of the wicked . . . shall rid their garments, and they shall be spotless before me" (D&C 61:33–34). Those who have fulfilled the charge to "declare the word" and have raised their voice of warning and witness to the world will stand "blameless before God at the last day" (D&C 4:2). They will have rid their garments of the blood and sins of the wicked (see Ezek. 33, 34).

During the dedicatory prayer of the Kirtland Temple, the Prophet pleaded that the Saints would be found with garments that were "pure" and would "be clothed upon with robes of righteousness" (D&C 109:76). The righteous are those who have rid their garments of the stain of sin, having washed them in the atoning blood of the Lamb who is without blemish, and are prepared to stand spotless in the presence of Deity.

President Joseph Fielding Smith noted that spotted garments are those "defiled by the practices of carnal desires and disobedience to the commandments of the Lord" (CHMR 1:163).

See also: Garments . . . Pure and White; Unspotted

Rigdon, Sidney

With the exceptions of Joseph Smith and Oliver Cowdery, the name of Sidney Rigdon appears more often in the Doctrine and Covenants than any other. After having served as a very popular preacher for the Baptists, Campbellites, and on his own, Rigdon became convinced of the truthfulness of the restored gospel by a careful and prayerful reading of the Book of Mormon. He was baptized on November 14, 1830, and many with whom he had previous religious association chose to follow Sidney's example in investigating this new faith.

Only a month later, his name appeared in one of the revelations wherein the Lord said to him, "I say unto you my servant Sidney, I have looked upon thee and thy works. I have heard thy prayers, and prepared thee for a greater work. . . . Thou was sent forth, even as John, to prepare the way before me" (D&C 35:3–6.) Thus, while previously not having had the complete truth, the Lord had used Sidney to prepare a people for the Restoration.

In March 1833, Sidney was set apart as a counselor to Joseph Smith in the Presidency of the Church (D&C 90:6). Sidney was a gifted orator and was called by revelation to be a "spokesman" for Joseph Smith (D&C 100:9).

This was the fulfillment of an ancient prophecy uttered by Joseph who was sold into Egypt, thousands of years prior to this time (2 Ne. 3:18; JD 25:126–27).

Early in his ministry, Joseph Smith said of his counselor: "Brother Sidney is a man whom I love, but he is not capable of that pure and steadfast love for those who are his benefactors, as should possess the breast of a president of the Church of Christ. This, with some other little things, such as selfishness and independence of mind, which, too often manifested, destroy the confidence of those who would lay down their lives for him— these are his faults. But, notwithstanding these things, he is a very great and good man; a man of great power and words, and can gain the friendship of his hearers very quickly. He is a man whom God will uphold, if he will continue faithful to his calling." Then, the Prophet added this plea: "O God, grant that he may, for the Lord's sake" (HC 1:443).

Unfortunately, in spite of all he suffered for the sake of truth, Sidney was not able to totally bend his will to that of the Lord's. In August 1843, Joseph accused Sidney of acts of betrayal and withdrew the hand of fellowship from him (HC 5:532). By October 1843, Joseph endeavored to "throw Sidney off his shoulders" and have him released from the First Presidency. Joseph indicated that Rigdon had been of little value to him as a counselor since the expulsion from Missouri. However, the conference voted to retain Sidney for yet another year. (HC 6:47–49.)

Following the martyrdom, Rigdon, who had been living in Pittsburgh, rushed back to Nauvoo with the suggestion that he be named as the "guardian" for the Church. At the memorable conference of August 8, 1844, Rigdon's eloquence could not prevail above the authority of the Twelve Apostles, and his bid for leadership failed.

Though he outwardly acquiesced, he secretly told many that he held "the keys of David" and that God had instructed him to take charge of the Church. Though he initially denied disloyalty to the Twelve, the truth was revealed and he was excommunicated from the Church on September 8, 1844. His efforts at organizing a following failed, fulfilling the prophetic words of Brigham Young: "All that want to draw a party from the Church after them, let them do it if they can, but they will not prosper" (SP, 7–18; see also HC 7:223–43).

See also: Pelagoram; Sidney; Spokesman

Riggs, Burr

Burr Riggs was one of several individuals called upon missions at a conference held in Amherst, Ohio, in January 1832 (D&C 75:17). A year later, his name appeared in the minutes of the proceedings of the high council at Kirtland, February 13, 1833.

Smith and Sjodahl wrote of this occasion: "He was charged with neglect of duty, and especially with failure to magnify his calling as a High Priest. He admitted the charge and expressed a desire to repent, but this he evidently failed to do, for he was severed from the Church on the 26th of the same month. In all probability, his neglect of duty began by failure to perform the mission to which he was called, or by neglecting his duties as a missionary." (SS, 436–37.)

Right Hand

In a symbolic sense, God has used the right hand to show privileged status. The Savior stands on the right hand of the Father (D&C 20:24; Moro. 7:27; Acts 7:56). The righteous, those whose names are recorded in the book of life, who take upon them the name of Christ and *know* him, are promised an eternal place at his right hand (Mosiah 5:9; 26:23–24; Alma 5:58).

President Joseph Fielding Smith explained that the "right hand is called the *dexter* . . . [which] means right . . . , *favorable* or *propitious*" (DS 3:108). "Showing favor to the right hand or side is not something invented by man but was revealed from the heavens in the beginning. . . . It is a symbol of righteousness and [is] used in the making of covenants." (AGQ 1:156.) The sacrament, for example, should be taken with the right hand. The

Lord declared, "I will uphold thee with the right hand of my righteousness" (Isa. 41:10).

See also: Left Hand

Righteous

As defined by scripture, the righteous are "the saints of the Holy One of Israel, they who have believed in the Holy One of Israel, they who have endured the crosses of the world, and despised the shame of it" (2 Ne. 9:18). These Saints live in a state of righteousness which Elder Joseph B. Wirthlin has described as "living a life that is in harmony with the laws, principles, and ordinances of the gospel" (En., May 1988, p. 81).

In this life, we "cannot always tell the wicked from the righteous" (D&C 10:37). However, the righteous are known unto God, "for the Lord seeth not as man seeth; for man looketh on the outward appearance, but the Lord looketh on the heart" (1 Sam. 16:7). When the Lord comes there will be "an entire separation" of the righteous and the wicked (D&C 63:54).

The Lord's purposes are righteous (D&C 17:4, 9), and he is a righteous Judge (Moses 6:57). He promises to gather the righteous on his "right hand unto eternal life" (D&C 29:27).

See also: Breastplate of Righteousness; Crown of Righteousness; Day of Righteousness; Offerings unto the Lord in Righteousness; Robes of Righteousness

Rights of the Priesthood

Through the Prophet Joseph Smith, the Lord declared "that the rights of the priesthood are inseparably connected with the powers of heaven and . . . cannot be controlled nor handled only upon the principles of righteousness" (D&C 121:36). The dictionary defines a right as "something, such as a power or privilege, to which one has a just or lawful claim." The only claims on the power or privileges of the priesthood are those guaranteed by righteous exercise of that authority. That is the principle upon which the rights of the priesthood rest, for to do otherwise is to grieve the Spirit of the Lord and lose claim to the priesthood (D&C 121:37).

The rights of the priesthood, therefore, encompass the privilege of living righteous lives and rendering unselfish service to one's fellowmen in behalf of God —to serve as His personal representative. As Elder Howard W. Hunter pointed out, "To love the Lord and our fellowmen is the key by which we unlock the power of the priesthood" (ACR, Aug. 1971, p. 98).

See also: Power of Priesthood

Rills

In a declaration of poetic prose, the Prophet invited the elements to proclaim the "wonders of your Eternal King." Among those so invited were the "rills"

(D&C 128:23). A rill is a very small stream or brooklet, the running forth of which would proclaim with gladness the goodness of God.

Ripe

In addition to variations of the term, the word *ripe* is found twice in the Doctrine and Covenants (D&C 29:9; 86:7). In the first instance the Lord speaks of the time when the earth shall be ripe, referring specifically to the time when it shall be so full of wickedness that it will be burned "and all the proud, yea, and all that do wickedly, shall be as stubble" (D&C 133:64; Mal. 4:1). The Lord has warned that "the world is ripening in iniquity" (D&C 18:6) and that there are people "who are well-nigh ripened for destruction" (D&C 61:31). Such people have fully developed (ripened) their iniquitous desires and habits.

The second occurrence of the word *ripe* is in an explanation of the parable of the wheat and tares (D&C 86:7; see also Matt. 13:24–32, 36–43). Wheat that is ripe is wheat that is ready to harvest — it is mature, fully developed, ready for those who will "thrust in their sickles."

See also: Cup of Mine Indignation; Earth Is Ripe; Field Is White Already to Harvest; Sheaves; Thrust in His Sickle

Robes of Righteousness

During the dedicatory prayer of the Kirtland Temple, the Prophet pleaded that on the day of resurrection the Saints would be "clothed upon with robes of righteousness" (D&C 109:76). These robes are also mentioned as the apparel to be worn by the Twelve Apostles who will stand at the right hand of the Savior upon his return (D&C 29:12).

Nephi petitioned the Lord to encircle him with the "robe of righteousness" worn by the Savior (2 Ne. 4:33). He later equated these robes with purity (2 Ne. 9:14). Robes of righteousness appear to be the same as those white robes which John saw being worn by those who have "washed their robes, and made them white in the blood of the Lamb" (Rev. 7:9–17).

Robes of righteousness are those white robes given celestial Saints, whose names are to be found in the book of life (Rev. 3:5), symbolizing their purity before God. They are "cleansed every whit from his iniquity" (3 Ne. 8:1). The whiteness of these robes testifies to the complete sanctification and purification of the Saints wearing them.

"And no unclean thing can enter into his kingdom; therefore nothing entereth into his rest save it be those who have washed their garments in my blood," said the resurrected Lord, "because of their faith, and the repentance of all their sins, and their faithfulness unto the end" (3 Ne. 27:19).

Rock

There are ten passages in the Doctrine and Covenants in which the Lord refers to the "rock" whereon mankind should build. For example, he said: "Build upon my rock, which is my gospel" (D&C 11:24). Twice the Savior mentions that his Church would be built "upon this rock" (D&C 33:13; 128:10), which is what Peter was told anciently (Matt. 16:15–18). Joseph Smith identified this "rock" as revelation (HC 5:258).

The Doctrine and Covenants refers to Christ as the "stone of Israel" (50:44), and the writings of Moses describe the Lord as the "Rock of Heaven," which is an appropriate title for one from whom revelation proceeds (Moses 7:53). Thus, in order to maintain "a sure foundation" (Hel. 5:12), one builds upon the rock of revealed truth emanating from the "Rock of Heaven."

See also: Revelation; Stone of Israel

Rod

Isaiah spoke of a "rod" that would come forth out of the "stem of Jesse" (Isa. 11:1). A rod is a straight or slender stick growing on or cut from a tree or bush. The rod from the stem of Jesse is an offshoot from his family tree.

The general identity of this rod was revealed by the Lord: "It is a servant in the hands of Christ, who is partly a descendant of Jesse as well as of Ephraim, or of the house of Joseph, on whom there is laid much power" (D&C 113:4). The specific identity of this servant is suggested by Sidney Sperry: "Joseph Smith must be the person referred to. . . . He is . . . the 'rod,' the servant in the hands of Christ. . . . We can, therefore, understand why Moroni would have occasion to quote all of Isaiah 11 to the young Prophet Joseph Smith." (DCC 617; JS—H 1:40.)

As used in Doctrine and Covenants 104:43, a rod is a measurement. One rod equals 5.5 yards or 5.029 meters.

See also: Jesse; Rod of My Mouth; Rods; Root of Jesse; Smith, Joseph, Jr.

Rod of My Mouth

The phrase "rod of my mouth" appears but once in the Doctrine and Covenants (D&C 19:15). The Lord warns the sinner to repent lest he be smitten with such a rod. Isaiah uses this phrase in conjunction with "the breath of [the Lord's] lips" (Isa. 11:4).

Smith and Sjodahl equate this expression with "the spirit of his mouth" (2 Thess. 2:8), and "the sword of [his] mouth" (Rev. 2:16; SS, 96). Reynolds and Sjodahl suggest that this phrase means the Lord's "word [or] his gospel" (CBM 1:358). The rod, as an instrument, is frequently associated with discipline or justice. Thus, if the unrepentant are to be smitten with the rod of the Lord's mouth, they will be punished or disciplined by the decree of his mouth. On the other hand, the rod of the Shepherd can be a device of comfort to those who hear and obey: "Thy rod and thy staff they comfort me," wrote the Psalmist (Psalm 23:4).

Rods

The dimensions of the lot for building the Kirtland Temple were described as "forty rods long and twelve wide" (D&C 104:43). A rod is a unit of length equal to 5.5 yards, 16.5 feet, or 5.029 meters. In measurement of yards, the temple lot was 220 yards long and 66 yards wide.

See also: Kirtland Temple

Rolfe, Samuel

Although the name of Samuel Rolfe appears only once in the Doctrine and Covenants, he is consistently mentioned as a stable, dedicated member of the Church in the Prophet's recorded history (D&C 124:142). The earliest mention of him is as a worker on the Kirtland Temple in 1835 (HC 2:206). Later that year he came to the financial aid of the Prophet and was one who agreed to help move the Saints from the troubled soils of Missouri (HC 2:327; 3:252).

Rolfe later presided over a quorum of priests in Nauvoo and worked as a carpenter on the Nauvoo Temple (HC 4:312; 7:326). In February 1844, when Joseph Smith sought volunteers for an exploring expedition in California and Oregon, Rolfe was among the few who willingly volunteered.

He was not called to travel west at that time but went later when the Saints were driven from Nauvoo. He served as a bishop in Winter Quarters and later served as a counselor in a stake presidency in Sycamore Grove, California. He died a faithful member in 1864.

Romney, Marion G.

In June 1978, a revelation received with great gladness throughout the world announced that the priesthood would be available to all worthy men who qualified to receive it (OD—2). Marion G. Romney was a member of the First Presidency at the time of this landmark revelation.

Born in Colonia Juarez, Mexico, on September 19, 1897, he was forced to flee the land of his birth during the Mexican Revolution in 1912. As the young man and his family were leaving, they were stopped by rebels who robbed and threatened to shoot them. Of this incident, President Romney recalled: "As I looked up the barrels of the rifles, they seemed very large to me. . . . I expected that they would shoot." (IE, Oct. 1962, p. 740.) Fortunately, the rebels did not shoot, for the Lord had plans for this young man. His patriarchal blessing promised that "the angels of your choice have been over you and watched over you for your good" (En., Nov. 1972, p. 26).

This same blessing promised that he would "be held in high honor and respect by the people, beyond your comprehension." His constant service to the Church has earned him honor and respect. He was called as one of the original five Assistants to the Council of the Twelve Apostles in 1941 and served in this capacity until his call as an Apostle in October 1951. Twenty-one years later, he was called to serve as a counselor in the First Presidency to President Harold B. Lee. He continued as a counselor when Spencer W. Kimball became the prophet. In 1985 he was called as the President of the Quorum of the Twelve Apostles.

Marion G. Romney's undeviating testimony of the gospel is exemplified in this declaration delivered in 1946: "I know the gospel is true. I doubt if I shall know it better, that is, with more certainty, when I stand before my Maker." (CR, Oct. 1946, p. 73.)

On May 20, 1988, President Romney joined the faithful prophets and Apostles who have preceded him in death and returned to his Maker. It is of significance to note that although he had been unable to speak for some weeks prior to his death because of physical infirmities, a day or two before his passing "he spoke, saying very audibly over and over again, 'Joseph,

Joseph.'" (CN, May 28, 1988, C–4.) There is no Joseph in the Romney family, and it is not inconceivable that President Romney may have experienced what Brigham Young did just prior to his death when he uttered those same words in reference to the Prophet Joseph Smith.

Root of Jesse

As was the case with the rod spoken of in Doctrine and Covenants 113:3–4, the Lord gives a general answer as to the identity of the "root of Jesse" spoken of in Doctrine and Covenants 113:5–6. He tells us it is one who is of mixed descent, coming both from the loins of Jesse, or Judah, and of Ephraim, or Joseph.

As was the case with the rod, Sidney B. Sperry suggests that Joseph Smith is the "root of Jesse." Thus, when Moroni quoted the eleventh chapter of Isaiah to Joseph Smith, he was citing the mission which this young Prophet was about to fulfill and which had been manifest in vision to the ancient Prophet Isaiah. (DCC, 617; JS—H 1:40.)

With respect to Joseph's lineage, Brigham Young declared he was "a pure Ephraimite" (JD 2:269). However, as Joseph Fielding Smith pointed out, "No one can lay claim to a perfect descent from father to son through just one lineage" (AGQ 3:61). Therefore, though Joseph's lineage may be traceable directly back to Ephraim through a given

line, of necessity there were inter-
marriages that took place, making it possible for his descent to
have also come from Jesse
through his forefather, Judah.

See also: Jesse; Rod; Smith,
Joseph, Jr.

Roundy, Shadrach

Although the name of Shadrach Roundy might not receive
high recognition among many,
his service and fidelity to the
Prophet Joseph Smith have
earned him lasting laurels in the
kingdom. Roundy was called by
revelation to the bishopric in
Nauvoo (D&C 124:141) and later
served as a bishop in the Salt Lake
Valley. However, he will be best
remembered for his courageous
defense of the Prophet. "His love
for the Prophet was so great that
he would have given his own life
freely in defense of his beloved
friend."

On one occasion when Jo-
seph's life had been threatened,
he personally asked Roundy to
help him. Brother Roundy single-
handedly kept a group of some
forty men from entering the
prophet's gate one night. They
had allegedly come to see the
mummies in Joseph's possession,
but the Prophet concurred with
Roundy's evaluation of their true
nefarious purposes.

Shadrach Roundy served as a
policeman in Nauvoo, as an officer in the Nauvoo Legion, and as
a bodyguard for Joseph. He had
the sad task of guarding Joseph
and Hyrum's martyred bodies on
the melancholy march returning
them to Nauvoo from Carthage.

He later served as a pioneer
leader during the crossing of the
plains and as a member of the
first Territorial legislature.
"Bishop Roundy died in Salt Lake
City, July 4, 1872, as a true and
faithful member of the Church."
(Jenson 1:642–43.)

Run Faster Than [Your] Strength

In 1828, the Lord counseled
Joseph Smith to "not run faster
or labor more than you have
strength" but he also cautioned
him to "be diligent unto the end"
(D&C 10:4). This qualifying
clause at the end should prevent
one from feigning being spiritually winded. King Benjamin gave
the Nephites similar counsel: "It
is not requisite that a man should
run faster than he has strength"
(Mosiah 4:27).

Elder Neal A. Maxwell offered
the following observation: "The
scriptural advice, 'Do not run
faster or labor more than you
have strength' . . . suggests *paced
progress,* much as God used seven
creative periods in preparing man
and this earth. *There is a difference,
therefore, between being 'anxiously engaged' and being over anxious and
thus underengaged.*" (CR, Oct.
1976, p. 14; italics added.) The
Prophet Joseph similarly cautioned the Saints to be wise: "By
being in haste," he said, "unreasonable sacrifices have been
made" (HC 1:279).

Rushing Mighty Wind

During the dedicatory prayer for the Kirtland Temple, Joseph Smith prayed that the "house be filled as with a rushing mighty wind, with thy glory" (D&C 109:37). The literal fulfillment of this prophetic plea occurred during the services "when a noise was heard like the sound of a rushing mighty wind, which filled the Temple, and all the congregation simultaneously arose, being moved upon by an invisible power; many began to speak in tongues and prophesy; others saw glorious visions; and I beheld the Temple was filled with angels," declared the Prophet. "The people of the neighborhood came running together (hearing an unusual sound within, and seeing a bright light like a pillar of fire resting upon the Temple), and were astonished at what was taking place." (HC 2:428.)

A similar expression is found in Joseph's description of the voice of Jehovah in that same temple, which was described as "the sound of the rushing of great waters" (D&C 110:3). This "rushing mighty wind" was evident on the day of Pentecost when the ancient Apostles received the Holy Ghost (Acts 2:1–4).

Regarding this special spiritual outpouring, Elder Bruce R. McConkie has written: "Some spiritual manifestations are so foreign to the experience of mankind generally that there is no way of describing them in words. They can only be felt and understood by the power of the Holy Ghost." (DNTC 2:34.)

Perhaps the closest description we have of such an experience was that of Lorenzo Snow. In a special moment of prayer, he said: "I heard a sound just above my head, like the *rustling of silken robes,* and immediately the *Spirit of God descended upon me completely enveloping my whole person,* filling me, from the crown of my head to the soles of my feet, and O, the joy and happiness I felt! . . . It was a *complete baptism—a tangible immersion in the heavenly principle or element, the Holy Ghost;* and even more real and physical in its effects upon every part of my system than the immersion by water." (BLS, 8; italics added.)

Ryder, Simonds

Simonds Ryder is mentioned but once in the Doctrine and Covenants (D&C 52:37), an occasion on which he was promised a blessing forfeited by another. His experience is a classic example that signs and wonders are not the means to lasting conversion. Ryder came into the Church as a result of an earthquake in China that some papers burlesqued as "Mormonism in China" (HC 1:158). When Ryder read of the account in the newspaper, "he remembered that six weeks before, a young 'Mormon' girl had predicted the destruction."

His departure from the Church came on just as shaky

ground. Sometime after his baptism, he was informed in a written communication from Joseph Smith and Sidney Rigdon that it was the will of the Lord that he should preach the gospel. However, inasmuch as his name was spelled "R-*i*-d-e-r" instead of "R-*y*-d-e-r," he apostatized, stating that if the Spirit of God did not know how to spell his name, it must have been the wrong spirit (HC 1:260–61, footnote).

Ryder's venom surfaced when on one occasion he led a mob that attacked the Prophet Joseph, leaving him tarred, feathered, and beaten (HC 1:264).

S

Sabbath Day

From sacred Sinai the Lord declared, "Remember the sabbath day, to keep it holy" (Ex. 20:8). Again, in our day, he has decreed: "And the inhabitants of Zion shall also observe the Sabbath day to keep it holy" (D&C 68:29). Although this latter command was specifically issued to the Saints in Missouri, the divine injunction applies to all men, especially those who claim membership in the society of Zion (see D&C 97:21).

The Sabbath day to Latter-day Saints is Sunday, the first day of the week, or the "Lord's day." "We admit without argument," said Elder James E. Talmage, "that under the Mosaic law the seventh day of the week, Saturday, was designated and observed as the holy day, and that the change from Saturday to Sunday was a feature of the apostolic administration following the personal ministry of Jesus Christ" (AF, 449).

By a revelation given on Sunday, August 7, 1831, the Lord designated Sunday as his Sabbath, or holy day. President Spencer W. Kimball made the following appeals regarding the Sabbath: "The failure to keep the Sabbath holy," he said, "is evidence of man's failure to meet the individual test set for each of us before the creation of the world, 'to see if they will do all things whatsoever the Lord their God shall command them' (Abr. 3:25)" (En., May 1975, p. 7).

"It would be wonderful if every family determined that henceforth no Sabbath purchase would be made. The Lord Jesus Christ said with, I think, some sadness, 'Why call ye me, Lord, Lord, and do not the things which I say?' (Luke 6:46.)" (En., Nov. 1975, p. 6.)

"The Sabbath is not a day for indolent lounging about the house or puttering around in the garden, but is a day for consistent attendance at meetings for the worship of the Lord, drinking at the fountain of knowledge and instruction, enjoying the family, and finding uplift in music and song. It is a day for reading the scriptures, visiting the sick, visiting relatives and friends, doing home teaching, working on genealogy records, taking a nap, writing letters to missionaries and servicemen or relatives, preparation for the following week's church lessons, games with the small children, fasting for a purpose, writing devotional poetry, and other worthwhile activities of great variety." (FPM, 270-71.)

Finally, a warning seems in order: "Are we not inviting eventual destruction as we desecrate all things holy and sacred," said President Kimball, "and make his holy day, the Sabbath, a day of work, of commercialism, and of pleasure-seeking?" (En., Nov. 1977, p. 6.)

See also: Lord's Day; Singleness of Heart

Sackcloth

According to Cruden, sackcloth is "a coarse cloth made of camel's and goat's hair. It was used for making the rough garments worn by mourners. It therefore became a symbol for sorrow and mourning." (Cruden, 556.)

The Lord proclaimed that one sign of his second coming will be to "clothe the heavens with blackness" and to "make sackcloth their covering" (D&C 133:69; Isa. 50:3; 2 Ne. 7:3). The context of this statement is a recounting of the miracles performed in leading the Israelites out of Egyptian bondage, which included the blackening of the skies (Ex. 10:21).

When Christ comes the second time, the skies will be blackened and the wicked will mourn as if in sackcloth (see JS—M 1:33-36).

Sacrament

The sacred ordinance of the sacrament was instituted by the Lord on the occasion known as the Last Supper (Matt 26:26-29; 1 Cor. 11:23-26). The resurrected Redeemer repeated this ordinance among his disciples in the Americas (3 Ne. 18:1-14, 28-32). Its purpose is outlined in the sacramental prayers found in both the Book of Mormon and the D&C (Moro. 4, 5; D&C 20:75-79).

An excellent summary of the purposes of the sacrament has been provided by Elder Dallin H. Oaks: "It causes us to renew the covenant we made in the waters of baptism to take upon us the name of Jesus Christ and serve him to the end. We also take upon us his name as we publicly profess our belief in him, as we fulfill our obligations as members of his Church, and as we do the work of his kingdom.

"But there is something beyond these familiar meanings, because what we witness is not that we *take* upon us his name but that we are *willing* to do so. In this sense, our witness relates to some future event or status whose attainment is not self-assumed, but depends on the authority or initiative of the Savior himself.

"Scriptural references to the name of Jesus Christ often signify the authority of Jesus Christ. In that sense, our willingness to take upon us his name signifies our willingness to take upon us the authority of Jesus Christ in the sacred ordinances of the temple, and to receive the highest blessings available through his authority when he chooses to confer them upon us.

"Finally, our willingness to take upon us the name of Jesus Christ affirms our commitment to do all that we can to be counted among those whom he will choose to stand at his right hand and be called by his name at the last day. In this sacred sense, our witness that we are willing to take upon us the name of Jesus Christ constitutes our declaration of candidacy for exaltation in the celestial kingdom. Exaltation is eternal life, 'the greatest of all the gifts of God.' (D&C 14:7.)

"That is what we should ponder as we partake of the sacred emblems of the sacrament." (CR, Apr. 1985, p. 109.)

The emblems of the sacrament are normally bread and water, however, the Savior instructed that "it mattereth not what ye shall eat or what ye shall drink when ye partake of the sacrament, if it so be that ye do it with an eye single to my glory" (D&C 27:2).

See also: Sacrament Meetings

Sacrament Meetings

Sacrament meetings are solemn occasions when the sacrament is administered to worthy members of the Church. In scripture, the term is mentioned only in Doctrine and Covenants 46:4–5. However, the implication for such a meeting is clear in other scriptures (D&C 20:75; 27:preface; 59:9–12; 62:4).

President Joseph Fielding Smith noted: "The Sacrament meeting of the Church is the most important meeting which we have, and is sadly neglected by many members. We go to this service, if we understand the purpose of it, not primarily to hear someone speak, important though that may be, but first, and most important, to renew this covenant with our Father in heaven in the name of Jesus Christ. Those who persist in their absence from this service will eventually lose the Spirit, and if they do not repent will eventually find themselves denying the faith." (CHMR 1:132; DS 2:340–

44.)

See also: Sacrament

Sacrifice

Although mentioned less than a dozen times in the Doctrine and Covenants, the principle of sacrifice permeates this entire book of revelations. "A religion that does not require the sacrifice of all things," said Joseph Smith, "never has power sufficient [to lead] unto life and salvation" (LF, 58).

Elder Bruce R. McConkie defined sacrifice as a willingness "to sacrifice all that we have for the truth's sake—our character and reputation; our honor and applause; our good name among men; our houses, lands, and families: all things, even our very lives if need be" (CR, Apr. 1975, p. 74). Implicit in every sacrifice is humble obedience; one must possess a broken heart and a contrite spirit (D&C 59:8; 97:8).

The Doctrine and Covenants speaks of burnt offering sacrifices (124:39), tests of faith (132:50–51), and tithing (97:12).

According to Smith and Sjodahl, the "day of sacrifice" spoken of in Doctrine and Covenants 64:23 has reference to tithing (SS, 394).

Brigham Young summarized: "If the people could see and understand things as they are, instead of saying, 'I have sacrificed a great deal for this kingdom,' they would understand that they had made no sacrifices at all" (JD 2:302).

See also: Offering unto the Lord in Righteousness

Saints

There are over two-hundred references to *Saints* in the standard works: The name has always been used to designate members of Christ's church here upon the earth. Paul, for example, referred to those who forsook the world and took upon them the covenants of the gospel as "fellow-citizens with the saints, and of the household of God" (Eph. 2:19). David sang of praising the Lord in "the congregation of saints" (Ps. 149:1).

In our day, the Lord has specifically designated the members of his Church as "Latter-day Saints" (D&C 115:3–4). These are they whom Daniel saw possessing the kingdom of the Most High (Dan. 7:22, 27).

Saints are those who put off the natural man and accept the atonement of Christ, becoming "submissive, meek, humble, patient, full of love," and "willing to submit to all things which the Lord seeth fit to inflict upon them" (Mosiah 3:19). They are "beloved of God" (Rom. 1:7) and "sanctified in Christ" (1 Cor. 1:2), believers in the Holy One of Israel and capable of enduring the "crosses of the world" (2 Ne. 9:18). The Prophet Joseph taught that "Saints should be a select people, separate from all the evils of the world—choice, virtuous, and holy" (TPJS, 202).

President Joseph F. Smith declared: "To be Latter-day Saints men and women must be thinkers and workers; they must be men and women who weigh matters in their minds; men and women who consider carefully their course of life and the principles that they have espoused. Men cannot be faithful Latter-day Saints unless they study and understand . . . the principles of the gospel that they have received." (GD, 114.) They must possess "the spirit of salvation," "the spirit of life," the "spirit of peace," and the "spirit of love for their fellow beings" (GD, 75).

The attributes of a Saint were further expounded by Elder George Q. Cannon, who said: "A Latter-day Saint! Think of the nature of the name. A Saint of God! Why, he should be next to an angel the most perfect of the human family. He should be perfect in his sphere, as God is perfect in His sphere. He should be free from fault. If he has a fault, he should seek daily and hourly to correct it and not rest satisfied as long as he is aware of the existence of a fault until he conquers it, pleading with the Father in the name of Jesus for strength to overcome his weakness, for power to put it away, carrying with him the spirit of love, the spirit of serenity, the spirit of peace, that when he appears in society, *no matter where he may be, all who come in contact with him may feel his influence and feel purified and strengthened by his example and by his words and by his very presence.* And

this is what God designs we should be as Latter-day Saints." (JD 20:290; italics added.)

Those members of the Church whose faithfulness manifests their desire and capacity to be Saints in more than name only, who "annihilate every selfish feeling" and "let love to God and man predominate" (TPJS, 178–79), will be those who will arise in the first resurrection (D&C 43:18), "inherit the kingdom of God," and whose "joy shall be full forever" (2 Ne. 9:18).

See also: Church of Jesus Christ of Latter-day Saints, The

Saints of God

See: Saints

Salem, Massachusetts

Although not mentioned within the text of a revelation, the town of Salem, Massachusetts, is referred to in the preface of section 111 as the town wherein the revelation was received. In late July 1836, Joseph and Hyrum Smith, Sidney Rigdon, and Oliver Cowdery left Kirtland on a short missionary journey that brought them to Salem in early August.

Joseph said that he "hired a house, and occupied the same during the month, teaching the people from house to house, and preaching publicly, as opportunity presented; visiting occasionally, sections of the surrounding country." He noted that "the fathers of Salem from 1692 to 1693, whipped, imprisoned, tortured, and hung many of their citizens for supposed witchcraft." (HC 2:464–65.)

During Joseph's stay in Salem, Brigham Young and Lyman Johnson, members of the Quorum of the Twelve, arrived for a short visit with the Prophet, where the latter remained until "some time in the month of September," when he returned to Kirtland.

It is of interest to note that Salem was the county seat of Essex County and that Robert Smith, the first of the Smith family line to settle in America, came to this very county to start his new life.

Salt Lake City, Utah

Known throughout the world as the capital of Mormonism, Salt Lake City is also the capital of the state of Utah. It has been the headquarters of The Church of Jesus Christ of Latter-day Saints since that momentous day on July 24, 1847, when the Lord's prophet, Brigham Young, declared: "This is the *right* place. . . . He had seen the valley before in vision, and upon the occasion he saw the future glory of Zion and Israel, as they would be, planted in the valleys of the mountains." (*Journal History*, July 24, 1880.)

The city is nestled in a valley bordered by mountains and is ad-jacent to the largest inland salt sea in the world—the Great Salt Lake. There is a religious significance to the abundance of salt and the name of the city which hosts the Lord's church. Elder Carlos E. Asay has noted that "the Organizer and Creator of this world understood perfectly the nature and importance of salt. More than thirty-five references to this substance are found in the scriptures. . . . The Savior referred to his disciples as the 'salt of the earth,' and charged them to retain their savor (Matt. 5:13). . . .

"I count it significant that the headquarters of The Church of Jesus Christ of Latter-day Saints is located in *Salt* Lake City. From this center of the Church flows the message of salvation to all the world. To this city of salt, men and women gather from all corners of the earth to receive instruction and edification. Such instruction, if accepted and practiced, will enable men to retain their *savor* and assist them in becoming *saviors of men.*" (En., May 1980, pp. 42, 44.)

Salt Lake City is the location where several revelations contained in the Doctrine and Covenants were received: President Wilford Woodruff received the revelation which led to the cessation of the practice of plural marriage in 1890 (see OD—1 plus accompanying excerpts from three of President Woodruff's addresses). In 1918, President Joseph F. Smith saw in vision the redemption of the dead (D&C

138). And, in June 1978, President Spencer W. Kimball and the Brethren of the First Presidency and the Twelve Apostles received a revelation making the priesthood available to *all* worthy males (see OD—2).

See also: Salt of the Earth

Salt Lake Temple

While not mentioned by name in the Doctrine and Covenants, the Salt Lake Temple was the location where the 1978 revelation on priesthood was received (OD—2). This temple is located on a ten-acre square in the center of Salt Lake City and was one of the first sites designated for special building purposes when the first main body of Mormon pioneers entered the valley on July 24, 1847. Four days later, Brigham Young marked the spot, proclaiming, "Here will be the Temple of our God" (ECH, 374).

On April 6, 1853, the day the cornerstone was laid, President Young said: "Five years ago last July I was here, and saw in the spirit the temple not ten feet from where we have laid the chief cornerstone. I have not inquired what kind of a temple we should build. Why? Because it was represented before me. I have never looked upon that ground, but the vision of it was there. I see it as plainly as if it was in reality before me." (DBY, 410.)

It appears that this temple was seen in vision by at least one other prophet, Isaiah, who spoke of "the mountain of the Lord's house [being] established in the top of the mountains" in the last days (Isa. 2:2–3). Elder LeGrand Richards identified the Salt Lake Temple as the "mountain of the Lord's house" of which Isaiah spoke (CR, Oct. 1975, p. 77).

The capstone of the temple was set in place on April 6, 1892, and the temple was completed one year later. Wilford Woodruff, fourth President of the Church, and the one who drove a stake to mark the spot designated by Brigham Young over forty years earlier, dedicated the temple and presided over services that lasted from April 6–24, 1893. In his prayer he said: "When thy people . . . are oppressed and in trouble, surrounded by difficulties or assailed by temptation and shall turn their faces towards this thy holy house and ask thee for deliverance, for help, for thy power to be extended in their behalf, we beseech thee, to look down from thy holy habitation in mercy and tender compassion upon them, and listen to their cries" (CN, March 16, 1986, C–7).

In addition to serving the regular functions of a temple, the Salt Lake Temple serves as a sanctuary for the General Authorities of the Church to meet and consider the affairs of the kingdom.

See also: Mountains of the Lord's House; Temple; Upper Room

Salt of the Earth

The expression "salt of the earth" is used in three of our

standard works. The New Testament scholar, Giuseppe Riciotti, said: "The expression 'salt of the earth' does not mean salt extracted from the earth but the *salt which is to preserve the earth, or mankind, against corruption just as it literally preserves flesh meat* and is sprinkled on the sacrifices offered in the Temple (Lev. 2:13). When this salt loses its strength, because it has been . . . adulterated in some way, then it must be thrown out of the house, that is, into the street, where all the refuse from a Palestinian house eventually lands." (Riciotti, 328; italics added; see Matt. 5:13; Mark 9:49–50; Luke 14:34; 3 Ne. 12:13; 16:15; D&C 103:1–10.)

The Savior decreed: *"When men are called unto mine everlasting gospel*, and covenant with an everlasting covenant, *they are accounted as the salt of the earth* and the savor of men" (D&C 101:39–40; italics added).

The "salt of the earth" consists of those members of the Church who are the true seasoning and preservatives of mankind. Their actions bring out the best in themselves and others and help guard against decay and corrosion in society.

See also: Salt Lake City; Savor of Men; Trodden

Salvation

The term *salvation* is one of the most frequently occurring words in the Doctrine and Covenants, appearing over fifty times. It is often used synonymously with the words *redemption* and *exaltation*; in each case its meaning can be ascertained by examining the context of the revelation in which it is found. In April 1829, the Lord equated salvation with the status of one who is "saved in the kingdom of God, which is the greatest of all the gifts of God" (D&C 6:13).

Joseph Smith declared: "Salvation is nothing more nor less than to triumph over all our enemies and put them under our feet. And when we have power to put all enemies under our feet in this world, and a knowledge to triumph over all evil spirits in the world to come, then we are saved, as in the case of Jesus, who was to reign until He had put all enemies under His feet, and the last enemy was death." (TPJS, 297, 305.)

As President Joseph Fielding Smith noted, however, there are two kinds of salvation: One is *unconditional*, the triumph over death which the resurrection will bring to *all*, and the other is *conditional*. Based upon one's worthiness, one will be "saved" in one of the three kingdoms of glory. The only ones not so *saved* will be sons of perdition. (D&C 88:21–32; DS 2:1–34.) In the ultimate sense, however, as Amulek pointed out: "How can ye be saved, except ye inherit the kingdom of heaven?" (Alma 11:37.) This latter salvation is *conditional* upon one's worthiness.

See also: Atonement; Redemption; Saved; Temporal Salvation

Sanctification

In the Doctrine and Covenants the term *sanctification* occurs only twice (D&C 20:31; 100:15), but the concept appears in several additional verses (D&C 39:18; 43:11; 133:62). Brigham Young said that "sanctification . . . consists in overcoming every sin and bringing all into subjection to the law of Christ. God has placed in us a pure spirit; when this reigns predominant . . . and triumphs over the flesh and rules and governs and controls as the Lord controls the heavens and the earth, this I call the blessing of sanctification." (JD 10:173.)

Thus, *sanctification is the process of becoming pure and spotless before God* through the power of the Sanctifier, who is the Holy Ghost. It is made possible through the grace of Christ. (D&C 20:31; 3 Ne. 27:19–20; Moro. 10:32–33.) It occurs when men yield "their hearts unto God" (Hel. 3:35).

Sanctification is brought to those whose complete repentance and love of that which is good have whitened their garments through the blood of Christ's atonement. These Saints have become "pure and spotless before God," being unable to "look upon sin save it were with abhorrence" (Alma 13:11–12).

One who is sanctified through the Spirit has "no more disposition to do evil, but to do good continually" (Mosiah 5:2). Elder Spencer W. Kimball said that the attitude which is basic to sanctification "is that the former trans-gressor must have reached a 'point of no return' to sin wherein there is not merely a renunciation but also a deep abhorrence of the sin—where the sin becomes most distasteful to him and where the desire or urge to sin is cleared out of his life" (MF, 354–55).

See also: Garments Pure and White; Holiness; Pure in Heart; Unspotted

Sanctuary

The word *sanctuary* appears once in the Doctrine and Covenants (D&C 88:137) and has reference to the house in which the School of the Prophets met. A sanctuary is a holy place generally associated with worship services. The Book of Mormon speaks of sanctuaries in which the people "began to assemble themselves before God . . . to worship God" (Alma 15:17; see also 21:6; 22:7).

See also: School of the Prophets

Sarah

The name *Sarah* appears in a revelation on marriage (D&C 132:34). Her name was Sarai, which the Lord changed to Sarah, meaning "Princess" (Gen. 17:15; LDSBD, 769). This latter name is most appropriate in terms of her serving as Abraham's queen throughout the eternities.

In addition to being Abraham's wife, Sarah was also his

half-sister (Gen. 11:29; 20:12). This latter relationship was an important factor in the deception foisted upon the Egyptians, when she was introduced as Abraham's sister rather than his wife. This was done in order to protect Abraham from possible assassination by those who would be fascinated by her and desire her for their own household, for she was a "very fair woman" (Abr. 2:21–25; Gen. 12:10–20).

In a similar stratagem involving King Abimelech, the Lord intervened to protect Sarah's virtue (Gen. 20). She died at the age of 127, 38 years before Abraham, and was later buried by him in the cave of Machpelah (Gen. 23:1–2, 19).

See also: Hagar; Law of Sarah

Satan

One of the names whereby the devil is known is Satan (D&C 10:5; 50:3; 64:17; 132:57). It is a formal Hebrew title for the devil and means the adversary or the opponent of the Lord (AF, 62–63).

See also: Devil

Saved

"Have you been saved?" is one of the most frequently asked questions by evangelical ministers. To many, to be "saved" is merely a matter of confessing a belief in Jesus Christ. To the Saints of God, however, the Savior declared, "And as many as repent and are baptized in my name, which is Jesus Christ, and endure to the end, the same shall be saved" (D&C 18:22).

Thus, in addition to the verbal expression of belief in Christ, there must be the active expression of one's belief by repenting and being baptized (D&C 3:20; 68:9), taking up "the cross" (denying oneself of all ungodliness), keeping the commandments (D&C 56:2; 100:17), and enduring to the end (D&C 53:7).

To "receive" the Savior means to receive his way of life and walk therein (D&C 49:5). All except the sons of perdition will be "saved" in *a* kingdom of God, be that telestial, terrestrial, or celestial. However, only in the latter kingdom will God and Christ dwell also (D&C 76:50–86; 88:21–32).

Again, to quote an ancient prophet, "How can ye be saved, except ye inherit the kingdom of heaven?" (Alma 11:37.) To be saved is not a matter of fervent declaration but rather of sustained spiritual progress along a well-defined but narrow path.

See also: Celestial; Glory; Mansions of My Father; Salvation; Telestial; Terrestrial

Savior

One of the most frequently used titles by which Jesus has been designated is "Savior." "Behold, I am Jesus Christ, the Savior of the world," he declared to

Joseph Smith (D&C 43:34). The title appears in each of the standard works.

Through Isaiah the Lord declared: "I, even I, am the Lord; and beside me there is no saviour" (Isa. 43:11). To the humble shepherds the heavenly heralds proclaimed, "For unto you is born this day in the city of David a Saviour, which is Christ the Lord" (Luke 2:11).

He is the Savior in two senses: first, he saves all mankind from the grip of the grave, for all will be resurrected (2 Ne. 9:6–11; 1 Cor. 15:20–22); second, the Savior saves us from the stain of sin *if* we will repent.

"He shall not save his people in their sins," said Amulek. "Therefore the wicked remain as though there had been no redemption made, except it be the loosing of the bands of death." (Alma 11:36–41.)

See also: Atonement; Jesus Christ; Redeemer; Redemption; Salvation; Saved

Savior unto My People

See: Saviors of Men

Saviors of Men

Only in the Old Testament (Obad. 1:21) and in Doctrine and Covenants 103:9–10 does one find the phrase *saviours on mount Zion* or *saviors of men*.

The Prophet Joseph identified the Latter-day Saints as these saviors and explained one way in which this title is applied is by the Saints "building their temples, erecting their baptismal fonts, and going forth and receiving all the ordinances, baptisms, confirmations, washings, anointings, ordinations and sealing powers upon their heads, in behalf of all their progenitors who are dead, and redeem them that they may come forth in the first resurrection and be exalted to thrones of glory with them" (TPJS, 330).

"But there are a great many things in which we can be saviors," declared President Charles W. Penrose. "We are to be saviors of men, too, in sending or carrying the gospel to every nation, kindred, tongue and people. That is imposed upon us; every Latter-day Saint, every man and woman and boy and girl born in the covenant or who has received it, is under obligation to do all that is possible for the sending forth of the word of the Lord to all nations of the earth." (CR, Apr. 1918, p. 17.)

The Lord specifically designated a bearer of the priesthood as "a savior" when he uses that priesthood to bless the lives of others (D&C 86:11). Through the saving ordinances administered by proper priesthood authority, one becomes eligible for exaltation.

Savor of Men

Those who are the true "salt of the earth" bring out the wholesome "savor of men" (D&C 101:39–40; 103:10; Matt. 5:13; 3 Ne. 12:13). Webster defines *savor* as a verb meaning "to have a specified taste or quality; a special flavor or quality." Faithful members of the Church, the true "salt of the earth," should provide a special quality in whatever social situation they find themselves. Their presence should be edifyingly *savory*, bringing out the best in others and adding to the righteous pleasure of all.

Elder Mark E. Petersen noted there can be a negative savor: "The savor that the wicked give off becomes a stench in [the Lord's] face." Elder Petersen suggested that one's positive savor is lost "by becoming casual in our obedience . . . , careless about attending our meetings . . . , if we neglect our prayers, our tithes and offerings . . . , if we do not share the gospel . . . , if we violate God's holy Sabbath . . . , if we are dishonest, unkind, or vengeful . . . , if we lose our virtue . . . , if we are guilty of infidelity in our family, or are otherwise cruel in our home . . . , if we oppose Church policies and defy our chosen leaders [and] if we withdraw from the Church and accept the destructive teachings of false prophets." (En., Nov. 1976, pp. 50–51.)

See also: Salt of the Earth

Scepter

References to a scepter, unless specifically identified as an actual rod or staff, are metaphorical expressions of supreme power. The scepter of Jesus Christ is one of righteousness (Heb. 1:8), and those who take the Holy Ghost as their constant companion are promised "an unchanging scepter of righteousness and truth" (D&C 121:46). In other words, such faithful ones are filled with great spiritual power and understanding.

Just as kings often have tangible scepters to demonstrate their earthly authority, those who hold keys of authority from the King of kings symbolically hold scepters of spiritual power (see D&C 85:7).

School in Zion

In August 1833, the Lord expressed his pleasure with the "school of Zion" which had been established and with his servant Elder Parley P. Pratt (D&C 97:3). Elder Pratt's autobiography reveals that this "school of Elders" was established in the latter part of the summer of 1833, when he was called to preside over it.

"This class, to the number of about sixty, met for instruction once a week. The place of meeting was in the open air, under some tall trees, in a retired place in the wilderness, where we prayed, preached and prophesied, and exercised ourselves in the gifts of the Holy Spirit. Here great blessings were poured out, and many great and marvelous things were manifested and taught. The Lord gave me great wisdom, and enabled me to teach and edify the Elders, and comfort and encourage them in their preparations for the great work which lay before us. I was also much edified and strengthened. To attend this school I had to travel on foot, and sometimes with bare feet at that, about six miles. This I did once a week, besides visiting and preaching in five or six branches a week." (APP, 93–94.)

School of the Prophets

One of the innovative institutions of the early Church was the "school of the prophets," presided over by the Presidency of the Church (D&C 88:117–141; 90:7–13). President Joseph Fielding Smith has described this school, as well as the "school of the Elders," as follows:

"There were two schools conducted in Kirtland. One was a school of the Elders where they carried out some of the provisions of this revelation (Sec. 88) in seeking knowledge of countries and kingdoms and languages, all such information as may be gained in the regular daily school. It was in this school where many of the Elders, then residing in Kirtland, hired Dr. Seixas, a learned Hebrew scholar, and under his direction studied the Hebrew language. This school was conducted for several months, and the Prophet, and others, became rather proficient in this language due to the guidance of the Lord as much as that of the Hebrew scholar. This school proved to be of great benefit to these brethren in later years.

"The other was the 'School of the Prophets,' and a very good description of this school and its purpose is given in this section of the Doctrine and Covenants, verses 117 to the end of the section. In a letter written by the Prophet Joseph to William W. Phelps in Zion, January 14, 1833, the following appears: 'You will see that the Lord commanded us, in Kirtland, to build a house of God, and establish a school for the prophets, this is the word of the Lord to us, and we must, yea, the Lord helping us, we will obey: as on conditions of our obedience he has promised us great things; yea, even a visit from the heavens to honor us with his own presence.' . . . The Prophet further writes: 'This winter (1832–3) was spent in translating the scriptures; in the School of the Prophets; and sitting in conferences. I had many glorious seasons of refreshing.' (D.H.C. 1:322.) This School of the Prophets and the schools where the ordinary branches were taught continued in Kirtland until the exodus from that place. It was for this school that the lectures on faith were prepared and which were delivered to the Elders. The idea has been expressed that Sidney Rigdon wrote these lectures, but they were compiled by a number of the brethren and the Prophet himself had the final revision of them. They contain a great deal of excellent teaching on the principle of faith.

"The 'School of the Prophets' is not something new to this dispensation. In ancient Israel, especially in the days of Samuel, Elijah and Elisha, there was such a school [1 Sam. 10; 2 Kgs. 2.]. . . .

"The object for which this school was organized is plainly stated in the revelation. None could join except he was clean from the blood of this generation. The only way he could be clean was to be obedient to the covenants of the Gospel and labor in behalf of his fellows for the salvation of their souls. Thus the preaching of the Gospel was a requirement made of those who desired to join this school. The School of the Prophets continued in Utah for several years under the administration of President Brigham Young, but after that time it was discontinued." (CHMR 1:372–73.)

Scott, Jacob

Among those called to travel two-by-two to Missouri, at the conference of June 7, 1831, was Jacob Scott (D&C 52:28). His traveling companion was Edson Fuller. No other mention is made of Scott in the Doctrine and Covenants.

He is reported to have left the Church in 1831 and does not appear to be either man mentioned in the minutes of a conference held on April 26, 1839, at Far West, Missouri, by the Twelve Apostles, where "Jacob Scott, Sen. and wife, Isaac Scott, Jacob Scott, Jun., [and] Ann Scott" were among those excommunicated from the Church (HC 3:336).

Scrip

On several occasions, the Lord has instructed those who went forth to preach to take neither purse (money) nor scrip (a bag of food), for the Lord would amply provide (D&C 24:18; 84:78, 86; Matt. 10:10; Luke 22:35–36).

"The Hebrew word (scrip) thus translated appears in 1 Sam. 17:40 as a synonym for the bag in which the shepherds of Palestine carried their food or other necessaries. The scrip of the Galilean peasants was of leather, *used especially to carry their food on a journey*, and slung over their shoulders. The English word 'scrip' is probably connected with . . . scrap, and was used in like manner for articles of food." (Peloubet, 598; italics added.)

See also: Purse

Scripture

The Lord has declared the Doctrine and Covenants to be a divine book of scripture (D&C 104:58), as well as the Bible and Book of Mormon (D&C 33:16; 42:12). The Pearl of Great Price, another book of scripture, was published and canonized following the death of Joseph Smith and is not mentioned in the Doctrine and Covenants. These four volumes of scripture comprise the standard works of the Church.

Additional revelations have since been added to these standard works and accepted as scripture (see En., May 1976, pp. 19, 127–29.)

Regarding the ongoing nature of scripture, Elder Bruce R. McConkie noted that "the canon of scripture is not now and never will be full. God speaks and his people hear. His words and his works are without end; they never close." (En., Aug. 1976, p. 8; see also Articles of Faith 1:9; 2 Ne. 28:27–30; 2 Ne. 29:9.)

Speaking of scripture which has come to us from times past, President Joseph Fielding Smith said: "Age has made it venerable to many because it is ancient. The word of the Lord delivered by the power of the Holy Ghost to the servants of the Lord today is also scripture, just as much as it was in ancient times." (CHMR, 1:258.) This is what the Lord declared in 1831 when he said that "whatsoever they [the presiding brethren] shall speak when moved upon by the Holy Ghost shall be scripture, shall be the will . . . , mind . . . , word . . . , voice of the Lord, and the power of God unto salvation" (D&C 68:4).

To the question "Whence cometh scripture?" we respond: *"When one of the brethren stands before a congregation of the people today,* *and the inspiration of the Lord is upon him, he speaks that which the Lord would have him speak. It is just as much scripture as anything you will find written in any of* . . . the standard works of the Church." (DS 1:186.)

Sea of Glass

When the earth is renewed by resurrection and becomes a glorified globe, a celestial sphere, it will be as a "sea of glass" (D&C 77:1; 88:16–26). "This is a figure of speech typifying the earth in its celestial form," wrote President Joseph Fielding Smith (CHMR 1:295).

Speaking of this change in our planet, Brigham Young said: "It will not then be an opaque body as it now is, but it will be like the stars of the firmament, full of light and glory; it will be a body of light. John compares it, in its celestial state, to a sea of glass." (JD 7:163.)

See also: Celestial; Sea of Glass and Fire

Sea of Glass and Fire

The Prophet Joseph Smith declared that the angels who minister to this earth "reside in the presence of God, on a globe like a sea of glass and fire" (D&C 130:5–7). Smith and Sjodahl suggest that "the Prophet is speaking of angels who have once belonged to this Earth; they reside on a glorified globe somewhere near where God dwells" (SS, 815).

Inasmuch as this heavenly habitation of angels manifests "all things past, present, and future" (D&C 130:7), and in its celestial state our earth "will be a Urim and Thummim to the inhabitants who dwell thereon" (D&C 130:9), it appears logical to assume these two globes share similar destinies. The first having already been glorified and the second not yet having fulfilled "the measure of its creation" (D&C 88:19). The latter shall become a "sea of glass" just as the former.

See also: Celestial; Heaven; Sea of Glass

Seal Them Up unto Eternal Life

A remarkable promise was given to some of the elders in November 1831 as they were authorized to "seal up unto eternal life" any whom the Father should reveal unto them (D&C 68:12). In essence, power was given these priesthood bearers, based upon receiving revelation, to say to a worthy recipient, "I seal you up to eternal life!"

There are recorded instances of this having been done (HC 1:322–34). However, some of those "sealed" did break their celestial contract and were delivered over to "the buffetings of Satan," as forewarned by the Prophet Joseph Smith. President Joseph Fielding Smith stated that *"All covenants are sealed based upon faithfulness"* (DS 2:98).

Therefore, even though a man may have received the promise of eternal life, his unrighteousness can nullify the covenant and he will be left as if the promise had never been made (D&C 121:34–38; 130:20–21; 132:7).

One other factor should also be considered. Prior to April 3, 1836, the *keys* of the sealing power had not yet been vested in mortal men in the dispensation of the fulness of times. It was not until that date that Elijah restored those powers to Joseph Smith and Oliver Cowdery in the Kirtland Temple (D&C 110:13–16). Therefore, "sealings" prior to that point were tentative, or, as Sidney Sperry said, "held in spiritual escrow . . . until the actual reception of the keys of Elijah" (DCC, 709).

Seal Up the Law/Testimony

See: Bind Up the Law/Testimony

Sealed by the Holy Spirit of Promise

Speaking of the inhabitants of the celestial kingdom, the Lord said they had been "sealed by the Holy Spirit of promise" (D&C 76:53). To be "sealed" is to have the Holy Ghost place a "stamp of approval" upon whatever ordinance has been performed in order to insure the promised blessing. His is the ratifying action.

Elder Melvin J. Ballard once said, "We may deceive men, but we cannot deceive the Holy Ghost, and our blessings will not be eternal until they are also sealed by the holy spirit of promise, the Holy Ghost, one who reads the thoughts and hearts of men and gives his sealing approval to the blessings pronounced upon their heads. Then it is binding, and of full force." (SMB, 237.)

Without this seal, all covenants "are of no efficacy, virtue, or force in and after the resurrection . . . ; for all contracts that are not made unto this end have an end when men are dead" (D&C 132:7).

See also: Holy Spirit of Promise; Sealing Blessings of My Church

Sealed His Mission . . . With His Own Blood

John Taylor's account of the martyrdom refers to the Prophet Joseph as having "sealed his mission and his works with his own blood; and so has his brother Hyrum. . . . The testators are now dead and their testament is in force." (D&C 135:3, 5.)

Thirty years after the martyrdom, Brigham Young made a similar statement: "We believe in Joseph the Prophet; he sealed his testimony with his blood, consequently we can, with impunity, believe on him a little better than if he were living. *When he was living, his testimony was not in force upon the people as it is now.*" (JD 18:242; italics added.)

Another prophet of the Church, Joseph Fielding Smith taught: "It was needful that these martyrs seal their testimony with their blood" (DS 1:219). "The shedding of their blood . . . bound that testimony upon an unbelieving world and this testimony will stand at the judgment seat as a witness against all men who have rejected their words of eternal life" (IE, June 1944, p. 364).

See also: Smith, Hyrum; Smith, Joseph, Jr.

Sealed . . . in Their Foreheads

One of the events preceding the Second Coming is the sealing to be placed in the foreheads of God's faithful servants (D&C 77:9; Ezek. 9:4). The Prophet Joseph taught that this sealing "signifies sealing the blessing upon their heads meaning the everlasting covenant, thereby making their calling and election sure. When a seal is put upon the father and mother, it secures their posterity, so that they cannot be lost, but will be saved by virtue of the covenant of their father and mother." (TPJS, 321.)

Elder Orson Pratt taught that this sealing also had reference to the "sealing blessing" pronounced upon the faithful who would go forth from the temple of the New Jerusalem to preach and minister to the inhabitants of the earth (JD 15:365–66).

Sealing and Binding Power

The Lord speaks of the "sealing and binding power" as being "the keys of the kingdom, which consist in the key of knowledge" (D&C 128:14). Elder Bruce R. McConkie wrote: "The keys of the kingdom are the power, right, and authority to preside over the kingdom of God on earth (which is the Church) and to direct all of its affairs. . . . These keys include the *sealing power*, that is, the power to bind and seal on earth, in the Lord's name and by his authorization, and to have the act ratified in heaven." (DNTC 1:389.)

"When the ordinances of salvation and exaltation are performed by or at the direction of those holding these keys, such rites and performances are of full force and validity in this life and in the life to come, that is, they are binding on earth and in heaven" (DNTC 1:424). Those same keys can, of course, loose previously promised blessings when covenants are broken (see D&C 124:93).

Sealing Blessings of My Church

In connection with his call as the Patriarch to the Church, Hyrum Smith was given the "sealing blessings" of the Church (D&C 124:124). Of these powers, Sidney Sperry said: "The Holy Spirit of promise is the seal of approval or acceptance placed upon a worthy person by the Holy Ghost after receiving ordinances and blessings. Every person, for example, who inherits exaltation is sealed by the Holy Spirit of promise. . . . *The Patriarch has the keys of that power by which men may be sealed up unto the day of redemption, that they may not fall notwithstanding the hour of temptation that may come upon them.* This doctrine is of deeply spiritual import and may be understood satisfactorily only by study and the enlightment of the Spirit." (DCC, 665; italics added. See D&C 91:4–6.)

It must be clearly understood, however, "that the president of the Church, not the patriarch, is appointed by God to preside," cautioned President John Taylor. "The *President of the Church presides over all patriarchs, presidents, and councils of the Church; and this presidency does not depend so much upon genealogy as upon calling, order, and seniority.*" (GK, 148; italics added.)

See also: Patriarchal Blessings

Season

The term *season* is used in various contexts within the Doctrine and Covenants. For example, "a season" is used to describe the few months in which Joseph lost his translating privileges (D&C 3:14), and also the time period in which he was commanded to stop translating (D&C 5:30). A short-term mission for Joseph Smith and Sidney Rigdon — which lasted a little over a month — is spoken of as "a season" (D&C 71:2–3). Thomas B. Marsh was commanded to remain in Missouri to publish for "a season" (D&C 118:2). In an epistle to the Saints, Joseph Smith indicates he is going into seclusion for a "short season" to avoid further persecution (D&C 127:1).

Products of the earth are spoken of as being "in the season thereof" (D&C 59:18; 89:11), and the Lord indicates that inhabitants of various kingdoms will be visited according to their order, or "in the season thereof" (D&C 88:58, 61). Judgment for the wicked is also reserved "in the season thereof" (D&C 121:24). Members of the Church are admonished to offer prayers "in the season thereof" (D&C 68:33). Elder Joseph Fielding Smith has said that "the season of prayer is in the morning before the family separates" (CR, Oct. 1919, p. 143).

The phrase "a little season," which appears thirteen times in the Doctrine and Covenants, connotes different time periods. The postmillennial period wherein Satan will be loosed to rage and reign is described as " a little season" (D&C 29:22; 43:31; 88:111). The phrase also refers to a short-term mission (D&C 42:5) and a short but unspecified time during which the Lord has asked certain people to remain in a given location (D&C 51:16; 63:42; 105:21).

People are admonished to ponder the preachments of missionaries for "a little season," which could have reference to their entire earthly lives (D&C 88:71). The chastisement of the people in Missouri and the ultimate redemption of this land is spoken of as "a little season" (D&C 100:13; 103:4; 105:9, 13). Joseph Smith believed this time period would be within a matter of several years, as did most of the early Church leaders (HC 2:145; JD 3:17).

Of this, Smith and Sjodahl have written: "The history of the Church shows us that the 'little season' extended over more than two years, or five, or even ten. Still, since the Spirit of revelation has characterized it as 'little,' we may hope that the redemption of Zion will not be postponed for a great while." (SS, 682.)

See also: In the Season Thereof; Little Season

Seat

One of the dictionary definitions of *seat* is "a place from which authority is exercised." An 1831 revelation proclaimed that the land of Zion was to be a "seat" (D&C 69:6). This *seat* was the *center place* for the Church, or the place from which the authority of the Church was to be exercised, namely Independence, Jackson County, Missouri (D&C 57:3).

The judgment seat of Christ (D&C 135:5; Ether 12:38) is symbolic of the seat from which he will exercise his authority as the Supreme Judge of this earth's inhabitants (D&C 76:68; 3 Ne. 27:16; John 5:26–27). The seat of the First Presidency (D&C 102:26–27, 33) has reference to the authority of the office or to the Quorum of the First Presidency.

Second Angel

He who will blow the "second trump," which will signal the resurrection of terrestrial beings, will be the "second angel" (D&C 88:99). At the end of the Millennium he will again blow his trump and "reveal the secret acts of men, and the thoughts and intents of their hearts, and the mighty works of God in the second thousand years" of earth's history (D&C 88:109). His identity is presently unknown.

See also: Second Trump

Second Coming

See: Curtain of Heaven; End of the World; First Caught Up to Meet Him; Great and Dreadful Day of the Lord; Great Sign in Heaven; Millennium; Moon Shall Be Turned into Blood; Pillar of Heaven; Presence of the Lord Shall Be As the Melting Fire; Seventh Angel/Trump; Stars Shall Fall from Heaven; Sun Shall Be Darkened; They Who Are in the North Countries; Those Who Are Christ's at His Coming; Tomorrow; Two Prophets; Two Shall Put Their Tens of Thousands to Flight

Second Death

The scriptures make it abundantly clear that "all" shall be raised from the grave, for "everybody who has tabernacled in the flesh shall again assume his body" (Alma 11:42–45; Morm. 9:13–14; Talmage, 391). "No matter what a man's sins may be, whatever crimes he may have committed, the resurrection of the mortal body is assured to him by the redemption of the Lord Jesus Christ. But after that comes the second death; and they who are sons of perdition will partake of that." (GT 1:34; D&C 76:37.)

The *second death* is a "spiritual banishment . . . by which those who partake of it are denied the presence of God and are consigned to dwell with the devil and his angels throughout eternity" (DS 1:49).

Speaking of those who are assigned to this awful fate, Joseph Smith said: "Those who commit the unpardonable sin are doomed to Gnolom—to dwell in hell, worlds without end" (TPJS, 361). Their fate is such that it is not to be revealed "save to those who are made partakers thereof" (HC 1:366; D&C 76:45–48).

See also: Blasphemy Against the Holy Ghost; Last Death; Resurrection of the Unjust; Shed Innocent Blood; Sons of Perdition; Spiritual Fall; Spiritually Dead

Second Elder

When The Church of Jesus Christ of Latter-day Saints was first organized, Oliver Cowdery was called by the Lord to be "an apostle of Jesus Christ" and "the second elder of this church" (D&C 20:3; HC 1:76–78). President Joseph Fielding Smith said: "We leave [Oliver] out in our list of Presidents of the Church . . . *but he was an Assistant President. Oliver Cowdery's standing in the beginning was as the 'Second Elder' [President] of the Church, holding the keys jointly with the Prophet Joseph Smith."* (DS 1:212.)

Because of transgression, Oliver lost his high calling and the Lord called Hyrum Smith to receive the "keys . . . and be crowned with the same blessing, and glory, and honor and priesthood, and gifts of the priesthood, that once were put upon him that was my servant Oliver Cowdery" (D&C 124:95; DS 1:216–22; 3:165–66).

With the sealing of Hyrum's testimony in blood, as a martyr of the kingdom, the position of "second elder," or second president, came to an end.

See also: Cowdery, Oliver; Smith, Hyrum

Second Man

"The second man," declared Paul, "is the Lord from heaven"

(1 Cor. 15:47; D&C 128:14). Inasmuch as Paul is comparing the "earthy" with the "heavenly," and the "first man" seems to refer to mortal man with his corruptible body of flesh and blood, patterned after the first man, Adam, it appears reasonable to conclude that the "second man" is of the Lord and refers to that *incorruptible, resurrected body which is patterned after He who was first to rise from the grave.*

This body is of a heavenly substance and is quickened by the spirit rather than by the blood, which is a corruptible, earthly element. For, wrote Paul, "as we have borne the image of the earthy, we shall also bear the image of the heavenly" (1 Cor. 15:49).

The heavenly, according to Bruce R. McConkie, is the "image of Christ or immortality, which is the natural inheritance of all men from Christ" (DNTC 2:402). Paul was teaching the reality of the resurrection to the Corinthians, "For as in Adam all die, even so in Christ shall all be made alive. But every man in his own order." (1 Cor. 15:22–23.)

See also: Resurrection

Second Priesthood

See: First Priesthood

Second Thousand Years

According to Doctrine and Covenants 77:6, this earth will pass through a temporal existence of seven thousand years.

"Temporal, by all interpretations," said President Joseph Fielding Smith, "means *passing, temporary or mortal.* This, then, has reference to the earth in its fallen state, for the earth was cursed when Adam, who was given dominion over it, transgressed the law. *Before that time this earth was not mortal any more than Adam was.*" (DS 1:78–81; 2 Ne. 2:22.)

The "second thousand years," spoken of in the Doctrine and Covenants, represent the second millennium of earth's temporal history, or the second thousand years from the time Adam was expelled from the Garden (D&C 77:7; 88:109).

At the end of the seventh of the one-thousand year periods, known as *the* Millennium, a series of seven trumps will be sounded by seven angels, each revealing "the secret acts of men, and the thoughts and intents of their hearts, and the mighty works of God" in their respective millennia (D&C 88:108–110). This will be comparable to opening the seven seals of the book which John the Revelator saw that contains the mysteries of the seven thousand years of earth's temporal existence (D&C 77:6–7; Rev. 5).

Second Trump

The "second trump" spoken of in Doctrine and Covenants 88:99 is the one which ushers in the resurrection of "those who are Christ's at his coming," but who will not have been caught up to meet him and descend in the fulness of his glory (D&C 88:98). This group will be of a terrestrial order.

Although their "honorable lives" qualify them for the first resurrection, for them this will occur when the second trump sounds on the afternoon of that glorious day, rather than in the morning (DS 2:296–97). The morning is reserved for the celestial beings who will answer the call of the "first trump."

See also: Those Who Are Christ's at His Coming; Second Angel; Terrestrial

Secret Chambers

From the time that Cain and Satan entered into their nefarious contract, which caused Cain to assertively say, "Truly I am Mahan, the master of this great secret, that I may murder and get gain," satanic schemes have been fostered in "secret chambers" (Moses 5:29–31).

This was true of the Gadiantons and their "secret works of darkness" (Hel. 8:4, 28), as well as of all "secret combinations . . . which are built up to get power and gain" (Ether 8:18–25). It was within such secret chambers that Judas bargained to betray the Savior.

In January 1831, the Lord warned the Saints in New York that "the enemy in secret chambers seeketh your lives" (D&C 38:13, 28). Evidently at that time there were those who in "Cainlike" fashion were conceiving satanic schemes against Joseph Smith and his faithful followers. The day will come when these rebellious conspirators shall have "their secret acts . . . revealed" (D&C 1:3).

See also: Secret Combinations

Secret Combinations

From the day Cain gloried in his wickedness, taking satanic pleasure in his evil alliance with the devil and declaring himself to be "Mahan, the master of this great secret" (Moses 5:31), similar alliances known as *secret combinations* have been upon the earth.

Anciently, the Nephite prophet Moroni warned of their destructive influence in our day and sadly reflected on the destruction of his own people as a result of secret combinations. "And whatsoever nation shall uphold such secret combinations . . . they shall be destroyed" (Ether 8:18-25). In a revelation given February 9, 1831, the Lord warned of the coming of "secret combinations" (D&C 42:64).

Elder Ezra Taft Benson has drawn a parallel between those combinations which destroyed the ancient Nephite and Jaredite civilizations and modern-day communism, which he says is nothing more than "the earthly image of the plan which Satan presented in the pre-existence" and against which we fought (CR, Sept. 1961, pp. 70-75).

President Joseph F. Smith warned against joining "secret societies" (GD, 109-11), and President David O. McKay voiced the following admonition: "Latter-day Saints should have nothing to do with the secret combinations and *groups antagonistic to the constitutional law of the land*" (GI, 306; italics added).

See also: Hidden Things of Darkness; Secret Chambers

Secret Parts

The Lord told several of the early leaders of the Church that their *secret parts* would not be discovered (D&C 111:4). This means that they would not be embarrassed or put to shame (see LDS edition of the King James Bible, Isa. 3:17, note a).

Secretary of the Interior

One of the key federal figures in overseeing the Territory of Utah was a member of the presidential cabinet, the secretary of the interior. The Utah Commission, a five-member board established by Congress to oversee election affairs in Utah, was required by the Edmunds Law of 1882 to report to the secretary of the interior (CHC 6:111). The accuracy of one of its reports regarding the practice of plural marriage was challenged by President Wilford Woodruff (OD—1).

See also: Utah Commission

Secrets of My Will

In the vision of the degrees of glory, the Lord declared, "I [will] make known . . . the secrets of my will" (D&C 76:10). These secrets, revealed to Joseph Smith and his scribe, Sidney Rigdon, touched upon "every law, every commandment, every promise, every truth, and every point touching the destiny of man, from Genesis to Revelation" (HC 1:252).

Speaking of the vision, Elder Charles W. Penrose said, "There is nothing in the . . . Bible that can compare with it" (JD 24:92). Some of that which was seen remains a secret, for Joseph and Sidney were not allowed to write all the sublime truths which their spiritual eyes beheld (D&C 76:114-119).

One can read the words describing this great vision in a matter of minutes; however, Joseph and Sidney were wrapped in the wonders of eternity for over an hour during the course of their experience (JI 27:304). Over a decade after this marvelous manifestation, the Prophet declared: "I could explain a hundred fold more than I ever have of the glories of the kingdoms manifested to me in the vision, were I permitted, and were the people prepared to receive them" (HC 5:402).

It appears, therefore, that the Lord's secrets will remain a mystery until the Saints are prepared to receive them. "There appears to be no point," said Elder Neal A. Maxwell, "in God's constantly illuminating the trail beyond where my eyes of faith can now see" (DSY, 1976, p. 190). The words of the Prophet Joseph should also be pondered: "The reason we do not have the secrets of the Lord revealed unto us," he said, "is because we do not keep them" (HC 4:479).

Sectarian

The Prophet Joseph stated that the belief "that the Father and the Son dwell in a man's heart is an old sectarian notion, and is false" (D&C 130:3). Sectarian refers to a belief promulgated by a sect or religious faction and generally has negative connotations. A sect is a dissenting or schismatic religious body, especially one regarded as extreme or heretical.

Sedition

We believe that "sedition and rebellion are unbecoming every citizen [who is] protected" in his "inherent and inalienable rights" by the government under which he lives (D&C 134:5-7).

Webster says that *sedition* is "incitement of resistance to or insurrection against lawful authority." This was one of the crimes charged against Barabbas, the wolf who was released by Pilate while the Lamb was given to the howling crowd who cried for his crucifixion (Luke 23:18–25).

See My Face

In 1833, the resurrected Redeemer said: "Verily, thus saith the Lord: It shall come to pass that every soul who forsaketh his sins and cometh unto me, and calleth on my name, and obeyeth my voice, and keepeth my commandments, shall see my face and know that I am" (D&C 93:1). Two years prior to this a similar promise had been given (D&C 67:10), and Joseph Smith and Sidney Rigdon became benefactors of the promise just several months later (D&C 76:22–24). The scriptures cite examples of others who have enjoyed this privilege (2 Ne. 11:2–3; Morm. 1:15; Ether 4:7; Moses 1:11; JST, Ex. 33:20).

"Seeing the Lord is not a matter of lineage or rank or position or place of precedence," said Elder Bruce R. McConkie. "The fact is that the day of personal visitations from the Lord to faithful men on earth has no more ceased than has the day of miracles. . . .

"All those who are now living in its entirety the law of the celestial kingdom—are already qualified to see the Lord. The attainment of such a state of righteousness and perfection is the object and end toward which all of the Lord's people are striving. We seek to see the face of the Lord while we yet dwell in mortality." (PM, 575–95.)

One who seeks the face of the Lord should keep in mind that the Lord "will unveil his face . . . in his own time, and in his own way, and according to his own will" (D&C 88:68).

Seed

The term *seed* has been used scripturally to represent one's posterity. Examples of this in the Doctrine and Covenants include Adam and his seed (D&C 29:42), Aaron and his seed (D&C 84:18), and the seed of Abraham (D&C 103:17). Anciently, mother Eve declared, "Were it not for our transgression we never should have had seed" (Moses 5:11).

Although it is not directly referred to in the Doctrine and Covenants, another important use of the term *seed* is its association with Christ. Speaking of the Savior, the Book of Mormon prophet Abinadi asked, "Who shall be his seed?" Answering his own query he said, "All those who have hearkened unto [the prophet's] words, and believed that the Lord would redeem his people, and have looked forward to that day for a remission of their sins . . . , these are his seed, or they are the heirs of the kingdom of God." (Mosiah 15:10–13; see also Isa. 53; En. May 1985, p. 10.)

See also: Fruit of . . . Loins; Offspring

Seed of Abraham

The meaning of the "seed of Abraham" is well illustrated in a confrontation Jesus had with some of the patriarch's proud descendants: "We be Abraham's seed," they boasted. To which the Master replied, "If ye were Abraham's children, ye would do the works of Abraham." (John 8:32–50.)

John the Baptist had previously cautioned the Jews to "think not to say within yourselves, We are the children of Abraham, and we only have power to bring seed unto our father Abraham; for I say unto you that God is able of these stones to raise up children into Abraham" (JST, Matt. 3:36).

Thus, heredity is insufficient in laying claim to kinship with father Abraham, for only the faithful are truly of his seed. These may include those who have literally descended from his loins as well as those who are adopted into his family through their faithfulness (Abr. 2:10, Gal. 2:29).

According to the Prophet Joseph, this latter group actually has their blood purged and becomes literally the "seed of Abraham" (HC 3:380). These are the "children of Israel" who are led out of the bondage of sin, through the power of the priesthood and by strict obedience to the laws and ordinances of the gospel (D&C 103:17). These are the "seed who will inherit celestial mansions with Abraham the father of the faithful" (D&C 84:34).

See also: Abraham; Works of Abraham

Seer

There are five instances in the Doctrine and Covenants where the Prophet Joseph Smith, or the presiding position he held, are referred to as "seer" (D&C 21:1; 107:91–92; 124:125; 127:12; 135:3). Additionally, Hyrum Smith is referred to by the same title (D&C 124:94). Anciently, Joseph, the son of Jacob, prophesied that Joseph Smith would be raised up as a great "seer" (2 Ne. 3:6–15).

According to the Book of Mormon, a seer is one who possesses or is commanded to use a Urim and Thummim (Mosiah 8:13; 28:13–16). He is a "revelator and a prophet" (Mosiah 8:16). He is one who can behold things "not visible to the natural eye" (Moses 6:36). In ancient times, prophets were referred to as seers (1 Sam. 9:9).

Elder John A. Widtsoe summarized the role of a seer as follows: "A seer is one who sees with spiritual eyes. He perceives the meaning of that which seems obscure to others; therefore he is an interpreter and clarifier of eternal truth. He forsees the future from the past and the present. This he does by the power of the Lord operating through him directly, or indirectly with the aid of divine instruments such as the Urim and Thummim. In short, he is one who sees, who walks in the Lord's light with open eyes." (ER, 258.)

The Church presently sustains the members of the First Presidency and Quorum of the Twelve Apostles as seers. The counselors in the First Presidency and the Apostles are subject to the authority of the senior Apostle, or President of the Church, who is *the* Seer. Joseph Smith specifically designated the counselors in the First Presidency and the Twelve Apostles as seers (HC 2:417). When there has been a Patriarch to the Church, he has also been sustained as a seer.

See also: Apostle; First Presidency of the Church; President of the High Priesthood; Urim and Thummim

Seneca County, New York

In the center of the state of New York lies Seneca County. From her bosom sprang the "stone cut out of the mountain without hands" that was destined to "roll forth until it has filled the whole earth" (D&C 65:2; 109:72–73; Dan. 2:34–35, 44). It was within the borders of Seneca County that the translation of the Book of Mormon was completed and the Three Witnesses thereto received manifestations from God (D&C 128:20). Here twenty sections of the Doc-

trine and Covenants were received and recorded, and the Church had its humble beginnings at the Whitmer home in Fayette (HC 1:75–80).

See also: Fayette

Sensual

By transgression of holy laws man becomes carnal, sensual, and devilish (D&C 20:20). As used in scripture, to be sensual is to focus one's energics on the lusts of the flesh, to unduly seek gratification of the senses, to concentrate on indulging one's appetites. It is to love Satan more than God (Moses 5:13).

Seraphic Hosts of Heaven

The terms *Seraphic hosts of heaven* and *Seraphs* each appear once in the Doctrine and Covenants (D&C 38:1; 109:79). The prophet Isaiah spoke of having seen "seraphim" in the presence of the Lord (Isa. 6:2; 2 Ne. 16:2).

According to Smith and Sjodahl, seraphim are the "attendants of Jehovah, reflecting His glory and majesty" (SS, 198). Another has said, "Seraphs are angels who reside in the presence of God, giving continual glory, honor, and adoration to him. 'Praise ye him, all his angels: praise ye him, all his hosts.' (Ps. 148:2.)

"It is clear that seraphs include the unembodied spirits of

preexistence, for our Lord 'looked upon the wide expanse of eternity, and *all the seraphic hosts of heaven, before the world was made.'* (D&C 38:1.) Whether the name seraphs also applies to perfected and resurrected angels is not clear. . . .

"The fact that these holy beings were shown to [Isaiah] as having wings was simply to symbolize their 'power, to move, to act, etc.' as was the case also in visions others had received. (D&C 77:4.)" (MD, 702–3.)

Seraphs

See: Seraphic Hosts of Heaven

Serpent, Old

Twice in the Doctrine and Covenants Satan is referred to as "that old serpent" (76:28; 88:110). The same terminology appears in the Book of Mormon (2 Ne. 2:18; Mosiah 16:3). *Cruden's Bible Concordance* says that "the Devil is called a *Serpent*, Rev. 12:9, both because he hid himself in the body of a real serpent when he seduced the first woman, and because of his serpentine disposition, being of subtil, crafty, and dangerous enemy to mankind" (p. 433).

The story of Satan's role as a serpent is best told in a revelation received by Joseph Smith in December 1830 (Moses 4:5–21). The motif of the serpent, as an enemy

to righteousness and as one who has been overcome by the devil, was represented in an interesting dream related by the Prophet Joseph Smith just two weeks before his martyrdom (TPJS, 368–69).

*See also:*Devil

Servants

The title of "servants" appears throughout the Doctrine and Covenants. Early in this dispensation the Lord declared that his words would be fulfilled, "whether by mine own voice or by the voice of my servants, it is the same" (D&C 1:38).

The title usually applies to those engaged in the ministry. John the Baptist called Joseph Smith and Oliver Cowdery his "fellow servants" (D&C 13), and the Lord frequently called specific people his servants (D&C 27:8; 49:1; 52:22–35).

There are two designations of servants in the scriptures: "1. Those who choose to serve the Lord and who keep his commandments are called his *servants*. After they have been tried and tested and are found faithful and true in all things, they are called no longer servants, but *friends*. (John 15:14–15.) His friends are the ones he will take into his kingdom and with whom he will associate to all eternity. (D&C 93:45–46.) They receive the adoption of sonship . . . ! Wherefore thou art no more a servant, but a son; and if a son, then an heir of God through Christ.' (Gal. 4:6–7.) Thus, those who are servants of God here gain exaltation hereafter.

"2. Those who do not choose to serve the Lord, who do not keep his commandments, and who do not receive the ordinances of his house, shall be *servants* to all eternity. (D&C 76:112.) They did not choose to be his servants here and so he will require ministering servitude from them in eternity." (MD, 705–6.)

See also: Bond Servants; Ministering Servants; Servants of Sin; Servants of the Most High

Servants of Sin

Those who falsely accuse the Lord's anointed have been divinely declared to be "servants of sin" (D&C 121:17). These are those whose lives are devoted to serving Satan, who cannot follow Christ (Moro. 7:11; see also 3 Ne. 13:24).

See also: Children of Disobedience

Servants of the Most High

Speaking of the inhabitants of the telestial kingdom, the Lord declared that "they shall be servants of the Most High; but where God and Christ dwell they cannot come, worlds without end" (see D&C 76:109–12). As Smith and Sjodahl so aptly explained, to be "servants of the Most High" is "an honorable position, indeed, but it is different to being 'king and priests,' " and receiving a *fulness* of God's glory (SS, 469; D&C 76:56; 84:33–38).

Speaking of the destiny of these "servants," President George Albert Smith said: "There are some people who have supposed that if we are quickened telestial bodies that eventually, throughout the ages of eternity, we will continue to progress until we will find our place in the celestial kingdom, but the scriptures and revelations of God have said that those who are quickened telestial bodies cannot come where God and Christ dwell, worlds without end" (CR, Oct. 1945, p. 172).

See also: Most High; Servants; Telestial

Servitude

Doctrine and Covenants 134 speaks of those "human beings . . . held in servitude" (D&C 134:12). This term is synonymous with slavery or bondage and is the state of being subject to another.

See also: Bond-Servants

Seth (Joseph)

During a period of time when pseudonyms were being used to disguise the identity of people mentioned in the revelations, Joseph, the son of Jacob, was referred to as "Seth" (D&C 96:7; pre-1981 edition). In most instances, only the names of the living were disguised, but in this case the identity of an Old Testament prophet long since deceased was hidden from the world (see HC 1:255). In current editions of the Doctrine and Covenants, only Jacob's actual name is shown.

See also: Joseph

Seth (Son of Adam)

Modern revelation provides additional insight into the life of Adam's noble son, Seth: He "was a perfect man, and his likeness was the express likeness of his father, insomuch that he seemed to be like unto his father in all things and could be distinguished from him only by his age" (D&C 107:43; Moses 6:10; Gen. 5:3). Seth was second only to Adam among the great patriarchs who met in the valley of Adam-ondi-Ahman, three years prior to Adam's death (D&C 107:53). He was an obedient son who "rebelled not, but offered an acceptable sacrifice, like unto his brother Abel" (Moses 6:3).

Seth was born when Adam was 130 years of age (Moses 6:10; Gen. 5:3–5), and was "ordained by Adam at the age of sixty-nine years" (D&C 107:42). Seth lived to be 912 years old and was survived by his son Enos, whom he taught "in the ways of God" (Moses 6:13, 16).

President Joseph F. Smith saw Seth as one of the "great and mighty ones" assembled in the "congregation of the righteous" at the time of the Savior's visit to the spirit world following his crucifixion (D&C 138:38, 40).

See also: Perfect Man

Seven Churches

In an explanation of some of the apocalyptic writings of John the Revelator, reference is made to "seven churches" which existed in Asia (D&C 77:5; Rev. 1:4). Joseph Fielding Smith suggested that these seven churches were branches of the Church in Asia Minor and "were all that were considered worthy of a standing in the Church at that time, indicating that the apostasy had at that day become extensive" (CHMR, 1:299–300).

Another writer indicated that the important thing to remember regarding these churches is that John held the keys of the kingdom upon the earth at that time and therefore had jurisdiction over the membership of each branch of the Church (DNTC 3:436).

Seven Seals

The seven seals binding the book which John the Revelator saw (Rev. 5:1) are identified in Doctrine and Covenants 77:7 as representing the seven periods of earth's existence. It is of interest to note the way in which this book was sealed. Ancient books frequently consisted of parchment rolled around a "stick" (see Ezek. 37:15–30). The book John saw consisted of seven parchments, each containing writing on both sides, and each being sealed separately. Thus, as one seal was broken and the parchment unrolled, the second seal would be exposed, and so on until all had been revealed. (See SS, 474.)

Seventh Angel/Trump

Prior to the ushering in of the Millennium, a series of trumps will be sounded by seven angels. The first sounding will signal the beginning of major events such as the destruction of the great and abominable church and the redemption of the dead (D&C 88:92–107). The seventh angel, or Michael, who is Father Adam, will proclaim that the Lamb of God has achieved his purposes.

Following this, a second series of trumps will commence to sound. Each in turn will reveal the secret acts, thoughts, and intents of men as well as the great works of God in a respective thousand-year period of earth's history. The first will proclaim the history of the first thousand years, the second will announce the second thousand years, and so on through the seventh angel. Michael, the seventh angel, will proclaim the binding of Satan during the seventh period of time, also known as the Millennium (D&C 88:108–10).

At the conclusion of the seventh thousand years, Satan will be loosed for "a little season," and Michael the archangel will gather together the hosts of heaven to victoriously do battle against the hosts of hell, as he did in the pre-earth war with the forces of evil (Rev. 12:7–9; D&C 88:111–115). Following this battle, Satan and his followers will be cast out forever.

See also: Adam; Ancient of Days; Archangel; Battle of the Great God; Dispensation of the Fulness of Times; Keys of Salvation; Michael; Thousand Years, The

Seventy, The

The office of seventy has traditionally been one of the ordained offices of the Melchizedek Priesthood. In October 1986, quorums of seventy were discontinued in the stakes of the Church. At the present time only those men who serve as General Authorities and have membership in the First Quorum of the Seventy belong to a quorum of Seventies (En., Nov. 1986, p. 48). These men are "especial witnesses" (D&C 107:25), "traveling ministers" (D&C 107:97), and constitute the third presiding quorum of the Church, following the First Presidency and the Quorum of the Twelve Apostles (D&C 107:26). The Seventies are "to bear record of [the Lord's] name in all the world," acting under the direction of the Apostles (D&C 124:139). Presently there is but one quorum, but as the Church grows this body of men could be expanded into additional quorums (D&C 107:95–96).

For many years the first quorum consisted only of seven men who were referred to as the First Council of Seventy (D&C 107:93–94). Commencing in October 1976, additional men were added to the quorum with the promise that it would "be gradually organized, eventually with seventy members" (CR, Oct. 1975, p. 3). One year later the twenty-one General Authorities who had previously been serving as Assistants to the Council of the Twelve were called to serve as members of the First Quorum of the Seventy.

"With this move," said President Spencer W. Kimball, "the three governing quorums of the Church defined by the revelations —the First Presidency, the Quorum of the Twelve, and the First Quorum of the Seventy— have been set in their places as revealed by the Lord" (CR, Oct. 1976, p. 10).

This organization was in fulfillment of the Lord's promise to an earlier prophet, John Taylor, that he would "reveal . . . from time to time everything that shall be necessary for the future development and perfection of my church." This revelation was in response to President Taylor's inquiry regarding the organization of the Seventies. (Pamphlet in the Church Historian's Office, dated April 13, 1883.)

See also: Equal in Authority; Especial Witnesses; General Authorities; Traveling Ministers

Shackles

See: Fetters of Hell

Shadow of Death

See: Region and Shadow of Death

Shaft of Death

The term *shaft of death* is not found in any scripture other than Doctrine and Covenants 85:8. The stem or body of an arrow as well as the long handle of a spear are referred to as shafts. The shaft of death is figurative language which represents death or destruction as a weapon such as an arrow or spear.

Shake Off the Dust of Thy Feet

The divine injunction to "shake off the dust of thy feet against those who receive thee not" was issued on several occasions to early missionaries of this last dispensation (D&C 24:15; 60:15; 75:20). Ancient missionaries shook the dust from their feet against those who rejected the gospel, for they "were to be considered as pagans with whom the Jews held no social intercourse. Even the dust of their dwellings and their cities, was to be treated as defilement, necessitating a cleansing." (SS, 126; Matt. 10:14; Acts 13:51.)

In other instances the elders have been admonished to "cleanse your feet even with water" as a testimony against those who reject the message (D&C 84:92; 99:4). Of these "ordinances," President Joseph Fielding Smith wrote: "The elders were to seek out from among the people the honest in heart and leave their warning testimony with all others, thus they would become clean from their blood. The cleansing of their feet, either by washing or wiping off the dust, would be recorded in heaven as a testimony against the wicked. This act, however, was not to be performed in the presence of the offenders, 'lest thou provoke them, but in secret, and wash thy feet, as a testimony against them in the day of judgment.' " (CHMR 1:223.)

Smith and Sjodahl gave further enlightenment on the subject of shaking the dust off one's feet: "The significance of this solemn act is made clear in Nehemiah 5:13. This prophet, after having taken a promise of the priests, shook his lap and said, 'God shake out every man from his house, and from his labor, that performeth not this promise, even thus be he shaken out and empty.' To shake the dust of the feet signified the same thing." (SS, 360.)

Shakers

See: Copley, Leman; Lee, Ann; Son of Man Cometh Not in the Form of a Woman

Shalemanasseh

W. W. Phelps was one of four individuals who were given code names in an 1832 revelation, their identity was not known until recent years (D&C 82:11, pre-1981 editions). These four, along with five whose real names were discovered earlier, constituted an association under the Order of Enoch. At the time of the revelation the Lord chose not to reveal the identities of any of the nine in order to keep this knowledge from coming into the hands of the enemies of the Church (HC 1:255). Current editions of the Doctrine and Covenants do not use these code names.

See also: W. W. Phelps

Sharper Than a Two-Edged Sword

The descriptive phrase "sharper than a two-edged sword" appears occasionally in scriptures to describe the power of God's word (D&C 6:2; 11:2; 12:2; 14:2; 33:1). A two-edged sword is one which has been sharpened on both sides to make it twice as effective. God's word and the still small voice of the Spirit are even sharper than this, for they are capable of piercing the most pernicious armament and of penetrating to the inner most depths of one's soul (D&C 85:6).

Paul wrote: "For the word of God is quick, and powerful, and sharper than any two-edged sword, piercing even to the dividing asunder of body and spirit, and of the joints and marrow, and is a discerner of the thoughts and intents of the heart" (JST, Heb. 4:12).

Sheaves

The term *sheaves* is used four times in the Doctrine and Covenants, each time relating to missionary labors (D&C 31:5; 33:9; 75:5; 79:3). Those who go forth in the ministry, faithfully proclaiming the gospel with all their souls, shall be "laden with sheaves," or, in other words, reap a harvest of souls. "He that goeth . . . bearing precious seed, shall doubtless come again with rejoicing, bringing his sheaves with him," declared the Psalmist (Ps. 126:6). The great missionary Ammon reminded his fellow laborers that their faithful efforts had produced a number of sheaves (Alma 26:5).

Sheaves is plural for *sheaf*, to which Webster gives as one definition, "any collection of things bound together." In the gospel sense, sheaves are collections of Saints bound together by their faith in the Lord Jesus Christ, the principles and ordinances of his everlasting gospel, the power and authority of the priesthood which makes those saving ordinances possible, and the Church which he established. "And I will gather my people together as a man gathereth his sheaves," said the resurrected Lord (3 Ne. 20:18).

See also: Field Is White Already to Harvest; Ripe; Thrash the Nations; Thrust in His Sickle

Shed Innocent Blood

The Apostle Peter reminds us that we are not redeemed with "corruptible things . . . but with the precious blood of Christ, as of a lamb without blemish and without spot" (1 Pet. 1:18–19). Christ stood in pure, undefiled innocence as his blood flowed in Gethsemane and on Calvary; thus, "innocent blood" was shed. Those who are "made partakers of the Holy Ghost" and then fall away "crucify to themselves the Son of God afresh" (Heb. 6:4–6; D&C 76:34–35); they "assent" unto his death (D&C 132:26–27), in the which they "shed innocent blood."

Elder Bruce R. McConkie has written that a son of perdition "commits murder by assenting unto the Lord's death, that is, having a perfect knowledge of the truth he comes out in open rebellion and places himself in a position wherein he would have crucified Christ knowing perfectly the while that he was the Son of

God. Christ is thus crucified afresh and put to open shame." (DNTC 3:161; see also AGQ 1:68–69.)

Elder Eldred G. Smith suggested another application of the phrase "shedding innocent blood." Referring to this expression, he said: "What do you think He's talking about? Is it possible that He was referring to abortion? Think about it! Is there more innocent life than that of the unborn child? And why is murder referred to when the Lord is talking about marriage?" (En., May 1978, p. 30.)

See also: Blasphemy Against the Holy Ghost; David; Murder; Second Death; Sons of Perdition;

Shederlaomach

In two revelations, one given March 15, 1833, in Kirtland, Ohio, and the other given April 23, 1834, at the same location, Frederick G. Williams was referred to as "Shederlaomach" (D&C 92:1–2; 104:27, 29; pre-1981 edition). In the first revelation, Williams is commanded to "be a lively number" of a united order and the latter revelation mentions his participation therein. The unusual name of Shederlaomach was a result of the secrecy that was necessarily employed at times in early Church history regarding people, places, and assignments (see HC 1:255). There is no other use of this name in recorded scripture; furthermore, it no longer is used

in current editions of the Doctrine and Covenants.

See also: Williams, Frederick G.

Shedolamak

The only mention of a place called Shedolamak is in a revelation on priesthood, given in March 1835 (D&C 107:45). Adam is reported to have been traveling to this place when he was met by his great-grandson, Cainan, upon whom he conferred the priesthood. Adam was at that point in his 412th year, for Cainan was ordained at age 87. No authoritative description of Shedolamak has been revealed.

Sheep

See: Good Shepherd

Shem

Among the "great and mighty" ones gathered in the "congregation of the righteous" visited by Jesus Christ in the spirit world was "the great high priest" Shem (D&C 138:38, 41). Shem was a son of Noah (Gen. 5:29–32; Moses 8:12) and his descendants are thought to be the Shemitic or Semitic races, which include the Hebrews, Phoenicians, Arabs, Aramaeans (Syrians), Babylonians, and Assyrians (LDSBD, 773). He is mentioned as one of the direct line ancestors of Joseph, husband of Mary the mother of Jesus (Luke 3:36).

Sheol, Benighted Dominion of

A word scripturally unique to the Doctrine and Covenants is *Sheol* (D&C 121:4). The Prophet Joseph Smith used this term in a pleading prayer from his confinement in Liberty Jail. It is a Hebrew word that translated in English in the King James Version of the Bible could mean "grave" (Gen. 37:35), "pit" (Job. 17:16), or "hell" (Ps. 16:10) (LDSBD, 773).

One writer has said that sheol "is the gloomy abode of departed spirits; it is the place the wicked go to await the day of their eventual resurrection . . . ; the connotation surrounding its usage is one of evil, sorrow, and anguish" (MD, 710).

See also: Benighted

Shepherd

See: Good Shepherd

Sherman, Lyman

Lyman R. Sherman was one of the original seven Presidents of the Seventy. Although his full name does not appear within the context of the revelations in the Doctrine and Covenants, it is in the preface of section 108, which contains a revelation directed to Sherman. The day after Christmas, 1835, he went to the home of the Prophet and requested a revelation: "For," said he, "I have been wrought upon to make known to you my feelings and desires, and was promised that I should have a Revelation which should make known my duty" (HC 2:345).

Sherman served as a member of Zion's Camp and as a member of the First Council of Seventy from February 28, 1835, until April 6, 1837, when he was released to serve as a high priest. He served on two high councils, one in Kirtland and one in Far West. (Jenson 1:190–91; HC 3:225.) He died at the age of thirty-four on January 27, 1839 (CA 1978, 117).

Sherwood, Henry G.

Although mentioned only twice in the Doctrine and Covenants, the name of Henry G. Sherwood is found frequently in the pages of Joseph Smith's history. His appearance in the Doctrine and Covenants is in connection with his being asked to pay stock in the Nauvoo House and as a member of the Nauvoo high council (D&C 124:81, 132). He also served on high councils in Kirtland and in the Salt Lake Valley.

When the Saints first moved to Commerce, Illinois, Sherwood was among those seriously stricken with malaria. Wilford Woodruff said that Sherwood "was nigh unto death." The Prophet Joseph commenced the work of healing the sick and "stood in the door of [Sherwood's] tent and commanded him in the name of Jesus Christ to arise and come out of his tent, and he obeyed him and was healed" (HC 4:4, footnote).

He was elected city marshal in Nauvoo and served as a delegate to the political convention which nominated Joseph Smith to the presidency of the United States (HC 6:389). On the pioneer journey west, he was appointed the "commissary general for the camp" and made the first survey drawing of Salt Lake City upon arrival in the valley. "Having no paper of suitable size, this important document was drawn on a prepared sheep's skin." He later moved to San Bernardino to survey a ranch which the Church had purchased, eventually becoming the surveyor for San Bernardino County. He died in that locale about 1862. (Jenson 4:717 – 18.)

Shield of Faith

In the war between good and evil, one must be protected with the "shield of faith" (D&C 27:17). An example of this shield of faith might be illustrated in the following home memories of Elder L. Tom Perry: "We were dressed in our home each morning, not only with hats and raincoats and boots to protect us from physical storm, but even more carefully our parents dressed us each day in the armor of God. As we would kneel in family prayer and listen to our father, a bearer of the priesthood, pour out his soul to the Lord for the protection of his family

against the fiery darts of the wicked, one more layer was added to our shield of faith. While our shield was being made strong, theirs was always available, for they were available and we knew it." (CR, Apr. 1974, pp. 140–41.)

Thus, this spiritual shield is that protective armament that becomes invincible through prayer, righteous obedience to all of God's commandments, searching and pondering the scriptures, and doing all within one's power to strengthen the power of faith. In addition, the Lord promises the righteous that he will be their "shield and their buckler" (D&C 35:14).

See also: Buckler

Shinehah

The name "Shinehah" appeared in three sections of pre-1981 editions of the Doctrine and Covenants. In two revelations it referred to the city or land of Kirtland (D&C 82:12, 13; 104:21, 40, 48). In the third revelation, it referred to the plains on which Adam dwelt (D&C 117:8).

The meaning of the name Shinehah was revealed anciently to Abraham. The Lord declared to this great prophet, "This is *Shinehah, which is the sun*" (Abr. 3:13; italics added). Thus, Shinehah, as applied to Kirtland, literally meant the "city of the sun." In view of the amount of celestial light which was revealed within this city, especially those rays of heavenly light restored within the walls of the Kirtland Temple, the name seems appropriate (see D&C 110).

See also: Kirtland

Shinelah

The verb "shinelah" was used once in pre-1981 editions of the Doctrine and Covenants (D&C 104:58). Its English meaning is "to print," but its origin is unclear. Based upon a discussion of the word *Shinehah*, by President Joseph Fielding Smith, one may assume that shinelah might be a word out of the Adamic language (CHMR 2:97). It is a variant of a word which means "sun" and therefore is appropriate when applied to the verb "to print"; for to print (shinelah) is to shed light upon a subject (Abr. 3:13).

See also: Shinelane

Shinelane

The word *shinelane* was found but once in scripture (D&C 104:63; pre-1981 editions). The meaning of the term as defined by the Lord is "printing," which is a derivative of the word *shinelah*, meaning "to print" (D&C 104:58). Both terms are variations of the word *Shinehah*, which means sun (Abr. 3:13). This term is no longer used in current editions of the Doctrine and Covenants.

See: Shinelah

Shod

See: Feet Shod with the Gospel of Peace

Shrink

In recounting his excruciating experience in Gethsemane, the Savior recalled how he desired "not [to] drink the bitter cup, and shrink" (D&C 19:18; see also Matt. 26:39; Mark 14:35–36; Luke 22:41–42). To shrink is to withdraw. For all who suffer moments of despair or discouragement and wish to withdraw from a difficult assignment, the words of the suffering Savior can provide great solace: "Nevertheless, glory be to the Father, and I partook and *finished*" (D&C 19:19; italics added).

See also: Atonement; Bitter Cup

Shule

During a period of time in which the names of men and places were being disguised, the lot where the ashery was located in Kirtland was referred to as "Shule" (D&C 104:39; pre-1981 edition, HC 1:255). This is the only use of that name in the Doctrine and Covenants, but it is also found in the Book of Mormon as the name of an ancient Jaredite king (Ether 7). According to Webster, an ashery is a place for ashes, or a place where wood is burned to ashes. Sperry indicated it was used for making soap

(DCC, 542). Shule is not used in current editions of the Doctrine and Covenants.

See also: Ashery

Sickle

See: Thrust in His Sickle

Sickness of the Land

In 1841, William Law was counseled to put his trust in the Lord "and cease to fear concerning his family, because of the sickness of the land" (D&C 124:87). Of this particular admonition, Smith and Sjodahl have written: "William Law is here instructed to trust in the Lord and not fear for the safety of his family, although there was sickness among the people. Fear is the great friend of disease-carrying microbes. It opens the door to them. If there is an epidemic abroad, it is certain to find the cowards. On the other hand, faith in God is an excellent foundation for both physical and moral health." (SS, 785.)

Sidney

The name of "Sidney" is used nine times in the revelations of the Doctrine and Covenants without an accompanying last name. In each instance, it refers to Sidney Rigdon (e.g., DBC 35:3; 100:1, 9).

Sift Him as Chaff

In 1831 Lyman Wight is warned that Satan desired to sift him as chaff (D&C 52:12). The Book of Mormon prophet Alma gives this same warning to his son Helaman (Alma 37:15). A similar warning was given anciently to the Apostle Peter and to the Saints in general, although the word *wheat* is used in the place of *chaff* (Luke 22:31; JST, Luke 22:31).

Chaff is the non-nutritious waste product of wheat and is separated from the grain by the wind when it is tossed into the air. This process is called sifting. Chaff is like a rudderless vessel that is driven at will by the wind. Satan desires to sift the Saints like chaff, to separate them from the soul-saving, nutritious grain of the gospel and carry them away in the winds of wickedness.

Signs

The term *signs* appears frequently in the Doctrine and Covenants, as well as in other scripture. Signs are supernatural manifestations whose power source is spiritual or beyond this world. The manifestations of signs usually defy a rational or logical explanation. Many signs are from God, for "signs follow those that believe" (D&C 58:64; 63:9–11; 84:65–73; 124:98–100).

On the other hand, signs may also be produced by the devil and his angels. Paul referred to these as "lying wonders" (2 Thess. 2:9).

Those who deliberately seek signs for purposes of personal amusement or gratification are not in good standing with God (D&C 63:7–11). "An evil and adulterous generation seeketh after a sign," said the Savior (Matt. 12:39), a principle also attested to by the Prophet Joseph (TPJS, 157, 278).

In response to the anti-Christ's request for a sign, Alma replied, "Thou hast had signs enough; will ye tempt your God? Will ye say, Show unto me a sign, when ye have the testimony of all these thy brethren, and also all the holy prophets? The scriptures are laid before thee, yea, and all things denote there is a God; yea, even the earth, and all things that are upon the face of it, yea, and its motion, yea, and also all the planets which move in their regular form do witness that there is a Supreme Creator." (Alma 30:44.)

The Doctrine and Covenants mentions "the signs of the coming of the Son of Man" (D&C 45:39), and we are informed that "it shall be given to know the signs of the times" (D&C 68:11). These signs will precede the second coming of the Savior and are scripturally catalogued in order that the faithful may discover the warnings. To the spiritually unaware, some of the less spectacular signs may pass by undetected, but to those with spiritual eyes the meaning will be clearly seen (D&C 63:9–11).

Silence in Heaven for . . . Half an Hour

See: Curtain of Heaven

Similitude

The Doctrine and Covenants contains three references to the word *similitude*. In the first instance the Lord speaks of the Nauvoo Stake as being "polished with the refinement which is after the similitude of a palace" (D&C 124:2). In this sense, the stake was to have the qualities that a palace might have: impressive, regal, well cared for—a place that would attract many.

In another revelation the Lord refers to "the baptismal font . . . as a similitude of the grave" (D&C 128:13). In this sense, it is symbolic or representative of the grave—one where the *old* man is laid down in preparation for the *new* man to come forth (see Rom. 6:3–6).

Finally, in the vision of the redemption of the dead, President Joseph F. Smith saw that the just "had offered sacrifice in the similitude [representation or type] of the great sacrifice of the Son of God" (D&C 138:13).

Sin

The revelations of the Doctrine and Covenants are replete

with admonitions to avoid sin. In his preface to this volume of scripture the Lord declared, "I the Lord cannot look upon sin with the least degree of allowance" (D&C 1:31).

Brigham Young gave a simple definition of sin when he said it "consisted in doing wrong when we know and can do better, and it will be punished with a just retribution, in the due time of the Lord" (JD 2:133). The Apostle John described sin as "the transgression of the law" (1 Jn. 3:4). Anciently, James wrote that "to him that knoweth to do good and doeth it not, to him it is sin" (James 4:17). Thus, sin can be the result of passive inaction as well as active transgression.

A modern-day prophet, Spencer W. Kimball, said: "Sin is an admission of surrender to the herd. It is a capitulation to the carnal in man and a rejection of joy and beauty in this life and in the worlds to come. . . . Sin is such sadness." (En., May 1978, p. 78.)

The sadness of sin was spoken of by another of the Lord's Apostles, Elder Neal A. Maxwell. He admonished those who seek pleasure in sin to "not look too deeply into the eyes of the pleasure-seekers about you, for if you do you will see a certain sadness in sensuality, and you will hear artificiality in the laughter of licentiousness" (CR, Oct. 1974, p. 14).

See also: Adultery; Apostates/ Apostatize; Backbiting; Blasphemy Against the Holy Ghost;

Carnal Desires/Mind; Craftiness of Men; Dead Works; Evil Speaking; Feigned Words; Filthy; Fornication; Garments Spotted with the Flesh; Greediness; Hypocrisy; Idolatry; Liars; Light-mindedness; Lust; Mind Became Darkened; Offerings of Cain; Pride; Secret Combinations; Sedition; Sensual; Servants of Sin; Shed Innocent Blood; Sinned Unto Death; Sorcerer; Stiffneckedness; Uncleanness; Vanities of the World; Whoremonger; Wicked

Singleness of Heart

Webster's *Unabridged Dictionary* defines *singleness* as "freedom from duplicity; purity of mind or purpose; sincerity; and singleness of purpose; singleness of heart." It is like being "singleminded." Therefore, when the Lord counsels every man who embraces the gospel to do so with "singleness of heart" (D&C 36:7), we are reminded that purity of mind and purpose must prevail.

There can be no duplicity of thinking, no double standards, for "a double minded man is unstable in all his ways" (James 1:8). There can be no half-hearted efforts. "We cannot survive spiritually with one foot in the Church and the other in the world," counseled Elder Bruce R. McConkie. "We must make the choice. It is either the Church or the world. There is no middle ground." (CR, Oct. 1974, p. 44.)

The admonition that the preparation of food on the sabbath is to be done with "singleness of heart" (D&C 59:13) reflects the necessity of prioritizing and keeping in perspective the purpose of this holy day. All else should be secondary to the worship of God.

See also: Eye Single to the Glory of God; Full Purpose of Heart

Sinned unto Death

An 1831 revelation declared: "I, the Lord, forgive sins unto those who confess their sins before me and ask forgiveness, who have not sinned unto death" (D&C 64:7). The nature of those who commit such a gross sin was defined as follows: "Those who turn from the light and truth of the gospel; who give themselves up to Satan; who enlist in his cause, supporting and sustaining it; and who thereby become his children—by such a course *sin unto death.* For them there is neither repentance, forgiveness, nor any hope whatever of salvation of any kind. As children of Satan, they are sons of perdition." (MD, 737.)

See also: Hosts of Hell; Kingdom Which Is Not a Kingdom of Glory; Outer Darkness; Resurrection of the Unjust; Sons of Perdition

Sixth Angel

A major portion of the book of Revelation is devoted to the missions of seven angels. The Doctrine and Covenants also speaks of seven angels who will sequentially sound their trumps prior to the occurrence of significant world events (D&C 88:98–110). The "sixth angel" will announce the fall of Babylon and reveal the secret acts and thoughts of the men who lived during the sixth period of earth's history (D&C 88:105, 109–10).

Inasmuch as this sixth period includes the dispensation of the fulness of times, in which we now live, Elder Wilford Woodruff said: "Joseph Smith, I expect, will sound the sixth trumpet. He will be at the head of this dispensation; or, if he does not blow the trumpet of this dispensation, I do not know who will." (JD 21:196.)

Slaves

The word *slaves* appears but once in the Doctrine and Covenants, that being in the context of a prophecy about war: "After many days, slaves shall rise up against their masters" (D&C 87:4).

Although this prophecy was fulfilled in part when the Negro slaves became a focal point in the American Civil War, President Joseph Fielding Smith has pointed out that these "slaves" may also refer to the downtrodden and oppressed of the nations of Mexico and Central and South America who have risen up and gained freedom from tyranny. "Let us not think that this prophecy has completely been fulfilled," he cautioned (CHMR 1:363).

Although a slave is normally considered to be one who is obligated to indentured servitude to another, further fulfillment of this prophecy may continue as "slaves"—the shackled citizens of communistic and dictatorial societies—rise up against their "masters" in an effort to gain freedom.

See also: Bond-Servants; Servitude

Sleep in the Dust

See: Dust of the Earth

Sleeping Dust

See: Dust of the Earth

Slothful

"He that is slothful shall not be counted worthy to stand," declared the Lord (D&C 107:100). The words *slothful* or *slothfulness* appear five times in the Doctrine and Covenants (D&C 58:26, 29; 90:18; 101:50; 107:100). They are also found in the Book of Mormon (Alma 37:46; 60:14), the Old Testament (Prov. 15:19; 19:15), and the New Testament (Matt. 25:26; Rom. 12:11; Heb. 6:12).

An appropriate description of one who is "slothful" comes from Elder A. Theodore Tuttle:

"The word *sloth* or *slothfulness* appears in scripture twenty-five times, generally to condemn *those who were slow to act.* . . . The Savior's reference to the sloth and slothfulness illustrates His displeasure and impatience with the person who is slow to act, who is slothful." (En., May 1978, p. 88; italics added.)

Smith, Alvin

For some, life's mission is of relatively short duration. So it was for Alvin Smith, eldest brother of the Prophet Joseph Smith. Born February 11, 1798, Alvin contracted what was diagnosed as "bilious colic" and died on November 19, 1823. The Prophet thought highly of his eldest brother and later remarked, "I remember well the pangs of sorrow that swelled my youthful bosom and almost burst my tender heart when he died. He was the oldest and noblest of my father's family. He was one of the noblest of the sons of men." (LMS, 333.) On another occasion the Prophet compared Alvin with father Adam and his son Seth, saying that Alvin "was a very handsome man, surpassed by none but Adam and Seth, and of great strength" (HC 5:247).

While in the Kirtland Temple on January 21, 1836, the Prophet had a vision of the celestial kingdom and saw his brother Alvin as an inhabitant of that heavenly home. Knowing that Alvin had died before the restoration of the keys of salvation, Joseph wondered at his brother's presence among the saved of God. Joseph was assured that all who died without opportunity to accept the gospel, but who would have accepted it, "shall be heirs of the celestial kingdom of God." (D&C 137:5–7.)

This revealed truth leads us to proclaim with Paul, "O death, where is thy sting? O grave, where is thy victory? The sting of death is sin." (1 Cor. 15:55–56.)

Smith, Don C.

Although mentioned but once in the Doctrine and Covenants (D&C 124:133), Don Carlos Smith, faithful younger brother of the Prophet Joseph, played an integral role in the early history of the Church. The best biographical sketch of Don Carlos would be that penned by the Prophet, who wrote the following under date of August 7, 1841:

"My youngest brother, Don Carlos Smith, died at his residence in Nauvoo this morning . . . in the 26th year of his age. He was born 25th March, 1816, was one of the first to receive my testimony, and was ordained to the Priesthood when only 14 years of age. The evening after the plates of the Book of Mormon were shown to the eight witnesses, a meeting was held, when all the witnesses, as also Don Carlos bore testimony to the truth of the latter-day dispensation. . . . He was one of the 24 Elders who laid the corner stones of the Kirtland Temple. . . . On the 15th of January, 1836, he was ordained President of the High Priests' quorum. . . . On the 26th September [1838] he started on a mission. . . . During his absence, his wife and two children were driven by the mob from his habitation, and she was compelled to carry her children three miles, through snow three inches deep, and wade through Grand river, which was waist deep during the inclement weather. . . .

"On Tuesday, 23rd July, 1839, I told Don Carlos and George A. Smith to go and visit all the sick, exercise mighty faith, and administer to them in the name of Jesus Christ, commanding the destroyer to depart, and the people to arise and walk; and not leave a single person on the bed between my house and Ebenezer Robinson's, two miles distant; they administered to over sixty persons, many of whom thought they would never sit up again; but they were healed, arose from their beds, and gave glory to God; some of them assisted in visiting and administering to others who were sick. . . .

"He was six feet four inches high, was very straight and well made, had light hair, and was very strong and active. His usual weight when in health was 200 pounds. He was universally beloved by the Saints." (HC 4:393–99.)

Smith, Eden

The ministerial labors of Eden Smith are mentioned twice in the Doctrine and Covenants (D&C 75:36; 80:2). Both of these revelations dealt with short-term missions he was called to serve in 1832.

In July 1833, he was in some difficulty, for the First Presidency of the Church prayed that his heart would be softened that he might obey the gospel. He had been serving as the president of the Eugene, Ohio, Branch of the Church, but had evidently sympathized with his disfellowshipped father and fallen into some erroneous ways (HC 1:369–71). That he saw his folly and turned back to the straight and narrow path is evidenced by his call to serve a mission to Pennsylvania in April 1843 (HC 5:349).

He did not travel west with the main body of the Church and died in Indiana in 1851 at the age of forty-five.

Smith, Emma

"When sorrows come, they come not single spies, but in battalions," wrote Shakespeare (*Hamlet*, act 4, sc. 5, lines 77–78). Such a statement might well describe the seventeen years of married life that Emma Hale Smith shared with her much maligned and persecuted prophet-husband. Even her betrothal to Joseph was anxiety laden, as her father, lacking a testimony of the Prophet's calling, opposed the union of his daughter to this visionary man. Yielding to her heart, Emma married Joseph Smith on January 18, 1827. This was the year in which Joseph completed his "apprenticeship" and received the plates from which the Book of Mormon was translated. Emma acted as the first scribe in Joseph's early efforts of translation. She was with the Prophet on several occasions when mobocrats vainly tried to steal the sacred records.

Her soul was scarred with the loss of four little ones who preceded her and Joseph to the other side of the veil. Her husband was forcefully torn from her side on a number of occasions and she was constantly deprived of the sustaining succor of his loving presence. Plural marriage became a severe test to this woman of sorrows, and her state of mind following the martyrdom of her beloved husband might well be described in Solomon's words: "By sorrow of the heart the spirit is broken" (Prov. 15:13).

When the Saints came west, Emma remained behind in Nauvoo. Although "every effort" was made to extend to her help in making the journey, "no amount of pleading, no amount of persuasion or kindness" could dissuade her from her chosen course (LJFS, 130).

It is ironic that during the same week in which Brigham Young officially became the President of the Church and reorganized the First Presidency, Emma married outside the faith. She became the wife of Lewis C. Bidamon, a resident of Nauvoo, on December 23, 1847, and died at Nauvoo on April 30, 1879.

Although in her later years she chose to remain separate from the Church founded by her prophet-husband, Emma's impact in the Church endured. Her call to compile the first hymnbook for the Church (D&C 25) and her service as the first president of the Relief Society are footnotes of faithfulness that cannot be erased. We shall best leave to futurity, and the just and benevolent judgment of an all-wise Father, to determine Emma's place in the eternities.

See also: Elect Lady

Smith, George A.

Cousin to the Prophet Joseph Smith, counselor to Brigham Young, and confidant of the Saints was George A. Smith. His name appears twice in the Doctrine and Covenants, once in a list of the Twelve Apostles (D&C 124:19), and once as an organizer of a company of pioneers (D&C 136:14). As a boy he was converted to the gospel through the Book of Mormon and spent more than half of his life in traveling and preaching the truths from that sacred volume.

George A. Smith was called to the holy apostleship on April 26, 1839, on the intended temple site at Far West, Missouri. At the October conference in 1868, he was called to serve as first counselor to Brigham Young in the First Presidency, in which position he faithfully served until his death September 1, 1875. He served as Church Historian and Recorder and helped to compile the documentary history of Joseph Smith. His memory supplied some of the missing details from that history, which his predecessor Willard Richards had prophesied by penning in the margins of that history, "to be supplied by George A. Smith."

Brigham Young paid Elder Smith the following tribute, "I have known Brother George A. Smith for forty-two years, have traveled and labored in the ministry with him for many years, and have believed him to be as faithful a boy and man as ever lived; and, in my opinion, he had as good a record on this and the other side of the veil as any man. I never knew of his neglecting or overdoing a duty; he was a man of sterling integrity, a cabinet of history, and always true to his friends."

He was further described as "humble and meek, yet full of courage and unbounded energy in the cause of right. He always had time to notice young people and children and leave his impress of love and kindness upon the tablets of their hearts." (Jenson 1:37–42.)

Smith, Hyrum

Sibling rivalry has existed since the days of Cain's venomous jealousy of his brother Abel (Moses 5:16–33). Other contentious kinsmen were Jacob and Esau, who struggled for supremacy even within their mother's womb (Gen. 25:22); Joseph and his brothers, who "could not speak peaceably unto him" and "hated him . . . for his dreams, and for his words" (Gen. 37); and Laman and Lemuel, who disdainfully said of their brother Nephi, "We will not that our younger brother shall be a ruler over us" (1 Ne. 18:10).

It is inspiring, therefore, that the annals of recorded history should contain this observation of another pair of brothers—Joseph and Hyrum Smith: "In life they were not divided, and in death they were not separated!" (D&C 135:3.) Though five years his senior, Hyrum Smith was ever solicitous of, and deferential to, his younger brother Joseph.

Throughout Hyrum's life, he "guarded his younger and more favored brother as tenderly as if the Prophet had been his son instead of his younger brother," wrote Joseph Fielding Smith. "He accepted the great mission of his brother Joseph in the most sacred and loyal spirit of humility." (HSP, 13.)

The Prophet himself said of Hyrum: "I could pray in my heart that all my brethren were like unto my beloved brother Hyrum . . . for I never had an occasion to rebuke him, nor he me" (HSP, 10). On another occasion, as he sought to write the names of those who had been faithful in the face of severe opposition, Joseph said: "There was Brother Hyrum who next took me by the hand—a natural brother. Thought I to myself, Brother Hyrum, what a faithful heart you have got! Oh may the eternal Jehovah crown eternal blessings upon your head, as a reward for the care you have had for my soul! O how many are the sorrows we have shared together. . . . Hyrum, thy name shall be written in the book of the law of the Lord, for those who come after thee to look upon, that they may pattern after thy works." (HC 5:107–8.) A guest in Hyrum's home once said of him, "He was really *a worthy brother of the Prophet*, and *together they were a worthy pair*" (HSP, 148; italics added).

The Lord's feelings for Hyrum were expressed in an 1841 revelation: "Blessed is my servant Hyrum Smith; for I, the Lord, love him because of the integrity of his heart, and because he loveth that which is right before me" (D&C 124:15). In a blessing received under the hands of his prophet-brother, Hyrum was told, "From generation to generation [you] shall be a shaft in the hand of . . . God . . . ; [you] shall not fail nor want for knowledge" (TPJS, 40–41). Surely, the fulfillment of this blessing has been evident in the generations of service faithfully rendered by Hyrum's posterity, among whom have been the Patriarchs to the Church and two Presidents.

Hyrum Smith held positions of prominence in the kingdom, serving as a counselor in the First

Presidency, as the Patriarch, and as an Assistant President of the Church. In this latter calling he was "crowned with the same blessing, and glory, and honor, and priesthood, and gifts of the priesthood, that once were put upon Oliver Cowdery" (D&C 124:94–95). If Hyrum had survived Carthage, he would have assumed the Presidency of the Church (DS 1:221; TS 5:683).

In the dedicatory prayer of the Provo Temple, Joseph Fielding Smith proclaimed: "We rejoice in the mission and ministry of the Prophet Joseph Smith and the Patriarch Hyrum Smith, who together held the keys of this final dispensation, and who sealed their testimony with their blood," which, according to the Doctrine and Covenants, was "the best blood of the nineteenth century" (CN, Feb. 12, 1972, p. 4; see D&C 135:6).

The brotherhood bond between Joseph and Hyrum Smith will endure eternally. Of his constant companion, the Prophet said: "My beloved brother Hyrum . . . possesses the mildness of a lamb, and the integrity of a Job, and in short, the meekness and humility of Christ; and I love him with that love that is stronger than death" (CN, Feb. 12, 1972, p. 3).

See also: Carthage Jail; Gems for the Sanctified; Gifts . . . Once Put upon Oliver Cowdery; Martyrdom; Office of Priesthood and Patriarch; Patriarch; Keys Whereby He May Ask and Receive; Sealed His Mission with His Blood; Sealing Blessings of My Church; Second Elder

Smith, John

The name of John Smith appears only in the minutes of the Kirtland High Council, which have become section 102 (D&C 102:3, 34). He was a member of that council along with other notable men such as Joseph Smith, Sr., Martin Harris, Oliver Cowdery, and the Prophet's brother Samuel. The Prophet had an uncle whose name was John Smith, who joined the Church in 1832 and came to Kirtland in 1833, where, on June 3, he was ordained a high priest. Inasmuch as the Kirtland High Council was organized on February 17, 1834, it appears reasonable to assume that the John Smith of the high council and the John Smith who was the Prophet's uncle were one and the same.

Uncle John served as an assistant counselor to Joseph Smith, as president of three stakes, and as Patriarch to the Church. He served in the latter position from January 1, 1849, to the day of his death, May 23, 1854. (Jenson 1:182–83.)

Smith, Joseph, Jr.

The man whose thread of life binds the pages of the Doctrine and Covenants was the Prophet Joseph Smith. Of him, John Taylor wrote: "Joseph Smith, the

Prophet and Seer of the Lord, has done more, save Jesus only, for the salvation of men in this world, than any other man that ever lived in it" (D&C 135:3; see also JD 18:326–27).

The Lord himself bore personal witness of Joseph's eternal influence in the destiny of mankind: "The ends of the earth shall inquire after thy name. . . . The pure in heart, and the wise, and the noble, and the virtuous, shall seek counsel, and authority, and blessings constantly from under thy hand. . . . Thy voice shall be more terrible in the midst of thine enemies than the fierce lion, because of thy righteousness; and thy God shall stand by thee forever and ever." (D&C 122:1–4.)

The significance of Joseph's status in the plan of salvation was attested to by President Joseph Fielding Smith: "If Joseph Smith was verily a prophet, and if he told the truth when he said that he stood in the presence of angels sent from the Lord, and obtained keys of authority, and the commandment to organize the Church of Jesus Christ once again on the earth, then this knowledge is of the most vital importance to the entire world. *No man can reject that testimony without incurring the most dreadful consequences, for he cannot enter the kingdom of God.* It is, therefore, *the duty of every man to investigate* that he may weigh this matter carefully and know the truth." (DS 1:189–90.)

During his thirty-eight years of mortality, this prophet of God set in motion the "stone" which was destined to roll forth and fill the earth, literally making this entire sphere the mountain of the Lord (Dan. 2:34–35, 44; D&C 65:2; 109:72–73). From the humble beginnings of the six-member church, organized in the obscure town of Fayette, New York, has come a kingdom of God which has literally touched the four corners of the earth.

Millions have come to know the Lord Jesus because of the Church he established through an unlettered farm boy. Joseph's learning was not of this world: "I am a rough stone," he wrote. "The sound of the hammer and chisel was never heard on me until the Lord took me in hand. I desire the learning and wisdom of heaven alone." (HC 5:423.)

On another occasion he boldly proclaimed: "I am learned, and know more than all the world put together. The Holy Ghost does, anyhow, and he is within me . . . and I will associate myself with him." (HC 6:308.) John Taylor observed that Joseph "was ignorant of letters as the world has it, but the most profoundly learned and intelligent man that I ever met in my life." (JD 21:163).

Among his heavenly tutors were the following: God the Father of all, and his Son Jesus Christ (JS—H 1:14–20); Moroni, keeper of the "stick of Ephraim" from whence the Book of Mormon was translated (JS—H 1:28–54); John the Baptist (D&C 13; JS—H 1:66–72); Peter, James, and John, the Lord's chief Apostles and keepers of the keys of the kingdom (D&C 27:12; 128:20; JS—H 1:72); Moses (D&C 110:11); Elias, or Noah who is also Gabriel (D&C 110:12; AGQ 3:138–41); Michael, or Adam (D&C 128:20); Raphael and . . . divers angels, from . . . Adam down to the present time" (D&C 128:21); Mormon and Nephi "and others of the ancient Prophets who formerly lived on this Continent" (JD 17:374); Alma (JD 18:47); Seth, the son of Adam (HC 5:347); the three Nephites (DOH, 162); Abraham, Isaac, Jacob, Enoch, "and the apostles that lived on this continent as well as those who lived on the Asiatic continent. He seemed to be as familiar with these people as we are with one another," observed John Taylor. (JD 21:94; see also TPJS, 180.)

The results of his having been tutored by those dwelling in the halls of heaven are evident in the penetrating truths revealed through his pen. Elder Bruce R. McConkie made the following observation of the Prophet: "Here is a man who has given to our present world more holy scripture than any single prophet who ever lived; indeed, he has preserved for us more of the mind and will and voice of the Lord than the total of the dozen most prolific prophetic penmen of the past" (En., May 1976, p. 95).

Joseph's divine mission, and even his name, were foretold in ancient prophecy (2 Ne. 3:6–15, 24). He stood among the noble spirits foreordained in pre-earth celestial councils to direct the work of the mortal ministry (HC 6:364; Abr. 3:22–23). Joseph Fielding Smith has expressed a conviction that the Prophet Joseph even assisted in the creation of this earth (DS 1:75). The Lord carefully watched over Joseph's ancestors, cultivating the right environment in which to place his anointed prophet (IE, Nov. 1964, pp. 923, 998).

A prophet of God; a true friend; a man of unsurpassed faith, courage, and conviction, who was "strong as a lion, but as gentle as a lamb;" serious, yet not one to take himself too seriously—such are the descriptions of Joseph Smith. He did not claim personal perfection, freely admitting his faults, but he was unflinching in assuming his prophetic mantle. He once cautioned, "The Saints need not think because I am familiar with them and am playful and cheerful, that I am ignorant of what is going on. Iniquity of any kind cannot be sustained in the Church, and it will not fare well where I am; for I am determined while I do lead the Church, to lead it right." (TPJS, 307.)

The results of his righteous leadership are readily observed in the church he established. Contrary to the excited declaration of a major newspaper of his time, which upon learning of his death proclaimed, "Thus Ends Mormonism," The Church of Jesus Christ of Latter-day Saints continues to fill the earth with the saving principles of the gospel. This is not a church of man, neither Joseph Smith's nor Mormon's. In the words of Elder Orson F. Whitney, it "is no mere nineteenth century religion; it is not merely a religion of time. It is the religion of the eternities." (CR, Apr. 1908, p. 89.)

Born in humble circumstances, December 23, 1805, Joseph Smith rose to spiritual heights honored by heaven and hated by hell. "He lived great, and he died great in the eyes of God and his people; and like most of the Lord's anointed in ancient times, has sealed his mission and his works with his own blood" (D&C 135:3). A mindless mob ended his life on June 27, 1844; and unwittingly provided the Prophet with a martyr's crown. Bullets, swords, and slander do not put an end to that which is of an eternal nature—neither the work nor the man.

See also: Apostle; Babes and Sucklings; Baurak Ale; Book of Mormon; Carthage Jail; Dispensation of the Fulness of Times; Doctrine and Covenants; Enoch (Joseph Smith); First Elder; First Presidency of the Church; Gazelam; Gems for the Sanctified; Gift Possessed by Joseph Smith; Innocent Blood; Joseph; Keys Whereby He May Ask and Receive; Manuscript (116 Pages); Martyrdom; Nauvoo; "O, Lord My God"; Presidency of the High Priesthood; Presidency of the School of the Prophets; President of the High Priesthood; Presiding Elder; Presiding High Priest; Promulgate; Prophet(s); Restoration, The; Revelator; Rod; Root of Jesse; Sealed His Mission . . . with His Blood; Seer; Sixth Angel; Special Witness; Translator; Unlearned; Warsaw; Weak Things of the Earth/World

Smith, Joseph, Sr.

"A man faithful to his God and to the Church in every situation and under all circumstances through which he was called to pass"—such was the descriptive eulogy of Joseph Smith, Sr., at his funeral (HC 4:192). His name was revealed anciently (2 Ne. 3:15), and he was the faithful father of the two prophets who stand at the head of the dispensation of the fulness of times—Joseph and Hyrum Smith. Surely the Lord must have had great confidence in the capacity of Joseph, Sr., to faithfully fulfill his fatherly role. He, alongside his noble sons, stood among the great in the pre-earth celestial councils.

Born on July 12, 1771, Joseph lived to be sixty-nine years of age. During those eventful, and often painful, years he gave great service to the Lord. It was to him that young Joseph first related the story of the angel Moroni's special visit, whereupon the father unhesitantly replied "that it was of God" (JS—H 1:48–50; see also LMS, 79.) The father dutifully deferred to his prophet-son, whom he served as an assistant counselor in the First Presidency (HC 2:509), as well as the first Patriarch to the Church. (HC 2:379–80.)

"Father Smith," as he was affectionately called by the Saints, served on the first high council of the Church (D&C 102:3, 34) and was one of the eight special witnesses to view the gold plates from which the Book of Mormon was translated. The revelation he received in February 1829 has become a classic guide for all who labor in the ministry (D&C 4).

Joseph's feelings for his father are expressed in the following reminiscent words: "I have thought of my father who is dead, who died by disease which was brought upon him through suffering by the hands of ruthless mobs. He was a great and a good man. . . . *He was of noble stature and possessed a high, and holy, and exalted, and virtuous mind.* His soul soared above all those mean and groveling principles that are so congenial to the human heart. I now say that he never did a mean act, that might be said was ungenerous in his life, to my knowledge. I love my father and his memory; and the memory of his noble deeds rests with ponderous weight upon my mind, and many of his kind and parental words to me are written on the tablet of my heart.

"Sacred to me are the thoughts which I cherish of the history of his life. . . . Let the memory of my father eternally live. . . . With him may I reign one day in the mansions above." (HC 5:125–26; italics added.)

Four months after his death on September 14, 1840, the Lord revealed that Joseph Smith, Sr., was sitting at the right hand of Abraham, "and blessed and holy is he, for he is mine" (D&C 124:19).

Smith, Joseph F.

Son of the patriarch-martyr, Hyrum Smith, and nephew of the prophet-martyr, Joseph Smith, Jr., Joseph F. Smith was but five years of age when a malicious mob took the lives of his father and uncle. He was born on November 13, 1838, during the days of mob rule in Missouri. He suffered the perils of persecution throughout his life. As an infant, his life was miraculously preserved when intruders ransacked his home, overturned his bedding, and left him to an almost sure suffocation beneath it.

When not quite eight years old, he drove an ox team from Montrose to Winter Quarters, Iowa, after a mob had driven his family from their home in Nauvoo, Illinois. Later he drove the wagon of his widowed mother, Mary Fielding Smith, across the plains from Iowa to the Salt Lake Valley. Along the way he was schooled in the faith of his mother.

On one occasion, her son observed how her faith and prayers led to the discovery of their lost oxen after others had given up the search. Of this experience, the boy would later say: "It was one of the first practical and positive demonstrations of the efficacy of prayer I had ever witnessed. It made an indelible impression upon my mind, and has been a source of comfort, assurance, and guidance to me throughout all of my life." (LJFS, 132–34.)

On another occasion, when her oxen suddenly fell and appeared to be in the throes of death, Joseph's faithful mother called upon the priesthood to rebuke the destroyer (LJFS, 150). This experience left its impact upon the boy regarding the power of the priesthood, which he himself would use so effectively throughout his life.

At the age of fifteen, he commenced a four-year mission to the Sandwich (Hawaiian) Islands and later served special missions both in those islands and in the British Isles. In 1866, at the age of twenty-seven, he was ordained an Apostle. He served as a counselor to presidents Brigham Young, John Taylor, Wilford Woodruff, and Lorenzo Snow. On October 17, 1901, he became the sixth President of The Church of Jesus Christ of Latter-day Saints—the Lord's prophet, seer, and revelator upon the earth.

Just a month before his death, he received a marvelous vision wherein he saw the ministry of the Savior to the spirits of the dead following His crucifixion (D&C 138). This vision, although previously accepted by the leading councils of the Church as revelation, was not presented to the membership of the Church to be accepted as scripture until April 3, 1976. The vision was a marvelous climax to the ministry of one who had spent his life declaring the doctrines of God to Saint and sinner, Jew and Gentile. His spirit left his mortal tabernacle on November 19, 1918, to take up his ministry in the world of the deceased which he had so recently viewed in vision.

Smith, Lucy Mack

To be the mother of prophets, one must surely have a great depth of personal spirituality and a capacity for instilling this same characteristic in her children. Such was Lucy Mack Smith, mother of the Prophet Joseph Smith and his patriarch-prophet brother, Hyrum.

Her prophet-son saw her in vision as a future inhabitant of the celestial kingdom of God (D&C 138:5). Lucy's writings reveal a deep spirituality and commitment to the Lord. She was a regular reader of the Bible and at a relatively young age had a spiritual experience which had a lasting impact on her. In 1802, as the mother of two small children, she was confined to bed with what the doctors diagnosed as "confirmed consumption." Men of medicine and the ministry gave her no chance of surviving, but the God of heaven had different ideas.

The special events of one restless night she recorded in her journal: "During this night I made a solemn covenant with God that if He would let me live I would endeavor to serve him according to the best of my abilities.'' Shortly thereafter a voice from heaven gave her the comfort she sought, and from that moment she gained both physical and spiritual strength. (LMS, 33–34.) She lived to bear eight more children, including he who was foreordained to be the prophet of the Restoration.

It is of interest that the mother of the man selected to restore God's Church should be born just four days after the day which gave birth to the nation that should host that church. Lucy was born on July 8, 1776, in New Hampshire, one of the original thirteen colonies of the United States.

She married the man whose name was known to at least one ancient prophet (2 Ne. 3:15 [6–15]), a spiritual giant himself. Joseph Smith, Sr., married Lucy on January 24, 1796. They lived as worthy companions until Joseph's death. Lucy rejoined her eternal companion upon her death on May 5, 1855.

Smith, Samuel H.

Born March 13, 1808, Samuel H. Smith was the younger brother of the Prophet Joseph. He is mentioned in six sections of the Doctrine and Covenants. The first four of these refer to his missionary labors, in one of which the Lord expressed his pleasure with Samuel's efforts (D&C 52:30; 61:35; 66:8; 75:13).

Samuel's missionary efforts are legendary, for he is credited with taking the first missionary journey for the Church. As a result of this initial effort, one of the copies of the Book of Mormon he distributed came into the possession of Brigham Young's family and was instrumental in converting him and his friend Heber C. Kimball, also a future Apostle (ECH, 88–89).

Samuel was the third person to be baptized in this dispensation, following his brother Joseph and Oliver Cowdery. His zeal for the Book of Mormon also allowed him to be one of the eight witnesses to that sacred volume of scripture. (Their testimony of having seen the plates from which it was translated is now contained in the forepart of that book.)

Samuel became a member of the first high council of the church at Kirtland (D&C 102:3, 34), and later served in a bishopric in Nauvoo (D&C 124:141).

He participated in the Battle of Crooked River, where Apostle David W. Patten received his martyr's crown. Following the battle, Samuel was among those who were pursued by mob forces and who were saved by the intervention of a miraculous snowstorm which separated the two groups. During this period, they were deeply concerned about the safety of their families and the Prophet, and were suffering severely for want of food. Samuel, as the appointed leader of the group, received the following revelation: "Thus saith the Lord, my servant Joseph is not injured, nor any of his brethren that are with him, but they will all be delivered out of the hands of their enemies; your families are all well, but anxious about you. Let your hearts be comforted, for I the Lord will provide food for you on the morrow.'' The next day, Samuel was led directly to an Indian camp where bread and meat were provided to them.

On the day a malicious mob murdered his brothers, Joseph and Hyrum, Samuel was relentlessly pursued by a contingent of that mob. Because of the severe fatigue brought on by that chase, a fever was contracted which, according to John Taylor, ''laid the foundation for his death, which took place on the 30th of July, [1844],'' (HC 7:111). Of him it was written, ''If ever there lived a good man upon the earth, Samuel H. Smith was that person.'' (Jenson 1:278–82.)

Smith, Sylvester

One of the members of the first high council of the Church was Sylvester Smith (D&C 75:34). He was a member of the famous Zion's Camp, although his ''quarrelsome spirit'' created a few problems on that march. Nevertheless, he was chosen as one of the seven Presidents of the Seventy in February 1835 and served in that capacity until 1837 when he was placed in the high priests quorum.

Smith experienced an outpouring of the Spirit during a solemn meeting at Kirtland in January 1836, when the heavens were opened and he leaped to his feet and exclaimed, ''The horsemen of Israel and the chariots thereof'' (Jenson 1:191). Several days later, in a meeting with the Apostles and the Seventies, he ''saw a pillar of fire rest down and abide upon the heads of the quorum [of the Seventy]'' (HC 2:386).

Sylvester Smith was one of the spiritual casualties that fell in troubled times in Kirtland between November 1837 and June 1838. His spiritual seeds had not taken proper root and were scorched by the sun of adversity (see Matt. 13:1–9); consequently, he lost his place in the kingdom.

Smith, William

The only mention of William Smith in the Doctrine and Covenants is as a member of the Quorum of the Twelve Apostles (D&C 124:129). Unfortunately, the spirit of this holy calling did not seem to penetrate his pride nor subdue his temperament, for he frequently found himself at odds with his prophet-brother Joseph, whom he physically attacked on several occasions.

William was suspended from fellowship on May 4, 1839, at a general conference near Quincy, Illinois. However, through the intercession of Joseph and Hyrum he was restored to his former standing in the Church.

By right of lineage, William received the office of Patriarch to the Church on May 24, 1845. However, because of a printed line in the *Times and Seasons* which stated he was patriarch "over" the whole Church, William attempted to exercise authority which he did not possess and was rejected both as an Apostle and as a patriarch by the general conference of the Church in October 1845. (For an excellent discussion of this issue, see GK, 146–49.)

William's bitterness continued, and he was excommunicated on October 19, 1845. He later became a patriarch in the church of James J. Strang, but was also excommunicated from that organization. In 1848, he assumed the "right" of presidency and attempted to gather Saints to Palestine Grove, Illinois. Little became of this and in 1850 he organized a church at Covington, Kentucky, based on the doctrine of lineal descent, declaring himself as president pro tem, with Lyman Wight and Aaron Hook as counselors. He finally deserted this organization and became nominally connected with the "new organization," which became the foundation for the Reorganized Church in 1860.

William Smith died at Osterdock, Clayton County, Iowa, on November 13, 1893. The tragedy of his life might well be expressed in the Old Testament proverb, "Pride goeth before destruction, and an haughty spirit before a fall" (Prov. 16:18).

Snider, John

In the early part of 1841, the name of John Snider (sometimes spelled "Snyder") emerges in several public documents of the Church. In January he is mentioned as a member of the Nauvoo House Building Committee (D&C 124:22, 62, 70). In February, his name appears among those who served on the personal staff of Lt. General Joseph Smith of the Nauvoo Legion.

Snider served as an assistant aide-de-camp and as a special guard (HC 4:296). He traveled to England to collect funds for the construction of the Nauvoo House and Temple and later helped in disposing of the properties of the Saints who left Nauvoo for the West. Snider came to the Salt Lake Valley in 1850, where he resided until his death in 1875.

Snow, Erastus

Perhaps no more dedicated missionary of the Church has ever lived than Erastus Snow. The only mention of his name appears in connection with his call to help organize the pioneers in their western trek (D&C 136:12). However, as one reads his history, the zealous service which he gave to the Church in its formative years is very apparent.

Erastus joined the Church at age fourteen, being baptized February 3, 1833. By June 1834, he was in the mission field where he diligently labored for the next four years. In June 1838, he heeded the call to go to Missouri to help build the Church in Zion.

The following February, he was visiting with the Prophet and Hyrum during their incarceration at Liberty, Missouri, when an escape attempt was foiled. As a consequence, Erastus was confined along with the other brethren in the jail. A militant mob threatened all kinds of physical violence and torture to the prisoners. At the height of the disturbance, Joseph prophetically promised his fellow prisoners that "not a hair of their heads should be hurt, and that they should not lose any of their things, even to a bridle, saddle, or blanket; that everything should be restored to them; they had offered their lives for their friends and the gospel; that it was necessary the Church should offer a sacrifice and the Lord accepted the offering" (Jenson 1:106).

Acting upon Joseph's recommendation, Erastus served as his own lawyer and was readily acquited. Following this, the lawyers gathered around him and desired to know where he had received his training, for they claimed to have never heard a better plea. True to the promise of Joseph, everything that was taken from the men was restored: "nothing was lost, although no two articles were found in one place" (Jenson 1:106).

In 1847, Erastus Snow and Orson Pratt were the first two men to enter the Salt Lake Valley, three days ahead of the main pioneer company. On February 12, 1849, he was called to serve as an Apostle in the Quorum of the Twelve. In addition to the numerous missions he fulfilled in the United States, he labored several years in Denmark and was responsible for the translation of the Book of Mormon and Doctrine and Covenants into the Danish language. He died on May 27, 1888, in the seventieth year of his life, having spent close to sixty of those years in the service of the Master.

Snow, Lorenzo

Although he is not specifically mentioned in any of the revelations in the Doctrine and Covenants, Lorenzo Snow's name appears at the conclusion of the document known as the Manifesto (OD—1). As the President of the Council of the Twelve Apostles, President Snow was the one who proposed that the Church accept Wilford Woodruff's declaration of the cessation of plural marriage as binding upon the Church.

Lorenzo Snow was born in Mantua, Ohio, on April 3, 1814, and joined the Church in 1836. Shortly thereafter, he received a patriarchal blessing in which he was promised that he "would become a mighty man. . . . There shall not be a mightier man on earth than thou." (IE, June 1919, p. 655.) The fulfillment of this blessing came when Lorenzo Snow became the prophet, seer, and revelator of the Lord on earth. On September 13, 1898, he was sustained as the President of The Church of Jesus Christ of Latter-day Saints.

Just prior to his being sustained as the President of the Church, he was visited by the Savior in the Salt Lake Temple. This visitation appeared to be, at least in part, a fulfillment of a previous patriarchal promise that he would "have power to rend the [veil] and see Jesus Christ" (IE, op. cit.).

He was the first to put into words the doctrine that man could become as God: "The destiny of man is to be like his Father—a god in eternity. This should be a bright, illuminating star before him all the time—in his heart, in his soul, and all through him.

As man now is, God once was:
As God now is, man may be.
A son of God, like God to be,
Would not be robbing Deity."
(IE, June 1919, p. 651.)

President Snow passed away on October 10, 1901, at the age of eighty-seven.
See also: Gods

Soften the Hearts

When the Lord promises to soften hearts, it is indicative of his making them pliable and receptive to the message he intends them to receive (D&C 104:80–81; 105:27; 124:9). The righteous have soft and receptive hearts for things of the Spirit while the hearts of the wicked are hardened and are difficult to penetrate with spiritual truths and promptings.
See also: Harden Their Hearts; Heart

Solemn Assemblies

Special, sacred meetings of the Church are designated as "solemn assemblies." These meetings were mentioned in revelation as early as November 1831, and appear eight times in the Doctrine and Covenants (D&C 88:70, 117; 95:7; 108:4; 109:6, 10; 124:39; 133:6). On the occasion of his being sustained as the President of the Church, Spencer W. Kimball made the following remarks regarding the nature of such solemn assemblies: "Solemn assemblies have been known among the Saints since the days of Israel. They have been of various kinds but generally have been *associated with the dedication of a temple or a special meeting appointed for the sustaining of a new First Presidency or a meeting for the priesthood to sustain a revelation*, such as the tithing revelation to President Lorenzo

Snow. . . . Joseph Smith led the first solemn assembly, and after closing his discourse, he called upon the several quorums, commencing with the presidency, to manifest by rising, their willingness to acknowledge him as the prophet and seer and uphold him as such by their prayers and faith. All the quorums in turn cheerfully complied with this request. He then called upon all the congregation of Saints also to give their assent by rising to their feet." (CR, Apr. 1974, pp. 64–65; italics added.)

Solemnities of Eternity

The phrase "solemnities of eternity" appears only once in the Doctrine and Covenants (43:34). Following a discussion of the keys of the kingdom and the Millennium, the Lord declared: "Treasure these things up in your hearts, and let the solemnities of eternity rest upon your minds."

The word *solemnity* appears in three other revelations in the Doctrine and Covenants. Admonition is given to "remain steadfast in your minds in solemnity and the spirit of prayer" (84:61), to declare the gospel "in solemnity of heart, in the spirit of meekness" (100:7), and to do "all things . . . in order and in solemnity" (107:84). Webster defines solemnity as the quality of character of being solemn, especially of being serious, dignified, or awe-inspiring.

Thus, to let the "solemnities of eternity" rest upon one's mind is to let the sacred, serious, dignified, and awe-inspiring truths of the gospel permeate one's thought processes, leaving no room for the sordid stains of worldly thoughts. An ancient prophet exemplified this principle when it was said of him, "So much was his mind swallowed up in other things that he beheld not the filthiness" (1 Ne. 15:27).

Solomon

In discussing the principle of plural marriage, the example of Solomon is cited, with the Lord indicating that he had justified Solomon's "having many wives and concubines" (D&C 132:1, 38). This ancient king of Israel was the son of David and Bathsheba (2 Sam. 12:24). His early reign was marked by the wisdom which had been granted him by God as a result of Solomon's special request, "Give . . . thy servant an understanding heart to judge thy people, that I may discern between good and bad" (1 Kgs. 3:9). One of his first uses for this gift came when he was asked to determine the true mother of a living and a dead child. This has become a classic story of wisdom. (1 Kgs. 3:16–27.)

He is well known for his splendid temple, which took seven years to construct (1 Kgs. 6:38). However, his changing value system from spiritual wisdom to worldly wealth may be reflected in the thirteen years it took to complete his own house (1 Kgs. 7:1).

His love of "strange women" and "other gods" caused him to slip spiritually, thus losing the glory of both earthly and heavenly kingdoms (1 Kgs. 11).

Some of One and Some of Another

"Is Christ divided?" asked the Apostle Paul (1 Cor. 1:13). Although he knew the answer to that question, he raised it to illustrate the point that Christ is the central figure in the gospel—the one to whom allegiance should be rendered rather than to the individual preacher. Some are as concerned with the name or reputation of the individual who teaches them or performs an ordinance in their behalf that they forget the authority that authorizes such action.

In the vision of the three degrees of glory, those who inhabit the telestial kingdom are described as "they who say they are some of one and some of another —some of Christ and some of John, and some of Moses . . . ; but received not the gospel, neither the testimony of Jesus, neither the prophets, neither the everlasting covenant" (D&C 76:98–101). "Some of one and some of another" is representative of misled religious factions

whose authority is vested in man rather than in divine revelation.

Son, The

See: Jesus Christ; Only Begotten Son

Son Ahman

Among the four books of scripture used by Latter-day Saints, the Doctrine and Covenants is unique in its use of the term *Son Ahman* (D&C 78:20; 95:17). Elder Bruce R. McConkie has given the following information regarding the origin and meaning of this title:

"In the pure language spoken by Adam—and which will be spoken again during the millennial era (Zeph. 3:9) —the name of God the Father is *Ahman,* or possibly *Ah Man,* a name-title having a meaning identical with or at least very closely akin to *Man of Holiness.* (Moses 6:57.) God revealed himself to Adam by this name to signify that he is a *Holy Man,* a truth which man must know and comprehend if he is to become like God and inherit exaltation. (1 John 3:1–3; D&C 132:19–24.)"

"Since *Ahman* is the name of God the Father in the pure language spoken by Adam, *Son Ahman* is the name of his Only Begotten Son." (MD, 29, 740.)

(For an interesting discussion by Elder Orson Pratt of an uncanonized revelation regarding the meaning of this name, see JD 2:342.)

See also: Jesus Christ; Son of Man

Son of God

See: Jesus Christ; Only Begotten Son

Son of Man

In sharp contrast to "the sons of men" (D&C 93:4), Christ is "the Son of Man" (D&C 45:39). That is, he is the Son of the "Man of Holiness" (Moses 6:57).

President Joseph Fielding Smith has written: "In each of the four gospels we read where the Savior frequently refers to himself as 'the Son of man.' Invariably in the New Testament, the common noun, 'Man,' is printed with a lower case 'm.' This is very likely due to the fact that the scholars who did the translating did not understand the significance of this expression. . . . The expression should be written, 'Son of Man,' with a capital 'M,' meaning Son of God." (AGQ 1:10–12.)

The Doctrine and Covenants correctly uses this sacred term in several sections (D&C 45:39; 49:6, 22; 58:65; 63:53; 64:23; 65:5; 68:11; 76:16; 109:5; 122:8; 130:12, 14, 15, 17).

See also: Jesus Christ; Son Ahman; Son of Man Cometh Not in the Form of a Woman

Son of Man Cometh Not in the Form of a Woman

The interesting statement, "the Son of Man cometh not in the form of a woman" (D&C 49:22), must be understood in light of the circumstances precipitating this revelation. In March 1831, converts from the sect called the "Shaking Quakers" were coming into the Church, but some were retaining several of the false notions previously taught to them (HC 1:167). One of these spurious teachings regarded the nature and gender of God.

President Joseph Fielding Smith made the following observation: "Since the Shakers held that God was both male and female, it was easy for them to believe in 'Mother' Ann Lee as 'the female principle in Christ,' and to believe that in her Christ had made his second appearance. The Lord corrects this foolish idea and says that the Son of Man cometh not in the form of a woman . . . but when he shall appear it shall be as the Only Begotten Son of God, full of power, might and dominion, who will put all enemies under his feet." (CHMR 1:210.)

See also: Lee, Ann; Son of Man

Son of the Morning

The title "son of the morning" is found three times in scriptural writings, although the Book of Mormon reference is taken from biblical records (D&C 76:26; Isa. 14:12–16; 2 Ne. 24:12–16). The title is always associated with Lucifer, who was cast out of heaven for rebellion.

President George Q. Cannon said: "Some have called him 'the' son of the morning, but here it is 'a' son of the morning—one among many, doubtless. This angel was a mighty personage. . . . He occupied a very high position, . . . he was thought a great deal of . . . , he was mighty in his sphere. . . . His plan . . . was so plausible and so attractive that out of the whole hosts of heaven one-third accepted his plan and were willing to cast their lot with him." (GT 1:4–5.)

Just as Jesus was the "firstborn" spirit child of our Father (D&C 93:21), so Lucifer appears to be one of those who was an early born spirit child, "a" son of the morning.

Elder Bruce R. McConkie has added that *"Lucifer, son of the morning*, also apparently signifies *son of light* or *son of prominence*, meaning that Satan held a position of power and authority in pre-existence" (MD, 744). "Just what authority Lucifer held before his rebellion we do not know," said President Joseph Fielding Smith, "but he was an angel of light, his name, Lucifer, meaning torchbearer" (CHMR 1:281).

See also: Devil; Lucifer

Song of the Lamb

"The song of the Lamb" as recorded in Doctrine and Covenants 133:56 is unique among latter-day scripture, although in ancient writ reference is made to this song in the Apostle John's writings (Rev. 14:1–3; 15:2–4). The Lamb, of course, is Christ (D&C 76:85; John 1:29, 36). The song—to be sung by the celestial Saints, who will inhabit the celestialized sphere which is as "a sea of glass mingled with fire"—is at least partially identified by the Revelator (Rev. 15:2–4):

Great and marvellous are thy works,
Lord God Almighty;
Just and true are thy ways,
Thou King of saints.
Who shall fear thee, O Lord,
And glorify thy name?
For thou only art holy:
For all nations shall come
And worship before thee;
For thy judgments are made manifest.

See also: Jesus Christ; Lamb

Sons of Aaron

In one sense, the sons of Aaron are those who are descendants of Aaron, the brother of Moses. However, in the sense in which it is used in section 84, it refers to those faithful brethren who are ordained to hold the Melchizedek Priesthood by those who themselves hold that power and authority and who then magnify that priesthood (DS 3:93; D&C 84:33–34).

Not all who are ordained unto this priesthood will be called the sons of Aaron and the sons of Moses. Only those who valiantly serve will be so called eternally. They will be sanctified and receive a renewed body that will allow them entrance into a celestial sphere where only the righteous will dwell. (D&C 84:33; 88:21–22.) They shall receive *all* that God himself has (D&C 88:33–38).

See also: Melchizedek Priesthood; Sons of Moses

Sons of God

While all who will sojourn upon this earth are the spiritual offspring of our Heavenly Father, only those who receive him through the teachings of his Only Begotten Son, Jesus the Christ, will receive the power to become true sons and daughters of God in an eternal sense (D&C 11:30; 35:2; 39:1–6; 45:8; John 1:12). This power is found only in The Church of Jesus Christ of Latter-day Saints (D&C 1:30; JS—H 1:5–20).

President Joseph Fielding Smith has written: "The destiny of the faithful man in this Church and the faithful woman is to become a son and daughter of God" (DS 2:37). The ultimate destiny of such an individual is to receive "all" that God possesses, or, in other words, to become as God is, to become gods themselves (D&C 76:58; 84:33–38).

Those who reject the invitation to become joint heirs in the household of God will not receive the keys nor have access to his house. They shall be as servants and strangers, standing upon the street, for "they were not willing to enjoy that which they might have received" (D&C 88:32).

Smith and Sjodahl said: "There is a difference between the status of a son, or daughter, appearing before a father, and a stranger standing as a transgressor before a judge" (SS, 471). The key to becoming a son or daughter of God is obeying the principles of the gospel and following the promptings of the still, small voice. "For," said Paul, "as many as are led by the Spirit of God, they are the sons of God" (Rom. 8:14).

See also: Children of God; Church of the Firstborn; Fulness of the Glory of the Father

Sons of Jacob

The "sons of Jacob" are referred to in the Doctrine and Covenants only in the dedicatory prayer of the Kirtland Temple (D&C 109:58). The context in which it is found appears to identify these "sons" as servants of the Lord—missionaries—charged with the responsibility of gathering out the righteous from among the nations of the earth (D&C 109:54–58). These "sons of Jacob" are sent forth by the great Jehovah, even Jesus Christ, to proclaim his truths.

The term *sons of Jacob* also appears in Malachi's writings in the Old Testament, but appears to have a general application to the whole House of Israel (Jacob), not merely those engaged in the ministry (Mal. 3:6; 3 Ne. 24:6).

Sons of Levi

In a broad sense, a son of Levi is one who is of the posterity of Levi, the son of Jacob and the father of that tribe of Israel charged with the responsibility of ministering the priesthood to the other tribes (Gen. 29:34; Num. 3:12; 8:14–26). More specifically, however, sons of Levi are those brethren who hold the priesthood in our day (DS 3:93; DCC, 81). At some future day, these "sons" will be called upon to reinstate the law of sacrifice in order that the "restoration of all things" may be accomplished (TPJS, 172–73; DS 3:94; Acts 3:19–21).

See also: Levi; Levitical Priesthood; Memorials for Your Sacrifices; Offering unto the Lord in Righteousness; Priesthood; Sons of Aaron; Sons of Moses

Sons of Men

The title "sons of men" appears in two sections. In Doctrine and Covenants 93:4 reference is made to Christ's coming to earth to dwell "among the sons of men." This might be interpreted as the Divine coming to dwell among the mortal.

In Doctrine and Covenants 124:49 reference is made to commandments which are issued from God to the "sons of men." In both instances, there appears to be a clear distinction made between divine Deity and mortal man, thus emphasizing the spiritually superior position of the one over the other.

Anciently, those referred to as "sons of men" represented those among whom "works of darkness" prevailed (Moses 5:52–57) and who would not hearken to the voice of God (Moses 8:15). In contrast, Noah and his sons were referred to as "the sons of God," because they "hearkened unto the Lord, and gave heed" (Moses 8:13). President Joseph Fielding Smith implied that the "sons of men" were those who did not hold nor honor membership in Christ's Church nor his priesthood, in contrast to the "sons of God," who held and honored both (AGQ 1:136–37).

Sons of Moses

In one sense, the sons of Moses are those who are literal descendants of this great prophet of Israel. However, in the sense in which it is used in section 84, it refers to those faithful brethren who are ordained to hold the Melchizedek Priesthood by those who themselves hold that power and authority, and who then magnify that priesthood (DS 3:93; D&C 84:33–34).

Not all who are ordained unto this priesthood will be called the sons of Moses and of Aaron. Only those who valiantly serve will be so called in the eternities. They will be sanctified and will receive a renewed body that will allow them entrance into a celestial sphere where only the righteous will dwell (D&C 84:33; 88:21-22). They shall receive *all* that God himself has (D&C 88:33-38).

See also: Melchizedek Priesthood; Sons of Aaron

Sons of Perdition

The title "sons of perdition" is found only in one section (D&C 76:32, 43). However, these pitiful people are also referred to by other descriptions (D&C 132:27). The consequences of their devilish deeds are likewise recorded (D&C 76:31-48).

Joseph Smith described how one qualifies for this fate from which there is no redemption. "He must receive the Holy Ghost, have the heavens opened unto him, and know God, and then sin against Him. . . . He has got to say that the sun does not shine while he sees it; he has got to deny Jesus Christ when the heavens have been opened unto him, and to deny the plan of salvation with his eyes open to the truth of it." (TPJS, 358.)

"A man must have sufficient knowledge to make him a God in order to be a devil," declared President George Q. Cannon (GT 1:120-21). Sons of perdition became "angels of the Devil," said Brigham Young, and it takes just as much preparation to enter the devil's domain as it does to prepare for celestial salvation; but, of course, the two are opposite extremes (JD 8:154; 3:93).

A son of perdition "commits murder by assenting unto the Lord's death, that is, having a perfect knowledge of the truth he comes out in open rebellion and places himself in a position wherein he would have crucified Christ knowing perfectly the while that he was the Son of God. Christ is thus crucified afresh and put to open shame." (DNTC 3:161; see also Heb. 6:4-6.)

Paul referred to "the man of sin" as a "son of perdition" (2 Thess. 2:3), and Joseph Smith identified "the man of sin" as the devil (HC 1:175). Jesus alluded to Judas Iscariot's being a son of perdition in his great intercessory prayer (John 17:12), and Elder James E. Talmage implied that Judas did qualify for this dubious distinction because "he had received the testimony that Jesus was the Son of God; and in the full light of that conviction he turned against his Lord, and betrayed Him to death" (Talmage, 649-51).

At the end of the Millennium, when Satan is once again loosed, "Men will again deny the Lord, but in doing so they will act with their eyes open and because they love darkness rather than light . . . ; they *become sons of perdition*" (DS 1:87).

See also: Blasphemy Against the Holy Ghost; Crucified Him Unto Themselves; Hosts of Hell;

Kingdom Which Is Not a Kingdom of Glory; Ordained unto This Condemnation; Outer Darkness; Resurrection of the Unjust; Sinned unto Death; Spiritual Fall; Spiritually Dead; Third Part of the Hosts of Heaven; Those Who Are to Remain Until the Great and Last Day; Vessels of Wrath; Worm That Dieth Not

Sorcerer

Condemnation is pronounced upon "liars, and sorcerers, and adulterers, and whoremongers" as well as the "fearful and the unbelieving" (D&C 63:17; 76:103). To place "sorcerers" in this category indicates the serious sin of fooling with sorcery and witchcraft of any kind.

Sorcery has been defined as the "use of power gained from the assistance or control of evil spirits. . . . In effect a sorcerer worships Satan rather than God and uses such power as Satan can give him in a vain attempt to imitate the power of God." (MD, 747.) The existence of sorcery in biblical, Book of Mormon, and modern times has been attested to by scripture (Ex. 7:11; Isa. 47; Mal. 3:5; Acts 8:9–11; Rev. 9:20–21; Alma 1:32; Morm. 1:19). Those who use this satanic source of power will find themselves without the kingdom of God (D&C 76:103; Rev. 22:14–15).

See also: Spirits of Men Who Are to Be Judged and Are Found Under Condemnation

Soul

The word *soul* is one of the most frequently used terms in religious parlance and appears throughout scripture. The Lord speaks of his children as "precious souls" (D&C 18:10–16). His own soul delights in "the song of the heart" (D&C 25:12). He admonishes those engaged in the ministry to "thrust in your sickle with all your soul" (D&C 31:5).

Satan is spoken of as endeavoring to destroy souls (D&C 64:17), but "every soul who forsaketh his sins" shall see the face of Christ (D&C 93:1). One must basically look at the context of the passage in which the word is used, for it may refer to a premortal spirit (Abr 3:23); mortal man whose spirit is housed in a temporal tabernacle of flesh (Abr. 5:7; D&C 138:9); a disembodied spirit of one awaiting resurrection (Alma 40:11–14, 23); or the resurrected spirit and body inseparably reunited (D&C 88:15–16).

When the Lord commands a man to labor with all his soul, he is asking that the full energy of his emotions, feelings, thoughts, and strength be brought to bear on the task at hand (D&C 31:5; see also Hel. 7:11; Morm. 3:12).

Sound of a Trump

A trump is a musical instrument, a trumpet. The sounding of various angelic trumps will announce at the beginning of the Millennium the retelling of great events in the earth's history (D&C 88:92–110). The "sound of a trump" is also used to describe the manner of voice that should be used in preaching the gospel (D&C 24:12; 29:4; 30:9; 33:2; 34:6; 36:1; 42:6; 75:4; 124:106).

The righteous resonance in the voices of those called to declare the message of salvation should be as clear as the tones of the trumpet. Just as the sonorous sound of Joshua's trumpeters caused the wicked walls of ancient Jericho to tumble, so should the divine message of God's servants destroy the sanctuaries of sin inhabited by the wicked of our day (Josh. 6). "For if the trumpet give an uncertain sound, who shall prepare himself . . . ?" (1 Cor. 14:8.)

South Carolina

As recorded twice in the Doctrine and Covenants, the Prophet Joseph prophesied that the commencement of "wars" and "difficulties which will cause much bloodshed previous to the coming of the Son of Man will be in South Carolina" (D&C 87:1; 130:12).

The first prophetic utterance occurred as a result of fervent prayer on December 25, 1832, and the second was a reiteration of this on April 2, 1843. The fulfillment of this remarkable prophecy commenced on December 20, 1860, when South Carolina became the first of eleven states to announce its secession from the Union that formed the United States.

The first shot of the American Civil War was fired on April 12, 1861, when the Union garrison at Fort Sumter, South Carolina, was attacked by confederate forces, and a four year war was under way. Of this war, the *Encyclopedia Britannica* said: "The American Civil War has been called by some the last of the old-fashioned wars; others have termed it the first of the modern wars of history. Actually it was a transitional war, and it had a profound impact, technologically, on the development of modern weapons and techniques." (15th ed., 4:681.)

Joseph Smith's prophetic powers went beyond merely announcing the forthcoming Civil War in America, for he spoke of "wars" that "will be poured out upon all nations beginning at this place," which was South Carolina. Sperry has written: "Men may quibble over this prediction by saying that wars have been among the nations for ages, but the fact remains that wars have broken out at frequent intervals since our great American Civil War, and today we commonly speak of World War I and World War II and are currently apprehensive of a World War III. The end of the matter is not yet." (DCC, 419).

See also: Southern States

South Countries

In January 1832, William E. McLellin was commanded to change his mission from the East and to go into the "south countries" (D&C 75:6–8). This charge did not include territory foreign to the United States, but merely meant he was to go into the southern states, or, that country which was *south* of his present location. Similarly, Major Ashley and Burr Riggs were sent into the "south country" (D&C 75:17).

Southern States

Almost three decades before the outbreak of the Civil War, the Prophet Joseph Smith prophesied that such an event would come to pass (D&C 87:3). Of the thirty-four states in the Union at the time the hostilities commenced, eleven states from the South formed their own confederacy. These seceding states were: South Carolina, Mississippi, Florida, Alabama, Georgia, Louisiana, Texas, Virginia, Arkansas, Tennessee, and North Carolina. The total population in these states was about 9,000,000, of which about 3,500,000 were Black slaves.

See also: Missouri; South Carolina

Sovereign

A sovereign is one who rules with supreme power over an established sphere, such as a king or monarch who rules over a particular country. In an August 1835 "declaration of belief regarding governments and laws in general," Church leaders af-firmed that civil officers are to enforce appropriate laws whether under the rule of a republic or a sovereign (D&C 134:3).

Speak Peace to Your Mind

One means whereby one may feel the flow of inspiration is that the Lord will "speak peace to your mind" (D&C 6:23). Oliver Cowdery used a similar phrase when commenting on the experience he and Joseph had when visited by the resurrected John the Baptist: "On a sudden, as from the midst of eternity, the voice of the Redeemer spake peace to us, while the veil was parted and the angel of God came down clothed with glory, and delivered the anxiously looked for message" (TS 2:202). This peace is a sense of spiritual tranquility and well-being that is entirely free of mental conflict or stupor of thought.

See also: Bosom Shall Burn; Feel; Revelation; Stupor of Thought

Speak with Tongues

"And again, it is given to some to speak with tongues," declared an 1831 revelation (D&C 46:24). To speak with tongues is to express oneself in a language that is not native to one's background. "Tongues were given for the purpose of preaching among those whose language is not understood; as on the day of Pentecost, etc., and it is not necessary for tongues to be taught to the Church particularly, for any man that has the Holy Ghost, can speak of the things of God in his own tongue as well as to speak in another; for faith comes not by signs, but by hearing the word of God" (TPJS, 148–49).

The Apostle Paul stated the principle well: "I had rather speak five words with my understanding, that by my voice I might teach others also, than ten thousand words in an unknown tongue" (1 Cor. 14:19).

See also: Gift of Tongues; Interpretation of Tongues

Speaking After the Manner of the Lord

In successive revelations given in 1831, the phrase "speaking after the manner of the Lord" is used (D&C 63:53; 64:24). In both revelations, events associated with the Millennium are enumerated, and such terms as *today*, *tomorrow*, and *nigh at hand* are used to express the time frame of such events. To speak after the manner of the Lord is to not only use his terminology but also in an ultimate sense to speak in the manner in which he would have his servants speak.

Such language would be edifying and uplifting, for what would be spoken would be what the Lord himself would have said. (See D&C 84:85; 88:64; Hel. 5:18; 8:3; 10:5.) In a sense, one speaking after the manner of the

Lord would also be speaking the language of the angels, who "speak by the power of the Holy Ghost" (2 Ne. 31:13; 32:2–3).

See also: Nigh at Hand; Today; Tomorrow

Special Witnesses

"All men may, by virtue of the priesthood and the gift of the Holy Ghost, become witnesses for Christ," declared President Joseph Fielding Smith. "In fact that is just what *every elder* in the Church should be, but *there is a special calling which is given to the Twelve special witnesses that separates them from other elders of the Church in the nature of their calling as witnesses.* These twelve men hold the *fulness of authority, keys,* and *priesthood,* to open up the way for the preaching of the gospel to every nation, kindred, and tongue." (DS 3:146.) The Twelve Apostles are *the* "special witnesses of the name of Christ in all the world," decreed the Lord (D&C 107:23).

Occasionally some will ask whether it is necessary for an Apostle to see the Savior in order to receive that sacred office. A man who served over sixty years in the Quorum of Twelve Apostles, President Joseph Fielding Smith, responded to this question: "It is their privilege to see him if occasion requires, but the Lord has taught that there is a stronger witness than seeing a personage, even of seeing the Son of God in a vision. Impressions on the soul that come from the Holy Ghost are far more significant than a vision." (IE 69:979.)

"The witness," declared Elder Boyd K. Packer, "does not come by seeking after signs. It comes through fasting and prayer, through activity and testing and obedience. It comes through sustaining the servants of the Lord and following them." (CR, Apr. 1971, p. 124.)

See also: Apostle; Testimony of Jesus

Spirit (#1)

"For man is *spirit*," declared the Lord (D&C 93:33; italics added). Premortal man was a spirit child of our Father in Heaven (Heb. 12:9) and was created "spiritually" before he came "naturally upon the face of the earth" (Moses 3:5). This spirit was "in the likeness of his person" (D&C 77:2).

Concerning this likeness, Parley P. Pratt wrote: "The spirit of man consists of an organization of the elements of spiritual matter, in the likeness and after the pattern of the fleshly tabernacle. It possesses, in fact, all the organs and parts exactly corresponding to the outward tabernacles." (KT, 124.)

This likeness is also in the image of our Father in Heaven (Moses 2:26–27). Regarding this, Elder Gordon B. Hinckley said: "That man who knows that he is a child of God, created in the im-

age of a divine Father and gifted with a potential for the exercise of great and godlike virtues, will discipline himself against the sordid, lascivious elements to which all are exposed" (CR, Oct. 1975, p. 57).

Joseph Smith proclaimed that "the spirit is a substance; that it is material, but that it is more pure, elastic and refined matter than the body; that it existed before the body, can exist in the body; and will exist separate from the body, when the body will be mouldering in the dust; and will in the resurrection, be again united with it" (TPJS, 207). This is in keeping with the instruction he gave in 1843 that spiritual matter "can only be discerned by purer eyes" (D&C 131:7–8).

The spirit of man comes to earth to receive and dwell in a temporal tabernacle, which he will leave upon death and reenter in a refined state at the time of the resurrection. Thus the Lord declared that "the spirit and the body are the soul of man" (D&C 88:15).

Those spirits who chose to rebel against God and follow Satan were cast out of heaven and will be forever denied the privilege of obtaining an earthly body (D&C 29:36–38; Abr. 3:27–28; Rev. 12:7–9; WTP, 34).

Spirit (#2)

Throughout the Doctrine and Covenants, whenever the term

Spirit is used with a capital *s* it refers to Deity. For example, in section 84 the Lord proclaims that "whatsoever is light is Spirit, even the Spirit of Jesus Christ" (D&C 84:45). In this particular instance the term *Spirit* is used to refer to the Light of Christ. Such phrases as "my Spirit" (D&C 1:33), "his Spirit" (D&C 20:77), and "that Spirit which leadeth to do good" (D&C 11:12) also refer to the Light of Christ.

In section 45, the Lord speaks of those who take "the Holy Spirit for their guide" (D&C 45:57). Elder Marion G. Romney indicated that this had reference to the Holy Ghost (CR, Sept. 1961, p. 60).

The "Spirit of God" mentioned as being the giver of the gifts of God (D&C 46:11) has likewise been identified by Elder Romney as the Holy Ghost (CR, Apr. 1956, pp. 68–70). Joseph Smith stated that these gifts "cannot be enjoyed without the gift of the Holy Ghost" (TPJS, 243).

When Joseph Smith and Sidney Rigdon referred to their "being in the Spirit" (D&C 76:11), they "were in a state of *spiritual rapture*, as was John on Patmos (Rev. 1:10), or Ezekiel (3:12), or Paul (2 Cor. 12:2–4). The veil was lifted from their mortal senses, and they could see and hear things spiritually, with their spiritual senses." (SS, 447.)

See also: Spirit of the Lord

Spirit of Jesus Christ

See: Light of Christ

Spirit of Man Was Innocent

Because the doctrine of original sin is so prevalent among the philosophies of men, it is important to understand the truth that "every spirit of man was innocent in the beginning" (D&C 93:38). The doctrine of original sin holds that all descendants of Adam must be regarded as being of a perverted or depraved nature. This thinking has led to the practice of infant baptism, which the prophet Mormon denounced as "mockery before God. . . . For awful is the wickedness to suppose that God saveth one child because of baptism, and the other must perish because he hath no baptism." (Moro. 8:9, 15; see 8:4–23.)

Spirits are born into this world, clothed with a tabernacle of flesh, free from the stain of sin. As the second article of faith declares, "We believe that men will be punished for their own sins, and not for Adam's transgression."

Indeed, children who die before reaching the age of accountability "are saved in the celestial kingdom of heaven" (D&C 137:10). The "age of accountability" has been defined by the Lord as "eight years old" (D&C 68:25; JST, Gen. 17:11).

See also: Accountable Before Me; Infant State; Little Children

Spirit of Prophecy

Twice in the Doctrine and Covenants the "spirit of prophecy" is mentioned (11:25; 131:5). According to the Prophet Joseph, "Salvation cannot come without revelation; it is in vain for anyone to minister without it. No man is a minister of Jesus Christ without being a Prophet. *No man can be a minister of Jesus Christ except he has the testimony of Jesus; and this is the spirit of prophecy."* (TPJS, 160; italics added.) John the Revelator declared, "The testimony of Jesus is the spirit of prophecy" (Rev. 19:10).

The Apostle Paul observed that "no man can say that Jesus is the Lord, but by the Holy Ghost" (1 Cor. 12:3). Thus, possessing the spirit of prophecy necessitates receiving revelation from the Holy Ghost that Jesus is the Christ. One who has this knowledge and who acts in accordance with that witness has the "testimony of Jesus."

See also: Testimony of Jesus

Spirit of Revelation

The Lord speaks of "the spirit of revelation" in Doctrine and Covenants 8:3. The previous verse defines this "spirit" as follows: "Yea, behold, I will tell you in your mind and in your heart, by the Holy Ghost, which shall come upon you and which shall dwell in your heart" (D&C 8:2). Thus, the Holy Ghost is the spirit of revelation.

Speaking of this spirit, the Prophet Joseph Smith taught: "A person may profit by noticing the first intimation of the spirit of revelation; for instance, when you feel pure intelligence flowing into you, it may give you sudden strokes of ideas, so that by noticing it, you may find it fulfilled the same day or soon. . . . Thus by learning the Spirit of God and understanding it, you may grow into the principle of revelation, until you become perfect in Christ Jesus." (HC 3:381.)

See also: Holy Ghost; Revelation; Still Small Voice

Spirit of the Lord

One challenge in understanding the phrase "the Spirit of the Lord" is that of comprehending the sense in which it is used. It may at times refer to the Light of Christ (D&C 1:33; 63:32), and on other occasions it may be used synonymously with the Holy Ghost (DS 1:50). Additionally, it may refer to the premortal spirit body of Jesus Christ (Ether 3).

Elder Bruce R. McConkie gave the following explanation: "To gain a sound gospel understanding, the truth seeker must determine in each scriptural passage what is meant by such titles as *Spirit, Holy Spirit, Spirit of the Lord, Spirit of God, Spirit of truth.* In many instances this is not difficult; in some cases, however, abbreviated scriptural accounts leave so much room for doubt that nothing short of direct revelation can identify precisely what is meant." (MD, 752.)

For example, in the case of D&C 121:37, the Lord indicates that the Spirit of the Lord is "withdrawn" from one who dishonors his priesthood. Because such a person would have received the gift of the Holy Ghost prior to his ordination to the priesthood, it appears that in this instance the withdrawal of the Spirit could refer to the Holy Ghost. But it likely has a double meaning, because as one degenerates from God, the Light of Christ diminishes and withdraws (D&C 1:33; TPJS, 217). Thus, one who violates priesthood covenants loses the companionship of the Holy Ghost as well as celestial current from the Light of Christ.

See also: Holy Ghost; Light of Christ; Spirit (def. #2); Spirit of Truth

Spirit of Truth

In the Doctrine and Covenants, the title "Spirit of truth" may apply either to the Lord, who proclaimed himself to be the "Spirit of truth" (D&C 93:26), or to the Holy Ghost (D&C 107:71), whose mission it is to testify of the truth (Moro. 10:5). The missionaries, and all others who teach the gospel, are instructed to do so "in the Spirit of truth" (D&C 50:13–22). That is, they are to testify of Jesus Christ—whose "voice is Spirit" and whose "Spirit is truth" (D&C 88:66)— and of the truths embodied in his gospel. The Holy Ghost, the truth testifier, bears witness of the Savior's divinity (John 15:26) and carries the testimony of the truths spoken into the hearts of the listeners (2 Ne. 33:1).

One must look carefully at the context in which the phrase "Spirit of truth" is used in order to determine its exact meaning. However, inasmuch as the Holy Ghost "bears record" of the Son (3 Ne. 11:32) and is "one" with him (1 John 5:7), it does not seem critical to always be able to properly differentiate between them in this sense.

See also: Holy Ghost; Jesus Christ; Spirit of the Lord

Spirit World

President Joseph F. Smith saw the spirits of those who had lived and died prior to the Savior's death anxiously waiting in the spirit world for the Son of God to arrive following his death on Calvary (D&C 138:16). The spirit world is the abode of those who have passed through the portals of death and are awaiting resurrection. It can be a place of happiness or misery, depending upon how the individual has lived in mortality (Alma 40:11–14, 20–21).

When Christ arrived in the spirit world, he did not go among the wicked and ungodly but instead confined his ministry to the righteous, organizing them into missionary task forces to go among the unrepentant and uninformed (D&C 138:20, 29–37). This short organizational ministry of the Savior bridged the gulf which had previously separated the righteous from the wicked in the spirit world (see Luke 16:19–26).

According to President Joseph Fielding Smith, the phrase *taken home to God* (Alma 40:11) "simply means that their mortal existence has come to an end, and they have returned to the world of spirits, where they are assigned to a place according to their works with the just or the unjust, there to await the resurrection" (AGQ 2:85).

Elder Orson Pratt took a different view. He suggested that upon death all spirits return to their ancient home in the presence of the Lord, albeit for perhaps a short period of time, because the wicked and the righteous would be separated (JD 16:332–33).

Both President Brigham Young and Elder Parley P. Pratt taught that the spirit world is behind the veil right here on this earth (JD 3:368–69; KT, 132–33). Elder Pratt said: "As to its location, it is here on the very planet where we were born; or, in other words, the earth and other planets of a like sphere, have their inward or spiritual spheres, as well as their outward, or temporal. The one is peopled by temporal tabernacles, and the other by spirits. A veil is drawn between the one sphere and the other, whereby all the objects in the spiritual sphere are rendered invisible to those in the temporal."

Spirits of Men Who Are to Be Judged, and Are Found Under Condemnation

At the end of the Millennium, a third trump shall sound and "then come the spirits of men who are to be judged and are found under condemnation" (D&C 88:100–101). These are those whose glory will be of a telestial nature (D&C 76:81–85, 102–6). They are "liars, and sorcerers, and adulterers, and whoremongers, and whosoever loves and makes a lie" (D&C 76:103; DS 2:297–98).

See also: Telestial; Third Trump

Spiritual Authorities of the Church

The term *spiritual authorities of the church* is a singular expression found in a revelation on priesthood (D&C 107:32). It appears to have reference to the three presiding quorums of the Church, namely the First Presidency, the Quorum of the Twelve Apostles, and the First Quorum of the Seventy. If any of these quorums should make a decision in "unrighteousness," an appeal could be made to the general assembly of the collective quorums. This group would constitute the spiritual authorities of the Church.

See also: General Authorities

Spiritual Body

The term *spiritual body* (D&C 88:27; 1 Cor. 15:44) must not be confused with the spirit body (D&C 77:2; 130:22; Eth. 3:16). The "spiritual body," declared Elder Joseph Fielding Smith, is the resurrected body "quickened by the spirit" instead of blood.

"After the resurrection from the dead our bodies will be spiritual bodies, but they will be bodies that are tangible, bodies that have been purified, but they will nevertheless be bodies of flesh and bones, but they will not be blood bodies, they will no longer be quickened by blood but quickened by the spirit which is eternal and they shall become immortal and shall never die." (CR, Apr. 1917, pp. 62–63.)

The term *spiritual body* has also been used in a limited sense to refer to the condition of Adam prior to the Fall. President Joseph Fielding Smith said: "When Adam was placed on the earth . . . , there was no blood in his body, but he had a spiritual body until it was changed by the fall. A spiritual body is one which is not quickened by blood, but by the spirit. Before the fall, Adam had a physical, tangible body of flesh and bones, but it was not quickened by blood. The partaking of the forbidden fruit caused blood to exist in his body and thus the seeds of mortality were sown and his body then became temporal, or mortal, subject to the vicissitudes of mortal change." (CHMR 1:231.)

See also: Adam; Fall; Resurrection

Spiritual Fall

The context in which *spiritual fall* is used in the Doctrine and Covenants appears to refer to something more serious than the general *Fall* to which all men are subject (D&C 29:44). Christ speaks of those who "cannot be redeemed from their spiritual fall, because they repent not." The Savior imploringly requested repentance of all, so that they might partake of the efficacy of his atonement. He suffered "for all, that they might not suffer *if they would repent.*" But, he warned, "if they would not repent they must suffer even as I." (D&C 19:15–20; italics added.) Thus, one derivative of the term *spiritual fall* may be the description of those who refuse to repent and consequently suffer in their own "Gethsemane."

Another facet, obviously, has to refer to those "sons of perdition" who have lost the will to repent, thus denying the luster of light at noonday and becoming incapable of accepting either Christ's Gethsemane or their own. They "cannot be redeemed." (D&C 76:32–38; DS 1:49.)

See also: Atonement; Second Death; Sons of Perdition

Spiritual Things

A contrast is frequently drawn between "spiritual things" and those of a temporal nature (D&C 29:31–34; 70:12). The Melchizedek Priesthood in particular is to administer in the "spiritual things" of the Church (D&C 107:8–12). Those who "labor in spiritual things" are those who are involved in "administering the gospel and the things of the kingdom unto the church, and unto the world" (D&C 72:14).

Although a distinction is drawn between the spiritual and the temporal, the Lord declared that "all things unto me are spiritual" (D&C 29:34). Of this statement, President Joseph Fielding Smith said: "All things to him are spiritual, or in other words *intended to be eternal*. The Lord does not think in temporal terms; his plan is to bring to pass the immortality and eternal life of man. In his eyes, therefore, all the commandments that have to do with our present welfare, are considered to be but steps on the way to his eternal salvation." (CHMR 1:307–8; italics added.)

Spiritually Dead

When Adam and Eve were cast out of the Garden, they became "spiritually dead," which means "they were cut off from the presence of the Lord" (D&C 29:41; Alma 42:7–11). There are two stages of spiritual death in the Lord's plan—one is eternal, the other potentially temporary. When Lucifer and his followers rebelled and were cast from God's presence, they experienced spiritual death, which in their case will be of an eternal nature. They are forever banished from divine dwellings (D&C 29:36–37; Rev. 12:7–9; 2 Ne. 2:17–18).

As previously mentioned, our first parents suffered the "first death" when banished from Eden. Likewise, all mortals suffer this death, after arriving at the "age of accountability," when they commit sin. This death can be overcome by removing the stains of sin through the "fruits of repentance" and by following those divine procedures which lead to one's being "born again" (Moro. 8:25–26; D&C 5:16; John 3:3–8; DS 2:273). Those who refuse to follow these procedures remain subject to the "first death."

The searing sentence of the "second death" will be pronounced upon the sons of perdition, whose rebellion in this life subjects them to the same eternal banishment to which Lucifer and his premortal followers are consigned (D&C 76:32–37). They have "sinned unto death" (D&C 64:7). They are "cut off . . . as to things pertaining to righteousness" (Hel. 14:16–18). They are "filthy still" and shall dwell eternally with "the devil and his angels" (2 Ne. 9:16).

See also: Death; Fall; First Death; Harden Their Hearts; Last Death; Sons of Perdition

Spokesman

An ancient prophecy by Joseph, one of the twelve sons of Jacob, identified the forthcoming mission of a great prophet whose name was to be Joseph (JST, Gen. 50:24–38). This future prophet was to have a "spokesman" (2 Ne. 3:18). In October

1833, the Lord declared that Sidney Rigdon was to be that "spokesman" for the Prophet Joseph Smith (D&C 100:9–11). Eight years later, after slipping somewhat, Sidney was reminded of this special calling (D&C 124:104).

President George Q. Cannon once proclaimed, "Those who knew Sidney Rigdon, know how wonderfully God inspired him, and with what wonderful eloquence he declared the word of God to the people. He was a mighty man in the hands of God, as a spokesman, as long [as] the prophet lived, or up to a short time before his death." (JD 25:126.)

See also: Rigdon, Sidney

Spotted

See: Garments Spotted with the Flesh

Spring Hill

While exploring the country north of Far West, Missouri, in anticipation of finding property upon which the Saints could settle, Joseph Smith and a small band of colleagues passed by Lyman Wight's home, which rested at the foot of a place known as Tower Hill. The Prophet gave the location this name because of "an old Nephite altar or tower that stood there."

A short distance from this historic place, the brethren endeavored to lay claim to a city plat near Wight's Ferry in Daviess County, township 60, ranges 27 and 28, and sections 25, 36, 31, and 30. They called the place Spring Hill, but the Prophet renamed it Adam-ondi-Ahman, because he said it was to be the location where Adam would sit in council prior to the Second Coming (D&C 116; HC 3:34–35; Dan. 7:9–14).

See also: Adam-ondi-Ahman

St. Louis, Missouri

In 1831, one of the major intersections of travel from east to west was St. Louis, Missouri. Following a conference of elders in Jackson County, Missouri, the Lord instructed many of the elders to return to the East by way of St. Louis. From this juncture, several of the leaders were to make their way to Cincinnati, Ohio, and the rest were to travel in twos in other directions. (D&C 60.)

Staff of Life

In the Word of Wisdom, the Lord mentions that "all grain is ordained for the use of man and of beasts, to be the staff of life" (D&C 89:14). According to Webster a "staff" is something which sustains or supports life, such as used in the common expression, "Bread is the staff of life."

Stakes

The clarion call to "enlarge" and "strengthen" the stakes of Zion was given anciently to Isaiah (Isa. 54:2), repeated to the Nephites (3 Ne. 22:2), and reiterated in our day (D&C 109:59; 133:9). A stake is an ecclesiastical unit of The Church of Jesus Christ of Latter-day Saints and covers a specific geographical area. According to the Lord, stakes are "curtains or the strength of Zion" (D&C 101:21). They are places where the Saints of God may be instructed more perfectly in the doctrines of salvation.

A stake is usually composed of a minimum of several thousand people, who are divided into smaller units known as wards. The first use of the term in modern times was when Kirtland, Ohio, was consecrated on April 26, 1832 as a place for a stake of Zion (D&C 82:13).

Each stake is presided over by a president and two counselors, who are called to their positions by revelation under the direction of a General Authority of the Church. Elder Harold B. Lee noted that a stake is "the most perfect administrative organization that the Lord has yet given us" (CN, Aug. 26, 1961, C-10).

See also: Standing Presidents

Stand by the Wall

The Lord declared that the enemies of his Prophet and "their posterity [would] be swept from under heaven . . . , that not one of them is left to stand by the wall" (D&C 121:15). This may be a euphemism ("the substitution of an agreeable or inoffensive expression for one that may offend") for a similar phrase found in the Old Testament (see 1 Kgs. 14:10). In this sense those who stand by the wall essentially means every male; thus, this passage alludes to the destruction of a family or household (1 Kgs. 16:10–12).

Stand Fast

To stand fast is to be firm, resolute, or unwavering. Those called to serve in the ministry should stand fast in their callings (D&C 9:14; 54:2). Disciples of Christ should stand fast in keeping the commandments of God (Alma 1:25).

See also: Continueth in God; Endure to the End; Valiant in the Testimony of Jesus

Standard for My People

In March 1831, the Lord reminded the Prophet Joseph that his "everlasting covenant" had been sent into the world to be a light and a "standard" (D&C 45:9). The Old Testament prophet Isaiah made a similar statement (Isa. 49:22), which the Book of Mormon prophet Jacob later quoted (2 Ne. 6:6). "This

Church," said Elder Marion G. Romney, "is the standard which Isaiah said the Lord would set up for the people in the latter days" (CR, Apr. 1961, p. 119).

See also: Church of Jesus Christ of Latter-day Saints, The; Ensign

Standard of Peace

In 1833 the Lord counseled his people to "lift a standard of peace" to any "people, nation, or tongue" that should seek to wage war against them (D&C 98:34). This "standard of peace" is synonymous with the "ensign of peace" (D&C 105:39); however, there may be a further meaning to consider.

It appears that the Lord is reiterating the doctrine of turning the other cheek and going the extra mile in seeking peace with an adversary (Matt. 5:38–48; 3 Ne. 12:38–48). Rather than being quick to strike a retaliatory blow, one should proclaim the message of peace. For, as an ancient government leader discovered, "the preaching of the word [of God] had a great tendency to lead the people to do that which was just —yea, it had [a] more powerful effect upon the minds of the people than the sword, or anything else" (Alma 31:5).

See also: Ensign of Peace

Standing High Councils

In March 1835, a great revelation on priesthood and church government was received which spoke of the "standing high councils" of the Church (D&C 107:36). "At the time this Revelation was given, there were two standing High Councils in the Church: One in Kirtland, organized February 17th, 1834, and one in Clay County, Mo., organized July 3rd, the same year" (SS, 702). The council in Kirtland was presided over by the First Presidency of the Church, which made it unique.

Today, there is a "standing high council" in every stake of the Church, presided over by a stake presidency, and jurisdictionally confined to the areas in which they are located.

See also: Council; High Council

Standing Ministers

It is the duty of those called to serve as elders in the Melchizedek Priesthood "to be standing ministers at home; to be ready at the call of the presiding officers of the Church and the stakes, to labor in the ministry at home [or] to go out into the world, along with the Seventies, to preach the Gospel to the world" (CR, Oct. 1904, pp. 3–4; see also D&C 124:137).

Perhaps there is another implication to the meaning of being a standing minister. Should he not be one who is alert or standing at his post rather than lying down and spiritually asleep in his calling? President George Q. Cannon illustrated this principle: "I ask myself, can I *stand* in this position and look upon the face of

God without feeling condemned . . . , that I have been a faithful minister of the Lord, a faithful shepherd of the flock of Christ, *a watchman who has never slept at his post,* who has never failed to utter the cry of warning when danger has menaced the Zion of God? *This is a feeling it seems to me every man who bears the holy Priesthood ought to have."* (GT 1:269; italics added.)

See also: Ministers; Watchman

Standing Presidents

A listing of the various quorums of the priesthood in Nauvoo, with their attendant officers, is found in section 124. Among the offices listed is the presidency of the high priests quorum, which "is instituted for the purpose of qualifying those who shall be appointed *standing presidents or servants over different stakes* scattered abroad" (D&C 124:133–35; italics added).

It appears that one of the major functions of this priesthood quorum was to train brethren to serve in administrative functions, one of which was that of stake president. Members of high councils and bishoprics also serve in the capacity of high priests. "It is the duty of the High Priests quorum to teach the principles of government," said President Joseph F. Smith. (PCG, 124.)

At the present time, the stake presidency serves as the presidency of the high priests quorum of that stake over which they preside.

See also: Stakes

Stanton, Daniel

Following the Amherst, Ohio, conference of January 1832, a number of elders received calls to preach the gospel, two-by-two. Among these was Daniel Stanton (D&C 75:33). This is his only mention in the Doctrine and Covenants, but his service to the Church can readily be traced through the Prophet Joseph's writings.

Elder Stanton served as a branch president in Missouri in 1833 and also as a counselor to Bishop John Corrill (HC 1:363, 409). He was later chosen to serve on the high council at Adam-ondi-Ahman and at Lima (HC 3:38; 5:427). He was chosen to preside over the Quincy, Illinois Stake, where a future Apostle, Ezra T. Benson, served as one of his counselors (HC 4:233).

The last mention of this faithful elder in the official history of the Church is his call to preside over a special district following the martyrdom of Joseph Smith (HC 7:305). He was with the main body of the Church that moved to the Rocky Mountains. Daniel Stanton died in Panaca, Nevada, in 1872.

Stars Roll upon Their Wings

See: Earth Rolls upon Her Wings

Stars Shall Fall from Heaven

One of the signs preceding the Second Coming will be that "the stars shall fall from heaven." (D&C 29:14; 45:42; 88:87; 133:49; Isa. 13:10; Matt. 24:29; Rev. 6:13.) A *possible* explanation of this phenomenon might be gleaned from an understanding of the history and destiny of our planet. Brigham Young said: "When the earth was framed and brought into existence and man was placed upon it, it was near the throne of our Father in heaven. And when man fell . . . the earth fell into space, and took up its abode in this planetary system, and the sun became our light." (JD 17:143; see also JD 9:317.)

On February 1, 1842, the official publication of the Church— the *Times and Seasons*—proclaimed that following the transgression of Adam, "the earth no longer retained its standing in the presence of Jehovah; but was hurled into the immensity of space; and there to remain till it has filled up the time of its bondage" (TS 3:672).

"This earth," said the Prophet Joseph, "will be rolled back into the presence of God" (TPJS, 181). To be "rolled back" implies that the earth at one point was "rolled away" from God's presence. The tenth article of faith states, "We believe . . . the earth will be renewed and receive its paradisiacal glory" (see also HC 5:61; Isa. 13:13).

From the above statements, it appears possible that this earth will be "renewed" and "rolled back" to its previous paradisiacal, planetary orbit near the abode of God. This will entail its removal from its present location within our solar system. In the process of such a move, as the earth hurtles through space, it could well appear that the stars are falling from the heavens.

Another possibility to explain these falling stars is found in the writings of the Prophet Joseph Smith and of Elder Parley P. Pratt, both of whom compared meteor showers to this great event (HC 1:439–40; APP, 110). Sperry also suggested that the falling stars spoken of "are probably not the distant suns we see in space, but the falling of bodies that will create tremendous light when they pass through the layers of our earthly atmosphere" (DCC, 434).

See also: Moon Shall Be Turned to Blood; Sun Shall Be Darkened

Steward

"For it is required of the Lord, at the hand of every steward, to render an account of his stewardship, both in time and in eternity" (D&C 72:3; 104:11–13). A steward is one to whome a responsibility has been delegated. The welfare of that someone or something for which he is responsible is his stewardship.

President George Q. Cannon said, "God our Eternal Father has placed all . . . possessions and blessings—that is, the possessions of the earth and the blessings connected with the earth—He has placed them in our hands merely as stewards, and we hold them subject to Him—in other words, in trust for Him" (GT 1:353). Thus, we will be held accountable for the way in which we utilize our earthly possessions (Mosiah 4:21–23), develop our talents (Matt. 25:14–30), magnify our callings (D&C 4:2; 84:33–41; Ezek. 3:19–21), teach our families (D&C 68:25), and conduct our own personal lives.

"And whoso is found a faithful, a just, and a wise steward shall enter into the joy of his Lord, and shall inherit eternal life" (D&C 51:19).

See also: Stewardship

Stewardship

"Thou shalt stand in the place of thy stewardship," declared the Lord (D&C 42:53). The concept of stewardship is specifically mentioned in eleven sections of the Doctrine and Covenants frequently referring to one's responsibility as a participant in the law of consecration or the united order (e.g., D&C 92; 104). But the principle of stewardship permeates every revelation given by the Lord. This principle rests upon the truth contained in the psalmist's proclamation, "The earth is the Lord's and the fulness thereof" (Ps. 24:1), and reflects the initial injunction given to our first parents to "dress the garden."

President George Q. Cannon declared, "the Lord has entrusted us all with a stewardship. He has placed under the control of man the elements of the earth, to do with them as seemeth good to him. This stewardship—that is, its extent or its value—may vary and does vary in each individual case. Some of us as stewards have large possessions and a large share of the elements which belong to the earth. Others have a smaller share. But we are all stewards, and undoubtedly will be required at some time in the future to account for the manner in which we use these stewardships." (GT 2:303; D&C 72:3; 104:11–13; Matt. 25:14–30.)

Perhaps stewardship is summed up in the concept of present responsibility and future accountability for everything and everyone that is placed within our trust.

See also: Consecration; Steward; Talent; United Order

Stick of Ephraim

The Lord declared that Moroni held "the keys of the record of the stick of Ephraim" (D&C 27:5). This stick (record) is the stick of Joseph spoken of by the prophet Ezekiel (Ezek. 37:16). President Joseph Fielding Smith declared that the "*Book of Mormon* is the record of Joseph. It contains the history of the descendants of Joseph on this land, both of Ephraim and of Manasseh. It was in the hands of Ephraim when it was given to Joseph Smith, and it is still in the hands of Ephraim when our missionaries go forth proclaiming its truths to the world, for *they also are of Ephraim*."

(DS 3:210.) He further stated that the "Book of Mormon came to Ephraim, for *Joseph Smith was a pure Ephraimite*" (DS 3:253).

In 1979 the Church published a new edition of the King James Version of the Bible (record of Judah), with extensive cross-reference aids that significantly increased the potential for gospel scholarship. In 1981 a new edition of the triple combination (Book of Mormon, Doctrine and Covenants, and Pearl of Great Price) was published, which also contained significant new study aids.

Speaking of the far-reaching impact of these new editions of the scriptures, Elder Boyd K. Packer said: "The stick or record of Judah—the Old Testament and the New Testament—and the stick or record of Ephraim—the Book of Mormon, which is another testament of Jesus Christ—are now woven together in such a way that as you pore over one you are drawn to the other; as you learn from one you are enlightened by the other. They are indeed one in our hands. Ezekiel's prophecy now stands fulfilled." (En., Nov. 1982, p. 53; see also 2 Ne. 3:12.)

See also: Book of Mormon; Ephraim; Moroni

Stiffneckedness

References to stiffneckedness are found only twice in the Doctrine and Covenants (D&C 5:8; 56:6). However, the word is found as a description of those who resist the promptings of the Spirit in both the Bible (Ex. 32:9) and the Book of Mormon (Alma 9:5).

The martyr Stephen indicated that stiffnecked people "resist the Holy Ghost" (Acts 7:51). Jacob taught that stiffnecked people "despised the words of plainness and killed the prophets, and sought for things that they could not understand" (Jac. 4:14). Stiffnecked people are also those who cannot "be governed by the law nor justice" (Hel. 5:3).

According to Webster, one who is stiffnecked is stubborn and inflexibly obstinate. Such are they who bow not their heads to be taught by the Spirit, but whose collars of sin keep their necks stiff and their heads haughtily erect in defiance of Deity. A stiff neck does not turn in the direction of divine guidance. By contrast, the Lord promises to "feel after" (search after) those who "stiffen not their necks" (D&C 112:13).

Still Small Voice

The term *still small voice* is used once in the Doctrine and Covenants (D&C 85:6), once in the Book of Mormon (1 Ne. 17:45), and once in the Old Testament (1 Kgs. 19:12). This "still small voice" is the Holy Ghost as it speaks to our "mind and heart" (D&C 8:2-3). This voice is generally *felt* rather than heard, although words may actually be revealed within one's mind, as was the case with the prophet Enos (Enos 1:10).

The ancient prophet Nephi chided his brothers for being "past feeling, that [they] could not feel his [the angel's] words" (1 Ne. 17:45). In 1829, the Lord indicated that when we pray about something that is right for us we should "feel that it is right" (D&C 9:8–9).

This feeling was described by Elder S. Dilworth Young in the following words: "If I am to receive revelation from the Lord, I must be in harmony with him by keeping his commandments. Then as needed, according to his wisdom, his word will come into my mind through my thoughts, accompanied by a feeling in the region of my bosom. It is a feeling which cannot be described, but the nearest word we have is 'burn' or 'burning.' Accompanying this always is a feeling of peace, a further witness that what one heard is right." (CR, Apr. 1976, p. 34.)

Underscoring the importance of the still small voice are the words of President Wilford Woodruff: "I have had visions; I have had revelations; I have seen angels; but the greatest of all is that still small voice" (JGK, 304). On another occasion he said, "I have never found anything that I could place more dependence upon than the still small voice of the Holy Ghost" (JD 21:196).

See also: Feel; Holy Ghost; Quake; Revelation; Testimony

Stir Up the Hearts

"Satan doth stir up the hearts of the people to contention," declared the Lord (D&C 10:63). One who is contentious stirs up the hearts of others by seeking to provoke or incite them to act in a sullen or discordant manner. It should be remembered, however, that men "are free to act for [them]selves" (2 Ne. 10:23) and do not have to respond in robotlike fashion to the contentious proddings of one who seeks to provoke them (see 2 Ne. 2:26–29).

See also: Anger; Contention; Reviling Not Against Revilers

Stone Cut Out of the Mountain

Anciently, the prophet Daniel interpreted the famous dream of King Nebuchadnezzar in which a stone "cut out without hands" rolled forth and destroyed all other kingdoms, while it became a mountain itself (Dan. 2:34–35, 44). This "stone" is also mentioned in an 1831 revelation (D&C 65:2). Joseph Smith further referred to this stone, or kingdom, in the dedicatory prayer of the Kirtland Temple, and identified that stone as the Church (D&C 109:72–73; see also HC 6:364–65).

More recently, President J. Reuben Clark, Jr., stated that "this work of the Lord is to roll forth as the stone cut out of the mountain without hands, and fill the whole earth. . . . *This is The Church of Jesus Christ of Latter-day Saints*, and its destiny as well as its mission is to fill the earth and to bring home to every man, woman and child in the world the truths of the Gospel." (CR, Oct. 1937, p. 107; italics added.)

See also: Church of Jesus Christ of Latter-day Saints, The; Kingdom of God on Earth; New York (State)

Stone of Israel

In an 1831 revelation, Christ identifies himself as the "stone of Israel" (D&C 50:44). This title can also be found in the Old Testament (Gen. 49:24). He is "the stone which the builders refused," but which became "the head stone of the corner" (Ps. 118:22; Matt. 21:42). Moses described the Lord as the "Rock of Heaven." Thus, if men build upon this "stone" or "rock," they are on a "sure foundation, a foundation whereon if men build they cannot fall" (Hel. 5:12; see also Jac. 4:14–16).

See also: Jesus Christ; Rock

Stone, That

In 1830, Hiram Page professed seership qualities from a "certain stone" which he pos-

sessed. His claims to prophetic powers led the Lord to give the revelation now known as section 28. Page claimed to know the location of the future city of Zion and had misled many to believe that the mind of the Lord had been made known through him.

The Lord rebuked Page and emphatically stated that "those things which he [Page] hath written from *that stone* are not of me and . . . Satan deceiveth him" (D&C 28:11; italics added). President Joseph Fielding Smith referred to this stone as a *peep-stone*, which is merely a satanic substitute of a genuine seer stone (CHMR 1:134).

See also: Page, Hiram

Storehouse, Lord's

"The Church storehouse system is an organization of physical warehouses and transportation facilities, with operating and managing personnel," said President Ezra Taft Benson. "This system is set up to receive, store, transport, exchange, and distribute food and nonfood commodities to those in need.

"A fundamental unit of the Church storehouse system is the local bishops storehouse. Bishops storehouses are Church-owned facilities from which local bishops obtain food, clothing, and other commodities to care for the poor and needy who are unable to care for themselves. . . .

"The Lord, by revelation, has commanded that storehouses be

established. The surpluses, or 'residue,' from the consecrated properties under the united order were to be kept in the storehouses 'to administer to the poor and the needy.' (D&C 42:34.) Later, the Lord instructed that the Presiding Bishop 'appoint a storehouse unto this church; and let all things both in money and in [food], which are more than is needful for the wants of this people, be kept in the hands of the bishop.' (D&C 51:13.)

"Today . . . bishops storehouses . . . are used for almost the identical purpose they were used for under the united order. Members consecrate their time and talents and means to produce, process, package, manufacture, and purchase commodities to care for those in need. . . .

"Storehouses are only established to care for the poor and the needy. For this reason, members of the Church have been instructed to personally store a year's supply of food, clothing, and, where possible, fuel." (En, May 1977, p. 82.)

See also: Consecration; United Order

Storm

In commenting on the value of some small things, the Prophet refers to the advantage a ship in a storm has when its helm is very small (D&C 123:16). Although in this sense, a literal storm is meant, the word *storm* is used metaphorically in several other references to imply an existing or pending fierce disturbance or doom (D&C 90:5; 115:6; 127:1).

See also: Defense and . . . a Refuge

Straightway

On several occasions in the scriptures the word *straightway* is used to denote an immediate action, something that occurs at once (1 Sam. 9:13; Matt. 4:20; Acts 9:20; Alma 14:28; D&C 136:25). One man fell away from the Church because "straightway Satan tempted him" (D&C 40:2).

By contrast, the servant in the parable of the vineyard "went straightway, and did all things whatsoever his lord commanded him" (D&C 101:62).

Strait

Many are familiar with the phrase, "strait is the gate, and narrow the way that leadeth unto [life or] the exaltation" (D&C 132:22; see also Matt. 7:14; Luke 13:24; 3 Ne. 14:14). Strait means narrow or constricted. President Spencer W. Kimball noted that strait is "not the shortest distance between two points. Strait means hard, difficult, exacting." (DSY, 1973, 265.)

Strange Act, My

In 1833, the Lord severely rebuked the Saints for neglecting

568 / Strangers and Pilgrims on Earth

the building of a temple in which, he said, his "strange act" would be brought to pass (D&C 95:4). The meaning of this "strange act" is expressed by Smith and Sjodahl: "The expression quoted is from the Prophet Isaiah (28:21), where it refers to the fact that God would fight against His own people, because of their apostate condition. 'Shall I not, as I have done to Samaria and her idols, so do to Jerusalem and her idols' (Isa. 10:11)? That was, in the estimation of the Jews, who did not realize their apostate condition, 'strange.' But in this dispensation our Lord was to perform an equally strange act, in revealing His marvelous plan of salvation and making war upon an apostate church which is boasting of its intimate relations with Deity. He was now waiting for the Saints to build that house, in which His messengers were to be prepared for that strange war and endowed with power from on High (v. 8). No wonder that He rebuked them for their tardiness!" (SS, 603.)

Strangers and Pilgrims on Earth

The unique phrase "strangers and pilgrims on the earth" appears in Doctrine and Covenants 45:13. A pilgrim is a traveler in alien lands. "The people of the city of Enoch, because of their integrity and faithfulness, were as pilgrims and strangers on the earth. This is due to the fact that they were living the celestial law in a telestial world, and all were of one mind, perfectly obedient to all commandments of the Lord." (CHMR 1:195.)

See also: Enoch; Enoch and His Brethren

Strong Drink

The revelation known as the "Word of Wisdom" specifically prohibits the use of "strong drinks," which are "not for the belly, but for the washing of your bodies" (D&C 89:5, 7). The leaders of the Church have consistently defined "strong drinks" as *any alcoholic beverage.*

The Patriarch Hyrum Smith offered the following counsel: "Some will say, 'I know that it did me good, for I was fatigued, and feeble, on a certain occasion, and it revived me, and I was invigorated thereby, and that is sufficient proof for me': It may be for you, but it would not be for a wise man, for every spirit of this kind will only produce a greater languor when its effects cease to operate upon the human body. But you know that you are benefited, yes, so does the man who has mortaged his property, know that he is relieved from his present embarrassments; but his temporary relief only binds the cords of bondage more severely around him." (TS 3:800.)

Stubble

"They that do wickedly shall be as stubble," declared the Lord

(D&C 29:9; see also Ex. 15:7; Isa. 5:20–24; Mal. 4:1; 1 Ne. 22:15; JS—H 1:37). Stubble is that part of the stalk of grain-producing grasses that is left after the grain has been harvested. The righteous are as the grain that is harvested for useful purposes, while the wicked are left to burn as waste.

See also: Burn; Great and Dreadful Day

Stupor of Thought

In righteously seeking an answer from the Lord, one may meet with the spiritual sensation of a burning bosom if the thing sought for is right, or with a stupor of thought if it is wrong (D&C 9:7–9). Just as a right answer will bring an enlargement of one's understanding, so will a wrong answer cause a diminution of spiritual feelings. Such a "stupor" can cause a literal numbness of feeling or suspension of thought.

According to Elder Melvin J. Ballard, when one experiences a "stupor of thought," the "heart will be turned away from that thing" which is wrong (CR, Apr. 1931, pp. 37–38).

See also: Bosom Shall Burn; Speak Peace to Your Mind

Subscription

Sidney Rigdon was commanded by the Lord to prepare "a statement of the will of God, as it shall be made known by the Spirit unto him; and an epistle and subscription to be presented unto all the churches" (D&C 58:50–51). The subscription as used here refers to a signed document which gives consent, sanction, or authorization to a proposed course of action.

Succor the Weak

An 1832 revelation counseled one who had just been called into the Lord's service to "succor the weak" (D&C 81:5). To *succor* is to go to the aid of one in want or distress, to administer relief. One called to service by the Lord is a spiritual shepherd.

The *weak* in the faith are those who lack the spiritual strength to stand alone against the winds of adversity and temptation. The Apostle Paul said that the "strong ought to bear the infirmities of the weak" (Rom. 15:1). He further counseled that "if a man be overtaken in a fault, ye which are spiritual, restore such an one in the spirit of meekness" (Gal. 6:1).

Sucklings

See: Babes and Sucklings

Summer

At the present time, the harvest of souls is proceeding with great urgency as missionaries go forth to labor in the fields. Just as the end of summer signals the end of the growing season, and thus the time for harvest, so has the Lord symbolically represented the time for the harvest of souls.

We are presently in a spiritual "summer," which will soon come to an unexpected end, leaving many unprepared (D&C 35:16; 45:2; 45:37, 56:16). The term *summer*, as used in these references, is synonymous with "today," which is that period of time preceding the coming of the Savior (SS, 393). When "tomorrow" comes, "summer" will be ended and the harvest completed.

Summum Bonum

In an epistle written by Joseph Smith and containing directions regarding salvation for the dead, the Prophet said that the "*summum bonum* of the whole subject" consisted "in obtaining the powers of the Holy Priesthood." Hereby, one could obtain a knowledge of this great work (D&C 128:11).

The term *summum bonum* is Latin and means "the supreme or highest good." Thus, the supreme good of salvation work for the dead is vested in the powers of the holy priesthood. Such powers supply the authority as well as the doctrinal foundation of such work.

Sun

See: Army with Banners; Fair as the Moon/Sun; Sun Shall Be Darkened

Sun Shall Be Darkened

The promised premillennial darkening of the sun, when it shall hide its face and refuse to give light, is one of the signs preceding the Second Coming (D&C 29:14; 34:9; 45:42; 88:87; 133:49; Isa. 13:10; Joel 2:31; Matt. 24:29; Rev. 6:12). For the sun to hide its face means that its frontmost part will no longer be visible.

A possible means whereby this could be accomplished is found in a statement by Brigham Young: "When man fell . . . , the earth fell into space and took up its abode in this planetary system, and the *sun became our light*" (JD 17:143; italics added). When the earth is "rolled back" into its former paradisiacal planetary orbit, its source of light will be from God's presence rather than from the solar rays of our sun. In this sense, the face of the sun will be hidden or darkened.

Another possible way in which the sun might be darkened is by being obscured by heavy clouds of volcanic ash, such as what might have occurred in ancient America at the time of the crucifixion (3 Ne. 8:20–23), or because of smoke from great fires caused by warfare.

See also: Moon Shall Be Turned into Blood; Stars Shall Be Darkened

Sundry Times

The Prophet speaks of having heard "the voice of God . . . at sundry times, and in divers places'' (D&C 128:21; see also Heb. 1:1). *Sundry* simply means various. Thus, God's voice has been heard on various occasions and in different places.

Supper of the House of the Lord

The "supper of the house of the Lord" (D&C 58:9) is that great offering of food and drink "which perisheth not, neither can be corrupted," and in whose "fatness" our souls should "delight" (2 Ne. 9:51). It is the combination of the "living water," which shall forever quench one's thirst (John 4:10–14), and the "living bread," which allows one to live forever (John 6:48–51).

In other words, it represents the fulness of the gospel, which we are commanded to "feast" upon (2 Ne. 31:20; 32:3). "And blessed are all they who do hunger and thirst after righteousness," declared the Savior, "for they shall be filled with the Holy Ghost" (3 Ne. 12:6).

This supper can only be enjoyed by those with the appropriate spiritual appetite. The words of President Hugh B. Brown illustrate this principle: "As the relish with which one enjoys a meal depends upon the appetite he brings to the table more than upon the quality and variety of food placed before him, so the degree of enjoyment and assimilation of spiritual refreshment will depend upon whether or not we 'hunger and thirst,' as en-

joined by the Savior, and be promised the reward of satisfaction" (CR, Apr. 1963, p. 6).

It appears that those who properly partake of this supper will be those who are invited to the great "marriage supper of the Lamb of God" (D&C 58:6–11).

See also: Feast of Fat Things; Marriage of the Lamb

Supper of the Lamb

See: Marriage of the Lamb

Supreme Being

Inasmuch as the Father has bestowed upon the Son *all* that he has (D&C 93:16–17), both bear the title of "Supreme Being" (D&C 107:4). To be supreme is to hold the highest rank or authority, to hold or exercise power which cannot be exceeded or overruled. Such is the divine position held by these two Supreme Beings, for they are not exceeded nor overruled by any other power. They are omnipotent (D&C 19:3; 61:1; Matt. 28:18; 1 Ne. 9:6; Mosiah 4:9; Alma 12:15; 26:35; Morm. 5:23; Ether 3:4).

See also: God; Father, The; Jesus Christ

Susquehanna County, Pennsylvania

Susquehanna County, Pennsylvania, is the area where the city of Harmony is located. It was from the bosom of Susquehanna

County, Pennsylvania, that Joseph received his wife, Emma; the priesthood of God; and fifteen of the revelations found in the Doctrine and Covenants. Additionally, somewhere in the wilderness north of Harmony, Susquehanna County, the Savior's three chief Apostles visited with Joseph Smith and Oliver Cowdery (D&C 128:20).

See also: Harmony, Pennsylvania

Susquehanna River

Although the restoration of the Aaronic Priesthood occurred near the banks of the Susquehanna River, in Harmony, Pennsylvania (HC 1:39–41), the river's name does not appear in the revelations until 1842 (D&C 128:20). This river runs through the lower portion of New York state and the upper portion of Pennsylvania, where the city of Harmony is located near its banks.

It was at this location that Joseph and Emma Smith made their home for a time on land purchased from Emma's father, Isaac Hale. On the banks of this river, mighty Michael detected the devil's design to deceive the Prophet Joseph. It was also on this river's historic banks that Peter, James, and John restored the Melchizedek Priesthood to the earth. (See ''The New York–Ohio Area'' map on page 296 of the 1981 edition of the D&C.)

Sweet, Northrop

The full name of Northrop Sweet does not appear in the context of a revelation, for he is merely referred to as ''my servant Northrop'' (D&C 33:1). His full name now appears in the preface to that revelation. Of him, Joseph Fielding Smith has written: ''Northrop Sweet came in the Church at the time of the preaching of the Lamanite missionaries. On October, 1830, [he was] called by revelation to enter the ministry and hearken to the voice of the Lord. . . . It was not long after this that Northrop Sweet left the Church and, with some others, formed what they called 'The Pure Church of Christ,' an organization that soon came to its end.'' (CHMR 1:152.)

Swine

See: Pearls . . . Cast Before Swine

Sword

See: Bathed in Heaven; Sharper Than a Two-edged Sword; Sword of Laban; Sword of Mine Indignation; Sword of My Spirit

Sword of Laban

The sword of Laban was an exceedingly fine sword with a

hilt of pure gold and a blade of the most precious steel, originally possessed by a Jewish citizen named Laban. It was this sword that the Spirit constrained Nephi to use in slaying the wicked Laban, thus delivering a sacred record into the hands of the righteous (1 Ne. 4). The prophet Nephi used this sword and others modeled after its likeness in defending his people (2 Ne. 5:14; Jac. 1:10). King Benjamin, another Nephite prophet-leader, wielded the sword in defense of his people and before his death passed it on to his son King Mosiah (W of M 1:13; Mosiah 1:16).

Nothing more is mentioned of the sword until 1829, when the Lord promised David Whitmer, Martin Harris, and Oliver Cowdery a view of it (D&C 17:1). In a visit made to David Whitmer in 1878, Elder Orson Pratt and Joseph F. Smith were told that the Three Witnesses had seen not only the plates of the Book of Mormon but also the Brass Plates, many other records, the Urim and Thummim, the Liahona, and the sword of Laban (LJFS, 242).

Additionally, Oliver related an experience he and Joseph Smith had of going into a cave filled with "many wagon loads" of plates such as those from which the Book of Mormon had been translated. On the wall of this cave hung the sword of Laban. However, on visiting the place a second time, they found the sword had been taken down, unsheathed, and laid across the gold plates. On it were these words: "This sword will never be sheathed again until the kingdoms of this world become the kingdom of our God and his Christ." (JD 19:38.)

See also: Laban; Three Witnesses

Sword of Mine Indignation

The Lord has promised that "the sword of mine indignation" will fall "in behalf of my people" (D&C 101:10). This statement was made at a time when the Saints were suffering severe persecution at the hands of their enemies. Smith and Sjodahl suggest that this sword of indignation refers to the numerous wars which are to befall mankind, commencing with the Civil War in the United States (SS, 639).

President Joseph Fielding Smith said: "The sword of indignation commenced to fall upon the enemies of the Saints shortly after the Saints were driven from Missouri, and from time to time it has fallen, both in this land and in foreign lands, and we may truly say that it fell upon the nations during the World War. However, it has not fallen 'without measure,' but this is shortly to come, for the nations are filling the cup of their iniquity which must be full before Christ comes." (CHMR 1:460.)

See also: Cup of Mine Indignation

Sword of My Spirit

One of the spiritual weapons with which one must arm himself is what the Lord calls "the sword of my Spirit" (D&C 27:18). "This is the word of God (Heb. 4:12; D&C 6:2)," wrote Smith and Sjodahl. "In this conflict [with the powers of darkness] the defenders must be well versed in the Scriptures, and be in touch with the Spirit of Revelation, in order to expound the truth." (SS, 138.)

Synagogue

On three occasions the Lord instructed latter-day missionaries to go to synagogues (D&C 63:31; 66:7; 68:1). A synagogue is generally thought of as a place of worship for Jews, such as the ones in which Jesus taught (Luke 4:16–38; see also LDSBD, 778). The ancient Nephites also built places of worship called synagogues (Alma 16:16). However, as used in the Doctrine and Covenants, the word *synagogue* does not appear to be restricted to a particular religious body, but to gatherings of worshipers in general.

T

Tabernacle

The "tabernacle" of which the Lord spoke in section 124, verse 38, refers to the portable "house of the Lord" which served ancient Israel as their temple (Ex. 34:26; Josh. 6:24). It is the sanctuary that Moses was commanded to construct in order that sacred ordinances not be performed before the eyes of the world (Ex. 25:8). This portable "temple," its construction, contents, and the ceremonies to be performed therein, are described in the Old Testament (Ex. 25–40).

Once a permanent temple was built by Solomon, the significance of the tabernacle disappeared, for it had "fulfilled the measure of its creation." It is important to recognize that any holy edifice is special *not* because of the beauty or nature of materials used in its construction, but because of the sacred purposes for which it was constructed.

See also: Tabernacle of God

Tabernacle of God

A revelation given in May 1833, stated that "the elements are the tabernacle of God; yea, man is the tabernacle of God, even temples" (D&C 93:35). Smith and Sjodahl state that "God dwells in the material universe, through His Spirit which pervades everything; not in the pantheistic sense of indwelling, which denies any distinction between matter and mind, body and spirit, God and the world, and affirms, to all intents and purposes, that the universe is God, and God the universe; but in the sense in which we say that God dwelt in the Tabernacle in the wilderness. He dwells in the material world as king in his palace." (SS, 596.)

Man's body becomes the temple or tabernacle of God as it is kept virtuous and clean as an abode for both man's spirit and God's Spirit (D&C 133:5; 1 Cor. 3:16–17; 6:19). Those who defile their "temples" will find themselves banished from God's presence, which is spiritual "destruction."

See also: Temple

Taken to Heaven Without Tasting Death

Among the marvelous manifestations in the Kirtland Temple was the appearance of Elijah, he "who was taken to heaven without tasting death" (D&C 110:13). The Old Testament records that Elijah's ascent to heaven was in a "chariot of fire and horses of fire" (2 Kgs. 2:11). Elijah's ascent was from a telestial to a terrestrial order, placing him among those whom we call "translated beings."

The Prophet Joseph declared: "Many have supposed that the doctrine of translation was a doctrine whereby men were taken immediately into the presence of God, and into an eternal fullness, but this is a mistaken idea. Their place of habitation is that of the terrestrial order, and a place prepared for such characters He held in reserve to be ministering angels unto many planets, and who as yet have not entered into so great a fullness as those who are resurrected from the dead." (TPJS, 170.)

Elijah was not allowed to taste of death during his mortal sojourn on earth, in order that he could perform ordinances belonging to this earthly sphere. God "reserved Elijah from death that he might . . . bestow his keys upon the heads of Peter, James, and John" on the Mount of Transfiguration (DS 2:110–12; AGQ 2:43).

Those who are "translated beings are still mortal and will have to pass through the experience of death, or the separation of the spirit and the body, although this will be instantaneous" (AGQ 1:165). Among those who have been translated were Enoch and his city (D&C 45:11–12; Moses 7:69), Melchizedek and the people of Salem (JST, Gen. 14:32–34), Moses (Alma 45:19), the Three Nephites (3 Ne. 28), and the Apostle John (D&C 7; 3 Ne. 28:6–7).

See also: Elijah; Enoch; Melchizedek; Translated

Talent

The word *talent* has often been associated with money or with the goods of this world (D&C 82:18; 104:69, 73). In ancient times, talents were, in fact, coins of considerable value. However, the parable of the talents (Matt. 25:14–30) has a broader application than mere money. For example, the Lord chastised early missionaries for hiding the talent with which they had been blessed, "because of the fear of man" (D&C 60:2, 13). This talent was the precious message of the restored gospel.

"Every man and woman that has talent and hides it will be called a slothful servant," declared Brigham Young. "Improve day by day upon the capital you have. In proportion as we are capacitated to receive, so it is our duty to do." (JD 7:7.) Whether our talents be gifts of the Spirit (D&C 46:11–26; Moro. 10:8–18) or talents of music, speech, artistic creativity, or capacity to think and reason, we are expected to not only improve them but also to use them for the benefit and edification of others (see D&C 82:18).

Elder Neal A. Maxwell made the following insightful observations regarding talents: "The gross size of our talent inventories is less important than the net use of our talents. . . . God does not begin by asking us about our ability, but only about our availability, and if we then prove our dependability, he will increase our capability!" (En., July 1975, p. 7.) Basically, the principle governing the possession and utilization of talents is that of stewardship: blessings (talents) are bestowed and an accounting thereof will be required.

See also: Stewardship

Tanner, Nathan Eldon

The man who presented the June 1978 revelation on priesthood for the sustaining vote of the Church at the 148th Semiannual General Conference was N. Eldon Tanner. This revelation is identified in the Doctrine and Covenants as Official Declaration—2.

N. Eldon Tanner had a distinguished career in education, government, and business before being called to devote the last twenty-two years of his life to full-time Church service. He was born on May 9, 1898, and was raised in Canada. Following his formal education he spent several years as a teacher and principal before serving in the legislature and provincial cabinet of the Canadian government. He later turned his talents to business enterprises, ultimately directing the construction of the two thousand-mile pipeline across Canada from Alberta to Montreal. He earned the nickname of "Mr. Integrity" because of his undeviating adherence to strict standards of honesty in his dealings.

In 1960, he was called to serve as a General Authority of the Church as an Assistant to the Council of the Twelve Apostles. In 1962 he was called to join the Council of the Twelve, and in 1963 he became a member of the First Presidency. He spent nineteen years in the highest quorum of the Church, serving four Presidents of the Church until his death on November 27, 1982.

His life exemplified the following statement from his own lips: "The greatest achievement in life is not the acquisition of money, position, or power. In my opinion, it is to come to the end of one's day having been true and loyal to his ideals. I can think of no achievement greater than that." (En., Jan. 1983, p. 6.)

Tannery

See: Lot of Tahhanes

Tares

In 1831, the Lord said that "the angels are waiting the great command to reap down the earth, to gather the tares that they may be burned" (D&C 38:12). A later revelation identified "that great church, the mother of abominations" as "the tares of the earth" (D&C 88:94). The term is used in Doctrine and Covenants 38, 86, 88, 101, and was also used by the Savior during his mortal ministry (Matt. 13:24–43). The tares represent the wicked, who will be destroyed at the coming of Christ (JST, Matt. 13:38–44). Joseph Smith also identified the tares as the "corruptions of the Church" (TPJS, 98).

Tares are noxious, poisonous weeds which resemble wheat. They are also referred to as "bastard wheat," which is "so much like true wheat that until the corn is in the ear the two cannot be distinguished. Hence any attempt to root up the tares would result in rooting up the wheat also." (Dummelow, 673; see also LDSBD, 780.)

"Traditionally, tares have been identified with the darnel weed, a species of beared ryegrass which closely resembles wheat in the early growth period and which is found in modern Palestine. This weed has a bitter taste; if eaten in any appreciable amount, either separately or when mixed with bread, it causes dizziness and often acts as a violent emetic." (DNTC 1:296.) Section 86 of the Doctrine and Covenants explains the parable of the wheat and tares, with an application to the latter days.

See also: Wheat

Taste of Death

The phrase *taste of death* is found in the Doctrine and Covenants (D&C 42:46), the Book of Mormon (3 Ne. 28:7, 25, 37, 38; Ether 12:17), and in the New Testament (Mark 9:1; John 8:52), and it is used in at least two different ways: First, those who have lived righteously will not taste of death (experience spiritual suffering) when their spirit takes flight from the flesh, for it will *taste* sweet rather than bitter to them. Second, those who have been granted an extension of their earthly experience by being translated do not taste of death in the normal sense. When the day of their death occurs, it will be in the twinkling of an eye (3 Ne. 28:8).

Taylor, John

John Taylor occupies the rare position of having authored a section in the Doctrine and Covenants (D&C 135). Called to the holy apostleship in 1838, Elder Taylor faithfully served as a member of that quorum of special witnesses and later ultimately served as the prophet and President of the Lord's Church here on earth (D&C 118:6; 124:129).

It was John Taylor's melodic voice which helped bring peace to the troubled minds of Joseph and Hyrum Smith only short minutes before their lives were brutally taken. Having accompanied the brethren to Carthage, John Taylor had offered to tear the jail down if only Joseph would give the word (LJT, 135). He was severely wounded in the attack which claimed his companions' lives, but he lived to bear powerful testimony of the truth for which the men had earned martyrs' crowns. Of his preservation, Elder Taylor wrote: "I felt that the Lord had preserved me by a special act of mercy; that my time had not yet come, and that I had still a work to perform upon the earth" (LJT, 150).

As a young man in England, John Taylor had exhibited an interest in things of the Spirit, including supernatural experiences that led him to America and the restored gospel. One such experience involved seeing a vision of an angel sounding a trumpet to the nations, and having the thought impressed upon his mind that he was to preach the gospel in America (LJT, 28; see Rev. 14:6–7). Upon immigrating to Canada, he became active as a lay preacher, but soon discovered that the doctrines of men did not coincide with the principles of truth taught within the Bible. His conversion was the result of the missionary efforts of Parley P. Pratt, who had received a revelatory blessing regarding the fruits of that mission and their future impact upon the Church (LJT, 35).

John Taylor joined the Church on May 9, 1836, with the following resolve: "When I first entered upon Mormonism, I did it with my eyes open. I counted the cost. I looked upon it as a life-long labor, and I considered that I was not only enlisted for time, but for eternity." (LJT, 48.)

Elder Taylor quickly became known for his courage and forthrightness in defending truth and liberty. Such an attitude earned for him the title, "Champion of Freedom and Liberty." In fact, one of the most prominent floral arrangements at his funeral was a large one with a banner reading, "Champion of Liberty."

He was also known for the zeal with which he pursued anything of either a temporal or spiritual nature. "If a thing is done well," he once said, "no one will ask how long it took to do it, but who did it." On another occasion he said, "I prefer a faded coat to a faded reputation."

His position was firm and well understood. Said one biographer, "Every Latter-day Saint always knew beforehand, on occasions when firmness and courage were needed, where President John Taylor would be found and what his tone would be" (LJT, 411).

His magnanimity is expressed in this plea to all who would call themselves Saints: "If you find people owing you who are distressed, if you will go to work and try to relieve them as much as you can, under the circumstances, God will relieve you when you get into difficulties" (ECH, 587). Though he arduously labored with pen and the spoken word to defend the Church, he was also quick to turn the other cheek when necessary. Of those who tried to provoke anger or hatred on the part of the Saints, Elder Taylor quipped: "They offer themselves to be kicked. Don't do it, have some respect for your boots." (LJT, 316.)

On July 25, 1887, John Taylor died a martyr's death, as the result of the severe persecution heaped upon him by the enemies of the Church, and he occupies what B. H. Roberts described as "the place of double martyr" (LJT, 414). True to the trust that had been placed in him, Elder Taylor died exemplifying the words he had often spoken: "I do not believe in a religion that cannot have all my affections, but I believe in a religion that I can live for, or die for" (LJT, 421).

See also: Carthage Jail; Martyrdom

Teachers

As most frequently used in the Doctrine and Covenants, the term *teacher* refers to the second office in the Aaronic Priesthood (D&C 18:32; 20:38–64; 38:40; 42:12; 84:30, 111; 107:10, 62–63, 86; 124:42). The scripturally outlined duties of this office are to: watch over and strengthen the Church; see that there is no iniquity in the Church, neither hardness with each other, neither lying, backbiting, nor evil speaking; see that the Church meet together often; see that all members do their duty; take the lead of meetings in the absence of higher authority;

warn, expound, exhort, teach, and "invite all to come unto Christ" (D&C 20:53–59). Other duties may be designated by the bishopric, who preside over the Aaronic Priesthood.

A second way in which the term *teacher* is used is in reference to he who presided as *the* teacher at the School of the Prophets, organized in Kirtland, Ohio, in February 1833. This teacher was the Prophet Joseph Smith (D&C 88:122–35).

See also: Aaronic Priesthood; School of the Prophets

Telestial

The term *telestial*, as found in sections 76 and 88, is unique to Mormon theology. There is a glory of the hereafter known as the telestial world or kingdom (D&C 76:98; 88:21), which is inhabitated by those whose resurrected bodies are "quickened by a portion of the telestial glory" (D&C 88:31; 76:109). There are also telestial laws which govern telestial worlds and their inhabitants (D&C 88:24).

The Apostle Paul described the bodies to be possessed by the inhabitants of the three kingdoms of glory in the hereafter, but our present King James Bible only refers to two of them by name— the celestial, or glory of the sun, and the terrestrial, or glory of the moon (1 Cor. 15:39–42). Nevertheless, Paul spoke of the glory of the stars, which glory is that of a telestial order (D&C 76:81, 98).

The Prophet Joseph Smith, in his inspired version of the Bible, used the term *telestial* to identify the glory of those resurrected bodies who inhabit such a kingdom (JST, 1 Cor. 15:40).

This glory is described by Elder James E. Talmage as follows: "This is for those who received not the testimony of Christ, but who, nevertheless, did not deny the Holy Spirit; who have led lives exempting them from the heaviest punishment, yet whose redemption will be delayed until the last resurrection. In the telestial world there are innumerable degrees comparable to the varying light of the stars. Yet all who receive of any one of these orders of glory are at last saved, and upon them Satan will finally have no claim. Even the telestial glory 'surpasses all understanding; And no man knows it except him to whom God has revealed it.' " (AF, 92–93; see D&C 76:81–112; 88:24, 31.)

President Joseph Fielding Smith informed us that the present status of our earth is that of a telestial order, which came about as a result of the fall of Adam (DS 1:82–85). The paradisiacal, or Garden of Eden, state of the earth was that of a terrestrial order, which order will return at the Second Coming and remain throughout the Millennium. At the end of this period, the earth will be celestialized.

See also: Glory; Last Resurrection; Mansions of My Father; Salvation; Saved; Servants of the Most High; Some of One and

Some of Another; Third Trump; Vengeance of Eternal Fire

Temperance

The Lord admonished that we be "temperate in all things" (D&C 12:8). According to Webster, temperance is "habitual moderation in the indulgence of the appetites or passions."

Although the word has usually been associated with abstinence from alcohol, it has other implications. The virtue of temperance, which is to be possessed by all who serve in the ministry (D&C 4:6; 107:30), is "not just refraining from drinking liquor!" said President Joseph Fielding Smith. It means to "be temperate in . . . language and in . . . actions — not make extravagant statements." (SYE, 356.)

Temple

References to temples in the Doctrine and Covenants pertain to houses of the Lord found in several locations. For example, the Savior refers to the temple which stood in Jerusalem at the time of his mortal ministry (D&C 45:18, 20). The site for the temple to be built in the New Jerusalem at Independence, Missouri, is mentioned in several sections (D&C 57:3; 58:57; 84:3). A great outpouring of revelation and heavenly visitations occurred at the Kirtland Temple in Ohio (D&C 110). This latter temple may be the one spoken of by the Lord when he promised to "come suddenly" to his temple (D&C 36:8; 42:36; 133:2; Mal. 3:1). Finally, the Nauvoo Temple is mentioned in several epistles written by the Prophet Joseph Smith (D&C 127:4, 9; 128:24).

Temples are sacred sanctuaries in which the Saints of God enter into covenants of salvation and receive inspired instruction. "Participating in temple ordinances is just as essential as baptism. Ultimately there will be no exaltation for anyone who does not receive the fullness of the gospel as it is administered in the temple." (CN, March 16, 1986, p. C–24.)

In temples, Latter-day Saints may receive what is known as an endowment, which Elder John A. Widtsoe described as follows: "The temple endowment relates the story of man's eternal journey; sets forth the conditions upon which progress in the eternal world depends; requires covenants or agreements of those participating to accept and use the laws of progress; gives tests by which our willingness and fitness for righteousness may be known, and finally points out the ultimate destiny of those who love truth and live by it" (PC, 178).

"The ordinances of the temple are so sacred that they are not open to the view of the public. They are available only to those who qualify through righteous living. . . . Their sacred nature is such that discussion in detail out-

side the temple is inappropriate."
(NE, June 1971, p. 27.)

See also: Anointing; Baptism for the Dead; Endowment; Endowment House; Fulness of the Priesthood; Holy House; Kirtland Temple; Mountains of the Lord's House; Nauvoo Temple; New and Everlasting Covenant of Marriage; Ordinances; Records; Salt Lake Temple; Tabernacle of God; Upper Room; Washings

Temporal Death

Temporal death is the "death in the flesh" which the Savior voluntarily experienced and to which all mankind are subject (D&C 29:42; see also 18:11; John 10:15–18; 1 Cor. 15:21–22). It is also referred to as "natural death" (D&C 29:43).

President Joseph F. Smith made the following observation: "In this natural body are the seeds of weakness and decay, which, when fully ripened or untimely plucked up, in the language of scripture, is called 'the temporal death' " (JD 23:169).

Temporal death is the temporary separation of body and spirit (James 2:26). The spirit takes flight to realms unseen by mortal eyes and the lifeless body is returned to mother earth to await the day of resurrection. President Smith taught further that "the body may be dissolved and become extinct as an organism, although the elements of which it is composed are indestructible and eternal" (JD 23:171). These

elements will be perfectly organized in one's resurrected body, and the spirit will be united with that body "never to be divided" (Alma 11:44–45).

"Death is a kind of graduation day for life," said Elder Sterling W. Sill (CR, Oct. 1976, p. 65). "Where the true Saints are concerned there is no sorrow in death except that which attends a temporary separation from loved ones," said Elder Bruce R. McConkie. "Birth and death are both essential steps in the unfolding drama of eternity." (CR, Oct. 1976, p. 158.)

Temporal Salvation

In giving the revelation known as the Word of Wisdom, the Lord referred to it as "the order and will of God in the temporal salvation of all saints in the last days" (D&C 89:2). The guidelines in this revelation stand as a code of health, intended to preserve and strengthen the temporal, or physical, body.

Nevertheless, as the Lord earlier declared, "All things unto me are spiritual, and not at any time have I given unto you a law which was temporal; . . . for my commandments are spiritual" (D&C 29:34–35). Thus, although the temporal or physical salvation of man is the most obvious benefit of following the counsel given in the Word of Wisdom, the ultimate benefits are spiritual.

President Joseph Fielding Smith noted that "the temporal

salvation of the children of men is a most important thing, but sadly neglected by many religious teachers. The truth is that the spiritual salvation is dependent upon the temporal far more than most men realize. The line of demarcation between the temporal, or physical, and the spiritual, cannot be definitely seen. . . . To men some of these commandments may be temporal, but they are spiritual to the Lord because they all have a bearing on the spiritual or eternal welfare of mankind." (CHMR 1:383.)

Temporal Things

Throughout the scriptures a distinction is drawn between those things which are of a spiritual nature and those which are of a temporal nature (D&C 29:30–35; 70:12). Webster defines *temporal* as that which pertains to time or is of an earthly nature. Thus, temporal things are those which are presently confined to this earth and are limited by man's time. Temporal things are carthy and pertain to mortality, whereas spiritual things have an eternal verity.

See also: Earthy

Ten Virgins

The term *ten virgins* is referred to with two separate meanings in the Doctrine and Covenants. In the first instance (D&C 45:56), reference is made to the parable of the ten virgins, five of whom were caught without oil in their lamps at the crucial moment of the wedding feast (Matt. 25:1–13).

Of these virgins, Elder James E. Talmage has written: "The virgins typify those who profess a belief in Christ, and who, therefore, confidently expect to be included among the blessed participants at the feast. The lighted lamp, which each of the maidens carried, is the outward profession of Christian belief and practice; and in the oil reserves of the wiser ones we may see the spiritual strength and abundance which diligence and devotion in God's service alone can insure. The lack of sufficient oil on the part of the unwise virgins is analogous to the dearth of soil in the stony field, wherein the seed readily sprouted but soon withered away. . . . The unwise five suffered the natural results of their unpreparedness." (Talmage, 578–79.) Section 63, verse 54, equates these "unwise" and "foolish virgins" with the wicked, who will be separated from the righteous at the coming of the Lord.

The second sense in which the term *ten virgins* is used is in conjunction with the principle of plural marriage. The ten virgins spoken of here are ten maidens designated to become brides in the celestial order of marriage (D&C 132:62, 63).

Tenets

The dictionary defines the word *tenet* as a dogma, belief, or opinion that is held to be true. The Lord cautioned an early exponent of the gospel, Martin Harris, not to preach about tenets, but to confine his preaching to the first principles—faith, repentance, baptism, and the gift of the Holy Ghost (D&C 19:31). This counsel is still applicable to teachers of the gospel in our day.

In the words of President Joseph Fielding Smith: *"We should keep our feet on the ground and not get off in the realm of the mysterious, the speculative, the things which the Lord has not yet made plain. . . .*

"The fundamental principles of the gospel—all that has to do with the salvation of man—are very clear and can be understood by those with ordinary intelligence. To spend time discussing useless questions which have no bearing on our salvation, and have no relationship to the commandments and obligations required of us by the plan of salvation, is just a useless pastime." (DS 1:305–6.)

Rumors and speculative stories could be classified as tenets, which President Harold B. Lee specifically pleaded with the Saints to cease promoting, referring to them as "the works of the devil" (CR, Apr. 1970, p. 56; see also CR, Oct. 1972, p. 125).

Terrestrial

The term *terrestrial* appears once in the Bible (1 Cor. 15:40) and a dozen times in sections 76 and 88 of the Doctrine and Covenants (76:71–98; 88:21–30). There is a terrestrial kingdom, or world (D&C 76:71), which is to be inhabited by resurrected beings whose bodies are of a terrestrial order or glory (D&C 76:78) and who live by terrestrial laws (D&C 88:23). The terrestrial kingdom is a secondary order of glory, falling below that of the celestial glory but being above that of the telestial glory. These degrees differ in brightness and luster, even as the sun, moon, and stars differ from one another.

The scriptures reveal that the celestial kingdom is divided into three heavens or degrees (D&C 131:1–4) and that the telestial kingdom likewise is subdivided into varying glories (D&C 76:98). Therefore, "we conclude that a similar condition prevails in the Terrestrial. Thus the innumerable degrees of merit amongst mankind are provided for in an infinity of graded glories." (AF, 409.) "God will give to every man a glory that will be suited to his condition" (GT 1:97).

The inhabitants of the terrestrial kingdom are described as follows: "1. Accountable persons who die without law (and who, of course, do not accept the gospel in the spirit world under those particular circumstances which would make them heirs of the celestial kingdom); 2. Those who reject the gospel in this life and who reverse their course and accept it in the spirit world; 3. Honorable men of the earth who are blinded by the craftiness of men and who therefore do not accept and live the gospel law; and 4. Members of The Church of Jesus Christ of Latter-day Saints who have testimonies of Christ and the divinity of the great latter-day work and who are not valiant, but who are instead lukewarm in their devotion to the Church and to righteousness" (MD, 784; D&C 76:71–80).

The term *terrestrial* is used in one other sense in Latter-day Saint discussion. According to the tenth article of faith, "the earth will be renewed and receive its paradisiacal glory." This refers to the terrestrial condition that will prevail during the Millennium, when only those who abide at least the law of this order will be allowed to inhabit our earth (DS 1:84–86). The dictionary, as one might suspect, defines the term *terrestrial* as that which is "of or relating to the earth or its inhabitants; earthly or mortal."

See also: Glory; Honorable Men of the Earth; Mansions of My Father; Paradisiacal Glory; Presence of the Son; Salvation; Saved; Second Angel; Second Trump; They Who Are Not Valiant; They Who Died Without Law

Territory of Iowa

In March 1841, the will of the Lord was sought regarding the Saints in the Territory of Iowa (D&C 125:1). At about this time the Saints began locating in the area surrounding the common border shared by Illinois and Iowa.

Dr. Isaac Galland had befriended the Saints and suggested they locate in Iowa, which had become a territory of the United States in 1838. Galland "thought they would be more likely to receive protection from mobs under the jurisdiction of the United States, than they would in a state of the Union, 'where murder, rapine and robbery are admirable (!) traits in the character of a demagogue; and where the greatest villains often reach the highest offices.' He also wrote to Governor Robert Lucas of Iowa, who had known the 'Mormon' people in Ohio, and who spoke very highly of them as good citizens." (ECH, 220.)

The Territory of Iowa originally included most of what is now the state of Minnesota as well as what we now know as the state of Iowa. It was a territory from 1838 until 1846, when it was admitted to the Union as the twenty-ninth state.

See also: Galland, Isaac; Iowa

Testimony

The Savior admonished early disciples of this dispensation to "bear testimony in every place, unto every people" (D&C 66:7). "According to the dictionary," said President Joseph Fielding Smith, "a testimony is a 'Statement or affirmation of a fact, as before a court; evidence, proof. . . .

"In relation to the gospel, a testimony is a revelation to the individual who earnestly seeks one by prayer, study, and faith. It is the impression of speaking of the Holy Ghost to the soul in a convincing, positive manner. It is something which is far more penetrating than impressions from any other source, but it cannot be fully described." (AGQ 3:28; see pp. 28–31.)

In the words of President Hugh B. Brown, "A testimony of the Gospel of Jesus Christ is a product more of the heart than of the head" (CN, Apr. 10, 1965, C–13). It is in this context that an ancient prophet spoke when he said, "when a man speaketh by the power of the Holy Ghost the power of the Holy Ghost carrieth it unto the hearts of the children of men" (2 Ne. 33:1). A modern-day prophet, Elder George Albert Smith, in like manner declared: "No matter how gifted we may be, or how choice our language, it is the spirit of our Father that reaches the heart and brings conviction of the divinity of this work" (CR, Oct. 1904, p. 66).

Elder Marion G. Romney described eight components which the testimony of a true Latter-day Saint should include: (1) a witness that there is a personal God; (2) a belief in God's plan of salvation, with Jesus Christ as the central figure; (3) a belief that Joseph Smith conversed with Deity in the Sacred Grove; (4) a conviction that the Book of Mormon is sacred scripture from God; (5) a witness that heavenly beings bestowed the authority upon Joseph Smith that is necessary to enable men to gain exaltation; (6) a knowledge that The Church of Jesus Christ of Latter-day Saints is the *only* repository of that authority; (7) a conviction that *every* man who has presided over this Church has had that authority; (8) the witness that the living prophet is just as much a prophet as was Joseph Smith. "The possession of a sure testimony," added Elder Romney, "is the most valuable possession a person can have." (LTG, 36–37.)

The formula for gaining a testimony was expressed by Elder John A. Widtsoe as a four-part process: (1) Cultivate the desire. "It must be insistent, constant, over-whelming, burning. It must be a driving force." (2) Recognize your limitations. (3) Put forth an effort to learn the gospel. Study must be constant, as well as prayer. (4) Weave the gospel into the pattern of your life. (ER, 15–17.) "To hold his testimony," cautioned Elder Spencer W. Kimball, "one must bear it often and live worthy of it" (CR, Oct. 1944, p. 46). To *bear* a testimony is not merely to express gratitude, a testimony must be "a declaration, a witness" (TYD, 275).

See also: Holy Ghost; Revelation; Still Small Voice; Testimony of Jesus; Testimony of the Jews; Testimony of the Just; Testimony of Their Fathers

Testimony of Jesus

Those who inherit the celestial kingdom must be active possessors of "the testimony of Jesus" (D&C 76:51). Those who dwell in terrestrial glories are they "who received not the testimony of Jesus in the flesh, but afterwards received it" and "are not valiant in the testimony of Jesus" (D&C 76:74, 79). Telestial kingdom inhabitants are they who "received not the gospel of Christ neither the testimony of Jesus" (D&C 76:82, 101). The testimony of Jesus is one of the gifts of the Spirit (D&C 46:11–14).

A modern-day Apostle has described the meaning of this phrase: "I have what is known as 'the testimony of Jesus,' " declared Elder Bruce R. McConkie, "which means that I know by personal revelation from the Holy Spirit to my soul that Jesus is the Lord; that he brought life and immortality to light through the gospel; and that he has restored in this day the fullness of his everlasting truth, so that we with the ancients can become inheritors of his presence in eternity" (CR, Apr. 1972, p. 133). According to John the Revelator, "the testimony of Jesus is the spirit of prophecy" (Rev. 19:10; see also TP.JS, 160).

See also: Jesus Christ; Spirit of Prophecy; Testimony; Valiant in the Testimony of Jesus

Testimony of the Jews

An ancient Nephite prophet spoke of "a record of the Jews, which contains the covenants of the Lord, which he hath made unto the house of Israel; and it also containeth many of the prophecies of the holy prophets" (1 Ne. 13:20–29). This record is the same as the "testimony of the Jews" spoken of in modern revelation (D&C 3:16).

The Lord identified this record (testimony) as the Bible. The world "shall have a Bible; and it shall proceed forth from the Jews, mine ancient covenant people," God declared (2 Ne. 29:4). The knowledge of the *promised* Messiah has generally come to the world through the Old Testament, and the knowledge of the *mortal ministry* of the Savior has come through the New Testament.

See also: Bible

Testimony of the Just

A bishop is to "judge his people by the tesimony of the just" (D&C 58:18). That which is just is fair, reasonable, and righteous. Thus, the testimony of the just is an unbiased and correct portrayal of the facts involved in the situation under consideration.

Testimony of Their Fathers

Based upon a careful reading of verses 16–20 in section 3, "the testimony of their fathers" refers to the records or plates from which the Book of Mormon was translated. These records would bear special testimony of the Savior to all who had descended from the ancient inhabitants of the Americas. These descendants are known today as Lamanites.

However, as the title page of the Book of Mormon points out, it is "written [not only] to the *Lamanites* . . . [but] also to the convincing of the *Jew* and *Gentile* that JESUS is the CHRIST" (italics added).

See also: Book of Mormon; Lamanites

Thankfulness

The Lord declared that "he who receiveth all things with thankfulness shall be made glorious" (D&C 78:19). To possess the quality of thankfulness is to be grateful, to show gratitude through acts of service and obedience as well as in expressions of prayerful praise. We are commanded to "thank the Lord [our] God in all things" (D&C 59:7).

President Joseph F. Smith observed that "one of the greatest sins of which the inhabitants of the earth are guilty today is the sin of ingratitude" (GD, 270).

That Man

In a revelation that—because of misinterpretation on the part of those who lacked the Spirit—has spawned a number of apostate offshoots from the true Church, the Lord spoke of removing "that man" and replacing him with "one mighty and strong" (D&C 85:7–8). "That man" refers to Bishop Edward Partridge, who at the time was being reprimanded in a letter written from Kirtland by the Prophet Joseph to W. W. Phelps in Missouri.

However, Edward Partridge repented of his erroneous ways to such an extent that following his death the Lord proclaimed that the bishop was among those who shared the presence of Deity (D&C 124:19).

See also: Edward Partridge; One Mighty and Strong

That Wicked One

In section 93, the Lord speaks of "that wicked one [who] cometh and taketh away light and truth, through disobedience, from the children of men, and because of the traditions of their fathers" (D&C 93:39). Satan is "that wicked one" who "in his rebellion and hatred of all things righteous, desires to destroy the souls of men, therefore he tries to take from them light and truth that they may be left in spiritual darkness" (CHMR 1:402).

See also: Devil

Thayre, Ezra

The name of Ezra Thayre appears in several revelations (D&C 33:1; 52:22; 54:preface; 56:5, 8; 75:31). In three of these he is admonished to take up the labors of missionary work, and in one he is rebuked for his pride and selfishness. There is also mention of his membership being in question in

1835, based upon a complaint signed by another Elder (HC 2:221). Thayre himself had previously brought charges against another member because his method of preaching was thought to be unbecoming (HC 2:33).

His later service included being a member of Zion's Camp (HC 2:185), a member of the First Quorum of the Seventy (SS, 307), and a high councilor at Adam-ondi-Ahman (HC 3:39). He became a member of the political governing body known as the Council of Fifty and campaigned in behalf of Joseph Smith's presidential bid in 1844.

Thayre did not remain faithful to the Church following the martyrdom of the Prophet and later affiliated with the Reorganized Church. (BYUS 20:163–97.)

See also: Thompson, Ohio

They Who Are in the North Countries

One of the intriguing issues discussed by gospel scholars and historians is the whereabouts and status of the lost ten tribes of Israel. Although lost to mankind's knowledge, their identity and location are known to God (1 Ne. 22:4; 3 Ne. 15:15). This body of Northern Israelites was led away captive by the Assyrian king Shalmaneser about 721 B.C. (2 Kgs. 17). An apocryphal book gives a description of the tribes' escape into "a further country, where never mankind dwelt." The journey allegedly took a year

and one-half to complete. (2 Esdras 13:39–47.)

The resurrected Redeemer visited the lost tribes following his postmortal ministry among the inhabitants of ancient America (3 Nephi 16:1–3; 17:4). At that time they were a distinct body of people, and the Savior established his Church among them (WTP, 131). We anticipate a future day when the scriptural records of the lost tribes will come forth and be added to the already existing scriptures of Judah (the Bible) and Ephraim (the Book of Mormon), thus completing "a triad of truth" (2 Nephi 29:13; En., Nov. 1986, p. 52).

One of the basic beliefs of Latter-day Saints is the "restoration of the Ten Tribes" (Articles of Faith 1:10) temporally to their homeland in Palestine and other places and spiritually to the gospel of Jesus Christ (3 Ne. 21:27–28; Mill M, 324). In 1831 the Prophet Joseph Smith declared that the Apostle John was then with the lost tribes preparing them for their return (HC 1:176, footnote). The scriptures tell us they will return from the *north* countries (Jer. 3:18; 16:14–15; 23:7–8; 31:8–9; Ether 13:11; D&C 133:26–34).

Elder Bruce R. McConkie identified this return as a Millennial event that will occur only after these people have accepted the Book of Mormon and the restored gospel of Jesus Christ (Mill M, 216, 325; ANW, 520–21; 529–30). Elder McConkie suggests that "there will be no prophets among them except the elders of Israel who belong to The Church of Jesus Christ of Latter-day Saints'' (ANW, 520).

A frequently expressed thought by General Authorities of the Church is that the lost tribes are intact as a body of people in some yet unknown location (WTP, 130; ST, 186; CR, Apr. 1916, p. 130; JD 4:231–32; 18:68). However, one authority wrote that these tribes ''are scattered in all the nations of the earth, primarily in the nations north of the lands of their first inheritance'' (ANW, 520; see also Mill M, 216).

An 1831 revelation tells us that the return of the ten tribes will be accompanied by the casting up of a highway ''in the midst of the great deep'' (D&C 133:27). This highway could be a literal road whereon the returning tribes will travel; it could be symbolic of a highway of holiness (Isa. 35:8), which one scholar has identified as the strait and narrow path (Mill M, 327); or a combination of the two pathways. In either event, we know that the returning tribes will receive the fulness of their priesthood blessings, including those of the temple, from the hands of Ephraim (D&C 133:32; Mill M, 325–29). Upon their return, the leaders (''prophets''; see D&C 133:26) of the tribes and all those who choose to follow the Lord will be subject to the priesthood direction of the President and prophet of The Church of Jesus Christ of Latter-day Saints—he who holds *all* keys of priesthood authority, in-

cluding those of directing the return of the lost tribes (D&C 28:20; 42:11; 110:11).

See also: Ephraim; Everlasting Hills; Highway Cast Up in the Midst of the Great Deep; Ice Shall Flow Down at Their Presence; Restoration of the Scattered Israel; Treasures

They Who Are Not Valiant

Among those who will not qualify for the fulness of the celestial kingdom but instead will be consigned to the terrestrial kingdom are those ''who are not valiant in the testimony of Jesus'' (D&C 76:79). To be valiant is to be courageous.

Elder Bruce R. McConkie taught that to be valiant in the testimony of Jesus ''is to be courageous and bold; to use all our strength, energy, and ability in the warfare with the world; to fight the good fight of faith. . . . The great cornerstone of valiance in the cause of righteousness is obedience to the whole law of the whole gospel.

''To be valiant . . . is to 'come unto Christ and be perfected in him'; it is to deny ourselves 'of all ungodliness,' and 'love God' with all our 'might, mind and strength.' (Moro. 10:32.)

'' . . . [It is] to believe in Christ and his gospel with unshakable conviction. . . .

''It is more than believing and knowing. We must be doers of the word and not hearers only. It is more than lip service. . . .

"To be valiant is to 'press forward with a steadfastness in Christ.' . . .

"[It is] to bridle our passions, control our appetites, and rise above carnal and evil things. . . .

"To be valiant in the testimony of Jesus is to take the Lord's side on every issue. It is to vote as he would vote. It is to think what he thinks, to believe what he believes, to say what he would say and do what he would do in the same situation. It is to have the mind of Christ and be one with him as he is one with his Father." (CR, Oct. 1974, pp. 43–47.)

Those who do not do these things are "they who are not valiant."

See also: Terrestrial; Valiant in the Testimony of Jesus

They Who Died Without Law

Among those who will inherit the terrestrial kingdom will be "they who died without law" (D&C 76:72). President Joseph Fielding Smith referred to these as inhabitants of the "heathen nations," who never knew the law of the gospel (CHMR 1:276; D&C 45:54).

Sperry suggested that "those in this category must include millions of people throughout the earth who never heard the Gospel of Christ and most of whom, even if they had heard it, would not have comprehended it or accepted it. Let me hasten to add," he cautioned, "that all men will hear the Gospel in the Spirit World, and some of those who die without law will doubtless accept it and become heirs to the Celestial Kingdom. But in His infinite mercy and foresight, the Father, knowing the spiritual capacity of His children, does not place a moral responsibility upon them in this life greater than they can bear. (Cf. Alma 29:8.) By reason of His great knowledge of men in the pre-mortal state, God segregated them to a large extent in mortality and fixed 'the bounds of their habitation.' (Cf. Deut. 32:7–9; Acts 17:26.) As a result, 'the heathen nations . . . and they that knew no law shall have part in the first resurrection; and it shall be tolerable for them.' (D&C 45:54.)" (DCC, 351.)

"Wherefore, he has given a law; and where there is no law given there is no punishment. . . . But wo unto him that has the law given, yea, that has all the commandments of God, . . . and that transgresseth them, and that wasteth the days of his probation, for awful is his state!" (2 Ne. 9:25–27.)

See also: Terrestrial

Thief in the Night

The Lord has warned that "desolation shall come upon this generation as a thief in the night" (D&C 45:19). He also reminded us that his second coming shall be "as a thief in the night" (D&C 106:4–5; see also 1 Thess. 5:2–8; JS—M 1:46–48).

He who comes as a "thief in the night" comes unexpectedly.

There may be previous signs or warnings given regarding his future arrival, but the event itself will come suddenly, without notice. They who are always prepared will be ready for the occasion, but the slothful and unrepentant, those who procrastinate, will be caught off guard and be unprepared.

Third Part of the Hosts of Heaven

Of all the spirit children of our Father in Heaven, one-third chose to rebel and follow Lucifer (D&C 29:36–38; Abr. 3:27–28; Rev. 12:7–9). They are referred to as devils (D&C 24:13), evil spirits (D&C 46:7), unclean spirits (Mark 3:11), angels of the devil (D&C 29:37), and "they who are filthy" (2 Ne. 9:16).

Those who chose this perditious path are committed to the destruction of God's purposes and exercise an everlasting hatred toward him and all who choose his ways (Moro. 7:12). They have become "sons of perdition because they are in rebellion against the Father and are denied the privilege of receiving bodies because they kept not their first estate" (WTP, 34).

So intense is their desire to possess a physical body that some even implored the Savior to cast them into the bodies of swine for they "prefer a swine's body to having none" (Mark 5:2–13; TPJS, 181). They traverse this telestial sphere taunting and tempting, hoping to secure even a temporary abode in a temporal tenement. There are numerous examples of these "unclean spirits" or "devils" being cast from the presence of the righteous by priesthood authority, which they are bound to recognize and obey (Mark 1:23–27; Luke 4:33–36; D&C 24:13; 34:9; 84:67; 124:98; HC 1:82–83).

This one-third of our Father's children, together with those whom they have successfully conquered, will be eternally banished from God's presence and suffer the fateful consequences of their sordid actions.

See also: Devils; Hosts of Hell; Sons of Perdition

Third Trump

Section 88 reveals that two series of seven trumps will sound, beginning with the return of the Savior at the beginning of the Millennium and ending with the last great battle between the forces of good and evil at the end of that thousand-year period. The "third trump" of the first series will sound at the end of the Millennium, announcing the resurrection of those of a telestial glory (D&C 88:100–101; DS 2:297–98).

See also: Spirits of Men Who Are to Be Judged; Telestial

This Land

See: America

Thomas (B. Marsh)

Occasionally in the Doctrine and Covenants, the Lord will refer to a man only by his first name. In most instances, the identity of the individual is understood through previous verses or the preface to that section.

In D&C 118:2 the name *Thomas* is given without these identifying qualities. Nevertheless, the revelation is addressed to "the Twelve," of whom Thomas B. Marsh was the President. He was the only member of the Twelve with the given name of Thomas.

See also: Marsh, Thomas B.

Thompson, Ohio

One of the locations where Joseph Smith received revelation was Thompson, Ohio. Elder B. H. Roberts described the nature of this settlement: "The Saints comprising the Colesville [New York] branch, when they arrived at the gathering place, in Ohio, were advised to remain together and were settled at Thompson, a place in the vicinity [northeast] of Kirtland. On their arrival Bishop Edward Partridge urged the Prophet Joseph to inquire of the Lord concerning the manner of settling them, and providing for them. Whereupon the Prophet inquired of the Lord and received the revelation. . . . [D&C 51.] It will be seen from that revelation that the Saints of the Colesville branch were to be organized under the law of consecration and stewardship. . . . It is evident that some of the brethren already living at Thompson, had agreed to enter into the law of consecration and stewardship with the Saints from Colesville; and that afterwards they broke this covenant. Among these were Leman Copley and Ezra Thayre." (HC 1:180, footnote.)

Newel Knight was sent to Joseph Smith to find out what course of action the Thompson Saints should take, and Doctrine and Covenants 54 is the Lord's response. Knight's previous appointment to take a missionary journey was canceled, and he was commanded to forsake the "stiffnecked" people and lead the "contrite" Saints of Thompson to Missouri (D&C 56:5–8).

See also: Colesville, New York; Copley, Leman; Thayre, Ezra

Thompson, Robert B.

The name of Robert B. Thompson appears but once in the Doctrine and Covenants (D&C 124:12). The Lord indicated his pleasure with the man's conduct. Thompson "was born in Great Driffield, England, October 1, 1811. For a number of years he was a Methodist preacher, but he embraced the gospel in Canada and was baptized in 1836. He lived in Far West when the fires of persecution were kindled, and was compelled to flee for his life." (SS, 769–70.)

Thompson died an early death on August 27, 1841. Of his passing Joseph Smith wrote: "Elder Robert Blashel Thompson died at his residence in Nauvoo, in the 30th year of his age, in the full hope of a glorious resurrection. He was associate editor of the *Times and Seasons*, colonel in the Nauvoo Legion, and had done much writing for myself and the Church." (HC 4:411.)

Those That Die in Me

See: Dead That Die in the Lord

Those Who Are Christ's at His Coming

When the second trump sounds in the afternoon of the first resurrection, "those who are Christ's at his coming" will be resurrected (D&C 88:99). These are those of a terrestrial order who "died without law," "who are honorable men of the earth" and "received not the testimony of Jesus in the flesh, but afterwards received it" (D&C 76:71–80). These are they "who were not worthy to be caught up to meet him [Christ], but who are worthy to come forth to enjoy the millennial reign" (DS 2:296–97).

See also: Second Trump; Terrestrial

Those Who Are to Remain Until the Great and Last Day

The fourth trump to sound, announcing the last order of res-

urrected beings, will be the call of condemnation. For "those who are to remain until that great and last day, even the end, . . . shall remain filthy still" (D&C 88:102). These are they to whom the notes of the trumpet will not be soothingly melodic but rather terrifyingly condemnatory, for they will signal eternal banishment from the glories of God to the outer reaches of darkness. These are the "vessels of wrath" known as sons of perdition. (D&C 76:31–38; 88:32.)

See also: Sons of Perdition

Those Who Have Fallen

In section 118 the Lord appointed four members of the Quorum of the Twelve Apostles to "fill the places of those who have fallen" (D&C 118:1, 6). The four "fallen" men were original members of the first Quorum of the Twelve established in this last dispensation. These four were William E. McLellin, excommunicated May 11, 1838; Luke S. Johnson, excommunicated April 13, 1838 (he was rebaptized in 1846 and died in Salt Lake in 1861); John F. Boynton, excommunicated December 1837; and Lyman E. Johnson, excommunicated April 13, 1838. (ECH, 575–76; CHMR 2:98.)

Thoughts

"God . . . is a discerner of the thoughts and intents of the heart" (D&C 33:1). Because he knows our very thoughts (D&C 6:16), we will be held accountable for them; if they are not found spotless, they will "condemn us" (Alma 12:14). Thus, the commandment is given to "cast away . . . idle thoughts" (D&C 88:69) and to "let virtue garnish thy thoughts unceasingly" (D&C 121:45).

"He approaches nearest the Christ spirit," said President David O. McKay, "who makes God the center of his thoughts" (CR, Oct. 1953, p. 10). Elder J. Thomas Fyans noted that "just as rivers are colored by the substances picked up as they flow along, so the streams of our thoughts are colored by the material through which they are channeled" (CR, Apr. 1975, p. 130).

Along this same vein, Elder Sterling W. Sill observed that "the mind, like the dyer's hand, is colored by what it holds. If I hold in my mind and heart great ideas of faith and enthusiasm, my whole personality is changed accordingly." (En., May 1978, p. 66.)

One must control the raw material that goes into the factory of the mind in order to ensure that the finished product is of a celestial quality. "You are today where your thoughts have brought you," said Bishop Thorpe B. Isaacson. "You will be tomorrow, and the next day, and every day where your thoughts will take you." (CR, Oct. 1956, p. 12; see also Prov. 23:7; Isa. 14:24.)

See also: Desire of Their Hearts; Willing Mind

Thousand Years, The

The "thousand years" spoken of wherein peace will reign, Satan will be bound, and Christ will rule the earth is the seventh period of earth's history known as the Millennium (D&C 29:11, 22; 77:12; 88:101, 110).

See also: Millennium; Seventh Angel/Trump

Thrash the Nations

The ministers of the Lord are called upon "to thrash the nations by the power of [His] Spirit" (D&C 35:13; 133:59). Smith and Sjodahl equate thrashing with threshing and offer the following explanation of this expression, which is also found in Habakkuk 3:12: "Threshing, in olden times, was done by treading out the grain on a threshing-floor. The going forth of the messengers of the gospel among the nations is like trampling the wheat sheaves on the hard floor. The valuable kernels are carefully gathered up; the straw is left." (SS, 186.) Thus, to "thrash the nations" is to preach the gospel to them and gather in the Lord's kernels (converts).

See also: Field Is White Already to Harvest; Sheaves; Thrust in His Sickle

Three Witnesses

In March 1829, Joseph Smith was promised that in addition to his testimony, "the testimony of three" would go forth regarding the truth of the Book of Mormon (D&C 5:11, 15). These three had been spoken of by ancient prophets (2 Ne. 11:3; 27:12; Ether 5:2–4), and their experience was verified by modern revelation (D&C 128:20).

The three chosen witnesses were Oliver Cowdery, Martin Harris, and David Whitmer. They beheld by the power of God the plates from whence the Book of Mormon was translated, as well as the heavenly messenger in whose care they are now kept, and they heard the voice of God declare the record to be true. (HC 1:52–57.)

"The object of this witness," wrote President Joseph Fielding Smith, "was that the world might be placed under obligation before the Lord, for these witnesses were to bear testimony 'by the power of God' " (CHMR 1:45). In addition to viewing the plates, the witnesses viewed the sword of Laban, the Liahona, the Urim and Thummim, and other records (D&C 17:1; LJFS, 242).

See also: Book of Mormon; Cowdery, Oliver; Harris, Martin; Liahona; Sword of Laban; Urim and Thummim; Whitmer, David; Wilderness of Fayette, Seneca County

Throne

The following discussion of thrones has been provided by Elder Bruce R. McConkie: "In the eternal sense, *thrones* are reserved for exalted persons who rule and reign as kings and queens in the highest heaven of the celestial world. It is in such a sphere that 'God, even the Father reigns upon his throne forever and ever.' (D&C 76:92; Rev. 20:11.) After Christ has presented up the kingdom to his Father, 'Then shall he be crowned with the crown of his glory, to sit on the throne of his power to reign forever and ever.' (D&C 76:108.)

"Then shall all those who are joint-heirs with him—who have been 'crowned with the glory of his might,' and 'made equal with him' (D&C 88:107)—then shall they also sit upon their thrones and even sit down with our Lord on his throne. . . .

"In token of their kingship, sovereignty, and dominion, exalted beings shall sit on thrones in eternity." (MD, 794; D&C 121:29.)

Those who are worthy to inherit such thrones will not use them as recliners of rest, for their very nature will impel them to be *anxiously engaged* in good causes (D&C 58:27–28). Celestial thrones are symbols of righteous power and the diligent use thereof; they are not seats for lethargic lounging.

See also: Blazing Throne of God

Thrust in His Sickle

There are a dozen occasions in the Doctrine and Covenants

when the Lord invites the laborers in his field to thrust in their sickles (e.g., D&C 4:4; 6:3; 14:3, 4; 33:7). A sickle is an agricultural instrument consisting of a curved metal blade fitted on a short handle. It is a common instrument for reaping crops in nonindustrialized nations. The Lord uses the analogy of thrusting in the sickle to illustrate the work required to harvest souls.

See also: Field Is White Already to Harvest; Ripe; Sheaves; Thrash the Nations

Time

An oft-quoted phrase in Latter-day Saint culture is "for time and for all eternity." This sacred statement is spoken of in connection with the holy ordinance of temple marriage, in which those words are used by the authorized officiator. The priesthood promise is given a worthy couple that their marriage will endure "for time and for all eternity" (D&C 132:7).

Time is based on a measurement of the position of the planet whereon one resides and would therefore differ from one sphere to another. As used in the temple, "time" refers to the period of one's mortal existence upon this earth.

When one passes through the veil of death, earthly time ceases to be part of one's experience and all contracts based upon this "time" are terminated. Contracts

for eternity transcend the veil and extend into a never-ending period of futurity.

See also: Angel's Time; Fulness of Times; God's Time; Meridian of Time; New and Everlasting Covenant of Marriage; Times of the Gentiles

Times of the Gentiles

The expression "times of the Gentiles" is found in two volumes of scripture (D&C 45:25, 28, 30; Luke 21:24). Of this phrase, President Joseph Fielding Smith has said: "The times of the Gentiles commenced shortly after the death of our Redeemer. The Jews soon rejected the Gospel and it was then taken to the Gentiles. The times of the Gentiles have continued from that time until now." (CHMR 1:196.)

The gospel was first taken to the Jews and only later to the Gentiles, that is, those not of the house of Israel, particularly of Judah. In fact, it took a dramatic vision to Peter to convince him that the "times of the Gentiles" had arrived (Acts 10).

The gospel is not presently being preached in an organized fashion to the Jews, for they who were "first" to hear it in the days of the Savior, shall be "last" to hear it in our day (Matt. 20:16; D&C 90:9). We are still in the "times of the Gentiles." When this time has been fulfilled, then Judah will again receive the gospel.

See also: Gentiles

Tithing

At the present time, the Lord's financial law of sacrifice and obedience is *tithing*. This law is mentioned in four sections of the Doctrine and Covenants (64:23; 85:3; 97:11–12; 119) and is a concept known in both the Bible (Mal. 3:8–11; Luke 18:12) and the Book of Mormon (Alma 13:15; 3 Ne. 24:8–11). Tithing has been defined by a former Presiding Bishop of the Church, Joseph L. Wirthlin, as follows: "The very word itself denotes one-tenth. A tithe is one-tenth of the wage earner's *full income.* . . . A tithe is one-tenth of the farmer's net income and also one-tenth of the produce used by the farmer to sustain his family which is a just and equitable requirement, as others purchase out of their income such food as is needed to provide for their families. A tithe is one-tenth of the dividends derived from investments. A tithe is one-tenth of net insurance income less premiums if tithing has been paid on the premiums." (CR, Apr. 1953, 98; italics added.)

Those who quibble over the amount, rationalize, or endeavor to justify less than one-tenth are guilty of "robbing God" (Mal. 3:8). Those who give "grudgingly" are committing sin (Moro. 7:6–8). "God loveth a cheerful giver," said Paul (2 Cor. 9:7). Brigham Young declared, "We do not ask anybody to pay tithing unless they are disposed to do so; but if you pretend to pay tithing, pay it like honest men" (IE, May 1941, p. 282).

The complete consecration of all we have to the Lord — which is required under the higher law — is not ours to live at the present time. Tithing is a schoolmaster for the day when we will give our all. "No man is forced to pay one-tenth of that which he receives, but no man is *entitled* to the blessings of the celestial kingdom who refuses to pay his honest tithing, and who has tithing to pay" (WTP, 276). "For he who is not able to abide the law of a celestial kingdom cannot abide a celestial glory" (D&C 88:22).

Today

The word *today* is used in two senses in the Doctrine and Covenants. It is used to represent that day in which we live, this moment of our existence. It is this meaning which applies to the declaration that God is "the same *today* as yesterday, and forever" (D&C 20:12; 35:1; italics added).

The other use of the term is defined by Smith and Sjodahl: " *'To-day'* is *the time before the coming of the Lord.* The expression is found in Psalm 95:7, and Heb. 3:13. The psalm referred to was sung at the dedication of the second temple, and it means, *now,* that we [have] had this manifestation of the goodness of God, 'harden not your heart.' The introduction of this phrase here is a prophetic allusion to the building of the Kirtland Temple and the manifestations there to be given, if the Saints would not harden their hearts." (SS, 393– 94; italics added.)

See also: Summer

Tomorrow

The single use of the word *tomorrow* occurs in section 64, verse 24, where the Lord refers to his second coming. "For after today cometh the burning—. . . for verily I say, tomorrow all the proud and they that do wickedly shall be as stubble; and I will burn them up," said the Lord.

Inasmuch as today in this sense is the time before the coming of the Lord (SS, 394), "tomorrow" is the day *of* his coming. Tomorrow is that time when "the summer shall be past, and the harvest ended" (D&C 45:2; 56:16).

See also: Today

Tongue

The tongue of every mouth will ultimately confess the glory of God and the name of his Only Begotten. "Seek not to declare my word, but first seek to obtain my word, and then shall your tongue be loosed," said the Lord (D&C 11:21). To have one's tongue loosed is to cause one to speak fluently or convincingly on the subject at hand (3 Ne. 26:14; D&C 88:104; Philip. 2:10). The Lord

warned the wicked that "their tongues shall be stayed that they shall not utter against me" (D&C 29:19). To stay one's tongue is to bind it or to prevent it from speaking.

When the scriptures speak of "nations, kindreds, tongues and people," reference is being made to nations or people who share a common language (D&C 7:3). To speak in one's own tongue is to speak in one's own language (D&C 90:11).

See also: Cloven Tongues as of Fire; Gift of Tongues; Speak with Tongues

Traditions of Their Fathers

The *traditions of their fathers* is a phrase generally used in scripture in a negative sense to indicate that children are following the bad examples of their fathers (D&C 93:39; see also Jer. 16:19; Alma 3:8; En., May 1981, p. 35).

Transfigured

See: Day of Transfiguration

Translated

There are several ways in which the word *translated* is used in the revelations. The first refers to the process which Joseph Smith used in rendering the language of the ancient Nephites into English (D&C 1:29; 10:10). The

Lord also referred to Joseph Smith's work in rendering plainer explanations of biblical passages as a translation (D&C 45:60).

Yet another meaning of *translated* refers to the condition whereby God alters the physical condition of selected mortals, thus making them temporarily impervious to the frailties of the flesh, including death (D&C 7; 107:49; 3 Ne. 28:4–12; Moses 7:69; JST, Gen. 15:32–34). At the appropriate future time, each of these translated beings will pass through an instantaneous death and be resurrected.

See also: Elijah; Enoch; John the Apostle; Melchizedek; Moses; Taken to Heaven Without Tasting Death

Translation

See: Book of Mormon; New Translation; Seer; Translated; Translation of My Scriptures; Translation of the Prophets; Translator; Urim and Thummim; Work of Translation

Translation of My Scriptures

See: New Translation

Translation of the Prophets

See: New Translation

Translator

On three occasions in the Doctrine and Covenants, the Prophet Joseph's presiding position is referred to with an enumeration of some of the roles associated with that position. The role of "translator" is mentioned in all three (D&C 21:1; 107:91–92; 124:125.)

Although one of Joseph's responsibilities was translating, that assignment does not appear to have been given to those who have since worn the prophet's mantle, nor are they sustained as "translators" in Church conferences. Elder John A. Widtsoe explained, "In current practice, the word 'translator' is omitted, since should records appear needing translation, the President of the Church may at any time be called, through revelation, to the special labor of translation" (ER, 256).

Traveling Bishops

The original revelation in Doctrine and Covenants section 20 was given in 1830, but verses 65–67 were added in 1835. These verses reflected the expansion of the Church government, adding such offices as "traveling bishops, high councilors, [and] high priests" (D&C 20:66–67).

On February 4, 1831, Edward Partridge was called to be the first bishop of the Church, with jurisdictional responsibilities in Zion [Missouri]. He was the presiding high priest to whom all looked for leadership in the Jackson County period of Church history. (CHC 2:367–68.)

Subsequently other bishops were called. Before the days of

Nauvoo, these bishops were not confined to a particular area and might well be classified as "traveling bishops." Later, men were called to serve as bishops of wards in Nauvoo, and in 1847 a Presiding Bishop of the Church was designated (CA 1978:123).

John A. Widtsoe identified three classifications of bishops: the Presiding Bishop of the Church, traveling bishops, and local or ward bishops (PCG, 126). It appears that "traveling bishops" have not been used since the early days of the Church when they were needed to regulate the newly organized branches.

See also: Bishop

Traveling Councilors

See: Traveling Presiding High Council

Traveling Elders

The phrase "traveling elders" appears but once in the Doctrine and Covenants (D&C 124:139) and refers specifically to the First Quorum of the Seventy, who are to be "traveling ministers" (D&C 107:97) under the direction of the First Presidency and the Twelve Apostles. In other words, theirs is not a "standing" ministry, but they are to travel throughout the world in their ministry. The Twelve Apostles, who are a "Traveling Presiding High Council," are in a general sense considered as traveling elders (D&C 124:39, footnote a; 107:33).

See also: Seventy; Traveling Ministers

Traveling High Council

See: Traveling Presiding High Council

Traveling High Priests

On February 17, 1834, the first permanent high council of the Church was organized at Kirtland, Ohio. The Prophet earnestly sought the Lord's guidance, and "a form and constitution" of all future high councils was prepared and approved two days later (HC 2:31).

Among the terms used in this "form and constitution" was that of "traveling or located high priests" (D&C 102:29). This had reference to the members of the high council who were to be distinguished from the "traveling high council," which consists of the Twelve Apostles (D&C 102:30). Traveling high priests act under the direction of the stake presidency as these men travel among the wards and branches within the jurisdictional boundaries of their respective stakes.

See also: High Council

Traveling Ministers

The Lord indicated that the "seventy are to be traveling ministers" (D&C 107:97). These men are General Authorities of the

Church who act under the direction of the First Presidency and the Quorum of the Twelve Apostles (HC 2:201–2). Theirs is not a standing ministry confined to one location but extends throughout the earth as they travel in ministering to the needs of the Saints and extending the blessings of the gospel to Jew and Gentile.

See also: Ministers; Seventy; Traveling Elders

Traveling Presiding High Council

In section 102, the Twelve Apostles are referred to as the "traveling high council" (D&C 102:29–30). They are referred to as "traveling councilors" and the "traveling Presiding High Council" in section 107 (D&C 107:23, 33). Historians have pointed out that the Twelve "served as a traveling high council, authorized to set in order Church affairs anywhere in the world outside the stakes of Zion. In 1841 their authority was expanded to include conduct of affairs within the stakes."(SLS, 80, 164.)

Thus, the Twelve received their authority "line upon line, precept upon precept," until they received a fulness of authority and keys under the hands of the Prophet Joseph Smith, prior to his death (DS 1:259; TS 5:650, 651, 698). It is in their authority as Apostles, holding the keys of the kingdom and acting under the direction of the First Presidency,

that they are a "Traveling Presiding High Council," with jurisdiction over all stakes and missions of the Church.

See also: Apostle; Prophet; Revelator; Seer; Special Witnesses; Twelve, The

Treasures

Treasures are generally thought of in a temporal sense, with visions of worldly wealth filling one's mind. Such treasures can be lost to thieves, rust, or other elements of the earth, and we have been warned about pursuing them to the exclusion of treasures with eternal staying power (Matt. 6:19–21; 3 Ne. 13:19–21; D&C 19:38). The Lord counseled that a "good" desire would be "to lay up treasures for yourself *in heaven*" (D&C 6:27; italics added).

One source suggested that "treasures in heaven are the character, perfections, and attributes which men acquire by obedience to law. Thus, those who gain such attributes of godliness as knowledge, faith, justice, judgment, mercy, and truth, will find these same attributes restored to them again in immortality. . . . The greatest treasure it is possible to inherit in heaven consists in gaining the continuation of the family unit in the highest heaven of the celestial world." (DNTC 1:239–40; see also Ps. 127:3–5; Alma 41:13–15; D&C 130:18.)

One reference to treasures in the Doctrine and Covenants indicates that when the lost tribes return from the north countries "they shall bring forth their rich treasures" (D&C 133:30). Although these separated children of Israel will undoubtedly bring with them tangible treasures of a temporal nature, such as were brought out of Egypt centuries earlier (see Ex. 12:35–36), they will also bring with them treasures of a spiritual nature, such as their own scriptures (2 Ne. 29:13) and the spiritual strength of a people of God.

Another interesting use of the term *treasures* occurs in Doctrine and Covenants 111. In 1836 the Prophet Joseph Smith and several traveling companions arrived in Salem, Massachusetts, as part of a short missionary journey. In addition to seeking converts, they also hoped to find a means of alleviating some of the financial distress the Church was then experiencing.

A man by the name of Burgess had told them he could locate a "hidden treasure" in Salem, but was unable to fulfill his promise. While in Salem, the Lord revealed to the Prophet that "there are *more treasures than one* for you in this city" (D&C 111:10; italics added).

These additional "treasures" had specific reference to the precious souls of the inhabitants of that city. However, the Lord indicated that he would gather them "in due time for the benefit of Zion" (D&C 111:2). It is interesting to note that while Joseph Smith's initial visit to Salem was unsuccessful in gathering either temporal or spiritual treasures, the promise of the Lord was at least partially fulfilled several years later. In 1843 the Prophet told Erastus Snow that he felt the "due time" of the Lord had arrived and sent Elder Snow to Salem. During the next several years he was able to baptize over one hundred people in that historic town. (Erastus Snow Journal [1841–1847], pp. 3–5.)

See also: Hidden Treasures of Knowledge; Riches of Eternity

Tree

See: Age of a Tree; Ax Is Laid at the Root of the Trees; Box-Tree; Fig Tree; Olive-Trees

Tribe of Judah

An 1831 revelation promised that the tribe of Judah would yet stand in the presence of their Messiah, the Lord Jesus Christ (D&C 133:35). Judah was one of the twelve sons of Jacob (Israel) and is the namesake of one of the twelve tribes of Israel.

Following the break-up of the United Kingdom, wherein all twelve tribes had been united under kings Saul, David, and Solomon, the tribe of Judah ruled the territory of Palestine known as the Southern Kingdom, which included Jerusalem. When the Romans destroyed Jerusalem in A.D. 70, the tribe of Judah became scattered to the four corners of the earth. The Jewish people have since reclaimed a portion of Palestine and established their present-day homeland, the nation of Israel.

The Savior was born through the lineage of Judah and proclaimed to the Samaritan woman, "salvation is of the Jews" (John 4:22); i.e., He who would provide the plan of salvation for mankind is of the tribe of Judah.

See also: Children of Judah; House of David; Israel; Jacob; Jews; Kingdom of the Jews; Tribes of Israel

Tribes of Israel

The "Tribes of Israel" represent the descendants of Israel (Jacob) through his twelve sons and their posterity. The original twelve tribes were named after each of Israel's sons through his four wives. These sons and their respective mothers were: Reuben, Simeon, Levi, Judah, Isaachar, and Zebulun, sons of Leah; Dan and Naphtali, sons of Bilhah; Gad and Asher, sons of Zilpah; and Joseph and Benjamin, sons of Rachel. (Gen. 29; 30.)

The Lord, through Jacob, gave Joseph's two sons, Ephraim and Manasseh, an inheritance among the tribes of Israel (JST, Gen. 48:5–6). In answer to the question, "Who was then eliminated from the twelve tribes?" Joseph Fielding Smith said: "It was Levi and Joseph who were not numbered as tribes in Israel. Joseph received a double portion through his sons, each inheriting through their adoption by their grandfather, and Levi's descendants becoming the ministers to all the other tribes of Israel." (AGQ, 1:115; Num. 3:12–13.)

See also: Ephraim; Israel; Jacob; Judah; Manasseh; They Who Are in the North Countries; Tribe of Judah

Trodden

The Lord warned those who had entered into the covenant of the United Order that if they transgressed or broke their covenant they would be "cursed . . . and shall be trodden down by whom I will" (D&C 104:5). To be trodden down is to be walked upon or trampled by another's feet. It is symbolic of being subdued, repressed, oppressed, and suffering misfortune at the hands of another.

On several occasions the wicked or wayward are compared to salt that has lost its savor and is "good for nothing only to be cast out and trodden under the feet of men" (D&C 101:40; 103:10; Matt. 5:13; 3 Ne. 12:13).

In another usage of the word, the Savior speaks of his having "trodden the wine-press alone," which refers to the atoning sacrifice which he alone wrought (D&C 76:107; 88:106; 133:50).

See also: Red in His Apparel; Salt of the Earth

Trump of the Angel of God

The "trump of the angel of God" is the signal to be given at the time of the Second Coming which will bring to pass the resurrection of those celestial Saints whose bodies had already been laid to rest in mother earth, as well as those of the same glory who are living at the time of Christ's coming. This latter group will pass through death and resurrection in a "twinkling of an eye" (D&C 43:32; 88:98). These combined groups will be "caught up to meet him" (Christ) and will then descend with him upon his return (DS 2:296).

See also: First Angel; First Fruits; First Resurrection; Lifted Up

Truth

The Lord declared, "Truth is knowledge of things as they are, and as they were, and as they are to come" (D&C 93:24; see also Jacob 4:13). Additionally we are told that "truth abideth forever" (D&C 1:39; 88:66) and "is light" (D&C 84:45). The challenge of God's Saints is to declare the truth of the restored gospel of Jesus Christ to all the world (D&C 58:47), not bragging, but in soberness (D&C 18:21), by the power of the Comforter (D&C 50:13–25).

The Savior desires all who are willing to be saved "to come unto a knowledge of the truth" (JST, 1 Tim. 1:3–5). He who is "the way,

the truth, and the life" (John 14:6) declared that "the Book of Mormon . . . contains the truth" (D&C 19:26) and that The Church of Jesus Christ of Latter-day Saints is "the only true and living church upon the face of the whole earth" (D&C 1:30). While most churches and religions have some truths, and obviously many good members, only in Christ's restored Church will the complete truth of the saving ordinances and principles of the gospel be found (TPJS, 316).

See also: Spirit of Truth; Word of Truth

Twelve, The

In June 1829, the Lord revealed the forthcoming selection of "the Twelve . . . who shall desire to take upon them my name with full purpose of heart" (D&C 18:26–37). These Twelve are men called and ordained to the holy apostleship and set apart as members of the Quorum of the Twelve Apostles (D&C 107:26, 33).

With one exception, the phrase "the Twelve" in the Doctrine and Covenants refers to Apostles of the dispensation of the fulness of times. In section 29, verse 12, the Lord makes reference to "the Twelve which were with me in my ministry at Jerusalem." These men, with the exclusion of Judas Iscariot, will stand at the "right hand" of Jesus at his coming, and "judge the whole house of Israel" (D&C 29:12; 1 Ne. 12:9; Morm. 3:18).

In our day, when the First Presidency is dissolved by the death of the President, if the two counselors had previously served as members of the Quorum of the Twelve Apostles, they revert back to that Quorum and it temporarily contains fourteen men until a new First Presidency is organized (CR, Apr. 1970, p. 118; Oct. 1972, p. 29).

See also: Apostle; Equal in Authority; Prophet; Revelator; Seer; Special Witnesses; Traveling Presiding High Council

Twinkling of an Eye

The descriptive phrase "changed in the twinkling of an eye" appears three times in the Doctrine and Covenants and has reference to the instantaneous change from life to death to resurrection that will occur to those who are righteous at the Lord's coming and to those who will live during the millennial period of earth's history (D&C 43:32; 63:51; 101:31). There will be no funerals and burials for these people, for their change to immortality will occur in no more time than it takes one to blink an eye. This phrase was used by the resurrected Lord when he spoke to the three Nephites who will remain on earth until his coming (3 Ne. 28:8), and Paul referred to it in his epistle to the Corinthians (1 Cor. 15:52).

See also: Resurrection

Two Prophets

In response to inquiries regarding the meaning of some aspects of the book of Revelation, Joseph Smith was informed that the "two witnesses" that John saw were "two prophets" to be raised up to the Jewish nation (D&C 77:15; Rev. 11:1-14). These two will have "power to shut heaven, that it rain not in the days of their prophecy: and have power over waters to turn them to blood, and to smite the earth with all plagues, as often as they will."

A massive Gentile army, which at some future day will encompass Jerusalem, "shall be hindered from utterly destroying and overthrowing the city, while these two Prophets continue" (VW, 41–42). However, "when they shall have finished their testimony," they will be allowed to be slain and their bodies will be left lying in the street for three and one-half days, while the wicked of the world make merry and rejoice over their deaths. Nevertheless, the prophets shall then be resurrected and respond to the invitation to ascend up to heaven. At this point, a great earthquake will separate the Mount of Olives, providing a valley of escape to the beleaguered Jewish people. The Savior's appearance will then be imminent. (Ezek. 38:17–23; ST, 170–72.)

The "two witnesses" were described by Elder Bruce R. McConkie: "These two shall be followers of that humble man,

Joseph Smith, through whom the Lord of Heaven restored the fulness of his everlasting gospel in this final dispensation of grace. No doubt they will be members of the Council of the Twelve or of the First Presidency of the Church. Their prophetic ministry to rebellious Jewry shall be the same length as was our Lord's personal ministry among their rebellious forebears." (DNTC 3:509–10.)

See also: Two Shall Put Their Tens of Thousands to Flight

Two Shall Put Their Tens of Thousands to Flight

In a series of pronouncements regarding premillennial happenings, including the appearance of the resurrected Lord, mention is made of "two [who] shall put . . . tens of thousands to flight" (D&C 133:58). It is not unreasonable to assume that this may refer to the "two prophets" who shall be raised up to the Jewish nation at some future point, and successfully humiliate and hold at bay the armies of the Gentiles that shall be encompassing Judah (Rev. 11:1–14; D&C 77:15). For a period of forty two–months, these two shall successfully "put tens of thousands to flight."

See also: Two Prophets

U

Unbeliever

The Apostle Paul said that the unbelieving wife or husband is sanctified by the believing spouse (1 Cor. 7:10–16; D&C 74:1). An unbeliever is one who has not accepted the gospel of Jesus Christ and is outside the faith. Unbelievers may also hold membership in Christ's church but lack the commitment to practice the beliefs espoused by that church.

See also: Believers

Uncleanness

The Lord has counseled "keep slothfulness and uncleanness far from you" (D&C 90:18; see also Eph. 5:3). Elder Bruce R. McConkie defined uncleanness as "moral filthiness, obscenity, or unchastity; any unholy or impure practice, as masturbation" (DNTC 2:517).

The Saints have been specifically counseled to keep anything that is unclean from polluting and defiling holy places of worship (D&C 94:8–9; 97:15–17). We are reminded that "the kingdom of God is not filthy, and there cannot any unclean thing enter into the kingdom of God" (1 Ne. 15:34).

President Marion G. Romney observed that "each person is therefore unclean to the extent to which he has sinned, and because of that uncleanness is banished from the presence of the Lord so long as the effect of his own wrongdoing is upon him" (En., May 1982, p. 8).

See also: Adultery; Filthy; Fornication; Garments Spotted with the Flesh; Lust; Sin; Whoremonger

Under His Feet

When the Son of Man comes he will "put all enemies under his feet" (D&C 49:6; see also 76:61; Ps. 66:3). This simply means that the wicked will no longer have free reign in their pursuit of evil but will instead be in subjection to Christ and his Father.

Understanding of the Prudent

In the great vision of the degrees of glory, the Lord manifested that "the understanding of the prudent shall come to naught" (D&C 76:9; see also 2 Ne. 27:26). In the same sense that the "wisdom of the wise shall perish," so shall it be with those who are "prudent [think they are

wise] in their own sight" (2 Ne. 15:21; Isa. 5:21). That is, those whose prudence and wisdom do not lead them to understand the things of an eternal verity—to reach to heaven—will find themselves mired in mortal matters, far short of the mark of eternal life (Jacob 4:14–16). Their "understanding . . . shall come to naught."

See also: Prudent; Wisdom of the Wise; Wise

Unfeigned

See: Love Unfeigned

Unfruitful in the Knowledge of the Lord

The Lord promised the presiding quorums of the Church that if they are righteous, godly, and full of the virtues which should characterize servants of God, "they shall not be unfruitful in the knowledge of the Lord" (D&C 107:30–31). In other words, they would not lack in understanding and testimony of the Lord Jesus Christ and the gospel that bears his name. This same phrase was used by the Apostle Peter in his writings (2 Pet. 1:4–9).

Elder Bruce R. McConkie has written: "None can comprehend the knowledge of God, of Christ, and of the gospel unless he himself possesses the attributes of godliness, for the knowledge of spiritual things comes only by revelation, and until a person gains godly attributes he cannot receive the Spirit from whom revelation comes" (DNTC 3:354).

Ungodly

See: Wicked

United Order

According to Elder Marion G. Romney, "The United Order, the Lord's program for eliminating the inequalities among men, is based upon the underlying concept that the earth and all things therein belong to the Lord and that men hold earthly possessions as stewards accountable to God.

"On February 9, 1831, the Lord revealed to the Prophet what His way was. (D&C 42.) In his way there were two cardinal principles: (1) consecration and (2) stewardship.

"To enter the United Order, one consecrated all his possessions to the Church by a 'covenant and deed which' could 'not be broken.' That is, he completely divested himself of all of his property by conveying it to the Church.

"Having thus voluntarily divested himself of title to all his property, the consecrator received from the Church a stewardship by a like conveyance. This stewardship could be more or less than his original consecration, the object being to make 'every man equal according to his family, according to his cir-cumstances and his wants and needs.' (D&C 51:3.)

"This procedure preserved in every man the right to private ownership and management of his property. At his own option he could alienate it or keep and operate it and pass it on to his heirs.

"The intent was, however, for him to so operate his property as to produce a living for himself and his dependents. So long as he remained in the order he consecrated to the Church the surplus he produced above the needs and wants of his family. This surplus went into a storehouse, from which stewardships were given to others and from which the needs of the poor were supplied." (LTG, 218–19.)

President J. Reuben Clark declared: "The United Order and communism are not synonymous. Communism is Satan's counterfeit of the United Order." As to the history of the original order, President Clark said: "The Lord tried us for three years to see if we could not set up the United Order; we could not. So then at Fishing River on June 22, 1834, following the dissolution of Zion's Camp, the Lord told us that we should give up the United Order and that he would not reestablish it until Zion was redeemed, and that time has not yet come." (MFP 6:199–200.)

See also: Order of Enoch; Steward; Stewardship; Storehouse, Lord's; United Order of the City of Zion; United Order of the Stake of Zion

United Order of the City of Zion

On February 9, 1831, the Lord revealed the basis of the United Order (D&C 42). This was the law of the Church for the next three years, although all did not subscribe to the conditions thereof and ultimately the law was repealed (MFP 6:200).

Several months before its demise, the Lord instructed the Saints to become organized in two major "orders." One was to be established in Missouri and another in Ohio. The former was to be called the United Order of the City of Zion, which encompassed the Saints in the "land of Zion," Missouri (D&C 104:47–50; see also D&C 57:1–2).

See also: United Order; United Order of the Stake of Zion

United Order of the Stake of Zion

The United Order of the Stake of Zion was the financial system which the Lord established in Kirtland, Ohio (D&C 104:47–50; MFP 6:199–200). In 1834, this was the eastern stronghold of the Church and was to be separate from the "order" established in the "City of Zion," or Missouri. Prior to this time, one "order" had encompassed the entire Church, although not all had faithfully subscribed thereto.

The Saints in Missouri were suffering severe persecution at this time; Smith and Sjodahl suggest that "the brethren in Kirt-land were not to suffer on account of the losses inflicted by the mob on the Saints in Zion. As an independent organization, they would be in a position to render financial aid to the exiles. As a part of the organization in Zion (under the previous singular system), the financial disaster engendered by mob rule would have affected them also, and they might have been unable to come to the aid of their brethren." (SS, 674.)

See also: United Order; United Order of the City of Zion

United States

The United States of America is only referred to directly once in the Doctrine and Covenants (D&C 135:7), although its landmark charter — the Constitution — is mentioned several times (D&C 98:5– 6; 101:80; 109:54; OD—1). "The United States of America grew from a group of English colonies established along the east coast of North America in the 17th and early 18th centuries" (*Encyclopedia Brittanica*, 15th ed., 1974, 18:946).

At the time of its mention in Elder John Taylor's account of the martyrdom (1844), the organized states of the country extended from the Atlantic Ocean westward to Iowa, Missouri, Arkansas, and Louisiana. The unorganized Indian Territory extended further west.

Ancient prophecy recorded the future birth of this nation as it was "delivered by the power of

God out of the hands of all other nations'' (1 Ne. 13:15–19). It is a ''land which is choice above all other lands'' (1 Ne. 13:30) because it is the birthplace of the restoration of the gospel; from its borders the message of salvation will go to every other nation (HC 4:540).

''The true destiny of America is *religious*, not political,'' declared President Alvin R. Dyer; ''it is *spiritual*, not physical'' (CR, Oct. 1968, p. 106). President N. Eldon Tanner noted: ''Only as we accept and live the teachings of the gospel can the destiny which God planned for America be realized and the world united in peace and brotherhood'' (En., May 1976, p. 51).

See also: America; Constitution (#1); Zion

Unjust

To be unjust is to act contrary to the ways of justice and righteousness (D&C 134:12). Those who so act are condemned by the Lord (D&C 101:90). He who was the perfect example of justice, ''suffered for sins, the just for the unjust, that he might bring us to God'' (D&C 138:7).

Those who refuse to accept Christ's atonement and the plan whereby they can become clean from their unjust acts will remain filthy and shall come forth in the resurrection of the unjust (D&C 76:17; 88:35, 102).

See also: Resurrection of the Unjust

Unlearned

See: Weak Things of the Earth/ World

Unquenchable Fire

In four places in the Doctrine and Covenants, the wicked are warned that they shall be cast into an ''unquenchable fire'' (D&C 43:33; 63:34, 54; 101:66). According to President Joseph Fielding Smith, ''This unquenchable fire is, of course, the torment which comes to the wicked who do not repent and who have failed to keep the covenants and commandments. It will be the torment of the mind and soul.'' (CHMR 1:232.)

This definition is in keeping with statements by two Book of Mormon prophets who spoke of the ''unquenchable fire'' that fills the breast of the guilty (Mosiah 2:38; Morm. 9:5).

See also: Everlasting Punishment; Vengeance of Eternal Fire

Unspeakable Gift of the Holy Ghost

The unique phrase ''the unspeakable gift of the Holy Ghost'' is found in what President Joseph Fielding Smith refers to as ''one of the greatest letters ever written'' (CHMR 2:176, 179; D&C 121:26). As an adjective, *unspeakable* denotes something that is inexpressible or unutterable. As a noun, it refers to ''a being or thing beyond the power of language to describe.''

Experiences with the Spirit of the Holy Ghost are frequently unspeakable in that they are beyond one's capacity to describe in mortal words. To quote Elder Neal A. Maxwell, ''the tongue cannot tell all it knows'' (En., May 1976, p. 26).

Unspotted

In order to remain ''unspotted from the world,'' the Saints are counseled to regularly worship in sacrament services (D&C 59:9). The spots of the world are the taints of the temptations to which one succumbs, the stains of sin. The unrepentant sinner will not stand without blemish.

See also: Garments . . . Pure and White; Garments Spotted with the Flesh; Marriage of the Lamb; Rid Their Garments

Untoward Generation

Webster defines *untoward* as ''difficult to manage, stubborn, or troublesome.'' Thus, when the Lord cries, ''Save yourselves from this untoward generation,'' he is admonishing all to step away from any leanings toward rebelliousness against his holy ways (D&C 36:6; 109:41). An ''untoward generation'' is a ''rebellious generation which refuses to change its ungodly course'' (DNTC 2:42).

A footnote reference in the LDS edition of the King James Bible to ''untoward generation'' indicates the meaning in Greek as a ''crooked'' generation (Acts 2:40, footnote b).

Upbraid Him Not

The term *upbraid* might be one of the most used and least understood words among Latter-day Saints. The passage of scripture which led Joseph Smith to the Sacred Grove was James's admonition: ''If any of you lack wisdom, let him ask of God, that giveth to all men liberally, and *upbraideth* not; and it shall be given him'' (James 1:5; italics added; JS—H 1:11, 26; D&C 42:68). Webster states that to ''upbraid'' means to charge, accuse, or reprove reproachfully, to scold. One who approaches the Lord in faith will not be reproached or scolded. Those with evil hearts, however, are to be upbraided, or reproved.

Upper Room

In announcing the revelation received on granting the priesthood to ''all worthy male members of the Church,'' the First Presidency said this revelation had come after they had spent ''many hours in the Upper Room of the Temple supplicating the Lord for divine guidance'' (OD—2). The temple referred to is the Salt Lake Temple. This house of the Lord has special rooms set aside for meetings of the First Presidency, Council of the Twelve Apsotles, and other General Authorities of the Church. Weekly meetings of the First Presidency and the Council of the Twelve are held in one of these special rooms.

One who was present on the occasion of the revelation said: "President Kimball brought up the matter of the possible conferral of the priesthood upon those of all races. This was a subject that the group of us had discussed at length on numerous occasions in the preceding weeks and months. The President restated the problem involved, reminded us of our prior discussions, and said he had spent many days alone *in this upper room* pleading with the Lord for an answer to our prayers." (P, 127; italics added.) Following further discussion in which hearts were knit in unity, prayerful petitioning of the Lord on the matter brought the sought-for answer.

See also: Cloven Tongues of Fire; Kimball, Spencer W.

Upright in Heart

The Lord has warned that only the "upright in heart" will participate in going up to the land of Zion. (D&C 61:16.) Webster's unabridged dictionary states that one who is upright is erect in position, pointing upward. An upright person such as Job (Job 1:1) is morally correct, honest, and just. If one's heart is upright, it is "pointing upward," lifted toward God, and receptive to the life-giving sustenance of the Spirit.

See also: Walk Uprightly

Uriah

In citing examples of authorized plural marriages, the Lord indicated that David's wives had been given him through prophetic sanction: "and in none of these things did he sin against me save in the case of Uriah and his wife; and, therefore he hath fallen from his exaltation" (D&C 132:39). There is a definite message in that statement to those who contract or consummate plural marriage without the authorization of the one who holds the keys of this power—the living prophet of The Church of Jesus Christ of Latter-day Saints (D&C 132:7).

President Spencer W. Kimball, twelfth prophet of this last dispensation, emphatically declared: "We warn you against the so-called polygamy cults which would lead you astray. Remember the Lord brought an end to this program many decades ago through a prophet who proclaimed the revelation to the world. . . . It is wrong and sinful to ignore the Lord when he speaks. He has spoken—strongly and conclusively." (CR, Oct. 1974, p. 5.)

Uriah, the man spoken of in the revelation regarding plural marriage, was the legal husband of Bathsheba, the woman with whom David committed adultery and for whom he had the faithful Uriah slain (2 Sam. 11). The martyr Uriah had such integrity that when called home from the battlefield to have an audience with the king, Uriah refused to sleep or receive refreshment in the luxury of his own home, for his colleagues were yet encamped in open fields and tents.

Just as surely as David's star lost its luster and fell into infamy, Uriah's star soared into eternal integrity and honor, for which he shall always be remembered.

See also: David; Law of Sarah

Urim and Thummim

The early revelations contained in sections 3, 6, 7, 10, 11, 12, 14, 15, 16, and 17 were received by Joseph Smith through use of the Urim and Thummim. "A Urim and Thummim consists of two special stones called *seer stones* or *interpreters*. The Hebrew words *urim* and *thummim*, both plural, mean *lights* and *perfections*. Presumably one of the stones is called Urim and the other Thummim. Ordinarily they are carried in a breastplate over the heart." (MD, 818.)

"The history concerning the Urim and Thummim, or 'Interpreters' . . . is not very clear. Abraham had the Urim and Thummim by which he received revelations of the heavenly bodies, as he has recorded in the Book of Abraham. (Abr. 3:1–4.) What became of these after his death we do not know. Aaron also had the Urim and Thummim, and these were, evidently from the reading of the Bible, handed down among the priests of Aaron from generation to generation. (Ex. 28:30; Lev. 8:8; Num. 27:21; Deut. 33:8; 1 Sam. 28:6; Ezra 2:63; Neh. 7:65.) The Lord gave to the brother of Jared the Urim and Thummim which he brought with him to this continent. These were separate and distinct from the Urim and Thummim had by Abraham and in Israel in the days of Aaron. (Ether 3:22–28.)" (AGQ 1:159.)

It was this latter Urim and Thummim that came into the possession of Book of Mormon prophets and were deposited with the plates that centuries later would be entrusted to the Prophet Joseph Smith (Ether 3:23–28; 4:1–5; Mosiah 28:11–16; JS—H 1:34–35). This instrument of spiritual discernment is mentioned in the text of several early revelations as the means whereby the Book of Mormon was translated (D&C 10:1) and as one of the ancient artifacts the three special witnesses of the Book of Mormon were to view (D&C 17:1).

Elder John A. Widtsoe said, "Clearly the Urim and Thummim were used in official communication with the Lord. Beyond that, little is known of them.

"While the Prophet was undoubtedly required to place himself in the proper spirit and mental attitude before he could use the Urim and Thummim successfully, yet it must also be concluded that the stones were essential to the work of translation.

"The 'stones in silver bows' seemed . . . to have possessed the general power of making spiritual manifestations understandable to Joseph Smith.

"The Prophet did not always receive revelations by the aid of the Urim and Thummim. As he grew in spiritual power, he learned to bring his spirit into such harmony with divinity that it became, as it were, a Urim and Thummim to him and God's will was revealed without the intervention of external aids." (ER, 89–90.)

Although the prophets and Apostles who are sustained as "seers" have the right to use the Urim and Thummim if necessary, it appears that the instruments have not been in the hands of Church leaders since Joseph Smith delivered them back to Moroni along with the sacred records from which the Book of Mormon was translated. President Joseph Fielding Smith emphasized that accounts of its use *after* that time "are evidently errors" (DS 3:225).

We are informed that "the place where God resides is a great Urim and Thummim," and the celestialized earth "will be a Urim and Thummim to the inhabitants who dwell thereon." The celestialized Saints who dwell thereon will possess their own personal Urim and Thummim. (D&C 130:8–10.) This may have

implications to the omniscience of God as well as to the light and perfection which emanates from him and those who faithfully follow him.

Utah

In 1847 President Brigham Young led a group of pioneers into the Great Basin area of what is now the western part of the United States but which at the time included territory claimed by Mexico. The Saints immediately began the colonization of a large territory they called "Deseret," which was a Book of Mormon name meaning "honeybee" (see Ether 2:3). The initial territory covered some 210,000 square miles, reaching from the Rocky Mountains on the east to the Sierra Nevada Mountains on the west and from the Columbia River on the north to the Gila River in Arizona on the south. (*Encyclopedia Britannica*, 15th ed., 18:1102.)

In 1850 Congress passed a bill organizing the Territory of Utah, discarding the Saints' chosen name of Deseret. "Brigham Young was appointed governor, a position he had held in the 'Provisional State of Deseret' " (ECH, 392). The "Territory" spoken of in Official Declaration—1 is the Territory of Utah.

Repeated efforts to achieve statehood were turned aside by the Congress, mainly because of falsehoods and misinformation circulated against the Saints and because of the public opposition to the Saints' practice of plural marriage. With the issuance of the Manifesto by Wilford Woodruff, calling an end to polygamy, Congress was more favorable to granting statehood for Utah. This became a reality on January 4, 1896, when the whittled-down Territory of Utah (now only 84,916 square miles) became the forty-fifth state of the Union. (SLS, 413–18.)

The state capital of Utah is Salt Lake City, headquarters of The Church of Jesus Chirst of Latter-day Saints. Three revelations in the Doctrine and Covenants were recorded in this place (D&C 138; OD—1; OD—2).

See also: Salt Lake City

Utah Commission

In 1882 the United States Congress passed the Edmunds Act. This law "made punishable the contracting of plural marriage, [and] also polygamous living, which was designated as 'unlawful cohabitation' " (ECH, 482). In addition the law "declared vacant all offices in the Territory of Utah connected with registration and election duties, and established a board of five commissioners, to be appointed by the president, to assume these functions" (SLS, 394).

This group of men arrived in Utah in August of 1882 and energetically went about their work, often "beyond the scope of the law," imposing many procedures which were unjust to the majority population—the Mormons (ECH, 483). Their reports to the secretary of the interior were often erroneous or false and biased against members of The Church of Jesus Christ of Latter-day Saints (OD—1).

See also: Manifesto; Secretary of the Interior

V

Vain

The word *vain* can have several meanings. When the Lord declares that one's "faith is vain," it means his faith is with-out any merit and is worthless (D&C 104:55). To be vain is to be conceited, and the Lord warns against vain ambition (D&C 121:37). Those who "take the name of the Lord in vain" are violating one of the basic commandments issued on the summit of Sinai (D&C 136:21; Ex. 20:7).

With regards to this last usage, to take the name of the Lord in vain is to profane or to blaspheme, to show utter disrespect for Deity. The Lord's name can also be taken in vain when one violates sacred covenants entered into at baptism, through priesthood ordinations, in holy temples, and through participation in sacrament services (see D&C 20:37, 75–79; 84:33–42).

President Spencer W. Kimball counseled that "it is not enough to refrain from profanity or blasphemy. We need to make important in our lives the name of the Lord." (CR, Oct. 1978, p. 7.)

There is another way in which the name of the Lord may be used in vain. This is done when one invokes God's name in unauthorized ordinances, "having not authority" (D&C 63:62). No matter how sincere an individual may be, unauthorized ordinances are without validity (see D&C 22). Of course to deliberately deceive by pretending to possess proper authority is a most serious sin.

Valiant in the Testimony of Jesus

Those "who are not valiant in the testimony of Jesus" lose the promised crown of glory in God's kingdom (D&C 76:79). President Ezra Taft Benson has noted: "Not to be valiant in one's testimony is a tragedy of eternal consequence. These are members who know this latter-day work is true, but who fail to endure to the end. Some may even hold temple recommends, but do not magnify their callings in the Church. Without valor, they do not take an affirmative stand *for* the kingdom of God. Some seek the praise, adulation, and honors of men; others attempt to conceal their sins; and a few criticize those who preside over them." (En., May 1982, p. 63.)

"The great cornerstone of valiance in the cause of righteousness," said Elder Bruce R. McConkie, "is obedience to the whole law of the whole gospel" (En., Nov. 1974, p. 35).

See also: Continueth in God; Endure to the End; Stand Fast; Testimony of Jesus

Van Buren County, Missouri

The name of Van Buren County, Missouri, appears only in the preface of section 101, which revelation was received following the expulsion of the Saints from Jackson County late in 1833. Under the date of December 12, 1833, four days before this revelation was received, Joseph Smith wrote: "An express arrived at Liberty, from Van Buren county, with information that those families, which had fled from Jackson county, and located there, were about to be driven from that county, after building their houses and carting their winter's store of provisions, grain, etc., forty or fifty miles. Several families are already fleeing from thence. The contaminating influence of the Jackson county mob, is predominent in this *new county of Van Buren*, the whole population of which is estimated at about thirty or forty families. . . . The continued threats of deaths to individuals of the Church, if they make their appearance in Jackson county, prevent the most of them . . . from returning to that county, to secure personal property, which they were obliged to leave in their flight." (HC 1:456–57; italics added.)

Although called Van Buren County as early as 1833, the state legislature did not officially create it as such until 1835, when a southern portion of Jackson County was officially partitioned away. Later its name was changed to Cass County, by which it is presently known.

See also: Missouri

Vanities of the World

Following his sacred interview with both the Father and the Son, Joseph Smith "was entangled again in the vanities of the world" (D&C 20:5). *Vanity*, according to Webster, is something that is of no real value, useless, or empty.

The "vanities" with which Joseph had become "entangled," were the valueless, "foolish er-

rors . . . and weakness[es] of youth." They were not "great or malignant sins;" but, rather, the "levity" which the young Prophet felt was "not consistent with that character which ought to be maintained by one who was called of God" (JS—H 1:28).

If pursued, vanity can bring condemnation (D&C 84:55). This may have something to do with the Lord's admonition to make proper use of one's stewardship of time and talents, to be "anxiously engaged" in good causes (D&C 58:26–28; 88:118–24), rather than to waste either time or talent on frivolity, carnality or other valueless pursuits of this life.

Veil

The origin of the veil is described by Elder Orson Pratt: "The Fall [of Adam] has let down a vail between us and our Father. . . . This vail does not prevent the eye of the Almighty from seeing and discerning the conduct of his children, but it prevents us, while in this state of mortality, from beholding his presence, unless we rend the vail by our faith and obedience and, like the brother of Jared, are permitted to come back into his presence. . . . We are now laboring under the imperfections of the fall, and because of that fall a vail shuts us from his presence." (JD 16:364; Ether 3.)

The nature of this veil is discussed by Elder Parly P. Pratt: "A veil is drawn between the one sphere and the other, whereby all the objects in the spiritual sphere are rendered invisible to those in the temporal. To discern beings or things in the spirit world, a person in the flesh must be quickened by spiritual elements, the veil must be withdrawn, or the organs of sight, or of hearing, must be transformed, so as to be adapted to the spiritual sphere. . . . The elements and beings in the spirit world are as real and tangible to spiritual organs, as things and beings of the temporal world are to beings of a temporal state." (KT, 126–27.)

In January 1831, the Lord promised that the "veil of darkness" would soon be rent and the "purified" would see him (D&C 38:8). The promise was repeated in November of that same year, and the Lord indicated the experience would not be with the "carnal neither natural mind, but with the spiritual" (D&C 67:10). One source suggests this promise was fulfilled when the veil was rent at the dedication of the Kirtland Temple and marvelous manifestations occurred (SS, 406–7; HC 2:427–28; JD 11:10).

A dramatic rending of the veil occurred shortly after the dedication of the temple in Kirtland when Joseph Smith and Oliver Cowdery were visited by the resurrected Lord and other heavenly messengers in the temple (D&C 110).

A further fulfillment of this promise indicates that "all flesh" shall see the Savior together when the "veil of the covering of his temple . . . which hideth the earth, shall be taken off" (D&C 101:23). Joseph Smith said, "Could we all come together with one heart and one mind in perfect faith the veil might as well be rent today as next week, or any other time" (TPJS, 9).

The rending of the veil is not reserved for a select few with special ecclesiastical callings. It is available to all the righteous. Elder Bruce R. McConkie has said: "The Lord wants all his children to gain light and truth and knowledge from on high. It is his will that we pierce the veil and rend the heavens and see the visions of eternity." (En., Nov. 1978, p. 61.)

See also: Revelation; Vision

Veils

See: Breastwork of the Pulpit

Vengeance of Eternal Fire

Speaking of those who will be consigned to the telestial glory in the hereafter, the Lord revealed that they will "suffer the vengeance of eternal fire" and be "cast down to hell" (D&C 76:105–6). Such eternal vengeance is decreed by Him whose name is Endless (D&C 19:10) and whose ways are eternal. That which is eternal will always be in existence, although one may not always be subject to its effects. Hence telestial beings will suffer the effects of their mortal misdeeds in the "vengeance of eternal fire" until the day of their redemption (resurrection) at the end of the Millennium; but the existence of the "eternal fire" will continue. In other words, the "prison" remains even after the individual "prisoner" has paid the price and has been set free (GT 1:144).

Although the wicked will be "burned" at the coming of Christ (D&C 64:24), the "fire" to which they will be subjected during their sojourn in hell is not literal. This "fire" is the anguish of their tormented spirits, as they experience the displeasure of Deity and suffer the consequences of their wicked ways (Mosiah 2:38; see also Alma 15:3; 36:12–13).

See also: Everlasting Punishment; Telestial; Unquenchable Fire

Vessels of the Lord

The dictionary defines a "vessel" as a receptacle or "a person regarded as one into whom some quality is infused." Those individuals who take upon themselves the name of the Lord are vessels who should be "infused," or filled, with a special quality of righteousness. The Lord declared, "Be ye clean that bear the vessels of the Lord" (D&C 38:42; 133:5; 3 Ne. 20:41; Isa. 52:11).

That which is carried within the "vessels" of the Lord, or "vessels of mercy" as Paul called them, should be of the highest quality, pure and undefiled, pouring forth a continuous stream of "living water" (Rom.

9:23; see also John 4:10; D&C 63:23). Such a person accepts Paul's counsel to "be a vessel unto honour, sanctified and meet for the master's use, and prepared unto every good work" (2 Tim. 2:21; see also 1 Thess. 4:3–4). These righteous receptacles are the true "vessels of the Lord."

Vessels of Wrath

Those who commit the "unpardonable sin" are designated as "sons of perdition," or "vessels of wrath, doomed to suffer the wrath of God, with the devil and his angels in eternity" (D&C 76:33). The term *vessels of wrath* appears only one other time in scripture, and it is contrasted with "vessels of mercy" (Rom. 9:22–23).

In this latter context, Elder Bruce R. McConkie has defined "vessels of wrath" as "the rebellious and disobedient; those, as the seed of Esau, who waste the days of their probation and walk in carnal paths." The "vessels of mercy" are contrasted as being "obedient and righteous persons, those, as the seed of Israel, who were foreordained in the premortal life to receive that glory which is eternal life." (DNTC 2:277.)

In the context of this definition, it would appear that not all "vessels of wrath" will become "sons of perdition." However, all "sons of perdition" are and will be "vessels of wrath," that is, they will be recipients of the wrath of God and suffer the torment thereof.

See also: Sons of Perdition

Vicarious Baptism

See: Baptism for the Dead

Vineyard

The term *vineyard* is a frequent expression found in the literature of the Lord. The great parable known as the allegory of Zenos, which gives the history of Israel, uses the term extensively to refer to the *world in which we live* (Jacob 5; AGQ 4:203–6).

The meaning of *vineyard* is very evident in the three dozen times it is found in the Doctrine and Covenants, of which the following is an example: Speaking of the world in which we live, the Lord said, "And my vineyard has become corrupted" (D&C 33:4). Again, the Lord said: "Thou art called to labor in my vineyard, and to build up my church, and to bring forth Zion" (D&C 39:13).

See also: Prune My Vineyard

Vipers

See: Generation of Vipers

Virgins

A revelation on marriage speaks of virgins (D&C 132:61–63). Specifically the term applies to one who has never had sexual intercourse. In a more general sense it may apply to an unmarried woman.

See also: Ten Virgins

Vision

Several Church Presidents have writings in the Doctrine and Covenants that came through the spiritual medium of a vision. Joseph Smith experienced the glorious vision which described the kingdoms of glory (D&C 76), and he spoke of his experience in the Kirtland Temple with heavenly messengers as a vision (D&C 110). In addition, he was given a vision showing the heirs of the celestial kingdom (D&C 137).

President Wilford Woodruff said "the Lord showed me by vision and revelation exactly what would take place if we did not stop this practice [of plural marriage]." (Excerpts from Three Addresses by President Wilford Woodruff Regarding the Manifesto, 1981 edition of the D&C, p. 293.) Furthermore, Joseph F. Smith had a vision of the redemption of the dead (D&C 138).

Elder Bruce R. McConkie explained, "Through supernatural means, by the power of the Holy Ghost, devout persons are permitted to have *visions* and to see within the veil. They are enabled to see spiritual personages and to view scenes hidden from ordinary sight. These visions are gifts of the Spirit. . . .

"Visions serve the Lord's purposes in preparing men for salvation. By them knowledge is revealed (2 Ne. 4:23), conversions are made (Alma 19:16), the gospel message is spread abroad, the church organization is perfected (D&C 107:93), and righteousness is increased in the hearts of men. And visions are to increase and abound in the last days, for the Lord has promised to pour out his 'spirit upon all flesh,' so that 'old men shall dream dreams,' and 'young men shall see visions.' (Joel 2:28–32.)" (MD, 823–24.)

See also: Revelation; Veil

Voice of . . .

Several scriptural citations concerning events preceding or accompanying the Second Coming speak of the voices of thunderings, lightnings, tempests, earthquakes, hailstorms, famines, pestilences, judgment, mercy, glory, and honor (D&C 43:21–25; 88:90; 133:50; Joel 2:11; Rev. 8:5). In addition to the voice of his servants (D&C 1:38),

God speaks a warning voice to earth's inhabitants through the elements and forces of nature.

Brigham Young said: " 'Do you think there is calamity abroad now among the people?' Not much. All we have yet heard and all we have experienced is scarcely a preface to the sermon that is going to be preached. When the testimony of the Elders ceases to be given, and the Lord says to them, 'Come home; I will now preach my own sermons to the nations of the earth,' all you now know can scarcely be called a preface to the sermon that will be preached with fire and sword, tempests, earthquakes, hail, rain, thunders and lightnings, and fearful destruction." (JD 8:123.)

Voice of a Trump

See: Sound of a Trump

Voice of Warning

See: Day of Warning

W

Waiting . . . on the Lord

The concept of waiting on the Lord is found in three volumes of scripture (Prov. 20:22; Isa. 40:31; 1 Ne. 21:23; D&C 98:2). The word *wait* in Hebrew means hope for or anticipate. Nephi tells us that "the people of the Lord are they who wait [hope] for him" (2 Ne. 6:13). One who waits upon the Lord places his trust in him and lives in accordance with his will in anticipation of his coming.

Wakefield, Joseph

The brief story of Joseph Wakefield is one of spiritual tragedy. In an 1831 revelation, the Lord indicated he was "well pleased" with Wakefield (D&C 50:37). At this time he was called to labor in the ministry with Parley P. Pratt. Shortly thereafter, he was called to go on a mission with Solomon Humphrey, which mission resulted in Wakefield's baptizing a future Apostle, George A. Smith (D&C 52:35; SS, 294).

While the convert Smith grew in spiritual stature, the missionary Wakefield diminished. The story is told that he became critical of the Prophet Joseph because Wakefield observed the Prophet leaving his study, where inspired work was taking place, and immediately playing with children. Wakefield did not see the activity of playing with children as being compatible with the role a true prophet should occupy, and thus became disaffected with the Church.

Walk in Crooked Paths

Latter-day scripture attests that "God doth not walk in crooked paths" (D&C 3:2; Alma 7:20). A crooked path is symbolic of deviousness or deceitfulness. God is incapable of being deceitful. His course is set and will not vary.

See also: One Eternal Round

Walk Uprightly

The Lord promised Joseph Smith that "all things shall work together for your good, if ye walk uprightly" (D&C 90:24). To walk uprightly is to walk erect; to be morally correct, honest, and just; and to be "pointing upward," according to Webster. It is the opposite of being stooped in sin. One who has walked uprightly can enter the presence of the Lord with a humble head held erect.

Parents are specifically commanded to teach their children to "walk uprightly before the Lord" (D&C 68:28).

See also: Upright in Heart

Walked with God

The Lord gave Enoch great power over temporal things, but he also gave the prophet a significant invitation when he said, "Thou shalt abide in me, and I in you; therefore walk with me" (Moses 6:34). We are told that Enoch "walked with God three hundred and sixty-five years" (D&C 107:49; see also Gen. 5:20–24; Moses 7:69).

Dummelow suggested: "In Jewish tradition Enoch's walking with God was taken to mean initiation into the mysteries of the universe, and the secrets of the past and future" (Dummelow, 13). However, to walk with God goes beyond gaining new knowledge. It is to walk in his ways.

To walk with God is to "walk not after the flesh, but after the Spirit" (Rom. 8:1); it is to "walk worthy of the Lord . . . being fruitful in every good work, and increasing in the knowledge of God" (Col. 1:10); it is to "walk in the light" (1 Jn. 1:7); it is to "walk in truth" (3 Jn. 1:4); it is to "walk guiltless before God" (Mosiah 4:26); it is "walking in his ways and keeping his commandments" (Mosiah 23:14); it is to "walk circumspectly before God" (Hel. 15:5).

To walk with God is to follow in the footsteps of him who said,

"What manner of men ought ye to be? Verily I say unto you, even as I am." (3 Ne. 27:27.) It is to seek perfection (Matt. 5:48; 3 Ne. 12:48).

See also: Enoch; Perfect

Ward

The term *ward* did not appear in the Doctrine and Covenants until an 1842 revelation (D&C 128:3), although it had been used in Nauvoo since October 1839. At this earlier date, Nauvoo was divided into three areas of Church jurisdiction, known as the upper, middle, and lower wards. According to Allen and Leonard, "This introduced the bishop's ward as a geographical subdivision of the Church. Not yet a fully developed administrative unit, the ward was simply a convenient division for administering financial and welfare concerns. In many American cities the term 'ward' had been used to designate political precincts, and the first Latter-day Saint ecclesiastical wards were apparently created with this precedent in mind." (SLS, 161–62.)

Elder John A. Widtsoe gave a further clarification of the term: "The Ward is the outgrowth of what was known in early days as 'branches' or 'churches.' These separate organizations were then spoken of as 'the church at Fayette,' 'the church at Colesville,' 'the church at Harmony,' 'at Kirtland,' and so on, and meant then about what ward means now, though the organizations referred to were not so complete as are our wards." (PCG, 318.)

The nature of a "ward" today is explained by Elder LeGrand Richards: "A ward organization is the unit that deals directly with the membership of the Church residing within ward boundaries, and is presided over by a bishop and two counselors, with a clerk or clerks to assist them. The bishopric directs the work of the Aaronic Priesthood quorums, keeps all quorums and auxiliaries fully organized, and sees that all the members are given an opportunity to labor in whatever capacity they are best qualified for, according to their special gifts and talents. The bishopric in the ward has the responsibility of the buildings and grounds, all temporal affairs, including the care of the poor and the underprivileged." (MWW, 166.)

See also: Bishopric

Warsaw, Illinois

In an 1841 revelation, William Law was commanded to let his testimony be heard in a number of cities, including that of Warsaw, Illinois (D&C 124:88). This was a town less than twenty miles south of Nauvoo on the Mississippi River. In the spring of 1841, some Saints settled just outside of Warsaw in a place they called Warren, but hostility from the residents of Warsaw soon caused them to withdraw to Nauvoo and other locations. At the time of the martyrdoms of Joseph and Hyrum Smith, the population of Warsaw was about five hundred.

Its significance in the early days of the Church lies in its newspaper, the *Warsaw Signal,* whose editor, Thomas C. Sharp, ran an open warfare against the Church. John Hay, the secretary of state for Illinois, officially referred to Warsaw as "the headquarters of the anti-Mormons" (CHC 2:236). On May 19, 1841, Sharp fired the opening volley in his long series of printed attacks on the Church and its leaders. His conduct led to Joseph Smith's canceling his subscription to the paper. Under date of June 1, 1841, Joseph wrote: "Discontinue my paper — its contents are calculated to pollute me — to patronize the filthy sheet — that tissue of lies — that sink in iniquity — is disgraceful to any moral man."

It was to Warsaw that part of the mob fled following their devilish deeds of June 27, 1844, and from its inflammatory newspaper came these words regarding the martyrdom: "THREE CHEERS to the brave company who shot him (Joseph) to pieces!"

See also: Martrydom

Washing Feet

See: Ordinance of the Washing of Feet; Shake Off the Dust of Thy Feet

Washings

The term *washings* is used in only one section of the Doctrine and Covenants and refers to a sacred ordinance performed only within a temple of the Lord (D&C 124:37, 39). The Savior said, "How shall your washings be acceptable unto me, except ye perform them in a house which you have built to my name?" This ordinance must be received by all who enter into exaltation within the celestial kingdom.

Watchful

One of the most important admonitions one should follow is to "be watchful" (D&C 61:38). Amulek exhorted the Nephites to "be watchful unto prayer continually" (Alma 34:39), as did Moroni (Moro. 6:4). Elder Howard W. Hunter suggested that "prayerful watching does not require sleepless anxiety and preoccupation with the future, but rather the quiet, steady attention to present duties" (En., May 1974, p. 18).

Watchmen

Two revelations refer to "watchmen," who were to occupy positions as lookouts over designated "vineyards." Section 101 refers to conditions in Missouri in which the Lord's designated vineyard, Jackson County, had been overrun by mob elements, forcing the Saints to seek refuge in other locations (D&C 101:43–62). Zion's Camp was an organized effort on the part of the Saints to set their own "watchmen" back upon the towers from whence they had been evicted (D&C 105).

Elder George Q. Cannon described the "officers of the Church of Jesus Christ of Latter-day Saints" as "watchmen" (GT 1:269). Speaking as one of the Lord's chosen servants, President Spencer W. Kimball said, "We continue to warn the people and plead with them, for we are watchmen upon the towers, and in our hands we have a trumpet which we must blow loudly and sound the alarm" (CR, Oct. 1975, p. 8).

Elder Cannon further noted: "They must stand and give warning of the approach of danger. They tell the people to prepare to escape threatened evil. If they are not watchful and vigilant, trouble may fall upon those whom they are appointed to guard and care for." (GT 1:269.) President John Taylor warned of the consequences accruing to those "watchmen" who fail in their sacred stewardship: "God will hold you responsible for those whom you might have saved had you done your duty" (JD 20:23).

See also: Standing Ministers; Watch-Tower

Watch-Tower

In the parable of the redemption of Zion, the Lord commands that "watchmen" be set upon a "watch-tower" lest the "enemy" come in and spoil the "vineyard" (D&C 101). Historically, a watch-tower has been used as a fortification for communities threatened by hostile forces. From its lofty perch, an alert watchman could sight the enemy before he made a surprise attack on an unprepared or defenseless people.

The psalmist described the Lord as a "high tower" (Ps. 18:2) and a "strong tower from the enemy" (Ps. 61:3). Solomon declared, "The name of the Lord is a strong tower: the righteous runneth into it, and is safe" (Prov. 18:10). Thus, the Tower upon which all mankind should stand is the Lord. Those who rely upon God and are alert and sensitive to the Spirit will be warned of pending attacks by the enemies of righteousness.

See also: High Tower; Watchmen

Waters

During the course of a journey that included travel by canoe, a small group of elders was warned about the "destructions upon the waters; yea, and especially upon these waters" (D&C 61:4-5). Sperry said that "these waters" refers specifically to the Missouri and Mississippi rivers (DCC, 255).

The Lord warned that in the last days he had "cursed the waters" (D&C 61:14-19). President Joseph Fielding Smith suggested that the curse upon the waters has been manifest not only in floods and storms but also in warfare, "especially by submarine" (CHMR 1:224).

See also: Canal, The; Deep Water Is What I Am Wont To Swim

Waters of Life

See: Well of Living Water

Wax Cold/Old/Strong

To wax means to come to be or to increase in size, strength, or intensity. Thus, to "wax strong" is to increase in strength or capacity (D&C 45:58; 121:45; Mosiah 18:26). To "wax old" is to increase in years, grow old, or even useless (D&C 1:16; 2 Ne. 7:9). Jesus gave counsel to seek after things "which wax not old" (Luke 12:33). Those who allow their love of men to "wax cold" lose the warmth of love—it becomes cold and lifeless.

See also: Love of Men Shall Wax Cold

Weak Things of the Earth/World

There is a difference between the weak (D&C 84:106) and the weak things of the earth or world (D&C 1:19; 35:13; 133:59). The former are those whose faltering faith needs strengthening, while the latter are they whose spiritual strength confounds the so-called wise and strong of the world. The Prophet Joseph Smith was considered unlearned, unlettered, and weak by the world, but through him the Lord showed forth his wisdom (D&C 124:1; 2 Ne. 3:13). The Lord does not work after the expectations or ways of the world (see 1 Cor. 1:26–31).

Elder Bruce R. McConkie has provided an excellent example to illustrate this point:

"Question: Who is better qualified to preach the gospel, a fifty-year-old college president of world renown who has many scholastic degrees, or a nineteen-year-old high school graduate who has no scholastic stature whatever?

"Answer: The one who has a testimony of the gospel and who is so living as to have the companionship and guidance of the Holy Spirit.

"Question: How is it that the weak things of the earth confound the mighty and strong?

"Answer: True religion is not a matter of intellectuality or of worldly prominence or renown, but of spirituality; and they are not weak but strong in the realm of spiritual things." (DNTC 2:316.)

Commenting upon those who are called to positions of leadership within the Church, Elder Spencer W. Kimball said: "I would not say that those leaders whom the Lord chooses are necessarily the most brilliant, nor the most highly trained, but they are chosen, and when chosen of the Lord they are his recognized authority, and the people who stay close to them have safety" (CR, Apr. 1951, p. 104).

"For my thoughts are not your thoughts, neither are your ways my ways, saith the Lord" (Isa. 55:8).

Weary in Mind

To be weary is to be tired or fatigued, usually because of an exertion of physical, mental, or spiritual energy. To be weary in mind is to be mentally fatigued. Among the promises the Lord gave to those who go forth in his work and "fail not to continue faithful in all things" was that they "shall not be weary in mind" (D&C 84:80).

He goes on to counsel those engaged in the ministry that they should "take [no] thought beforehand what ye shall say; but treasure up in your minds continually the words of life [the scriptures], and it shall be given you in the very hour that portion that shall be meted unto every man" (D&C 84:85). Thus, those who faithfully search the scriptures (see D&C 11:21) and continue faithful in their ministry will not suffer mental fatigue but will feel a freshness of thought as their minds are enlightened by the Spirit.

Well of Living Water

Anciently, the prophet Isaiah declared, "Therefore, with joy shall ye draw water out of the wells of salvation" (Isa. 12:3; 2 Ne. 22:3). A similar phrase was used by the Savior in conversing with the Samaritan woman at Jacob's well. She was promised "living water" which, if she drank, would cause her to never thirst again; for it would be in her "a well of water springing up into everlasting life" (John 4:5–15).

In the Doctrine and Covenants the Lord speaks of "waters of life" and of a "well of living water" (D&C 10:66; 63:23). Of such waters, Elder Bruce R. McConkie has written: "For the thirsty and choking traveler in a desert wilderness to find water, is to find life, to find an escape from agonizing death; similarly, the weary pilgrim traveling through the wilderness of mortality saves himself eternally by drinking from the wells of living water found in the gospel.

"*Living water* is the words of eternal life, the message of salvation, the truths about God and his kingdom; it is the doctrines of the gospel. Those who thirst are invited to come unto Christ and drink. (John 7:37–38.) Where there are prophets of God, there will be found rivers of living water, wells filled with eternal truths, springs bubbling forth their life-giving draughts that save from spiritual death." (DNTC 1:151–52; italics added.)

Welton, Micah B.

In January 1832, a number of elders were called into missionary service. Among these was Micah B. Welton (D&C 75:36). It is assumed that this man remained faithful during those

early days of the Church, for in April 1844 M. B. Welton is listed among those who received mission calls to the state of Kentucky (HC 6:338).

According to Church genealogical records he received a temple endowment in Nauvoo in 1846. There is an "M. Welton" who is listed as a citizen of Clay County, Missouri, at the time the Saints were asked to leave. This man, however, was part of a "citizens" committee appointed to see that the Saints left the area, and it appears unlikely that he would have been a member of the Church (HC 2:455). No further references on the family of Weltons is found in published Church records.

Western Countries

On two occasions in the Doctrine and Covenants, missionaries are commanded to travel and preach in the "western countries" (D&C 45:64; 75:15). The first revelation referred to the area of the United States which was west of New York, and the second referred to the country west of the state of Ohio.

Wheat

The parable of the wheat and the tares was expounded by the Savior during his mortal ministry and again by revelation to Joseph Smith (Matt. 13:24–30, 36–43; D&C 86:1–11). The Prophet said that the wheat represented the

Church (TPJS, 98). The "wheat," said the Savior, shall be gathered and "secured in the garners to possess eternal life, and be crowned with celestial glory" (D&C 101:65).

See also: Church of Jesus Christ of Latter-day Saints, The; Field Is White Already to Harvest; Ripe; Sheaves; Tares; Thrust in His Sickle

Whit

The term *whit* is used four times in the Bible, eight times in the Book of Mormon, and only once in the Doctrine and Covenants (e.g., 2 Cor. 11:5; Hel. 11:19; D&C 33:4). In the latter reference, the Lord spoke of his vineyard having "become corrupted every whit."

Smith and Sjodahl offer this explanation: " 'Whit' means a very small part of a thing, a particle, and when the Lord says that His vineyard has become corrupted, 'every whit,' He teaches us that the corruption is total: that there is not a spot in all the world that has not been affected by the apostasy from His sovereignty. Hence the urgent necessity of faithful laborers at this, the eleventh and last hour." (SS, 173.)

White Stone

The "white stone" mentioned in Doctrine and Covenants 130:10–11 is best described in those verses.

See also: Urim and Thummim; Wonders of Eternity

Whitlock, Harvey

Although he is mentioned but once in the Doctrine and Covenants, that being in conjunction with a missionary assignment (D&C 52:25), Harvey Whitlock has the distinction of being one for whom Joseph Smith received a special revelation. He had come into the Church prior to June 1831 but had gone astray prior to September 1835, when he imploringly wrote to Joseph Smith to find out the will of the Lord regarding himself. In the letter he referred to his being led astray by the "allurements of many vices" and described himself as "a poor, wretched, bewildered, way-wanderer to eternity."

Joseph's letter of response included a revelation directed to Whitlock in which the Lord promised him forgiveness and told him that he would "be counted worthy to stand among princes, and . . . yet be made a polished shaft in my quiver for bringing down the strongholds of wickedness" if he remained faithful. The Prophet invited Whitlock to return to Kirtland and participate in the School of the Prophets (HC 2:313–16). His rebaptism and ordination to the priesthood are mentioned in January 1836 (HC 2:388).

Several years prior to this, he and another man had their tongues bound by the devil, whereupon Joseph commanded the evil one to depart, much to the "joy and comfort" of all present (HC 1:175, footnote). Whitlock's ability to persevere was lacking, and he left the Church on several occasions, finally joining the Reorganized Church and losing the promised blessings of the Lord.

Whitmer, David

Among the most prominent participants of the early period in Church history was David Whitmer. He was one of the six original members of the Church, as well as one of the three privileged to see the angel Moroni, behold the gold plates from which the Book of Mormon was translated (among other ancient artifacts), and hear the voice of God bearing personal testimony to the truthfulness of the ancient record of holy writ.

Along with Oliver Cowdery and Martin Harris, he was charged with the responsibility of seeking out the twelve men who would occupy the first apostolic chairs of this dispensation (D&C 18:37). He was the recipient or corecipient of four revelations in the Doctrine and Covenants (14; 17; 18; 30) and received a mission call in yet another revelation (D&C 52:25).

It was David Whitmer who brought transportation to Harmony, Pennsylvania, to transport Joseph and Emma Smith, together with Oliver Cowdery, up to Fayette, New York, where

Joseph and Oliver completed translating and transcribing the Book of Mormon at the home of David's father. He was called to serve as "a president" of the Church in Missouri, where he served about four years. During a brief period from July 1834 to December 1834, he was the designated successor to Joseph Smith, if the Prophet's life had been taken (HC 3:32, footnote).

Oliver Cowdery's ordination as Assistant President of the Church superseded David's previous appointment, but the latter seemed confused on this issue after that point. Following Whitmer's rejection as "a president" of the Church in Missouri, he refused to accept the jurisdiction of the high council and continued to identify himself as "President of the Church of Christ." For this and other "unchristianlike conduct," he was excommunicated on April 13, 1838. His efforts to attract a following failed.

In April 1887, he published a booklet entitled, "An Address to All Believers in Christ by a Witness to the Divine Authenticity of the Book of Mormon." The title, of course, bore continued witness of his firm belief in the divine manifestation which had been his, but the contents exhibited his differences with the divine Church of which he had been an original member.

Unfortunately, the warning of the Lord in 1830 had not taken root: "Behold, I say unto you, David, that you have feared man and have not relied on me for strength as you ought. But your mind has been on the things of the earth more than on the things of me, your Maker, and the ministry whereunto you have been called." (D&C 30:1–2; see Jenson 1:263–71.)

See also: Book of Mormon; Three Witnesses

Whitmer, John

"Next to his brother David, John was the most prominent and able man among the Whitmers, and rendered efficient service to the Church in various ways, as long as he remained faithful," said Andrew Jenson. He was the recipient of four revelations in the Doctrine and Covenants (D&C 15; 26; 30; 47) and is the major benefactor of instructions in another (D&C 69:2–8). His name also appears among a select group of men in Doctrine and Covenants 70:1.

John was affiliated with the Church in its beginning stages, being baptized by Oliver Cowdery within a month after the latter received this authority from a heavenly messenger. He accompanied the Prophet Joseph on his first missionary trips to Colesville, New York, and became the first regularly appointed Church Historian. He became one of the presiding officers of the Church in Missouri and served on the high council in Kirtland, where he also attended the temple dedication. In November 1837, some objec-

tions were raised as to his leadership in Missouri; and in February 1838, he and several others were rejected by the assembled Saints.

On March 10, 1838, he was excommunicated by action of the high council at Far West, Missouri, "for persisting in unchristianlike conduct." After his spiritual severance, Whitmer refused to deliver up the Church records and documents that were in his possession. He remained in Far West, but in spite of his bitterness and antagonism against the Saints, he never denied the reality of the experience which would make his name known to generations thereafter. He, as one of the Eight Witnesses to the Book of Mormon, had seen the plates from which that sacred book was translated. Even among the worst enemies of the Church, John Whitmer would continue to affirm the truthfulness of America's second witness for Christ. (Jenson 1:251–52.)

See also: Book of Mormon; Horah

Whitmer, Peter, Jr.

Joseph Smith described Peter Whitmer, Jr., as a "zealous friend and assistant in the work" of translating the Book of Mormon (HC 1:49). Section 16 of the Doctrine and Covenants was personally addressed to him and he was a corecipient of section 30. In addition to these, he was called in a later revelation to go on a mission among the Lamanites (D&C 32:2).

It was this mission that took him to Missouri, where he took an active part in Church affairs and suffered the persecution of mobocracy. Perhaps as a result of this suffering, he died in Liberty, Missouri, on September 22, 1836, just a few months after being called to serve on the high council.

Other than remaining faithful to the gospel, his most notable achievement was probably as one of the Eight Witnesses to the Book of Mormon. In this capacity he saw and handled the sacred gold plates from which this ancient book of scripture was translated. (Jenson 1:277.)

See also: Book of Mormon

Whitmer, Peter, Sr.

The name of Peter Whitmer, Sr., does not appear within the context of the revelations that comprise the Doctrine and Covenants. However, he is mentioned in the preface of section 21 and is referred to as "old Father Whitmer" in section 128, verse 21. It was at the home he built at Fayette, New York, that the Church was organized on April 6, 1830. Of his seven children who lived to adulthood, all were intricately involved in the early history of the Church. David was one of the Three Witnesses to the Book of Mormon, and his sister Elizabeth Ann was married to Oliver Cowdery, another of the Three Witnesses. Christian, Jacob, John, and Peter, Jr., were four of the

Eight Witnesses to the Book of Mormon, and their sister Catherine's husband, Hiram Page, was a fifth witness.

Unfortunately, during the trials of the Missouri persecutions, nearly the entire family turned away from the Church. Nothing more is recorded of "old Father Whitmer" except the date and place of his death—August 12, 1854, in Richmond, Ray County, Missouri, at the age of eighty-one. (Jenson 1:282–83.)

See also: Chamber of Old Father Whitmer; Old Father Whitmer

Whitney, Newel K.

Mentioned in ten sections of the Doctrine and Covenants, Newel K. Whitney was an important cog in the wheels which moved the Church forward in its early days (D&C 63:42; 64:26; 72:8; 78:9; 82:11; 84:112, 93:50; 96:2; 104:39–41; 117:1, 11). Born on February 5, 1795, Whitney was almost ten years senior to the Prophet, whom he faithfully served.

After joining the Church in November 1830, Newel and his wife had a remarkable vision in which they were told to "prepare to receive the word of the Lord, for it is coming." Shortly thereafter, a sleigh of strangers pulled up to Newel's store in Kirtland, Ohio. One of the occupants alighted from the vehicle and strode up the stairs of Whitney's establishment. "Newel K.

Whitney, thou art the man!" exclaimed the stranger. To this friendly greeting, Newel replied, "You have the advantage of me. I could not call you by name as you have me." "I am Joseph, the Prophet," said the stranger. "You've prayed me here; now what do you want of me?" Thus began a long and cherished friendship.

The Prophet remained at Whitney's home, where he was hospitably treated, and under whose roof some of the revelations now contained in the Doctrine and Covenants were received. Joseph's trust in Newel extended beyond the financial finesse which the latter possessed, for the Prophet often entrusted his friend with some of his most secret thoughts and revelations. Among these was the principle of plural marriage. It was Newel K. Whitney who preserved the written revelation on plural marriage which eventually was given to Brigham Young to be had in the archives of the Church, and it was Elder Whitney who performed the ceremony in which his own daughter became the first plural wife by divine authority in this dispensation.

In December 1831, he was called as the second bishop of the Church (D&C 72). He functioned in this office in Ohio and Illinois before being called as the Presiding Bishop of the Church on April 6, 1847. He served faithfully until his death on September 23, 1850. Of him, the *Deseret News* said: "Thus in full strength and mature years, has one of the oldest, most exemplary, and most useful members of the Church fallen suddenly by the cruel agency of the King of Terrors. In him, the Church suffers the loss of a wise and able counselor and a thorough and straightforward business man. It was ever more gratifying to him to pay a debt than to contract one, and when all his debts were paid he was a happy man, though he had nothing left but his own moral and muscular energy. He has gone down to the grave, leaving a spotless name behind him" (Jenson 1:222–27).

See also: Ahashdah; One Wife

Whore of All the Earth

Destruction by "devouring fire" will be the ultimate destiny of "the great and abominable church, which is the whore of all the earth" (D&C 29:21; see also Rev. 17:16; 19:2). A whore is one who prostitutes her body, selling sexual favors for some kind of remuneration. The whore of all the earth is symbolic of Babylon or everything that is evil and contrary to the gospel of Jesus Christ (D&C 86:3). It is "the church of the devil . . . the mother of abominations" (1 Ne. 14:10).

This church does not represent a particular organization but includes all people who fight "against Zion" (the pure in heart) (2 Ne. 16:10; see also D&C 97:21).

See also: Babylon; Great and Abominable Church; Wine of the Wrath of Her Fornication

Whoremonger

Webster defines a "whoremonger" as one who is a lecher or one given to whoring. In other words, such a one is groveling amidst the filth and degradation of illicit sexual thoughts and relations. These are they who will "suffer the vengeance of eternal hell" (D&C 63:17; 76:103–5; Rev. 21:8; 22:15). "For this ye know, that no whoremonger, nor unclean person, nor covetous man, who is an idolater, hath any inheritance in the kingdom of Christ and our God" (Eph. 5:5).

See also: Spirits of Men Who Are to Be Judged, and Are Found Under Condemnation; Uncleanness

Wicked

The term *wicked*, or the references to *wickedness*, appear so frequently in holy writ that scriptural concordances include hundreds of such citations. The wicked are obviously the opposite of the righteous (D&C 10:37), and their evil deeds will earn them a destination far removed from the presence of God (D&C 29:27, 41).

The attitude of Deity towards the wicked might be summed up in this statement: "I, the Lord, am angry with the wicked" (D&C 63:32). We are admonished to "cease . . . from all . . . wicked doings" (D&C 88:121). One who is wicked engages in things contrary to the ways of God. Thus, he is described as *ungodly*.

The label of "wickedness" need not be confined to those who either openly or surreptitiously *seek* sin, but also to those procrastinators who passively pursue its siren call. For, as James said, "to him that knoweth to do good, and doeth it not, to him it is sin" (James 4:17; see also Alma 34:33–36). An all-encompassing definition of the "wicked" was given by President Joseph Fielding Smith, who said that this meant "all who had not repented and received the Gospel" (CHMR 1:258).

See also: Wicked Man, A; Wicked Men

Wicked Man, A

As a result of his having lost an early Book of Mormon manuscript containing 116 pages of translation, Martin Harris was called a "wicked man" by the Lord (D&C 3:12; 10:1). "At heart, Martin was not wicked and desired to do what was right. . . . His wickedness consisted in his selfish desire to gratify his own wish contrary to the will of the Lord, after he had been denied this request twice before it was granted. Moreover, he was wicked in that he violated a most sacred and solemn covenant and trust which he made with the Lord through the Prophet Joseph Smith. From his wicked act, or acts, he humbly repented and again found favor with the Lord to the extent that he was privileged to stand as one of the special three witnesses of the Book of

Mormon, and to behold the plates in the presence of the holy angel. He was deprived, however, from ever again acting as scribe in the translation of this sacred record of the Nephites." (CHMR 1:28.)

See also: Harris, Martin; Manuscript (116 Pages)

Wicked Men

The Prophet Joseph spoke of "wicked men" being upon the earth during the thousand years of peaceful existence known as the Millennium (TPJS, 268–69). Inasmuch as those who inhabit the millennial earth will be of either a celestial or terrestrial order, an explanation is in order.

Elder Joseph Fielding Smith said: "In using the term 'wicked men' . . . , the Prophet did so in the same sense in which the Lord uses it in the eighty-fourth section of the Doctrine and Covenants, 49–53. The Lord in this scripture speaks of *those who have not received the Gospel* as being under the bondage of sin, and hence 'wicked.' However, many of these people are honorable, clean living men, but they have not embraced the Gospel. The inhabitants of the terrestrial order will remain on the earth during the Millennium and this class are without the Gospel ordinances." (TPJS, 268–69, footnote; italics added.)

Wicked One

See: Devil

Wide Expanse of Eternity

The Savior said he was the One who "looked upon the wide expanse of eternity . . . before the world was made" (D&C 38:1). According to one commentary, the wide expanse of eternity "would, if a Hebraism, mean, 'the wide, eternal expanse,' or 'boundless space,' which is different from the expanse (*raquia*) of Genesis 1:6–8, that appeared on the second day of the creation. The grand truth conveyed here is, that our Lord existed before the world was made, and that, with some object in view, He surveyed space and all it contained." (SS, 198.)

Wight, Lyman

The name of Lyman Wight appears in three sections of the Doctrine and Covenants (52:7, 12; 103:30, 38; 124:18, 62, 70). He was baptized in 1830 and was one of the first to receive the office of high priest. At a conference in Kirtland in June 1831, he testified to seeing the Savior in vision. His faithfulness and courage in the early days of the Church seemingly knew no bounds. When others hesitated, he stepped forth to offer his all. During the persecution of the Saints in Missouri, he was described as "a dread to his enemies and a terror to evil doers."

Wight shared the confines of the Liberty Jail with Joseph and Hyrum Smith during their six months of incarceration and was ever ready to defend his leader with his life. Once, when asked to betray the Prophet in order to save his own life, Wight responded: "Shoot and be damned!"

Although not polished in speech and sometimes rough in appearance, Lyman Wight could bear a powerful testimony. During a mission to Cincinnati, he worked as a fisherman by day and preached by night. "One evening he went from the fish net to the court house, and stood on the top of a stove barefooted with his trousers rolled up to his knees, and his shirt sleeves up to his elbows, and preached two hours. Some of the people remarked, 'He preaches the truth, though he does not look much like a preacher.'" On April 8, 1841, he was called to join the select ranks of the Twelve Apostles, filling a vacancy created by the martyrdom of David W. Patten.

The "wild ram of the mountains" is how Joseph Smith referred to Lyman Wight (HC 7:435). He was one of those fearless men of great physical courage whose fidelity to the Prophet was unquestioned. Yet, as Joseph died on that fateful day in June 1844 and his physical body began the process of natural decay, in a similar fashion a spiritual decay began to take effect in Lyman Wight, for he found it impossible to transfer his loyalties from the man Joseph to the cause for which he stood.

Wight resisted the leadership of Brigham Young, stating he did not believe "the death of Joseph gave one of the twelve a supremacy over the others" (BYUS 17:109–10). "The day was when there was somebody to control me," declared this errant Apostle, "but that day is past." Unfortunately, this 1831 warning of the Lord was disregarded: "And let my servant Lyman Wight beware, for Satan desireth to sift him as chaff" (D&C 52:12). Contrary to counsel, Lyman led a colony to Texas and was excommunicated from the Church on December 3, 1848 (Jenson 1:93–96). He died on March 31, 1858.

See also: Wight's Ferry

Wight's Ferry

About thirty miles northwest of Far West, Missouri, stood the home of Lyman Wight. It was situated at the foot of a place which Joseph Smith called Tower Hill, because of the remnants of an old Nephite tower or altar which he had found upon the hill (HC 3:34–35). About one-half mile up the river from this location was Wight's Ferry, named after the man who operated it and owned the house at the foot of the hill.

It was near here that the Prophet identified the location of Adam-ondi-Ahman and the valley of Adam (D&C 116).

See also: Spring Hill; Wight, Lyman

Wilderness

The term *wilderness* is used in several senses in the Doctrine and Covenants. The basic definition of *wilderness* is that it is an uncultivated, uninhabited, desolate region. This is the way in which it is applied to the areas which Lehi (D&C 17:1) and Moses (D&C 84:23) traversed. It is descriptive of the area in which the Lamanites were formerly found (D&C 32:2; 49:24), and was the type of area in which God chose to restore the priesthood to earth (D&C 128:20).

Its unique usage, however, is in relation to the Church, which is said to have been "called forth out of the wilderness" (D&C 5:14; 33:5; 86:3; 109:73; Rev. 12). This wilderness is the wasteland of apostasy. President Joseph Fielding Smith offered the following observation: "In the book of Revelation, Chap. 12, we have a very vivid symbolical description of the Church being driven into the wilderness by the great dragon. 'And to the woman (Church) were given two wings of a great eagle, that she might fly into the wilderness' . . . Now in the Dispensation of the Fulness of Times, the Church is again called forth from the wilderness, and her man-child (the Priesthood) is restored to her again." (CHMR 1:153–54.) Another gospel scholar has suggested that the "man-child" to which the "woman" (Church) gives birth is the Kingdom of God "which shall hold sway during the Millennial Era" (DNTC 3:511).

See also: Wilderness of Fayette

Wilderness of Darkness

In all scripture, the only place the phrase *wilderness of darkness* is found is in the dedicatory prayer of the Kirtland Temple. The Prophet prayed that the "church may come forth out of the wilderness of darkness" (D&C 109:73), which represented a place lacking the light of the gospel or a place of persecution. Joseph Smith wanted the Church to "shine forth" in all her glory.

The Prophet's plea is reminiscent of John the Revelator's description of the Church as a woman fleeing into the wilderness during the dark days of apostasy (Rev. 12:1–17). Joseph Smith was called to "lay the foundation of this church, and to bring it forth out of obscurity and out of darkness" (D&C 1:30).

Wilderness of Fayette

Two revelations were received in 1829 which promised the forthcoming fulfillment of ancient prophecy (2 Ne. 27:12; Ether 5:3–4) regarding the calling of three special witnesses to the Book of Mormon (D&C 5; 17). The latter revelation was received in Fayette, New York, home of one of the Three Witnesses, David Whitmer.

Joseph Smith and Oliver Cowdery completed the translation of the sacred book of scripture at the house of David's father. Shortly thereafter, the Three Witnesses — Whitmer, Cowdery, and Martin

Harris—received the promised view of the plates in the wooded wilderness near the Whitmer home at Fayette in Seneca County (D&C 128:20).

On this sacred occasion the voice of God spoke from heaven saying, "These plates have been revealed by the power of God, and they have been translated by the power of God. The translation of them which you have seen is correct, and I command you to bear record of what you now see and hear." (HC 1:52–57.)

See also: Book of Mormon; Three Witnesses

Williams, Frederick G.

The earliest mention of Frederick G. Williams in the Doctrine and Covenants is in a revelation received in September 1831, in which he is counseled not to sell his farm at Kirtland (64:21). Although section 81 was originally received in behalf of Jesse Gause, an inconspicuous man who served as a counselor to Joseph Smith but who silently left the stage of Church involvement and entered obscurity, Frederick G. Williams's name is printed as the recipient of the revelation because he was called to the same position, and the same counsel applied to him (BYUS 15:362–64).

Although Williams and Sidney Rigdon were serving as counselors to the Prophet, the First Presidency was not officially organized until the following year

(D&C 90:6; CHMR 1:312). For divine purposes the Lord referred to Frederick as "Shederlaomach" on several occasions. (D&C 92:1–2; 104:27, 29; pre-1981 edition.) In May 1833, Williams was severely chastised by the Lord for not having his own house in order (D&C 93:40–43).

He traveled to Missouri as a member of Zion's Camp, acting as the paymaster for that body. He was actively involved in the building of the Kirtland Temple, and during its dedicatory services saw an angelic being within its holy walls. Unfortunately, he became recreant in his responsibilities and was rejected as a counselor in the First Presidency during a conference at Far West, November 7, 1837 and was later excommunicated.

One year later, at Nauvoo, Frederick G. Williams returned to the Church seeking forgiveness and rebaptism. His confirmation in the Church was recorded in Joseph's journal as having taken place on August 5, 1838. He again fell away, and his excommunication followed on March 17, 1839. He was extended the hand of fellowship in April 1840, and "died as a faithful member of the Church, October 10, 1842, at Quincy, Illinois." (Jenson 1:51–52.)

See also: Gause, Jesse; Shederlaomach

Williams, Samuel

In an 1841 listing of the priesthood leaders in Nauvoo, Samuel

Williams is mentioned as a member of the presidency over the elders (D&C 124:137). His ordination as an elder appears under date of October 6, 1839, in the minutes of a conference at Commerce, Illinois (HC 4:13). The previous January his name appeared among those who covenanted to assist the Saints in removing from Missouri (HC 3:252).

Sometime prior to October 1844, Williams was sustained as the president of the elders quorum in Nauvoo and was unanimously upheld in this office at the important conference held a little over three months after the martyrdom (HC 7:297). He came west with the main body of the Church, and an 1850 census showed him to be a resident of Salt Lake City. No additional information is currently available on him.

Willing Mind

"Behold, the Lord requireth the heart and a willing mind," declared Deity (D&C 64:34). The mind is that part of the individual that feels, perceives, thinks, wills, and reasons. To have a "willing mind" is to be favorably inclined toward the things of the Spirit, to be open and receptive thereto, and to rejoice therein. It is to recognize that "to be learned is good if [we] hearken unto the counsels of God" (2 Ne. 9:29). It is to know that "to be carnally-minded is death, and to be spiritually-minded is life eternal" (2 Ne. 9:39). It is to be in a state of readiness to do the will of God.

The Apostle Paul noted, "As there was a readiness to will, so there may be a performance" (2 Cor. 8:11).

See also: Desire of Their Hearts; Thoughts

Wilson, Calves

Following an important conference at Amherst, Ohio, in January 1832, a number of elders received mission calls. Among these were Asa Dodds and Calves Wilson, who were told to go "unto the western countries," or the western part of the United States (D&C 75:15). Nothing more is recorded of Wilson or his companion in published Church records.

Wilson, Dunbar

The only mention of Dunbar Wilson in the Doctrine and Covenants is as a member of the Nauvoo High Council (D&C 124:132). Family records identify him as Lewis Dunbar Wilson. He affiliated with the Church as early as 1836 and followed the Saints from Ohio to Missouri and Illinois and then on to Utah, where he died on March 11, 1856.

Wine

The sacramental prayers refer to the use of wine as an emblem to remind us of the blood shed by the Savior in our behalf (D&C 20:40, 78–79; Moro. 5:1–2). An 1830 revelation informed the Prophet Joseph Smith that it was not necessary to use wine, "for it mattereth not what ye shall . . . drink when ye partake of the sacrament, if it so be that ye do it with an eye single to [God's] glory" (D&C 27:2). The present practice of the Lord's Church is to use water instead of wine in sacramental services.

The Lord has specifically enjoined his Saints not to partake of wine or strong drink, which has been interpreted by his prophets to mean alcoholic beverages (D&C 89:5–7). The value of refraining from the use of such drinks was shown anciently by Daniel and his three friends (Dan. 1) and has been substantiated by science in our day.

See also: Pure Wine; Red in His Apparel; Sacrament; Wine of the Wrath of Her Fornication; Wine on the Lees; Wine Press/Vat; Word of Wisdom (#2)

Wine of the Wrath of Her Fornication

Three times in the Doctrine and Covenants the Lord speaks of Babylon making "all nations drink of the wine of the wrath of her fornication" (D&C 35:11; 88:94, 105). A reference to the nations drinking of the "cup" of Babylon is also found (D&C 86:3).

Babylon, the symbol of the wicked ways of the world, offers to all nations the cup of her iniquity, or the wine of fornication. Anything that is crass, degrading, or evil becomes part of the ingredients which make up such a "drink," from which all nations of the earth have partaken. Upon those who drink will the wrath of God descend—thus the plea to "go . . . out from Babylon" (D&C 133:5, 7) and partake not of the bitter dregs of her wine.

See also: Babylon; Whore of All the Earth

Wine on the Lees

In 1831, the Lord admonished the elders to bear testimony that the foundation of Zion might be laid and that a "feast of fat things, of wine on the lees well refined" might be prepared (D&C 58:6–8). Commenting on this passage, Sidney B. Sperry said: "The 'fat things' and 'wine on the lees' were to the ancient Hebrews a representation of prosperity. 'Wine on the lees' is wine matured by resting on the lees or dregs at the bottom of the wine cask, hence 'well refined.' The 'fat things' and 'wine on the lees' at the feast are therefore a representation of the offering of the rich things of the Gospel at the Lord's table." (DCC, 237.)

See also: Feast of the Fat Things; Wine

Wine-Press/Vat

See: Red in His Apparel

Wings

See: Eagles' Wings; Earth Rolls upon Her Wings; Hen Gathereth Her Chickens

Winter Quarters

Following the exodus from Nauvoo, which began in February 1846, the Saints located in temporary settlements on the plains of Iowa and Nebraska. One of these locations, Winter Quarters, was where the revelation now known as section 136 was received. During the summer of 1846, the United States government called upon five hundred "able-bodied men" from the Mormons to enlist in the army and take their march through the southwestern part of the country. This group of soldiers became known as the Mormon Battalion.

Because of the weakened condition in which this left the pioneers, the government secured permission from the Indians for the Saints to locate temporarily on lands belonging to these native Americans. A site was chosen on the west bank of the Missouri River on what is now known as Florence, Nebraska, near the Iowa border.

"A committee of twelve men was appointed to arrange the temporary city into wards, over which bishops were chosen to preside. . . . Every family labored diligently to construct some kind of a house in which they could find shelter, although many of these were merely dugouts built in the side of the hill. The place was named Winter Quarters and was laid out regularly into streets." (ECH, 339–40.) "By December of 1846, there were 548 log houses, 38 sod houses, with 3,483 inhabitants" (LDS 1:520).

It was at Winter Quarters, in December 1847, that the Lord called Brigham Young to preside over the Church and the First Presidency was reorganized. The settlement was finally abandoned in the summer of 1848.

See also: Omaha Nation

Wisdom

"Seek not for riches but for wisdom," declared the Lord (D&C 6:7). Again, "treasure up wisdom in your bosoms" (D&C 38:30). It was seeking after wisdom that directed young Joseph Smith to seek God in prayer, which brought about the great theophany of 1820 (JS—H 1:11–20; see also D&C 42:68). The Saints are instructed to teach one another words of wisdom out of the best books in order to increase faith (D&C 88:118; 109:7).

The essence of wisdom might be expressed in this comparative description by Elder James E. Talmage: "Knowledge is to wisdom what belief is to faith, one an abstract principle, the other a living application. Not possession merely, but *the proper use of knowledge constitutes wisdom.*" (AF, 100; italics added.)

See also: Word of Wisdom (#1)

Wisdom of the Wise

The "wisdom of the wise," which shall be surpassed by the wisdom of the righteous (D&C 76:9), is the learning of the world which is transitory and not of an eternal nature. It consists of the learning of those who "hearken not unto the counsel of God, for they set it aside, supposing they know of themselves, wherefore, their wisdom is foolishness and it profiteth them not" (2 Ne. 9:28).

See also: Arm of Flesh; Prudent; Understanding of the Prudent; Wise

Wise

The term *wise* is used in both a positive and a negative way in the Doctrine and Covenants. In a negative sense, the Lord said that the wisdom of the righteous shall cause the "wisdom of the wise" to perish (D&C 76:9). In an earlier revelation, those who criticized the Prophet Joseph were challenged to select "the most wise" among them and see if he could write a revelation comparable to those received by the Prophet (D&C 67:6). That same month the Lord said, "The weak shall confound the wise" (D&C 133:58). And, a decade later, Joseph Smith indicated that the things of God "have been kept hid from the wise and prudent" (D&C 128:18).

The nature of these "wise" people was expressed by the Prophet when he said: "There are a great many wise men and women . . . in our midst who are too wise to be taught; therefore they must die in their ignorance, and in the resurrection they will find their mistake" (TPJS, 309).

The Nephite prophet Jacob spoke in a similar vein: "O the vainness, and the frailties, and the foolishness of men!" he said. *"When they are learned they think they are wise, and they hearken not unto the counsel of God, for they set it aside, supposing they know of themselves, wherefore, their wisdom is foolishness and it profiteth them not. And they shall perish."* (2 Ne. 9:28; italics added.) Thus, the "wise" spoken of in the above citations are those who "are learned" (at least in temporal things) and, therefore, "they *think* they are wise," but "they hearken not unto the counsel of God."

Webster defines *wise* as "discerning and judging soundly concerning what is true or false, proper or improper; discreet, as opposed to foolish." This is the sense in which the term is applied to the righteous throughout the scriptures.

"And he that is a faithful and wise steward shall inherit all things" (D&C 78:22; see also 51:19; 72:4; 101:61). An earlier revelation said, "For *they that are wise and have received the truth, and have taken the Holy Spirit for their guide, and have not been deceived* —verily I say unto you, they shall not be hewn down and cast into the fire, but shall abide the day" (D&C 45:57; italics added). The documents that Joseph Smith brought forth are spoken of as being "wise"; they are true and lead one to God (D&C 135:3).

The proper state of being "wise" is stated by Jacob: "But to be learned is good *if* they hearken unto the counsels of God" (2 Ne. 9:29; italics added). Or, as Paul admonished Timothy, "Study to shew thyself *approved unto God*" (2 Tim. 2:15; italics added).

See also: Babes and Sucklings; Prophet; Wisdom of the Wise

Withal

The word *withal* means therewith or thereby (D&C 46:16).

Wo

The word *wo* denotes distress, affliction, or something of an adverse nature. "Wo unto him" simply means that adversity will befall the individual upon whom or about whom the "wo" is spoken (D&C 11:15; 38:6).

Woe

The Lord declared, "woe shall come unto the inhabitants of the earth if they will not hearken unto my words" (D&C 5:5). Webster tells us that a woe is "a condition of deep suffering from misfortune, affliction, or grief."

Wolves

Although the word *wolves* is only used once in the Doctrine

and Covenants (D&C 122:6), its use as a symbol of predatory people who seek to take advantage of and to destroy the sheep of the Good Shepherd is also found in other scriptures (Matt. 7:15; 10:16; Luke 10:3; Acts 20:29; Alma 5:60; 3 Ne. 14:15).

Wonders of Eternity

The phrase *wonders of eternity* is used but once in the Doctrine and Covenants (D&C 76:8), but the term *wonders* appears in connection with the phrase *signs and wonders* (35:8; 45:40; 63:12), and the *wonders of your Eternal King* (128:23). Among the cross-references to "wonders of eternity" listed in pre-1981 editions of the Doctrine and Covenants are references to the "mysteries" of the kingdom of God, and to "all things that pertain unto the kingdom of God" (D&C 76:7; 88:78).

Smith and Sjodahl state that the "wonders of eternity" include the "history of the past and events yet to come" (SS, 446). In an ultimate sense, the righteous, to whom the "wonders of eternity" will be revealed, will be those who obtain the celestial kingdom and become possessors of the "white stone" whereby all things will be made known (D&C 130:10–11).

In a general sense, wonders are miracles or extraordinary manifestations.

Wont

See: Deep Water Is What I Am Wont to Swim

Woodruff, Wilford

Beset by brutal accidents from an early age, one would almost believe Wilford Woodruff was afflicted with malignant misfortune. "On 27 distinct occasions," he once remarked, "I have been saved from dangers which threatened my life." "The devil has sought to take away my life from the day I was born," continued Elder Woodruff. "I seem to be a marked victim of the adversary. I can find but one reason for this: the devil knew if I got into the Church of Jesus Christ of Latter-day Saints, I would write the history of that Church and leave on record the works and teachings of the prophets, of the apostles and elders." "Whenever I heard Joseph Smith preach, teach, or prophesy, I always felt it my duty to write it; I felt uneasy and could not eat, drink, or sleep until I did write." (WW, 5–12, 476–77.)

This "hungering and thirsting after righteousness" was typical of Wilford's whole life. In his later years he said, "I labored to find this Church, I may say, from my childhood up, and many a midnight hour have I [pleaded] . . . that the Lord would let me find a people who contended for the faith once delivered to the Saints. . . . I prayed to the Lord to let me live to find such a people,

and he promised that I should." (JD 18:40.)

On December 29, 1833, two elders came to Wilford's town and scheduled a meeting in the schoolhouse. Wilford's reaction is recorded in his journal: "Upon my arrival home [from work] . . . I immediately turned out my horses and started for the schoolhouse without waiting for supper. On my way I prayed most sincerely that the Lord would give me His spirit, and that if these men were the servants of God I might know it, and that my heart might be prepared to receive the divine message they had to deliver." (WW, 33.)

Following the meeting, Wilford rose to his feet and bore the testimony which the Spirit had urged him to do, confirming the message of the elders. In like manner, pages of the Book of Mormon bore witness to his soul of the truths he had heard and was reading. On New Year's Eve, 1833, with three feet of snow on the ground, Wilford Woodruff entered the "warm" waters of baptism; said he, "the water was mixed with ice and snow, yet I did not feel the cold."

He participated in the march of Zion's Camp the following year and then spent two years in the southern states as a missionary, while holding the office of a priest. In 1891 he was to say, "I desire to impress upon you the fact that it does not make any difference whether a man is a Priest or an Apostle, if he magnifies his calling. . . . Never in my life, as an Apostle, as a Seventy, or as an

Elder, have I ever had more of the protection of the Lord than while holding the office of Priest. The Lord revealed to me by visions, by revelations, and by the Holy Spirit, many things that lay before me." (MS 53:628–29.)

His apostolic calling came while he was serving a mission in the eastern states and Fox Islands (D&C 118:6). He is mentioned twice more in the Doctrine and Covenants, once as a member of the Twelve (D&C 124:129) and once as a leader of the pioneers westward movement (D&C 136:13). His missionary experiences are legendary and his life exemplifies an exacting faith in God. On many occasions his life or property, and that of others, was saved by his being in tune to the whisperings of the Spirit.

One of his spiritual highlights was the apearance to him of the signers of the Declaration of Independence, and other notable men of history, in the St. George Temple, where they demanded that he perform the ordinances of the temple in their behalf (CR, Apr. 1898, pp. 89–90; JD 19:229).

On April 2, 1889, he was set apart as President of The Church of Jesus Christ of Latter-day Saints, the Prophet, Seer, and Revelator of the Lord upon the earth. In this capacity, he received divine direction to bring to an end the practice of polygamy, and accordingly issued the famous "Manifesto" (OD—1). This was not "done without earnest prayer before the Lord," he said.

"For me to have taken a stand in anything which is not pleasing in the sight of God, or before the heavens, I would rather have gone out and been shot. . . . I say to Israel, the Lord will never permit me nor any other man who stands as the President of this Church to lead you astray." (WW, 567–72.) "Wilford the Faithful," as he was called by Joseph Smith, passed away on September 2, 1898, to pursue his course of righteousness in yet another sphere.

See also: Manifesto

Word, The

It is evident that the use of the term *Word* in an 1833 revelation refers to Christ (D&C 93:8–11). Similar statements are found in the Gospel of John (John 1:1–14). One commentary states: "Christ is the Word or Messenger of Salvation. . . . The gospel itself is *the word* [D&C 11:21], and it is because the gospel or word of salvation is in Christ that he, on the principle of personification . . . , becomes the Word." (DNTC 1:71.)

See also: Jesus Christ

Word of Knowledge

The "word of knowledge," spoken in Doctrine and Covenants 46:18, *"refers to the gift to instruct others.* There is a difference between wisdom, knowledge, and ability to instruct. According

to Coleridge, 'common sense in an uncommon degree' is what men call *wisdom*. It is almost a direct operation of intuition. *Knowledge* is a carefully-stored-up supply of facts, generally slowly acquired. The *ability to instruct* is the gift to impart of this supply to others. Each is a gift of God." (SS, 274; italics added.)
See also: Knowledge

Word of My Power

The "word of my power" (D&C 29:30; Jacob 4:9; Moses 1:32) is a title that signifies that the Son of God carries with him the power, authority, and words of the Father (MD, 844).

Word of Truth

The "word of truth" mentioned in Doctrine and Covenants 50:19 is "that which comes from the Spirit of God . . . comes through the channels He has appointed. This is *one* sure sign of a true doctrine or any divine manifestation." (SS, 292.)
See also: Truth

Word of Wisdom (#1)

Among the gifts of the Spirit is the "word of wisdom" (D&C 46:17). This "gift" was defined by Elder Stephen L Richards as "the beneficent application of knowledge in decision [making]." However, cautioned Elder

Richards, *"I do not believe that true wisdom can be acquired or exercised in living without a sound fundamental knowledge of the truth about life and living. . . .* The fundamental knowledge which the Church brings to you will bring you understanding. Your testimony, your spirit, and your service will direct the application of your knowledge; that is wisdom." (CR, Apr. 1950, pp. 163–64; italics added.)
See also: Wisdom

Word of Wisdom (#2)

Section 89 is known as the Word of Wisdom, which the Lord gave for the benefit and "temporal salvation of all saints in the last days." Although it entails laws of health that specify both what should and should not be consumed, the major emphasis has been upon the abstinence of alcoholic beverages, tobacco, tea, coffee, and, most recently, drugs. President Spencer W. Kimball stated: "Certainly numerous young people have been damaged or destroyed by the use of marijuana and other deadly drugs. We deplore such." (En., Nov. 1974, p. 6.)

Initially the Word of Wisdom was given as a "greeting" rather than by "commandment or constraint." President Joseph F. Smith said, "The reason undoubtedly why the Word of Wisdom was given—as not by 'commandment or restraint' was that at that time, at least, if it had been given as a commandment it would have brought every man, addicted to the use of these noxious things, under condemnation; so the Lord was merciful and gave them a chance to overcome, before He brought them under the law" (CR, Oct. 1913, p. 14).

In 1838, the Prophet Joseph declared: "No official member in this Church is worthy to hold an office after having the word of wisdom properly taught him; and he, the official member, neglecting to comply with and obey it" (TPJS, 117). On September 9, 1851, President Brigham Young publicly proclaimed, "The Word of Wisdom is a commandment" (IE, Feb. 1956, p. 78).

It is of interest to note a statement by President Spencer W. Kimball: "We have no intent to take away from our friends, and the other people of the world, their agency in the use of these prohibited things. But we believe that the Lord, when he gave the Word of Wisdom, was *speaking to all the people in the world.*" (En., May 1975, p. 7; italics added.)

Elder Russell M. Nelson stated: "Self-mastery comes from obedience to the Word of Wisdom. . . . As you develop courage to say no to alcohol, tobacco, and other stimulants, you gain additional strength. You can then refuse conspiring men—those seditious solicitors of harmful substances or smut. You can reject their evil enticements to your body." (En., Nov. 1985, p. 31; see D&C 89:4.)

See also: Conspiring Men; Destroying Angel; Herbs; Hidden Treasures; Hot Drinks; In the Season Thereof; Man That Sheddeth Blood or Wasteth Flesh; Pure Wine; Staff of Life; Strong Drink; Temporal Salvation

Work of the Gathering

The "work of the gathering" is mentioned twice in the Doctrine and Covenants, and in both instances refers to the process of gathering to Missouri—the land of Zion (58:56; 101:20; see also 63:24). In the latter revelation the Lord reaffirmed this location as the place he had appointed for the gathering of his Saints. However, the day is yet to come when the "Center Stake" of Zion will be established in Missouri (JD 11:324).

See also: Center Place; City of Zion; Independence, Missouri; Jackson County; Zion

Work of Translation

The phrase *work of translation* occurs four times in the revelations. In the first two instances, it refers to the work being done on the plates from whence the Book of Mormon came (D&C 10:3, 34). In the latter two references, the Prophet's work on revising the Bible is the "work of translation" (D&C 73:4; 76:15).

See also: Book of Mormon; New Translation; Seer; Translator; Urim and Thummim

Works of Abraham

"In the scriptural meaning there will be thousands of the literal descendants of Abraham, Isaac, Jacob, and Joseph, who will never be called by Abraham's name or be of the house of Israel. This will be because they have rebelled against the truth and have not placed themselves in harmony with the covenants which are required in order that they may inherit as *sons* and *daughters*. In other words, to become a son or daughter of Abraham, the individual must 'do the works of Abraham.' The Lord recognized the fact that the Jews were *descendants* of Abraham, but they could not be classed as the *children* of Abraham." (DS 3:249–50; John 8:33–59; Rom. 9:1–8; see also Alma 5:22–24.)

The "works of Abraham," which the Saints are admonished to pursue (D&C 132:32), must include two traits for which the ancient patriarch was renowned—faith and sacrifice. The Prophet Joseph proclaimed, "The sacrifice required of Abraham in the offering up of Isaac, shows that *if a man would attain to the keys of the kingdom of an endless life; he must sacrifice all things*" (TPJS, 322; italics added).

See also: Abraham; Seed of Abraham

Workways

The Prophet wrote that "a very large ship is benefited very much by a very small helm in the time of a storm, by being kept workways with the wind and the waves" (D&C 123:16). *Workways* is a nautical term which means keeping the bow of the ship headed into the wind. This is the safest course during times of storm.

World

There are over two hundred references to the term *world* in the Doctrine and Covenants. It can be used interchangeably with the term *earth* (D&C 1:23; 38:1), or it may mean the *inhabitants* of this telestial turf (D&C 1:19–20; 46:3).

A reference to the "world" frequently means the life-style of the vast majority of the earth's inhabitants. This mode of living places emphasis upon pleasure seeking and upon the tangible treasures of the earth as opposed to values of an eternal verity. The Savior warned us that we cannot serve God at the same time we are seeking for worldly riches (Matt. 6:19–24; 3 Ne. 13:19–24). In like fashion, the Apostle John cautioned the early Saints against loving "the world" and "the things that are in the world," for this attitude diminishes their devotion to Deity (1 John 2:15–17).

In our day, a modern Apostle has said: "We cannot survive spiritually with one foot in the Church and the other in the world. We must make the choice. It is either the Church or the world. There is no middle ground.'' (Bruce R. McConkie, CR, Oct. 1974, p. 44.)

See also: Babylon; Earth; Idumea; Kingdoms of the World; Spirit World; Weak Things of the World; Worlds, The

Worlds, The

The Doctrine and Covenants attests that this earth is not the only globe generated by the power of God. The Prophet Joseph Smith and Sidney Rigdon declared that ''the worlds are and were created'' by Jesus Christ (D&C 76:23–24; see also 93:10). He is the same ''who was in the bosom of the Father before the worlds were made'' (D&C 76:39). Moses heard the divine decree that ''worlds without number have I created; and . . . by the Son I created them, which is mine Only Begotten'' (Moses 1:33).

The following graphically describes the number of these worlds created by Christ: ''Worlds without number! Innumerable unto man! There is no finite way to envision the extent of the worlds created by Christ at the behest of his Father. Count the grains of sand on all seashores and Saharas of the world, add the stars in the firmament for good measure, multiply the total by like sums from other worlds, and what do we have? Scarcely a dot in the broad expanse of an infinite universe—all created by Christ.'' (PM, 55.)

See also: Creator; Jesus Christ

Worm Dieth Not

Speaking of the sons of perdition, the Lord indicated they would ''reign with the devil and his angels in eternity, where their worm dieth not'' (D&C 76:44). This phrase is also found in the Old and New Testaments, as well as the apocryphal book of Judith (Isa. 66:24; Mark 9:43–48; Judith 16:17).

Dummelow said: ''These words may be intended to refer to the literal destruction of their corpses, or may also include *the torment of the spirits of the ungodly.* Jewish interpretation adopted the latter view.'' (Dummelow, 453; italics added.)

Perhaps the creeping feeling of spiritual corruption will be as real to those destined to suffer this fate as the crawling of worms in the flesh of corruptible bodies. ''Woe to the nations that rise up against my kindred! The Lord Almighty will take vengeance of them in the *day of judgment,* in putting fire and *worms in their flesh; and they shall feel them, and weep for ever.*'' (Judith 16:17; italics added.)

See also: Sons of Perdition

Worship

In his confrontation with the tempter, Jesus scuttled Satan's plea for servitude with this rebuke: ''Thou shalt worship the Lord thy God, and him only shalt thou serve" (Matt. 4:10; Luke 4:8). To worship is to adore, honor, reverence, serve, pay homage to, and pray to Deity. It is to place God uppermost in one's thoughts and to follow his ways.

A true pattern for worship can be found in section 93 of the Doctrine and Covenants in which we are taught that Christ received a fulness of the Father by following him and that we too may receive that fulness by emulating the Savior's example. Elder Bruce R. McConkie noted that "true and perfect worship consists in following in the steps of the Son of God" (CR, Oct. 1971, p. 168). Worship is not seen in spoken words alone but in service rendered.

Although we seek to follow a prophet's counsel in believing in Christ (2 Ne. 25:28–29) and in worshiping the One who wrought the atonement in the sense that we reverence, respect, and desire to follow him, we recognize the Eternal Father as the ultimate focus of true worship. The First Presidency has reminded us that "the sole object of worship, God the Eternal Father, stands supreme and alone, and it is in the name of the Only Begotten that we thus approach Him" (IE, Apr. 1912, p. 485; see also D&C 18:40).

See also: Reverence

Wounds

See: Prints of the Nails

Wrest the Scriptures

Webster states that to wrest is to "turn or twist; to ascribe a wrong meaning or intent to; to deliberately misinterpret or distort." The Lord warned against wresting the scriptures (D&C 10:63).

President Joseph Fielding Smith gave the following counsel regarding wresting or misinterpreting the scriptures: "It is wrong to take one passage of scripture and isolate it from all other teachings dealing with the same subject. We should bring together all that has been said by authority on the question. If we were to make a photograph, it would be necessary for all of your rays of light to be focused properly on the subject. If this were not done then a blurred picture would be the result. This is the case when we try to obtain a mental picture, when we have only a portion of the facts dealing with the subject we are considering." (DS 2:95.)

The Prophet Joseph gave the key whereby scriptures are to be interpreted: "What is the rule of interpretation?" he asked. "Just no interpretation at all. Understand it precisely as it reads. I have a key by which I understand the scriptures. I enquire, what was the question which drew out the answer, or caused Jesus to utter the parable?" (TPJS 276–77.)

See also: Scripture

Y

Year of My Redeemed

The Lord, through Isaiah, spoke of "the day of vengeance" and the "year of my redeemed" (Isa. 63:4). This latter phrase is also used within the context of the Second Coming in the Doctrine and Covenants (D&C 133:52). As one studies those verses which both precede and follow the use of the phrase "year of my redeemed," both in Isaiah and in the Doctrine and Covenants, the signs of the second coming of the Savior and the ushering in of the Millennium are very evident.

Inasmuch as the "day of redemption" has specific reference to the day of resurrection, it appears that the "year of my redeemed" is that special time when "they who are Christ's at His Coming" will be redeemed from the bondage of death through the resurrection (D&C 88:16; DS 2:97).

Referring to "the year of the Lord's redeemed," Elder Bruce R. McConkie has written: "To the righteous who have waited for him and kept his laws, the Second Coming will be a day devoutly to be desired, a day of peace and redemption, a day when in justice will cease and wickedness be banished, a day when the vineyard will be cleansed of corruption and its rightful Ruler reign in the midst of his saints." (MD 696.) Thus, this special time will also be one in which mankind will be *redeemed* from the sinful subtleties of Satan and the wickedness of the world.

See also: Day of Redemption; Second Coming

Years of Accountability

See: Accountable Before Me; Infant State; Spirit of Man Was Innocent

Yesterday, Today, and Forever

The phrase *yesterday, today, and forever* (D&C 20:12; 35:1; Heb. 13:8; 1 Ne. 10:18) simply means the past, present, and future. When God is spoken of as being the same yesterday, today, and forever, it means that he is unchanging, never varying in his course (DNTC 3:238).

See also: Today

Yoke

The word *yoke* is frequently used metaphorically in scriptures to describe subjection or a heavy burden that is placed upon one (1 Kgs. 12:4, 9–11; Isa. 9:4; 1 Ne. 13:5). In his dedicatory prayer of the Kirtland Temple, the Prophet Joseph pleaded with the Lord to relieve his suffering Saints from the yoke they had borne (D&C 109:31–32, 47, 63).

In the traditional sense, a yoke is a wooden bar or frame by which two animals are joined at the heads or necks for working together. Webster indicates that the term also identifies an arched device formerly laid upon the neck of a defeated person.

Young, Brigham

Perhaps in the same sense that Joseph Smith's name was to be "had for good and evil" (JS—H 1:33), the name of Brigham Young evokes similar responses. He would eventually say, "I regret that my mission is not better understood by the world, [but] the time will come when I will be understood, and I leave to futurity the judgment of my labors and their result as they shall become manifest." (POC, 82–83.)

The world has since recognized Brigham's superb skills in colonizations, but many still lack the spiritual wisdom to see his prophetic mantle. At the unveiling of the Brigham Young statue in the Rotunda at Washington, D.C., Elder Albert E. Bowen said: "He possessed in superlative de-

gree qualifications that always go with greatness: intelligence, loyalty, faith, courage. It is possible to disagree with his religious belief, but it is not possible, on the record of history, to question his sincerity nor his superb statesmanship." (ASBY, 15.)

Of his conversion to the Church, to which he gave his all, the following has been said: "Never a credulous man, nor one to be hurried in his judgments, Brigham subjected the new religion over a period of two years to the test of careful study, scriptural comparison, and critical analysis. On April 14, 1832, he was baptized and became a member of the church at the age of thirty-one. From that day until the day of his death he trod a thorny path mid scenes of turbulence and violence of which for over thirty years he was the central figure." (ASBY, 13.) In his own words, he embraced the gospel "for all day long." Whatever Brigham Young did was done with full commitment, for, said he, "I have believed all my life that that which was worth doing was worth doing well" (NE, Sept. 1977, p. 17).

Two years after his baptism, he was ordained one of the original members of the Quorum of the Twelve Apostles in this dispensation. It is as a member of this august body that he is first mentioned in the Doctrine and Covenants (124:127). His loyalty to the Prophet Joseph knew no bounds. "I have lain upon the floor scores and scores of nights," he said, "ready to receive the mobs who sought his [Joseph's] life" (JD 18:361).

Brigham was noted for "his *strict obedience* to the Prophet. Brother Joseph never made any requirements of him that he did not strictly comply with," said George Q. Cannon. (JI 20:222.) The Lord's feelings for this faithful man are expressed in this revelatory salutation: *"Dear and well-beloved brother,* Brigham Young" (D&C 126:1).

Joseph and Brigham's relationship was strong from the beginning. It was from Brigham's mouth that the Prophet first heard the Adamic tongue, which Joseph declared was from God; "the time will come," he said, "when brother Brigham Young will preside over this Church" (MS 25:439).

Following Joseph's death, the question of succession was resolved at a conference held on August 8, 1844, in Nauvoo. That the mantle of Joseph was indeed upon Brigham Young was both spiritually and physically manifest. "It was necessary that there should be some manifestation of the power of God," said John Taylor. "No sooner did President Young arise than the power of God rested down upon him in the face of the people. It did not appear to be Brigham Young; *it appeared to be Joseph Smith* that spoke to the people—Joseph in his *looks,* in his *manner,* and in his *voice;* even *his figure was transformed so that it looked like that of Joseph,* and everybody present, who had

the Spirit of God, saw that he was the man whom God had chosen to hold the keys now that the Prophet Joseph had gone behind the veil." (JD 23:363–64; italics added.)

At Winter Quarters, Brigham told Wilford Woodruff that Joseph had visited him the previous night and told him to tell the people to get the Spirit of God in order to sustain them in their work. On his deathbed, Brigham's last words were, "Joseph! Joseph! Joseph!"

He presided over the Church as President of the Twelve Apostles from 1844 until 1847, when the First Presidency was once again organized, with Brigham Young as President. Here he remained until his death on August 29, 1877. He was "resistant as the granite mountains to evil, injustice, or falsehood," and his prophetic mantle of leadership was always worn with great visibility. Nevertheless, he disclaimed perfection (JD 10:212), and understood the source from whence his power flowed (D&C 59:21).

"Men talk about what has been accomplished under my direction, and attribute it to my wisdom and ability," he remarked, "but it is all by the power of God, and by intelligence received from him. . . . What I know concerning God, concerning the earth, concerning government, I received from the heavens, not alone through my natural ability, and I give God the glory and the praise." "I am no better, nor any more important than another man who is trying to do good." (JD 16:46; 6:275–76.)

Young, Joseph

On February 28, 1835, Joseph Young became one of the Seven Presidents of the Seventy—a General Authority of the Church. He is mentioned in the Doctrine and Covenants in conjunction with this office (D&C 124:138). Joseph was baptized a week before his elder brother, Brigham Young, entering those sacred waters on April 6, 1832. His previous enthusiasm for Methodism was easily transferred to his new-found faith, for his was "a genuine love of truth, rather than bigoted devotion to a sectarian creed."

Joseph served a number of missions, marched with Zion's Camp, and was miraculously preserved in the slaughter of Saints that took place at Haun's Mill, Missouri. Joseph Smith's prediction that Joseph Young would preach in the "old world" was fulfilled in 1870 when he visited the British Isles. He was described as "a benevolent and merciful man, full of kindness and good works, and full of integrity to the cause he espoused." He died in full fellowship of the Church on July 16, 1881. (Jenson 1:187–88.)

Youward

Thomas B. Marsh and the other members of the Quorum of the Twelve were reminded by the Lord that Joseph Smith held the keys of the kingdom, but that they were also given "to you-ward" (D&C 112:15). This simply meant to(ward) you.

See also: Apostle

Z

Zacharias

Zacharias was a descendant of Aaron, holding the right to the priesthood of his illustrious fore-father (TPJS, 272–73). He be-longed to the eighth of the twenty-four courses of priests established by King David (1 Chr. 24:10). This course was named after Abijah, or Abia. Robert J. Matthews said: "This does not mean necessarily that Zacharias was a direct descendant of Abijah, but only that he belonged to the course that was named after him" (ABL, 18).

While functioning in his priestly responsibilities within the temple, he received the divine decree from the angel Gabriel that though "well stricken in years," he and his wife, Elisabeth, would have a son. This son's name was to be John and his mission was to prepare for the coming of the Lord (D&C 27:7; Luke 1:5–19). Though stricken dumb at the time of this marvelous manifestation, Zacharias's voice was restored on the day the infant was to be named and "was filled with the Holy Ghost, and prophesied" (Luke 1:20–23, 57–79).

When Herod issued his death decree upon all male infants under the age of two (Matt. 2:16), Zacharias hid his young son from the executioners. Upon refusing to disclose the hiding place, he "was slain by Herod's order, between the porch and the altar, as Jesus said" (TPJS, 261; Matt. 23:35).

According to apocryphal writings, when faced by Herod's threat, Zacharias said: "I am a martyr of God if thou sheddest my blood: for my spirit the Lord shall receive, because thou sheddest innocent blood in the forecourt of the temple of the Lord" (Montague Rhodes James, trans., *The Apocryphal New Testament* [Oxford: The Clarendon Press, 1953], p. 48).

Zarahemla

The city of Zarahemla, originally located in the Territory of Iowa, is mentioned by the Lord in Doctrine and Covenants 125:3. "This settlement was founded by the Saints in 1839, on the uplands about a mile west of the Mississippi River, near Montrose and opposite Nauvoo, Ill. The Church had bought an extensive tract of land here. At a conference held at Zarahemla, August 7, 1841, seven hundred and fifty Church members were represented, of whom three hundred and twenty-six lived in Zarahemla. But when the Saints left for the Rocky Mountains, that city was lost sight of." (SS, 796.)

The name *Zarahemla* is not new to students of the Book of Mormon, for within the pages of that sacred book it was used to identify a land (Omni 1:12), a people (Omni 1:14), a man (Omni 1:18), and a city (Alma 2:26).

Zion

There are over two hundred references to "Zion" in the Doctrine and Covenants. In most instances, reference is made to a particular location—the state of Missouri; and more specifically to Jackson County, even the city of Independence (D&C 57:1–3). This is where the future "Center Stake of Zion" will be organized and a great temple built prior to the coming of Christ. The Prophet Joseph Smith declared, "The whole of America is Zion itself from north to south" (TPJS, 362). Zion is also used to describe the ancient *city* of Enoch (D&C 38:4; Moses 7:19); a *hill* (D&C 76:66); and, most important, a *people* (D&C 97:21; Moses 7:18). A *place* of Zion will only be established when a *people* of Zion are ready for occupancy.

President Spencer W. Kimball declared, "*Zion* is a name given by the Lord to his covenant people, who are characterized by purity of heart and faithfulness in caring for the poor, the needy, and the distressed" (En., Nov., 1977, p. 78). He further stated, "Zion can be built up only among those who are the pure in heart, not a people torn by covetousness or greed, but a pure and selfless people. Not a people who are pure in appearance, rather a people who are pure in heart. Zion is to be in the world and not of the world, not dulled by a sense of carnal security, nor paralyzed by materialism. No, Zion is not things of the lower, but of the higher order, things that exalt the mind and sanctify the heart."

President Kimball then suggested three fundamental things that must be done in order to bring about a Zion; "*First*, we must eliminate the individual tendency to selfishness that snares the soul, shrinks the heart, and darkens the mind. . . . *Second*, we must cooperate completely and work in harmony one with the other. There must be unanimity in our decisions and unity in our actions. . . . *Third*, we must lay on the altar and sacrifice whatever is required by the Lord.

We begin by offering a 'broken heart and a contrite spirit.' We follow this by giving our best effort in our assigned fields of labor and callings. We learn our duty and execute it fully." (En., May 1978, p. 81; italics added.)

See also: America; Beautiful Garments; Center Place; Children of Zion; City of Zion; Daughters of Zion; Goodly Land; Holy One of Zion; Independence, Missouri; Jackson County; Land of Zion; Pure in Heart; United States; Work of the Gathering; Zion of Enoch; Zion's Camp

Zion of Enoch

At a conference of the Church in 1831, the Lord declared that he had "taken the Zion of Enoch into mine own bosom" (D&C 38:4). Smith and Sjodahl gave the following explanation of the "Zion of Enoch": "This city called 'Zion' because its inhabitants were all righteous and 'pure in heart' (D&C 97:21) will return when the Millennial reign is come. (Moses 7:63.)

"Enoch, the seventh from Adam (Jude 14) built a city called Zion, after the people of God, so named by the Lord, because they were united, righteous, and prosperous. This city of Enoch flourished for three hundred and sixty-five years and then the Lord, by some process not know to us, took it with all its inhabitants, 'to His bosom,' thus saving them from destruction in the flood that was to come. 'And from thence went forth the saying, Zion is fled' (Moses 7:18, 19, 68, 69). The building up of another Zion in the latter days was predicted by the prophets of old. David, for instance, says, 'When the Lord shall build up Zion, he shall appear in his glory.' (Psalm 102:16.) That the people of God in the latter days should be found in a mountain region, was also foretold. 'O Zion, that bringest good tidings, get thee up into high mountain' (Isa. 40:9; see also Ezek. 40:2)'' (SS, 199–200).

Elder Orson Pratt added this commentary: "It was called a city of holiness, for God came down and dwelt with that people; he was in their midst, they beheld his glory, they saw his face, and he condescended to dwell among them for many long years, during which time they were instructed and taught in all of his ways . . . [and] when they were fully prepared, having learned the doctrine of translation, were caught up into the heavens, the whole city." (JD 17:147.)

See also: Enoch; Zion

Zion's Camp

As part of the plan to alleviate the suffering and persecution of the Saints in Missouri, the Lord revealed to the Prophet Joseph Smith a plan that called for the coming of an expedition of from one hundred to five hundred "of the strength of my house." The forming of this expedition was previously revealed by the Lord in a parable (D&C 101:55–60). The Saints in Missouri had been driven from their homes by mob action and were desirous of knowing when "Zion" (Jackson County, Missouri) should be "redeemed" (HC 2:61–62). This expedition, known as Zion's Camp, was the Lord's response.

The camp included contingents from Ohio and Michigan and eventually had a strength of 205 men and 25 wagons. The first group left Kirtland on May 1, 1834, and the camp was ultimately disbanded on June 25, near Rush Creek in Missouri. (HC 2:64–114.)

Some of their experiences included the following: the discovery of the skeletal remains of a "white Lamanite" named "Zelph"; an outbreak of cholera that afflicted sixty-eight persons and claimed fourteen lives, partly due to the rebellious spirit shown by some members of the camp; and the divine protection afforded the men when the elements preserved them from mobocracy.

Upon arriving in Missouri, the Lord informed the Prophet Joseph, who was commander-in-chief of the expedition, that in consequence of transgression, the time for Zion's redemption was not yet at hand (D&C 105). Though many were disappointed, and some even looked upon the march as a failure, it had served a providential purpose.

As Elder Neal A. Maxwell once said, "those who marched

in Zion's Camp were not exploring the Missouri countryside but their own possibilities" (CR, Oct. 1976, p. 16). From this group came many of the men who were chosen to be the Apostles and other leaders of the early Church.

Zombre

One of the code names used by the Lord to disguise the real identity of individuals was that of "Zombre" (D&C 96:6; 104:24, 34; pre-1981 edition; HC 1:255). This name was applied to John Johnson in June 1833, and again in April 1834. This name is no longer found in current editions of the Doctrine and Covenants.

See also: Johnson, John

Zoramites

The Lord promises that a knowledge of him should come to the Zoramites (D&C 3:17). Zoram was the servant of an influential Jewish citizen, Laban, who lived in Jerusalem around 600 B.C. He took an oath to follow Father Lehi's expedition into the wilderness and ultimately crossed oceanic waters to the American continent (1 Ne. 4; 18). His descendants were known as Zoramites, although in a general sense they were known as Nephites—as were all those who lived under the Nephite system of government (Jacob 1:13–14; 4 Ne. 1:36; Morm. 1:8).

Perhaps one of the greatest compliments Zoram could have received was a prophet's declaration that Zoram was a true friend unto the prophet Nephi "forever" (2 Ne. 1:30). Through intermarriage, his blood lineage has been preserved through the Lamanites of our day.

Bibliography

Acceptance of the Statue of Brigham Young. Washington, D.C.: United States Government Printing Office, 1950.

Allen, James B. & Leonard, Glen M. *The Story of the Latter-day Saints.* Salt Lake City: Deseret Book, 1976.

Area Conference Reports. Salt Lake City: The Church of Jesus Christ of Latter-day Saints.

Backman, Milton V. Jr., *The Heavens Resound.* Salt Lake City: Deseret Book Co., 1983.

Bible Dictionary. Cambridge, England: Cambridge University Press, n.d.

Bible Dictionary. Salt Lake City: The Church of Jesus Christ of Latter-day Saints, 1979.

Book of Mormon, The: Another Testament of Jesus Christ. Salt Lake City: The Church of Jesus Christ of Latter-day Saints, 1981 ed.

Brigham Young University Studies. Provo, Utah: Brigham Young University Press.

Brooks, Melvin R. *LDS Reference Encyclopedia.* 2 vols. Salt Lake City: Bookcraft, 1960.

Burton, Theodore M. *God's Greatest Gift.* Salt Lake City: Deseret Book, 1976.

Cannon, George Q. *Gospel Truth.* 2 vols. Compiled by Jerreld L. Newquist. Salt Lake City: Deseret Book, 1974.

Church News. Salt Lake City: The Church of Jesus Christ of Latter-day Saints.

Conference Reports. Salt Lake City: The Church of Jesus Christ of Latter-day Saints.

Corbett, Pearson H. *Hyrum Smith: Patriarch.* Salt Lake City: Deseret Book, 1963.

Cowley, Matthias F. *Wilford Woodruff.* Salt Lake City: Bookcraft, 1964.

Cruden, Alexander. *Cruden's Complete Concordance.* Grand Rapids, Michigan: Zondervan Publishing House, 1968.

Deseret News 1978 Church Almanac. Salt Lake City: Deseret News Press, 1978.

Devotional and Fireside Speeches. Provo Utah: Brigham Young University.

Devotional Speeches of the Year. Provo, Utah: Brigham Young University.

Diary of Oliver B. Huntington. (Manuscript located in the Historical Department of The Church of Jesus Christ of Latter-day Saints.) n.d.

Doctrine and Covenants, The. Salt Lake City: The Church of Jesus Christ of Latter-day Saints (various editions).

Dummelow, J. R. (ed). *The One Volume Bible Commentary.* New York: Macmillan Publishing Co., 1936.

Dyer, Alvin R. *Who Am I?* Salt Lake City: Deseret Book, 1966.

Encyclopedia Americanna, 1985 ed.

Encyclopedia Britannica, 15th ed., 1974.

Ensign. Salt Lake City: The Church of Jesus Christ of Latter-day Saints.

Evans, Richard L. *Unto the Hills.* New York: Harper, 1940.

Gunn, Stanley R. *Oliver Cowdery: Second Elder and Scribe.* Salt Lake City: Bookcraft, 1962.

Hinckley, Bryant S. *Sermons and Missionary Services of Melvin J. Ballard.* Salt Lake City: Deseret Book, 1949.

Holy Bible. King James Version.

Holy Scriptures: Inspired Version. Independence, Missouri: Herald Publishing House, 1944.

Hymns of The Church of Jesus Christ of Latter-day Saints. Salt Lake City: The Church of Jesus Christ of Latter-day Saints, 1985.

Improvement Era. Salt Lake City: The Church of Jesus Christ of Latter-day Saints.

Instructor. Salt Lake City: The Church of Jesus Christ of Latter-day Saints.

Jenson, Andrew. *LDS Biographical Encyclopedia.* 4 vols. Salt Lake City: Western Epics, 1971.

Journal of Discourses. 26 vols. London: Latter-day Saints' Book Depot, 1854–86.

Juvenile Instructor. Salt Lake City: The Church of Jesus Christ of Latter-day Saints.

Kimball, Spencer W. *Faith Precedes the Miracle.* Salt Lake City: Deseret Book, 1978.

Kimball, Spencer W. *The Miracle of Forgiveness.* Salt Lake City: Bookcraft, 1969.

Larsen, Gustive O. *The "Americanization of Utah for Statehood.* San Marino, CA: Huntington Library, 1971.

Lee, Harold B. *Stand Ye In Holy Places.* Salt Lake City: Deseret Book, 1974.

Lee, Harold B. *Youth and the Church.* Salt Lake City: Deseret Book, 1953.

Matthews, Robert J. *A Burning Light: The Life and Ministry of John the Baptist.* Provo, Utah: Brigham Young University Press, 1972.

Maxwell, Neal A. *We Will Prove Them Herewith.* Salt Lake City: Deseret Book, 1982.

McConkie, Bruce R. *A New Witness for the Articles of Faith.* Salt Lake City: Deseret Book, 1982.

McConkie, Bruce R. *Doctrinal New Testament Commentary.* 3 vols. Salt Lake City: Bookcraft, 1965–73.

McConkie, Bruce R. *Mormon Doctrine.* 2d ed. Salt Lake City: Bookcraft, 1966.

McConkie, Bruce R. *The Millennial Messiah.* Salt Lake City: Deseret Book, 1982.

McConkie, Bruce R. *The Mortal Messiah.* 4 vols. Salt Lake City: Deseret Book, 1979–1981.

McConkie, Bruce R. *The Promised Messiah.* Salt Lake City: Deseret Book, 1978.

McKay, David O. *Ancient Apostles.* Salt Lake City: Deseret Book, 1964.

McKay, David O. *Cherished Experiences.* Compiled by Clare Middlemiss. Salt Lake City: Deseret Book, 1965.

McKay, David O. *Gospel Ideals.* Salt Lake City: Improvement Era, 1957.

Messages of the First Presidency. 6 vols. Compiled by James R. Clark. Bookcraft, 1965–75.

Millennial Star. Manchester, England: The Church of Jesus Christ of Latter-day Saints.

New Era, The. Salt Lake City: The Church of Jesus Christ of Latter-day Saints.

Nibley, Preston. *The Presidents of the Church.* Salt Lake City: Deseret Book, 1941.

Oaks, Dallin H. & Hill, Marvin S. *Carthage Conspiracy.* Urbana, Illinois: University of Illinois Press, 1975.

Packer, Boyd K. *Teach Ye Diligently.* Salt Lake City: Deseret Book, 1975.

Palmer, Lee A. *The Aaronic Priesthood Through the Centuries.* Salt Lake City: The Church of Jesus Christ of Latter-day Saints, 1967.

Pearl of Great Price, The. Salt Lake City: The Church of Jesus Christ of Latter-day Saints.

Peloubet, F. N. *Peloubet's Bible Dictionary.* Philadelphia: Universal Book and Bible House, 1947.

Petersen, Mark E. *Adam: Who Is He?* Salt Lake City: Deseret Book, 1976.

Petersen, Mark E. *Moses: Man of Miracles.* Salt Lake City: Deseret Book, 1977.

Pratt, Parley P. *A Voice of Warning and Instruction to All People.* New York: W. Sandford, 1837.

Pratt, Parley P. *Autobiography of Parley P. Pratt.* Salt Lake City: Deseret Book, 1966.

Pratt, Parley P. *Key to the Science of Theology.* Salt Lake City: Deseret Book, 1965.

Priesthood. Salt Lake City: Deseret Book, 1981.

Reynolds, George C. & Sjodahl, Janne M. *Commentary on the Book of Mormon.* 7 vols. Arranged by Phillip C. Reynolds. Salt Lake City, 1955.

Richards, Claude. *J. Golden Kimball.* Salt Lake City: Bookcraft, 1966.

Richards, Franklin D. & Little, James. *A Compendium of the Faith and Doctrines of The Church of Jesus Christ of Latter-day Saints.* Liverpool, England: Orson Pratt, 1857.

Richards, LeGrand. *A Marvelous Work and a Wonder.* Salt Lake City: Deseret Book, 1950.

Riciotti, Guiseppe. *The Life of Christ.* Translated by Alba I. Zizzamia Milwaukee: Bruce Publishing Co., 1947.

Roberts, B. H. *A Comprehensive History of The Church of Jesus Christ of Latter-day Saints.* 6 vols. Provo, Utah: The Church of Jesus Christ of Latter-day Saints, 1930.

Roberts, B. H. *The Life of John Taylor.* Salt Lake City: Bookcraft, 1963.

Roberts, B. H. *Succession in the Presidency of the Church.* Salt Lake City: Deseret News Press, 1894.

Romney, Marion G. *Look to God and Live.* Compiled by George J. Romney. Salt Lake City: Deseret Book, 1971.

Shapiro, R. Gary. *An Exhaustive Concordance of the Book of Mormon, Doctrine & Covenants, Pearl of Great Price.* Salt Lake City: Hawkes Publishing, 1977.

Sill, Sterling W. *The Upward Reach.* Salt Lake City: Bookcraft, 1962.

Smith, Hyrum M. & Sjodahl, Janne M. *Doctrine and Covenants Commentary.* Salt Lake City: Deseret Book, 1960.

Smith, Joseph. *History of the Church of Jesus Christ of Latter-day Saints.* 7 vols. 2d. ed. rev. Edited by B. H. Roberts. Salt Lake City: The Church of Jesus Christ of Latter-day Saints, 1932–51.

Smith, Joseph. *Lectures on Faith.* Compiled by N. B. Lundwall. Salt Lake City: N. B. Lundwall, n.d.

Smith, Joseph. *Teachings of the Prophet Joseph Smith.* Selected by Joseph Fielding Smith. Salt Lake City: Deseret Book, 1938.

Smith, Joseph F. *Gospel Doctrine.* 5th ed., Salt Lake City: Deseret Book, 1938.

Smith, Joseph Fielding. *Answers to Gospel Questions.* 5 vols. Compiled by Joseph Fielding Smith, Jr. Salt Lake City: Deseret Book, 1957–66.

Smith, Joseph Fielding. *Church History and Modern Revelation.* 2 vols. Salt Lake City: The Council of the Twelve Apostles, 1953.

Smith, Joseph Fielding. *Doctrines of Salvation.* 3 vols. Compiled by Bruce R. McConkie. Salt Lake City: Bookcraft, 1954–56.

Smith, Joseph Fielding. *Essentials in Church History.* Salt Lake City: Deseret Book, 1979.

Smith, Joseph Fielding. *The Life of Joseph F. Smith.* Salt Lake City: Deseret Book, 1969.

Smith, Joseph Fielding. *Man: His Origin and Destiny.* Salt Lake City: Deseret Book, 1954.

Smith, Joseph Fielding. *Seek Ye Earnestly.* Compiled by Joseph Fielding Smith, Jr. Salt Lake City: Deseret Book, 1970.

Smith, Joseph Fielding. *The Signs of the Times.* Salt Lake City: Deseret Book, 1961.

Smith, Joseph Fielding. *The Way to Perfection.* Salt Lake City: Deseret Book, 1931.

Smith, Lucy Mack. *History of Joseph Smith.* Edited by Preston Nibley. Salt Lake City: Bookcraft, 1958.

Snow, Eliza R. *Biography of Lorenzo Snow.* Salt Lake City: Deseret News Co., 1894.

Sperry, Sidney B. *Book of Mormon Compendium.* Salt Lake City: Bookcraft, 1968.

Sperry, Sidney B. *Doctrine and Covenants Compendium.* Salt Lake City: Bookcraft, 1960.

Sperry, Sidney B. *Themes of the Restored Gospel.* Salt Lake City: Bookcraft, 1950.

Talmage, James E. *The Articles of Faith.* 37th ed. Salt Lake City: Deseret Book, 1958.

Talmage, James E. *The House of the Lord.* Salt Lake City: Deseret Book, 1968.

Talmage, James E. *Jesus the Christ.* 25th ed. Salt Lake City: Deseret Book, 1956.

Talmage, James E. *The Vitality of Mormonism.* Salt Lake City: Deseret Book, 1919.

Taylor, John. *The Gospel Kingdom.* Selected by G. Homer Durham. Salt Lake City: Bookcraft, 1964.

Taylor, John. *Mediation and Atonement.* 1882. Reprint. Salt Lake City: Deseret News Press, 1964.

Times and Seasons. Nauvoo, Illinois: The Church of Jesus Christ of Latter-day Saints.

Utah Genealogical and Historical Magazine. Salt Lake City: Utah Genealogical Society.

Webster's Third New International Dictionary. Unabridged. Springfield, Mass.: G&C Merriman Co., 1961.

Welker, Roy A. *Spiritual Values of the Old Testament.* Salt Lake City: LDS Department of Education, 1952.

Whitney, Orson F. *Life of Heber C. Kimball.* 3rd ed. Salt Lake City: Bookcraft, 1945.

Widtsoe, John A. *Evidences and Reconciliations.* Arranged by G. Homer Durham. Salt Lake City: Bookcraft, 1960.

Widtsoe, John A. *Priesthood and Church Government.* Salt Lake City: Deseret Book, 1939.

Widtsoe, John A. *Program of the Church.* Salt Lake City: LDS Department of Education, 1936.

Woman. Salt Lake City: Deseret Book, 1979.

Young, Brigham. *Discourses of Brigham Young.* Selected by John A. Widstoe. Salt Lake City: Deseret Book, 1975.

General Authorities Cited

Asay, Carlos E.	First Quorum of the Seventy (1976–)
Ashton, Marvin J.	Asst. to the Quorum of the Twelve (1969–1971); Quorum of the Twelve Apostles (1971–)
Ballard, M. Russell	First Quorum of the Seventy (1976–1985); Quorum of the Twelve (1985–)
Ballard, Melvin J.	Quorum of the Twelve Apostles (1919–1939)
Benson, Ezra Taft	Quorum of the Twelve Apostles (1943–1985); President of the Church (1985–)
Brown, Hugh B.	Asst. to the Quorum of the Twelve (1953–1958); Quorum of the Twelve Apostles (1958–1961; 1970–1975); First Presidency (1961–1970)
Burton, Theodore M.	Asst. to the Quorum of the Twelve (1960–1976); First Quorum of the Seventy (1976–)
Cannon, George Q.	Quorum of the Twelve Apostles (1860–1873; 1877–1880; 1887–1889); First Presidency (1873–1877; 1880–1887; 1889–1901)
Christiansen, ElRay L.	Asst. to the Quorum of the Twelve (1951–1975)
Clark, J. Reuben, Jr.	First Presidency (1933–1961); Apostle (1934)
Clawson, Rudger	Quorum of the Twelve Apostles (1898–1943); First Presidency (1901)
Cowley, Matthias F.	Quorum of the Twelve Apostles (1897–1905)
Dunn, Paul H.	First Council of the Seventy (1964–1975); First Quorum of the Seventy (1975–)
Dyer, Alvin R.	Asst. to the Quorum of the Twelve (1958–1968; 1970–1976); Apostle (1967); First Presidency (1968–1970); First Quorum of the Seventy (1976–1977)
Evans, Richard L.	First Council of the Seventy (1938–1953); Quorum of the Twelve Apostles (1953–1971)
Faust, James E.	Asst. to the Quorum of the Twelve (1972–1976); First Quorum of the Seventy (1976–1978); Quorum of the Twelve Apostles (1978–)

Fyans, J. Thomas · Asst. to the Quorum of the Twelve (1974–1976); First Quorum of the Seventy (1976–   )

Hales, Robert D. · Asst. to the Quorum of the Twelve (1975–1976); First Quorum of the Seventy (1976–1985); Presiding Bishop (1985–   )

Hanks, Marion D. · First Council of the Seventy (1953–1968); Asst. to the Quorum of the Twelve (1968–1976); First Quorum of the Seventy (1976–   )

Hart, Charles H. · First Council of the Seventy (1906–1934)

Hinckley, Gordon B. · Asst. to the Quorum of the Twelve (1958–1961); Quorum of the Twelve Apostles (1961–1981); First Presidency (1981–   )

Hunter, Howard W. · Quorum of the Twelve Apostles (1959–   )

Isaacson, Thorpe B. · Presiding Bishopric (1946–1961); Asst. to the Quorum of the Twelve (1961–1965); First Presidency (1965–1970)

Kimball, Heber C. · Quorum of the Twelve Apostles (1835–1847); First Presidency (1847–1868)

Kimball, Spencer W. · Quorum of the Twelve Apostles (1943–1973); President of the Church (1973–1985)

Lee, Harold B. · Quorum of the Twelve Apostles (1941–1970); First Presidency (1970–1972); President of the Church (1972–1973)

Lyman, Francis M. · Quorum of the Twelve Apostles (1880–1916)

McConkie, Bruce R. · First Council of the Seventy (1946–1972); Quorum of the Twelve Apostles (1972–1985)

McKay, David O. · Quorum of the Twelve Apostles (1906–1934); First Presidency (1934–1950); President of the Church (1951–1970)

McKay, Thomas E. · Asst. to the Quorum of the Twelve (1941–1958)

Maxwell, Neal A. · Asst. to the Quorum of the Twelve (1974–1976); First Quorum of the Seventy (1976–1981); Quorum of the Twelve Apostles (1981–   )

Nelson, Russell M. · Quorum of the Twelve Apostles (1984–   )

Nibley, Charles W. · Presiding Bishop (1907–1925); First Presidency (1925–1931)

Oaks, Dallin H.   Quorum of the Twelve Apostles (1984–   )
Packer, Boyd K.   Asst. to the Quorum of the Twelve (1961–1970);
                   Quorum of the Twelve Apostles (1970–   )

Penrose, Charles W.   Quorum of the Twelve Apostles (1904–1911); First
                       Presidency (1911–1925)

Perry, L. Tom   Asst. to the Quorum of the Twelve (1972–1974);
                Quorum of the Twelve Apostles (1974–   )

Petersen, Mark E.   Quorum of the Twelve Apostles (1944–1984)

Peterson, H. Burke   Presiding Bishopric (1972–1985); First Quorum of the
                     Seventy (1985–   )

Pratt, Orson   Quorum of the Twelve Apostles (1835–1842;
               1843–1881)

Pratt, Parley P.   Quorum of the Twelve Apostles (1835–1857)

Reynolds, George   First Council of the Seventy (1890–1909)

Richards, George F.   Quorum of the Twelve Apostles (1906–1950); Acting
                       Patriarch (1937–1942)

Richards, Franklin D.   Quorum of the Twelve Apostles (1849–1899)

Richards, LeGrand   Presiding Bishop (1938–1952); Quorum of the Twelve
                    Apostles (1952–1983)

Richards, Stephen L   Quorum of the Twelve Apostles (1917–1951); First
                      Presidency (1951–1959)

Roberts, B. H.   First Council of the Seventy (1888–1933)

Romney, Marion G.   Asst. to the Quorum of the Twelve (1941–1951);
                     Quorum of the Twelve Apostles (1951–1972; 1985–
                     1988); First Presidency (1972–1985)

Sill, Sterling W.   Asst. to the Quorum of the Twelve (1954–1976); First
                     Quorum of the Seventy (1976–1978); General Author-
                     ity Emeritus (1978–   )

Smith, Eldred G.   Patriarch (1947–1979); General Authority Emeritus
                    (1979–   )

Smith, George A.   Quorum of the Twelve Apostles (1839–1868); First
                    Presidency (1868–1875)

Smith, George Albert   Quorum of the Twelve Apostles (1903–1945); President
                        of the Church (1945–1951)

Smith, Hyrum   First Presidency (1837–1841); Patriarch (1841–1844);
               Associate President of the Church (1841–1844)

Smith, Hyrum M.	Quorum of the Twelve Apostles (1901–1918)
Smith, Joseph, Jr.	Prophet and President of the Church (1830–1844)
Smith, Joseph F.	First Presidency (1866–1877; 1880–1887; 1889–1901); Quorum of the Twelve Apostles (1877–1880; 1887–1889); President of the Church (1901–1918)
Smith, Joseph Fielding	Quorum of the Twelve Apostles (1910–1970); First Presidency (1965–1970); President of the Church (1970–1972)
Snow, Lorenzo	Quorum of the Twelve Apostles (1849–1898); First Presidency (1873–1877); President of the Church (1898–1901)
Stapley, Delbert L.	Quorum of the Twelve Apostles (1950–1978)
Talmage, James E.	Quorum of the Twelve Apostles (1911–1933)
Tanner, Nathan Eldon	Asst. to Quorum of the Twelve (1960–1962); Quorum of the Twelve Apostles (1962–1963); First Presidency (1963–1982)
Taylor, John	Quorum of the Twelve Apostles (1838–1880); President of the Church (1880–1887)
Teasdale, George	Quorum of the Twelve Apostles (1882–1907)
Tuttle, A. Theodore	First Council of the Seventy (1958–1975); First Quorum of the Seventy (1975–1986)
Wells, Daniel H.	First Presidency (1857–1877); Special Counselor to the Twelve Apostles (1877–1891)
Wells, Rulon S.	First Council of the Seventy (1893–1941)
Whitney, Orson F.	Quorum of the Twelve Apostles (1906–1931)
Wirthlin, Joseph B.	Asst. to the Quorum of the Twelve (1975–1976); First Quorum of the Seventy (1976–1986); Quorum of the Twelve Apostles (1986–)
Wirthlin, Joseph L.	Presiding Bishopric (1938–1952); Presiding Bishop (1952–1961)
Woodruff, Wilford	Quorum of the Twelve Apostles (1839–1889); President of the Church (1889–1898)
Young, Brigham	Quorum of the Twelve Apostles (1835–1847); President of the Church (1847–1877)
Young, S. Dilworth	First Council of the Seventy (1945–1975); First Quorum of the Seventy (1975–1981)